For Marco and Françoise
to whom I owe so much

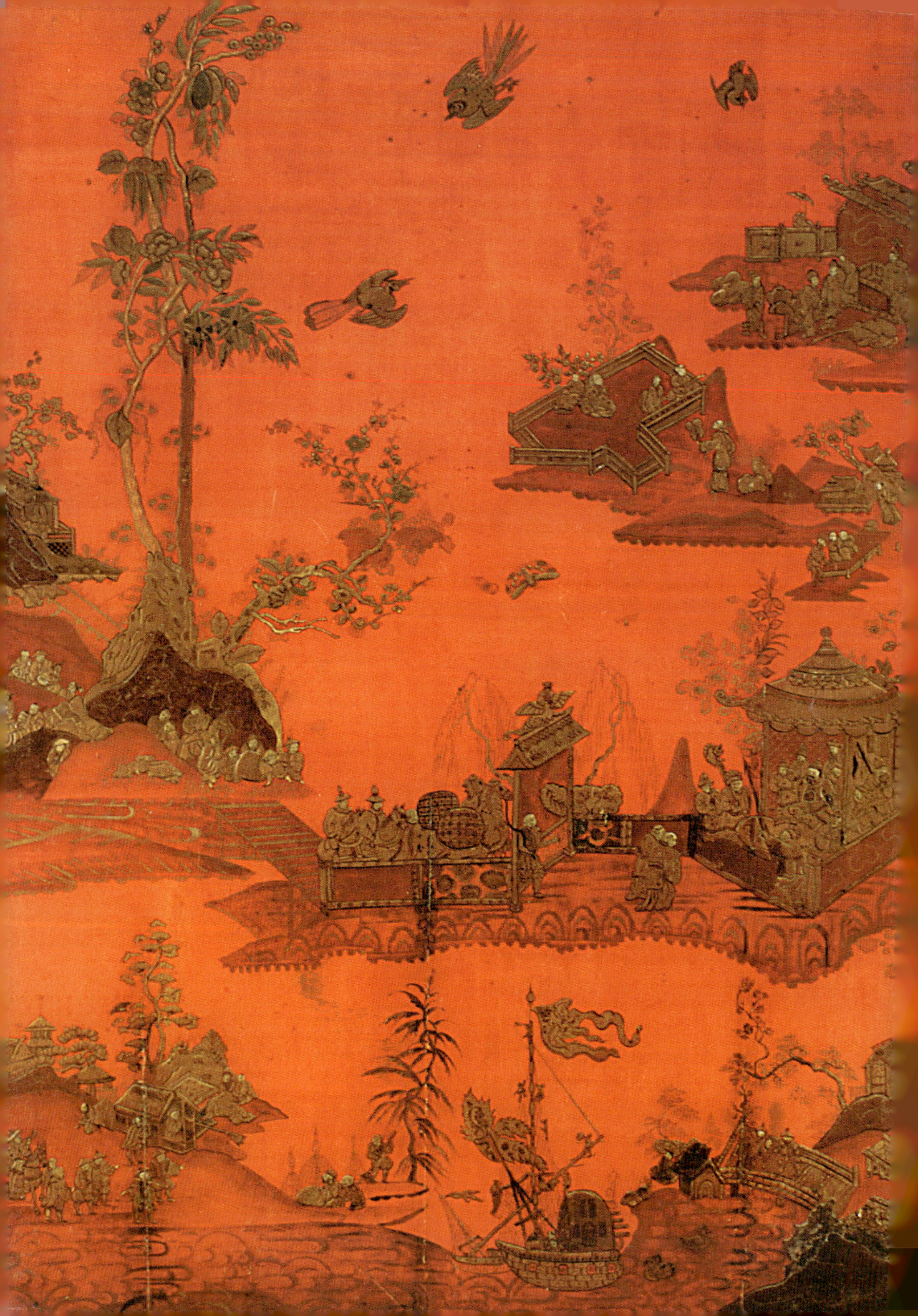

Francesco Morena

Chinoiserie

The Evolution of the Oriental Style in Italy from the 14th to the 19th Century

Translated by *Eve Leckey*

Centro Di

Francesco Morena
Chinoiserie. The Evolution of the Oriental Style in Italy from the 14th to the 19th Century
translated by Eve Leckey

Italian edition:
Francesco Morena
Cineseria. Evoluzioni del gusto per l'Oriente in Italia dal XIV al XIX secolo
ISBN 978-88-7038-450-5

della Edifimi srl, Firenze
edizioni@centrodi.it
www.centrodi.it
ISBN 978-88-7038-451-2
Printed by Alpi Lito, Florence,
September 2009
Printed in Italy

Cover:
Anonymous Sicilian artists, Details of the Chinese-style wall paintings. Palermo, Palazzina Cinese
(see Fig. 163).

Page 2:
Detail of the central panel in the Chinese Room, originally in Turin, now in the Nelson-Atkins Museum of Art, Kansas City (Missouri).

Contents

Chinoiserie: From Ornamentation to Architecture

Almost fifty years after the publication of Hugh Honour's fundamental volume describing the development of chinoiserie throughout Europe this book, patiently researched and written with verve by Francesco Morena, succeeds in bringing together the results of recent studies carried out by various scholars to provide a critical appraisal of the style in Italy from the 16th to the 18th centuries. It was in this period that oriental works of art, already passionately collected by princes and sovereigns, were gradually appropriated by the architects and decorators of Europe who modified the stylistic elements to create their own original interpretations.

Morena has become a recognised expert in the arts of the Far East and is highly knowledgeable concerning various historic periods of oriental civilizations and the artefacts they produced, now housed in public collections. In this latest study, he accompanies us on an evocative journey to distant lands far in the past, beginning in the Middle Ages and the Renaissance and continuing through the 16th century when elements of Chinese painting were often combined with decorative styles derived from Indian and Islamic art. The craftsmen of Venice are an example of this eclecticism as, despite the large quantities of porcelain and silk imported from China, during the mid 16th century they produced sumptuous furnishings entirely covered with decorations in coloured lacquer and gold recalling Indian and Persian designs, or strewn with a close inlay of ivory and mother-of-pearl that spread over the entire article creating a pattern in which geometric decoration and floral designs alternate, reflecting the designs of Turkish rugs and Iznik ceramics. Throughout this century and for part of the next, similar designs were abundantly painted on the furniture in the residences of the Tuscan grand dukes and on ceramics, especially those known as "porcellana medicea", made of a special clay and produced at the kiln established by Francesco I in the San Marco workshops in Florence. But it was during the 17th century that a greater awareness of and interest in Chinese art, at last unencumbered by references to the Ottoman and Indian civilizations, developed in western society as a result of both the more assiduous trade that took place between Europe and the Orient and the increasingly frequent missions organised by the church. These contacts encouraged not only the growth of private collections but also the diffusion of printed texts regarding the habits, customs and the architecture of China, often accompanied by engravings which were to provide the main source of inspiration for ornamentalists in the 18th century.

Following his overview, Morena briefly describes the diffusion of the style throughout Europe before proceeding to analyse the many forms that chinoiserie took in 18th-century Italy. Hugh Honour's publication had already made available a considerable amount of information; Morena makes a further contribution by describing more fully the dense web of cultural and artistic exchanges that took place the 1700s, a century during which the travels of a discerning nobility and scholars, and the increasing publication of printed texts with richly illustrated repertories gave rise to a vibrant flow of ideas and stimuli.

With the development of the *rocaille* style which developed at the French court, chinoiserie flourished into an international fashion, quickly evolving from simply a decoration on furnishings to emerge in the fields of painting and architecture. Even the natural landscape was affected, with the creation in England of gardens where the sedate and regular Renaissance style of layout gave way to a less inhibited planting arrangement. Indeed, within the parks of the 1700s complete buildings appeared emulating Chinese architecture, both with their decorative style and their pavilion-like structure. As Andreina Griseri has noted, it was during this period that the Italian courts tended to abandon the pompous baroque style of interior decoration with its stuccos and allegorical paintings. The solemn magnificence of the "animated metaphor" now surrendered to the imagination, to delicate, spontaneously meandering decorations, to a liberal interpretation of the gods and their passions, to fabulous tales of far-flung worlds whose traditions, as in the case of China, were recreated in styles of fashion, entertainment and architecture. From now on every palace had to have at least one room decorated with chinoiserie and every garden worthy of note had to have a building, bridge or ice house modelled on the architecture of China. Items of oriental art, previously displayed in *Wunderkammern* as fine rarities, now became part of everyday life, appearing in the inlay of wood panelling, as used by Juvarra in Piedmont, or mounted on gilded bronze. Craftsmen and decorators hastened to copy their whimsical forms and succeeded in creating many extraordinary items, the products of unbridled fantasy, an imagination freed of all stylistic restrictions. An unruly and carefree style took over; lines had become sinuous, leaping and darting in a flow which pauses only to be resumed again with even greater vivacity. The rules of composition based on the study of classicism were replaced by the creative inspiration of artists who sought to satisfy the fickle and often bizarre requests of their patrons at court, closely followed by those of the aristocracy who were all too anxious to keep up to date. In vogue throughout most of the 18th century, the paintings, gilded stucco and inlaid furnishings of these exotic interiors combined to create a "sublime artifice" which still today provokes in us the delightful sensation of being whirled from one wonder to another in a fabulous Far East where the distinction between reality and illusion vanishes amidst the playfully ambiguous images reflected in the mirrors.

Although Rococo was the style best suited to interpreting Chinese art, the fashion for creating rooms decorated with chinoiserie did not disappear altogether during the neoclassical period. Now, however, their conception was more structured and thus more faithful to the descriptions of architecture and decoration provided by foreign travellers. At the close of the 18th century this lively period of European chinoiserie began to fade and in the early 1800s exponents of the Empire style were more interested in rediscovering ancient Egypt's esoteric magnificence. During the Restoration an ephemeral revival of a 'neo-rococo' chinoiserie was soon superseded first by ornamentation deriving from the Arab world and later – towards the end of the century – by the fashion for Japanese art.

Concentrating his study on the 18th century, Francesco Morena has been able to fully analyse the many different forms of chinoiserie in Italy, presenting not only the most important interiors still in existence in the former royal palaces, but also the entire and vast range of furnishings – lacquer, porcelain, majolica, glass and fabrics – which Europe's sovereigns and scholarly collectors competed to acquire. It was no easy task to reconstruct a history of chinoiserie in Italy following the authoritative studies already mentioned, but Morena has cast light on the complex course of events during the 1700s, and the detailed overview of the situation in Italy which he provides in these richly documented pages represents an important contribution to the subject. Based on a profound knowledge of the literature, he has succeeded in providing a synthesis of the Italian scene, at the same time describing the evolution of a style that profoundly influenced society during the Age of the Enlightenment.

Enrico Colle

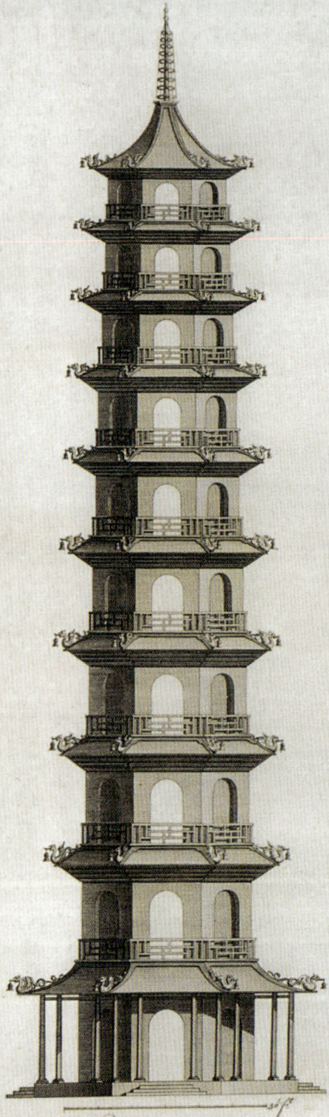

Elevation of The Great Pagoda as first Intended

Introduction

The study of art history can produce moments of intense pleasure. It is a wonderful experience to be able to hold an antique and it is just as exciting to discover its history and that of its former owners. Reading an art book is not simply educational but can be as gripping as a novel or as captivating as a more general work. The art book combines a range of factors – the specific subject, the style and approach, the illustrations – that capture the attention and stimulate thought as well as the imagination. An interaction is established with the author as one enjoys the literary style and the ability to reveal genuinely intriguing art-historical connections.

When I read *Chinoiserie. The Vision of Cathay* by Hugh Honour (1961) for the first time, as a university student, I immediately felt I had made a discovery which would influence the rest of my life. I was struck by the breadth of culture underlying the author's development of the subject, sweeping across history from Marco Polo to the 20th century and involving the most diverse geographical regions. At the same time, connections between disciplines that appear to be unrelated were revealed. The visual and the applied arts, theatre, literature, politics, economics: considered together these all contribute to creating the 'style' of society in a given period.

What also impressed me in Honour's work was the desire to create a 'bridge', a gateway between Europe and Asia, especially the most distant horizons where China and Japan are located. Despite claiming in the preface that "My book is intended for those who, like myself, have a nodding acquaintance with Chinese art", Honour went on to clarify some specific aspects of Far Eastern art and culture, especially the predominant role that they played in the development of an 'exotic' style in Europe. He described the adventures of European travellers who visited China in the 12th and 13th centuries and the arrival in the "Old Continent" of the first objects from the Far East; he presented a group of items made in the 16th and 17th centuries which exemplify the interpretation of exotic motifs in the West, and then proceeded to discuss the main argument of his study. He identified a 'baroque', a 'rococo' and lastly a 'neoclassical' chinoiserie. In the mid 1800s a Japanese style gained in popularity and in many ways was quite different from chinoiserie as it developed in a period when scientific progress had radically reduced distances both geographically and culturally between continents. The three subdivisions formulated by Hugh Honour thus suggested that chinoiserie as a stylistic phenomenon succeeded in adapting to a series of artistic periods as they developed over time, despite their quite evident

William Chambers, *The Pagoda in Kew Gardens*, London 1763 (see Fig. 78).

differences in style. He explained perfectly the versatility of chinoiserie, defining it as "the manifestation of the European vision of Cathay". It was not therefore an artistic style, but rather the transposition in visible form of an interest that had always fired the European imagination: distant, mysterious lands, the physical and cultural diversity and the artistic achievements of other peoples.

Anyone reading this book will immediately be aware of the debt I owe to Hugh Honour's study, read and re-read on many occasions, especially when I decided that my main areas of interest and specialization were the history of collecting *orientalia* in Italy and the study of Far Eastern antiques in particular. Before its publication in 1961, several general studies on international chinoiserie had appeared (Belevitch-Stankevitch 1910; Cordier 1910; Paris 1911), but Honour's book was a turning point for the subject to which all subsequent studies made reference, though each had its own particular approach (Impey 1977; Jarry 1981; Jacobson 1993; Paris 2007; Brighton 2008).

Honour's book and the other studies mentioned tend to suggest that Italian chinoiserie played a modest role, especially compared to development of the style in France, England, Holland and Germany – the countries where the style came into being before spreading elsewhere and assuming 'pan-European' characteristics. This is only partly true and to provide a context it seemed useful to introduce the chapters on Italian chinoiserie in the 1800s with a preliminary *résumé* of chinoiserie in Europe. Indeed, the research undertaken has confirmed that the style developed autonomously in Italy too, and was of considerable art-historical importance. Firstly, though in this case we are dealing with a 'taste for the exotic' rather than chinoiserie itself, it is not incorrect to state that the earliest experiments for applying oriental motifs to items produced in the west took place in Italy: on silk fabrics in the 14th century, majolica, milk glass and lacquer work in the 16th century. This tradition certainly influenced developments during the 1600s, 1700s and 1800s and mingled with initiatives from other countries where in the meantime 'China-mania' and chinoiserie had become all the rage. This combination of older indigenous elements – easily distinguishable among the various courts – and those more recently introduced from abroad may also explain why chinoiserie in Italy assumes regional aspects reflecting the political and geographical divisions of the country. Consequently chinoiserie in Italy during the 18th century is analysed according to the various states then existing in the peninsula, each of which had its own characteristics despite continual artistic contacts and exchanges. Indeed, this historical and geographic fragmentation of Italian chinoiserie is easily deduced from a review of the literature relevant to the subject and consulted in writing this volume: general studies have been published by Giuseppe Morazzoni, Alvar González-Palacios and Enrico Colle; Giuliana Ericani has written on the Veneto; for Piedmont a book has recently been published by Lucia Caterina and Cristina

Mossetti; the Kingdom of Naples is the subject of a work by Elio Catello; Hapsburg Lombardy is discussed in Paola Venturelli's study, while numerous other texts (see the *Bibliography* at the end of this volume) refer to chinoiserie in passing, within the context of other subjects and issues. In brief, it could be said that elements of the oriental style can be found in Italian artistic production in all regions and at all times. I have therefore limited myself to describing only part of the immense heritage that exists in Italy in the hope that a general, but clear and consistent picture has emerged, leaving room for further more specialized research.

I would like to thank Hugh Honour for having invited me to his home. Despite my nervousness we were able to discuss some aspects of Italian chinoiserie. I am deeply grateful to Enrico Colle who generously provided invaluable help and advice during the various stages of my research. His knowledge and skill were fundamental in planning the text as well as in resolving some more specific problems.
I would also like to thank Alessandra and Ginevra Marchi who believed in the publication from the beginning, encouraging me to complete it and offering their support and experience. Manola Miniati and Alberto Bartolomeo of Centro Di have provided professional and generous assistance during production of the publication.
My sincere thanks to Lucia Caterina who had the patience to read the text and alert me to some defects before going to print. Any errors that remain are purely my responsibility.
I am grateful to the director and all the staff at the Kunsthistorisches Institut in Florence where I carried out most of the bibliographical research.
Lastly, my thanks to the many friends and colleagues who have contributed in different ways to ensuring that the publication saw the light of day: Luisa Ambrosio, Nicoletta Baldini, Giuseppe Bertini, Ornella Casazza, Stefano Casciu, Marco and Françoise Chiarini, Silvia Ciappi, Daniela Di Castro, Riccardo Gennaioli, Donatella Germanò, Valeria Giubilato, Stefania Glori, Angela Guerra, Marco Lattanzi, Libreria del Porcellino, Anna Lo Bianco, Maria Rosaria Mancino, Linda Martino, Barbara, Ismael and Linda Morena, Rosanna Muzzi, Serena Padovani, Rita Pastorelli, Filippo Pedrocco, Patrizia Piergiovanni, Annalisa Porzio, Vladimiro Rusca, Maurizio Sammartini, Chiara Squarcina, Cecilia Spetia, Camillo Tonini, Silvio Varando.

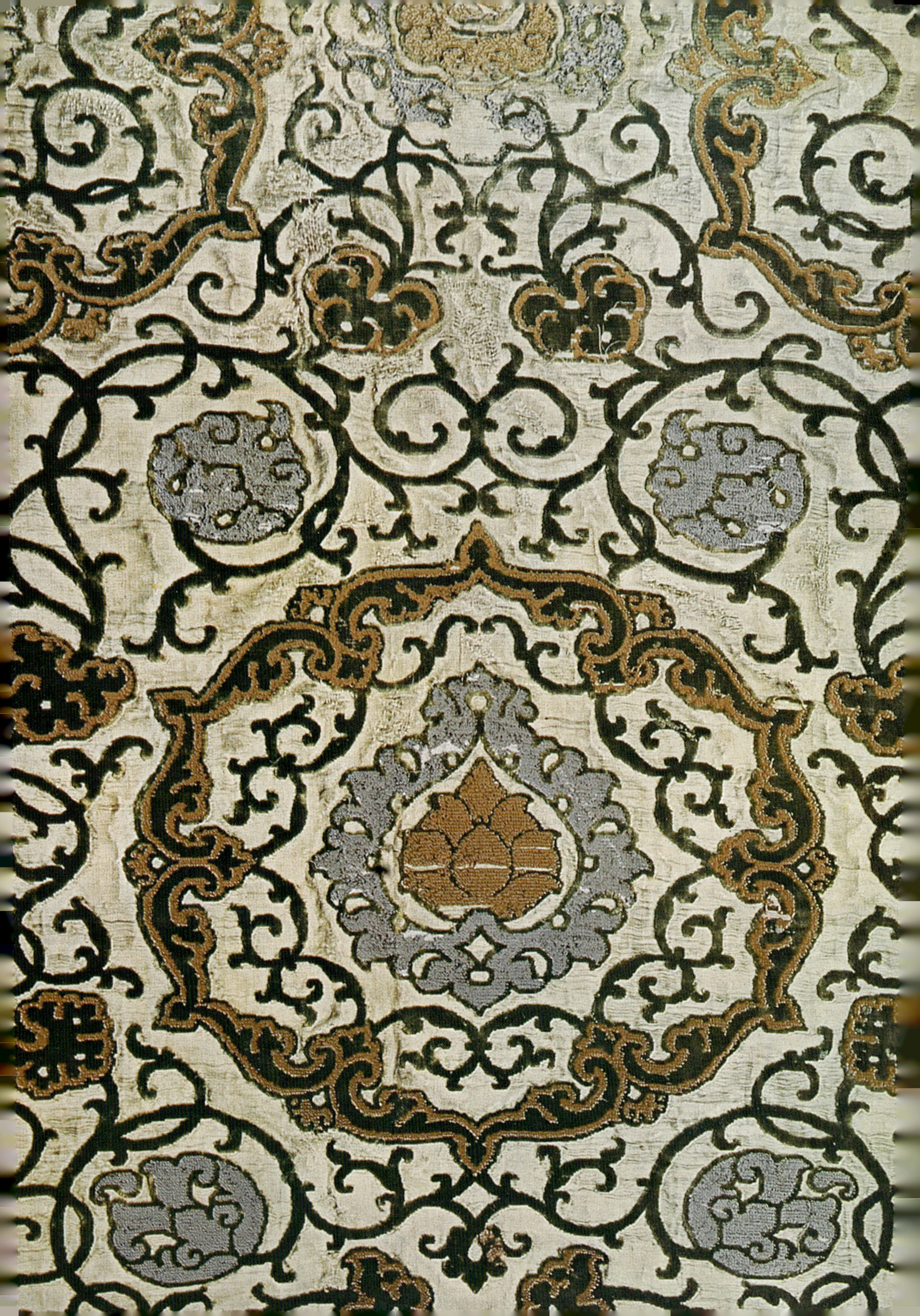

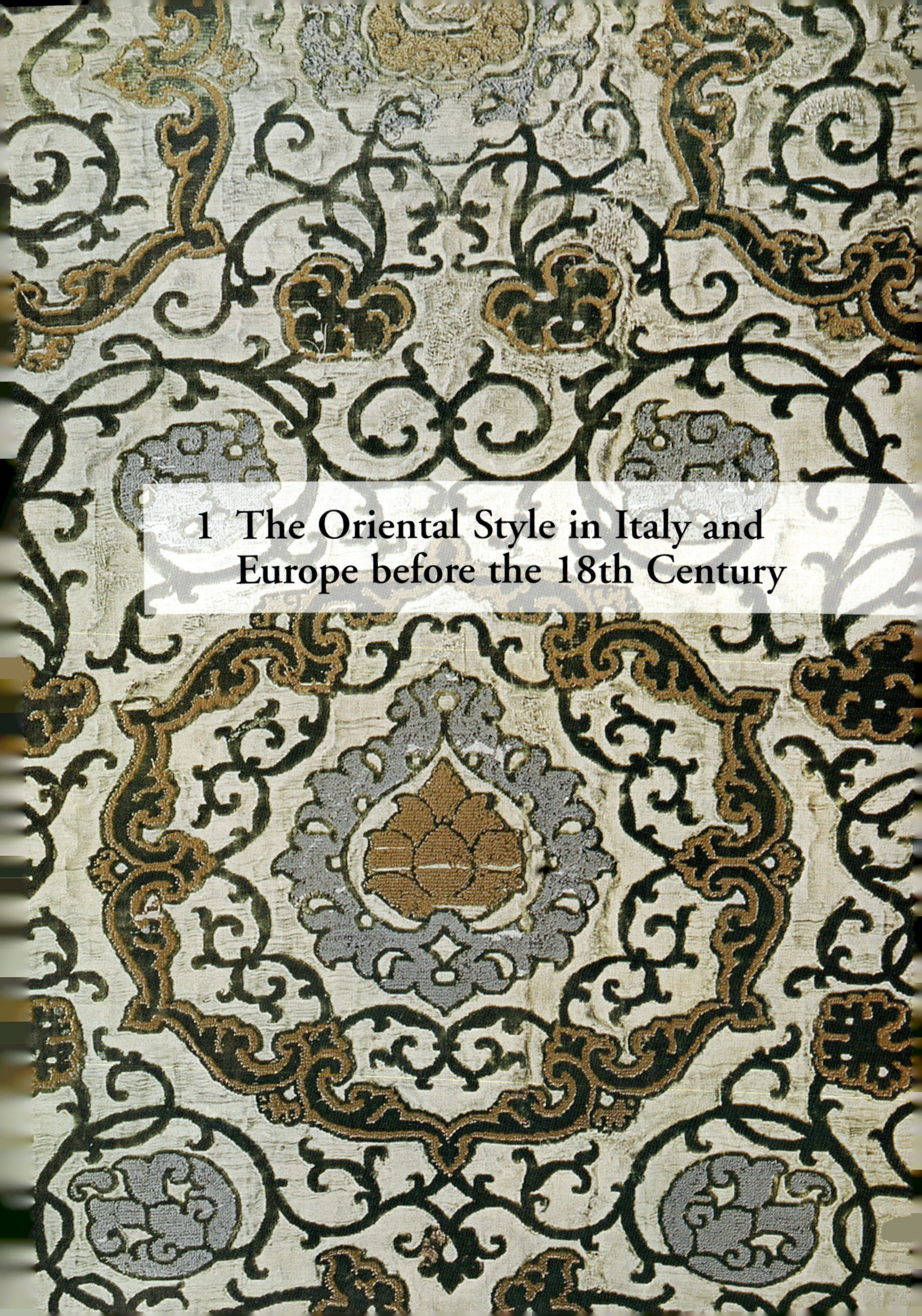

1 The Oriental Style in Italy and Europe before the 18th Century

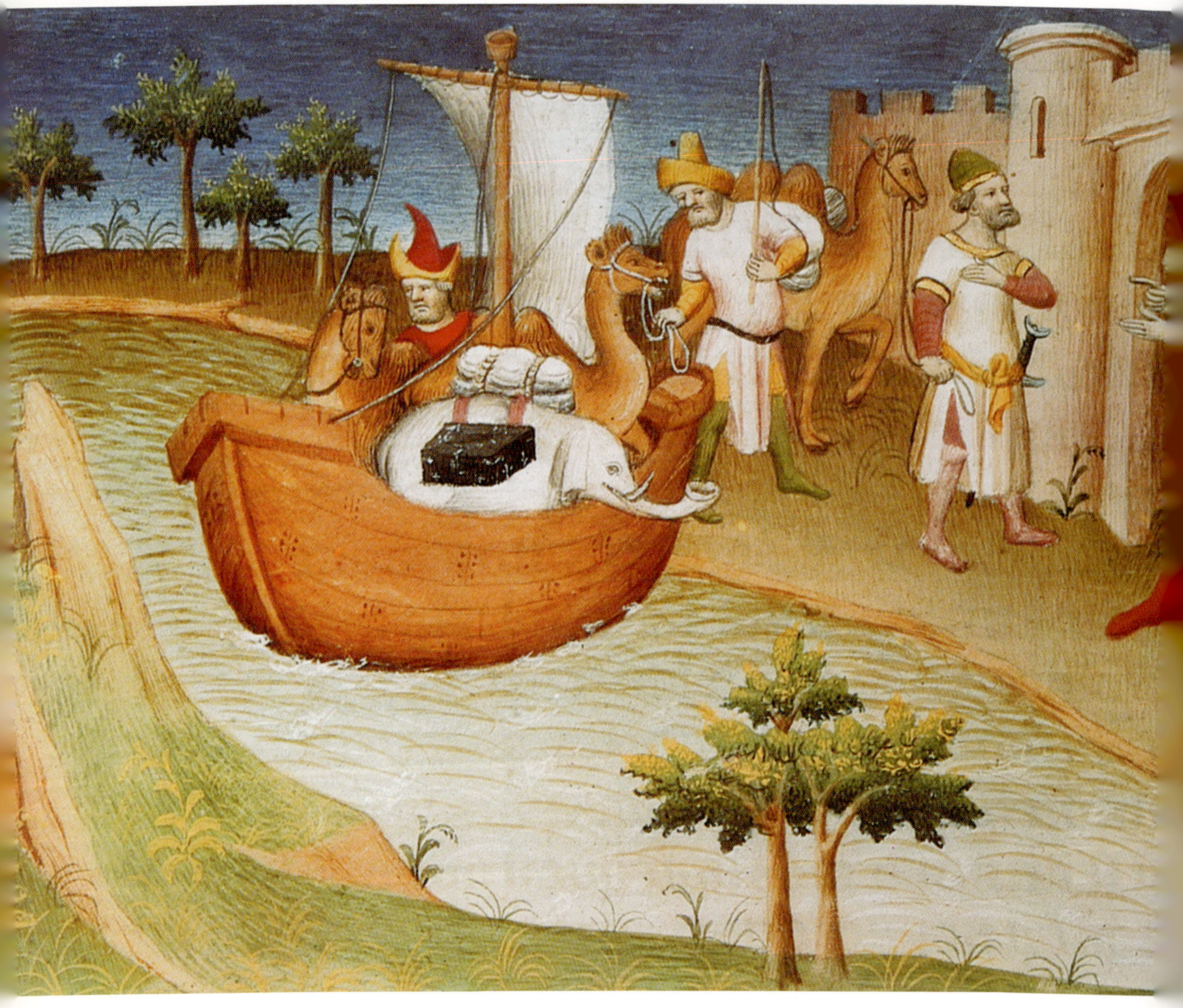

1. *The Arrival of Marco Polo at the Court of Genghis Khan,* miniature in the *Livres des Merveilles*, early 15th century. Paris, Bibliothèque Nationale.

This magnificent miniature appears in what must be the most luxurious edition ever produced of Marco Polo's *Travels* (*Il Milione*). The manuscript in the National Library, Paris (inv. ms. fr. 2810), belonged to Jean du Berry, the younger son of Charles V, king of France, and contains eighty-four miniatures illustrating the most important events during the sojourn of the Venetian traveller in China. With no visual source for an oriental subject available to them, the anonymous artists based themselves entirely on Marco Polo's descriptions.

Visions of the Orient from Antiquity to the 15th Century

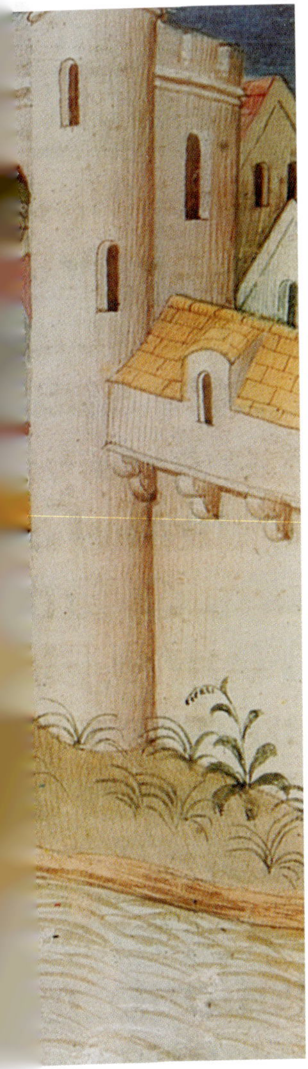

The Roman Empire and China under the Han Dynasty

The first contacts between China and the peoples of Europe took place several centuries before the beginnings of Christianity. Although some western travellers had succeeded in venturing as far afield as the regions of upper Indus before the expeditions of Alexander the Great (356-232 BC) between 326 and 324 BC, the development of real commercial and cultural contact between these two immense territories only became possible with the advent of more stable political conditions. This occurred when the expansion of the Roman Empire in the West coincided with the formation of the Han Empire in the East in 206 BC, despite the political and geographical barriers represented by the Parthians on the one hand and the arid expanses of the steppes of central Asia on the other. According to Chinese documents, a first Roman legation entered China in 166 AD when Marcus Aurelius (121-180 AD) was Emperor in Rome, while a second arrived some time between 280 and 289 AD. In both cases however, the 'delegations' were more likely to have been isolated initiatives by private merchants who thought they would be able to obtain greater economic advantages if they presented themselves as envoys from the glorious Empire in the west. On the other hand, according to information provided by the orator Florius at the end of the first century AD, it seems that Chinese envoys arrived in Rome at the time of Augustus, though this is not confirmed by any other source either Roman or Chinese. What is certain, however, is that in 97 AD the army official, Gan Ying, was sent to take charge of various military operations in central Asia. The opportunity to make formal contact with the Roman Empire could well have arisen at the time, but the Chinese officer had no real interest in advancing such an initiative and very probably was dissuaded by the Parthians who were most unwilling that any direct contact should be established between the two powers.[1]

The Romans knew China by the name of *Seres,* a word that originally referred to the Chinese product most sought after in the West – silk. Known in the East ever since the second millennium BC, this precious Chinese textile was highly prized by the Romans who were prepared to spend absolute fortunes to own some. Large amounts of Roman money were used to obtain the rare fabric, quite infuriating Pliny the Elder (23-after 79 AD) who reprimanded his spendthrift fellow citizens in his *Naturalis Historia* (XII, 84) "At the very lowest computation, India, the Seres, and the Arabian Peninsula, withdraw from our empire one hundred millions of sesterces every year".[2] Seneca (21-65 AD) too made similar comments in his *De beneficiis* during the same period.[3] Chinese silk had arrived in Rome during the first century BC under the Empire and trade continued to increase and flourish, always to the economic advantage of the Parthians who acted as intermediaries. It is unlikely, on the other hand, that western goods reached Chinese markets given that, as Pliny again records, "They shun all intercourse with the rest of mankind and await the approach of those who wish to traffic with them" (*Naturalis Historia:* VI, 88). Other sources from the Roman period provide many comments on the 'Seres', and despite their brevity, these accounts continued to feed the myth of a far country located on the edge of the known world where people of different customs, traditions and physical appearance lived. In the 3rd century AD, with the dissolution of the Han Empire and the progressive decline of the Roman Empire, the conditions that would have lead to an eventual historic meeting no longer existed. Consequently, until at least the 13th century, the histories of Europe and of the Far East progressed in different directions.[4] There is insufficient evidence to support the theory that during the centuries in which the Roman Empire dominated in the west and the Han Dynasty in the east, there was any awareness of oriental figurative arts or that they may have influenced those of Europe, despite the discovery in Rome of Chinese objects such as the bronze vase of the Zhou period (1045-221 BC). Now in the Museum of Stockholm, the vase contained a fragment of Chinese silk[5] which the Romans most probably appreciated more for the exquisite quality of the material than its decorative aspect.

Italy and Mongol China

By 1242 the devastating armies of Ghengis Khan (1162-1227), under the command of Batu (1205-1255), *khan* of Kiptchiaq (in southern Russia) had arrived at the gates of Vienna and Split in the Balkans. The peoples of Europe were awaiting the by now inevitable head-on clash when the invincible Mongol army halted their relentless advance to return to their homelands. The Great Khan Ögödäi (1186-1241) had died and tradition held that his successor could only be chosen from amongst those who were physically present at the assembly called to elect the new leader. Thus Europe was saved from danger, but not China; between 1279 and 1368 the country had to submit to the shame of foreign domination, a humiliation that was all the more grave since the Chinese had always considered the Mongols as no better than barbarians. The new dynasty was provocatively named Yuan, "the First", and the new Emperor to be elected was Kublai Khan (1214-1294). The immense Mongol empire consisted of a series of Asian regions, all with similar administrative structures and the Chinese government established by the heirs of Ghengis Khan did have some positive aspects, at least from the cultural point of view. Boundaries between the various regions of the continent

2. Fra Mauro, Map of the World, Venice 1459 (?). Venice, Biblioteca Nazionale Marciana.

A Camaldolite monk who lived on Murano, Fra' Mauro's world map was a fundamental achievement in the history of European cartography. The main sources for this complex undertaking were the accounts of travellers, especially *Il Milione* by Marco Polo for Asia, and information provided by Portuguese seafarers for Africa. Created with the help of the famous cartographer Andrea Bianco in 1448-1449, the map in the Marciana Library would seem to be a copy made by Fra Mauro in 1459 with the help of assistants.

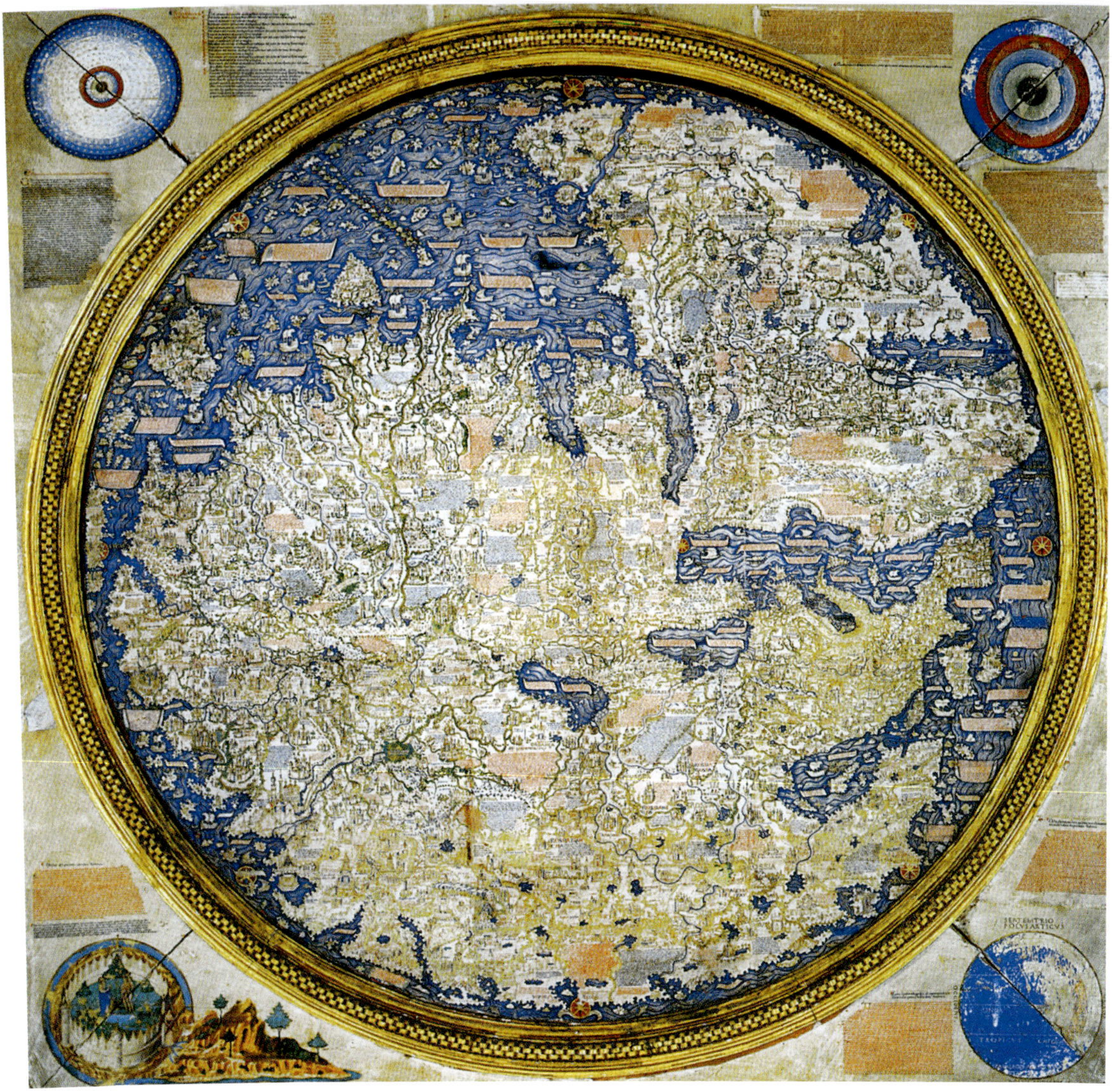

became more secure, thus protecting the safety of the increasingly numerous travellers journeying along the caravan routes crossing central Asia from China to the eastern coasts of the Mediterranean. Chinese cities, and in particular the capital Dadu, nowadays Beijing, were ready to welcome the many foreigners who began to arrive hoping to trade, but also to occupy the most important administrative offices from which the new Mongol government preferred to exclude the Chinese. Thus the *Pax mongolica* at last created the conditions that would bring about a meeting between the worlds of East and West.

Ever more frequently caravans of merchants travelled towards China to establish their businesses. From Italy in particular not only did the Genoese set forth, but in even greater numbers the Venetians who, already with active interests in the Near East, now turned their attention to ever further horizons.

The names of many of these travellers are known to us and some left written accounts of their travels.[6] The most famous is, without doubt, Marco Polo (1254-1324) who lived in China from 1275 to 1292 and on returning to Italy dictated his memoirs to Rustichello around 1298 when both were imprisoned in Genoa. Despite suspicions that his accounts are often rather fanciful, Marco Polo's book, *Il Milione* (The Travels of Marco Polo) enjoyed immense popularity as soon as it appeared. It is considered the most influential account of the customs and habits of the Chinese at the time and for many centuries provided the basis of European knowledge regarding the Far East. Despite clear omissions, obvious errors and heavy reliance on earlier literature and tales, *Il Milione* stimulated a host of travellers to take the initiative of following in his footsteps, not least Christopher Columbus (1451-1506).[7]

Other travellers had ventured along what subsequently became the Silk Road before the Venetian author and some had succeeded in reaching China. In 1245 Pope Innocent IV sent Giovanni dal Pian del Carpine (c. 1180-1252) to Karakorum in Mongolia to meet the Great Khan Güyük. The task before the Franciscan monk, representing the Vatican State and Christianity, was threefold: establish a relationship with the dreaded Tartars, prevent the risk of further attempted invasion and hopefully create an alliance against the feared Islamic peoples. He succeeded in none of these but he did produce the *Historia Mongolorum* which was to become a precious source of information regarding the habits and customs of the Mongols and other peoples under their control, including the Chinese.[8] In 1254 Louis IX of France despatched the Flemish Franciscan William de Rubruck (1220-1293) on a similar journey to meet the Grand Khan. In Karakorum Rubruck met Guillaume Boucher, a French jeweller who had gained fame at the court for his artistic inventions such as a centrepiece in the form of a fountain from which wine flowed.[9] But perhaps the first Italians to travel beyond Mongolia (where in fact Giovanni dal Pian del Carpine and William de Rubruck had stopped) and enter China around 1265-66 were the brothers Niccolò and Matteo Polo, respectively father and uncle of Marco, thus at least a decade before the more famous Venetian adventurer began his journey to the East. Giovanni da Montecorvino (1246-1328) reached Peking in 1294 after a journey of four years. An envoy of pope Nicholas IV, Giovanni translated some religious Christian texts into Chinese, made a series of converts, and on founding a church in China with the approval of Rome, was appointed archbishop of Peking. Between 1309 and 1313 he was joined by colleagues including Andrea da Perugia who was made bishop of Zayton (now Quanzhou) in 1323. In 1318 Odorico da Pordenone (1265-1331) left Italy to travel to China entirely independently, without any support from the church and without any specific commercial intent. Unlike other travellers before him, Odorico decided to take the sea route and resided in Dadu for three years from 1325 to 1328. On returning to Italy in 1330 he wrote his memoirs

entitled *Relatio*.[10] Giovanni de' Marignolli from Florence arrived in Peking around 1342, sent to China by pope Benedict XII to take responsibility for the spiritual welfare of the Mongol empire following the deaths of Giovanni da Montecorvino and Andrea da Perugia. Emperor Toghan Temür had requested the mission in a letter sent to the pope via a legation from Alanya in the Caucasus lead by Andalò da Savignone, a merchant from Genoa. Marignolle sailed for the East from Naples in 1339 in the company of the envoys who had by then toured the cities of Italy, bearing numerous gifts for the Mongol emperor sent both by the pope and by king Robert d'Anjou. While no trace is found in Chinese records of previous expeditions, Marignolli's was indeed documented, in particular the Neapolitan horse that the ambassador brought with him from Italy, which was not only portrayed by the court artist but also praised in a series of poems.[11]
Apart from these and similar accounts of journeys, during the 14th century a proliferation of purely imaginary tales set in the Far East appeared, including the *Mirabilia* by Jordan de Severac (1329) and Sir John Mandeville's *Travels* (1371). Mandeville's book in particular contributed greatly to the creation of

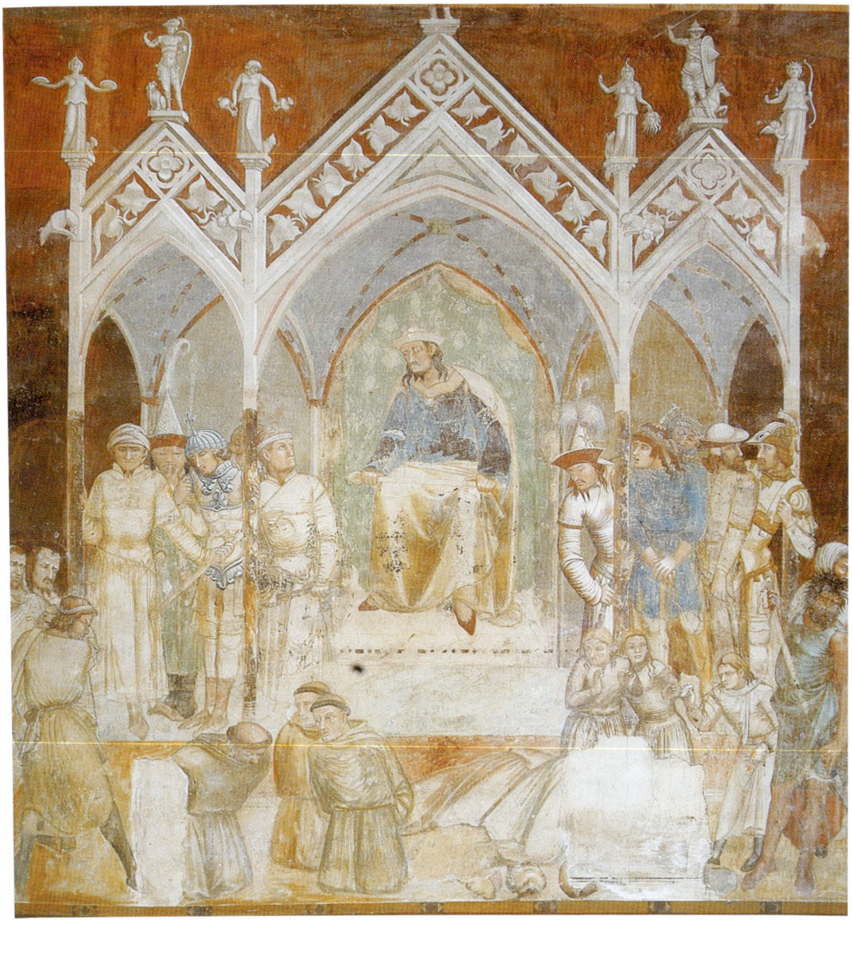

3. Ambrogio Lorenzetti, *The Martyrdom of the Franciscans at Tana*, c. 1336-1340. Siena, San Francesco Cloister.

News of the dramatic massacre of the Franciscans at Tana in 1321 was brought to Italy in 1330 by Odorico da Pordenone who had received the bodies of the monks while in India. The features, hairstyles and clothes portrayed are very similar to those of Far Eastern characters, suggesting that Lorenzetti had first-hand visual knowledge of the Mongols. The Asian features of the sultan seated in the centre of the fresco are less marked.

a fantastical vision of the mythical Cathay and relied greatly on descriptions from earlier texts which perhaps were easy for a wider public to understand.[12] Meanwhile in Italy the *Guerin meschino*, a chivalrous tale set in Asia and Africa, was written by Andrea da Barberino and appeared in Florence around 1400.[13]

While relatively large numbers of Italians and Europeans journeyed to China quite frequently, Mongols and perhaps even Chinese occasionally travelled in the opposite direction, from China to Europe. Evidence of these visitors is found in quite a significant number of paintings that include 'Mongol characters', particularly in the works of some 14th-century Italian, especially Tuscan, artists.[14] Ambrogio Lorenzetti (1290-1348) provides an example in his portrayal of the *Martyrdom of the Franciscans at Tana* in the church of San Francesco in Siena, dated around 1330, as well as Andrea da Firenze in the Spanish Chapel in Santa Maria Novella in Florence, and Altichiero in the *Martyrdom of the Saints* in St George's Oratory in Padova. Lastly, in the fresco of *St George and the Dragon* in the church of St Anastasia in Verona, Pisanello (c. 1395-c. 1455) accurately represented the severe and distinctive features of a Mongol archer – also portrayed in a drawing now in the Louvre – whom he had probably observed in the retinue of Emperor Sigismund on the occasion of his visit to Rome in 1432. The images of Mongols painted by Lorenzetti could perhaps have been based on written descriptions available at the time, such as Marco Polo's *Travels*. However, given the lifelike characterisation it is more than likely that he had actually seen and observed some Asian characters. During the papacy of Boniface VIII a Mongol mission lead by the Florentine Guiscardo de' Bastari arrived in Rome and just a year later, in 1301, a delegation from the Far East headed by Buscarello di Ghisolfi stopped in Siena on the way to the papal city. The Mongol official Kökodei and Tommaso Ugi from Siena were certainly part of this group and in 1305 Ugi was documented as a representative in Europe of the Khan of Persia, Oljäitü.[15] Lorenzetti, at the time an adolescent, perhaps had the opportunity then to study the visiting Asians at first hand, subsequently reusing the images in his fresco of the *Martyrdom*, despite the fact that the massacre was not carried out by Mongols, but by Indians.[16] The subject of Lorenzetti's fresco – the martyrdom of four Franciscan monks – required an oriental element of some kind, after all, as the event had taken place at Tana in India near today's Mumbai.[17] The Franciscans of Siena were clearly deeply affected by the death of their brothers, including a young man of the town named Pietro, and to commemorate their sacrifice, they immediately commissioned Lorenzetti to make a more detailed fresco cycle with the same subject for the cloister of the San Francesco monastery. Although these have been lost, Lorenzo Ghiberti (1378-1455) left us a full description of the paintings in his *Commentarii*.[18]

Chinese Wares in Italy in the 13th and 14th Centuries

Chinese merchandise began to arrive in Italy from the Far East with increasing frequency during the mid 13th century. Firstly ceramics, as fragments of Chinese porcelain have been discovered at a site near Lucera, in southern Italy, which existed during the rule of Frederick II, in 1223.[19] Possibly paintings and illustrated books or individual prints also arrived, as a use of space and structural composition typical of the Chinese style of painting, but unlike anything in earlier European artistic works, begins to appear. These compositional concepts can be seen in works such as Simone Martini's fresco, *Guidoriccio da Fogliano* (c. 1284-1344) in the Palazzo Comunale, Siena (originally situated approximately below the *Mappamondo* by Ambrogio Lorenzetti, now lost),[20] and on some of the details of the *Danza delle fanciulle* also by Lorenzetti (1337-1339) in the fresco representing *Gli effetti del Buon Governo in città e in campagna*, and also located in the Palazzo Comunale.[21]

However, as at the time of the Romans over one thousand years earlier, in 13th and 14th-century Europe the most desirable Chinese product was still silk. This preference is referred to, among others, by the Florentine Francesco Balducci Pegolotti, an employee of the Bardi company and director of its London branch from 1318 to 1321. In his *Pratica delle mercatura* published in 1339, he not only confirms that the land routes between the Mediterranean and Cathay had been made quite safe by the efficiency of the Mongols, but he also provides information regarding the merchandise that was easiest to sell in the East, (linen, clothes made of calf leather, tin, coral, amber, silver) and on the other hand the oriental products most requested in Italy – silk and spices in particular.[22] At the time trade in oriental fabrics was exclusively handled by the merchants of Genoa and Venice who, reluctant to deal through intermediaries in the Middle East, frequently travelled personally to China.[23] The names of some of these traders have come down to us: the Venetians, Pietro Lucalongo, in Peking in 1305, Luchetto Duodo, Franceschino and Giovanni Loredan, the latter of whom travelled to China for a Venetian company established in 1339;[24] Jacopo di Oliviero and Antonio Sarmane, who died in Peking in 1330, were from Genoa.[25] These merchants bought substantial quantities of raw silk, transported it to Europe and sold it to one of the numerous Italian factories specialised in manufacturing the fabric which the Genoese and Venetians had established in Greece, Spain and Turkey, as well as Italy.

Chinese silks were widely found in Italy and in many European countries, especially in the treasuries of several cathedrals (Danzig, Stralsund, Brandenburg, Åbo, Upsala, to name only a few).[26] Indeed the practice of wrapping relics in this precious foreign fabric turned out to be extremely useful, as consequently they were rarely handled and, saved from wear and tear, have survived to the present day in a good state of conservation and generally undamaged. Scholars may not all agree that the silk funerary clothing found in Verona in the sarcophagus of Cangrande della Scala (who died in 1329) is of Chinese or central Asian origin, probably having been imported to Venice,[27] but there is no doubt about the vestments that belonged to pope Benedict XI (1240-1304, elected pope in 1303). Dating from the late 13th century the silk garment is now preserved in the sacristy of the church of San Domenico in Perugia as a dalmatic,[28] while a fragment is also in the Metropolitan Museum of Art in New York. [29] The dalmatic is a combination of fabrics and was probably made in Rome. Images of the apostles are arranged in the centre, surrounded by broad strips of Chinese silk decorated with designs of birds, leopards and curling leaves which form a dense pattern, a traditional motif characteristic of the Mongol-Chinese period. The stoles were made in Lucca based on a Far Eastern design.[30] How and when this Chinese silk arrived in the Vatican is not documented though some inventory records of the day provide positive evidence that similar items did exist in the Holy See: "Item, listam de panno tartarico et aurum cum duobus leonibus de argento" (inventory of the possessions of Boniface VIII dated 1295); "Item, unum pannum tartaricum pro cortina indicum laboratum ad campassum factos ad modum pinarum; et in quolibet comparsu sunt vites et folia, et due aves sine dracones" (inventory of the possessions of Clement VIII dated 1311).[31] The floral pattern decorating the fabric of Benedict XI's liturgical vestments is found repeated on numerous other Chinese silks in Europe from the 14th century on. Interestingly it also appears on the clothing of the angel on the left

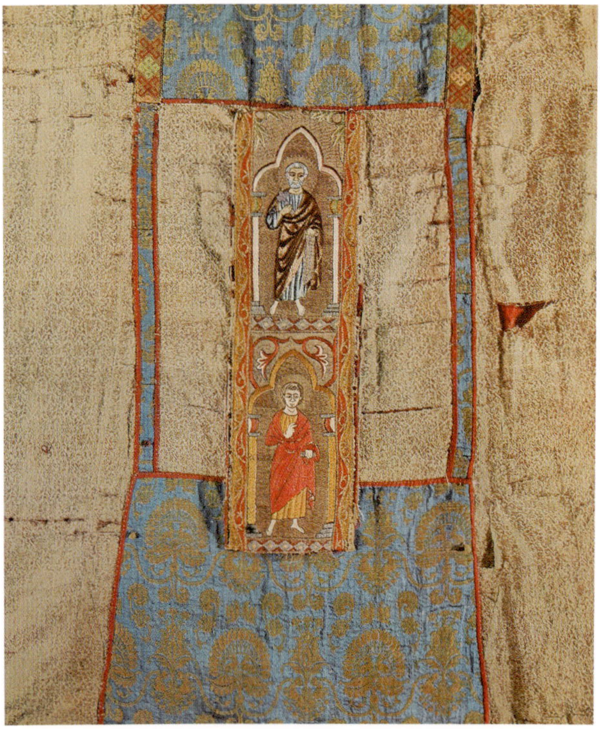

4. Dalmatic, late 13th century, detail. Perugia, Church of San Domenico, sacristy.

The vestment is partly composed of pieces of Chinese silk which arrived in Europe with other Far Eastern fabrics in the late 13th and early 14th centuries, at the height of the expansion of the Mongol Empire. Often, as in this case, oriental goods were sent to the West as gifts for important members of the European aristocracy. The popes too appreciated these rare fabrics which are documented in the Vatican as early as the 13th century.

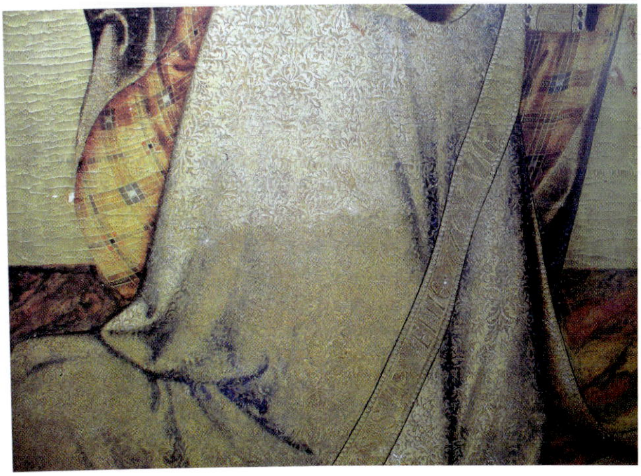

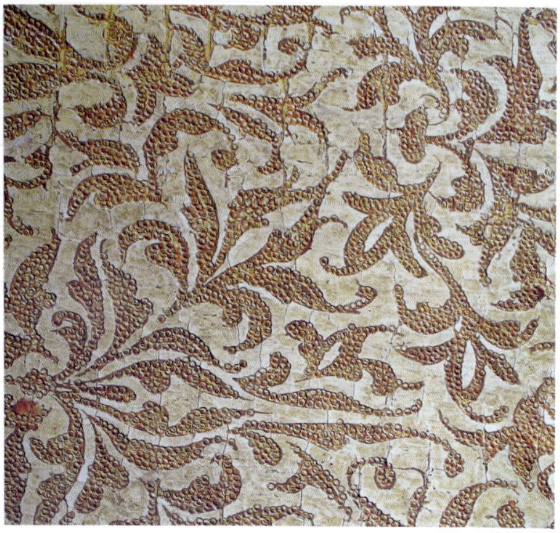

5a,b. Simone Martini, *Annunciation*, 1333. Detail of the angel's clothing. Florence, Uffizi Gallery.

Active in the late Middle Ages, Simone Martini's works reveal his fondness for elegant Chinese silks. Moreover, the rich colours of his paintings were ideal for illustrating the sophisticated patterns of fabrics originating from the Mongol Empire.

side of the *Annunciation* painted by Simone Martini in 1333 (Florence, Uffizi Gallery). One of the most important artists representing the European high gothic style in Italy, Martini was also one of the most enthusiastic admirers of the Chinese exoticism which had gained such great popularity in 13th and 14th century Europe.[32] In fact Italian painting of this period often reproduced original oriental patterns, providing an inexhaustible source of information regarding the types of fabric then in fashion, whether made in China or in Italy.[33] Simone Martini also used motifs of clearly Chinese origin for details of the vestments and accessories that appear in the painting of *St Louis of Toulouse*, now in the Capodimonte Museum in Naples. Active during the first half of the 14th century, Paolo Veneziano too had certainly seen many of the oriental fabrics which appear in the clothing of religious figures in his works, painted with great mastery and sophistication.[34] Followed by other Italian artists of the 14th century, Giotto (1267-1337) made use of *phags-pa* inscriptions on the clothes worn by some of the figures frescoed in the Scrovegni Chapel in Padova in 1304-1306. So precise and clear is the writing that there can be no doubt the great artist had some direct knowledge of this Asiatic script, which Kublai Khan had made obligatory for use in drafting official documents.[35]

Silk

For over two thousand years, until at least the 6th century AD, the art of making silk was a technical and cultural achievement known exclusively to the Chinese. Procopius (c. 500-c. 565 AD) in *De Bello Gothico* recounts that in 555 a group of monks arrived in Byzantium from India and presented the emperor Justinian with a gift of mulberry silk worms, urging him to establish production of the fabric in the West.[36] Some centuries later, in the mid 12th century, the necessary skills and knowledge for its manufacture travelled from Byzantium to Italy, or rather to Sicily which had been ruled by the Normans since 1072, though centuries of close contact with the world of Islam had ensured a strong and enduring Arabian influence. Even before several professional silk workers had migrated from Corinth to Palermo in 1146,[37] the Sicilians had been capable of producing artistic textile masterpieces such as the cloak for the coronation of Ruggero II (1095-1154) in 1133 (Kunsthistorisches Museum, Vienna).[38] However, no Chinese motifs appear on the fabrics produced in Palermo. At the time when textile manufacture was flourishing in Palermo the Mongols had not yet vanquished the Chinese territories, leading to the opening of commercial routes across the Asian continent, and the influence of Arab, Norman, Byzantine and Persian decorative repertories was, in any case, so strong that they continued to dominate Sicily's repertory of designs. However, eastern elements did appear, such as a group of natural motifs and a bestiary which was found throughout the entire immense Asian continent, and were indeed the harbinger of later, more Chinese, subjects. In addition, before finally arriving in Europe, various cultural elements that had their origins in China generally underwent various degrees of filter simply by passing through Central Asia and the Middle East, at least until the 17th century. Original Chinese works were also subject to Persian influences as, especially in the Tang period (618-907 AD), raw silks from the Far East were often sent to the Middle East where they were decorated before being sent back to China where the exotic motifs of western Asia were very popular. These continual cross currents and exchanges are just one of the reasons why it is so difficult to determine precisely how Far Eastern decorative motifs actually travelled to Europe. This is particularly true as regards Italian textile production in the 12th and 13th centuries when the style of decoration was based predominantly on parallel and symmetrical lines, the use of bands with flowing floral arabesques, and circular patterns enclosing two facing animals. This last feature, known by its original Sassanid term, *senmurv*, became highly popular in Italian textiles, perhaps as it combined harmoniously with heraldic motifs that were typical of the Romanesque style.[39]

The arrival of Chinese fabrics lead to the unprecedented use of less rigid patterns, no longer hemmed inside parallel bands, gradually abandoning symmetry and geometric arrangements for a less stylised and more naturalistic approach to both plant and animal designs.[40] The repertories of Italian craftsmen gradually began to assimilate the predominant subjects of oriental tradition including lotus flowers, pomegranates, peonies, florets linked by whirls and sprays, not to mention the phoenix, dragons, unicorns and other birds and animals, all of which were portrayed with a renewed attention to movement and fluidity. Sicily was only marginally interested in this change of style, but so intensely were the manufacturers of Lucca and Venice involved that their 14th-century production could well be defined as the first known form of chinoiserie.

Silk production in Lucca began about the middle of the 12th century when

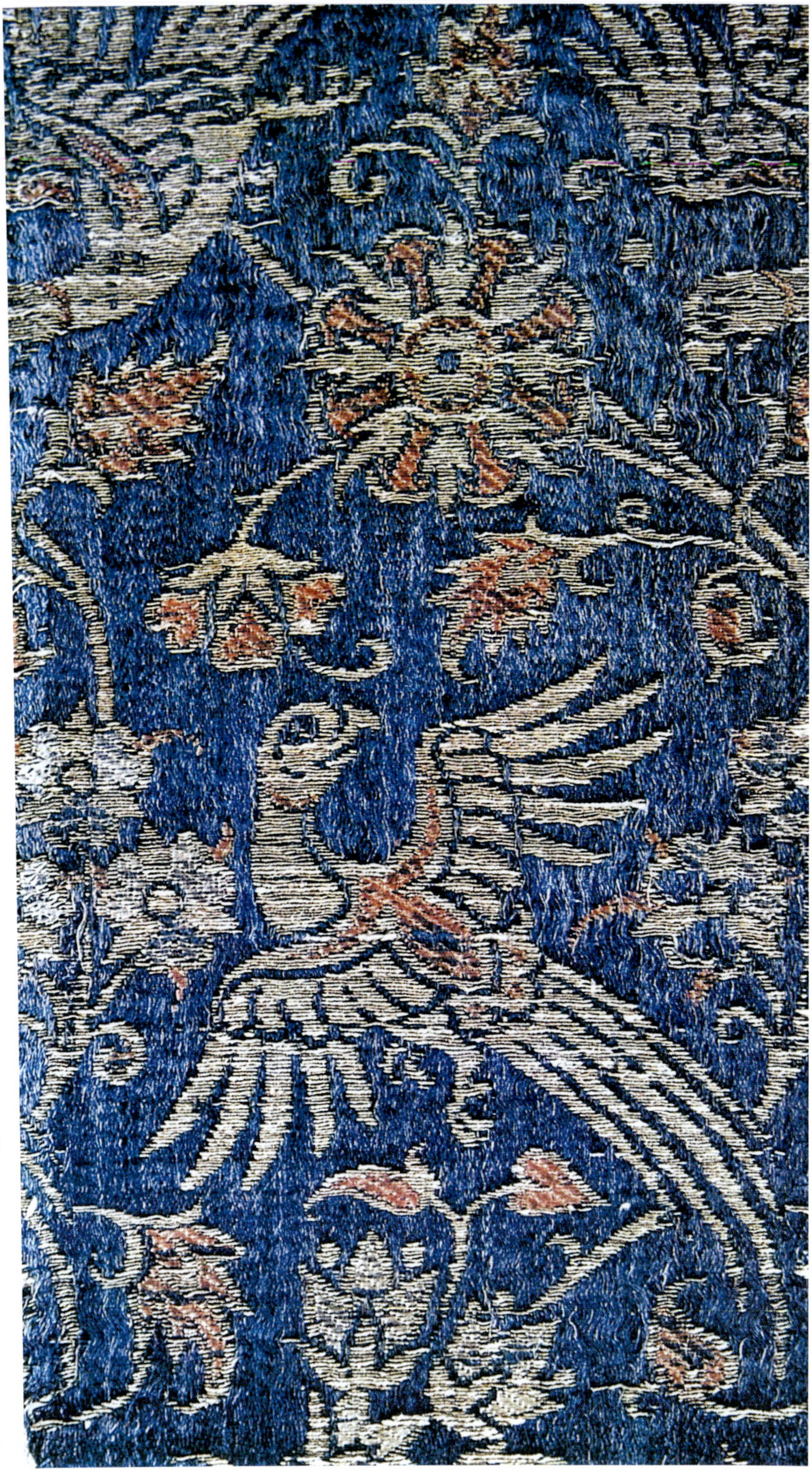

6. Fabric. Lucca, 14th century. Berlin, Kunstgewerbemuseum, Loewi Collection.

The phoenix is one of the most popular subjects in Asian art. In China this mythical bird had various symbolic meanings, often of female significance (it is the emblem of the empress, for example, while the dragon is the emperor's emblem). The motif of a bird taking flight amidst the dense foliage of lotus flowers and sprigs was used by many Italian textile factories and derived from the Chinese phoenix although probably reinterpreted by artists and craftsmen of western Asia who, as a result of their geographic proximity, more rapidly assimilated cultural developments originating in the great Celestial Empire.

Greek silk workers established the first workshops in the town. Raw silk and other necessary materials were mainly supplied from the East. As in Sicily, during the early phase of production manufacturers in Lucca made use of decorative themes derived mainly from the Byzantine and Persian repertories. As Chinese silks began to arrive in the country the ornamental repertory of Middle Eastern designs was gradually replaced by those of eastern Asia.[41] Silk production in Venice developed similarly and the close connections between the two cities were reinforced as, between 1307 and 1320, silk workers from Lucca migrated to Venice, setting up new textile workshops there, a trend that had occurred during the late 12th century in Florence and many other cities in Italy, France and England.[42] Chinese patterns, which "developed their own characteristics and could therefore be identified and recognised compared to the production of the rest of Italy",[43] were not introduced to Venice by mere accident. The city's most energetic phase of colonial and commercial expansion occurred during the 13th and 14th centuries and trade with countries to the east of the Mediterranean brought vast profits. In the inventory of the goods of Marco Soranzo made in 1371 there is a reference to textiles from 'Cathay', and in 1336 a Venetian merchant is known to have been selling Chinese silk in Montpellier.[44] Silk cocoons were mainly imported from the East, Sicily, the Abruzzi and Spain; spinning and most of the other phases of production were undertaken by skilled female employees who were trained in the art. Silks from Lucca and Venice were highly appreciated at the courts of Europe, thus contributing to the popularity and diffusion of the earliest form of chinoiserie in Italy.

7. Fabric. Venice, 15th century, first half. Prato, Museo del Tessuto.

The pomegranate motif was one of the most popular in 15th century Italy and numerous variations appeared in the following century. It was also frequently adopted as a pattern for ceramics (see Fig. 14). Although difficult to identify its precise origins, it is generally derived from one of the oldest oriental motifs. It may in fact be a stylised lotus flower, a design that was frequently used in China as a pattern to decorate silk fabrics exported to the West.

First references to a society of 'depentori' appeared during the second half of the 13th century. These 'painters' were in fact the forerunners of lacquer workers, or japanners, who worked in Venice during the 17th and 18th centuries. The *Giustichieri Vecchi*, who regulated the work of craftsmen, issued decrees in 1271 and 1283 stating that the 'depentori' could only consign their wooden items once they had been painted or varnished while items covered with leather, however, were only to be consigned three days after varnishing.[45] The order referred to almost all manufactured items, including weapons, which required greater protection. The varnish used consisted of a mixture based on sandarac, a resin which was quite different from traditional oriental lacquer, but in general both served the same purpose of protecting items from damage by external agents. There is no evidence as to whether – or how much – oriental lacquer might have influenced the early development of this Venetian trade, nor is it known if the Venetian 'depentori' were interested in the decoration of their wares in addition to its practical function. What is certain though is that Italian references to lacquering, a technique with its origins firmly rooted in the Far East, also appear in the late 13th century when European chinoiserie was beginning to develop.

During the late Middle Ages some highly unusual and rare oriental items were to be found in Europe, frequently mounted with precious or semi-precious

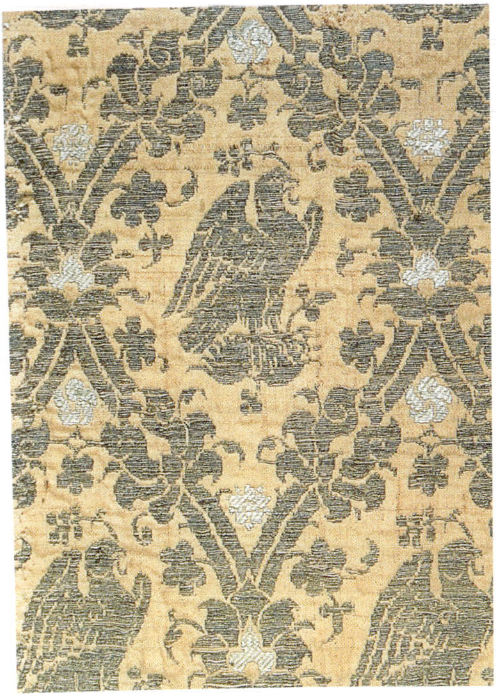

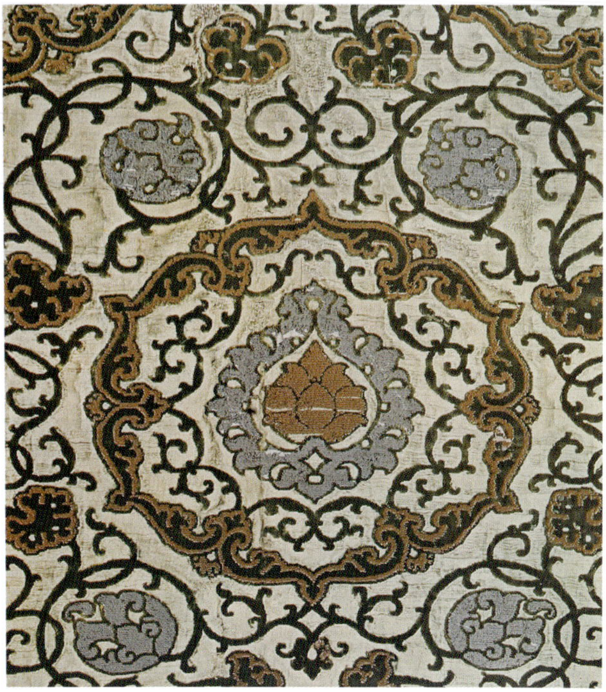

8. Fabric. Venice (?), 14th century. Lyons, Musée des Tissus.

Published on several occasions, the origin of this piece of lampas is still uncertain. Some believe it to be generically Italian, while others suggest a more specific origin (Sicily, Lucca, Venice). It undoubtedly recalls Far Eastern examples, however, especially evident in the motifs such as the lotus flower and birds, as well as the compositional style, which is less rigid compared to European designs.

9. Fabric. Florence, mid 16th century. Turin, Museo Civico.

The motif of stylised lotus flowers and entwining fronds of plants – typical of Italian 16th-century textiles – is clearly derived from Far Eastern designs, modified in Islamic countries. Eleonora di Toledo (1522-1562), duchess of Tuscany, wore a dress made from a velvet similar to this in the portrait by Agnolo Bronzino dated 1545 (Florence, Uffizi Gallery).

metals, a feature that perhaps represents a further facet of chinoiserie. Gold, silver and precious stones had been used since ancient times to shelter important Christian relics and the practice of enhancing exotic items with fine decorative mounts may be related to this tradition. Porcelain in particular, but also nautilus shells, coconuts, jade, lacquer work and other kinds of curiosities, inspired the artistry of gold and silversmiths, jewellers and watchmakers for a long time to come, reaching its height in 18th-century France.[46]

China's contribution to the evolution of European decorative arts continued during the 15th century, though compared to the previous century it was less predictable and is more difficult to trace. Without doubt, once assimilated, oriental motifs easily fitted into the western decorative repertory, integrating perfectly with existing elements. While some of their more truly exotic features may have been lost, the style became more flexible and the iconography more familiar. A prime example of this transformation and westernization of a Chinese decorative theme is the pomegranate motif, perhaps the most characteristic of Italian textile patterns from the 15th until the mid 16th century, often appearing amidst the foliage of parallel vertical rows of entwined leafy fronds. It is quite clearly a stylised evolution of the Chinese lotus flower, present in many textiles that were exported to the Middle East. A mutated ornamental motif used to decorate Italian silks, the design quite probably also influenced ceramic painters when they began to reproduce Chinese porcelain motifs in the late 15th and early 16th centuries.

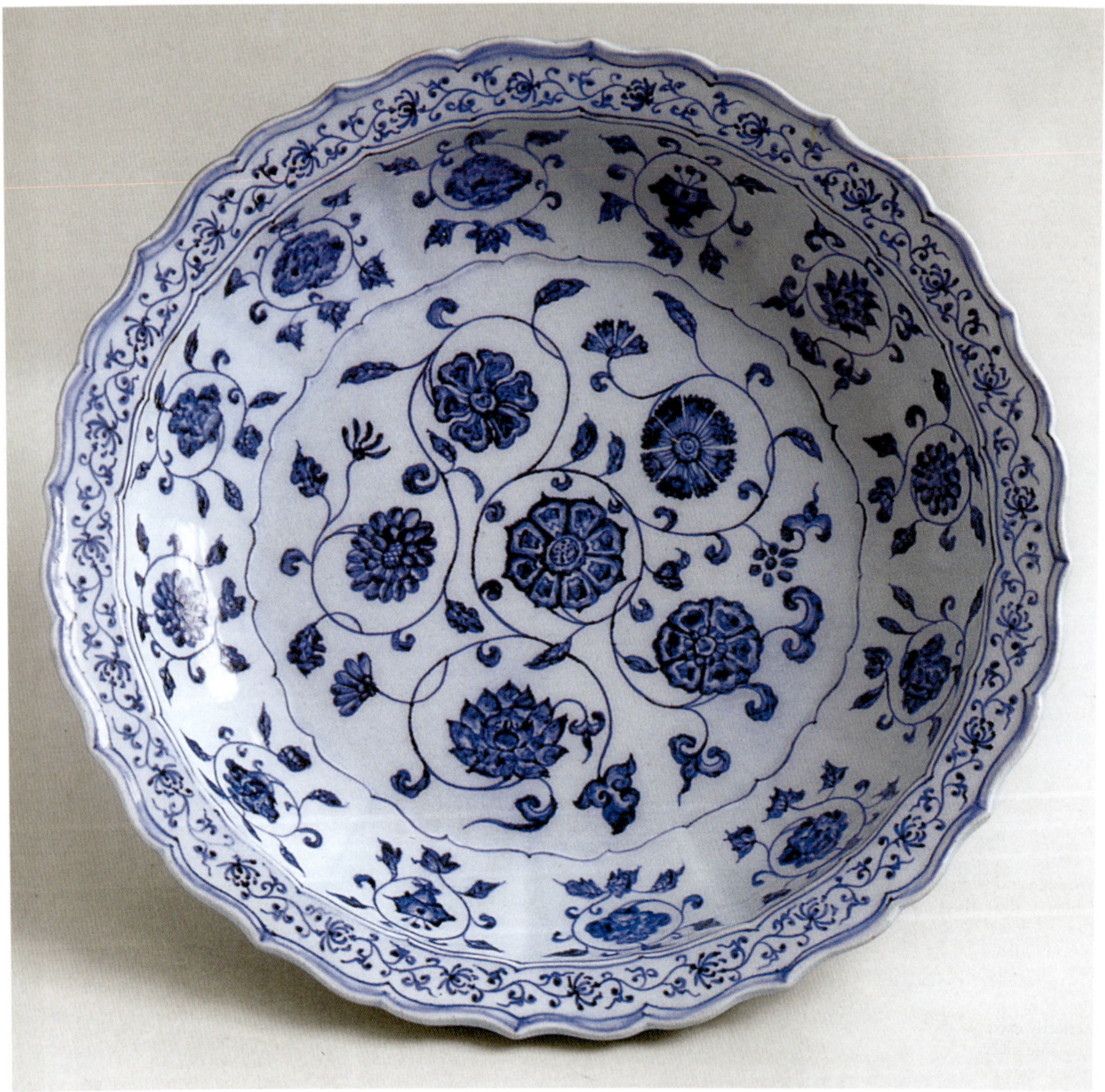

The Fashion for the Exotic in 16th-Century Italy

In 1368, after nearly a century of foreign domination, Chinese rebels succeeded in overthrowing the Mongol government and establishing the new Ming dynasty which was to reign continuously until 1644. The tolerant, liberal and cosmopolitan policies that had been introduced by the heirs of Kublai Khan were entirely reversed by the new rulers who restricted external contact with foreigners, preferring to promote only internal commercial and cultural development. Despite this, during the 15th century a reasonable amount of Chinese products continued to reach various destinations in Europe, East Africa and Western Asia, mainly through Arab merchants and traders. Direct contact between the West and countries under the influence of China recommenced at the end of the 15th century when the colonial period began. The Portuguese – undisputed masters of the Indian Ocean for the entire 16th century – were the first to establish the conditions for profitable trade between the 'East Indies' and Europe, followed by the Spanish who created the port of Manila in the Philippines, and then at the end of the century by the English and Dutch. At the same time the *conquistadores* were equally interested in the Americas, the 'Western Indies'. Many Italians travelled to the Far East in this early phase of colonialism, most often on the Portuguese ships which had been plying the routes between Europe and Asia since 1498.[47] One such was Filippo Sassetti (1540-1588) who left Lisbon in 1577 and was to die in Goa in 1588. A geographer in the service of Francesco I de' Medici (1541-1587), he sent a letter to the grand duke during his period in India, in which he recounted the technique used to make porcelain, thus helping to reveal this centuries-old 'mystery'.[48]

Apart from spices, the goods most highly prized in Europe were artistic items of all kinds. Fascinated by exotic rarities, European sovereigns sought all manner of curios including lacquer, ivory, fabrics and many other novelties. But the most desirable product was without doubt porcelain – pure, brilliant white, made of an extremely hard paste, light and tinkling, and usually decorated with arabesque floral motifs, painted in a particularly intense and brilliant cobalt blue. Only in China could this magnificent ware be found and Europeans sought their supply from the Celestial Empire. Chinese porcelain had existed in Europe previous to the 16th century and was generally imported from the Near East by enterprising Venetian merchants. Even before the collections of Ottoman and Persian sultans had been created, Lorenzo il Magnifico, for example, owned some fifty pieces which were listed in an inventory drawn up on his death in 1492.[49] The Portuguese already owned

10. Blue and white dish. China, early 15th century. Rome, Museo Nazionale d'Arte Orientale.

The principle characteristics of Chinese porcelain are perfectly exemplified in this exquisite piece: the fine and immaculate purity of the ceramic paste, the smooth glaze and the brilliance of the cobalt blue enamel used for the elegantly sinuous decoration. These were the features that enchanted Europeans, encouraging production of oriental style models in the West as early as the 16th century.

porcelain items in the early 16th century, even before they had established direct contact with Chinese merchants, most probably bought in the emporiums of Calcut in India, or perhaps given to the nobility as gifts, or acquired from Arab merchants who controlled all commerce with China at the time.

Ceramics

From a technical point of view, Italian ceramists who wished to imitate Chinese porcelain were faced with a series of apparently insurmountable problems. Firstly, the chemical composition of this oriental paste posed a complete conundrum and many, referring to the information provided by Marco Polo, believed it was not composed of a clay mixture, but rather a sort of finely ground shell. Other mysteries were the smoothness of the exterior, the absolute lack of porosity and lastly the resistance of the cobalt blue when fired. But Italian ceramists were not to be defeated and, with the means available to them at the time, attempted to resolve these problems as best as possible using a thickish layer of tin glaze on an extremely fine ceramic base. Although it was not possible to fire at the extremely high temperatures of Chinese porcelain – which produced both the vitrification of the alkaline content and the highly characteristic osmosis of the clay base, glazing and coloured pigment – nevertheless Italian cobalt blue did not loose its brilliance. The resulting majolica may therefore be considered as at least a fair surrogate of Chinese porcelain.

Italian manufacturers also attempted to imitate the motifs with which oriental pieces were decorated. About 1550 one of the plates in Cipriano Piccolpasso's (1524-1579) *I tre libri dell'arte del vasajo*,[50] illustrates the motif which he names 'alla porcellana' (porcelain style) – an arabesque of slender stems from which small, usually trilobate, leaves spring. This design could be used on any part of the majolica, although it appears mainly on the rim and the back of plates. The arabesque motif developed between the 1520s and 1550s and was used by almost all the ceramic workshops active at the time.

Venice was probably the first city to adopt this Chinese porcelain motif which then spread to other ceramic factories in north and central Italy. The development of the pattern is particularly interesting to observe on a group of plates commissioned between 1515 and 1530 by German and Venetian families from workshops in Venice.[51] Apart from the heraldic shields in the centre of all the plates, a purely Chinese-style foliate design dominates both the front and the back, delicately painted with great care and attention to the graphic detail. The undulating leafy scrolls, occasionally flowing freely, occasionally forming a chain, is only interrupted by a series of flower heads – often based on the lotus flowers or chrysanthemums painted by Chinese ceramic decorators in the 14th and 15th centuries. Many Chinese porcelain pieces were easily available for use as models in 15th-century Venice,

11. *Porcelan Tirata*, pl. 32 from *I tre libri dell'arte del vasajo* by Cipriano Piccolpasso Durantino, mid 16th century.

The plate illustrating the text on ceramic production techniques shows two variations of the 'alla porcellana' pattern. Evolution of the original Chinese model is already well advanced in this example. Although the curling volute is clearly oriental in style, the 'knot' on the right and the mannerist appearance of the plant fronds are typical features of traditional Italian decoration in the 16th century.

12. Majolica plate decorated in the 'alla porcellana' style and showing the arms of the Lamparten von Greiffenstein and Meuting families from Germany. Venice, c. 1515. Frankfurt am Main, Museum für Kunsthandwerk.

The minute plant scrolls and lotus flowers scattered around the border were inspired by Chinese blue and white porcelain. The Venetian ceramists who created this design did not copy the original model however, but chose to interpret it in a style that is closer to Renaissance tastes.

especially in the houses of nobility, including of course the Doges. The sultans of Egypt often sent such gifts to foremost citizens such as Francesco Foscarini (in 1442), Pasquale Malipiero (in 1461) and Agostino Barbarigo (in 1490).[52] Clearly the porcelain of these collections provided Giovanni Bellini (c. 1430-1516) with the models for the pieces he painted in 1514 in the *Feast of the Gods* now in the National Gallery in Washington.

In addition to Venice, other centres of ceramics in Italy made use of these Chinese porcelain patterns. Already active in the 13th century, producing goods mainly for sale in Florence and nearby towns, the workshops of Montelupo were well known in the late 15th century; their success in exporting goods to a large area that included most of the ports around the Mediterranean and Atlantic coasts continued until 1530.[53] Unlike Venetian ceramics, it is not so easy to trace the oriental inspiration for Montelupo's products decorated with 'Chinese porcelain' designs, although in general the decorative elements reflect the influence of Chinese ornamentation. The 'serrated crescent' design for example, typical of Montelupo's decoration from 1490, undoubtedly recalls contemporary Italian silks with the pomegranate motif – that stylization of the lotus flower which had evolved from its Chinese origins. The ceramists of Montelupo may not have had the opportunity to work from original Far Eastern examples, but the workers of the Cafaggiolo factory certainly did. Fragments of white Asian ceramics dating from about 1500 were found in soil layers relating to the 16th century at the Cafaggiolo kilns in the Mugello. Members of the Medici family, who originated from the area and remained strongly attached to both it and the local ceramic workshops, probably provided original models of Chinese porcelain for the workers there. Cafaggiolo's production provides firm

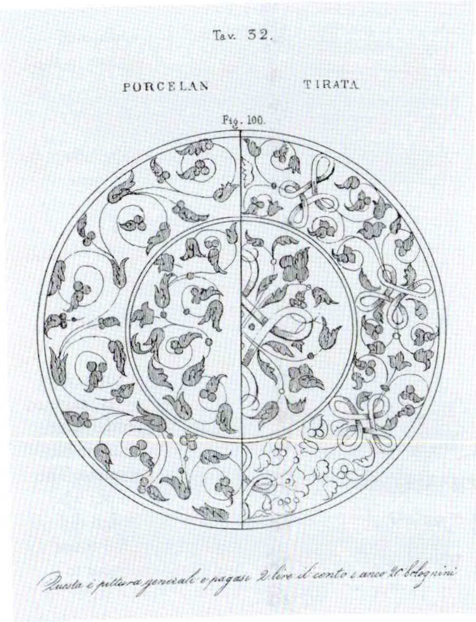

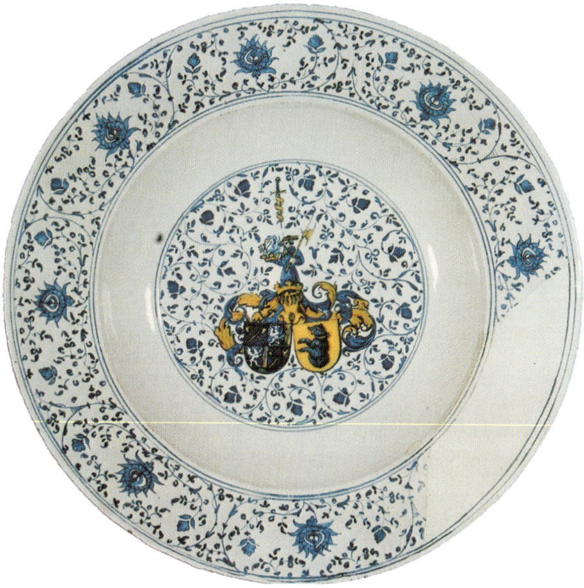

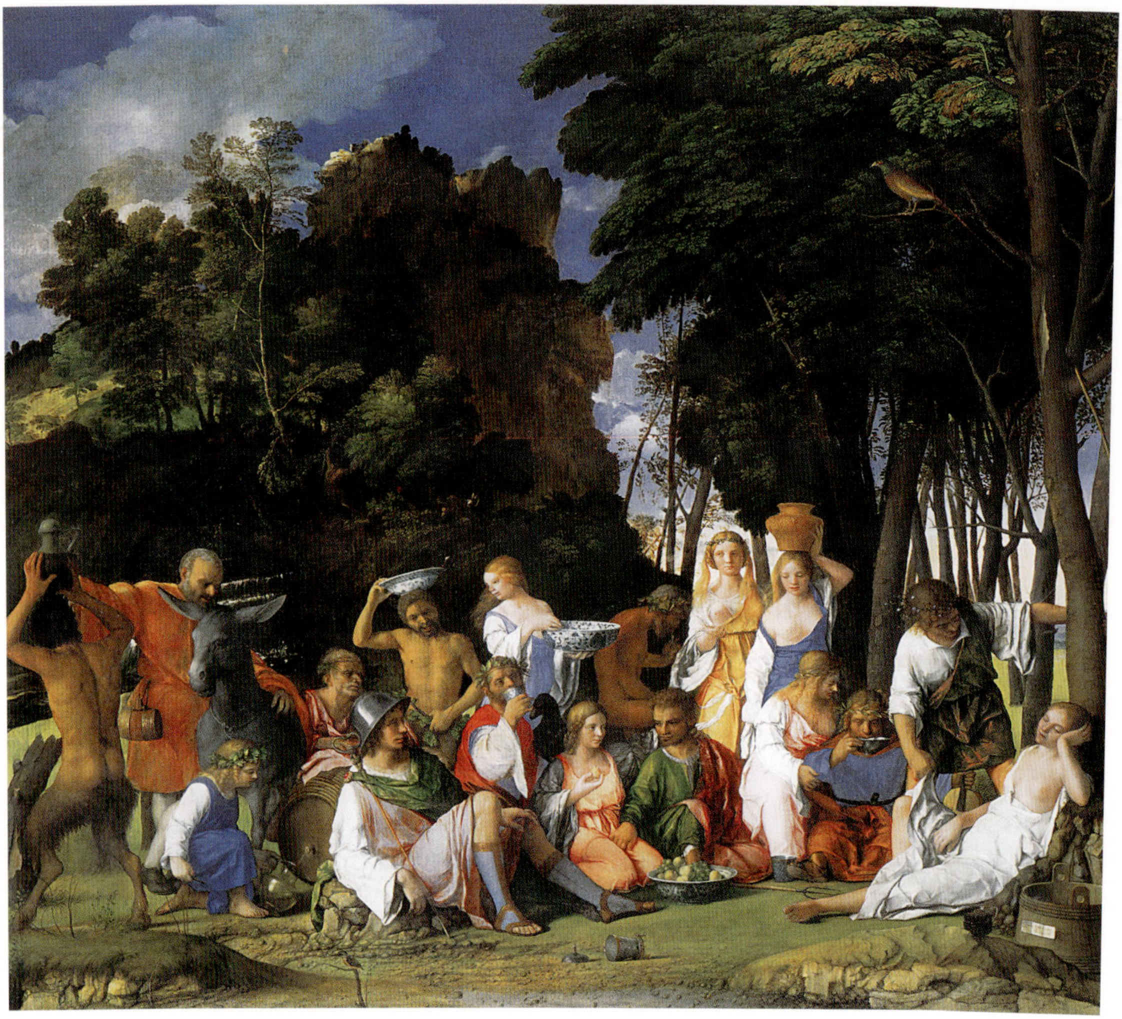

evidence of the influence of Chinese porcelain, particularly the 'alla porcellana' designs, the mesh of leafy fronds, the eight segments into which the edges of many pieces are divided and some decorative details such as the open diamonds which frequently occur in Chinese ornamentation.[54] A variant of this design developed in the workshops of Faenza, a town which was a voluntary and peaceful protectorate of Venice at this time. Faenza's production in the early decades of the 1500s clearly demonstrates a Chinese influence, especially in the floral arabesques.[55] Documents also reveal that Alberto Catani, a ceramic worker in the town of Lodi, also used Chinese motifs. Shortly before 1526 he was commissioned by Federico II Gonzaga (1500-1540), count of Mantova, to produce an entire majolica service in the 'Chinese style'.[56]

The Medici quest to produce porcelain played an important role in the history of Italian 16th-century chinoiserie. Francesco I, grand duke of

13. Giovanni Bellini (with later additions by Dosso Dossi and Titian), *The Feast of the Gods*, detail, c. 1514 (modified 1521-1522 and 1529). Washington, National Gallery of Art, Widener Collection.

The detailed precision with which Giovanni Bellini has painted the items of Chinese porcelain in this famous work reveals that he must have worked from the genuine article. In the early 16th century Venice was still an important trading centre between the Far East and Europe. Many exotic goods were acquired by the Venetians and by the courts of Europe.

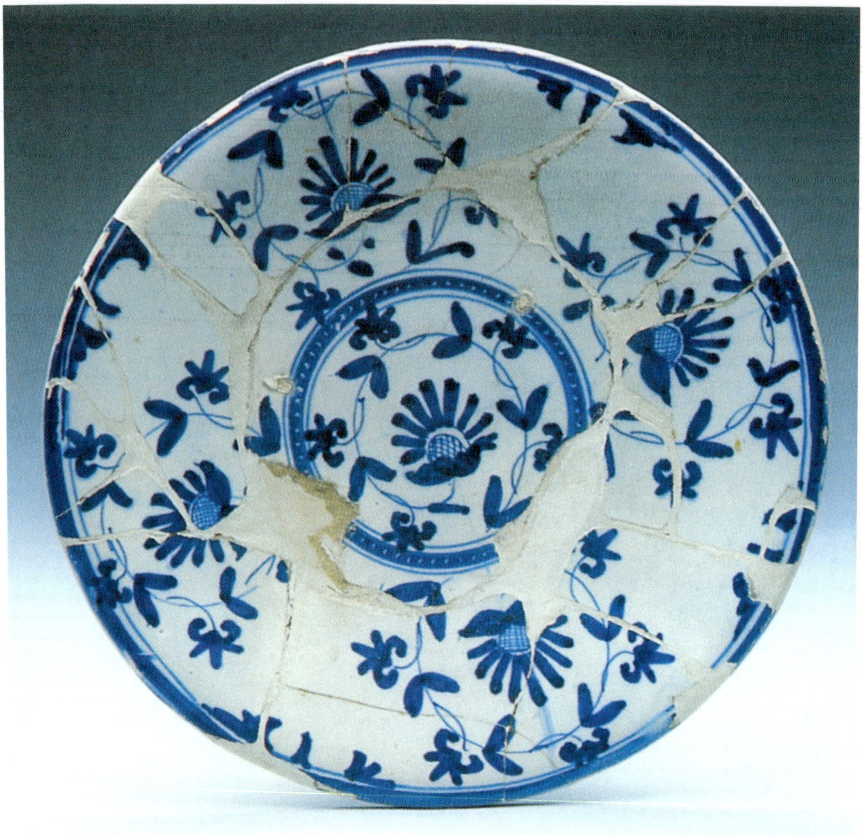

14. Majolica plate, Montelupo, c. 1510-1520. Montelupo (Florence), Museo della Ceramica.

The influence of Far Eastern decoration is combined here with similar motifs already in use in Italian textile factories in the 15th century (see Fig. 7), such as the stylised lotus flower of Chinese origin. This fan-like design was adopted by the ceramists of Montelupo towards the end of the 15th century.

Tuscany from 1574 to 1587 (though he effectively held power on behalf of his father from 1564) initiated this short-lived and much beleaguered project. The results achieved however, doubtless succeeded in satisfying Francesco's initial hopes. Like his illustrious forbears and his father Cosimo, he too was quite knowledgeable about Chinese porcelain and was the owner of a large collection. An impassioned alchemist and collector with sophisticated interests, the young grand duke created various art workshops in Florence, from semi-precious stones to jewellery, crystal and glass, as well as financing several kilns. The workshops were located in the 'Casino' in San Marco and were run by expert ceramic workers from Faenza. Their task, however, was not to produce majolica but to try to discover the secret behind porcelain which at the time, despite frenetic research in all of Europe, was still known exclusively to the Chinese. "At the time when the grand duke Francesco ruled, in his garden at the Casino ... he had summoned men skilled in all the arts ... and there were maestri who made beautiful vases of porcelain, noble vases decorated in fine and rare fashion", wrote the contemporary Agostino del Riccio.[57] Francesco was probably encouraged to further this research by the results achieved at the D'Este court in Ferrara. Here, under the patronage of Alfonso II (1533-1597), the talented team of Camillo and Battista da Urbino had succeeded in manufacturing what contemporary sources referred to as 'porcelain', though the production ceased on the death of Battista in 1574.[58] In 1568 Giorgio Vasari (1511-1574) records that Bernardo Buontalenti (1536-1608) had discovered "the way to fuse rock crystal and purify it" succeeding in "making porcelain vases that have all the perfection of the oldest and the best, and the most excellent maestro of this is now Giulio da Urbino, who is with the most illustrious Duke Alfonso II of Ferrara, and he makes wonderful things ... his porcelain being supremely elegant".[59] It is probable that Vasari mistook the names of the two artists from Urbino: addressed to Francesco I, a letter dated 25 August 1567 from Bernardo Canigiani, Florentine ambassador to Ferrara, confirms this, as he refers to

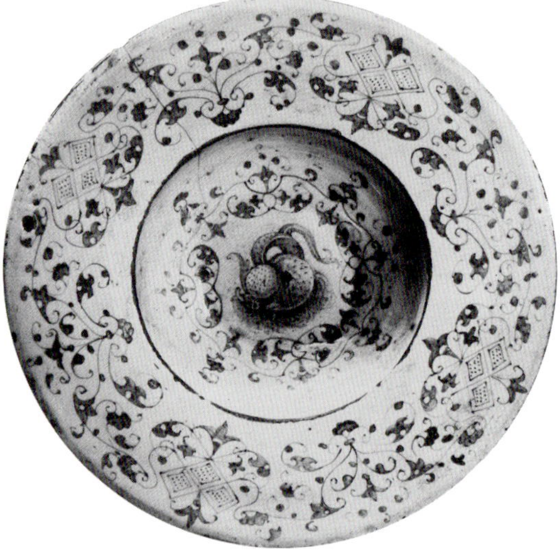

15. Majolica plate. Cafaggiolo, 16th century, first quarter. Florence, Museo Nazionale del Bargello.

Although the decoration of the central medallion is European in style, the dish also reveals Far Eastern themes in the floral arabesques around the border, divided by three losange shapes combining to form a diamond.

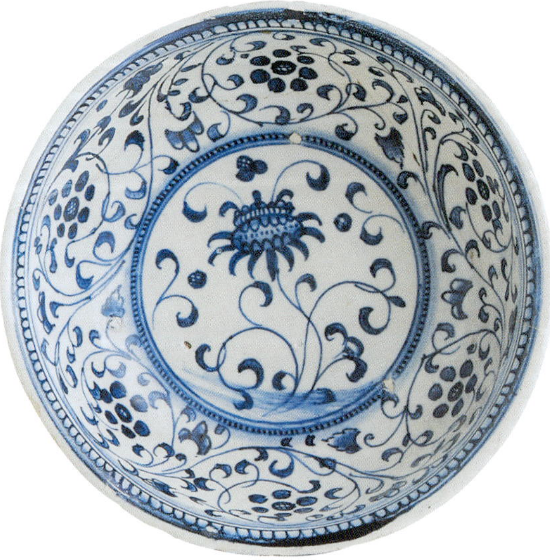

16. Majolica plate. Faenza, early 16th century. Faenza (Ravenna), Museo Internazionale della Ceramica.

A highly successful interpretation of an original Chinese model, with a delightful and quite individual decorative arrangement. The whirling leafy sprigs around the sides emphasie the ethereal flower in the centre, representing perhaps a stylised chrysanthemum, a motif often used by Far Eastern ceramists.

17. Pilgrim flask of 'Medici porcelain'. Florence, c. 1580. Paris, Musée du Louvre.

Clearly part of the early production, the decoration of this flask provides undeniable evidence of the extent to which Chinese porcelain influenced the ceramists of the Florentine factory. The decorative style of the late Ming period (1368-1644) is copied almost identically – the groups of rocks at the bottom, the pine tree in the centre, the deer on the left and the heron on the right are all features found on Far Eastern wares abundantly available in the Medici collections.

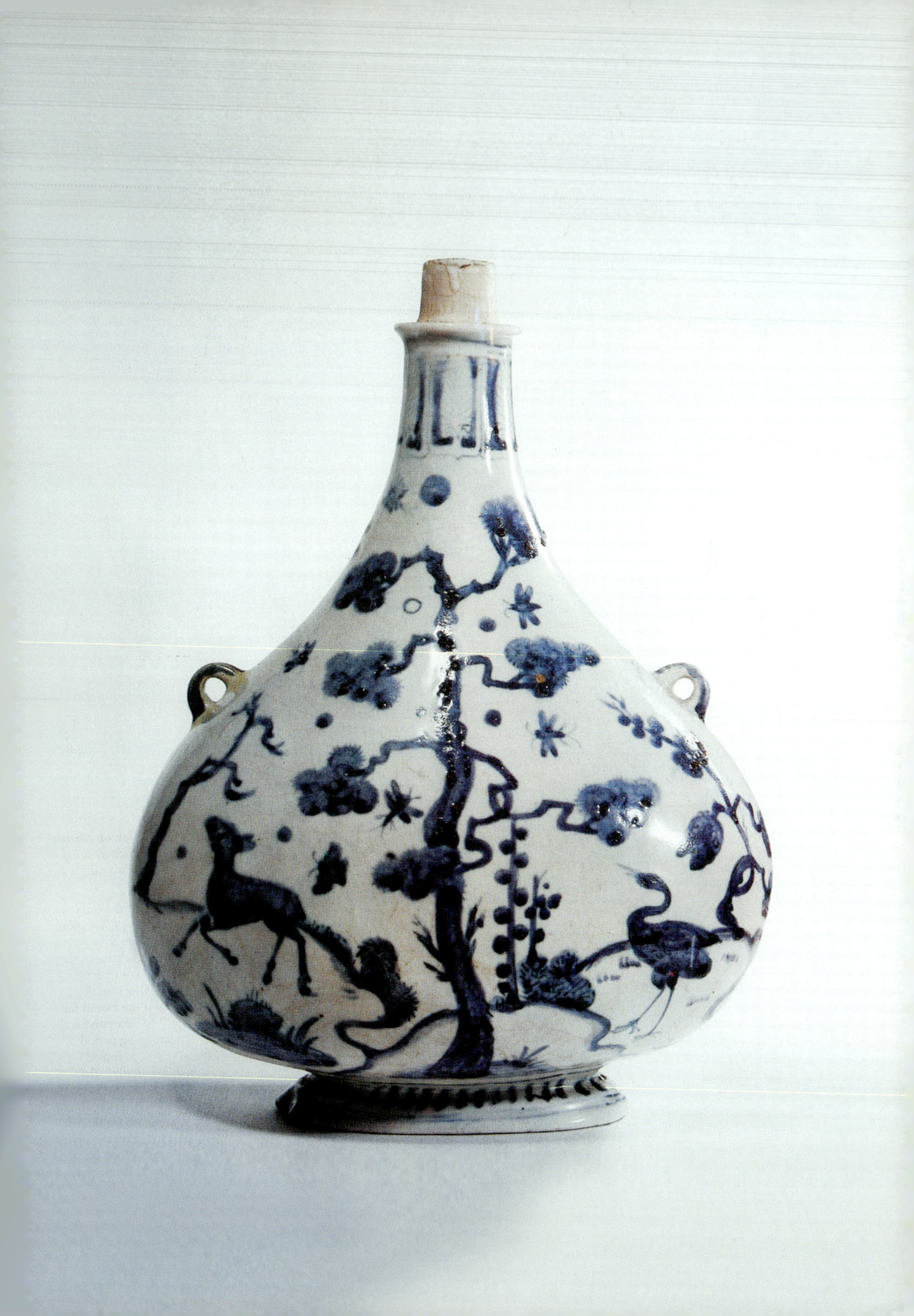

"Camillo da Urbino, a ceramist and painter, but really alchemist to HH, who is the modern discoverer of porcelain and a good friend of the Lord of Florence".[60] Sadly no examples of Ferrara's production have survived.[61] On the other hand a large amount of the Medici output is still in existence in both European and American museums. The paste used in these pieces is rather soft, but the white is brilliant enough for the final result to appear similar to Chinese porcelain. The decoration is painted with lead enamel, while cobalt blue is added to the backgrounds to render the colour, enclosed within a fine manganese surround, more brilliant. The motifs are generally floral though scenes with classical-style figures, often taken from engravings, are also present. An example is provided by two flasks in the Louvre, one of which bears the inscription 'prova' on the base which would suggest an early trial piece. The close relationship between these and examples of Chinese porcelain is very evident, especially in the choice of the plant motif such as the large pine tree which appears in the centre and the triumphant peony flower, but also the animals, the fawn, ducks and small birds so typical of the oriental repertory. Models were provided by goods exported during the Jaijing period (1522-1566), around mid century. In the early days of production, Chinese designs were carefully reproduced but subsequently sources became more 'Florentine' and the forms, which even at the beginning had not been rigorously oriental, began to be quite obviously influenced by contemporary designs for glass, metal, majolica and semi-precious stones. These Florentine experiments were unusually successful, especially considering that porcelain would still not be 'discovered' in Europe for a further century. Ulisse Aldovrandi (1522-1605), a doctor, naturalist and philosopher from Bologna who owned both original Chinese and Medici porcelain pieces, stated in the catalogue of his encyclopaedic collection, *Museum metallicum*, published posthumously in 1648, "Haec vasa [of Chinese porcelain] in nostris regionibus, deficiente tali argilla et aqua memorata, fabricari non possunt: nihilo-minus Magnus Hetruriae Dux aeternae mamoriae Franciscus huiusmodi vasa chinensibus non inferiori curavit".[62] At the end of the 17th century, Lorenzo Magalotti (1637-1712) was of the same opinion, according to a letter he wrote to Leone Strozzi, "regarding the porcelain pieces I can tell Your Holiness that they were made in Florence ... to sight and touch, the paste appears as good as and perhaps better than that of China. So that you might be convinced that they were made in Florence, on the bottom of the vase, painted in blue, you can see the dome of S. Maria del Fiore, which it is difficult to believe has an older sister in Canton or Peking".[63]

18. Pilgrim flask made of milk glass. Venice, c. 1510-1520. Baltimore (Maryland), Walters Art Gallery.

As with other existing examples of early 16th-century Venetian milk glass, the 'exotic' decorative element is mainly provided by the floral arabesques inspired by similar motifs found on Chinese porcelain, though they surround Renaissance images. These items were, however, intrinsically 'chinoiserie' pieces since they were produced as western surrogates of oriental items.

19. Glass pilgrim flask. Venice, late 16th – early 17th century. Milan, Museo Poldi Pezzoli.

The decoration of even the most classic transparent glassware was influenced by Far Eastern motifs in the 16th century. The floral sprigs engraved on this item obviously derive either from the motifs on Chinese porcelain, or contemporary Venetian ceramics in the oriental style.

Glass

Contemporary to the experiments with majolica, attempts were made in Venice to reproduce hard white oriental porcelain with the use of glass. Applying their technical skills and knowledge, the glass workers of Murano succeeded in producing an unusual material known as 'milk glass' for the white opacity obtained by adding bleaches to the frit of lead and tin. White glass had already been in use for some time to make mosaic tesserae. The use of milk glass as a surrogate for Chinese porcelain became a practical proposition only after Angelo Barovier (?-1480) had mastered the technique of glass blowing.[64] Experiments to reproduce porcelain using glass were probably already quite advanced by the mid 15th century as an inventory of Jacopo d'Angelo's workshop drawn up in 1457 includes, in addition to traditional crystal glass, pieces of "porcelain" which were almost certainly pieces of milk glass. In Venice around 1470 an alchemist known as Antonio was making "porcelain", described as "pieces of great perfection, because he has produced transparent and delightful porcelain ... which look as if they have come from the barbarians and are perhaps better".[65] Milk glass is quite frequently mentioned in early 16th-century documents, which often refer to it as "imitation porcelain". This particular development is confirmed in a

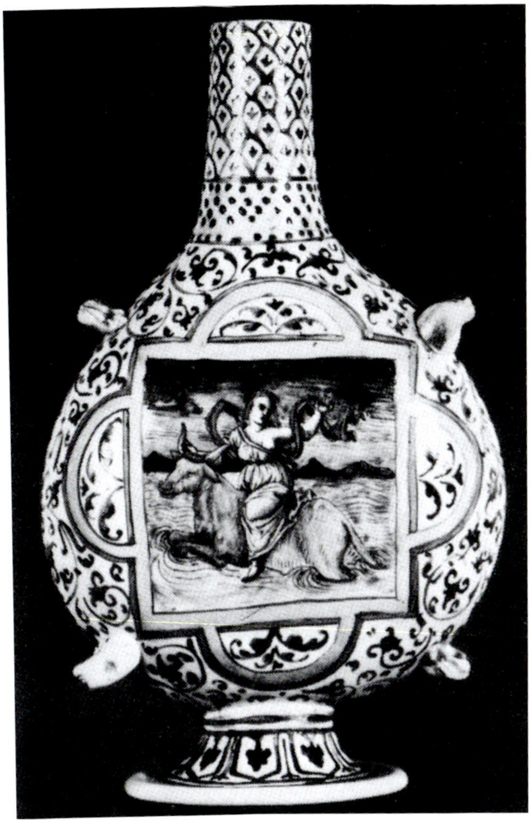

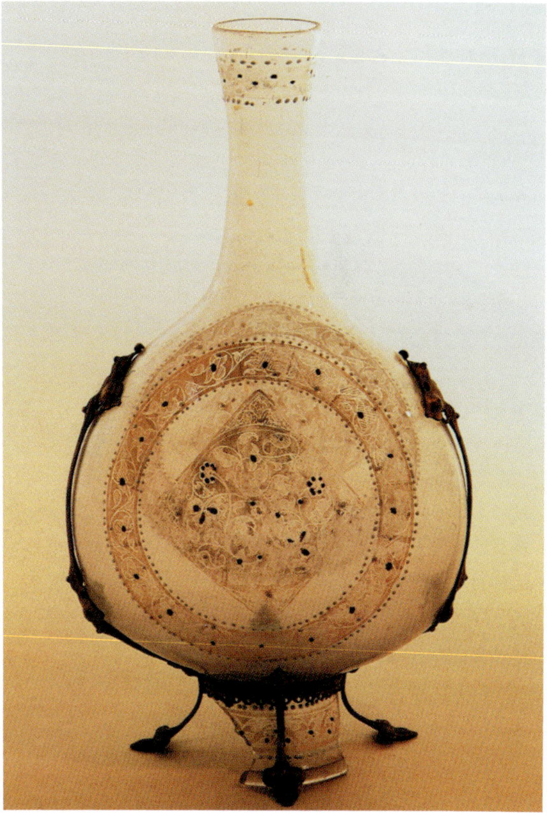

document dated 4 June 1518 in which the glass worker Leonardo Peringer announced to the Venetian Senate that he had discovered how to "make all kinds of porcelain, just like the transparent kind from the Levant".[66] "Imitation porcelain" was acquired in 1504 by Ercole d'Este and in 1519 by Jacopo Tebaldi for Alfonso I (1476-1534), duke of Ferrara.[67] Having already established the production of majolica in the city, Alfonso was eager to experiment with manufacturing Chinese-style porcelain and tried to persuade the artisan who had supplied the milk glass (perhaps Peringer?) to move to Ferrara, though unsuccessfully. Despite enjoying great popularity during the 16th century, only very few pieces of milk glass, all dating from the first decade of the 16th century, have survived until today.[68] As with majolica, milk glass items were heavily influenced by the Orient and both the form and subject of the items clearly reflect the most salient features of Chinese porcelain in the decorative motifs, the use of cobalt blue as the principle colour, and floral decoration based on oriental arabesques. Unlike majolica, however, Chinese plant motifs were not predominant but rather provided a setting for images belonging to the most classical Italian Renaissance repertories.[69]

Lacquer

Experiments to produce items imitating oriental lacquer began in the late 16th century. After silk and porcelain, lacquer too was a technical and artistic achievement of the Far East alone. Extracted as resin from the *Rhus vernicifera* plant, lacquer was already in use in China and Japan in the 4th millennium BC and was particularly admired for its qualities both as a polish and as protection against humidity and water. Oriental lacquered objects began to be imported to Europe during the first half of the 16th century, after Portuguese explorers had established contact with Asian merchants. In particular, Japanese lacquered items, made to satisfy the requests of an increasing number of foreign buyers, met with great success. The legendary Cipangu – Japan – of Marco Polo's tales only became a reality towards the middle of the 16th century when missionaries, including the Jesuit Francesco Saverio (1506-1552), arrived to convert the inhabitants. Oriental lacquer is first recorded in Europe during the early decades of the 16th century, but is mentioned more frequently towards the end of the century.

About the same time items of lacquered wood and leather began to be produced in Italy, and in particular in Venice, such as chests of drawers (with various forms and functions), musical instruments of different kinds, bucklers and other military harnesses, frames for paintings and mirrors, as well as tables and covers for books. All such pieces are clearly copied from examples of oriental origin.[70] Dating from the last quarter of the 16th century, the objects are covered with a varnish similar to lacquer, principally black in colour, but also red and green, and are decorated in gold usually with floral and geometric 'damascene' patterns. This kind of decoration was also produced on metal by Venetian craftsmen known as "azziministi", a term derived from the Arab *Al Agem* meaning Persia.[71] One such specialist was Paolus Ageminius, possibly the Paolo Rizzo who had a workshop in Ruga degli Orefici near Rialto around 1570 and who made a casket which belonged to the Trivulzio collection in Milan.[72] The finest masterpiece of Venetian 16th-century lacquer is "Laura's Harp" originally in the Este collections.[73]

Rather than Chinese or Japanese, the models for this kind of Venetian decoration were Middle Eastern, and in particular the artistic schools of Safavid Persia in Tabriz and Isfahan, and Ottoman Constantinople. Although Venice avoided involvement in the European colonial drive, the city did continue to develop close commercial contacts independently with the Middle East in the late 16th century. Every year items from the Orient were sold at a great market held in St Mark's Square and managed entirely by Venetians who acquired all foreign goods by pre-emption as they arrived in their state.[74] These items too were often decorated with motifs which originally were quite Chinese, although subsequently filtered by Persia before then being adopted by Venetian craftsmen. The decoration of the shield illustrated overleaf is a case in point;[75] its overall arrangement is entirely characteristic of 14-15th century blue and white porcelain with a central motif surrounded by an arabesque design of leaves and swelling flower heads,

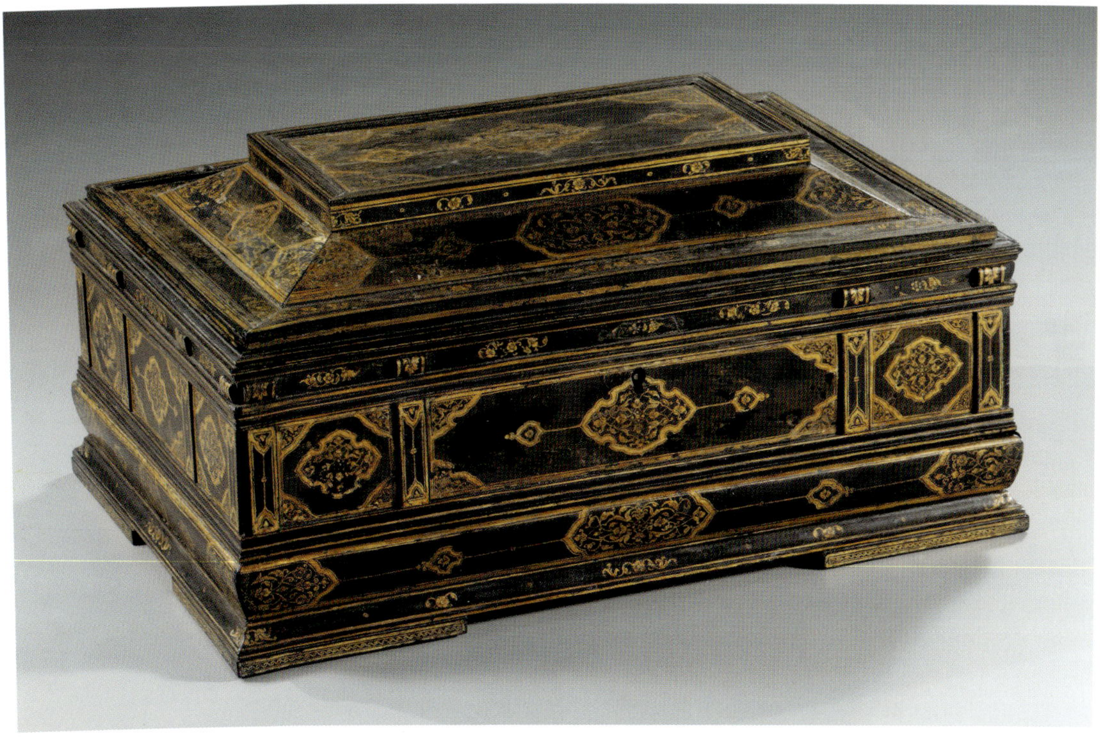

20. Writing box in lacquered wood with gold decorations. Venice, late 16th century. Private collection.

A typical example of late 16th-century Venetian lacquer work. Rather than Japanese or Chinese, the style of decoration is based on Middle Eastern models. However, even this damascene form of ornamentation reflects the influence of the Far East, particularly the use of a black background for the gold motifs, a feature and combination of colours found throughout a vast area of Asia.

clearly derived from the stylized oriental lotus flower pattern. The band with garlands of foliage winding around the outer edge is also typically oriental. The shield is one of a group of items which have a wood base, covered first with leather and then painted with coloured lacquer and decorated with gold. This piece belonged to the Odescalchi collection and is now in Palazzo Venezia in Rome, while similar pieces are housed in Palazzo Ducale in Venice, in the Bargello Museum in Florence and in Salzburg where the bishop of the city, Wolf Deitrich von Raitenau (1559-1617) commissioned various items of this kind towards the end of the 16th century.[76] The mingling of Near and Far East, Africa and the Americas is also evident in the most authoritative text on traditions in the late 16th century world, entitled *Habiti antichi et moderni di tutto il mondo, in Venetia presso G. G. Bernardo Sessa* written by Cesare Vecellio (1521-1601), and first published in Venice in

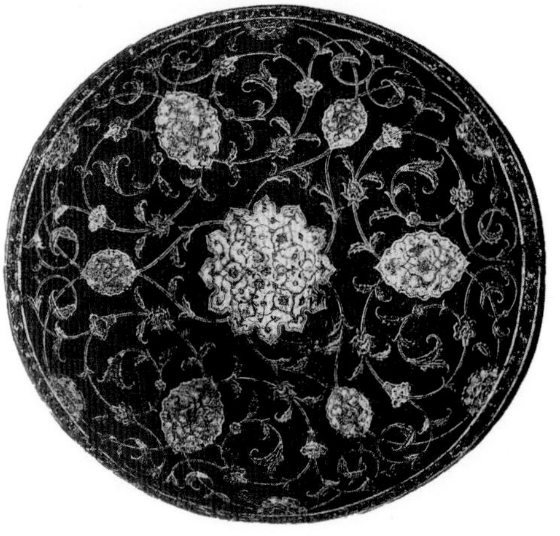

21. Wooden shield covered with leather and lacquered with gold and coloured decoration. Venice, 16th century, second half. Rome, Palazzo Venezia, Odescalchi Collection.

Although obviously reflecting the damascene style of decoration, the ornamentation of this shield – and numerous other similar examples still existing – is clearly based on classic Chinese porcelain designs, especially the overall pattern of stylised flower heads set amidst scrolling fronds with trefoil leaves.

1590. The volume contained abundant illustrations and these images were used not only to represent exotic styles but also to illustrate texts on ethnography and anthropology as late as the 19th century. A second edition of the book, revised and enlarged, was already published in Venice in 1598 and a third in 1664, and its continuing popularity lead to a Spanish edition in 1794 while it appeared in French in 1859-60.[77]

In a review of late 16th-century Venetian lacquer, Hans Huth suggested Venetian workmanship for a small folding table once in the collection of Ferdinand II of the Tyrol (1529-1595) in the castle of Ambras and now in the Kunsthistorisches Museum, Vienna.[78] His opinion was based not only on stylistic and technical factors, such as the decoration which is not entirely Chinese in appearance, and the use of a varnish not obtained from *Rhus vernicifera*, but he also took the history of the piece into consideration. The table was given to the archduke as a gift from his son, cardinal Andreas of Burgau, bishop of Brixen, who often visited Venice where most probably he

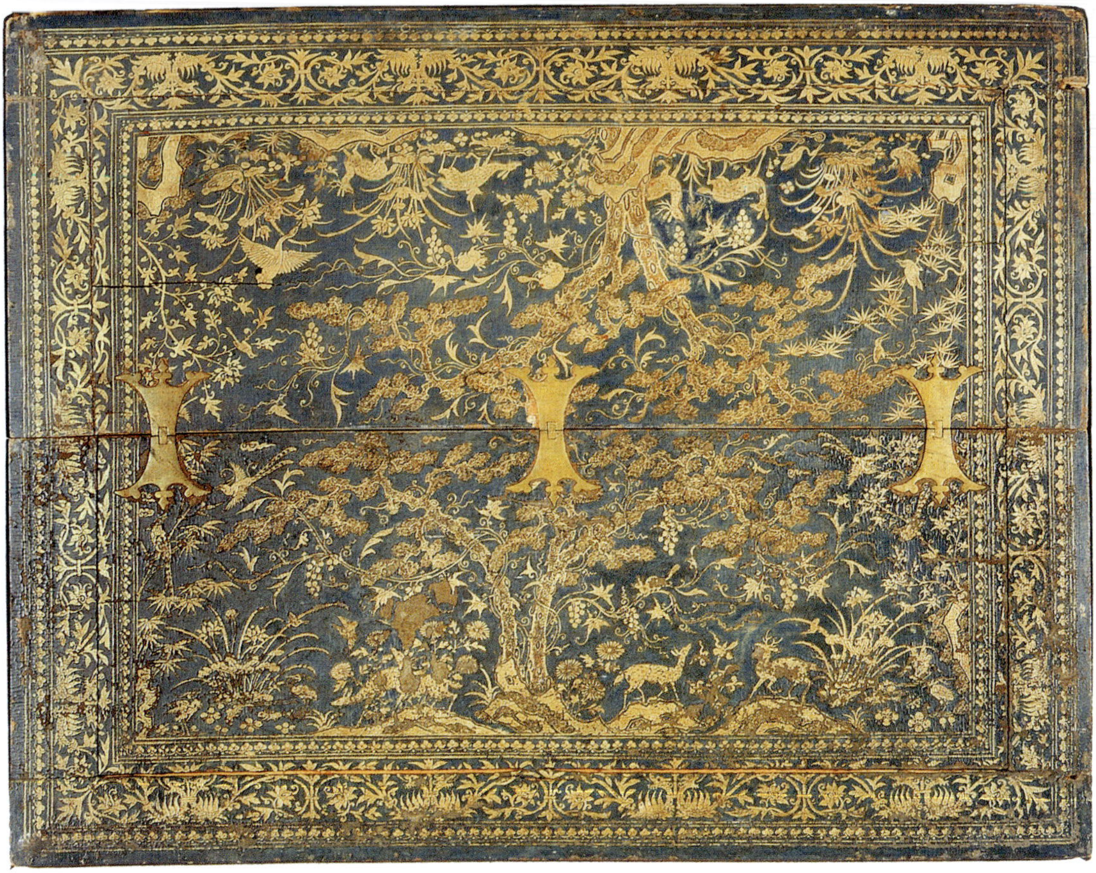

22. Table top in lacquered wood with gold decorations. Golconda (?) (India), 16th century, second half (before 1596). Vienna, Kunsthistorisches Museum, Kunstkammer.

Documented in 1596 in the collections of Ferdinand of the Tyrol, the importance of this item has lead to much speculation about its origins. In particular, during the 20th century some scholars suggested that it had been made in Europe, thus maintaining that it was one of the earliest examples of chinoiserie. However, the lacquer work is more probably Asian and provided a model and many oriental ideas for European craftsmen.

would have bought the piece. Schlosser too (1908)[79] believed that this famous table was one of the earliest examples of chinoiserie though for a long period the piece was considered to be an original Chinese work. Recently however, based on comparisons with some fabrics produced in the same city, manufacture of the table has been attributed to Golconda (southern India), capital of the Qutb Shahi dynasty from 1507 to 1589.[80] The theory is convincing although many of the decorative motifs, both animal and plant, are traditionally Chinese. However, the floral garland around the outer edge and the excessive symmetry of the arrangement are, in fact, extremely similar to the Timuride style. In his discussion of the table Huth provided an illustration of a similar work, without stating its provenance, for comparison suggesting that this too might be a late 16th-century Italian piece.[81] Consisting of scenes filled with plant motifs and animals set into the spaces between diagonal, horizontal and vertical bands, the decoration of the table illustrated does not appear to be particularly similar to the "cardinal's table" in Vienna. On the other hand there do seem to be some similarities to a table now in the Chigi Saracini collection in Siena. The slender top of this piece is supported on legs with circular and

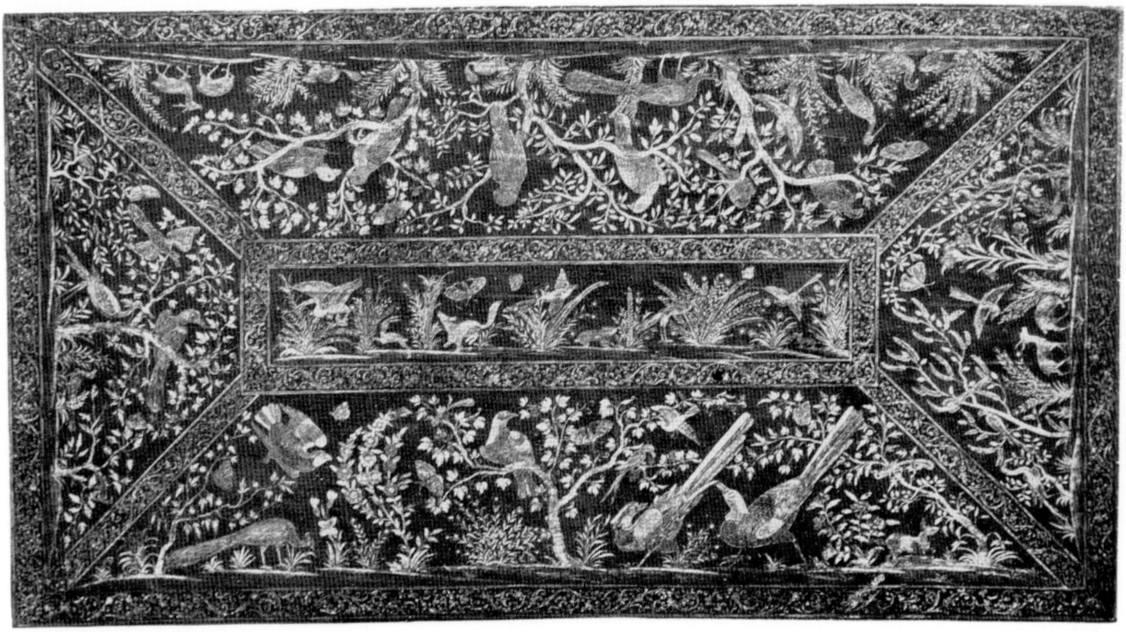

23. Table top in lacquered wood with gold decorations. Florence, late 16th -early 17th century (from Huth 1971, Fig. 30).
That oriental lacquer work inspired this work is evident not only in the use of a dark varnished background for the gold decoration but also for the decorative motifs of birds amidst dense arabesques of foliage enhancing the bands of the frames surrounding the naturalistic images. The inspiration here was not however, Far Eastern lacquer work, but that of Persia.

square sections, joined by a cross bar and the whole structure has a uniform layer of black varnish highlighted with gold ornamentation. The legs are decorated with sturdy branches of foliage and small birds while the top has the same design as the piece in Huth's illustration, the only difference being that the rectangle in the centre is larger. In addition, on all four sides a round medallion appears, framed by leafy arabesques similar to those running along the edges and in the bands that divide the internal scenes. Another, and perhaps much greater difference, is that the decoration presents not only monkeys, but also humans represented in groups of several figures hunting or simply seen in a landscape. Some of the clothes and various details of the scenes, such as the umbrella shading the group crossing a bridge on the back of a horse, are clearly of Chinese origin. According to Enrico Colle, who has published this work on several occasions,[82] the table is Florentine and dates from the early 17th century. This theory is supported by both the shape and especially by the frequent descriptions of 'Indian style' furnishings that appear in the Medici inventories from the end of the 16th century, including "a large bowl of Indian wood with gold illuminations" which arrived in Florence in 1587 from Rome amongst the items that cardinal Ferdinando I (1549-1609) had acquired while living in Rome.[83] In addition, two small tables "of black lacquer decorated with arabesques of powdered gold and figures, leaves, animals, birds and flowers in several colours in the Indian fashion" are documented in the Pitti Palace as early as 1595 and are attributed to "Samuel Sonagna, a Jew". The rather vague definition of "all'indiana" was applied indifferently to original Asian or American pieces, or even to Italian reproductions of exotic items and could not alone justify

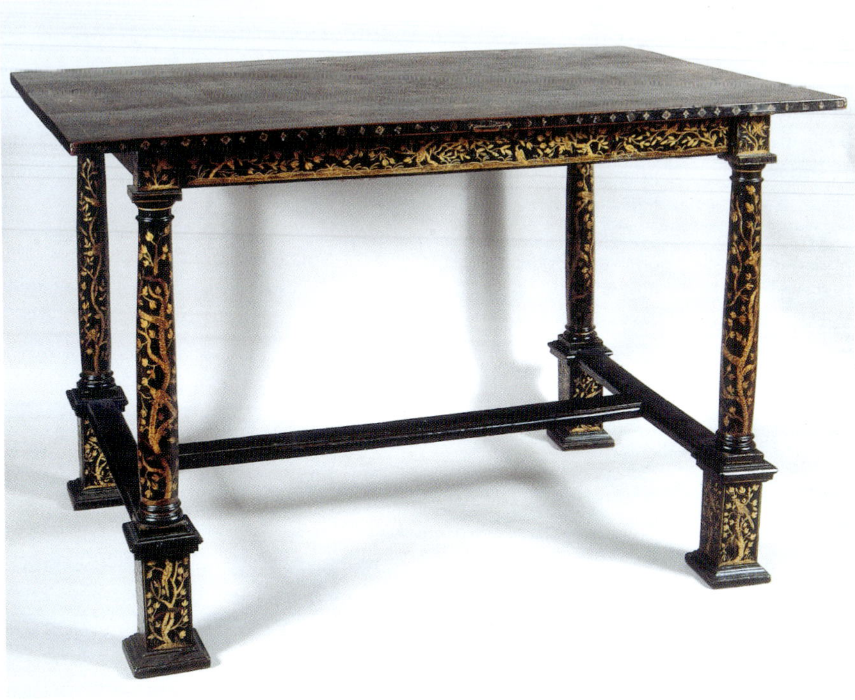

24a,b. Table in lacquered wood with gold decorations. Florence, late 16th – early 17th century. Siena, Chigi Saracini collection.

Although extremely similar to the table illustrated in Fig. 23, the iconography here is more markedly Chinese as can be seen from the characters who populate the landscapes.

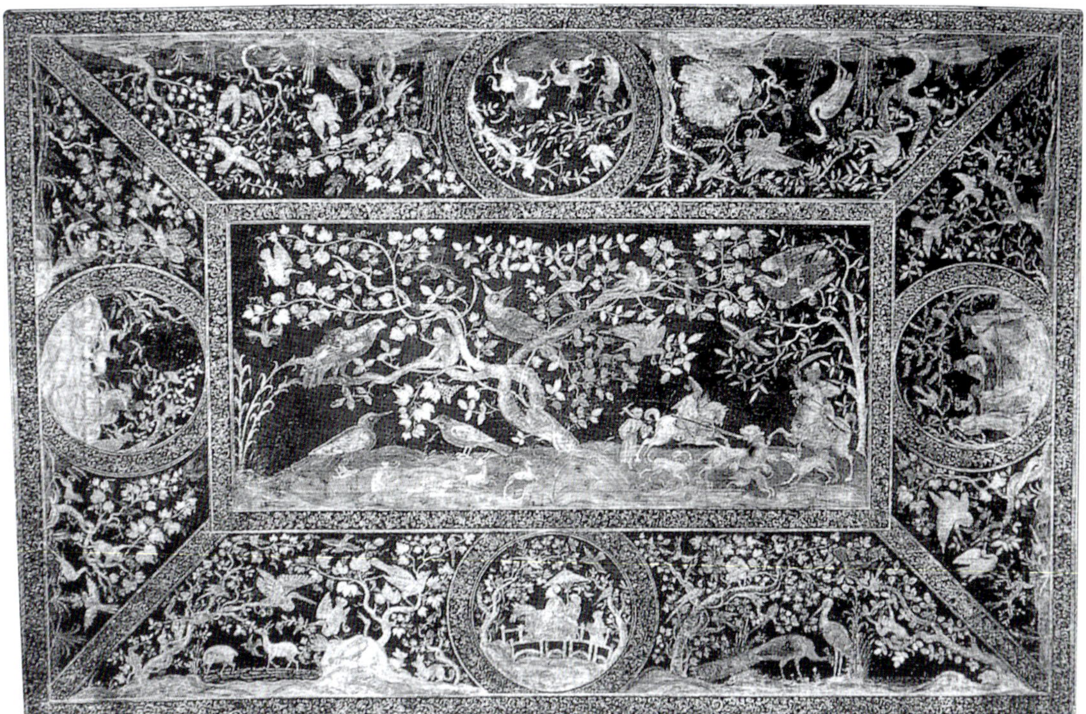

Colle's attribution. However, it is known that to satisfy the Medici's fascination with exotic scenes this type of decoration was quite commonly produced by the court craftsmen. The real composition of porcelain paste and the qualities of lacquer had been described to his Medici masters by Francesco Carletti, a Florentine (c. 1573-1636). While in Goa in 1599 he had seen extremely fine lacquered items, imported from China, in the houses of some of the most eminent Portuguese, "completely decorated with gold and strange arabesques on a black varnish made of a material taken from the bark of a tree, which becomes so hard and takes on such a wonderful brilliance that you can see yourself in it very well".

Moreover, in the first half of the 17th century recipes for producing oriental varnish were collected in Florence and are still conserved in the *Ricettari del Fondo Palatino*. Justus Lampe from Flanders was brought to Florence in 1618 to demonstrate his skill in decorating furniture with "all kinds of Indian-style" painting and was also asked to teach the technique to some pupils.

One such pupil, a certain Virgilio Lotti, immediately set to work on the decoration of "two columns for a bed" – an intriguing piece of information that brings to mind two bed posts housed in Palazzo Colonna in Rome and suggests that perhaps these too could be Florentine, or at least Italian, dating from the early 17th century. Both the technique and the decorative features are heavily influenced by Japanese lacquer which was explicitly made for exportation to the west, and referred to as *Nanban*.

In this group of Florentine lacquer pieces the six brackets presented in the exhibition *Magnificenza alla corte dei Medici* assume a particular importance.[84] Previously in Francesco I's 'studiolo' in Palazzo Vecchio, documents reveal that the six brackets were made to a design by Bernardo

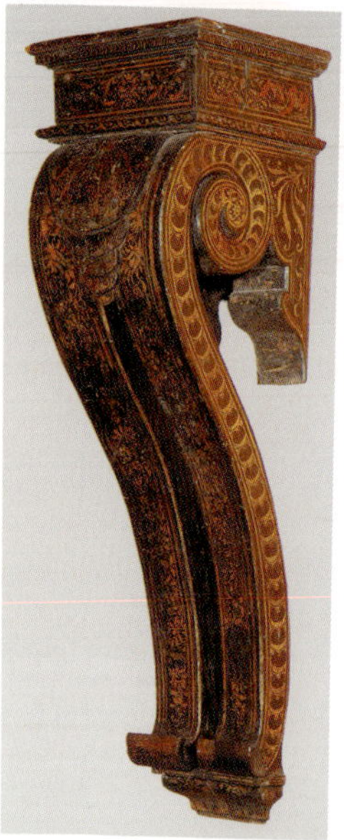

25. Dionigi di Matteo Nigetti and Bartolo da Venezia, Bracket, lacquered wood with gold decoration, c. 1586. Florence, Uffizi Gallery, store rooms.

Decorated by Bartolo da Venezia in Florence with Middle Eastern motifs in gold on a dark varnished background. Clearly Venetian craftsmen provided an important contribution to the development of 'Indian-style' lacquer techniques in Tuscany.

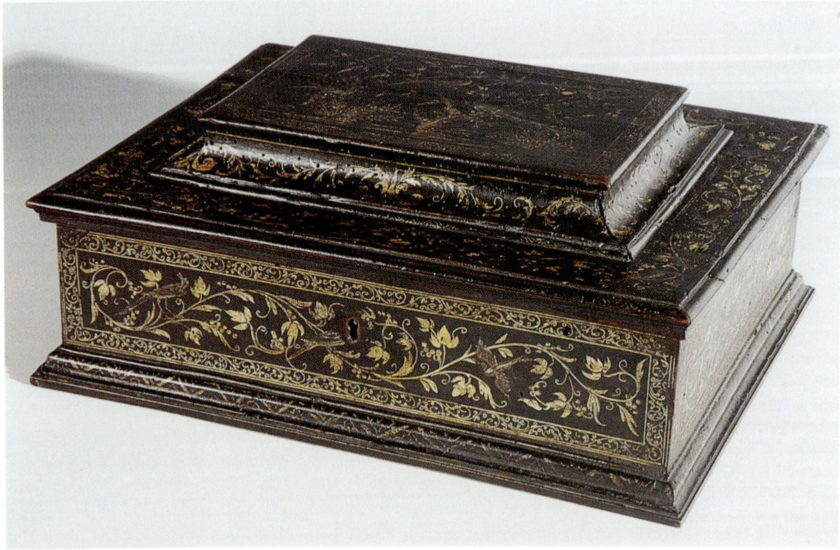

26. Writing box of lacquered wood with gold and colour decoration. Florence, late 16th century. Florence, Galleria di Palazzo Mozzi Bardini.

This extremely elegant box also reveals many similarities to 16th-century Venetian lacquer work, in its turn inspired by Middle Eastern items.

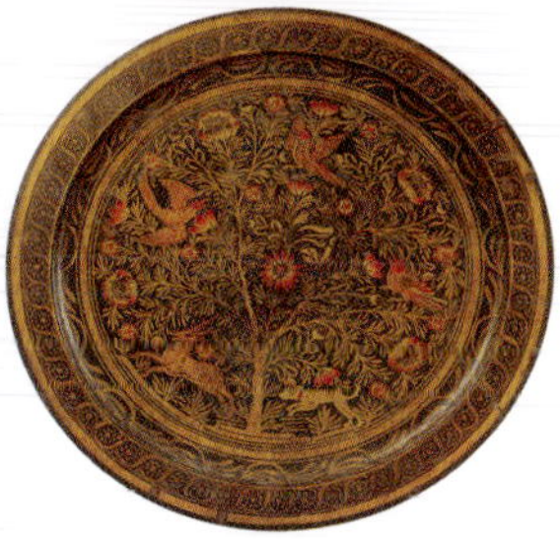

27. Lacquered wood dish with gold and colour decoration. Florence (?), late 16th – early 17th century. Venice. Private collection.

The dark background is decorated with traces of colour and motifs of wild animals, plants and trees; the plate belongs to a specific group of 'Indian-style' items made in Florence in the late 16th and early 17th centuries.

28. Cabinet. Florence (?), late 16th – early 17th century. Siena, Chigi Saracini Collection.

Buontalenti in 1586 to support the bronze statues in the Tribune of the Uffizi. They were carved by the Florentine Dionigi di Matteo Nigetti, and the gold decoration on a brown background was the work of a certain Bartolo da Venezia. This clearly confirms that the 'damascene' decoration, so finely produced by the Venetian craftsmen, became popular in Florence at an early date and was a further stimulus to developing local production of 'Indian style' decoration on a lacquer ground. There are at least three more lacquer works dating from the early decades of the 17th century and decorated in the 'exotic' style that may be identified as of Florentine origin: a writing box in the Galleria di Palazzo Mozzi Bardini in Florence,[85] a cabinet, also in the Chigi Saracini collection in Siena[86] and a dish in a private collection.[87]

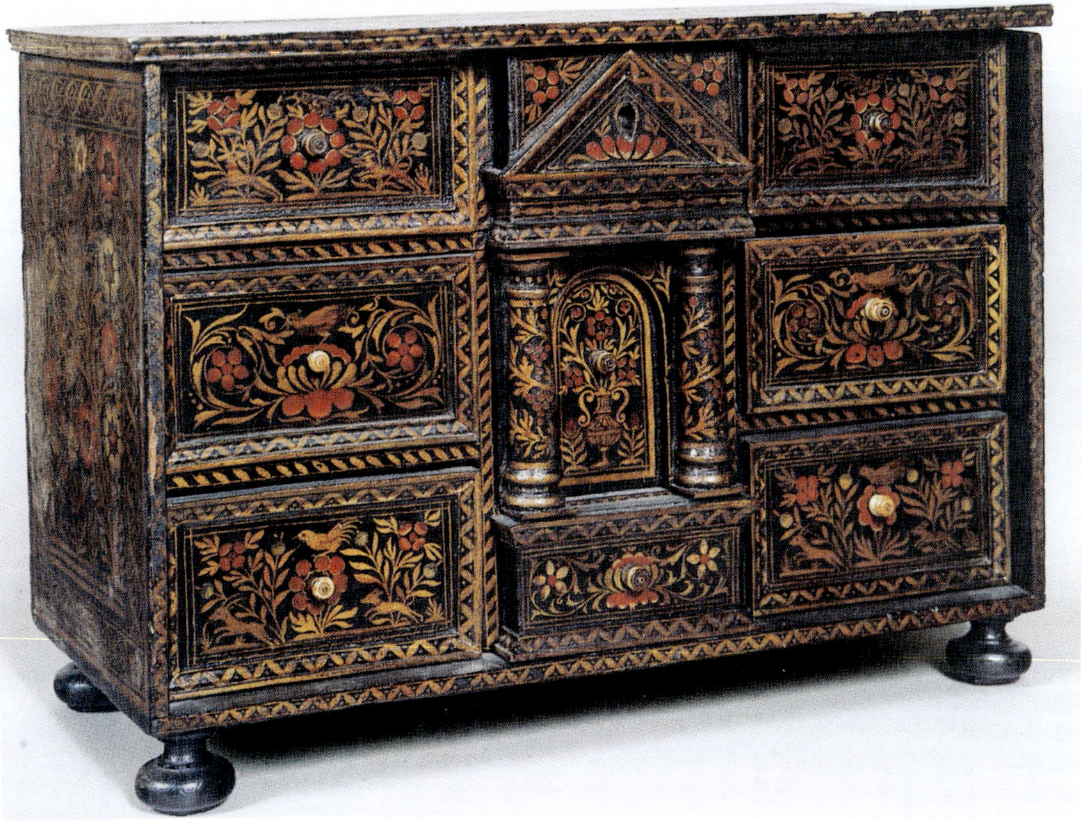

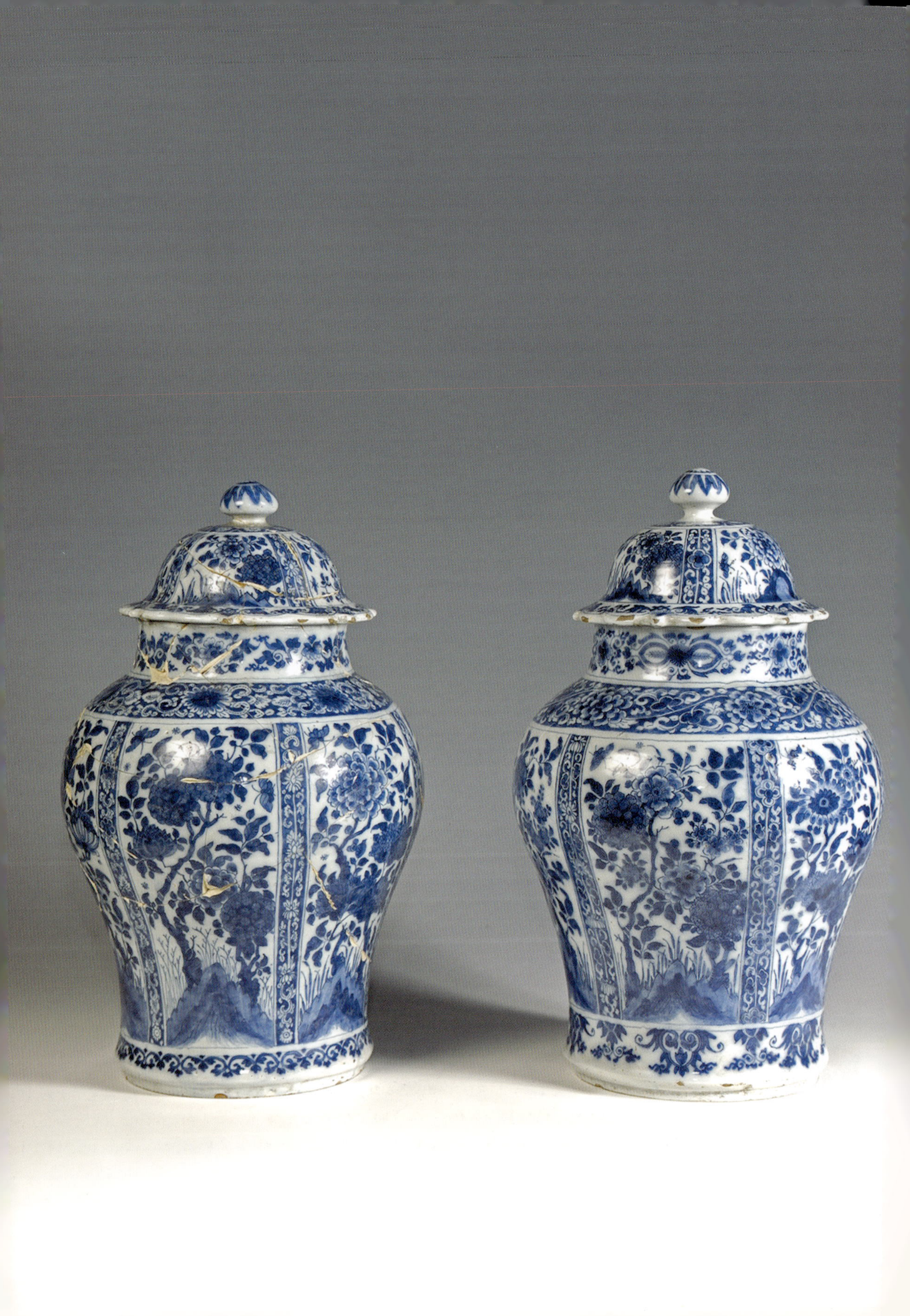

Oriental Curios in Europe and Italy in the 17th Century

29. Two majolica vases. Delft (Holland), early 18th century. Florence, Palazzo Pitti.

The ceramists of Delft based the form and decoration of these vases on Chinese porcelain made at the time of emperor Kangxi (1662-1722). Items such as these arrived in Amsterdam on the ships of the Dutch East India Company from the earliest years of the 17th century.

30. Cabinet (detail). England, c. 1620. London, Victoria and Albert Museum.

Black lacquer background painted with gold, silver and touches of colour. The decorative style recalls Islamic ornamentation seen on late 16th-century Venetian lacquer work. The floral motifs have an Indian appearance while the scenes on the inside of the doors are of Chinese inspiration such as the landscape arranged on different, parallel levels and the details of the clothes worn by various figures.

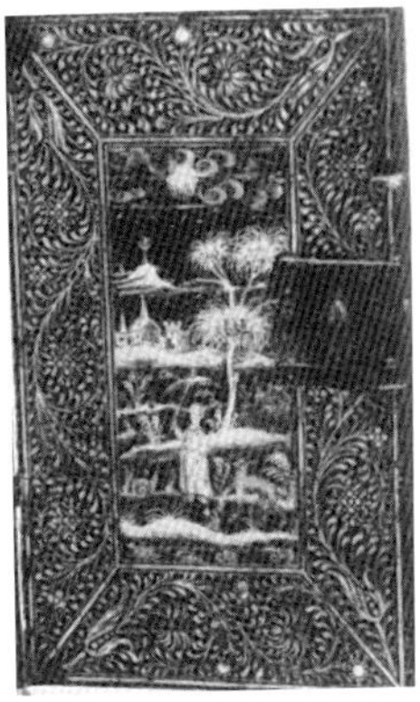

Europe

The production of lacquer in Venice and Florence was one of the earliest examples of Italian chinoiserie and developed at the same time as Dutch and English 'japanning'. Imitation of oriental lacquer was widely practiced from the early 17th century in Holland and indeed most of the many recipes for making varnishes in the famous manuscript of doctor Theodore Turquet de Mayerne from Geneva (1573-1655?) are Flemish.[88] In Amsterdam prior to 1610 a Society of Lacquer Workers (*lackwercken*) existed and a certain William Kick seems to have occupied a particularly important role in its ranks as a specialist in the production of Chinese lacquers; so well produced were they that it has been suggested that specialized workers were brought to Holland from Japan to teach the art to Europeans.[89] In 1612 the States General commissioned Kick to make a lacquer chest to send to the Turkish sultan Ahmed Khan as a gift and this was followed by a similar item made for the Palatine Countess.
Unfortunately no early examples of 'oriental-style' Dutch lacquer are known to have survived, but comparison with several pieces made in England during the second and third decades of the 17th century may provide some idea of their appearance as presumably such contemporary works presented various similarities of design and decoration.[90]
Both Portuguese and Dutch craftsmen reacted to the arrival on the market of large quantities of Chinese porcelain by producing goods in the 'Chinese style'. Although these could not achieve the inimitable quality of oriental pastes, they could at least reproduce the decorative designs with a similar use of cobalt blue on the white tin-glaze background and by copying the ornamental motifs taken from Far Eastern originals. In Portugal this kind of porcelain was already in production in the late 16th century, although it was most popular in the early decades of the 17th century when, even compared to later production, Chinese-style elements are more easily recognised, sometimes indeed even slavishly reproduced.[91] The same was true of ceramic decorators working in Delft where early chinoiserie majolica dates from 1620, a few years later than Portugal, given that the Dutch East India Company (VOC) began operating in 1600. The principle models for both Portuguese and Dutch production were provided by Chinese porcelain made in Jingdezhen (in the southern province of Jiangxi) in the late 16th and early 17th centuries, during the reign of emperor Wanli of the Ming dynasty (1573-1619). The decoration was mainly blue and white and the most traditional Chinese plant and animal motifs were

used, occasionally with the inclusion of the human figure. One of the styles most popular at this time was called 'kraak', a corruption of the Portuguese term 'caracca', a particular type of ship suited to travelling the oceanic routes. This style was identified by a purplish tone of the cobalt blue, a lack of precision in the ornamental detail, and a decoration arranged in radial panels. Both the techniques and styles produced in the city of Delft were later copied by most of the German ceramic factories, principally active in the second half of the 17th century. Hanau, Frankfurt, the Potsdam-Berlin factory, Kassel and Brunswich, Ausbach and lastly the factory in Plane an der Havel (Brandenburg) – all introduced Chinese subjects to their repertories.[92]

Ceramics in Italy

Chinese-style motifs were quite frequent on the wares produced in Turin from the early 17th century, even before an entrepreneur from Genoa, Captain Giovanni Bianchi, established the 'Regio Parco' workshop in 1646 with the authorization of Carlo Emanuele II of Savoy.[93] The animal, plant and geometric motifs used on several of these early products reveal the Far Eastern influence. A band presenting the tips of a *ruyi* sceptre, for example, was quite often used and was a common decoration on oriental porcelain made both for the internal market and for export to the west. The repertory of the Regio Parco factory extended to include a naturalistic style of decoration, clearly inspired by Chinese porcelain motifs, used from the second half of the 1500s to the early decades of the following century.[94] Following the closure of the factories in Genoa only Savona and Albisola remained active in Liguria becoming important centres of production with a fundamental role in the diffusion of oriental motifs in Italy during the 17th century.[95] Ligurian ceramics were already highly successful in the 16th century, much esteemed for the quality of the clay and brilliance and fineness of their white glaze. Large quantities were sold to the Italian courts, especially those in the Tyrrhenian basin, but were also exported to other European states and even

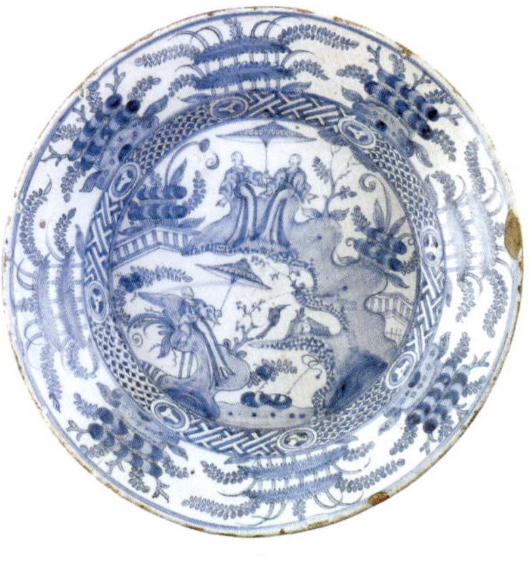

31. Plate. Portugal, 17th century, first quarter. Lisbon, Museo Nazionale di Arte Antica.

The groups of flowers around the border, the geometric pattern around the cavity, the use of blue and especially the central scene with figures, parasols, clumps of rocks and little fences – the entire decoration provides a typical example of how profoundly Chinese art influenced Portuguese ceramics from the late 1500s and throughout the 17th century.

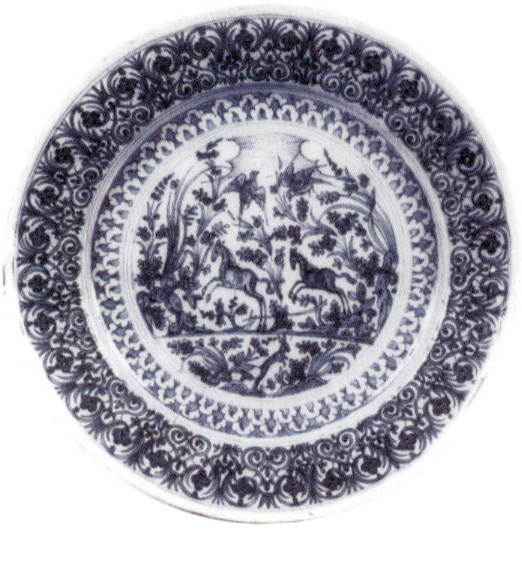

32. Majolica plate. Turin, 17th century, first half. Turin, Museo Civico.

Various details of the decoration were derived from porcelain produced in China during the final phase of the Ming dynasty (16th-17th century) such as the scene of plants and animals in the centre and the friezes around the border and edge. The band surrounding the central scene is formed by a series of *ruyi* sceptre points alternating with *lingzhi* – symbolizing eternal life.

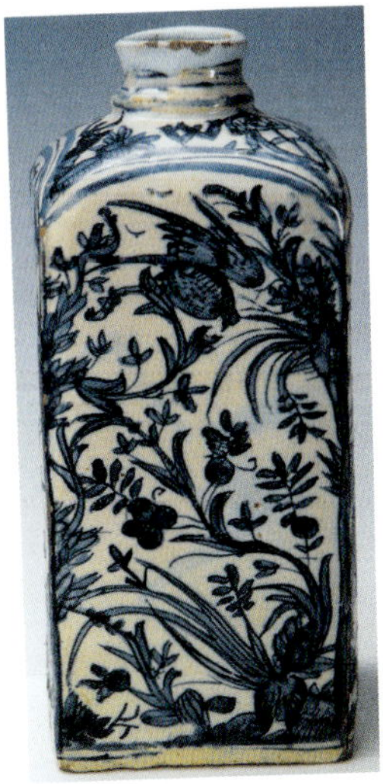

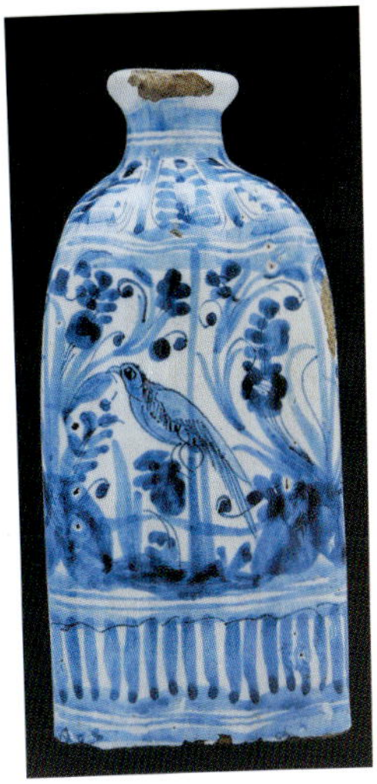

33. Majolica bottle. Turin, Manifattura del Regio Parco, 17th century, second half. Genoa, Palazzo Tursi.

34. Majolica bottle. Savona or Albisola, circa mid 17th century. Florence, Boncompagni Ludovisi collection.

central and north America. The influence of Chinese wares is clearly evident during this period, but Iznik designs, the lustre majolica of Manises and contemporary Venetian production all put in an appearance too. The use of the arabesque motif known as 'alla porcellana' was common to many other Italian factories and towards mid century this was combined with the closed form of the *ruyi* sceptre tips. In the 17th century however, Chinese decorative models became much more obvious on Ligurian products, stimulated both by increased importation of original items from the Far East, and by the example of Portuguese and Dutch factories, which exploited oriental motifs more intensely at the time.[96] In addition to the evident influence of Islamic, Turkish and Indo-Portuguese art, 17th-century Ligurian ceramics also adopted an elaborate naturalistic style of Chinese motif in use during the second half of the Ming dynasty – from the later 16th to the first half of the 17th century. The fauna motifs include a choice of pheasants, geese, ducks, phoenix, cranes, quails, horses, weasels, squirrels, deer, hares, locusts, lizards, frogs and the unicorn; the floral repertory included pines, willows, cherry trees, lotus plants, while the 'kraak' design provided the decorative divisions. Ligurian ceramic workers were indeed eager to imitate porcelain, albeit Portuguese, as Giovan Domenico Peri stated in his book on trading, *Il Negotiante* published in 1647. After the 1650s a degree of Chinese influence is also evident in Ligurian items which were decorated 'a tappezzeria' – an original and apparently casual arrangement of a floral decoration covering the entire surface of the item. In this case inspiration came from porcelain made in China during the "period of transition" (1620-1682), when the Imperial manufacturers were suffering a crisis caused by disorders arising from the succession of the Ming (1368-1644) and Qing (1644-1911) dynasties. Private producers came into their own at this time and developed their production to satisfy the increasing demands of European customers.

Elements of chinoiserie can also be seen in the decoration of two bowls currently in the Victoria and Albert Museum in London, dated respectively 1627 and 1638. Although the decorative style consisting of floral motifs, birds and scenic views, reflects 16th-17th century Iznik items, the two bowls are of particular importance as they represent perhaps the most successful attempt in 17th-century Italy to reproduce the most characteristic features of Chinese porcelain.[97] Once quite understandably thought to be Tuscan, the two bowls were instead made in Padova where the production of wares with floral motifs mainly based on Turkish and Ottoman models is well documented throughout most of the 17th century. The result was a soft, extremely fine china, decorated with cobalt blue and coloured enamels giving an overall appearance quite similar to Chinese works. The decoration copied from Turkish Iznik manufacturers, was in its turn derived from Chinese items.[98]

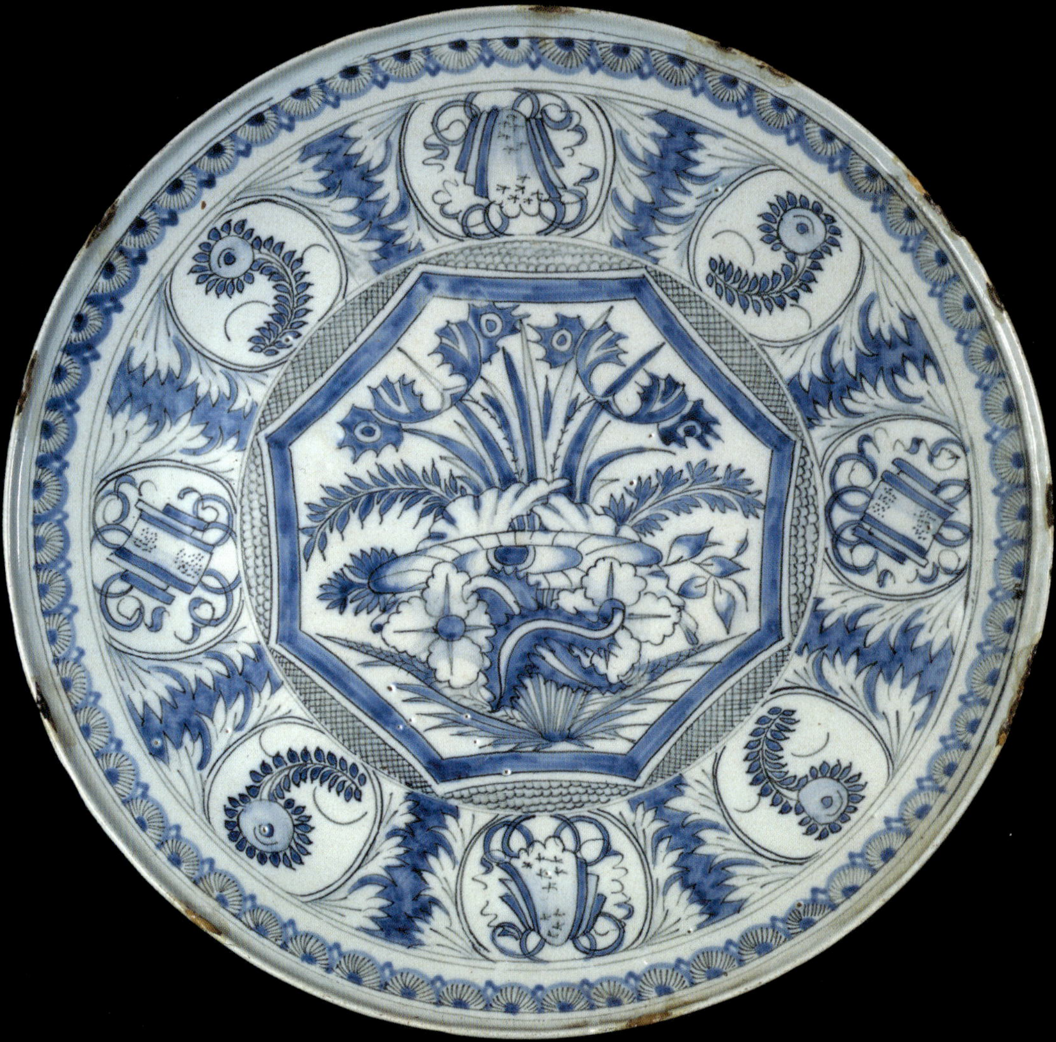

35. Majolica plate. Albisola (Savona), Grosso factory, 1683. Genoa, Fondazione Carige.

A highly important piece both in the history of Ligurian majolica in the 17th century and in the development of chinoiserie in Italy. Perhaps more than other pieces, this plate is an explicit example of decoration derived from blue and white Chinese porcelain and especially the *kraak* design produced in China from the late 16th to mid 17th centuries for export to south-east Asia and Europe.

Scientific Collections and Printed Books

As other scholars of chinoiserie have commented in the past, there are so few historical documents and artefacts available relevant to the period between roughly 1630 and 1670 that – as had occurred during the 1400s – it might seem the popularity of the East and its products was not as lively as it had been in the 16th and early 17th centuries. The situation was common throughout Italy and other European countries. Yet contacts between Asia and the West were particularly fruitful during the 17th century.

The 16th century was the century of Iberian colonialism – first on the part of the Portuguese, followed by the Spanish – and the common interests of the two states lead to the annexation of Portugal to Philip II in 1580. In the late 1500s however, the English and Dutch gained supremacy of the Asian seas. In 1600, with the consent of queen Elisabeth, the English had established an East India Company and two years later the Dutch followed suit. Between Asia and Europe the volume of commerce in exotic merchandise reached unprecedented levels in the 17th century with the importation mainly of spices, porcelain, fabrics and lacquered items as well as tea. Italy did not have direct links with the Far East, although Florence and Genoa had attempted to finance East India Companies along the lines of those of other European countries and with the possible logistic and technical support of the ports of Lisbon and Amsterdam. However, orientalia continued to arrive in the Italian courts, either acquired in the European emporiums, or sent as gifts to the most important aristocratic families. Collections of oriental artefacts, often of considerable size and quality, were naturally owned by royalty but also by private citizens including distinguished personages who created their own scientific cabinets or *wunderkammern*. In Italy these 'encyclopedic' collections first came into being in the 16th century, the work of scholars such as Ferrante Imperato (1550-1631) in Naples, Francesco Calceolari (c. 1521-?) in Verona, Michele Mercati (1541-1593) in Rome, the Gualdo family in Vicenza, Federigo Contarini (1538-1613), Andrea Vendramin and Girolamo Aleandro (1480-1542) in the Veneto, and above all Ulisse Aldrovandi in Bologna. The 17th century saw the development of two more collections belonging to Ferdinando Cospi (1606-1686) in Bologna, and to Manfredo Settala (1600-1680) in Milan, catalogued respectively in 1677 and 1664. These included numerous items from Asia selected both for their value as rarities and for their ethnographic interest as examples of the produce of those distant lands.[99]

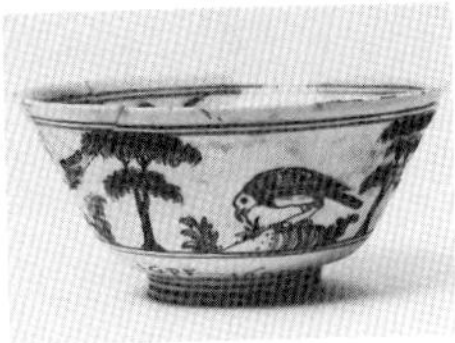

36. Small bowl of 'porcellana padovana' (Paduan porcelain). Padua, 1627. London, Victoria and Albert Museum.

The decoration is a copy of Turkish Iznik items produced in the late 16th and early 17th centuries. Both the Ottoman and Paduan ceramists attempted to produce majolica of a quality as near as possible to that of Chinese porcelain.

In the 17th century the religious orders that sent missions to the Far East all had their headquarters in Rome, seat of the papacy and of Christianity. There had been attempts to convert the Asian continent even before the formidable Mongol Empire came into being in the 13th century. Tales had circulated for several centuries claiming that a land of Christians existed beyond the Islamic dominions, founded by the legendary Father Gianni, a myth that continued even at the time of Marco Polo who was convinced he might come across him during his travels. During the 1500s, the ships of Catholic Spain and Portugal carried many missionaries to the 'Indies' – Franciscans, Dominicans, Carmelites and, especially, Jesuits. Members of the order founded by Ignazio di Loyola considered that preaching the Christian dogma outside Europe was an absolute priority and every means possible was used to convert the infidels. Some results were achieved – particularly in Japan which quickly became the most 'Christian' country of the continent, at least until 1637 when the shogun Tokugawa forbade foreigners to live in his land. The task of missions in China was much more difficult and complex despite the fact that many of the Jesuits who sought to convert the country were among the most renowned in the history of the order. For a lengthy period Matteo Ricci (1552-1610) lived in China at the court of the emperor Wanli (ruler from

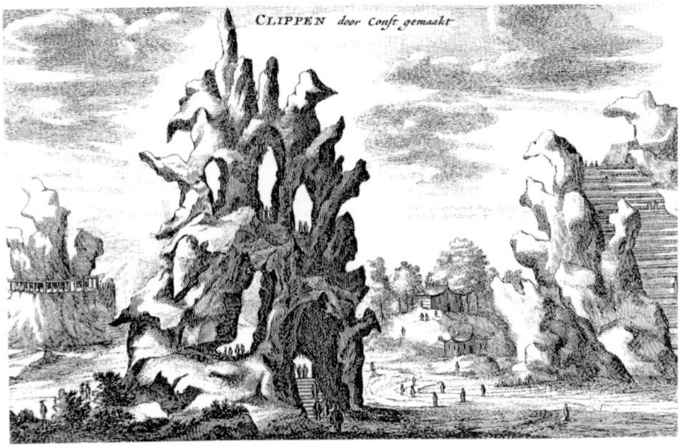

37. *Rocks,* engraving by Jan Nieuhoff, *Het gezantschap der Neerlantsche Oost-Indische Compagnie aan den grooten tartarischen cham,* Amsterdam 1665. Basel University Library.

Nieuhoff's engraving represents the 'Chinese rocks' motif and a similar composition appears in the volume by Von Erlach (1721, III, pl. 15). Extremely irregular in shape and with large oblong holes, the rocks are known in China as *taihu,* after mount Tai, where a great number of them are found. The Chinese believe these natural phenomena have the power to avert evil and they frequently appear as a motif in the decorative repertories of Chinese and Japanese art used on items for export to Europe.

1573 to 1619) and was more successful compared to the brothers who both preceded and followed him. A sinologist ahead of his time and a skilled cultural mediator, he understood that the only way in which to penetrate the Chinese culture was to create a dialogue at the highest levels of society and even the emperor himself – instead of approaching the lower levels, the tactic commonly used before him. Studying the most fundamental traditions of the Middle Kingdom, he acquired the necessary means for communication: the script, the literary classics, and the customs and traditions of the people in general. Gradually he was no longer considered to be a barbaric foreigner, but rather a new member of the Chinese cultural elite. And if there were any need to explain Chinese acceptance of a European in their midst, this most surely lies in the fact that he could impart western scientific knowledge from astrology to mathematics, from physics to geography.[100] Not only did Matteo Ricci explain the theories that he had learned during his training in Rome, keeping up to date through his correspondence with his homeland, but in particular he rendered them more acceptable and usable within the culture of the Chinese who tended to be cautious and even suspicious. Thus Ricci devised a globe with China at the centre, knowing that no Chinaman would ever have accepted seeing his country in a secondary position compared to Europe which in the 17th century was still considered on a level with the barbarian populations who remained beyond the boundaries of the Empire. Matteo Ricci's work in China was recounted partly in the five volumes of *De Christiana expeditione apud Sinas* by Father Nicolas Trigault, published in Rome in 1615, and partly in *Della Cina* (1663) by Daniello Bartoli (1608-1685), containing an account of the work of the Jesuits in Asia (*Dell'Istoria della Compagnia di Gesù in Asia*).[101] Despite strict Imperial controls, his achievements were continued by numerous other fellow priests who returned to Europe with a store of knowledge that often they put into writing and was sometimes published. The engravings in some of these publications were of particular importance for the development of chinoiserie and contributed to

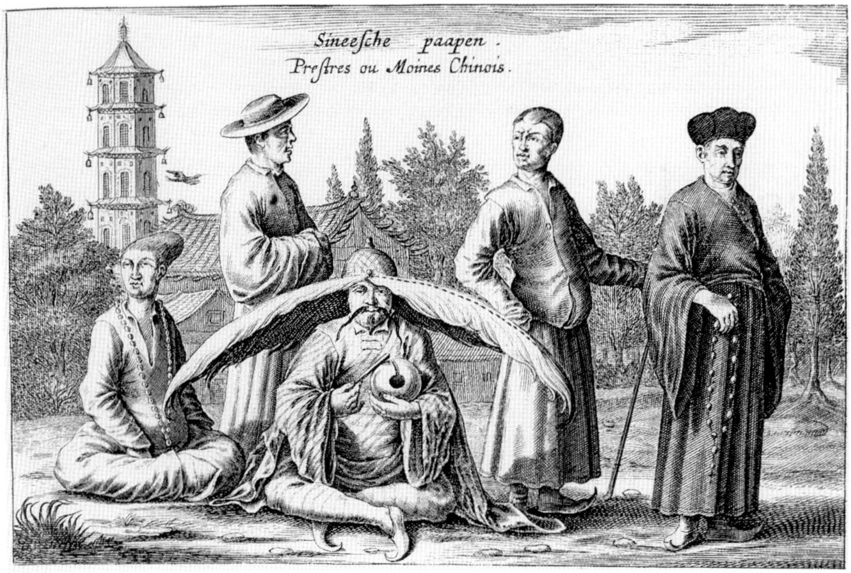

38. *Chinese priests or monks*, engraving by Jan Nieuhoff, *Het gezantschap der Neerlantsche Oost-Indische Compagnie aan den grooten tartarischen cham*, Amsterdam 1665. Basel, University Library.

Another image by Nieuhoff which inspired many chinoiseries. In addition to the pagoda that appears on the left, the exaggerated brim on the monk's headgear in the centre became a kind of icon of the 'vision of Cathay' that developed throughout Europe during the 18th century.

creating a truer and more precise idea of these distant places. Important information finally became available: the physical appearance of the inhabitants, the geographical structure of the land, the most typical customs and traditions, the most characteristic architectural styles, the most frequently used artistic and technical processes, even portraits of the emperors, and also included gross errors derived from the oldest texts. In the 17th century the notions that westerners had of oriental Asia were still rather fanciful – a peaceful, rich and receptive country, in some ways similar to the almost 'degenerate' image that had been common in the 14th century. Above all, Europeans looked to the East to satisfy their fascination with 'exoticism', rather than to improve their general knowledge. Consequently, fantastic tales and invented accounts of journeys to the Far East continued to circulate throughout Europe in the 18th century, a typical example being that of

George Psalmanazar published in London in 1704.[102] China was represented in its 'preferred form' on the artistic items that came from there (fabrics, lacquer, and especially ceramics) and in the illustrated texts of the Jesuits and European geographers.

Accounts of China and Japan had already been published in the 1500s, but without illustrations to accompany the texts. Compiled by Giovan Battista Ramusio (1485-1557) from Treviso, the volume *Delle Navigazioni et Viaggi* is a grandiose and varied collection of travellers tales concerning both the Far East and the Americas, published for the first time in Venice in 1550 and frequently reprinted until 1606.[103] In 1569 the Dominican priest Gaspar da Cruz (?-c. 1570), who had lived in China for some months about 1556, published his *Tractado* providing much information about the country. Some years later in 1585 on the explicit instructions of pope Gregory XIII, the Spanish Augustinian Father Juan González de Mendoza (c. 1540-1617) completed the *Historia de las cosas más notables, ritos y costumbres del gran Reyno de la China*, which was translated into numerous languages following the first edition.[104] The first, more analytical study, the *Historiarum Indicarum libri XVI* compiled by the Jesuit priest Giovanni Petri Maffei (1533-1603), appeared in Florence in 1588 and was largely based on the writings of Alessandro Valignano (1539-1606) who had lived in the Far East for much of his life.[105] Engravings, especially illustrating the India subcontinent, by Baptista van Doetecun made from drawings by the author, Jan Huyghen van Linschoten (1563-1611), were included in the volume *Itinerario: Voyage oft schipvaert von Jan Huygen voan Linschoten naer Oost ofte Portugaels Indien, 1579-1592*), published in Amsterdam in 1596.[106] Dated 1599, Richard Hakluyt's (1552-1616) *Voyages* is an English translation of a general work on the Jesuits in China. One engraving of an Indian deity and fourteen of Japanese divinities appeared in the 1615 edition of *Imagini delli Dei de gl'Antichi* by Vincenzo Cartari (1531-after 1571), a volume of the *Seconda Parte delle Imagini de gli dei Indiani*, compiled by Lorenzo Pignoria (1571-1631), an antique dealer from Padova.[107] Accompanied by an explanatory text based on information provided by returning missionaries, the drawings for these prints were by Girolamo Aleandro (1574-1629) who used original oriental statues housed in the Jesuit collections in Rome for his models.[108] It was still rare to find images of the Far East in Europe in 1642 when the Portuguese Jesuit Alvaro Semedo (1585-1658) published his work on China *Relatione della Grande Monarchia della Cina* containing only four engravings – two maps and two portraits.[109]

From the mid 17th century, publications on China, both by Jesuits and by Dutch Protestants, began to contain an increasing number of illustrations. Such was the public and critical success they achieved that many of the images of chinoiserie used throughout the 1700s were based on these illustrations.[110] One of the volumes most widely available and most frequently used was entitled *Het gezantschap der Neerlantsche Oost-Indische Compagnie aan den grooten tartarischen cham*, by Jan Nieuhoff (1618-1672), first published in Amsterdam in 1665 and

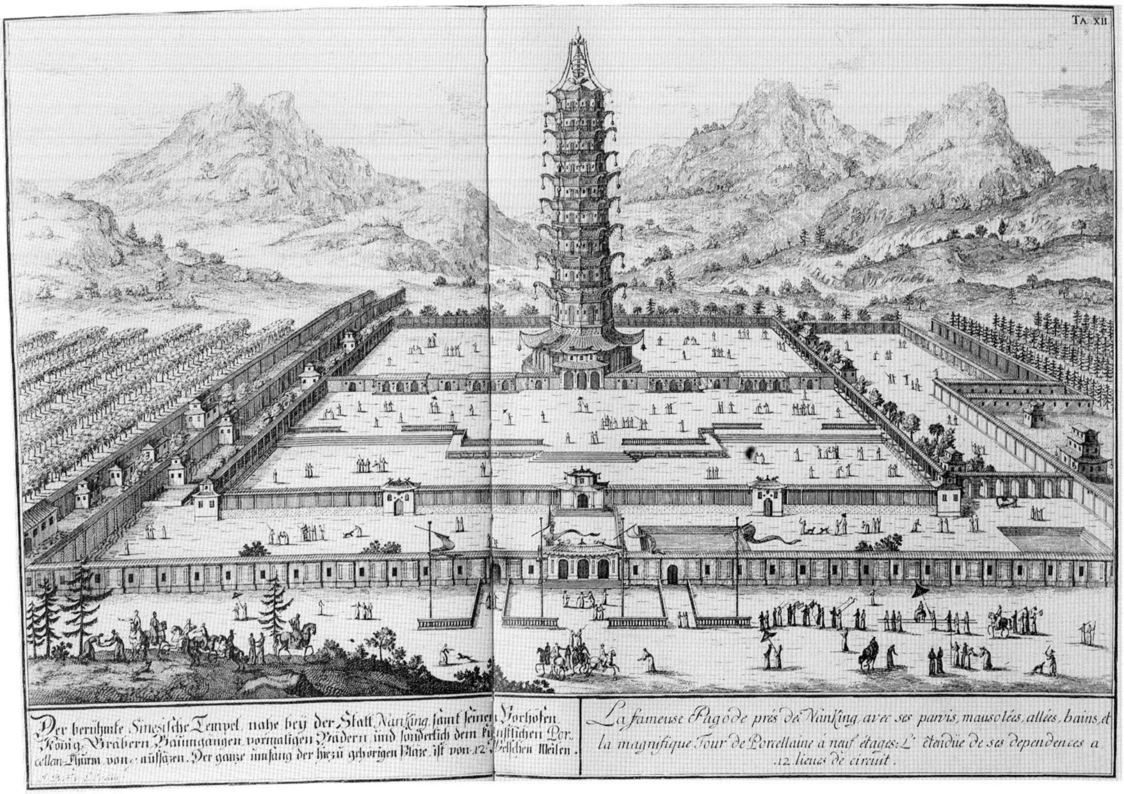

39. *The Nanking Pagoda*, engraving by Johann Bernard Fischer von Erlach, *Entwurf einer historischen Architektur*, 1721 (III, pl. 12). Basel, University Library.

Published in Vienna in 1721, the books written by the court architect Fischer von Erlach (1656-1723) on the fundaments of architecture, "Entwurff einer historischen Architektur" contain several engravings of China. The image of "La fameuse Pagode prés de Nanking…" illustrated here is obviously based on the print published over fifty years earlier by Nieuhoff (1665): both provided the model for 'Chinese' buildings which became highly fashionable in 18th century Europe.

quickly followed by translations into English and French. Nieuhoff had accompanied the Dutch diplomatic mission to China between 1655 and 1657 as a steward and his detailed account was supplemented by the sketches he had made at the time, transformed into engravings for the publication. Half genuine description, half romanticised reconstructions, the one hundred and fifty images in the volume provided the basis for many chinoiserie items, first and foremost the decorations on the boiserie Lackcabinett in the castle of Rosenborg in Denmark, commissioned by Frederick III (1609-1670) and completed by Francis de Bray before 1670.[111] In the same year Louis Le Vau (1612-1670), an architect employed to produce exotic works that would impress and amuse Louis XIV, designed the *Trianon de porcelain* in the park of Versailles. He based this on the *Porcelain Pagoda of Nanking* illustrated by Nieuhoff thus stimulating the building of a series of 'Chinese style' garden pavilions which continued uninterrupted until the 19th century. The illustrations in Nieuhoff's book also inspired Johann Bernard Fischer von Erlach (1656-1723), another architect, to publish some 'Chinese style' plates in his *Entwurf einer historischen Architektur* (1721), especially, in addition to the Nanking Pagoda, the artificial rocks erected in Shangai by Yu Yuan in 1559, and the Imperial Palace in Peking.[112]

In 1667 a renowned Jesuit father, Athanasius Kircher (1602-1680) published *China monumentis qua sacris qua profanis, nec non variis naturae et artis spectaculis, aliarumque rerum memorabilium argumentis illustrata*, more simply known as *China Illustrata*, in Amsterdam. The engravings in the volume are somewhere between truthful descriptions of oriental customs and memories somewhat embellished by distance, but were frequently used as the basis for chinoiserie decorations such as the Lacquer Room in Rosenborg dated 1670.[113] Despite the fact that Kircher's greatest wish was to go to the Far East and his emphatic requests before being sent to Italy in 1630, his superiors prevented such a mission and preferred him to remain in Europe.[114] A quick learner and endowed with a highly enquiring mind, Kircher studied the most disparate fields of scientific knowledge, ranging from mathematics to physics, from ethnography to astronomy and music. Believing that their origins stemmed from dynastic Egypt, his interest in extra European cultures was stimulated by both the information provided directly by other Jesuit Fathers on their return to Rome, and by studying texts on related subjects. In the preface to *China Illustrata* Kircher lists the principle sources for his work: *De Tartarico Bello Historiae* (Rome 1654), the *Novus Atlas Sinensis* (Amsterdam 1655) and *Sinicae Historiae Decas Prima* (Munich 1658), edited by Martino Martini (1614-1661), a Jesuit priest from Trento who was in China in 1643. The idea for the creation of a Museum in the Collegio Romano was the initiative of Kircher and it quickly became an obligatory point of reference for any intellectual visiting Rome. According to the description published in 1678 numerous oriental items were exhibited, many of which were chosen almost exclusively for their descriptive content, rather than any artistic quality or value as a 'curio'. The collections of contemporary *wunderkammern* on the other hand served an entirely different purpose.

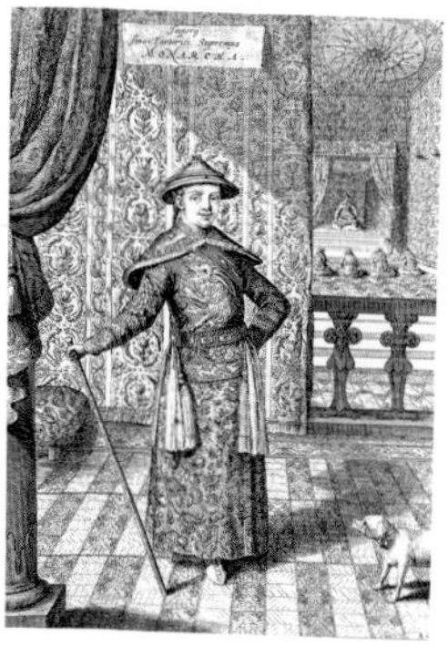

40. *The supreme sovereign of the Chinese empire*, engraving by Athanasius Kircher, *China Illustrata*, Amsterdam 1667. Basel, University Library.

Despite the Chinese subject, many details of the engraving are pure European Baroque. The monarch has little of the Orient about him, apart from his pointed hat and the dragon on his chest. However, the poet Jean de la Fontaine (1621-1695) wrote that Louis XIV decorated the walls of his private apartment with fabrics imported from China after having seen the engravings in Kircher's publication.

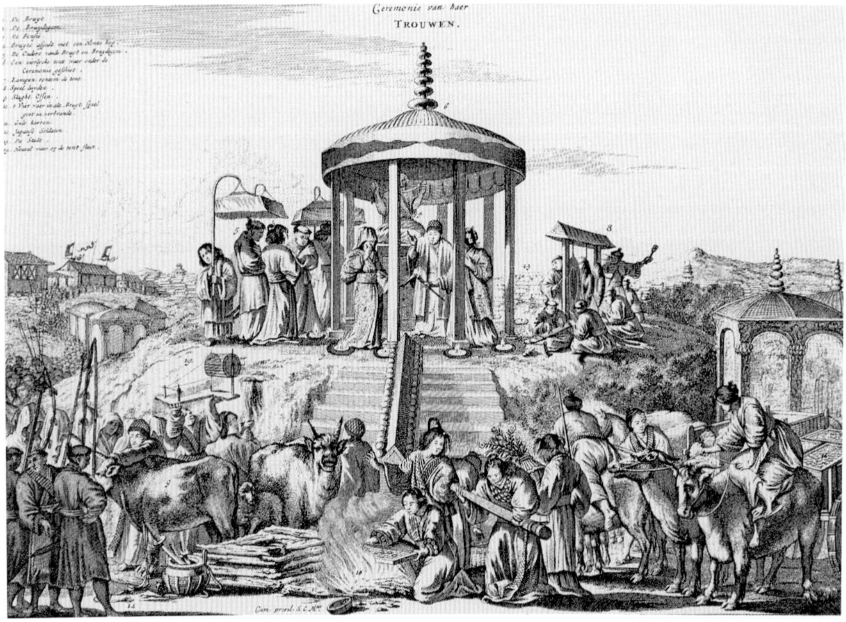

41. *The wedding*, engraving by Arnoldus Montanus, *Gedenkwaerdige Gesantschappen der Oost-Indische Maatschappy in't Vereenigde Nederland aan de Kaiseren van Japan*, Amsterdam 1669. Basel, University Library.

Although Montanus' publication was devoted to the customs and habits of Japan, many chinoiserie compositions were based on the images that accompanied the text. This portrayal of a *Wedding*, for example, is very similar to a painting of the same subject made by Boucher in 1740 (Besançon, Musée des Beaux-Arts), and subsequently used for a tapestry in the *Second Chinese Series*: certain details are almost identical.

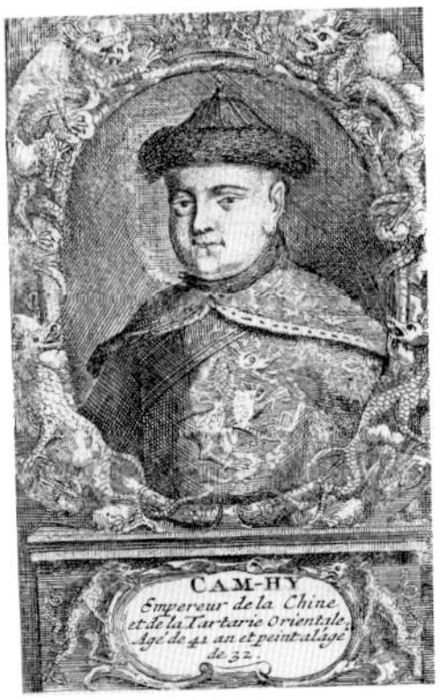

42. *Cam-Hy [Kangxi], Emperor of China and Eastern Tartary at the age of 41,* engraving by Louis-Danile Le Comte, *Nouveaux Mémoires sur l'Etat présent de la Chine,* 1696.

The text by the Jesuit priest, Louis-Daniel Le Comte published in 1696 on his return from his travels in the Far East, begun in 1685 as a member of the French delegation to Siam, was highly successful and by 1701 had already been published in English. As with Kircher several decades earlier (see. Fig. 40) the features and costume in this portrait are decidedly un-oriental. However, the dragon motif – one of the most characteristic of Chinese iconography and much used in European chinoiserie – does appear quite frequently.

Many images, frequently used for chinoiserie décor, accompanied the text by Arnoldus Montanus, the *Gedenkwaerdige Gesantschappen der Oost-Indische Maatschappy in't Vereenigde Nederland aan de Kaiseren van Japan* (Amsterdam 1669), which was immediately translated into English by John Ogilby and published in London in 1670 with the title *Atlas Japannensis.*[115] Like Nieuhoff's book this form of Dutch travel literature provided a secular alternative to contemporary publications of the Jesuits. Montanus (c. 1625-1683) had taken his degree in theology and philosophy in Leiden and had written numerous books on the history of Holland, Calvinist tracts and geography and was a leading member of the Protestant cultural elite. In 1650 he had already published *De wonderen van 't Oosten*, a compendium of information available at the time on the East. His book on Japan dated 1669 collected information provided by members of the Dutch East India Company following their travels there. The first part of the volume relates the events that took place during a diplomatic mission to the shogun Tokugawa Iemitsu in 1649-50. Andries Frisius also participated in the mission and also wrote an account of the journey though there are many discrepancies between the two. The second part assembles other accounts somehow garnered from the archives of the Dutch East India Company. Montanus' work was already widely read shortly after its first publication and some of the engravings were used throughout the 18th century by artists who specialized in chinoiserie. François Boucher was clearly inspired by the plates in Montanus' book, especially in 1740 when preparing the designs for the tapestries of the *Second Chinese Series* made by Beauvais.

Montanus' volume on Japan was published by the famous editor and engraver Jacob von Meurs (1619-1680) who was specialised in this kind of publication and had already collaborated on Nieuhoff's book. Von Meurs was planning a series of publications covering the geography of the entire world and the *Gedenkwaerdige Gesantschappen* was part of this project. Olfert Dapper (c. 1635-1689) also participated in the series and in 1668 had already

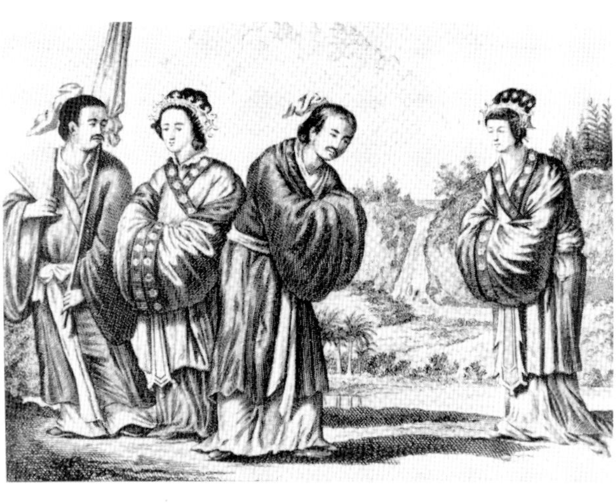

43. *The Arrival of a Lady,* engraving by Olfert Dapper, *Gedenkwaerding Bedryf der Nederlandsche Oost-Indische Meetschappye op de Kunste en in het Keizerrijk von Taising if Sina,* Amsterdam 1670.

The volume belongs to the ambitious series of geographical, ethnic and anthropological texts which included Nieuhoff and Montanus' books, all of which were published by the Dutch editor Von Meurs.

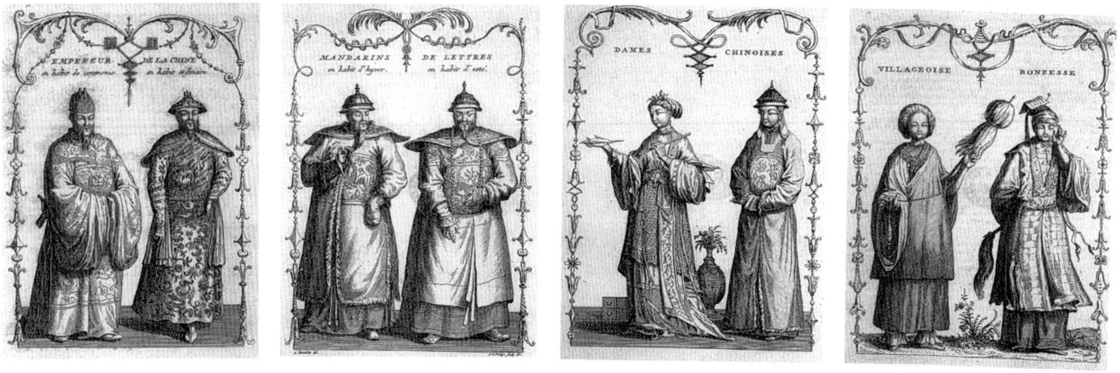

44a,b,c,d. Chinese characters, engravings by Jean-Baptiste Du Halde, *Description Géographique, Historique, Chronologique, Politique et Physique de l'Empire de la Chine et de la Tartarie Chinoise*, Paris-The Hague 1735-1736. Private collection.

The engravings that accompanied the text written by the Jesuit father, Du Halde provided models for many chinoiseries especially in the later part of the 18th century. In Italy they were used by Neapolitan and Sicilian artists at the end of the century and in the early 1800s for the decorative murals in the Favorita villa at Portici and the Chinese Palace in Palermo, for example.

contributed two important volumes on Africa. In 1670 he published *Gedenkwaerding Bedryf der Nederlandsche Oost-Indische Meetschappye op de Kunste en in het Keizerrijk von Taising if Sina*, later translated into English as the *Atlas Chinensis.* The book recounts the Dutch diplomatic mission to China in 1667 and included a considerable number of illustrations.[116] These too were used in the following decades as the basis for many chinoiserie decorations – Peter Schenk, for example, copied them in detail for his engravings of Chinese motifs published between 1700 and 1705.[117]
The quantity of such publications gradually increased as the West managed to establish cultural and commercial relations with the Far East on a more frequent and regular basis. Some of the volumes that most contributed to creating an image of China in Europe were a compilation by Father Joachim Bouvet (1656-1730) entitled *L'éstat present de la Chine en figures*, Paris 1697,[118] the *Histoire de l'Edit de l'Empereur de la Chine* (Paris 1698) by Father Charles Le Gobien (1653-1708), and especially *Nouveaux Mémoires sur l'Etat présent de la Chine* (Paris 1696) by the Jesuit priest Louis-Daniel Le Comte (1655-1728) in which the first critical comments on the Chinese 'paradise' appear.[119] Japan, its history and traditions were described instead in *The History of Japan* published on the initiative of Hans Sloane (1660-1753) in London in 1727 and based on the writings and drawings of Engelbert Kaempfer (1651-1716) who had lived in Japan for a lengthy period. So successful was the book that it was immediately translated into Dutch and French. Of the many Jesuit publications on China to have had a degree of influence on the development of chinoiserie, the *Description Géographique, Historique, Chronologique, Politique et Physique de l'Empire de la Chine et de la Tartarie Chinoise … ornée d'un gran nombre de Figures et des Vignettes* (Paris-The Hague 1735-1736) by Father Jean-Baptiste Du Halde (1674-1743) is particularly interesting for the engravings and texts that describe the traditional methods and techniques of Chinese art.[120]

1) Bertuccioli, Masini 1996, pp. 4-6.
2) Bussagli 1986, p. 41.
3) Surdich 2007, p. 11.
4) Bertuccioli, Masini 1996, pp. 10-17.
5) Bussagli 1986, p. 12.
6) Boothroyd, Détrie 1992.
7) Surdich 2007, p. 117.
8) Surdich 2007, pp. 65-67.
9) Impey 1977, p. 175.
10) Odorico da Pordenone 1982.
11) Bertuccioli, Masini 1996, pp. 62-73.
12) Krása 1983.
13) Chiappori 1981.
14) Tanaka 1985.
15) Chiappori 1981, pp. 284-285.
16) Prinz 1993, p. 416.
17) Frugoni 2002, pp. 186-190.
18) Prinz 1993, pp. 416-417.
19) Whitehouse 1966.
20) Honour 1961 (1963), p. 37.
21) Bussagli 1986, p. 124.
22) Bussagli 1986, pp. 107-108; Vercellin 1990, p. 33; Tanaka 1994, p. 129.
23) Surdich 2007, pp. 125-130.
24) Bussagli 1986, p. 108.
25) Vercellin 1990, p. 30.
26) Simmons 1956.
27) Magagnato 1983; Bussagli 1986, pp. 112-129.
28) Santangelo 1959, p. 15.
29) Simmons 1948, p. 23, fig. 29.
30) Santangelo 1959, pp. 15-16.
31) Curatola 1990, p. 46.
32) Cecchi 2001.
33) Klesse 1967.
34) Pedrocco 2003.
35) Tanaka 1984; Tanaka 1994, pp. 129-130.
36) Bussagli 1986, p. 46.
37) Bussagli 1986, p. 87.
38) Devoti 1976, p. XIII; Bussagli 1986, p. 88.
39) Romano 1994.
40) Simmons 1948.
41) Devoti 1989.
42) Bussagli 1986, p. 101.
43) Davanzo Poli, Moronato 1994, p. 20.
44) Vercellin 1990, p. 28.
45) Rispoli Fabris 1974, p. 143.
46) Impey 1977, p. 54.
47) Morena 2005, p. 39.
48) Lightbown 1969, p. 231.
49) Morena 2005, p. 17.
50) Piccolpasso Durantino 1879, pl. 32.
51) Alverà Bortolotto 1981, pp. 64-65, pls. XLVI-XLVIII.
52) Clarke 1974, pp. 25-26.
53) Berti 1986, pls. 27-34; Berti 1998, pp. 135-137.
54) Cora, Fanfani 1982; Alinari 1987.
55) Ravanelli Guidotti 1998, pp. 265-283, no. 60e.
56) Ferrari 2003, p. 35.
57) Cora, Fanfani 1986, pp. 15-16.
58) Campori 1879, pp. 35-36.
59) Cora, Fanfani 1982, p. 15.
60) Campori 1879, p. 38; Cora, Fanfani 1986, p. 15.
61) Righi Guerzoni, in Sassuolo 2000, pp. 69, 73-74.
62) Bertocchi 1988, p. 38.
63) Cora, Fanfani 1986, p. 16.
64) Dorigato 2002, p. 54.
65) Guasti 1902, cited in Cora, Fanfani 1986, pp. 14-15.
66) Clarke 1974, p. 27; Cora, Fanfani 1986, p. 15.
67) Campori 1879, pp. 23-24.
68) Clarke 1974.
69) Barovier Mentasti 1982, p. 69.
70) Huth 1971, pp. 2-10; González-Palacios 1986, pp. 307-309, 315; González-Palacios 1996, pp. 42-43; González-Palacios 2004, pp. 42-47; Grube 2006.
71) Huth 1971, p. 3.
72) Huth 1971, p. 3.
73) Huth 1971, p. 10, pls. 35-36; Durante, Martellotti 1982; Trionfi Honorati 1982.
74) Huth 1971, p. 2.
75) Franzoi 1990, p.83, no. 117, fig. 35 a p. 169.
76) Huth 1971, p. 4.
77) Berlin 1973, p. 206, no. J2a.
78) Huth 1971, pp. 4-5; Impey 1977, p. 114.
79) Schlosser 1908, p. 64.
80) De Moura Carvalho 2001.
81) Huth 1971, fig. 30.
82) Colle 1993, figs. 5-6; Colle in Mantova 2000, p. 147; Colle 2000, pp. 158-159, no. 34.
83) Morena 2005, p. 38.
84) Heikamp in Firenze 1997, p. 238, no. 190.
85) Scalini in Firenze 2005, p. 124, no. I.71.
86) Colle in Mantova 2000, p. 143, no. 125.
87) Santini 2003, fig. 6.
88) Gheroldi 1995, pp. 22-23.
89) Huth 1971, p. 14; Jacobson 1993, p. 43.
90) Huth 1971, pls. 38-44; Beevers 2008, p. 15.
91) Lisbon 1994.
92) Jarry 1981, pp. 71-88.
93) Farris 2004.
94) Pessa 2005, p. 56, no. 41.
95) Genoa 2004.
96) Cameirana 2004.
97) Ericani, Marini 1990, p. 237.
98) Mottola Molfino 1976, figs. 395-396.
99) Lightbown 1969, pp. 253-261.
100) Mignini 2005.
101) Lightbown 1969, pp. 250-251; Berlin 1973, p. 133, no. B5.
102) Innocenti 2007.
103) Berlin 1973, p. 153, no. E1.
104) Berlin 1973, p. 153, no. E2.
105) Alessandro Valignano 2008.
106) Berlin 1973, pp. 153-154, no. E3.
107) Lightbown 1969, pp. 242-248; Cartari 2004, pp. XIV-XXI, 377-400.
108) Lightbown 1969, p. 244.
109) Berlin 1973, pp. 155-156, no. E7.
110) Berlin 1973, pp. 158-159, no. E12; Ulrichs 2007.
111) Boesen 1979.
112) Berlin 1973, pp. 207-208, no. J7.
113) Berlin 1973, pp. 156-158, no. E10.
114) Lo Sardo 2001.
115) Hasselink 2002.
116) Berlin 1973, p. 161, no. E20.
117) Ducret 1966.
118) Berlin 1973, p. 162, no. E23.
119) Jacobson 1993, pp. 34-35; Détrie in Parigi 2007, p. 25.
120) Berlin 1973, p. 163, no. E29.

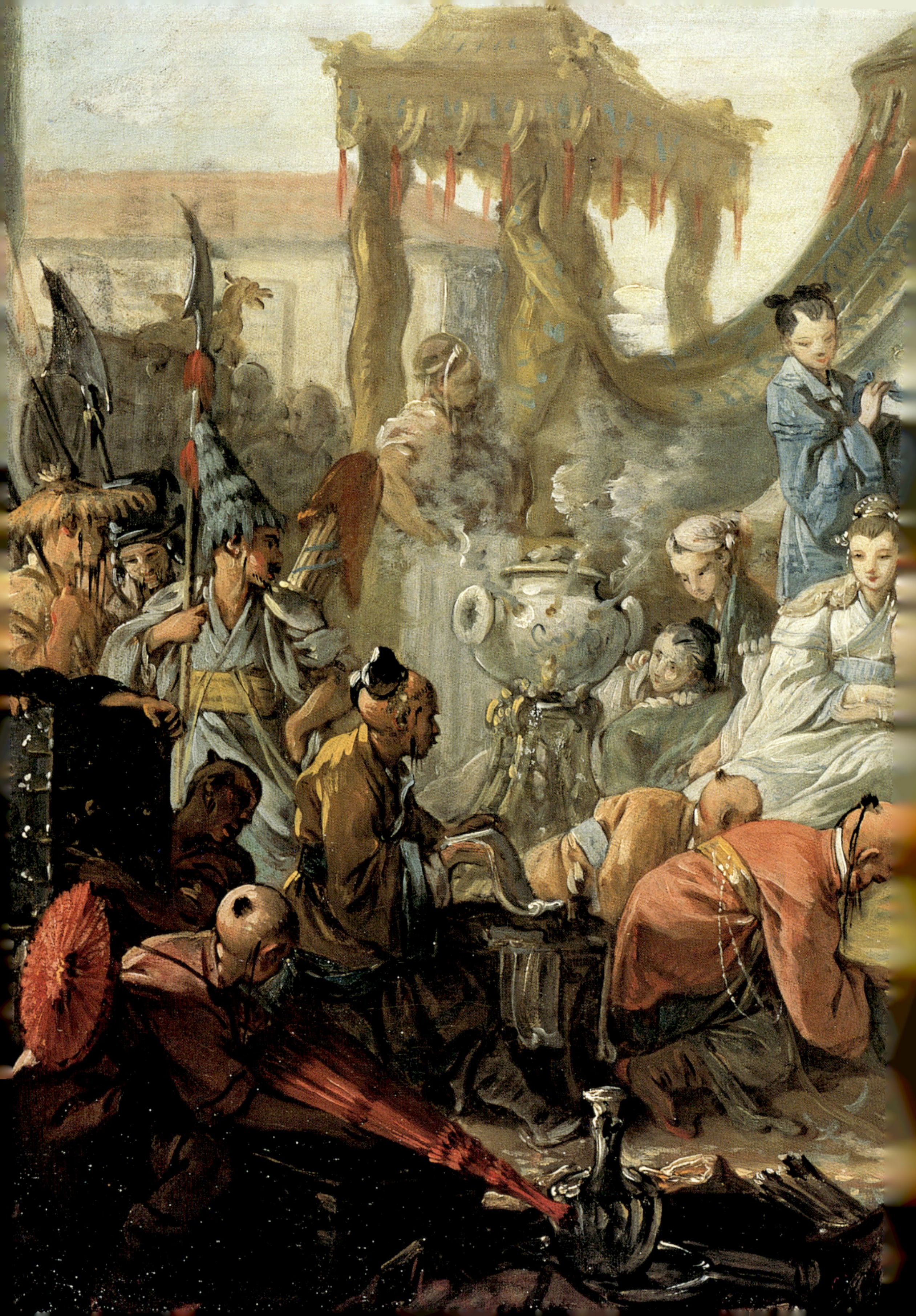

2 Chinoiserie in Europe in the 18th Century

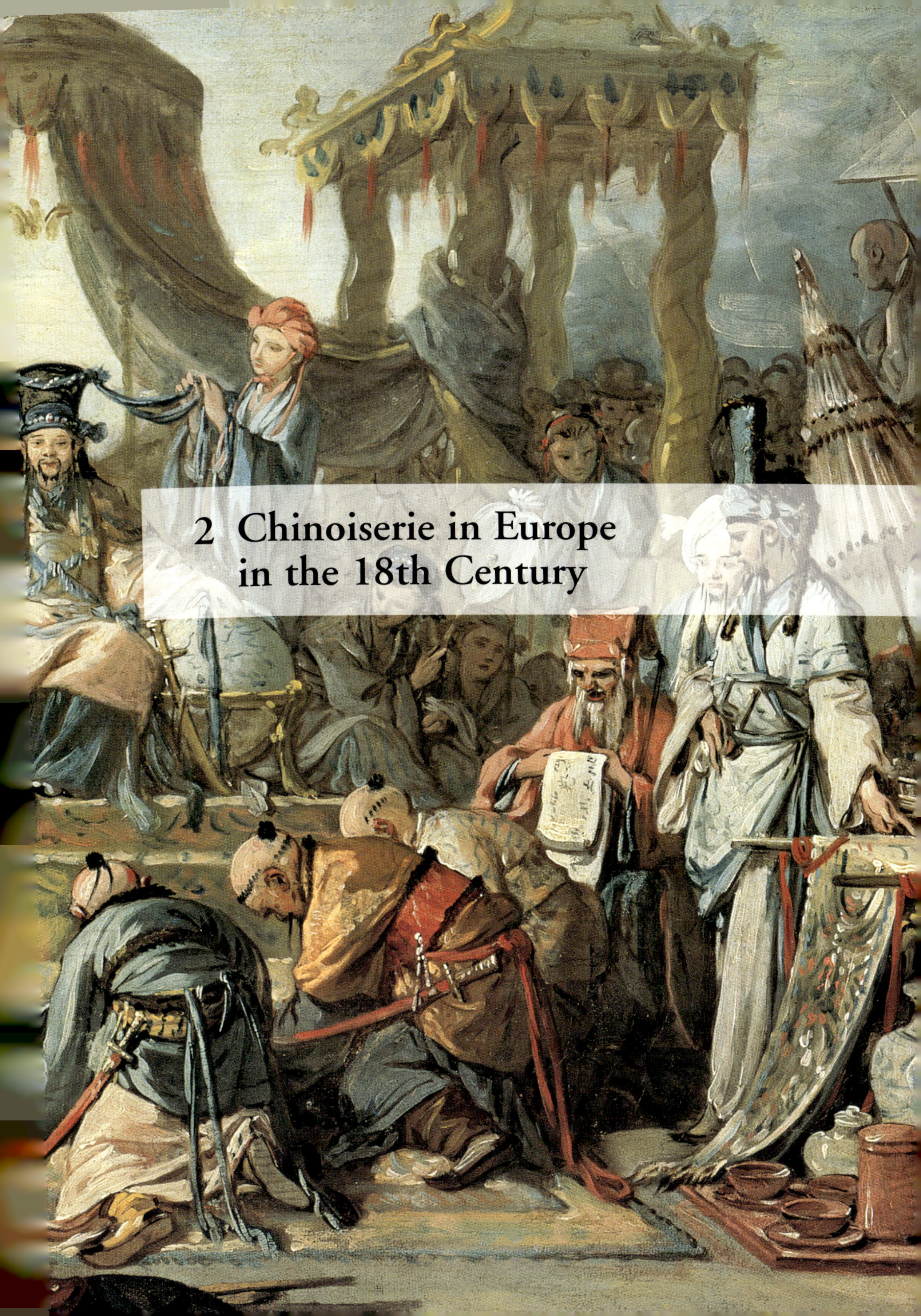

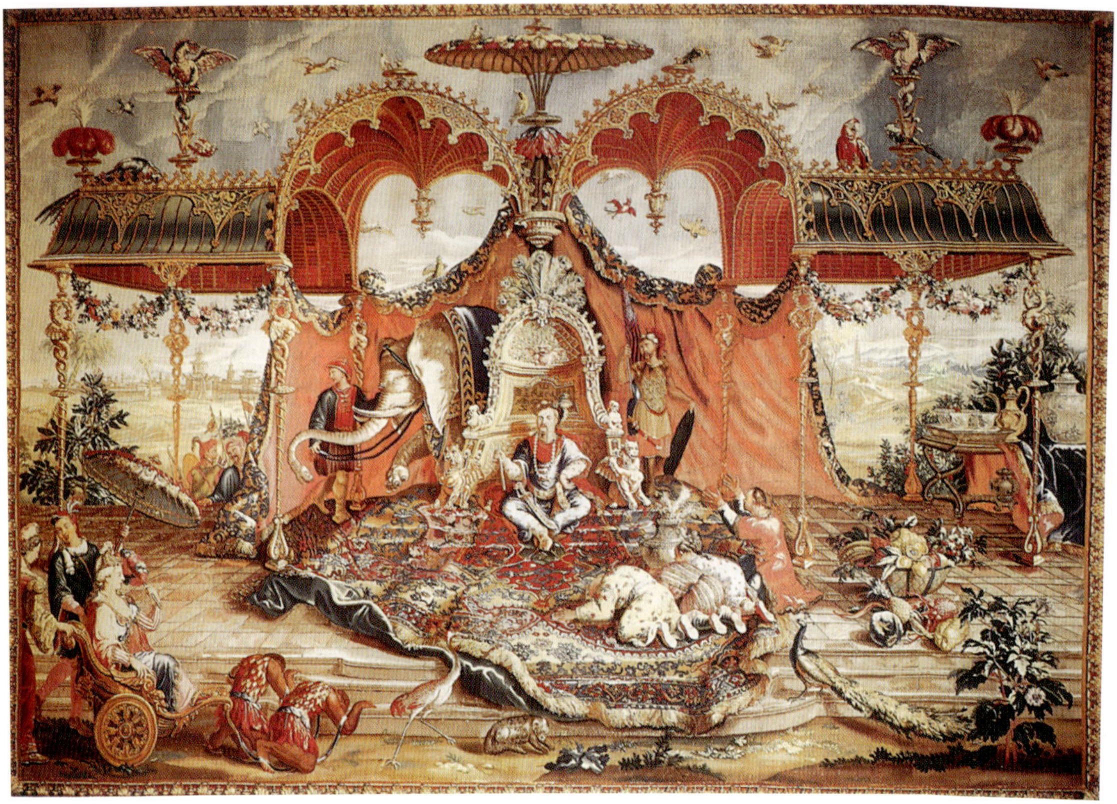

45. *The Emperor's Audience*, a tapestry from the suite *L'Empereur de Chine*, Beauvais tapestry, 1725-1730. Paris, Musée du Louvre.

The suite of tapestries made at the Beauvais factory from 1688 is one of the masterpieces of international chinoiserie during the baroque period. The elaborate design mixes a varied range of exotic elements providing an excellent example of the passion Louis XIV and his court had for the Orient, albeit entirely invented and far from representing a true image of the Asian lands.

France

Louis XIV and Baroque Orientalism

According to Hugh Honour, the development of 'baroque chinoiserie' began in 1670,[1] the year Louis XIV (1638-1715) commissioned the architect Louis Le Vau to build the *Trianon de porcelaine* in the park of Versailles as a gift for his current mistress, Mme de Montespan (1640-1707). Although it was said to be based on Nieuhoff's engraving of the famous *Nanking Pagoda*, it was in fact a single storey building with a thoroughly classical appearance that had little in common with Chinese structures. Indeed, even the external facing was made of ceramic tiles from Delft, Nevers, Rouen and Lisieux and was certainly not of porcelain. Despite this, writers of the day were at pains to describe it as a quite typically Chinese creation, probably for the characteristic prevalence of blue and white both inside and out, doubtless inspired by the porcelain with which the entire Orient was associated at the time. This fantastic construction was the first 'Chinese style' pavilion built in Europe, but so delicate was it that in 1687 it had to be demolished as the costs of maintenance became prohibitive. However, the arrival at court in 1684 and in 1686 of two diplomatic missions from Siam stimulated a renewed interest in the 'exotic style' which quickly became a complete mania. This French fashion developed in many different genres and included various kinds of collections, artistic production and culture in general.

One of the greatest exponents of Louis XIV chinoiserie was the royal decorator Jean Bérain (1637-1711) whose ornamental compositions contained evident references to the Far East and to China in particular. "The designer of a particular style of décor, somewhere between 16th-century grotesques and the complicated swags and garlands and cherubs characteristic of the Baroque",[2] Bèrain eagerly interpreted Louis's fascination with 'exoticism' by simply using figures of Chinamen, or monkeys and pagodas, in place of the fauns, classical statues and cherubs which at the time populated the French decorative repertory, and owed much to the Roman Baroque of Bernini, Pietro da Cortona and Borromini.[3] Bérain also organised numerous court celebrations some of which were inspired by China such as the *collation à la chinoise* hosted by the king at Versailles on 7 January 1700 and famed for the costumes, settings, and novelties, all devised in a Chinese style. The entire scenario was most probably based on original Chinese theatre, described in an account by Ambassador Isbrand, published in Hamburg, which had reached Versailles two years earlier in 1698. The

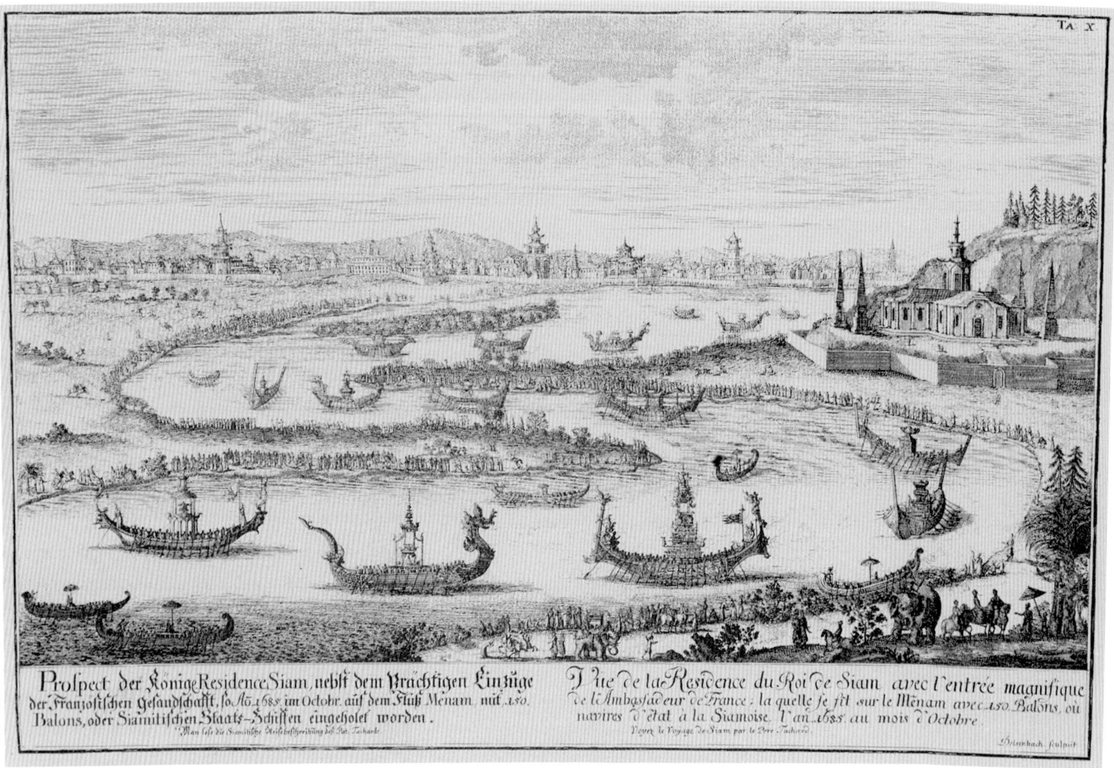

46. *View of the king of Siam's palace with the grand arrival of the French ambassador*, engraving by Johann Bernard Fischer von Erlach, *Entwurf einer historischen Architektur*, 1721. Basel, University Library.

Two Siamese delegations arrived in Paris in 1684 and 1686 stimulating a renewed interest in the Far East on the part of Louis XIV and the French court; in 1685 a French delegation travelled to Siam and their arrival is commemorated in this engraving.

performance of acrobats held to celebrate the arrival of the Siamese diplomatic mission in Paris was another memorable event,[4] and the Chinese theme continued to appear in other theatrical performances during this period, such as *Les Chinois* by Jean François Regnard (1655-1709) in 1692, the *Théâtre italien de Gherardi* in 1700 and in 1713 (*Foire*).[5] The baroque chinoiseries invented by Bérain provided a model for European artists for the entire 18th century.

The acquisition of goods from China boomed throughout France at this time – porcelain, textiles and lacquered Chinese, Japanese and Indian works were proudly exhibited in the houses of the most important and well-informed personalities and architects were requested to design new furnishings for their display. Such an immense quantity of goods was imported to France by the East India Company, established in 1664. The local manufacturers soon found themselves facing a serious economic crisis, and the only way in which to avoid complete collapse was to start producing works in the oriental style, a decision which obliged weavers, ceramic factories and furniture makers to adapt their output. At the end of the century, the ceramic factories of Nevers and Rouen were established, encouraged and supported by both royal commissions and the example of nearby Delft.[6] Nevers was set up on the initiative of some Italian ceramists in the retinue of Luigi Gonzaga (1539-1595) who had become duke of Nevers

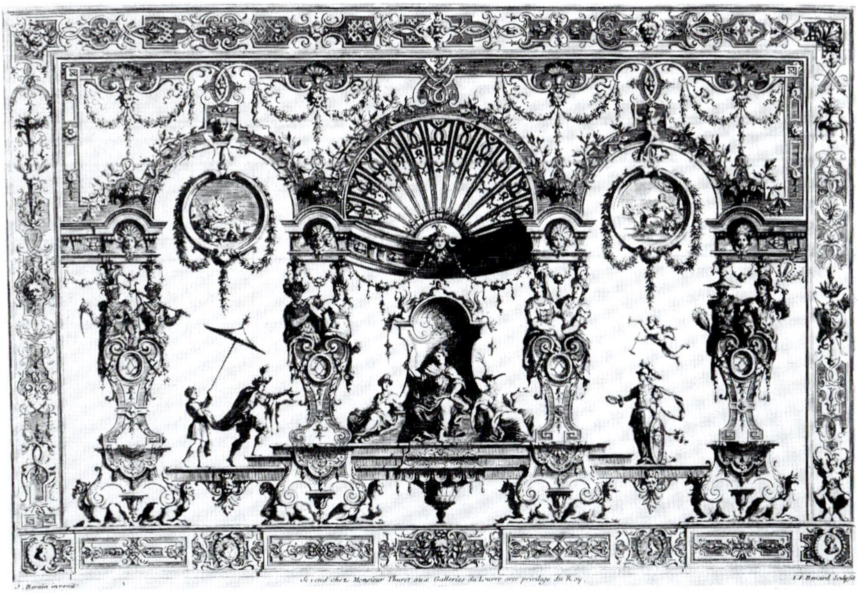

47. Jean Bérain, Grotesques with chinoiserie, engraving, late 17th century – early 18th century. London, Victoria and Albert Museum.

France's decorative repertory under Louis was established by Bérain who published numerous engravings. In this image the eastern theme is represented by the oriental figure of a supplicant on the left. The context is, however, classical in style and the ornamentation is based on 16th-century Italian decorative designs.

on marrying Henriette of Clèves (1542-1601). Thus, towards the end of the century Italian late Renaissance grotesque motifs grew in popularity and were not only applied to ceramics but were also utilised by decorators working for Louis XIV. The factory of Rouen received a great boost from the Sun King when, in an attempt to fill the badly depleted coffers of the state, he took the initiative of melting down his silver tableware and replacing it with the cheaper majolica, inviting his subjects to follow his example. In 1709 therefore, he commissioned an entire majolica dinner service from the Rouen factory.

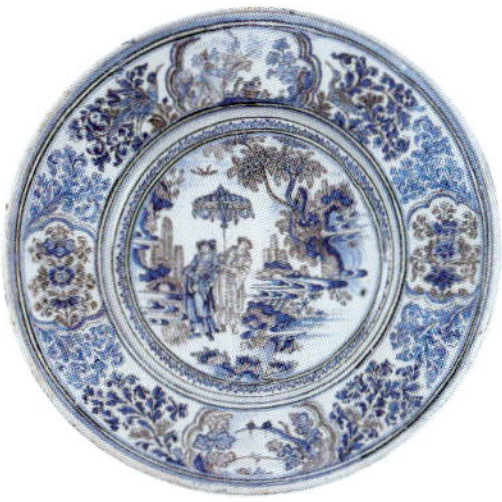

48. Plate. Nevers, late 17th century. Sèvres, Musée National de Céramique.

The origins of this scene do not lie in original Far Eastern ceramic decoration, but rather in the engravings of Chinese subjects (Nieuhoff, Kircher, Montanus, etc.) which became increasingly available in Europe after the 1650s. In this case however, the decorator has not simply copied the scene but has interpreted it with his own personal touch.

French furniture *au façon de la Chine* was also produced during this period, and the department of *ouvrages de la Chine* which Louis created at Gobelins under the direction of Charles Le Brun (1619-1690)[7] was responsible for making many pieces; examples of these works are now so rare that it is impossible to fully describe or appreciate their qualities.

However, the second *Livre commode*, dated 1692, mentions that "the Langlois family imitated the furniture of China extremely well ... master Essarts ... copied both the form and the relief work of *Lachinage*. The younger Mr Langlois excelled in producing figures and Chinese motifs",[8] while as early as 1674 Antoine d'Emery published recipes for the preparation of lacquers in *Recueil de Curiosités Rares et Nouvelles*; some years later, in 1688, the *Traité de mignature, les secrets de faire le vernis de la Chine* appeared while Father Louis Le Comte provided further information on the method followed in the Far East in his volume published in 1696.

The tapestry factories of Gobelins and Beauvais, founded respectively in 1662 and 1664, began production in the same period. The suite of the *History of the Emperor of China* was produced at Beauvais and became part of his repertory in 1688, remaining in the catalogue until at least 1731.[9] The series consisted of ten scenes although they were usually sold in sets of six panels.

The designs were made by three artists, Guy Louis Vernasal (1648-1729), Belin de Fontenay (1653-1715) and Baptiste Monnoyer (1634-1699), who clearly took their inspiration from the engravings that accompanied the texts of Nieuhoff, Dapper, Montanus, Martini and Kircher. The scene with *Les Astronomes* is a kind of graphic account of the work of two Jesuit fathers – Jean Adam Schall von Bell (1591-1666) and Ferdinand Verbiest (1623-1688) – who were famous for the achievements they had obtained during their mission in China. Verbiest was the author of *Astronomia Europaea sub Imperatore tartaro Sinico*, published in 1687, in which he described the installation of astronomical instruments in the Peking Observatory.[10] During the same period the Gobelins factory produced the *Tenture des Indes* suite, designed by some of the artists who had created the *Tenture chinoise*.[11]

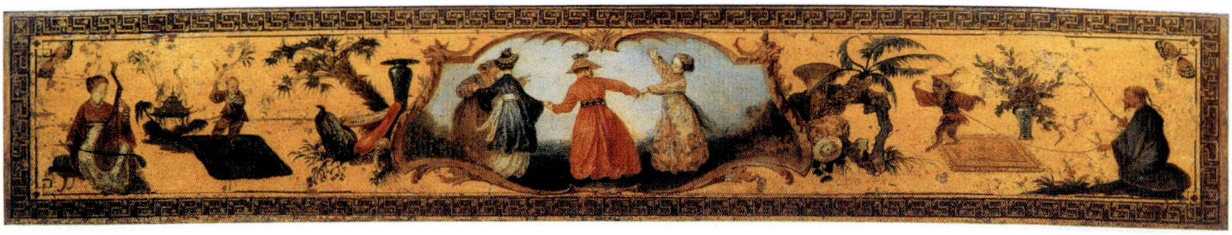

49a,b. Antoine Watteau, Chinoiserie. Florence, Fondazione Roberto Longhi.

Not all scholars agree with the attribution of this work to Watteau, but it is unanimously accepted that it is an early 18th-century French work. The panel was probably originally part of a boiserie decoration or piece of furniture (though it is unlikely to have been a harpsichord), dismantled at an unknown date. The reference to Watteau would date the piece to approximately the period when the Cabinet du Roi was made at the Chateau La Muette (c.1709).

Rococo

Bérain's decorative compositions provided a prototype for the future development of French chinoiserie, embraced and continued by many renowned artists. Around 1709 Antoine Watteau (1684-1721) decorated the *Cabinet du Roi* in the Château de La Muette.[12] No longer in existence, but illustrated in a series of engravings by François Boucher (1703-1770), Etienne Jeaurat (1699-1789) and Jean Aubert (c. 1680-1741), and first presented in the posthumous publication *Oeuvre Gravé* (1726-1735) edited by his friend Julien, Watteau's *Cabinet* may be considered the work on which all later international rococo chinoiserie was based.[13] Elegant yet with an air of melancholy, the scenes he devised perfectly integrated a Chinese element with the context of early 18th-century Europe, combining courtly and rural motifs with the sensuality of exotic subjects. Given the precision with which the Chinese names in the titles of these works are transcribed, it is probable that the artist was able to consult original Chinese paintings – perhaps the forty-nine volumes presented as a gift to Louis XIV in 1697 by a Jesuit on his return from China.[14] Compositions such as the *Divinité Chinoise*, for example, framed by elegant stylised sinuous scrolls in the style of Claude Audran III

(1658-1734), provided an inexhaustible source of inspiration for the chinoiserie developed by various French artists during the first half of the 18th century.

Many artists at work during the period when French Rococo was enjoying its greatest success (from 1725-1750) designed chinoiserie works: P.P. Bacqueville;[15] Gilles Marie Oppenordt (1672-1742), who introduced the Rococo in a series of six ornamental designs with elegantly slender scrolls; Nicolas Pineau (1684-1754), who produced a series of *Nouveaux desseins de plaques, consoles, torchères et médailles* between 1725 and 1730, as well as a drawing now in the Musée des Arts Décoratifs in Paris showing three models for *commodes* with chinoiserie motifs decorating the lacquer panels and probably intended as furnishings for a complete room in the Chinese style;[16] Alexis Peyrotte (1699-1769), who most probably was the author of a series of four panels dated 1725 of quite excellent quality and originally in the salon of

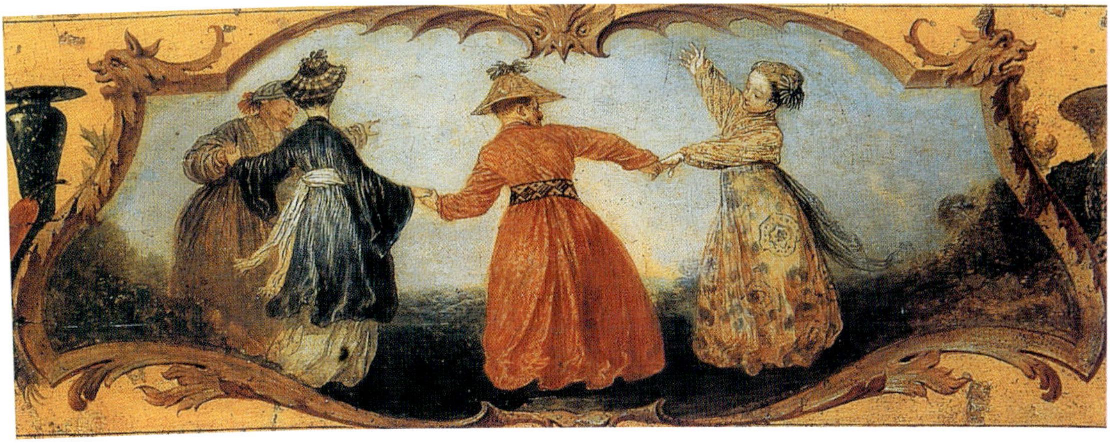

the residence of the prince of Thurn and Taxis in Frankfurt, designed by Robert de Cotte (1656-1735).[17] Many of Peyrotte's chinoiserie designs were published in Lyons between 1740 and 1743 by Robert-Menge Pariset in the *Suite de nouveaux cartouches chinois,* and from 1755 to 1758 he decorated two residences at Choisy in the oriental style.[18] In 1730 for a room in the Hôtel de Boulogne, now destroyed, Nicolas Lancret (1690-1743) made a series of panels now in the Musée des Arts Decoratifs in Paris, which provide a particularly fascinating example of the oriental theme, portrayed however by figures in clothes and attitudes that appear more Parisian than Eastern.[19] In addition to a panel with a *Pagoda and Exotic Fruits* (Paris, Bibliothèque Nationale de France),[20] in 1735 Jacques de Lajoüe (1686-1761) produced four designs with a Chinese subject (*Prosternation Chinoise*, *Divertissement Chinois*, *Observation Chinoise* and *Conversation Chinoise*) partly inspired by the creations of Nieuhoff and published after the death of the artist by Basan (1723-1797).[21] De Lajoüe also designed decorative motifs for silks and some

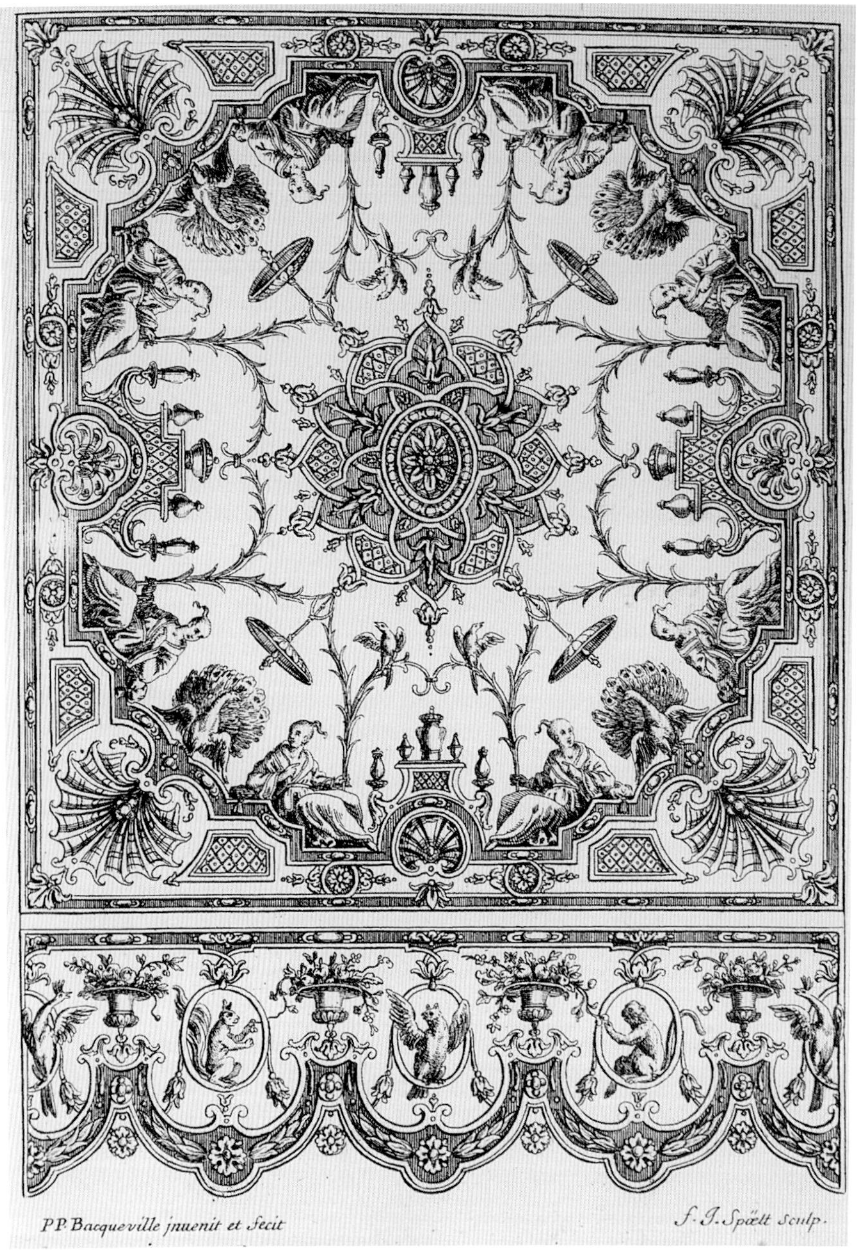

50. P.-P. Bacqueville, Grotesques and chinoiserie, 1720.

Author of the *Livre d'Ornements propre pour les meubles et pour le Peintres...*, in the early 18th century P.-P. Bacqueville created a range of ornamental compositions with the obligatory references to chinoiserie. In this engraving, figures of Chinamen, parasols, jars and vases set on shelves alternate with arabesques reminiscent of Italian Renaissance designs. Such scenes and images greatly contributed to the diffusion throughout Europe of the oriental style which originated in France.

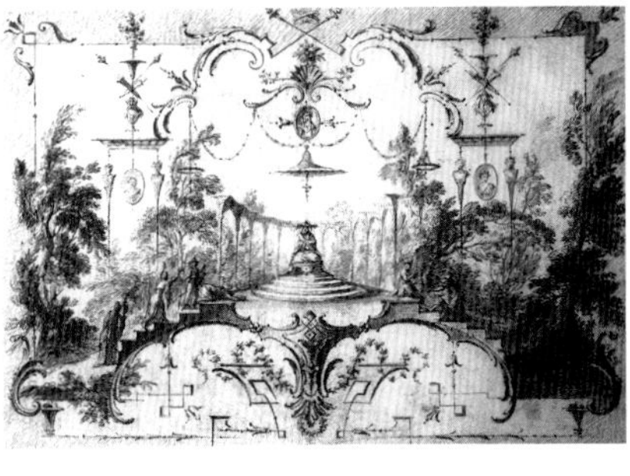

51. After Antoine Watteau (Gabriel Huquier ?), *Divinité chinoise*, 1729-1730. New York, Cooper Union Museum.

In this and the following illustration, Watteau represented the theme of homage to a deity, one of the most frequent in chinoiserie iconography during the 1700s. Hugh Honour attributed the engraving to Gabriel Huquier, based on a composition created by Watteau.

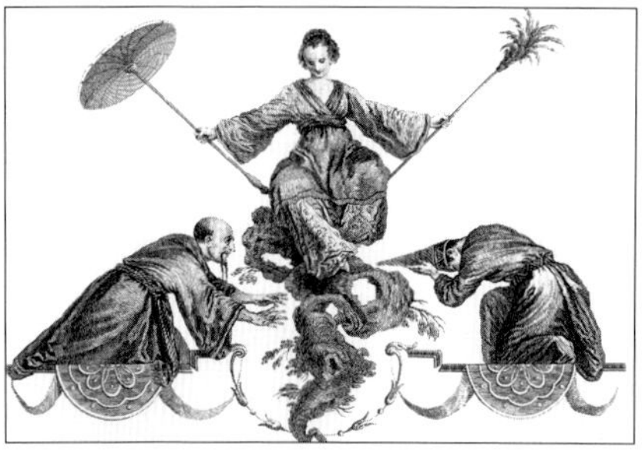

52. After Antoine Watteau, *Idole de la déesse Ki Mao Sao dans le Royaume de Mang au pays de Laos*, c. 1729.

One of Antoine Watteau's most famous chinoiseries, designed for the decoration of the Cabinet du Roi in the Chateau La Muette and engraved about 1729 by Aubert. The image was frequently used during the 18th century throughout Europe and Italy. A variation also exists entitled *La Déesse THVO-CHVU dans l'isle d'Haïnan.*

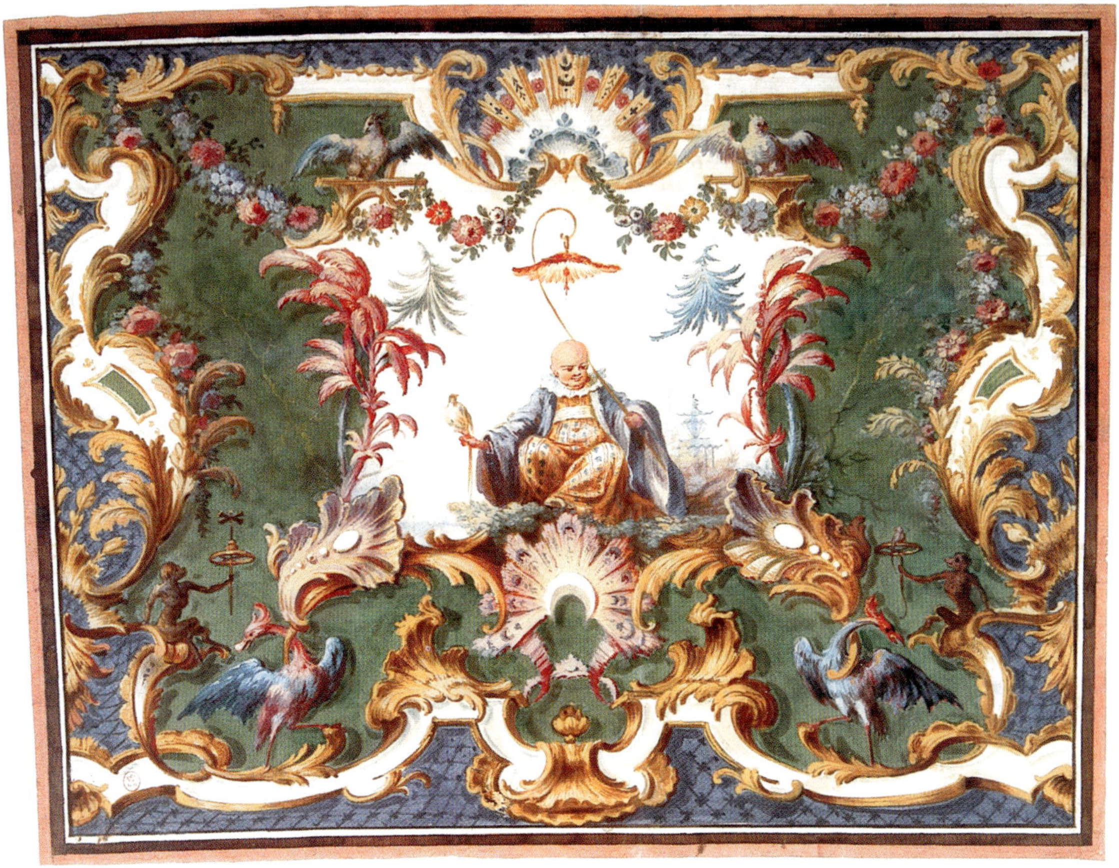

53. Alexis Peyrotte, Figure of a Chinaman framed by volutes, c. 1745-1752. Paris, Bibliothèque Nationale.

Peyrotte probably designed this composition for use on a screen: it is paired with a second sheet (Paris, Bibliothèque Nationale, Etampes, Hd 64 réserve, Folio, f. 12, no. 18), which portrays an equally exuberant decoration.

64 of his chinoiserie patterns for fabrics have survived, although it is not known if they were ever used by the factories of Tours and Lyons. The engraver and publisher Gabriel Huquier (1695-1772) worked for many famous artists, including those mentioned, and probably this frequent contact with Chinese subjects inspired him to publish his *Recueil des différentes especes d'oiseaux, fleurs, plantes et trophées de la Chine* in 1745.[22] Other artists who adopted the genre were Juste-Aurèle Meissonnier (1695-1750);[23] Jacques Caffiéri (1668-1755),[24] a bronze worker in Paris; François-Thomas Mondon (1709-1755), some of whose Chinoiserie designs were published in the *Quatrième Livre de formes rocailles* in 1736;[25] Pierre Quentin Chedel (1705-1763);[26] Gilliers, an engraver who in 1769 designed and published amusing table centrepieces with figures of Chinamen amidst bizarre *rocaille* settings;[27] the goldsmith Claude II Balliu (1661-1754) who created a magnificent centre-piece in gilded silver;[28] Claude Gillot (1673-1722) a contemporary of Watteau;[29] Jean Baptiste Pater (1695-1736).[30]

Set within the most classical French Rococo ornamental frames graced with scrolls, pavilions and shells in the *rocaille* style, Watteau's designs were re-used by Christophe Huet (1700-1759) in his most famous chinoiserie work – the

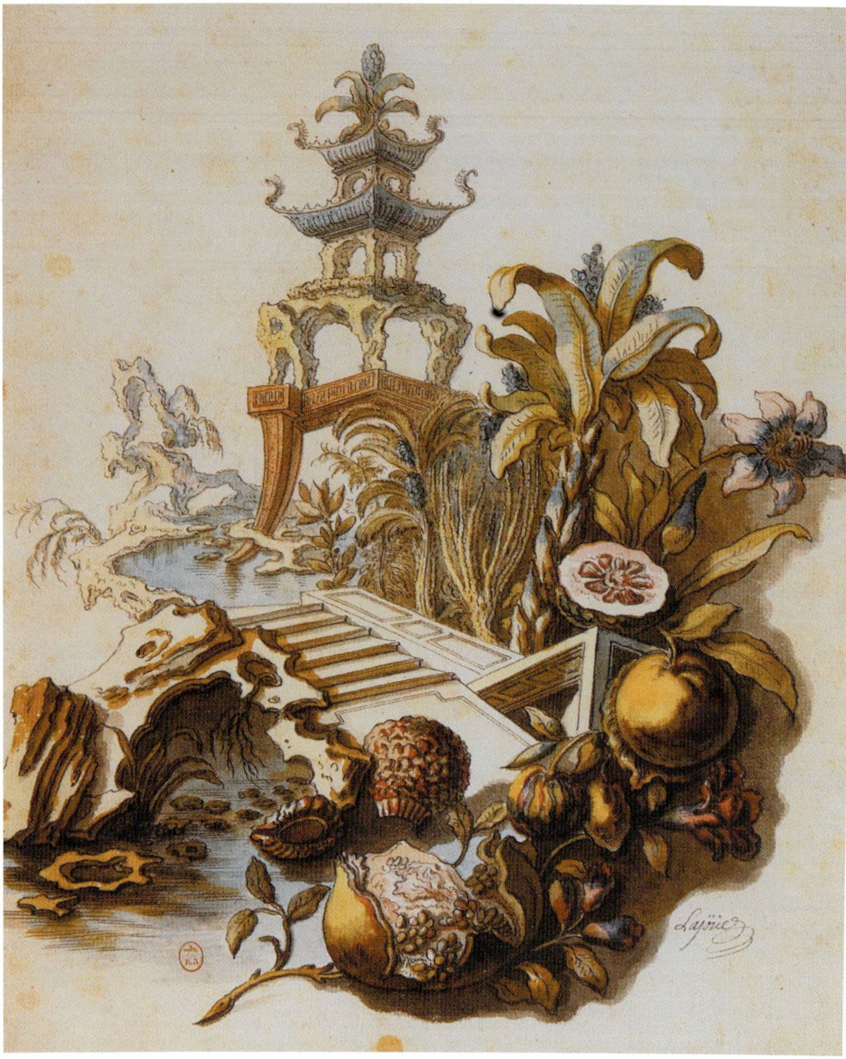

54. Jacques de Lajoüe, *Pagoda and Exotic Fruits*, c. 1734-1740. Paris, Bibliothèque Nationale.

Jacques de Lajoüe was one of the French ornamentalists to successfully experiment in combining Rococo and chinoiserie. This and a similar drawing also in the National Library, Paris (Estampes, Hd 64 réserve, Folio, f. 8, no. 12: cm. 53,2x39,4) was never reproduced as a print. It has been suggested that this particular composition decorated the fabric used in the bathroom of queen Maria Lesczinska in 1737.

55. Gabriel Huquier, *Vases with Flowers, Fruits and Peacock Feathers*, engraving from the *Recueil des différentes especes d'oiseaux, fleurs, plantes et trophées de la Chine*, c. 1745. Paris, Bibliothèque d'Art et d'Archéologie (J. Doucet Collection).

This highly elegant composition shows Gabriel Huquier's sensitivity and technical skill in portraying one of the most popular themes in Japanese and Chinese art – the flower basket. Perhaps based on an original Far Eastern painting or porcelain decoration, the artist has produced some of the most typical examples of Asian flora (peonies, cherry blossom, beets, peacock feathers) with considerable precision. The type of basket and the wooden stand are also rigorously Chinese.

Grande Singerie in the Château of Chantilly, completed in 1735.[31] This work is an example of '*singerie*' – a form of chinoiserie which replaced fauns and cherubs, and even Chinese figures, with monkeys. The *Petite Singerie*, also completed in 1735 at Chantilly, is the work that best represents Huet's skill in parodying the behaviour of his contemporaries disguised as monkeys, and a collection of these caricatures was later published in *Singeries, ou différentes actions de la vie humaine rappresentées par des singes.* Huet was also commissioned by the duke of La Vallière to decorate the Chinese Salon and the small salon in the Château des Champs, bought by Madame de Pompadour in 1757,[32] and between 1749 and 1752 he worked on the *boiseries* of the Hôtel de Rohan in Paris commissioned by cardinal Armand de Rohan (1717-1756). These he designed in the eclectic style combining elements of chinoiserie with '*singeries*' and Turkish motifs, adapting scenes from the

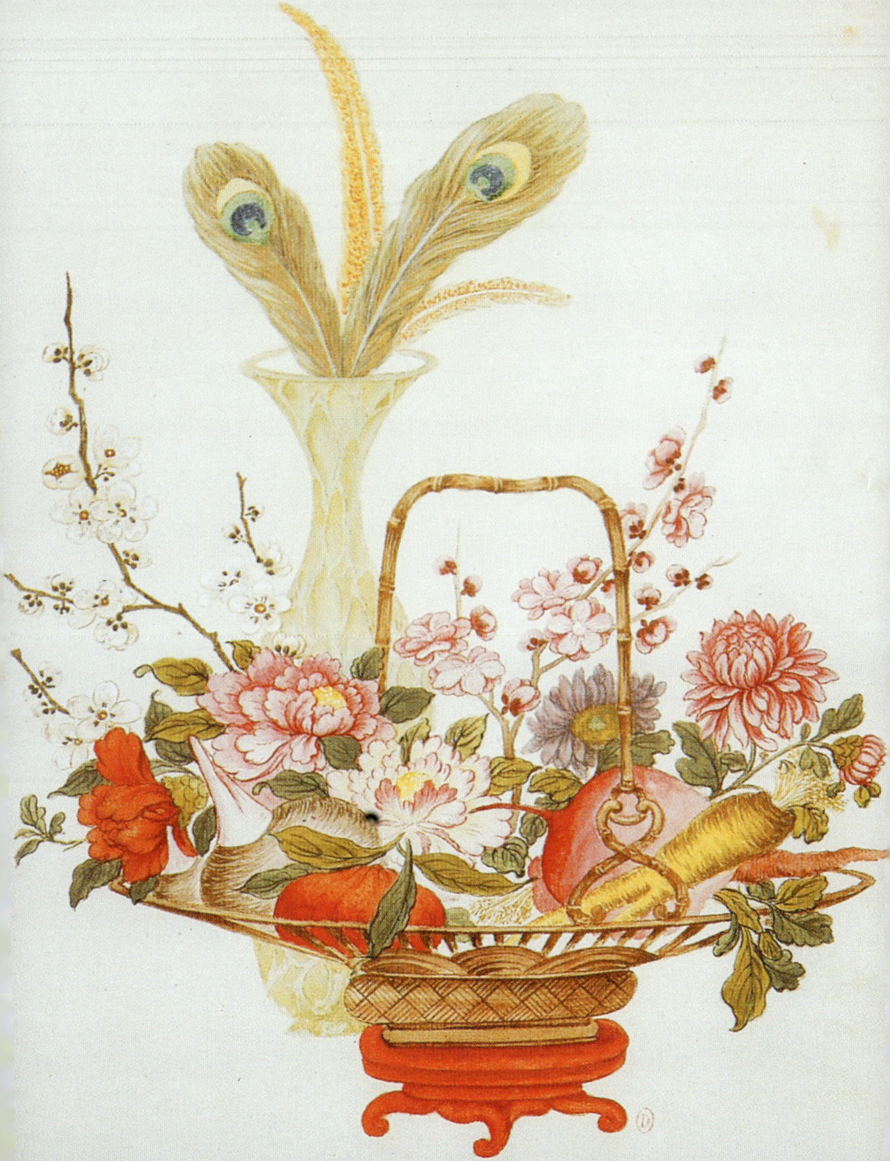

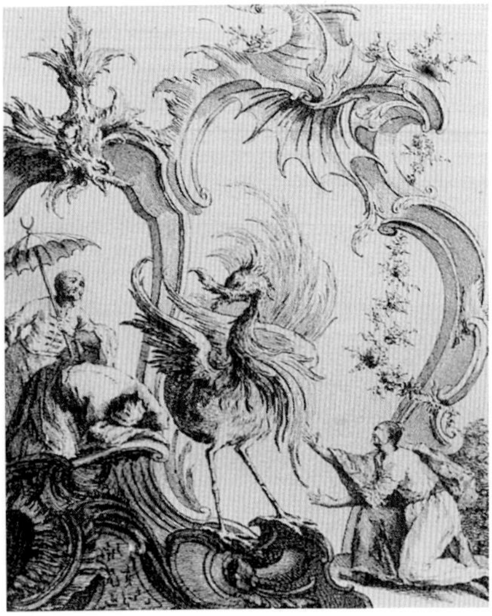
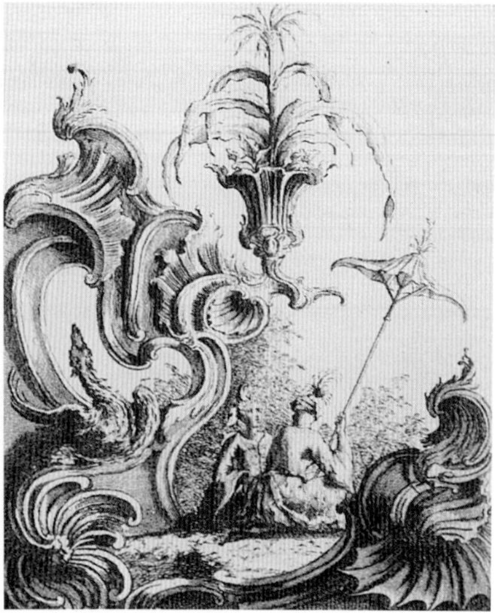

56a,b. François-Antoine Aveline, from François-Thomas Mondon, Scenes with chinoiserie, 1736. Private collection.

The engraving on the left is in the *Quatrième Livre de formes rocailles*, and on the right in the collection of *Ornements chinois*.
In 1736 Aveline published altogether six series of engravings of rococo ornamentation designed by Mondon, several of which included chinoiseries.

illustrated repertories of Kircher and Nieuhoff which he then framed with scrolls and volutes in the style of Gillot, Audran and Watteau. This work by Huet demonstrates the influence of François Boucher's creations, in particular those produced around 1740 as designs for the Beauvais tapestries.[33]
Following the enormous success of the suite of the *History of the Emperor of China*, the Royal tapestry works decided to produce a new series of chinoiserie scenes. The scope of these was to be quite different from the group of tapestries commissioned by J.B. Fleurian d'Armenonville in 1724 and designed in the oriental style by the artist Jacques Vigoureux Duplessis.[34]
During the 1740s the factory was directed by Jean-Baptiste Oudry (1686-1755) and Nicolas Besnier (1709-1754) who commissioned preparatory sketches from Jean-Joseph Dumons (1687-1779). Based entirely on Boucher's works, the 'Second Chinese Suite' consisted of six tapestries representing *A Chinese Meal, The Chinese Fair, Chinese Dance, Chinese Fishing, The Chinese Hunt* and the *Chinese Garden* and continued to be produced until 1775.[35] The royal household commissioned a set from the factory in 1759 and in 1763 it was delivered to the Minister of Foreign Affairs, Bertin, who sent it to the emperor of China as a gift. The set of tapestries was finally presented to Qianlong (1736-1795) by two missionaries in 1767 and was displayed in the Summer Palace in Peking. There it remained until 1860 when, following the sack of the city by the English, two pieces were brought back to Europe. The other four are most probably in Chinese collections.[36] Although only six were produced as tapestries, Boucher had prepared ten designs altogether for Beauvais including the *Chinese Wedding, Chinese Curio, the Bird of Fortune* and the *Audience of the Emperor of China* (Besançon, Musée des Beaux-Arts et d'Archéologie). Eight of the ten designs were exhibited at the Salon in 1742 and the entire cycle represents the finest example of chinoiserie created by Boucher, the most prolific artist of the genre working in the 1730s and '40s.

His Chinese scenes were invented mainly between 1735 and 1745 and several series of his engravings with this subject were published, such as *Scènes de la vie chinoise* dated 1737, produced by Gabriel Huquier, *The Five Senses* engraved by Pierre Aveline in 1740, the *Four Elements*, also by Huquier, and the *Chinese Figures* engraved by J. Ingram in 1744, to mention just a few of those readily available.[37] Some of Watteau's chinoiseries were also reproduced by Boucher and were probably his first introduction to the genre.[38] The atmosphere of Boucher's chinoiserie is quite idyllic, and the treatment is similar to his portrayals of European themes; his figures are both elegant and sensual; the clothes and expressions of the numerous 'Chinese' characters filling his designs reflect a countrified elegance but are entirely Parisian in style. Boucher was painter to Madame de Pompadour (1721-1764) and to the court of Louis XV (1710-1774), both of whom were passionately interested in the Orient, and the easy availability of his prints meant that his artistic works in the 'Chinese style' were imitated and used as models throughout Europe for many decades to come. He too was an enthusiastic collector of Far Eastern items and he owned quite a large number of works at least some of which he acquired from the Parisian antiquarian Gersaint. Possibly these provided Boucher with inspiration for his dreamy Chinese scenes. However, there are also strong parallels between his creations and the images in the volume *Gedenkwaerdige Gesantschappen* by Arnoldus Montanus which appeared in

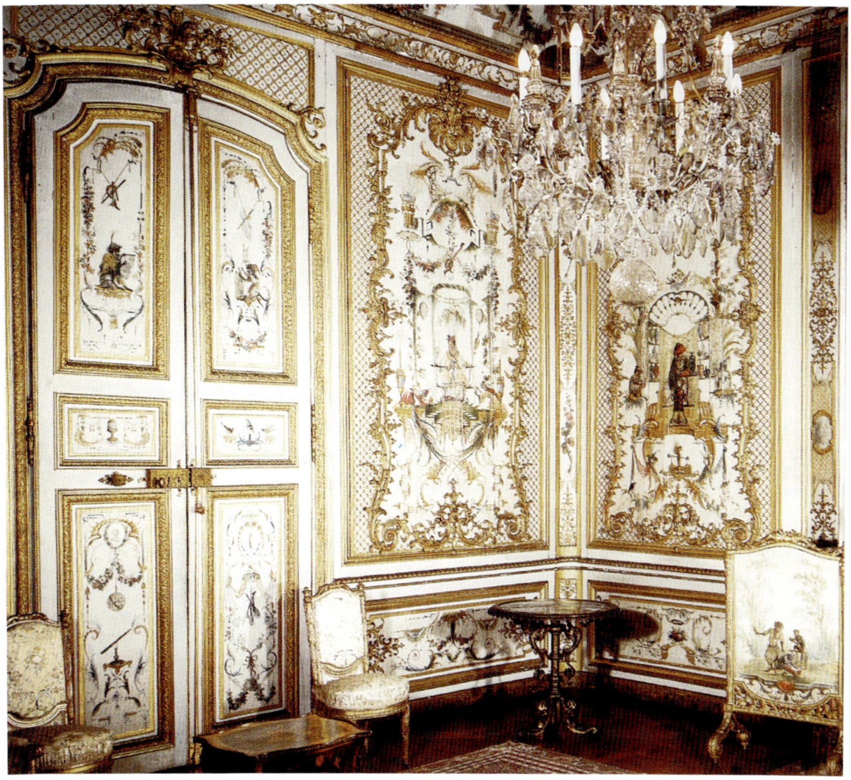

57. Christophe Huet, Chinoiserie decorations, c. 1735. Chateau de Chantilly, Grande Singerie.

The scenes that Huet painted for this room represent a kind of synthesis of early 18th-century French chinoiserie, before Boucher's later creations gave the genre a new vigour. Designed as a series of panels each surrounded by gilded wood rococo frames, the Grande Singerie inspired similar inventions. In Rome, for example, the Pozzi brothers based their Chinese Rooms in Palazzo Colonna on these works.

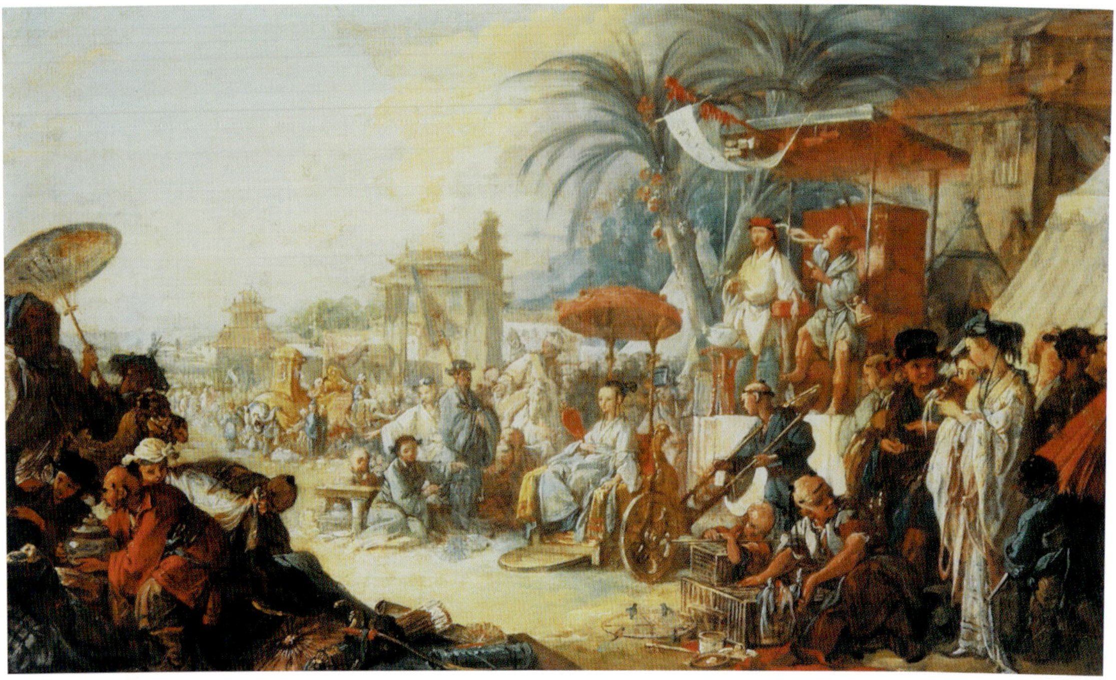

58. *The Chinese Fair*, tapestry after a painting by François Boucher. Beauvais, c. 1750. Turin, Palazzo Reale.

Boucher made the preparatory sketch for the Beauvais weavers to create this tapestry, part of the *Second Chinese Suite*. The detail of the lady seated in a rickshaw driven by a servant is taken from a print in Montanus' book dated 1669, in which however, the characters appear in Japanese costume.

1669 (actually describing the customs of Japan), as well as the illustrations in *La Galerie agréable du monde* (Leiden 1729) by Pieter van der Aa (1659-1733) and the designs for *Yuzhi Gengzhi Tu*, an encyclopedic work commissioned by the Chinese emperor Kangxi (1662-1722) from the artist Jiao Bingzhen and published in 1696.[39]

Yet even more widely available throughout Europe were the designs with oriental subjects created by Jean-Baptiste Pillement (1728-1808). Inspired by Watteau, Huet and Boucher, as well as by Johann Gregorius Höroldt (1696-1755), he was one of the most important artists responsible for diffusion of the genre throughout Europe and his designs,[40] whether scenes with figures or stylised Persian patterns, were adopted throughout the second half of the 1700s by most European manufacturers to decorate their fabrics, ceramics, furniture and almost everything else.[41] Both the easy availability of his prints and his numerous journeys to almost all the European courts contributed to the widespread use of his works and evidence of his artistic style is still to be found in Paris, Madrid, Lisbon, Vienna, Avignon, Warsaw, Switzerland, Holland, as well as Turin, Rome, Milan, and Florence which he visited between 1761 and 1763. He first trained at the Gobelins factory when Jean Baptiste Oudry was director of the decorators' department and both his experience here, and the fact that he came from Lyons, must in part explain why he was so adept at creating designs that were especially suited for transfer onto fabric. The Aubusson factory in particular used his designs on various suites of tapestries with Chinese motifs produced in the second half of the 18th century (*Œuvres de Fleurs, ornements, cartouches et figures et sujets chinois,*

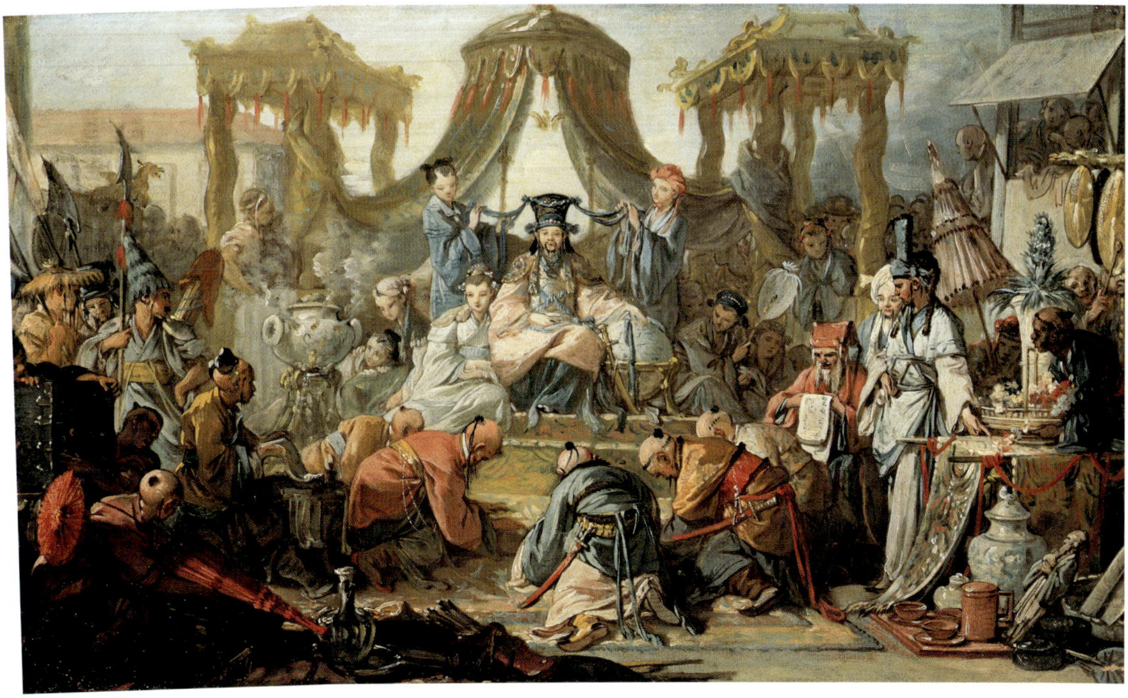

59. François Boucher, *The Chinese Emperor's Audience*, 1742. ©Besançon, Musée des Beaux-Arts et d'Archéologie (photo Charles Choffet).

One of the preparatory sketches made by Boucher in 1740 as a design for one of the *Second Chinese Series* of Beauvais tapestries. The theme of the Emperor's audience was a favourite from the 17th century on. It had already been used for a tapestry in the *First Chinese Series* produced by Beauvais in the late 1600s. Boucher's passion for the Orient is evident from the almost entirely faithful portrayal of Chinese and Japanese articles in this composition.

1776).[42] Pillement's first oriental designs appeared in 1755 when he collaborated with Mathias Darly and George Edward on the pattern book, *A New Book of Chinese Designs Calculated to Improve the Present Taste*. His first series of individual prints on the same subject was also produced in 1755 in London with the title *A New Book of Chinese Ornaments* while in 1757 similar publications followed, almost all engraved by P.C. Canot. Collaborating with Robert Hancock, Anthony Walker and others, almost 950 of his prints appeared in *The Ladies Amusement* and except for these, all the works he had published in England were reprinted in 1767 by Charles Leviez (1708-1776) in the collection entitled *L'Oeuvre de Jean Pillement, Premier Peintre du Roi de Pologne*. Extending well beyond the rococo period, Pillement's works continued to be used throughout the entire second half of the 18th century, coinciding more or less with the period during which chinoiserie was at the height of its popularity in France, and before the classical style made a triumphant return to fashion. The duration of the success of Pillement's designs – which clearly had more in common with the rocaille style than with neoclassicism – is rather surprising, as already in 1748 Abbé Gougenot in his *Lettre sur la peinture, la sculpture et architecture*, commenting on collectors and their collections stated, "another equally irritating thing about these 'cabinets' is that instead of being enhanced with an attractive drawing or fine piece of sculpture, on the whole they are full of pagodas and other figures of that kind that have no other merit than that of coming from distant lands. Our collectors are only interested, therefore in odd items of poor taste?"[43]

Textiles, Painted Paper, Ceramics, Lacquers and Gardens

Despite the changes in fashion that occurred throughout the 18th century, most French manufacturers of artistic wares concentrated on the oriental style. Apart from the royal tapestry factories, France was noted for its high quality textiles with the most important and flourishing centres in Tours and Lyons. Oriental patterns were a constant feature in their decorative repertories and were elaborated to satisfy the increasing requests of their customers. Although an edict was issued as early as 26 October 1686 prohibiting the sale of printed cotton cloth in France (known as *indiennes*), the importation of large quantities of original oriental fabrics did not diminish. The decree also prohibited the wearing of "cotton cloth printed in India or reproduced in the Kingdom" in order to fully protect the interests of traditional French textile factories, despite the fact that many of them had recently learnt, and even improved, the technique of printing cotton.[44] A further similar edict was issued in 1723 at the request of the by now distraught owners of factories in Lyons and Tours who, as documented by Savary des Bruslons in his *Dictionnaire universel du commerce* (1723-1730)[45] were no longer capable of resisting Chinese competition. However, printed oriental cottons were to be found on the black market and moreover, free-trade areas existed in Paris itself as printed fabrics could be produced within the precincts of monasteries where access was not permitted to the police.[46] Oriental influences are clearly evident on the 'bizarre silks' produced in France from the late 17th century and many producers later adopted the designs of artists such as Jean-Antoine Fraisse, Alexis Peyrotte and Jean-Baptiste Pillement. Far Eastern motifs are also seen in the highly naturalistic patterns produced by Jean Revel (1684-1751) who was the most important name in French textile design in the first half of the 18th century.[47] In his *Dictionnaire* Savary des Bruslons also refers to the popularity in late 17th-century France of *papier peints* – paper decorated and coloured with motifs of clearly oriental derivation. The fashion for decorating rooms with *papiers peints* enjoyed great success with much of French society as it provided an economic alternative to the more expensive oriental fabrics which had now become so difficult to obtain following the ban on importation issued in 1686. Oriental-style papers were made throughout Europe, including Italy, where the Remondini factory in Bassano del Grappa was particularly renowned for its production.

French ceramic factories also used Chinese designs throughout the 18th century. Until at least the 1750s Nevers and Rouen continued to produce their original motifs, as did the factories of Sinceny, Aprey, Lille, Moulins, La Rochelle, Marsiglia, Marignac, Strasbourg, Lunéville, Sceaux, Saint-Cloud, Chantilly, Vincennes and Sèvres all of which used oriental models or European derivations, both in their painted designs and their figurines.[48] The grotesque decorations – which also included more or less evident references to the Far East – produced by the Clerissy factory in Moustiers were closely

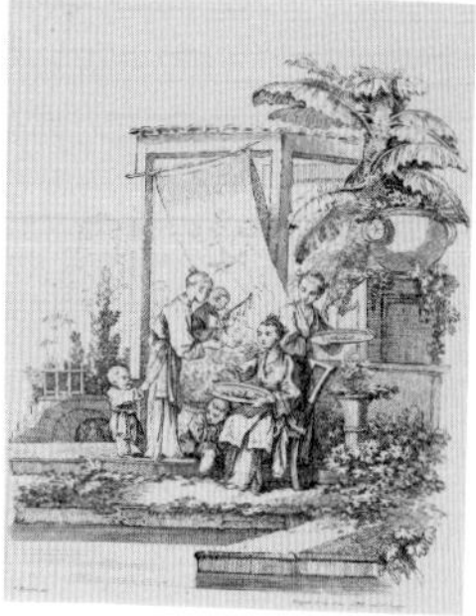

60. Gabriel Huquier after François Boucher, *Lady Seated with Children and Servants*, from the series *Scènes de la vie chinoise*, c. 1742. New York, The Metropolitan Museum of Art.

Comparison of this composition and the Chinese print opposite clearly reveals just how strong was the influence of original Far Eastern works on the development of Boucher's chinoiserie. However, he modified the subject of the Chinese print, representing silk weaving, to suit the more frivolous and idealised tastes of the European 18th century.

61. After Jiao Bingzhen, *The Second Moult of Silk Worms*, print from *Yuzhi gengzhi tu*. Peking 1696.

The print was made from a drawing by Jiao Bingzhen, part of a series commissioned directly by emperor Kangxi (1654-1722), who also wrote the verses accompanying the images, to illustrate the *Yuzhi gengzhi tu*. This encyclopaedic publication appeared for the first time in the 12th century. The compositions reproduced in the 1696 edition seem to indicate that the artist had some knowledge of the techniques of European painting. Perhaps for this reason Boucher felt they could be suitably adapted for a western public.

采桑初罢绿条稀
陌上归来日正迟
村舍家家簾幌静
春蠶新长再眠时

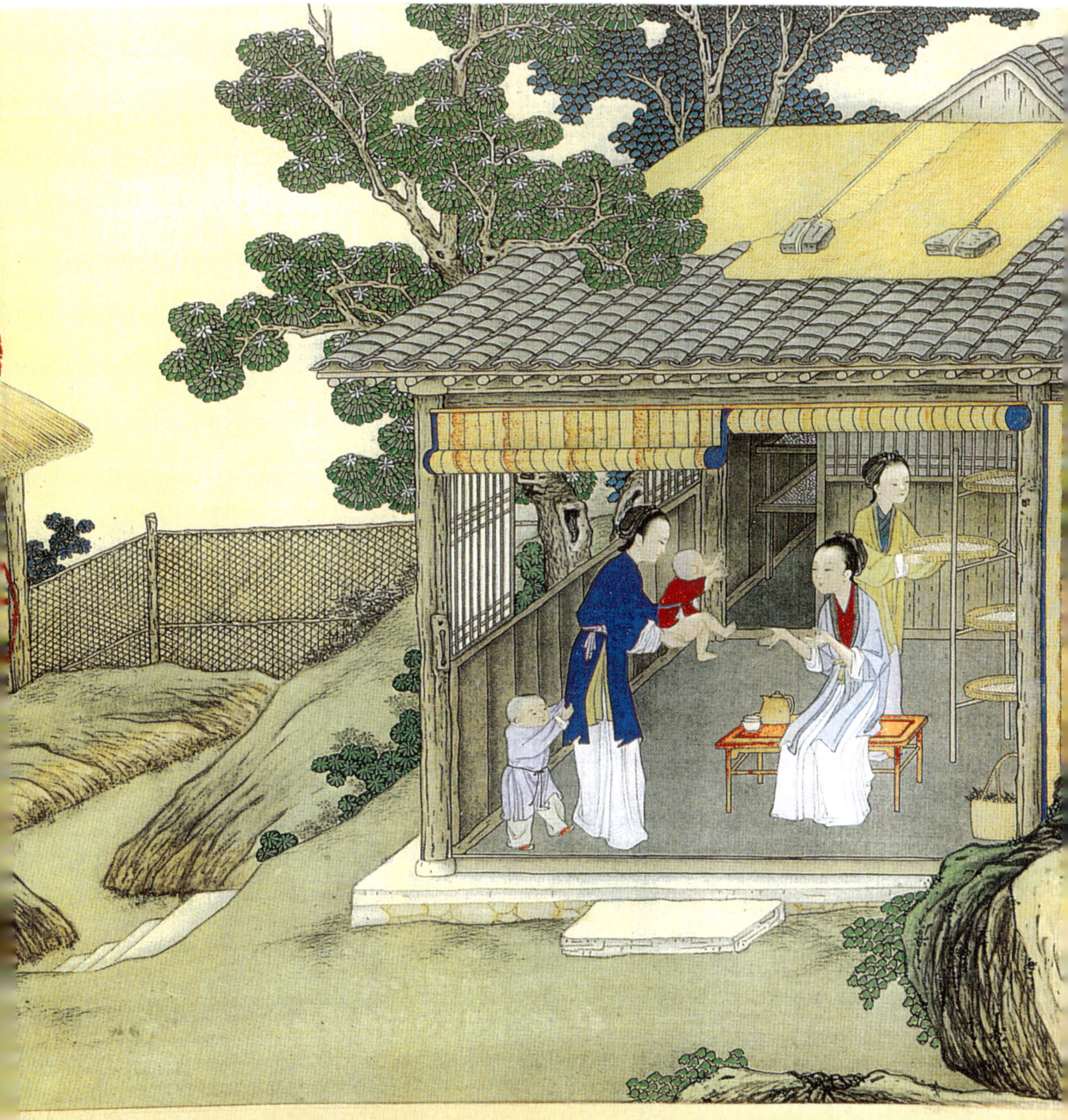

related to the designs Bérain had begun to develop in the later 17th century. These were widely adopted as a source of inspiration by the ceramic painters of Lombardy, Piedmont and the Veneto in the early 17th century. There is a strong resemblance in particular between the Moustiers ceramics and the decorations used by Rossetti both in Turin and Lodi after 1725.[49] A great collector of orientalia and especially Chinese and Japanese porcelain, Louis Henri di Bourbon (1692-1740), the seventh prince of Condé and cousin of Louis XV, created the Chantilly factory in 1725 under the direction of Cicaire Cirou (1700-1755).[50] In 1729 Jean-Antoine Fraisse (c. 1680-1738/39) became director of the department of decorators and his designs of Far Eastern subjects were principally inspired by items in the prince's collection. These were collected and published by Philippe-Nicolas Lattin (1685-1751) in 1735 in the *Livre de desseins chinois tirés d'après des originaux de Perse, des Indes, de la Chine et du Japon, dessinés et gravés en taille-douce, par Le Sr Fraisse, Peintre de S.A.S Monseigneur Le Duc* and, following the death of the artist Gabriel Huquier, edited the publication of a series of Fraisse's 'Chinese' prints between 1742 and 1750. Some editions of this work contain additional Chinese paintings which presumably also belonged to the prince of Condé.[51] Fraisse had added details of his own to these originals so that they could more easily be reproduced on porcelain as well as furniture and textiles which were also made by the Chantilly factory at the time.[52] 'Chinese' lacquered furniture was made by Jacques Dagly (1669-1729), brother of the more famous Gérard, who had moved to France in 1713. With the exclusive right to use lacquer varnishes for the next twenty years, the young Dagly collaborated with the painters Pierre de Neufmaison (1672-1752), who later became *Directeur des Ouvrages de la Chine* at Gobelins, and Claude III Audran. Known as "le vernis des Gobelins" he made items exclusively for the court and their quality was considered equal to that of the oriental originals. On his death, Neufmaison became director of the workshop, succeeded in 1752 by his son-in-law, Charles André Tramblin (1672-1742), who gradually almost entirely excluded chinoserie motifs from the decorative repertory.[53] Founded by the Martin brothers, the royal factory for production of '*vernis façon de la Chine*' was established in 1748.[54] At first specialising in copies of oriental lacquer wares, they eventually developed a highly successful decorative style of their own, receiving several prestigious commissions such as a cabinet for Versailles and furnishings for the Dauphine Marie-Josèphe of Saxony in 1748. Voltaire (1694-1778), a great enthusiast of all things Chinese, highly praised their works – "Et ces cabinets où Martin/ A surpassé l'art de la Chine".[55] Guillaume-Jean Martin (1713-1754) was responsible for creating at least two of the three lacquered rooms in the royal palace of Portici, dismantled in the 19th century, one of which was decorated with oriental scenes, while a further member of the family moved to Berlin in 1747.[56] Lastly, in 1772 the most important French manual for lacquer workers, *L'art du peintre Doreur et Vernisseur*, by Jean Felix Watin was published in Paris.[57] Watin, a great

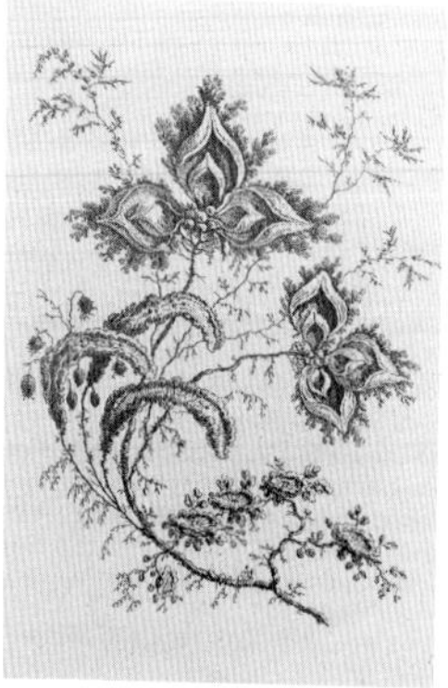

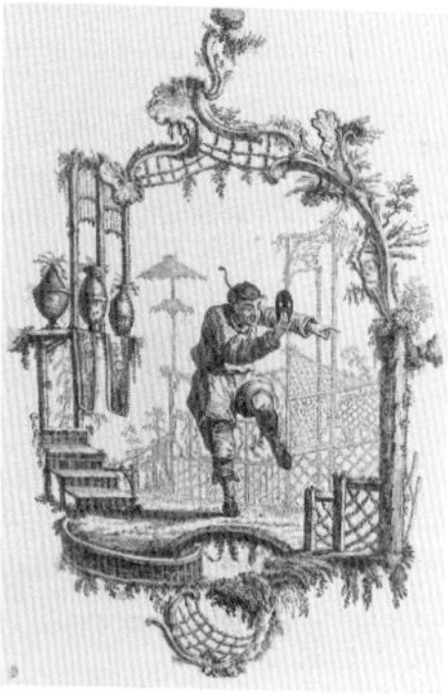

62. Jean-Baptiste Pillement, *Persian Flower*, from *Fleures Persannes*, c. 1760. Milan, Castello Sforzesco, Raccolta Bertarelli.

One of a series of six prints designed, drawn and engraved by Pillement. This style of floral decoration is only loosely based on original oriental collections, but it became one of the most characteristic motifs of Pillement's chinoiserie repertory.

63. Jean-Baptiste Pillement, *Chinese Dancer*, 1759. Milan, Castello Sforzesco, Raccolta Bertarelli.

This composition is an excellent example of Jean-Baptiste Pillement's vast repertory of chinoiseries. It was engraved by Canot who often reproduced the creative inventions of the French ornamentalist.

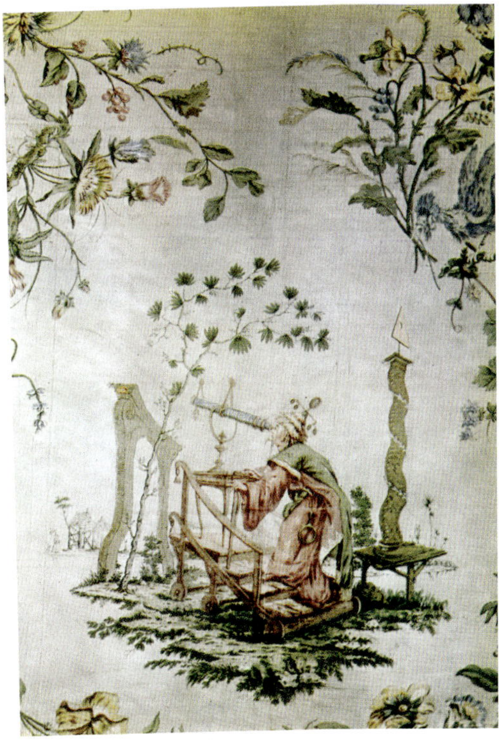

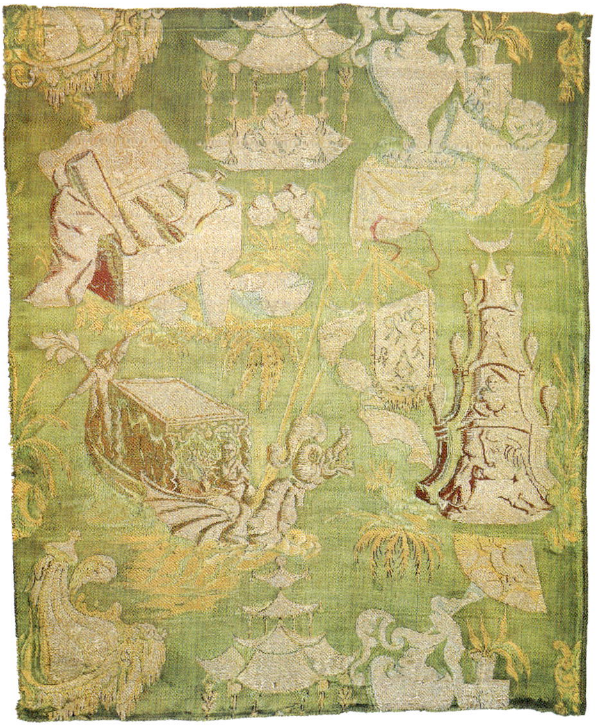

64. Chinoiserie fabric with motif in the style of Pillement. Lyons, c. 1750. Lyons, Musée des Tissus.

Known as the *Chinese Astronomer*, the motif in the centre of this fabric has often been published in texts on the oriental style as a typical example of 'Pillement' chinoiserie although the original source remains unknown. It is without doubt French and datable to the later 18th century.

65. Fabric. Lyons, c. 1735. Krefeld, Textilmuseum.

Some of the themes most often reproduced from the 18th-century repertory of chinoiserie are seen in the pattern of this fabric: porcelain items, pavilions, divinities, Chinese figures and, of course, the dragon.

collector of oriental lacquer work, a painter and gilder as well as a spice and dye merchant whose clients included the Martin, wrote his treatise based not only on his own professional experience but also information provided by the memoirs, published in 1760, of the missionary Father Pierre Nicolas d'Incarville (1706-1757) who had lived in Peking for a long period (*Mémoires de l'Académie française royale*, vol. XV).

During the 18th century the practice of inserting original Chinese or Japanese panels into their works was quite common among French cabinet makers. Examples of this had already existed in England in the 17th century, such as the series of furnishings now in the Victoria and Albert Museum, made in 1680 for Robert Spencer, second Earl of Sunderland. During the reign of Louis XV this special technique was developed by Bernard II van Risamburgh (c. 1696-c. 1766) who adapted oriental pieces already belonging to historical collections. Numerous craftsmen followed his example and successful works were later produced by Jean-Henri Riesener (1734-1806) and Adam Weisweiler (1744-1820) who made the furnishings for the chambers of Marie-Antoinette at Versailles.[58] The fashion for 'informal' gardens which had developed in England, arrived in France in the mid 18th century. *La Nouvelle Héloïse* by Jean Jacques Rousseau (1712-1778) published in 1761 contains numerous references to the vogue, mainly critical, however, rather than enthusiastic.[59] In 1749 the Jesuit Frère Attiret, who lived in Peking for many years, had provided a description of the imperial garden, called Yuan Ming

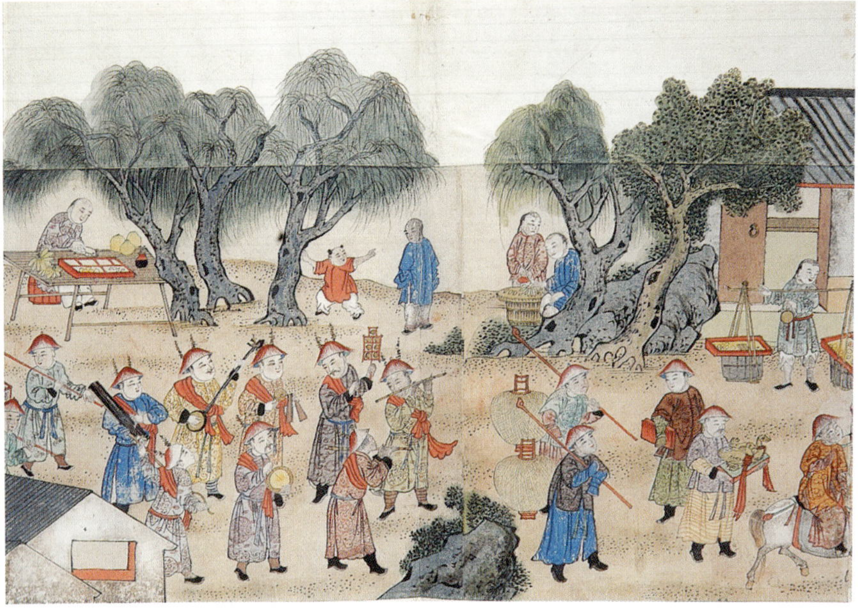

66. Jean-Antoine Fraisse, drawing from the *Livre de desseins chinois*, 1735. Paris, Bibliothèque Nationale de France.

The chinoieries produced by Jean-Antoine Fraisse were based on the many items in the collection of oriental art belonging to Louis Henri de Bourbon, mainly consisting of Chinese and Japanese porcelain. There were also some paintings such as this, however, which Fraisse slightly modified, adapting it to suit the requirements of decorators working for the Chantilly factories.

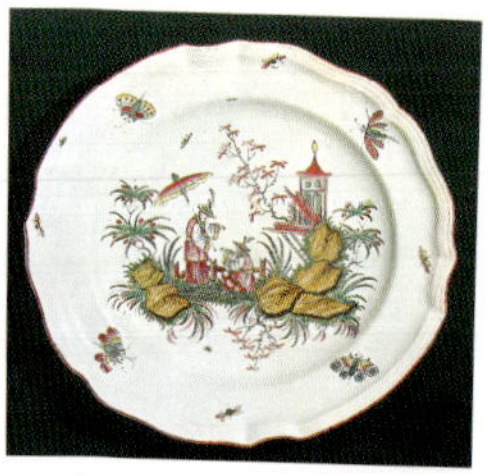

67. Plate. Luneville, c. 1770. Sèvres, Musée National de Céramique.

The style of chinoiserie that appeared on French ceramics in the later 18th century strongly influenced majolica production in northern Italy during the same period, such as that of Lodi.

Yuan.[60] His readers quickly linked this first hand information to news of innovations in garden layout taking place in England and various French architects became specialised in what was referred to as the 'jardin anglo-chinois'. Antoine Richard, for example, was responsible for designing the gardens of Versailles commissioned by Marie-Antoinette in 1774, Louis Carrogis (1717-1806) created the Parc Monceau for the duke of Orléans in the 1770s and Joseph Bélanger (1744-1818) became famous for his work on the Parc de Bolëil for the prince de Ligne.[61] Two of the most successful examples were the Jardins de Bagatelle and Saint-James, both in the Bois de Boulogne, the first laid out by Bélanger, while the second was begun in 1772 by the treasurer general of the French navy, Claude Baudard (1738-1787) who made

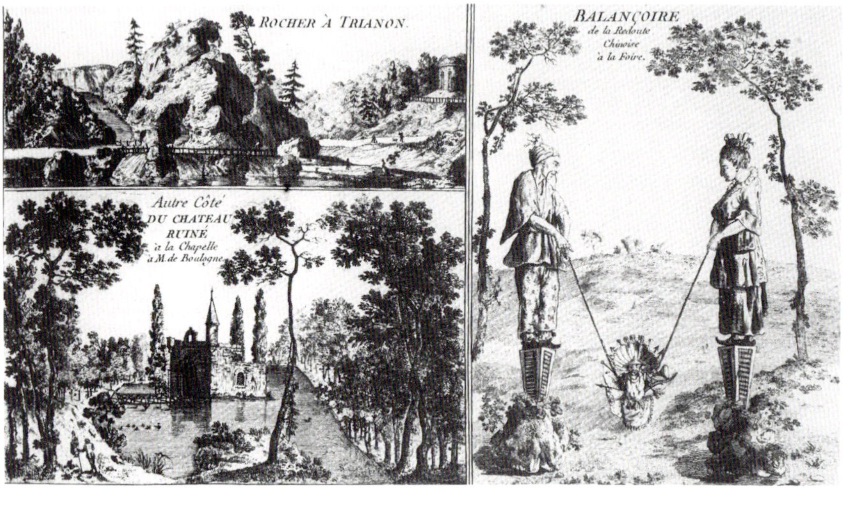

68. Three views of a panoramic garden, engraving by Georges Louis Le Rouge, *Détails de nouveaux jardins à la mode et 'jardins anglo-chinois'*, 1784. London, Victoria and Albert Museum.

Altogether twenty-one volumes, the monumental work by Le Rouge contained a large number of engravings related to more or less well-known *anglo-chinois* gardens created in 18th-century Europe.

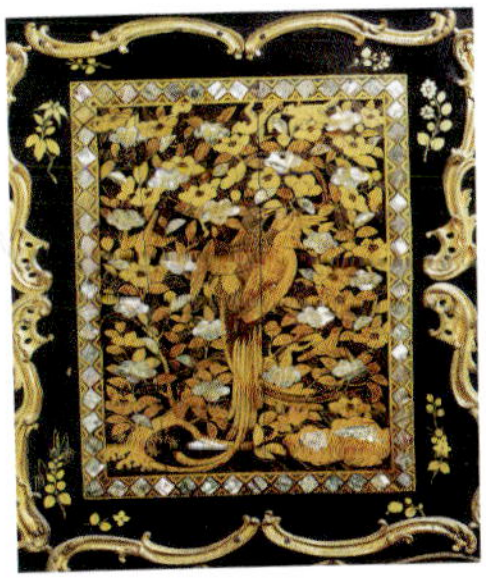

69a,b. Commode with drawers, mid 18th century. Florence, Pitti Palace.

Of French origin, the sides and front of this commode are decorated with panels taken from an original late 16th-century Japanese cabinet; the wood panels are lacquered and decorated with mother-of-pearl inlay. The fashion of inserting oriental lacquer panels into the framework of European furniture developed in France before 1750.

use of water from the Seine to create numerous enchanting water games.[62] Suggestions for creating gardens in the new *anglo-chinois* style were collected in *Détails de nouveaux jardins à la mode et "jardins anglo-chinois"* (1773-1788), a series of twenty-one volumes by Georges Louis Le Rouge (1722-1778), an engineer and royal geographer who is merited with first publishing a print revealing the real appearance of the Yuan Ming Yuan garden.[63] Based mainly on the work by William Chambers, printed in France by Laugier (1713-1769) in 1755 with the title *Essai sur l'architecture*,[64] Le Rouge's engravings included a series of 'Chinese' pavilions for gardens, some of which already existed such as those at Chantilly, Bonnelles, Cassan, Chanteloup and the "Désert de Retz" by Monsieur de Monville.[65] This immense work by Le Rouge is particularly interesting as it also provides an idea of the diffusion of the 'anglo-chinois' garden in Italy. Many of the engravings illustrate the plans of parks designed by Francesco Bettini for his Italian clients, discussed later.[66] At roughly the same time – in 1782 – the Abbé Jacques Delille (1738-1813) published *Les Jardins ou l'art d'embellir les paysages* in Paris. Now the initial enthusiasm had waned even the concept of landscape gardening began to be affected by the change in fashion, and a return to the harmony of classicism was rapidly gaining favour.[67]

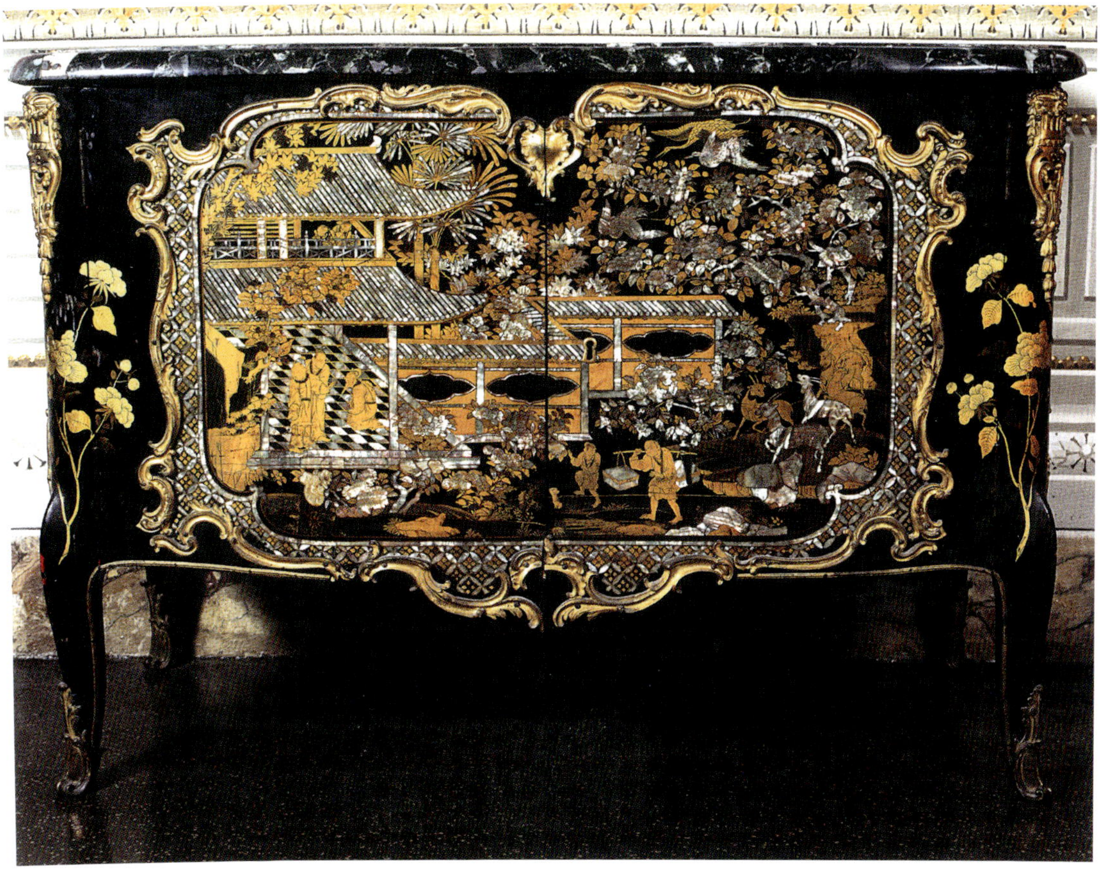

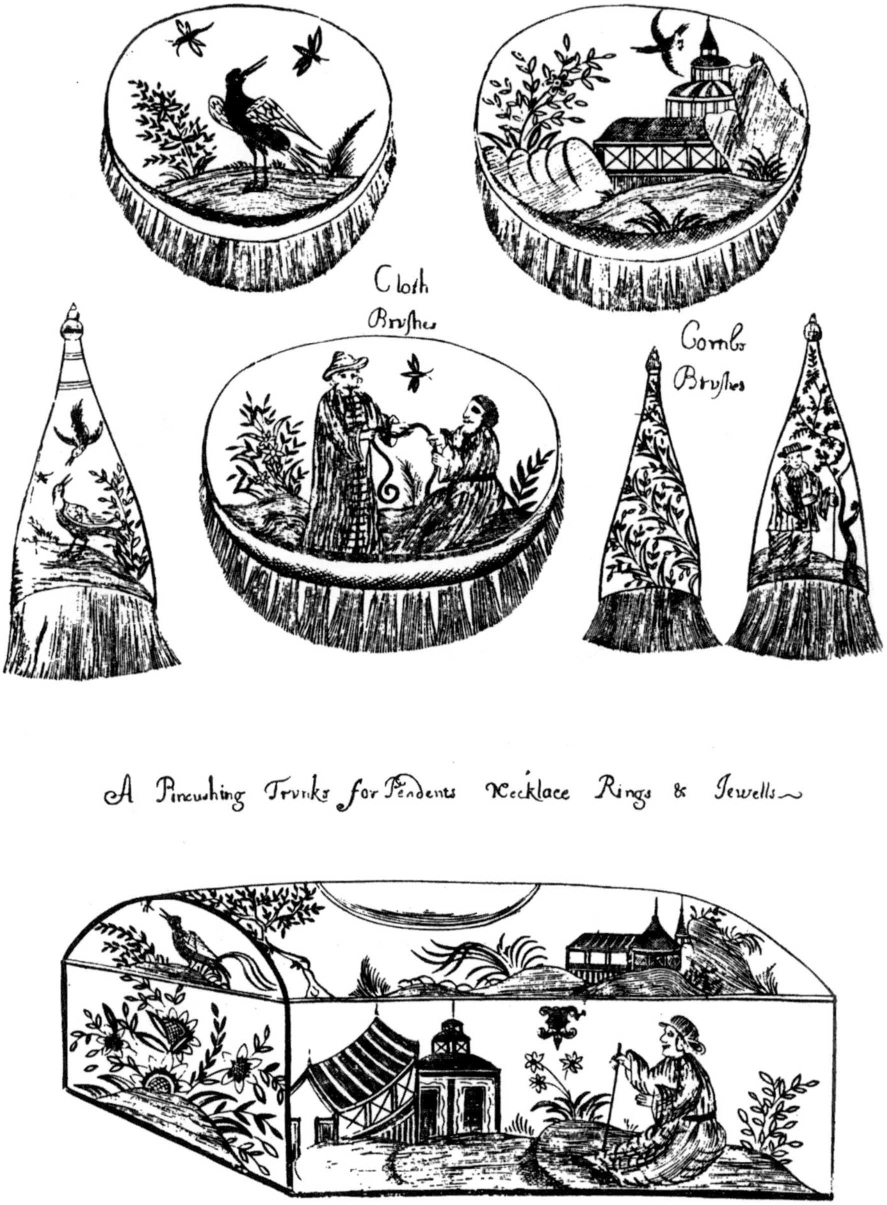

70. Lacquered items with chinoiseries, engraving by J. Stalker and G. Parker, *Treatise on Japanning and Varnishing*, Oxford 1688, pl. 4.

The *Treatise* by J. Stalker and G. Parker contained engravings with examples of ornamental motifs for decorating lacquered items, often in the oriental style. Although many original oriental items were abundantly available in England at the end of the 17th century and many illustrated texts on the more distant regions of Asia had been published in Europe, these chinoiserie designs still have an archaic air. The birds, flowers and figures clothed in long, sweeping robes and the imaginary buildings, all recall the oldest repertories, dating from at least the early 17th century.

England

The 17th Century

Daniel Marot (1660-1752) was a pivotal figure in the development of baroque chinoiserie in some three countries: France, Holland and England. French by birth, Dutch by adoption and from 1685 under the patronage of William of Orange (1650-1702), his architectural works were mainly accomplished after William became king of England. It was in England that he was able to fully develop the ideas he had formulated during his education in France, and frequently his plans incorporated the new element of chinoiserie, especially to please queen Mary (1662-1694) who was a passionate collector of orientalia and an enthusiastic sinophile. Marot's designs, especially those for interiors, were of fundamental importance for the spread of chinoiserie throughout Europe.[68] In particular he invented the *porzellan zimmern* which, from the end of the 17th to the middle of the 18th century, were created in various forms at all the European courts, including those of Italy.[69]

71. Daniel Marot, Design for a 'Chinese room' (*The China Closet*) in *Nouveaux livres de Portments*, c. 1700.

In this design, as well as in others with a similar theme, Daniel Marot has created a setting where – displayed to fine effect – the oriental porcelain is the most important element. Items are arranged inside the fireplace and on the shelves above, on numerous other shelves around the walls and on the cornice just below the vault of the ceiling around the entire room.

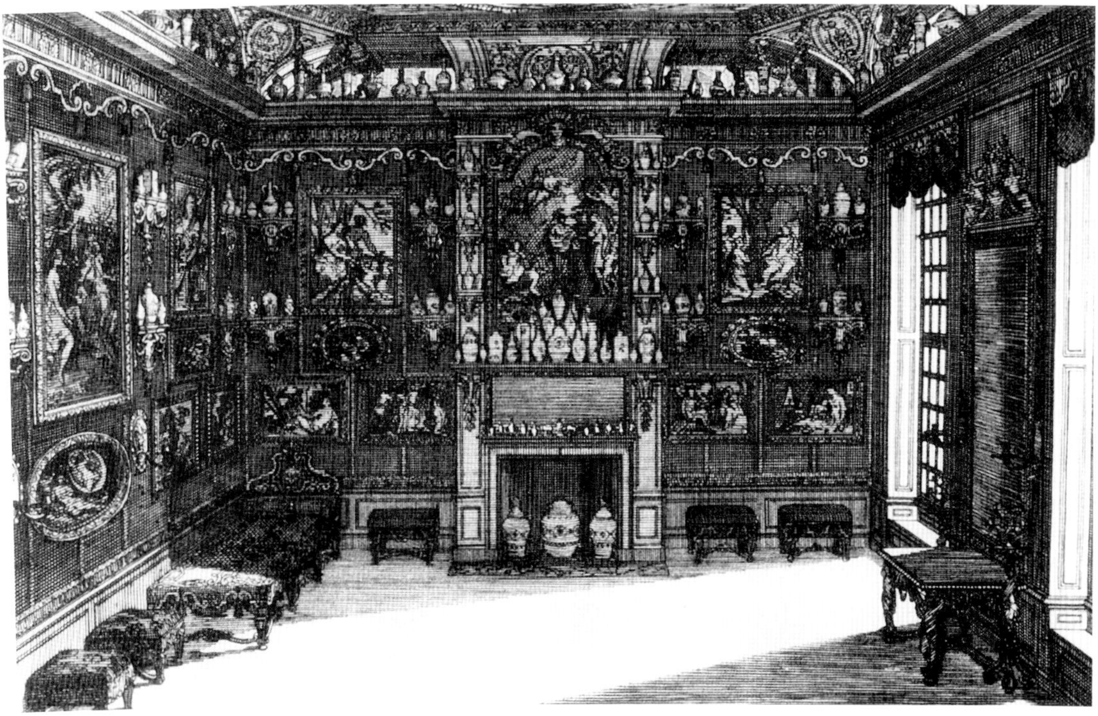

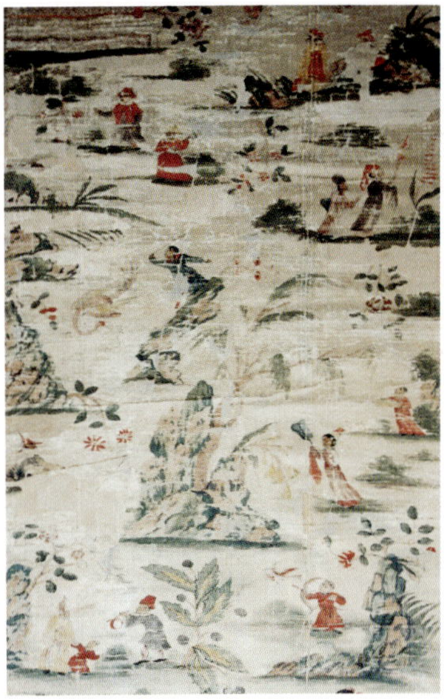

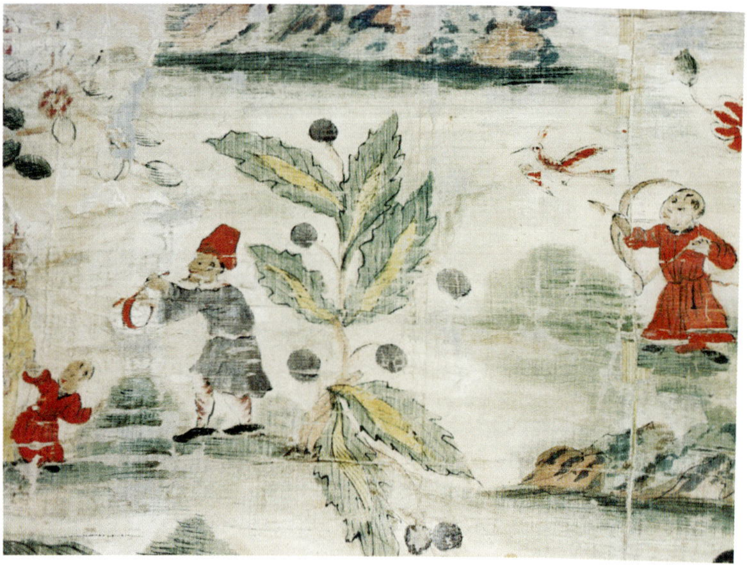

72a,b. Fabric. England (?), late 17th century. Florence, Museo Stibbert.

Probably English, the chinoiserie pattern of this fabric is baroque in style. The spirit and arrangement is close to subjects of a similar kind in Stalker and Parker's *Treatise*. Rather curiously, pieces of this fabric have been used together with fragments of an original Chinese cloth (dated early 18th century); clearly whoever made this 'patchwork' thought that the two fabrics (Chinese and European in an oriental style) were quite indistinguishable.

During the 1600s English chinoiserie was encouraged by a colonial tradition that had begun in the late 16th century and became institutionalised in 1600 with the foundation of the East India Company, authorised by queen Elisabeth. The Chinese theme already appeared in the early 17th century in plays by Ben Johnson (1572-1637) who considered the Far East to be a place of perdition.[70] The influence of the East is evident in English majolica, furniture and textiles throughout the 17th century and the designs were often copied by local craftsmen to satisfy the increasing requests for items decorated in the Chinese style as well as to combat the excessive power of merchants who imported oriental works.

The technique of applying lacquer was known as "japanning" in England, recalling the Japanese origin of the best lacquer available on the market at the time. In 1680 Charles II commissioned a Japanese style cabinet from the specialised craftsman, Gerreit Jensen to be presented as a gift to the emperor of Morocco.[71] At first original oriental models were copied without any variation or modification (of form, technique or decorative motifs), but towards the end of the 17th century some artistic individuality had begun to develop, especially following the publication in Oxford in 1688 of the *Treatise on Japanning and Varnishing* by John Stalker and George Parker. Although this was not the only volume of the kind to be used by English craftsmen at the time – William Salmon's *Polygraphice* had appeared in 1685 – Stalker and Parker's volume had the advantage that the text was accompanied by hundreds of images of decorative motifs to be used on japanned items and combined various exotic styles including Chinese, Japanese, Indian and Islamic, as well as European.[72] As the authors themselves stated in the introduction, far from being relevant exclusively to specialists, the *Treatise* was intended for all who were interested in trying their hand at japanning, which had developed into a

fashionable hobby. The success of Stalker and Parker's volume continued throughout the early decades of the 18th century, until at least 1742, when *The Handmaid to the Arts* by Robert Dossie (1717-1777) appeared. Reprinted in 1764 and again in 1796, the volume was welcomed especially for the greater clarity of its language compared to its illustrious predecessor. However, despite flourishing local production of a high quality, lacquer works imported from China and Japan continued to flood the English market, seriously threatening the survival of many workshops. In 1701 professional japanners asked the government to restrict the importation of oriental goods.[73]
Even stronger was the protest of textile manufacturers and especially those of Spitalfields.[74] Although oriental decorative patterns had been adopted by textile workers quite some time earlier and an edict limiting importations had been issued in 1670, the sector was suffering a grave crisis. The English public

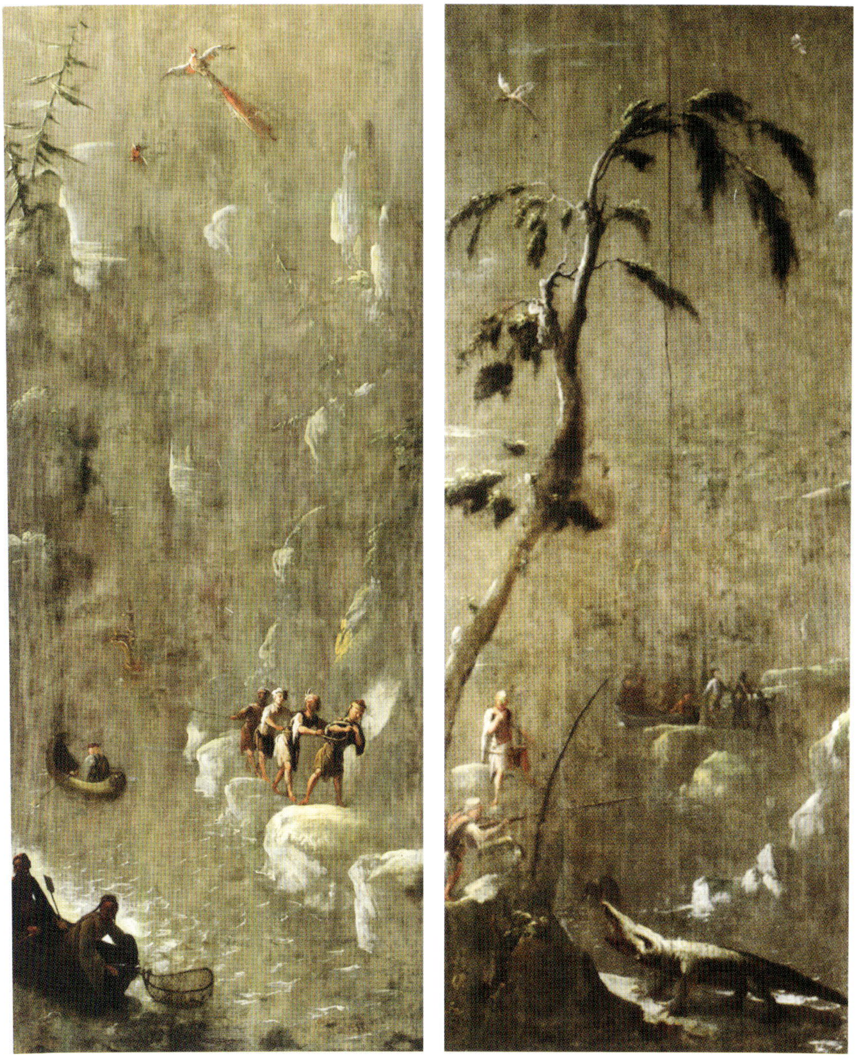

73a,b. Robert Robinson, Chinoiserie panels. London, 1694. London, Victoria and Albert Museum.

The panels were published by Hugh Honour and were in the London residence of Christopher Wren (1632-1732) in Botolph Lane, demolished in 1906. Originally thirty-one pieces existed, eleven of which have survived and are now in the Victoria and Albert Museum: one bears the date 1694. They are now unanimously accepted as the work of Robert Robinson, supported by comparison with the designs for the chinoiserie tapestries made by the Soho factory (see Fig. 74).

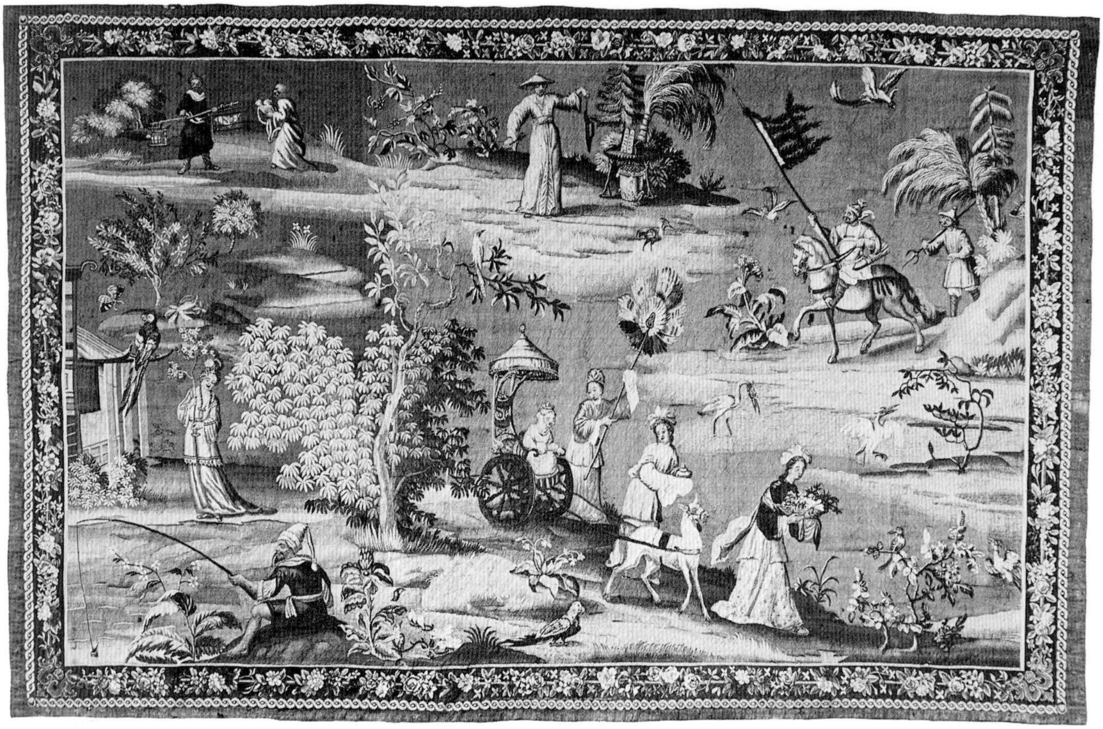

74. Tapestry. London, Soho, c. 1700. London, Victoria and Albert Museum.

This is one of a group of tapestries with 'exotic' motifs made by the Soho factory in London and probably designed by Robert Robinson. A first series, completed in 1699, was commissioned by Elihu Yale who had been governor of Madras; another set was made for Kensington Palace almost at the same time. The decoration of all the tapestries is a mixture of 'Chinese' elements and Indian art, probably based on the Mogul miniatures which Yale had brought back with him on returning to Britain.

favoured Indian chintz fabrics, both painted and printed, and one of the designs most in vogue was the Tree of Life which was immediately – and successfully – copied by Chinese manufacturers. Indian textiles, mainly used for furnishings, had been imported by England since 1618 and since about the middle of the century designs that were more acceptable to the European idea of exoticism had been sent to Asia for production by Indian craftsmen.[75] During the second half of the 17th century it became extremely popular to wear clothes made from this kind of material – a fashion that was highly criticised by Daniel Defoe (1660-1731) in 1708.[76] The first licence for manufacturing printed fabrics was granted to Will Sherwin in 1676[77] and production of this kind of eastern cloth was only completely liberalized in 1774.[78] Various English manufacturers made textiles with exotic designs including the Soho tapestry works directed by John Vanderbank. Around 1700 he produced a series of works in which heterogeneous oriental motifs were arranged in a layout forming separate groups, similar to lacquer decoration.[79] Altogether there were some fifty different designs; four of these hangings were bought by Elihu Yale (1649-1721), founder of the renowned American university. In almost the same period the fashion for fabrics with 'bizarre' patterns became popular in England, a trend most skilfully interpreted by the artist James Leman (1688-1749) who based his creations on original Chinese and Japanese textiles.[80]

In the late 17th and early 18th centuries chinoiserie – whether imitations of

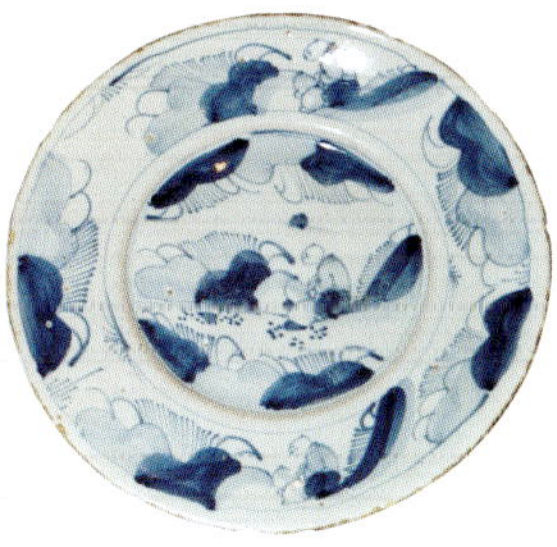

75. Majolica plate. England, late 17th century. London, Victoria and Albert Museum.

As in other European countries, in the late 17th century England too produced majolica with decorations emulating that of Chinese porcelain. Decorated with blue enamel on a white background, in the centre of this piece is a scene of children playing, quite a common motif on Far Eastern ceramics. The volutes around the border, on the other hand, were invented by the English decorator who used shades of blue to lend a choreographic effect to the design.

original oriental works or reinterpretations of an exotic theme – experienced a boom in the most disparate kinds of artistic production in England. Silverware, the ceramics of Southwark, Lambeth and Bristol, painted and printed textiles, paper wall coverings, *boiseries* and theatre scenery were all influenced by the new style. *The Fairy Queen* by Elkanah Settle (1648-1724) – an operatic version, including Chinese characters, of Shakespeare's *Midsummer-Night's Dream* – was performed in London in 1692. The scenery was most probably painted in oriental style by Robert Robinson, an artist specialised in this kind of design.[81]

'Eclectic' Chinoiserie

Towards the beginning of the 18th century the oriental theme began to be so over-exposed that it was heavily criticised by some English intellectuals such as Daniel Defoe, John Pope (1688-1744), Robert Morris and Lord Shaftesbury (1671-1713), who were the early advocates of the 'Palladian' neoclassical style that was soon to take over in Great Britain.[82] Contempt for the extravagancies of the 'Chinese' style did however, also have its roots in a stubborn hostility to the innovations taking place in France where chinoiserie was enjoying great favour, introduced to England by William de la Cour (1700-1768) with *First Book of Ornament.*[83] Despite this, in the mid 1700s when a resurgence of anti-chinoiserie attitudes occurred, the fashion forcefully returned to favour, enthusiastically appreciated by important personalities such as Horace Walpole (1717-1797) while at the same time the production of Chinese style works was encouraged by the publication of some influential decorative repertories.[84] Mathias Darly (c. 1720-1778) produced *A New Book of Chinese, Gothic and Modern Chairs* in 1751 and Mathias Lock and Henry Copeland published their *New Book of Ornaments in the Chinese Taste* a year later.[85] In 1754 Thomas Chippendale (1718-1779) published his fundamental work, the *Gentleman and Cabinet-Maker's Directory*. Containing 160 plates with engravings of designs for chairs, tables, cupboards and chests of drawers, many in fact created by Darly and Lock, the book can be considered the bible of English chinoiserie at the time ("a Large Collection of the most Elegant and Useful Designs of Household Furniture in the Gothic, Chinese and Modern Taste").[86] In the same year *The New Book of Chinese Designs Calculated to Improve the Present Taste* by Mathias Darly and George Edward appeared. Many of these compendiums were intended mainly for furniture makers and interior decorators, including John Linnell who designed the furnishings for the 'Chinese style' bedroom of the fourth duke of Beaufort in Badminton House (Victoria and Albert Museum, London). In open competition to Chippendale's works, the chinoiserie fantasies published by Thomas Johnson between 1756 and 1758 enjoyed great success. In 1757 Sir William Chambers published his *Designs of Chinese Buildings, Furniture, Dresses, Machines and Utensils*, compiled on his return from a lengthy sojurn

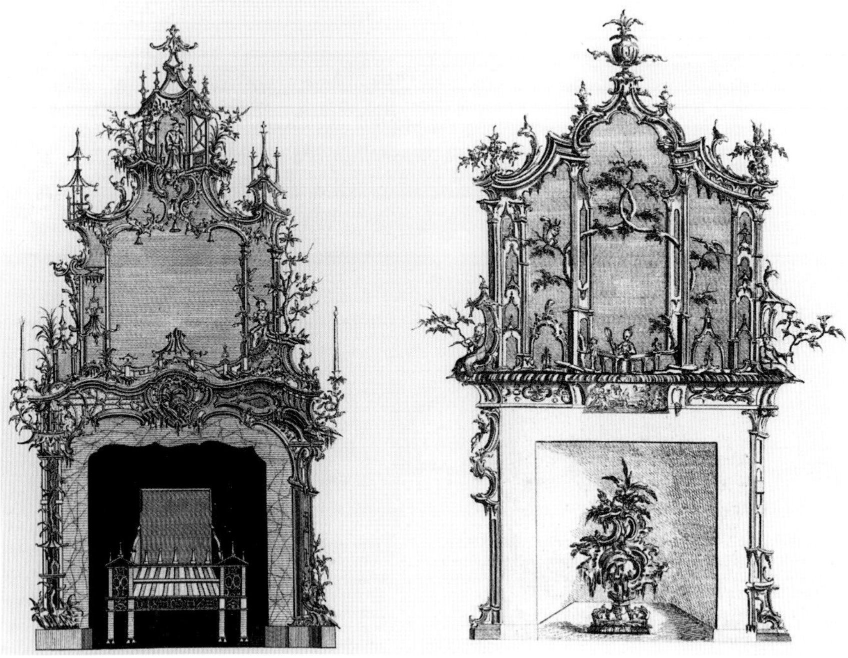

76a,b. Designs for chimney breasts with mirrors, left, from the *Collection of Designs* (1758) by Thomas Johnson; right, from the *Universal System of Household Furniture* (1762) by William Ince and John Mayhew.

The 18th-century English chinoiserie exemplified in these two designs for chimney breasts was in fact a hybrid, mingling stylistic details of various kinds and epochs. On the whole, the structure derives from French Rococo during the 1730s, which included characteristic features of international gothic architecture. The exotic element is provided by the appearance of oriental figures, pavilions and imaginary animals.

in the Far East.[87] Unlike its predecessors, this work provides a more analytical study of Chinese architecture and decoration, yet Chambers, together with Robert Adam (1728-1792), later became one of the most convinced advocates of the neoclassical style.[88] On the whole, however, English rococo chinoiserie was a hybrid which mingled elements of European gothic, French ornamental details of the 1700s, and motifs of Chinese origin.

In the same period *The Ladies Amusement or Whole Art of Japanning Made Easy*, was published in London by Robert Sayer in 1760. This volume contained around 1500 designs of which 900 were chinoiserie, many invented by Jean-Baptiste Pillement who was working in England at the time. One of the interiors of this period that fully reveals its debt to the inventions published in *The Ladies Amusement* is the bedroom made for the sinophile and famous actor, David Garrick (1717-1779) by Thomas Chippendale between 1772 and 1778 (Victoria and Albert Museum, London).[89] In 1769 Chippendale had designed a series of private rooms for Sir Rowland Winn at Nostell Priory in Yorkshire, entirely decorated with chinoiserie furniture, fabrics and painted paper wall coverings.[90] The most extraordinary English chinoiserie of the day, however, was to be seen at Claydon House and had been commissioned in 1769 by Lord Verney whose intention was to combine the classical Palladian exterior of the building with the most fantastic and extravagant oriental interiors.[91] Luke Lightfoot, a carver and woodworker, created highly original decorations consisting of a riot of pagodas, mandarins and fantastic birds in brilliantly coloured and exuberant compositions.

During the mid 18th century porcelain with Chinese designs was produced alongside more traditional items. Chelsea, Bow, Derby, Liverpool, Lowesoft, Bristol and Worcester made wares copying both Chinese and Japanese models, as well as items decorated with chinoiserie patterns adapted to European tastes.[92] Rather unusually, England was the only European country to produce silverware with 'Chinese' motifs surrounded by rococo scrolls and volutes.[93] Paul de Lamerie was a skilled silversmith who successfully combined elements of French *rocaille* with oriental motifs taken from ceramic decorations.[94]

The 'Jardin Anglo-Chinois'

The most typically English contribution to 18th-century chinoiserie was the garden that came to be known as 'anglo-chinois'. In complete contrast to the crisp precision of Renaissance and baroque Italianate gardens this English development made more natural use of both plants and structures in the landscape and preferred an irregular layout, believed to be a characteristic of Chinese gardens. In fact, this notion was based on the imaginary scenic views invented in the mid 17th century by artists such as Salvator Rosa (1615-1673) and Claude Lorrain (1600-1682) with the later addition of Chinese-style pavilions. However, it is probably also true that the fashion developed as a reaction to the success of the French garden as invented by André Le Nôtre (1613-1700), who had created both Vaux-le-Vicomte and Versailles.[95] The 'jardin anglo-chinois' originated about 1685 with the publication of Sir William Temple's book, *Upon the Gardens of Epicurus,* in which he claimed that irregularity in garden design was a Chinese invention, known in those distant lands as "Sharawadgi", meaning "not regular", "a graceful disorder";[96] the term was, in fact, a corruption of a Japanese word expressing a similar

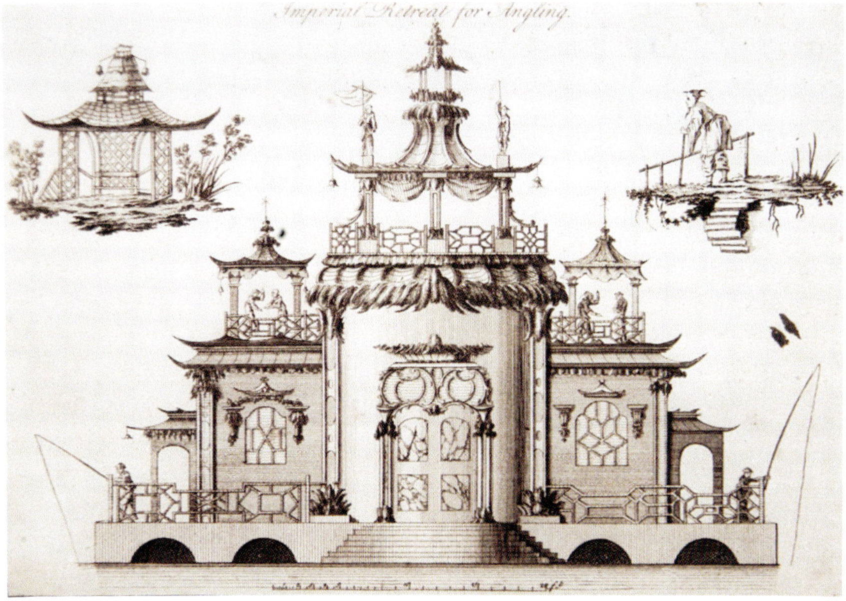

77. Matthew Darly and George Edwards, *Imperial Retreat for Angling*, engraving from *The New Book of Chinese Design Calculated to Improve Present Taste*, London 1754. London, Victoria and Albert Museum.

Darly and Edwards' publication provided numerous designs of furniture, fireplaces, and vase stands all in the chinoiserie style. The volume also contained plates with landscapes and 'Chinese style' decorations to be used to decorate lacquer work, porcelain and fabrics with oriental motifs. Some of these compositions were re-published in *The Ladies Amusement* in 1760.

concept, known to the Dutch since the 17th century.[97] Temple was ambassador to Holland and doubtless was familiar with Nieuhoff's publication, which contained an illustration of Yuan Ming Yuan, a large garden which surrounded the old Summer Palace, later destroyed. Further engravings illustrated 'Chinese' buildings. In general, the best-informed experts of landscape design successfully promoted the idea that "all the world is a garden" – including its natural disorder: in 1712 Joseph Addison (1672-1719) praised the Chinese garden for harmonizing so gently with its natural surroundings.[98] In 1715 Lord Burlington designed his garden at Chiswick House with the help of Alexander Pope and William Kent (c. 1685-1748), based on the illustrations by Matteo Ripa (1682-1746),[99] thus initiating a lively debate concerning landscape design that would later be termed 'picturesque'. But it was Lancelot 'Capability' Brown (1716-1783) who first achieved success transforming the classical garden into an elaborate park where pavilions of all kinds, based on classical antiquities as well as the Orient, were dotted around a landscape ideally created by the vagaries of nature.[100]

In England the earliest garden architecture in the oriental style was at Stowe (Buckinghamshire); documented in 1738, it was painted on the outside with exotic motifs by the Venetian decorator Francesco Sleter;[101] at Woburn (Bedfordshire) there was a similar and contemporary building designed by William Linnell;[102] in 1741 Richard Bateman had an entire farm built in the Chinese style on his Old Windsor estate in Berkshire while the Pavilion at Broughton House (Northamptonshire) was built for Lord Montagu in 1745.[103] In the same year the House of Confucius, designed by Joseph Goupy, was built in Kew. This was followed in 1747 by a pavilion built in Shugborough Park, Staffordshire for captain Auson who had lived in Canton for several years.[104] Immediately after the appearance of *Chinese and Gothic Architecture properly ornamented*, in 1750 William Halfpenny published his volume of *New Designs for Chinese Temples* with 60 engraved plates, followed by *Rural Architecture in the Gothik Taste* in 1752. Similar works were published by Edwards and Darly (1754), Paul Decker (*Chinese Architecture, Civil and Ornamental, Adapted to This Climate*, 1757), Edward Oakley and Charles Over (*Ornamental Architecture in Gothic, Chinese and Modern Taste*, 1758) and William Wright (1767), to mention only a few. William Chambers' volume of 1757 was of particular importance, however. An architect, he was responsible for building further exotic structures in Kew Gardens commissioned by Augusta the princess dowager of Wales and completed in 1762 a year before he published *The Garden and Buildings at Kew* (1763). One of the most famous buildings in the park was the pagoda which became the prototype for a style fashionable throughout Europe until the early decades of the 1800s. The building was based on the numerous engravings illustrating the Nanking pagoda which had been available for over a century in Europe and was built according to the rules of Chinese

78. William Chambers, *The Pagoda in Kew Gardens*, engraving from *Gardens and Buildings at Kew*, London 1763.

The great pagoda in Kew was built in 1762 and just a year later in 1763 the architect William Chambers published a volume – including this engraving – illustrating all the structures in the park at Kew. The Gardens were quite eclectic with buildings in various styles – Chinese, Moorish, classical and Egyptian. Chambers is merited with having introduced a style of chinoiserie that was much closer to the original models, less fanciful than the exotic style previously adopted in Europe.

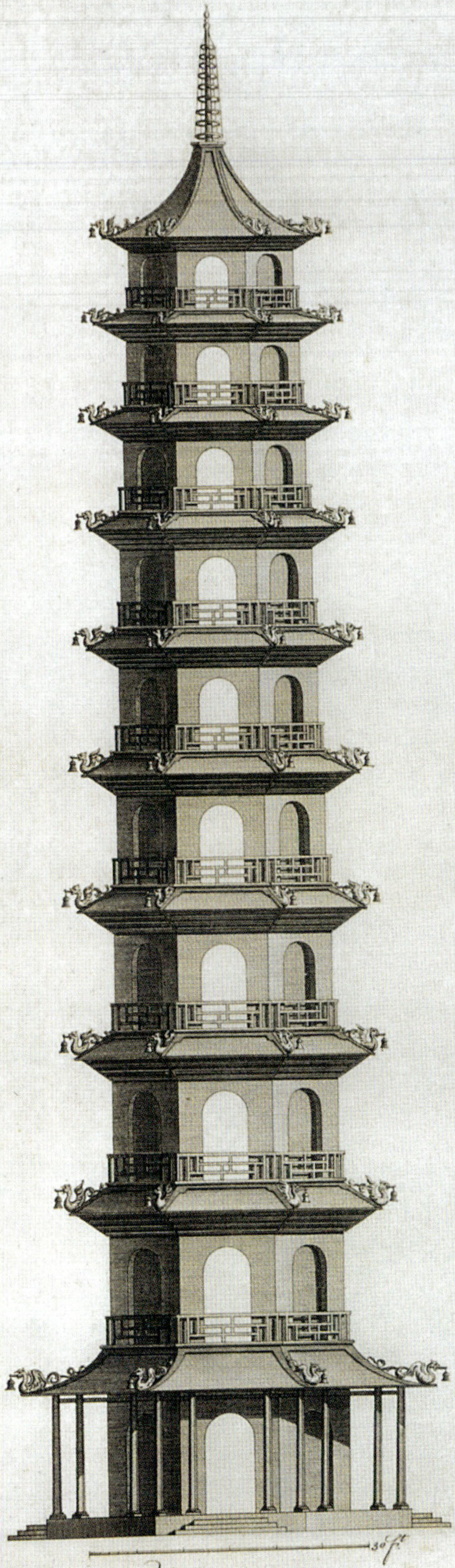

Elevation of The Great Pagoda – as first Intended

T. Miller sculp.

W. Chambers Architectus –

architecture that Chambers had learned while living in Canton. Although other similar buildings existed in England (such as Marybone House in Gloucester, built in the 1740s, and a wooden structure at Shugborough dated 1752),[105] the Kew Gardens pagoda provided the prototype for a style which became fashionable throughout Europe until the early decades of the 19th century.[106] In 1772 Chambers published *A Dissertation on Oriental Gardening* – a sequel to his famous *Designs of Chinese Buildings...* of 1757. Chambers heavily criticised the English garden which he claimed was a poor imitation of nature and praised the variety, charm and art of the Chinese garden.[107] He identifies three types of landscape – the pleasing, the horrid and the enchanted – all of which could be achieved by building pavilions, grottos and mountains intended to provoke a sense of wonder and excitement in the visitor. Another English architect, John Bush, invented and built a folly for Catherine the Great (1729-1796), Empress of Russia, consisting of no less than an entire Chinese Village with eighteen houses built around a pagoda and temple. The somewhat eccentric Catherine, revealed to be a fervent enthusiast of the English garden in a letter to Voltaire in 1772, had the village built in the grounds of her summer residence, Tsarskoe Selo overlooking the gulf of Sweden. Partly directed by the Italian, Antonio Rinaldi, work continued after Catherine's death in 1786 and was finally completed in 1818.[108]

The Brighton Pavilion was beyond any doubt the most extravagant building of its time.[109] Commissioned by George, prince of Wales (1762-1830), it was

79. Jean-Baptiste Pillement, Chinoiseries in *The Ladies Amusement*, 1760.

The Ladies Amusement was intended for the vast and heterogeneous public, enthusiasts of oriental decoration and not necessarily specialised decorators; it provided a vast range of ideas not only for the English, but for dilettantes throughout Europe. Many of the chinoiseries were devised by Pillement who frequently worked with London publishers at the time.

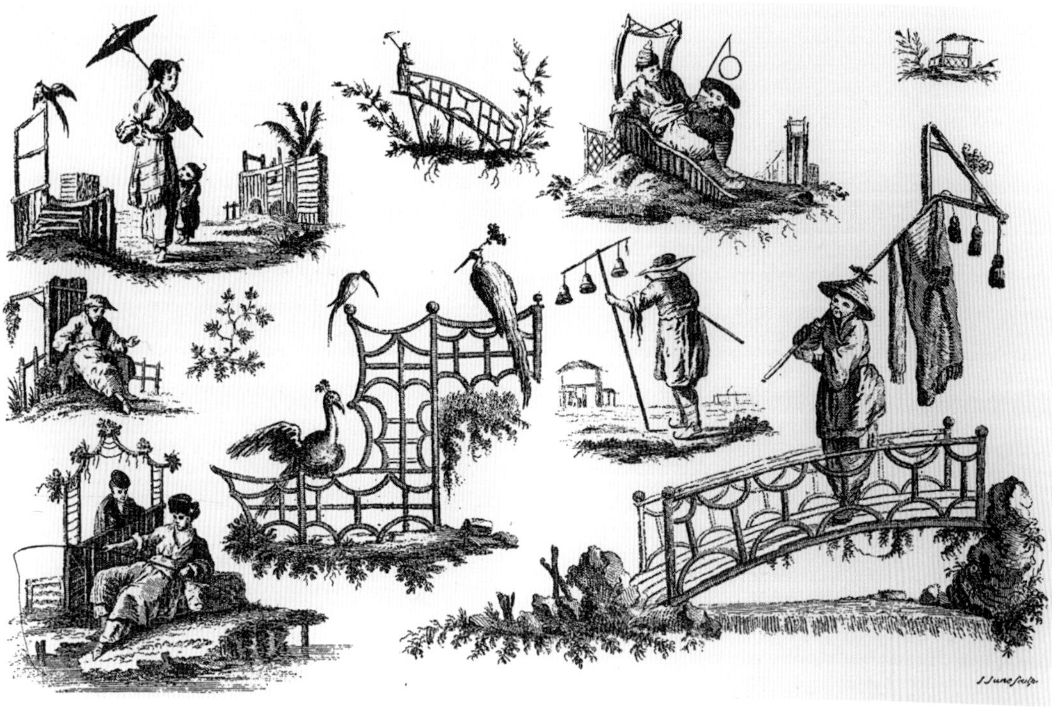

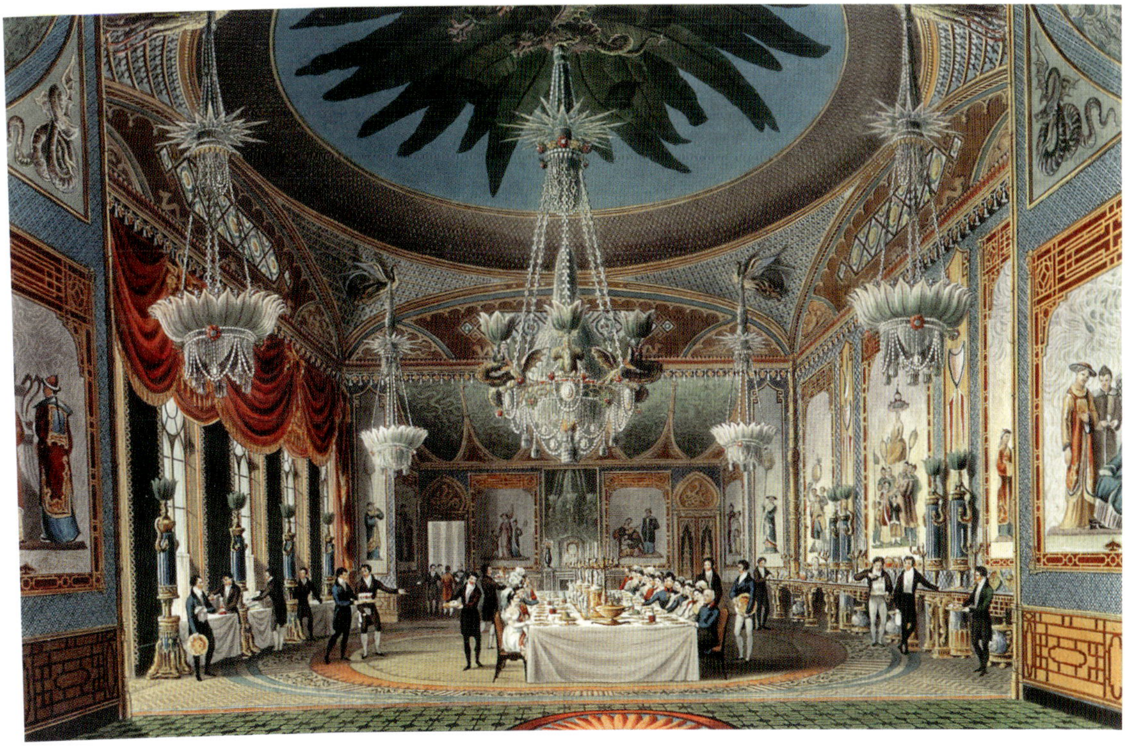

80. John Nash, *The Reception Hall of the Brighton Pavilion*, 1826. Brighton Museum and Art Gallery.

The Brighton Pavilion was completed in 1821 and is one of the last great works of chinoiserie in Europe. In fact, many of the external details of the Pavilion were derived directly from India, with its spires and onion domes. However, the interior decorations are quite Chinese with oriental figures and dragon motifs throughout.

begun by Henry Holland (1745-1806) and his pupil P.F. Robinson and was subsequently extended by Humphrey Repton (1752-1818) and John Nash (1752-1835) who completed the building in 1821; the interior decoration was carried out by members of the Crace family who drew much of their inspiration from the Cantonese paintings for exportation acquired by the prince.[110] Georgian chinoiserie was already in vogue in 1790 when the Chinese Room in Carlton House was designed for the prince of Wales,[111] and in the Brighton Pavilion is combined with the Indian style which had become so fashionable. Built in 1805 the pavilions at Sezincote were in the same style and had been greatly admired by the Prince Regent when visiting in 1807. The combination of these styles in the Brighton pavilion is most striking in the external elements where Mogul domes and pinnacles alternate with sweeping 'Chinese' roofs. Inside, however, the Chinese influence dominates – dragons, bundles of bamboo, banana trees and scenes filled with mandarins cover the columns, walls and ceilings, while the interior was decorated with ornamental chinoiseries and original works from the Far East. The rather eccentric Brighton Pavilion was the object of many satirical comments by contemporary critics and remained an isolated case as, in the early 1800s, European tastes were once more changing. Chinoiserie was becoming old-fashioned and the more classical styles of antiquity were returning to favour.[112]

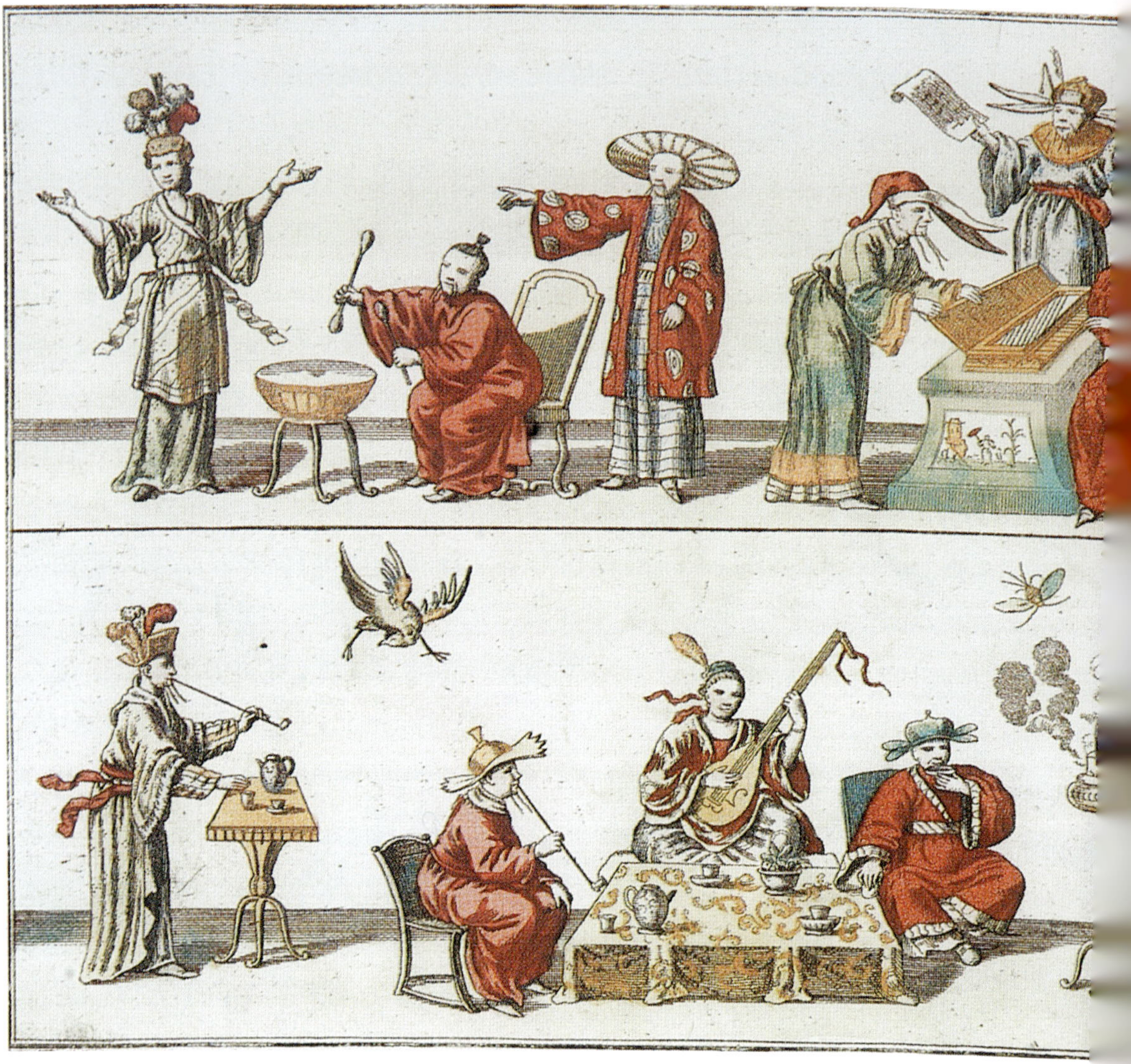

81. Martin Engelbrecht, Chinoiseries, c. 1720. Milan, Castello Sforzesco, Raccolta Bertarelli.

Engelbrecht's engravings with chinoiseries were widely available throughout Europe and provided ideas and designs for many decorators in all kinds of media from ceramics to lacquer work.

Germany

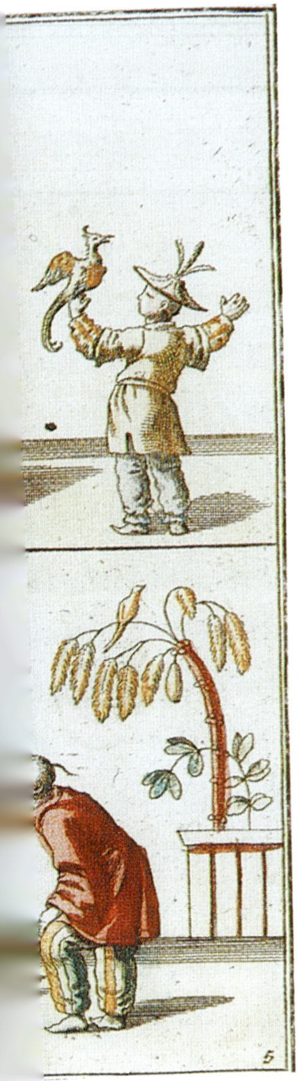

Chinoiserie developed later in Germany than in France and England and, although most of the stylistic features were imported, an autonomous style did in fact evolve and was often admired and imitated in other European countries. Politically and culturally the country was fragmented but the ruling families of the various states formed a network of family connections through marriage and consequently there was considerable cohesion in their artistic interests. The most influential collectors of chinoiserie and oriental objects were Augustus II the Strong, of Saxony (1670-1733), Frederick the Great of Prussia (1712-1786) and Max Emanuel of Bavaria (1662-1726), who set the fashion for all the other courts of Germany.

Many famous German architects, artists and decorators frequently made use of the Chinese style. Employed by the Elector of Brandenburg for most of his working life, Paul Decker the Elder (1677-1713) specialised in creating decorations for ceramics, fabrics and lacquer which were then published in *Entwürfe für Lackarbeiten* (Designs for lacquer work). His designs with oriental themes clearly reveal the influence of late 17th-century illustrated compendiums such as the works of Nieuhoff, and the scenes he designed were often surrounded by rather baroque ornamentation, similar to Bérain's works.[113] Many of the decorators working in nearby Augsburg made use of exotic subjects, such as Elias Baeck (1669-1747) whose chinoiserie designs were published by Jeremias Wolff (1663-1724),[114] as well as Joseph Sebastien (1700-1768) and Johann Baptist Klauber (1712-1787),[115] Caspar Neuner,[116] Johann Georg Pintz (1697-1767), and Martin Engelbrecht (1684-1756).[117] Johann Christoph Weigel (1654-1726)[118] also worked in Nurnberg and Johann Michael Hoppenhaupt was an interior decorator who worked at Charlottenburg, Potsdam, Berlin, Monbijou and Sans Souci.[119] Friedric Wilhelm Höder (? - c. 1761) from Berlin lived in France for several years learning the stylistic principles of French Rococo before working as a decorator and carver also at Sans Souci.[120]

Although he was born in Amsterdam and worked principally in Holland, the compositions created by Peter Schenk the Elder (1660-1718) were particularly successful in Germany. In 1702 he published a series of twelve reproductions entitled *Picturae Sinicae ac Surattenae* consisting of Chinese scenes taken from original works and including long explanatory inscriptions in Chinese, possibly copied from one of the many Chinese books imported to Europe in the 17th century.[121] Between 1700 and 1705, Schenk published a further series of prints with Chinese subjects, based on the volume by Olfert Dapper

(1670)[122] describing Japanese customs. Pieter Schenk the Younger (1698-1775) published a series of *Nieuwe geinventeerde Sineesen*[123] which were mainly prepared during the first two decades of the 18th century and were widely used by decorators throughout Europe from about 1725-30. Ignaz Preissler (1676-1741) of Kronstadt in Bohemia, decorator to count Von Kolowrat (1684-1753) from 1729 to 1739, for example, used them to ornament the various formats he worked on, especially porcelain and glass.[124]

Lacquer

The use of 'Chinese style' lacquer was already common in Germany in the late 17th century. Princess Sibylla Augusta of Saxe-Lauenburg and countess of Baden-Baden was an enthusiastic patron of the oriental arts and had commissioned the Lacquer Room in the Rastatt Palace as well as several *surtouts à la chinoise* – exuberant centrepieces published in Augsburg in 1729.[125] Shortly after the publication of Stalker and Parker's *Treatise* in 1688 she compiled a volume containing recipes for preparing oriental lacquers.[126] Some of the formulas most probably came from Holland where lacquer work had been well established already in the early 1600s. One of the most important centres for production was Spa, the Belgian town where Gérard Dagly (c. 1665-1715) had been born and learned the skill before moving to Berlin in 1686 to work for Frederick Wilhelm II, Elector of Brandenburg, subsequently becoming director of the most important workshop of Chinese lacquer in Germany.[127] Nominated 'court lacquer master', he immediately enjoyed international renown and in addition to Berlin worked in almost all the large German cities, including the court of the Palatine Elector in Düsseldorf. He was also for many years a close friend of Gottfried Leibniz (1646-1716) who was convinced that contact between the Chinese and

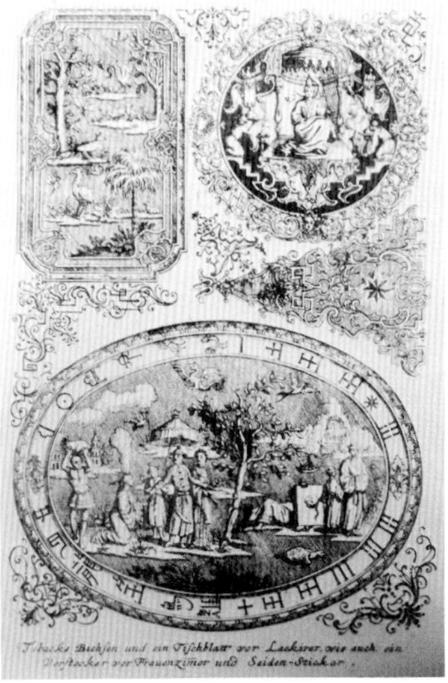

82. Paul Decker, Chinoiseries, engraving from *Entwürfe für Lackarbeiten*, c. 1710.

Entwürfe für Lackarbeiten (Designs for lacquer work), was a repertory of designs produced explicitly for decorators. Paul Decker mainly based his compositions with an oriental theme on illustrations in volumes describing Asia published during the second half of the 1600s (Nieuhoff, Montanus, Kircher, for example).

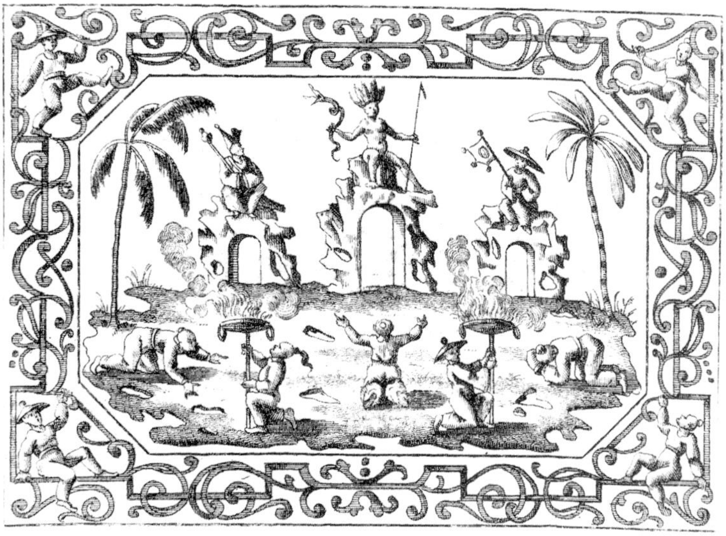

83. Elias Baeck (alias Heldenmuth), Chinoiseries, c. 1720.

Working in Augsburg, Baeck created numerous compositions mainly for use by jewellers and porcelain decorators. His chinoiseries were obviously based on images found in illustrated books that described far-flung lands, published in the second half of the 17th century (Nieuhoff in particular). The features of the deity in the centre of this image are clearly much closer to the iconography of North American characters than Chinese.

European cultures was vitally important (*Novissima Sinica*, 1697).[128] The lacquered works produced by Dagly were masterpieces, the smoothness and gloss almost perfectly reproducing the appearance of original oriental lacquer, while the attention to the detail of the decorative motifs, derived from Japanese and Chinese works, is exquisite. Almost certainly inspired by oriental porcelain, his works of white lacquer ornamented with coloured figures are especially delightful, such as the magnificent harpischord dated 1710 and now in the castle of Charlottenburg near Berlin.[129] Dagly's technique was also known in France, where his younger brother Jacques lived and worked.
Two other lacquer masters who were active in Germany in the early 18th century were Andreas Völkert and David Pennewitz.[130] In 1747 Jean Alexandre Martin, one of the famous Parisian family of lacquer workers, moved to Berlin to the court of Frederick II of Prussia and in 1755 worked on the Flower Room at Sans Souci. Another French craftsman, Sébastien Chevalier, moved to Potsdam in 1766 and shortly after established his own workshop there.[131] French artists and craftsmen had begun to arrive in Germany in the late 17th century following the Edict of Nantes in 1686, and brought with them the styles and fashions of Louis' France including the rage for chinoiserie. By 1686 Pierre Mercier, an employee at the Aubusson tapestry works, had established a factory in the capital of Prussia managed by Charles Vigne from 1720. The patterns used at the Berlin factory thus obviously included chinoiserie scenes and often these reproductions were more faithful copies of the original Chinese models.[132]
Augustus II the Strong also decided to establish a workshop to make lacquer

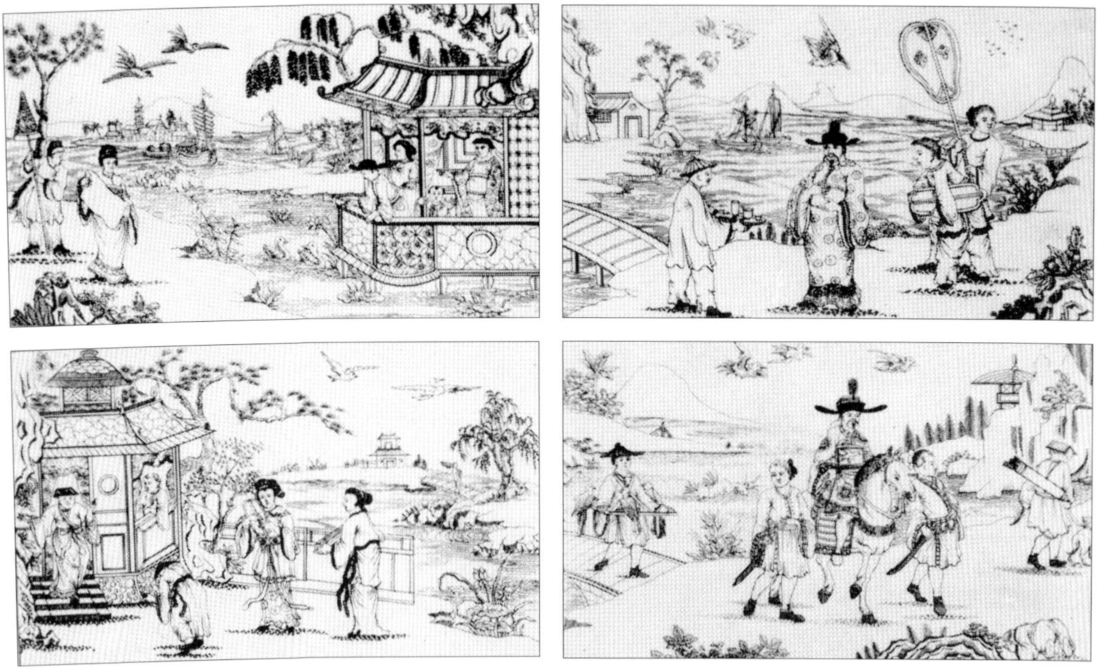

84a,b,c,d. Peter Schenk The Younger, Chinoiseries from *Nieuwe geinventeerde Sineesen*, c. 1725. Dresden, Kupferstich-Kabinett.

Compositions such as these by Schenk the Younger were used by many European ceramic factories for their chinoiserie designs.

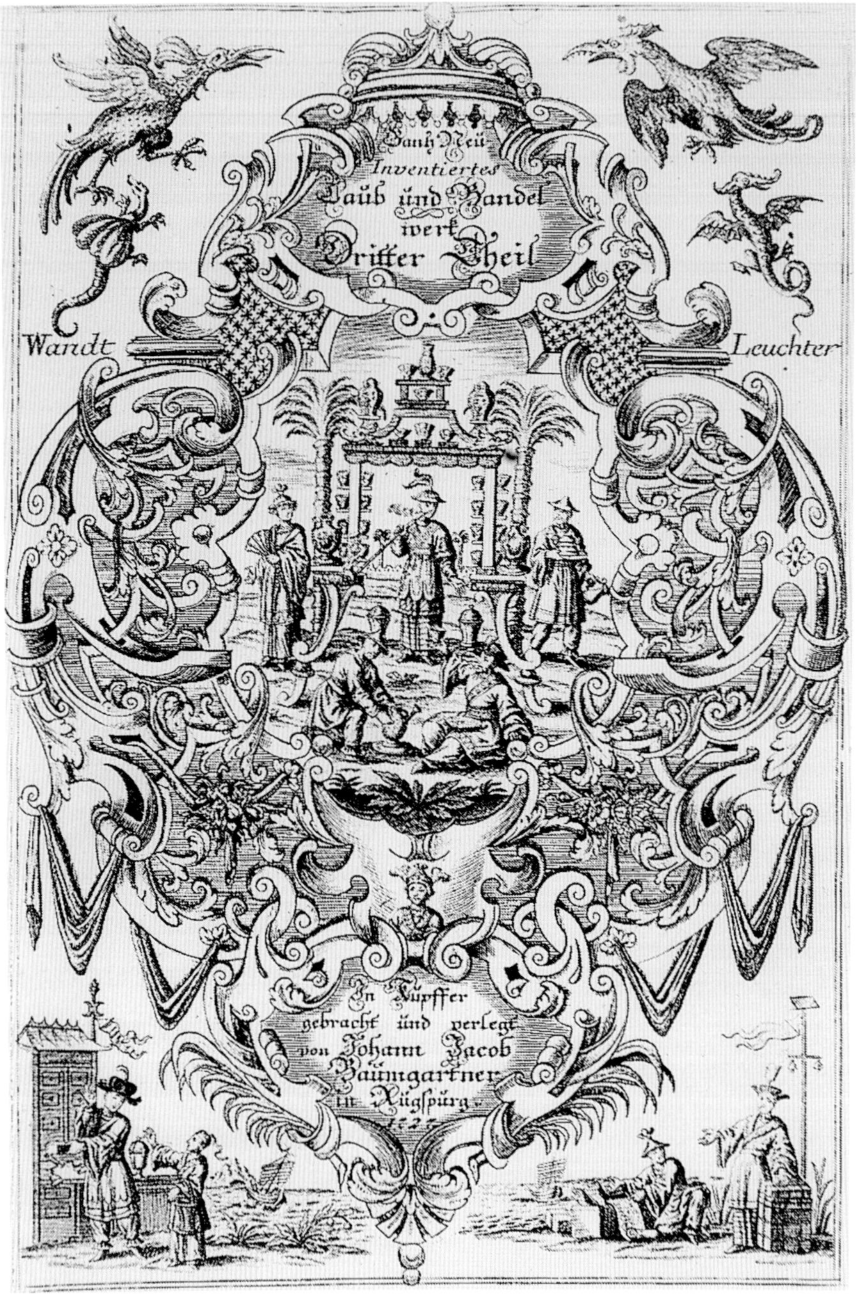

85. Johann Jacob Baumgartner, Chinoiserie in baroque cartouche, 1727. London, Victoria and Albert Museum.

J.J. Baumgartner was a noted decorative ornamentalist in Augsburg. In the centre of this engraving, in a cartouche that is still baroque in style, is a highly detailed chinoiserie scene while two simpler images appear below on the left and right. In the background of the main scene is a fireplace decorated with porcelain, a fashion first invented by Daniel Marot in the late 17th century (see Fig. 71).

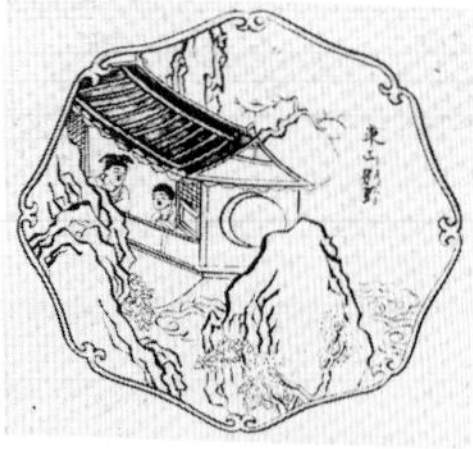

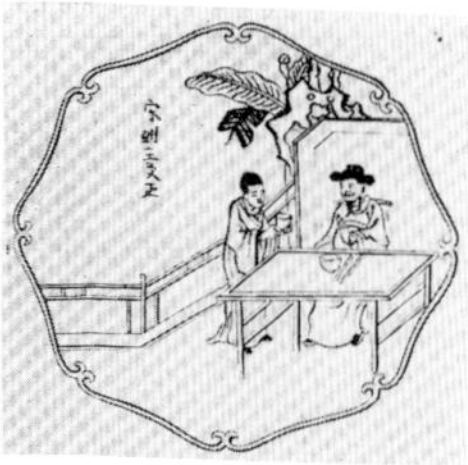

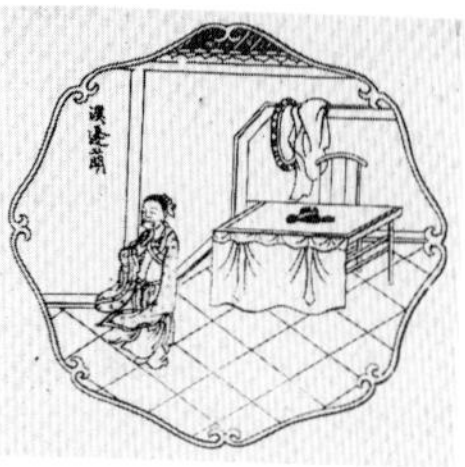

86a,b,c,d,e,f. Peter Schenk The Elder, Chinoiseries from *Picturae Sinicae ac Surattenae*, 1702. Dresden, Kupferstich-Kabinett.

This series of images by Schenk The Elder consists of twelve sheets, each of which contains two individual scenes. Schenk based his decorations on original Chinese works and reproduced even the ideogrammes of Far Eastern writing with complete precision.

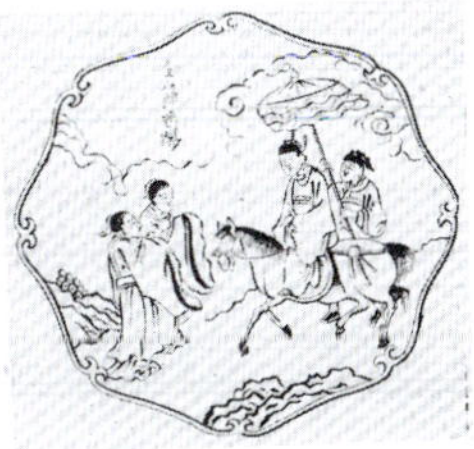

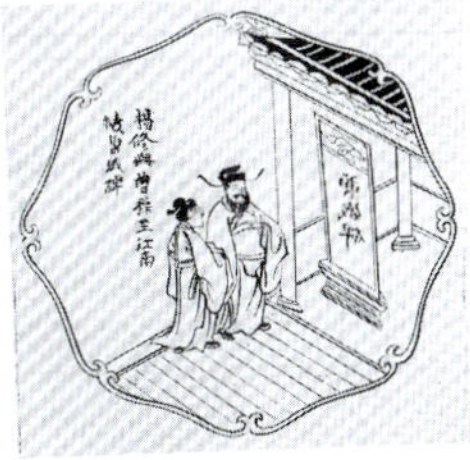

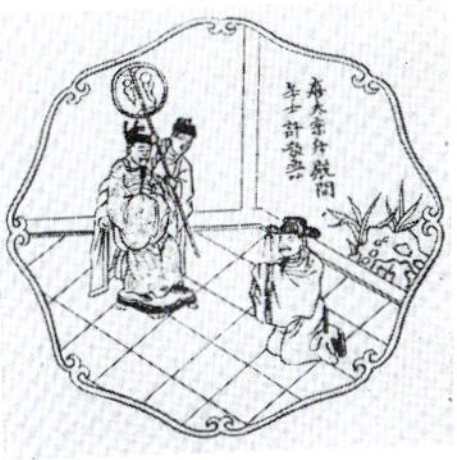

items in Dresden. Augustus had noted the works of Martin Schnell (1685-1740) in 1703 while he was working for Gérard Dagly in Berlin and in 1710 Schnell moved to Dresden where lacquer items had previously been made exclusively by Heinrich Teschau.[133] Schnell made numerous pieces for both the German aristocracy and Augustus II whose passion for all that was connected with Japan and China was at its height during this period. During his early days in Saxony however, records show that he was mainly involved in decorating the porcelain that was just beginning to be produced at the Meissen factory.

Described in 1694 by Christoph Pitzler (1657-1707), some of Gérard Dagly's most important creations were the lacquer panels made for a room in the Oranienburg castle (famous also for the *Porzellan Zimmer* made for Frederick I of Prussia between 1688 and 1695 and one of the first of its kind in Europe). The fashion for 'lacquer rooms' which had first begun at Rosenborg in Denmark some decades earlier, perhaps enjoyed most success in Germany. Enthused by Dagly's creations, in 1705 the Elector Franz von Schönbrun commissioned a series of lacquered panels, framed by garlands in the baroque style, for a room in his Neue Residenz at Bamberg.[134] The carved scrolls that frame the panels decorating the walls of the Lacquer Room at Ludwigsburg, created for the duke of Würtemberg between 1714 and 1722, are much lighter in appearance as the influence of early French Rococo began to be felt. Dodging around the numerous shelves arranged to display the porcelain items, Johann Jacob Saenger painted the oriental motifs of the *boiseries*.[135]

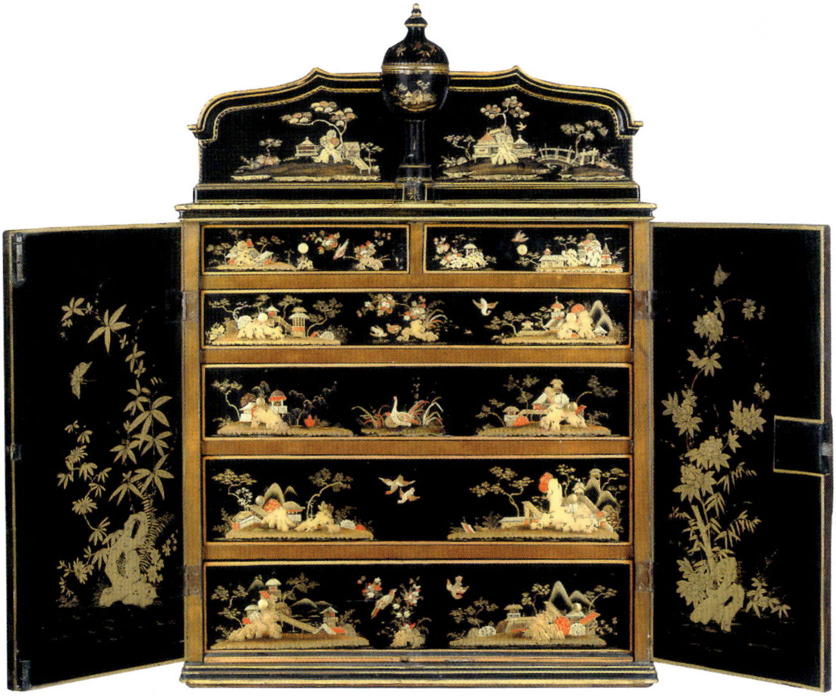

87. Cabinet of lacquered wood with gold and colour decoration. Holland, c. 1700. Vienna, Liechtenstein Collection.

For over two hundred years Holland was the only western country to have commercial relations with Japan. Imitations of the magnificent Japanese lacquer work were already being produced in Amsterdam in the early 17th century. This cabinet, one of a pair, demonstrates not only with what skill the Dutch craftsmen had learned the techniques of lacquer work but also the extent to which they had assimilated the decorative style.

A few years later Max Emanuel, Elector of Bavaria who had lived in France for several years where he had doubtless observed the new trends in decoration, commissioned the court architect to build a Chinese pavilion in the park of Nymphenburg. The interior was a combination of various forms of 'Chinese' decoration (lacquer panels, possibly made by a Bavarian craftsman, Delft tiles, original Chinese wallpaper) and favourite, traditional European motifs.[136] The building is clearly classical in form and reveals nothing of the 'exotic' vision that underlay its conception;[137] however, an early example of the Elector's fondness for chinoiserie are the rare panels of fabric (c. 1700) which decorate the walls of a study in the Munich residence, embroidered with scenes taken mainly from the engravings of Niuehoff, Dapper and Montanus.[138] Maximilian Emanuel's son, Karl Albrecht (1697-1745) was responsible for a second pavilion at Nymphenburg, decorated by François de Cuvilliés (1695-1768). Author of the *Livre d'ornements à diverses usages,* Cuvilliés created one of the finest examples of chinoiserie at the time, with a particularly sophisticated use of blue and white décor for the interior. Also at Nymphenburg, Cuvilliés decorated a room with original Coromandel lacquered panels from China. In 1735 he designed a similar room on the first floor of the Falkenlust hunting lodge in Brühl, using the panels of two Chinese screens with a gold decoration picked out on a black background;[139]

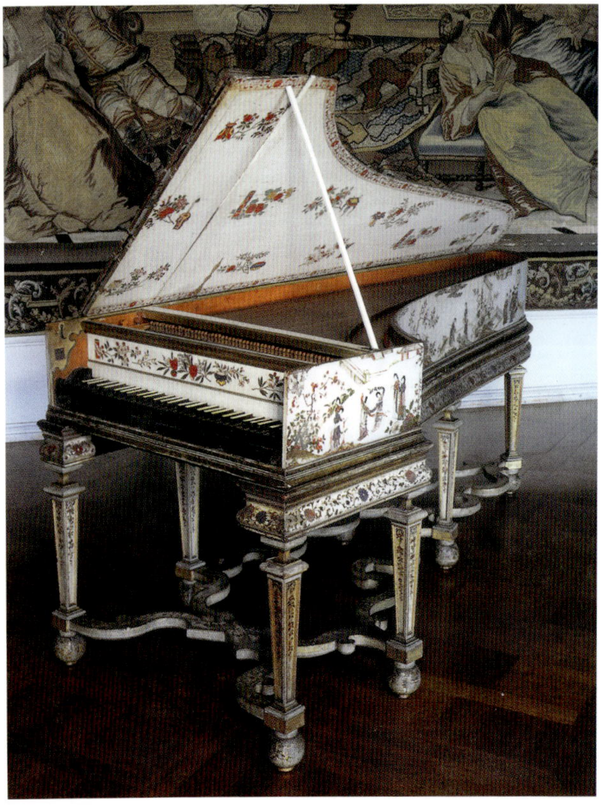

88. Harpischord, c.1700. Berlin, Schlöss Charlottensburg.

Gérard Dagly's workshop was responsible for the lacquer work of this harpsichord made about 1700. The white lacquer background for the decoration was a speciality of this lacquer master who based both the decoration and the technique of his works almost entirely on original oriental works. His model in this case was provided by the *famille verte* porcelain produced in China in the late 17th century, most of which was destined for export to European markets.

additional sections with a similar design were made in Europe, most probably in Paris.[140] Clemens August (1700-1761), the younger son of the Bavarian Elector and bishop of Cologne, was just as passionate about the Far East, and China in particular. It was he who rebuilt the castle at Brühl including many 'Chinese style' rooms. In 1750 Clemens August commissioned an entire *Chinesisches Haus* for the park at Brühl, which a series of contemporary engravings shows to be fairly similar in style to mid 18th-century French structures of the same kind.

Meissen Porcelain

The establishment of a ceramic factory at Meissen by Augustus II the Strong of Saxony represented an immense contribution to the development of arts in Europe. In this small city, not far from Dresden, Augustus employed professional workers and also provided the necessary financial investment to finally discover the 'secret' of porcelain after centuries of failed attempts. The technical contribution to this achievement was provided by Jean-Fréderic Böttger (1682-1719) – an alchemist who came to Dresden in 1701 after having laboured with little success for Frederick I of Prussia in Berlin – and the physicist and matematician Ehrenfried Walter de Tschirnhaus (1651-1708), who had earlier tried to improve the technical processes in the glass factories in Saxony. In 1709 they succeeded in producing a fine, hard red grés similar to the paste of the Chinese wares produced by the Yixing factories, huge quantities of which were imported to Europe at the time and copied in both Holland and England. It was then a short step to obtaining white porcelain

89. Sketch of chinoiseries, from the *Schulz Codex*, c. 1723-1726 Leipzig, Museum für Kunsthandwerke.

The *Schulz Codex* contains many chinoiseries designed by Johann Gregorius Höroldt, some of which were used to decorate Meissen porcelain. Höroldt was the factory's *hausmaler* and his 'exotic' inventions were delightfully elegant and sensual, derived from both the works of French artists and Far Eastern works in the Elector's enormous collection.

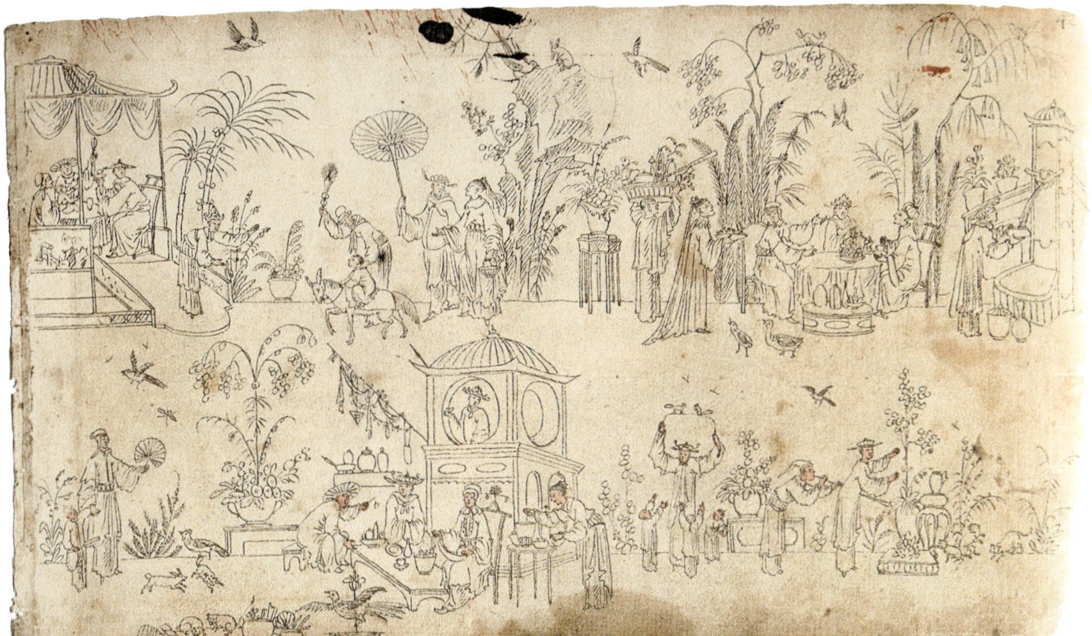

and the first results appeared just a few months later when it was discovered that the missing element was kaolin (china clay), a material quarried in fact not far from Meissen. The original intention of the factory was to reproduce Chinese and Japanese porcelain, and especially the characteristics of the paste.[141] Once this was achieved not only were the forms and decorations of some of the Chinese and Japanese pieces in the immense collection of Augustus II reproduced, but it was also decided to create some chinoiserie subjects.[142] At first the chinoiserie motifs were devised by painters active in the workshops of nearby Augsburg though from about 1725 the designs were mainly created in Meissen by Johann Gregorius Höroldt. In 1720 Höroldt had moved to the town from Vienna where he had worked in the Du Paquier factory (the second in Europe to begin producing porcelain) and quickly became expert at creating Chinese scenes and designs.[143] In 1726 he published a series of prints with oriental motifs, based on the compositions of Claude Gillot and Antoine Watteau, taken from an extensive series of designs some of which were collected in the *Schulz Codex*.[144] Höroldt's figures, elegantly elongated and always represented in refined poses and occupation, belong to an imaginary dream-world. His models for these compositions were provided not only by French artists, but also original works in the Elector's collection. Other painters who devised chinoiserie patterns and motifs at Meissen were Ehrenfried Stadler (1701-1741), Christian Friedrich Herold (1700-1779) from Berlin and Adam von Löwenfinck (1714-1754). However, the quite beautiful sculptural works produced by Johann Gottlieb Kirchner (1706-?) and Johann Joachim Kändler (1706-1775) made little use of oriental subjects. Following the death of Augustus II in 1733 chinoiserie decoration of Meissen porcelain came to an end.

Augustus' passion for the the Orient also gave rise to what Oliver Impey has described as the most successful chinoiserie work of the 18th century.[145] Made in 1702 by the goldsmith and jeweller Johann Melchior Dinglinger (1664-1731), the magnificent centrepiece known as "The Grand Mogul's Birthday" is a quite splendid work not only for the precious materials used but also for the extravagance of its subject and technical perfection. It is, moreover, a kind of synthesis of Europe's particular vision of the Orient – a summary of the entire evolution of chinoiserie. The atmosphere is dream-like with varied references to the cultures of India, Japan, China, the Near East and Europe itself, all distilled from the illustrations and models most widely available at the time - from those of Nieuhoff to Montanus and Dapper, but also Stefano Della Bella (1610-1664) who adapted Turkish motifs on more than one occasion.[146]

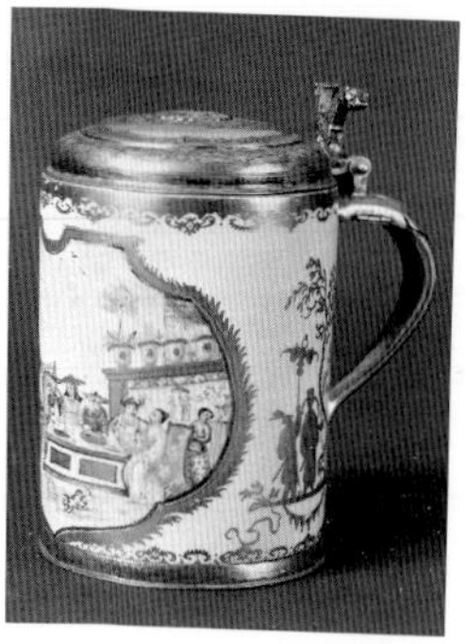

90. Beer tankard. Meissen, c. 1720-1730. Florence, Pitti Palace, Museo delle Porcellane.

The tankard (fired sometime between 1720 and 1725) was probably decorated in the workshop of either the Aufenwerth sisters or Bartholomäus Seuter, though certainly in Augsburg some time before 1731-1733 when Elias Adam added the metal mount. The chinoiserie scene is taken from f. 82 of the *Schulz Codex*.

Chinese Pavilions

The oriental-style pavilions built by Augustus the Strong at Dresden were the first in Europe after the porcelain *Trianon* at Versailles. In 1719 he decided to turn his 'Dutch' Palace, built just two years earlier, into a 'Japanese' Palace where he would house his extraordinary collection of oriental and Meissen porcelain which – even then – was so immense that it required a separate building to house it. However, if on the outside the only exotic features of the entire structure were the Chinese caryatids on the ground floor and the curvature of the roof,[147] the interior on the other hand boasted a sumptuous combination of original Far Eastern items and European chinoiserie.[148]
Augustus was also responsible for the *Indianisches Lustschloss* at Pillnitz, designed by Matthaus Daniel Poppelmann (1662-1737) and built between 1720 and 1732; the few oriental elements of the *Lustschloss* are slightly more obvious than those of the Japanese Palace, but they are just as superficial, although they do add a degree of liveliness to what would otherwise be an early neoclassical structure.[149]
The most important 'exotic' building in all of Germany however, was the Chinese Pavilion in the Sans Souci park. Approaching the French rococo style in appearance, Frederick the Great's building was inspired by *Le Trèfle* which had been commissioned by Stanislas Leszcynski (1677-1766), king of Poland and father-in-law to the king of France.[150] Leszcynski sent the plans of his pavilion to Frederick who commissioned the work from his architect Johann Gottfried Buring (1723-c. 1788). The Tea House at Potsdam is a masterpiece, representative of all European chinoiserie, in particular the whimsical, oniric atmosphere that pervades the building.[151] Various exotic elements are combined, from the gentle, Chinese-style forms of the structure itself such as the curving roof, to the lively colours of the exterior, the arrangement of life-sized statues of Chinese figures around the almost circular upper storey – and not forgetting of course that part of the Elector's immense collection of oriental porcelain was exhibited inside. The wooden Chinese pavilion given to Louisa Ulrika (1720-1782), Frederick the Great's sister, by her husband the king of Sweden as a birthday present in 1753 must have been quite similar to that of Sans Souci.[152] In the park of Drottningholm, just six kilometres from Stockholm, the building only survived for a decade to be replaced by a brick structure, still standing, designed by the court architect, Carl Frederick Adelcrantz (1716-1796).[153] The fragile building is perhaps more elegant than the Tea House at Potsdam and provided an ideal setting for the royal family to relax. Natural light flooded in through the large windows, reflecting and illuminating the bright colours of the wall decorations, while the rooms – the library, drawing rooms and salons – were designed for the queen and her children to indulge their favourite pastimes. The interior décor reflected the work of Boucher, Pillement and William Chambers, but also included original Chinese and Japanese items such as the painted wall papers,

numerous porcelain works, and lacquered panels used to cover the walls of the Yellow Room and the Red Room. So heterogeneous was the combination of features that the Pavilion has frequently been described as a true synthesis of the various European chinoiserie styles.[154]

Later buildings included the folly built by Frederich II of Hessen Kassel (1720-1785) consisting of an entire Chinese village built on the shores of a lake at Wilhelmshöhe, and christened Mulang. Work began in 1781 and ended in 1797 when, lacking any suitable Chinamen to occupy the place, a colony of negroes was imported. In addition to the similar experiment at Tsarskoe Selo initiated some years later by Catherine the Great (who was also German) a further Chinese village was built at Rosswald, near Trappau in Silesia. An 'anglo-chinois' garden was made in Count Ludwig's park at Steinfort near Münster in the 1780s shortly after the publication of *Geschichte und Theorie der Gartenkunst* (Leipzig 1779), a treatise on gardening by Christian Hischfeld (1742-1792), which became a reference work for the entire 19th century and was widely consulted in Italy too, where it was published in a reduced form edited by Luigi Mabil (1752-1836).[155]

1) Honour 1961 (1963), p. 61; Jacobson 1993, pp. 35-36.
2) Colle 2000, p. 10.
3) Honour 1961 (1963), p. 70.
4) Honour 1961 (1963), pp. 72-73; Jacobson 1993, pp. 36-38.
5) Catucci 2007, p. 54.
6) Jacobson 1993, p. 49.
7) Huth 1971, p. 87.
8) Honour 1961 (1963), p. 69.
9) Jarry 1981, pp. 16-24; Wolvesperges in Paris 2007, pp. 150-152.
10) Berlin 1973, pp. 138-143.
11) Jarry 1981, p. 16.
12) Macchia, Montagni 1968, pp. 92-93; Brunel in Paris 2007, p. 13.
13) Honour 1961 (1963), p. 103.
14) Honour 1961 (1963), p. 104.
15) Paris 2007, p. 124.
16) Fuhring 2005, pp. 108-109, no. 29.
17) Jarry 1981, p. 49; Gruber 1996, p. 284.
18) Fuhring 2005, pp. 180-185, nos. 63-65; Paris 2007, pp. 136-138.
19) Pacia 1990, p. 111.
20) Fuhring 2005, pp. 112-113, no. 31.
21) Fitz-Gerald 1964; Paris 2007, pp. 131-132.
22) Paris 2007, p. 130.
23) Fuhring 1999; Fuhring 2005, pp. 110-111, no. 30.
24) Fitz-Gerald 1963, no. 21.
25) Paris 2007, p. 133.
26) Fuhring 1999, p. 75, fig. 30.
27) Zenone Padula 1992, pp. 94-95.
28) Paris 2007, p. 125.
29) Paris 2007, p. 129.
30) Paris 2007, pp. 134-135.
31) Jacobson 1993, pp. 68-70.
32) Gruber 1996, p. 284.
33) Honour 1961 (1963), p. 107; Paris 2007, pp. 126-127.
34) Jarry 1981, p. 24.
35) Jarry 1981, pp. 24-28.
36) Forti Grazzini in Colorno 1998, pp. 194-198.
37) New York-Detroit-Paris 1986-1987, pp. 205-210, nos. 41-44.
38) Jacobson 1993, p. 68; Stein in Paris 2007, p. 86.
39) Stein 1996; Stein in Paris 2007, pp. 86-100.
40) Paris 2007, pp. 139-141.
41) Cionini 1993; Gordon-Smith 2000; Gordon-Smith 2004; Gordon-Smith 2005.
42) Jarry 1981, pp. 28-32; Paris 2007, p. 149.
43) Fuhring 1999, p. 77.
44) Bellezza Rosina, Cataldi Gallo 1993, p. 36.
45) Jarry 1981, pp. 37-41.
46) Bellezza Rosina, Cataldi Gallo 1993, p. 37.
47) Jarry 1981, p. 44.
48) De Rochebrune in Paris 2007, pp. 112-117; Paris 2007, pp. 148, 176-184, 201-205, 208-211, 222-260, 262-265, 269-275.
49) Ferrari 2003, p. 50.
50) Paris 2007, pp. 155-160.
51) Miller 1996.
52) Miller 2001.
53) Huth 1971, pp. 88-90.
54) Huth 1971, pp. 95-97.
55) Huth 1971, p. 96.
56) Porzio 2005.
57) Huth 1971, p. 55.
58) Baulez in Kopplin 2001, pp. 29-41.
59) Jacobson 1993, pp. 161-162.
60) Tagliolini 1988, p. 319; Mosser in Paris 2007, p. 83.
61) Jacobson 1993, pp. 166, 168.

62) Jacobson 1993, pp. 166-167.
63) Berlin 1973, pp. 354-355, no. R2.
64) Jacobson 1993, p. 162.
65) Impey 1977, pp. 150-152.
66) Heimbürger Ravalli 1981.
67) Tagliolini 1988, p. 320.
68) Marot 1892.
69) Murdoch in Paris 2007, pp. 42-43.
70) Beveers 2008, pp. 14-15.
71) Jarry 1981, p. 140.
72) Honour 1961 (1963), p. 83; Jacobson 1993, pp. 45-47.
73) Huth 1971, p. 38.
74) Honour 1961 (1963), p. 97; Jacobson 1993, p. 55.
75) Baldwin Beer 1970, pp. 24, 26-27.
76) Irwin, Brett 1970, p. 30.
77) Jarry 1981, p. 52.
78) Bellezza Rosina, Cataldi Gallo 1993, p. 35.
79) Jarry 1981, pp. 33-35.
80) Rothstein 1990, pp. 71-72, nos. 13, 16.
81) Honour 1961 (1963), pp. 89-90; Paris 2007, pp. 142-143.
82) Honour 1961 (1963), pp. 94-95; Jacobson 1993, pp. 124-125.
83) Impey 1977, p. 120.
84) Honour 1961 (1963), pp. 180-181; Impey 1977, pp. 120-122.
85) Jacobson 1993, p. 129.
86) Impey 1977, pp. 121-122; Jacobson 1993, p. 130.
87) Jacobson 1993, pp. 162-164.
88) Honour 1961 (1963), pp. 183-185.
89) Honour 1961 (1963), p. 220; Impey 1977, p. 125; Jacobson 1993, p. 141.
90) Jacobson 1993, pp. 141-142.
91) Honour 1961 (1963), pp. 159-160; Impey 1977, p. 172; Jacobson 1993, pp. 146-149.
92) Paris 2007, pp. 153, 161, 172, 261.
93) Honour 1961 (1963), p. 79,
94) Murdoch in Paris 2007, pp. 50-56.
95) Honour 1961 (1963), p. 170.
96) Honour 1961 (1963), p. 171.
97) Mosser in Paris 2007, p. 79.
98) Conner 2008, p. 55.
99) Jacobson 1993, p. 155.
100) Impey 1977, pp. 132-134.
101) Conner 2008, pp. 55-56.
102) Conner 2008, p. 56.
103) Conner 2008, pp. 56-57.
104) Honour 1961 (1963), pp. 178-179; Impey 1977, p. 149; Jacobson 1993, p. 160; Brighton 2008, pp. 59-60.
105) Conner 2008, pp. 56-57.
106) Impey 1977, pp. 143-146; Jacobson 1993, p. 162.
107) Jacobson 1993, pp. 163-164.
108) Jacobson 1993, pp. 163-164.
109) Honour 1961 (1963), p. 223; Impey 1977, pp. 155-157.
110) Conner 2008A, pp. 65-68.
111) Honour 1961 (1963), p. 222.
112) Parissien in Londra 2004, p. 359.
113) Berlin 1973, pp. 213-214, no. J17.
114) Berlin 1973, pp. 261-262, nos. L46-48.
115) Berlin 1973, p. 309, no. P38.
116) Berlin 1973, p. 300, no. P14.
117) Berlin 1973, pp. 262-263, nos. L50-54.
118) Berlin 1973, pp. 214-215, no. J18.
119) Berlin 1973, p. 308, no. P35a-c.
120) Berlin 1973, pp. 307-308, nos. P32-34.
121) Fontein, Den Blaauwen 1966; Berlin 1973, p. 246, no. K99.
122) Ducret 1966.
123) Den Blaauwen 1966; Berlin 1973, p. 247, no. K102.
124) Von Strasser, Spiegl 1989, pp. 218-220 e 226, nos. 73-76 e 81-82.
125) Grimm 2007.
126) Honour 1961 (1963), p. 73; Huth 1971, p. 79; Zenone Padula 1992, p. 94.
127) Huth 1971, pp. 66-72.
128) Kühn 1973; Kühn in Berlin 1973, pp. 174-194.
129) Honour 1961 (1963), pp. 72-73; Jacobson 1993, p. 42.
130) Huth 1971, pp. 72-73.
131) Huth 1971, p. 73.
132) Jarry 1981, pp. 28-32.
133) Huth 1971, pp. 74-77.
134) Honour 1961 (1963), p. 74; Jacobson 1993, p. 39.
135) Honour 1961 (1963), p. 74; Jacobson 1993, p. 41.
136) Götz 2007.
137) Honour 1961 (1963), p. 74; Jacobson 1993, p. 41.
138) Ulrichs 2008, pp. 51-56.
139) Honour 1961 (1963), p. 131; Jacobson 1993, 90.
140) Hansmann 2002, pp. 72-81.
141) Jacobson 1993, pp. 98-103; Pietsch in Paris 2007, pp. 57-62; Paris 2007, pp. 185-200.
142) Cassidy-Geiger 1996.
143) Cassidy-Geiger 1996, p. 104, figs. 14-16.
144) Modelli Meissen 1981.
145) Impey 1977, p. 177.
146) Pietsch in Paris 2007, p. 58.
147) Pietsch in Paris 2007, p. 59.
148) Schwarm 2007.
149) Impey 1977, p. 147.
150) Jacobson 1993, pp. 92-94; Mosser in Paris 2007, pp. 81-82.
151) Honour 1961 (1963), p. 132.
152) Honour 1961 (1963), p. 136.
153) Harris in Paris 2007, pp. 74-77.
154) Jacobson 1993, pp. 94-97; Harris 2007.
155) Tagliolini 1988, pp. 318-319.

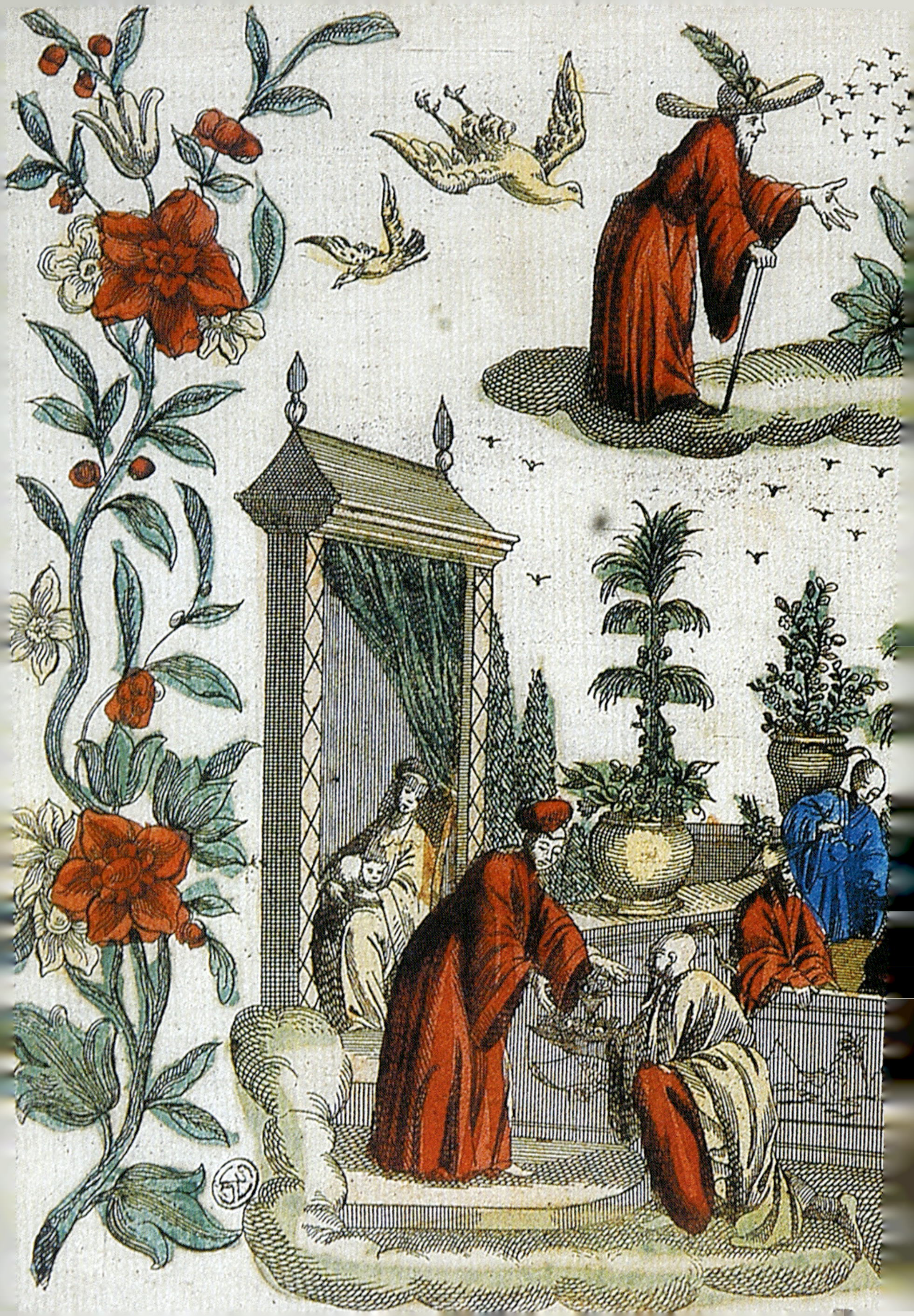

3 Chinoiserie in Italy in the 18th Century

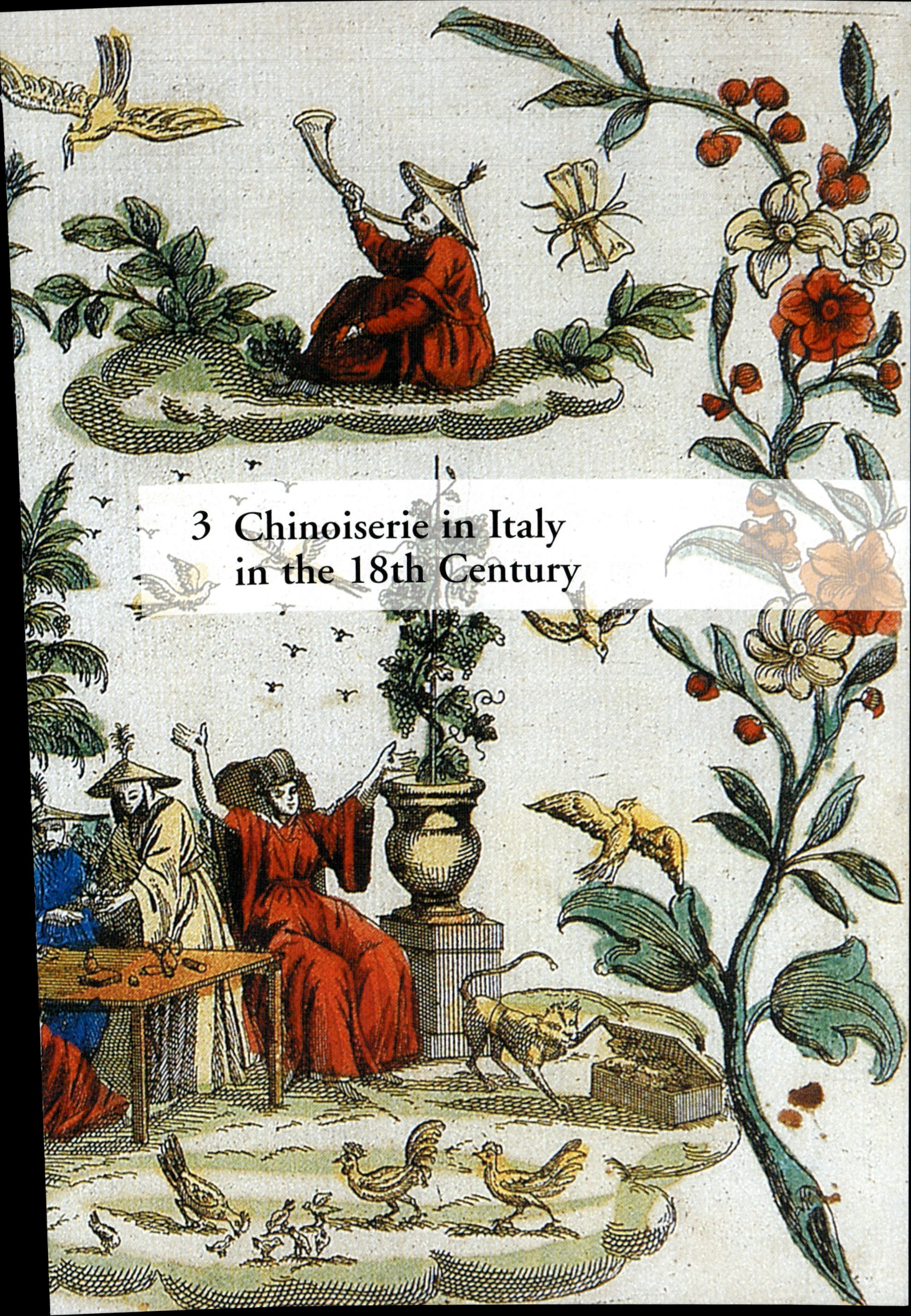

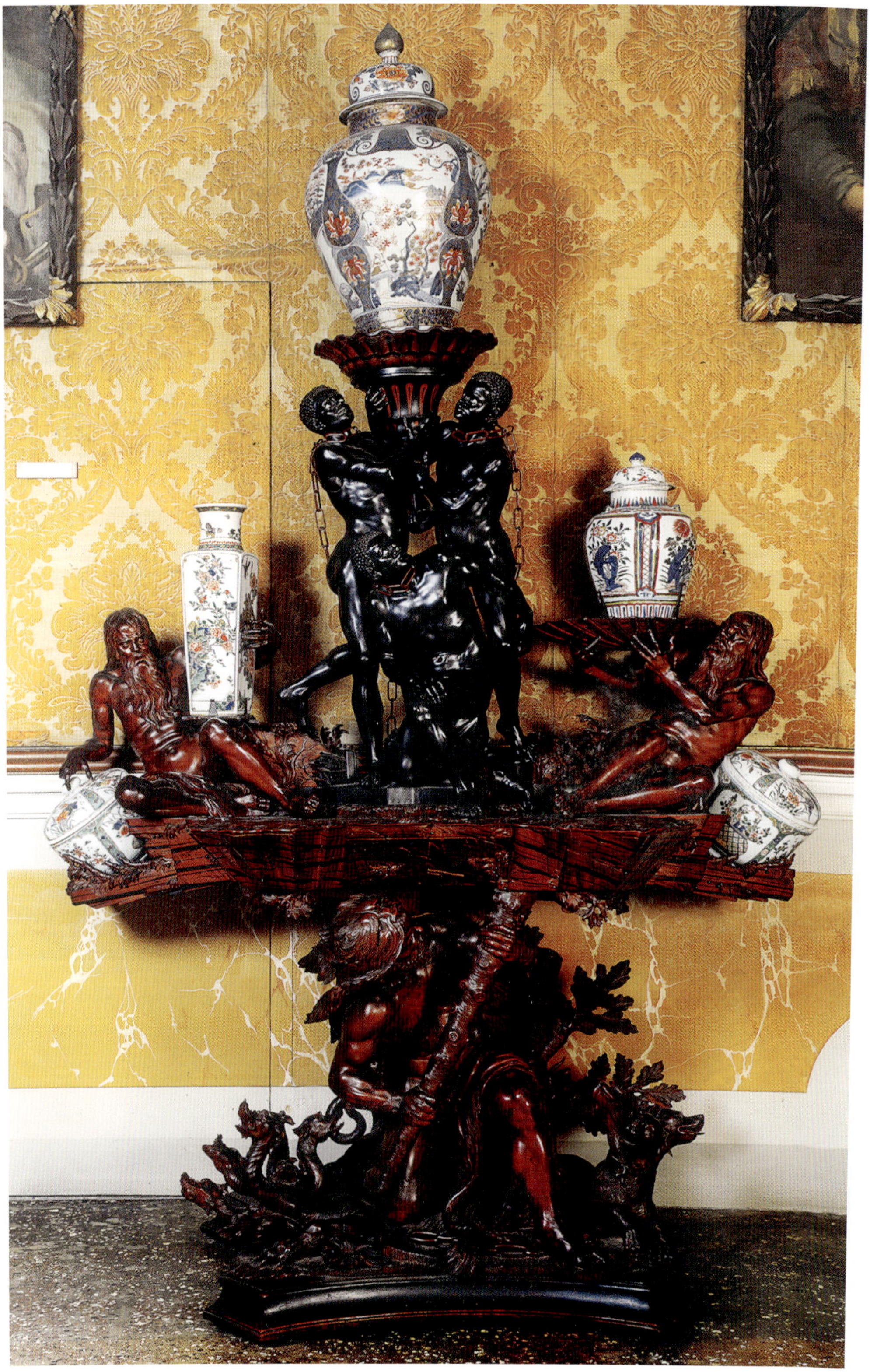

The Republic of Venice and the Veneto

Venice, the 'Gate of the Orient'. From ancient times until at least the Middle Ages – the period when the 'maritime cities' reigned over the seas of the Mediterranean – Venice rejoiced in this grandiose title, just one of the city's many glorious names. The long and glorious history of Venice seems to be governed by its inhabitants' almost genetic passion for the distant lands that lie beyond the Strait of the Dardanelles, beyond the shores of the eastern 'Mare Nostrum', a passion that influenced the development of the arts and many aspects of the city's culture. For Venice the Orient was a source of wealth and power, but it was also one of the factors that lead to the gradual loss of maritime control that had contributed so fundamentally to its grandeur. Decline set in when the Portuguese found alternative routes allowing them to establish more direct commercial contacts with ports in the south of Asia during the late 15th century. As a result the Venetians began to experience competition from more hardened rivals who were often supported in their ventures by the economy of an entire state. The industrious Venetian merchants were forced to carve out their own sector within the complex network of commercial and cultural relationships with the East, concentrating especially on the Near East which was less of a target for the colonizing countries. During the 16th and 17th centuries oriental goods from both the Islamic and the Far Eastern countries continued to arrive quite regularly in Venice whose merchants sold them on to other Italian and European cities, still impressed by the city's allure despite stiff competition from the East India Companies that now existed in other European countries. In 1602 some of the most important aristocratic families of Venice (Giustinian, Tiepolo, Barbaro and Zen) contributed large sums of money to the foundation of the Dutch East India Company. Thus Venetians were still in touch with the habits and customs of these exotic lands, and gradually the medieval image of China created by Marco Polo was replaced by more realistic and coherent information provided in the many accounts that appeared in the 17th and 18th centuries. The city – the 'Serenissima' – wavered somewhere between past glories and disastrous decline for the rest of its existence until, that is, the end of the 18th century when Napoleon's troops entered the city.

However, Venice remained one of the capitals of style and culture throughout the 18th century when chinoiserie was at its height. Influenced by original oriental works and open to developments that arrived from other European states, Venice succeeded in evolving its own 'Chinese style' partly

91. Andrea Brustolon, Stand for vases with Chinese and Japanese porcelain, c. 1700. Venice, Ca' Rezzonico.

Brustolon designed this monumental stand specially for Far Eastern porcelain works, probably the very same as those still displayed. The rounded vase with a lid at the top is an Imari piece made in Japan in the late 17th century. The four other pieces are Chinese: the oldest piece is above on the right and dates from the mid 17th century, while the other three – with coloured *famille verte* decorations – are more recent and date from the reign of emperor Kangxi (1662-1722).

due to the skill of the artists and artisans, and partly to the intuition of patrons and clients who appreciated the technical refinements of both decoration and form. Often the chinoiserie of the Serenissima was used as a model and was appreciated for its creative variety and for its unmistakable style.

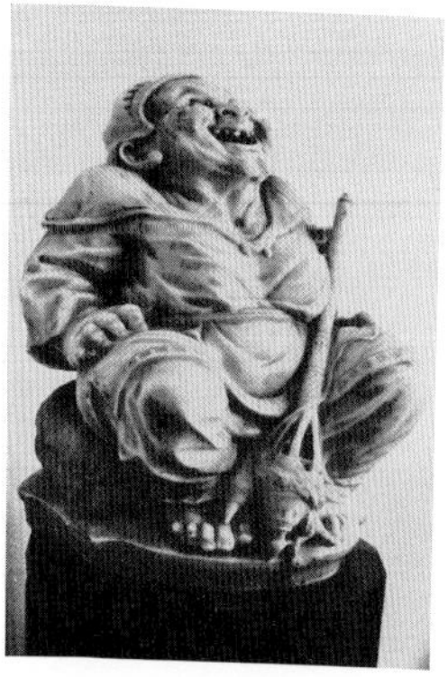

92. Giovanni Bonazza, Figure of a Chinaman, late 17th century. Padova, Biblioteca Universitaria.

Forming a matching pair, a statue of a Chinese lady by Bonazza is also housed in the University Library of Padova.

The Baroque Period

A new and more pronounced taste for chinoiserie in Venice developed in the late 17th and early 18th centuries. It was at this time that Venetians began to formulate a more specific image of China and its culture. In 1679 the various regions of the East still represented a vague and homogenous entity where Turks, Africans, Indians and Tartars were lumped together with little distinction, as is evident from the detailed description of a grand masquerade provided by Angelo Bottarello in his *Ragguaglio d'una Maschera a cavallo seguita il 27 Febraio 1679* (Account of a masquerade on horseback held on 27 February 1679) which appeared in the *Breve descrizione di Venezia, e de piacevoli trattenimenti, che godea prima, che s'introducessero i Teatri, e che tuttora gode, in tutte le quattro stagioni dell'anno, ed in particolare il tempo di Carnevale* (Brief description of Venice and its pleasant entertainments which were once enjoyed, introduced by the Theatres, and are still enjoyed in all four seasons of the year and especially at Carnival time) published in Venice in 1718. The costumes worn by the participants in the procession were not actually sufficiently precise to identify the native peoples represented and were often limited to feather headdresses and magnificent robes. Thus the Tartar-Chinaman portrayed by Francesco Morosini wore "Spanish 'gianelli' with mottled tips, four patterned pleats and an undershirt of the same colour, edged with lace, a collar of fur and brilliant orange sendal trimmed with lace, brocade breeches, embroidered boots on his feet, on his head an embroidered kerchief with a crest of red and white egret feathers, extremely expensive".[1] This confusion was shortly to change as illustrated texts specifically on China became increasingly available in Venice. Some, with accounts of the lives of the Chinese emperors were translated and published in the Veneto in the early years of the 18th century. In 1716 Albrizzi published the *Mappamondo istorico*, which "contained the Lives of the Emperors of China" while in Padova in 1710 the translation of Bouvet's text written in 1697 was printed with the title *Historia dell'Imperator della Cina*. Some years later in 1737, the *Storia del gran Gengis Cam primo imperatore degli antichi Mongoli e Tartari* by François Pétis de la Croix (1653-1713) was published in Venice.[2]

The theatre was also affected by the Venetians' increasing passion for Cathay and the fabulous world that those distant lands evoked in the early 18th century. In 1707 at the San Cassian theatre the *Taican re della Cina* was performed with music by Urbano Rizzi of Treviso, scenery by the Florentine

Angelo Rossi, and dances arranged by "Monsieur L'Eveque Dance Master of HH of Mantua" whose choreography most probably was based on the orignal Chinese theatre described in the accounts written by Everard Isbrand, "Of Black Indian Men and Women of the Court of Elmirena. Of Buddhist Priests, ministers of the temple of Foe. Of Noble Chinese Men and Women attending the coronation of Taicano" (the last title was revived in 1761 by Groppo in his *Catalogo di tutti i drammi per musica*). The intermezzos, entitled *Lisetta Cinese* and *Aristobalo indiano*, were written by Count Ludovico Widiman.[3] An illustration in the libretto provides some idea of how the stage must have appeared: parasols, winged dragons, gently swooping roofs, a pagoda in the distance which clearly owes much to the Nanking tower published by Nieuhoff in 1665, not to mention turbans and

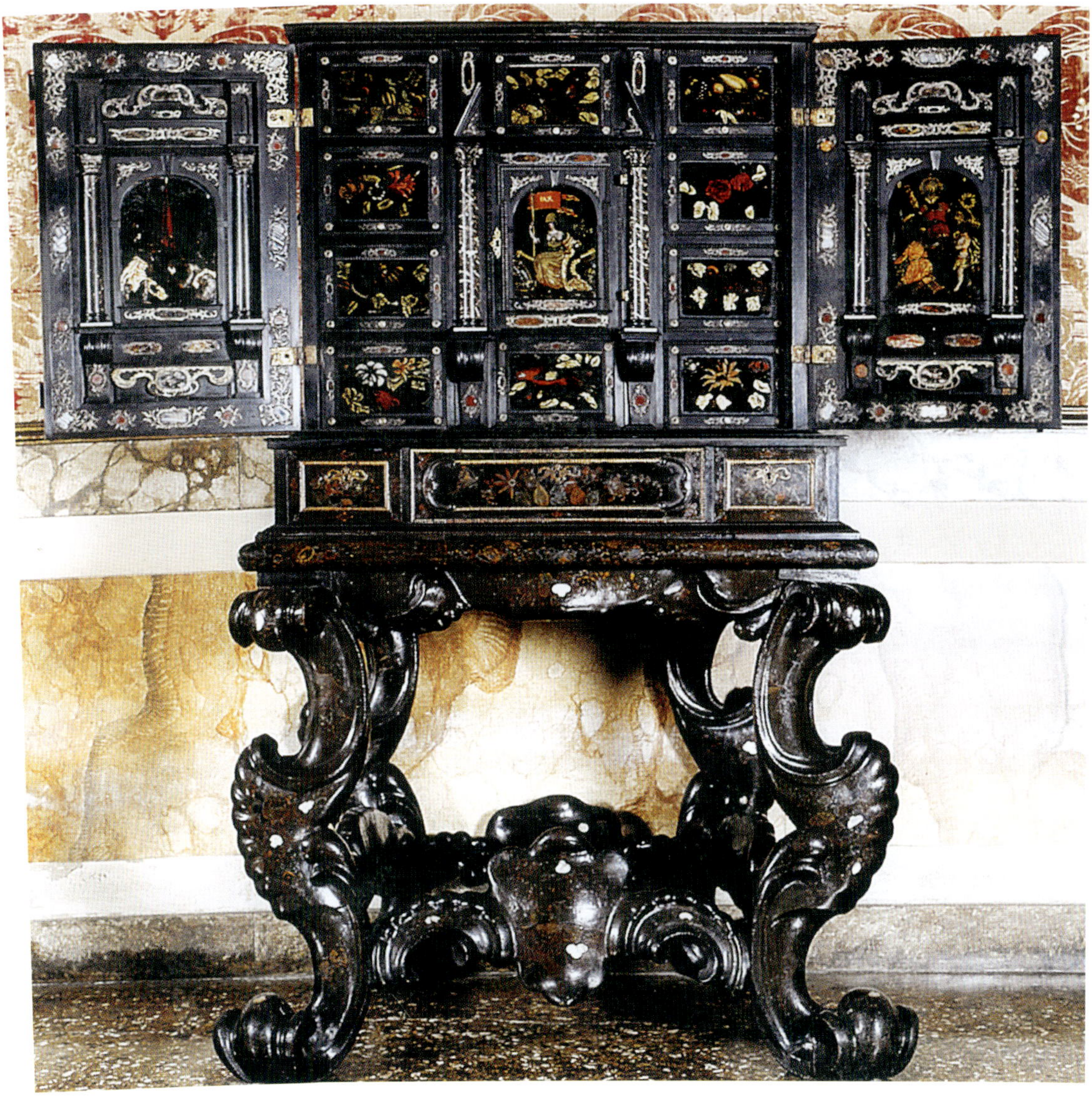

93. Table with cabinet. Venice, late 17th century. Venice, Ca' Rezzonico.

A typical example of a late 17th-century Venetian decorative technique in which lacquer and an inlay of mother-of-pearl are combined; often – as in this case – craftsmen used chinoiserie subjects and images. The cabinet standing atop the table is its contemporary, produced in Augsburg and also partly decorated with oriental vignettes.

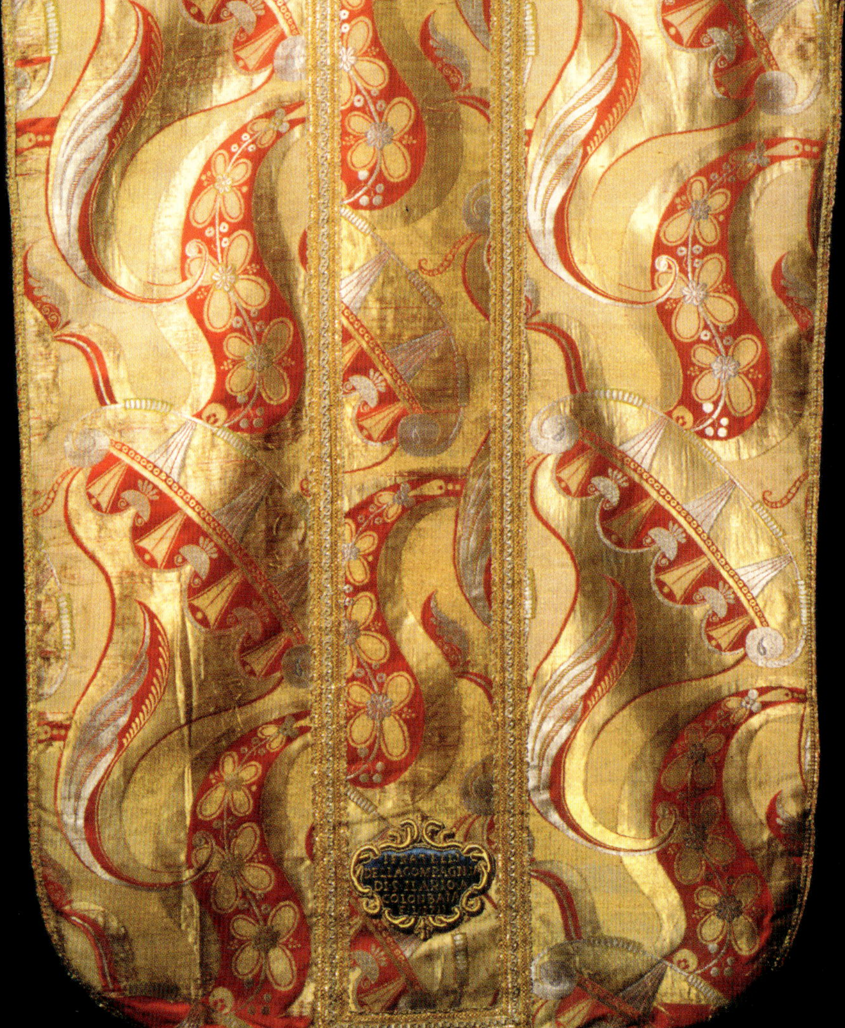

a form of dress which is nearer to the cross-bred image of an oriental figure than to Chinese costume. The libretto refers to the sources used for the costumes, scenery and even the tale itself, all principally derived from the best-known Jesuit texts on the subject, "So many tales have been told in such a short time about that country, and are all so similar that I will not dwell on further details of their habits. We know of their marriage practices, their funeral customs, ... descriptions of their factories and rarer things, superstitions surrounding their idols, preserved by the 'bonzi' who are priests, and other details that seem to both entertain and educate the spectator with foreign novelties. These are all taken from Kircher's 'Illustrated China', the accounts of P. Le Cont, the 'Istorie della Cina' by Bartoli and the writings of P. Samedio Portoghese which provided the fundamental history of this 'Tragedy'".[4] A scholar from Verona, Scipione Maffei (1675-1755), published *Della Scienza chiamata cavalleresca* in Rome in 1710 describing the lofty morality of the Chinese and the outstanding philosophy of Confucius, which heralded the enlightened ideas of Henri de Boulainvilliers (1658-1722) and Voltaire.[5]

From an artistic point of view, during this period Venice and the surrounding area absorbed widely different influences which were then filtered and modified according to local tastes; thus chinoiserie too became imbued with the Venetian spirit, at the time influenced by Roman-style baroque. The interiors of buildings in and around the Venetian lagoon were quite covered with gold and white stucco work, opulent fabrics enriched with threads of gold, collections of paintings and sculptures of the highest quality, and exotic works too abounded, in particular Chinese and Japanese porcelain. Venetians seemed to favour overcrowded and rather muddly interiors, heavily ornamented in high relief and generally rather theatrical in style – a taste that is reflected in the dramatic furnishings carved like veritable statues, a model developed by Bernini some decades earlier. From Belluno, Andrea Brustolon (1662-1732) was one of the best known interpreters of this trend in Venetian furniture and in 1700 he created a series of forty pieces commissioned by Pietro Venier (1647-1726) for his palace on Fondamenta San Vio and now in the Ca' Rezzonico Museum.[6] Brustolon's spectacular wooden sculptures supported a series of porcelain vases mainly dating from the second half of the 17th century, mostly Chinese and Japanese as well as some Dutch items in the oriental style. While on the one hand these brackets are indicative of the respect that Venetian collectors had for their oriental porcelain works, on the other they constitute a rare example of late 17th-century Venetian chinoiserie, similar in intent – if not grandeur – to the practice of embellishing exotic items with precious metallic mounts. Two supports for coats of arms in Palazzo Doria Pamphilj in Rome, dated 1675 and sculpted by Filippo Parodi (1630-1702) in the same naturalistic style as that of Brustolon,[7] served a similar purpose. The Chinese porcelain works currently displayed on the Roman brackets are

94. Chasuble. Venice (?), 1700-1710. Impruneta (Florence), Museo di Santa Maria.

Brocade lampas with 'bizarre' pattern. The chasuble is part of a set of vestments which includes a maniple and stole, donated to the sanctuary of Santa Maria all'Impruneta for the procession of the Brotherhood of Sant'Ilario a Colombaia. Also popular in France and Spain, this particular style of fabric design was so widespread that it cannot be attributed to Venice with any certainty.

later than the supports and date at least from the mid 1700s.[8]
Roughly contemporary to Brustolon, Giovanni Bonazza (1654-1736) was another important artist of the Venetian Baroque who created a style of sculpture that his own sons skillfully developed and perfected. Their sculptural works were highly inventive, although their particular idiom had its roots in traditions that were more popular than courtly.[9] Venetian by birth, Bonazza first gained fame on the mainland, especially in the area around Padova where the standard of local sculptural production was particularly poor at the time. Oriental caricatures provided one of Bonazza's most popular themes, such as the two figures of *Chinamen* blithely at ease with their almost deformed bodies and the exaggerated features of their grinning faces. These characters, and the series of garden sculptures portraying *Indians*, are part of a regional repertory which provided an alternative to the high classicism of early 18th-century sculpture in Venice. This more novel genre originated from images seen in the engravings of various travel books published during the second half of the 18th century and widely available throughout Europe (Nieuhoff, Montanus, Dapper, etc.).
In addition to their fame as carvers, Venetian furniture makers were renowned for their skilled use of protective varnishes, often enlivened by tortoise shell or mother-of-pearl inlay, an art that became fashionable in Venice in the later decades of the 17th century.[10] In 1668, Maxime Misson in his volume *Nouveau voyage de l'Italie*, refers to a healthy trade in lacquer work in Venice.[11] The two techniques of japanning and inlay were frequently used together and occasionally the scenes portrayed on the lacquered surface were Chinese, as in the case of the console table in the Ca' Rezzonico Museum.[12] The piece also supports a particularly interesting lacquered cabinet with chinoiserie scenes, attributed to an unknown craftsman from Augsburg in the 17th century. Just as there can be no doubt regarding the oriental origins of the lacquer, the mother-of-pearl inlay too derived from Asia, and was often used in Islamic items, or lacquered objects produced in India, China and Japan, especially those made for exportation to Europe. Several artists were skilled in the use of both the lacquer and inlay techniques, such as Domenico Rossetti (1650-1736), an architect, engraver and inlayer to the doge Francesco Morosini and, in the late 17th century, designer of "a room in the house of the grand chancellor, Angelo Nicolosi, which made use of various Chinese arts – lacquer work, carving and mother-of-pearl inlay: the finest of works both for its originality and the quality of the craftsmanship".[13] Rossetti also worked for the Elector Palatine in Düsseldorf as an engraver on copper and it was most probably in Germany that he first became interested in fine oriental-style lacquer items, expertly imitating both eastern originals and English, Dutch and German works. Rossetti used a transparent and impermeable varnish of sandarac for the lacquer, a formula that had long provided an excellent substitute in Venice for the resin of the *Rhus vernicifera* tree used in the Far East, but not

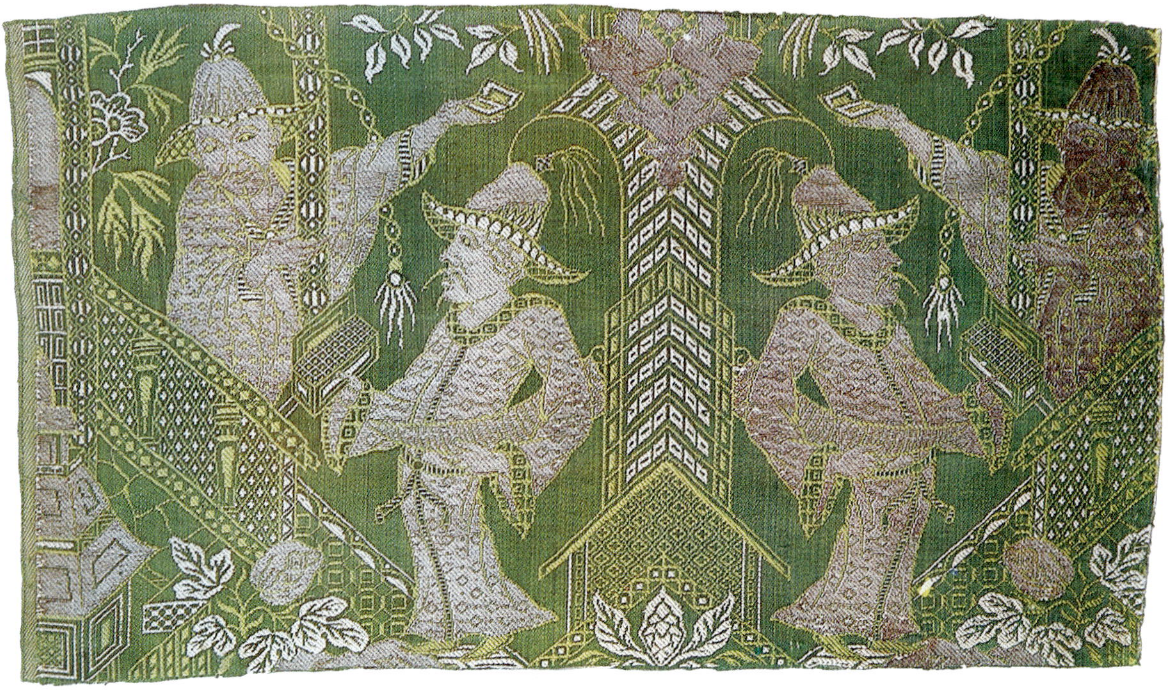

95. Fabric. Venice, c. 1700. Prato, Museo del Tessuto.

Specialists date this fragment of silk (cm 35x21) to the baroque period in Venice. It is difficult to identify a source for the scene represented, but it is most probable that it too was derived from the published compendiums of oriental subjects that circulated in Europe and Italy from the mid 17th century.

available in Europe. Father Vicenzo Coronelli (1650-1718), a lay brother who held the chair of cosmography at the university of Padova, provided the instructions - published first in his *Epitome Cosmografica* of 1693, while the recipe appeared in 1701 in the first volume of his encyclopedia *Biblioteca universale sacra e profana, antica e moderna.*[14] Coronelli made globes of the earth and heavens which he covered with a protective, smooth and glossy varnish obtained using his own recipe and method and it is more than likely that the same preparation was used by the lacquer masters of Venice to obtain the same quality and effect. Later, recipes were widely published in the numerous treatises on the preparation of lacquer available throughout Italy and Europe. From 1766, for example, Venetian lacquer workers could consult the recipe that appeared in the *Trattato di miniatura* published by the printer and bookseller, Garbo; in 1770, in his *Dizionario delle Arti e Mestieri*, Francesco Griselini (1717-1787) printed a recipe – most probably garnered from the Venetian craftsmen he frequented – for the preparation of a varnish which was a close imitation of the original Chinese one. Lastly, a Venetian edition of the *Nuovo Trattato per qualsivoglia sorte di vernici comunemente dette della China* by Angelo Maria Alberto Guidotti, published in Bologna in 1764[15] appeared in 1791, with the title *Metodo facile per formare qualunque sia sorte di vernici della Cina e del Giappone.*

Although its fame had to be shared with Lyons and Tours, in 1700 Venice still had an excellent reputation for textile production. Probably the development of chinoiserie designs in France at the time stimulated Venetian craftsmen to produce silks with 'Chinese-style' decorative motifs, though it is also possible that they were strongly influenced by printed compendiums of chinoiseries available throughout Europe, many published in Augsburg and Nurnberg. Of completely different origin were the textiles that the scholar Vilhelm Slomann aptly christened as '*bizarre silks*' in 1953. The designs are exotic in character, scattered with motifs that are often quite enigmatic – indeed bizarre – softly outlined and forming patterns that flow rhythmically in irregular compositions.[16] Many theories and suggestions have been proposed by Slomann and others as to the sources used by European craftsmen to compose these eccentric designs. The most plausible influence however, are the floral designs and especially the overall irregular arrangement of the motifs on Chinese and Japanese fabrics arriving on the European markets in quantity at the time.[17] Until relatively recently Venice was believed to be the birthplace of this kind of fabric design, beginning about 1680 and shortly followed by Spanish production – mainly in Valencia. Lyons and England began to produce the same style only in the early 18th century, when the fashion must already have been quite widespread in Europe as Daniel Marot chose to illustrate three examples in his series of engravings entitled *Patrons d'étoffes et de Velours*, published from 1702 to 1712.[18]

In the salon and rooms of the first floor of Villa Van Axel-Castelli at Altivole near Treviso the frescoed decorations of the overdoors are clearly derived from the fashions of early 18th century France.[19] In one a Chinese figure is seen driving a cart drawn by two camels, while portrayed in the others are oriental characters with parasols, fans and the inevitable cone-shaped hat; the images are all enclosed within late baroque scrolls similar to those seen in the engravings of the works of Bérain, Audran and Watteau. Although the quality is not outstanding, the scenes are, however, noteworthy for their early dating to the first decades of the 18th century. The use of both chinoiserie and characters of the Italian Commedia dell'Arte here is also of particular interest, introducing a fashion that was to continue throughout the 18th century. The town most active in the production of ceramics in the region during the late 17th and early 18th century was Bassano del Grappa where, shortly after 1650, the factory founded by Francesco Mainardi (1619-1701) had been granted the exclusive right to produce majolica wares by the Venetian senate.[20] The decorations were often based on those of other European factories and made use of a simple but effective range of colours with shades of blue, yellow and green with a faint darker outline and picked out with white enamel relief dots. The decorative motifs were mainly floral although figures were sometimes included. On a few rare occasions Chinese figures also appeared, though their attitudes and posture were more classical than informal. Works of this kind date from the early 18th century, and most certainly before 1730 when the factory succumbed to a prolonged crisis leading to its closure.[21]

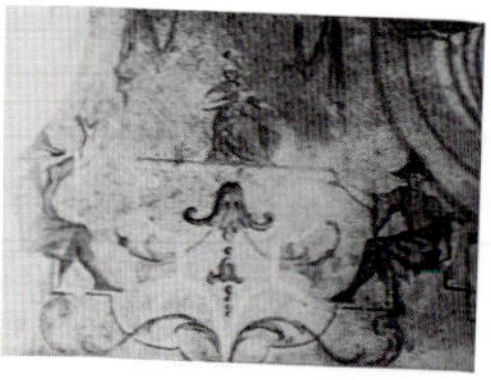

96. Anonymous Venetian decorative painter, Detail of a fresco with chinoiserie motifs, 1700-1725. Altivole (Treviso), Villa Van Axel-Castelli.

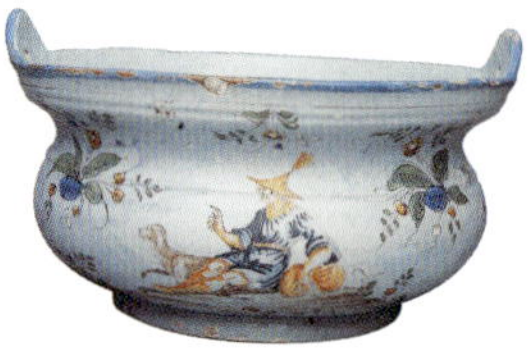

97. Cooler. Bassano del Grappa (Vicenza). Mainardi factory (?), early 18th century. Private collection.

Experts in Venetian ceramics propose Mainardi in Bassano del Grappa as the makers of this cooler. Consequently it would have been made before the 1730s when the factory closed down. The chinoiserie scenes decorating the piece echo the classical style, especially the courtly pose of the figure and the presence of a dog. The flowers and foliage surrounding the scenes are purely European.

The Rococo Style

In the course of the 18th century Venice ceased to hold any political ambition within Europe and both the city's present and future were conditioned solely by the glories of the past. Admired for its gaiety and the elegance of its citizens as well as its superb artistic heritage, Venice became a favourite destination on the Grand Tour and the numerous foreigners who arrived every year brought with them the latest European fashions. Venetians became 'Frenchified' and adopted the customs and habits of Parisian aristocrats during the reign of Louis XV, although a streak of cultural and artistic individuality was maintained. It was in this context that numerous architectural and decorative projects were begun, altering the appearance of the city. One of the leading forces in this renewal was the architect Giorgio Massari (1687-1766) who favoured the principles of French Rococo which were progressively replacing the outmoded baroque style. Once the bombastic gilding and rotundities of 17th-century décor had been removed, the interiors of Venetian palaces became lighter and more airy, enlivened by softer colours and more delicate ornamental structures, better suited to the newly fashionable developments in decorative painting represented by the work of Tiepolo in particular.

Life for the wealthy in 18th-century Venice was sophisticated, sociable and entertaining. Intimate little gatherings of a close circle of friends and acquaintances were highly popular, held in apartments known as 'casini' located on the mezzanine floors of Venetian palaces, referred to ironically by Montesquieu (1689-1755) during his journey through Italy in 1728.[22] It was in these low-ceilinged rooms, so perfectly portrayed by Pietro Longhi (1701-1785), that the most topical subjects of the day were discussed while sipping chocolate and listening to delightful music played on a spinet, and daring amorous affairs took place. The rooms were furnished with paintings, sculptures and ornaments in a pretty and fanciful decorative style, often reflecting a taste for the exotic, now much in vogue among the Venetian aristocracy and certainly far removed from the pomposity of the earlier baroque decorative style. It was during the 1750s that the taste for chinoiserie reached its peak in Venice and several works splendidly represent the extreme sophistication and variety of the 'Chinese style'. Chinoiserie spread over every kind of surface and invaded every possible kind of technique, from frescoes to lacquer work, from fabrics to stucco, perfectly complementing the numerous original oriental goods imported to the lagoon. From the mid 1700s, as the French influence gradually diminished and the neoclassical style began to take over, Venetians were attracted by the more eccentric English and German Rococo where elements of chinoiserie began to appear.

The visit of Augustus the Strong in 1716 was a crucial moment in the development of exotic tastes in Venice and a watershed between baroque and rococo chinoiserie. In honour of the sovereign, the city organized a floating procession headed by a regatta barge with the title *China arrives in triumph from Asia with the Homage of its Pages.* A contemporary engraving by Andrea Zucchi (1679-1740), from a sketch by Alessandro Mauro[23] portrays this extraordinary event. Mauro had worked for the Elector in Dresden for a period and was well aware that his tastes strongly favoured the Orient. In Germany he had seen the most recent developments in the fashion for chinoiserie – both French and German – and these were crammed into the decorations of the barge. In typical carnival spirit, the Venetians filled the barque with characters dressed 'alla cinese', wearing the inevitable cone-shaped hats and arranged in various postures in the little space available to them, while parasols dominated the entire scene. The two largest are placed fore and aft, supported by flying cherubs and crowned by two female allegorical figures. The atmosphere is lively and festive as befits such a masquerade; as in an improvisation by Watteau some years before, Harlequin, Pulcinella and the other characters of the Commedia dell'Arte have been replaced to make way for the first official appearance of a Chinaman interpreted à la Venise.

In addition to such masquerades, the Chinese theme was quite popular in the theatre in the mid 1700s. Already in 1735 Metastasio (1698-1782) had written *Le Cinesi* in Vienna, performed the same year during carnival with the future empress Maria Theresa (1717-1780), then aged only 18, her sister and a lady of the court improvising as actresses. The music was written by Antonio Caldara (1670-1736, a pupil of Legrenzi, 1626-1690) who in 1722 had already set *Camaide imperatore della China* to music with two intermezzos, *La Marchesina di Nanchin* and *Il conte di Pelusio.*[24] However, the opera was not represented in Venice at the time and only arrived in Italy between 1748 and 1750. At the specific request of Farinelli (1705-1782) adaptations were made by Metastasio in 1749 to include a fourth male character and this version was performed by the Paganini Company in Florence, Milan and Turin. With the new title of *La Festa Cinese* and music by Nicola Conforto (1718-1793), Metastasio's opera was performed in Spain at a celebration for Ferdinando VI (1713-1759), while in 1754, again in Spain, Conforto staged *L'Eroe Cinese.*[25] In 1737 Bettinelli published the "Arcisopratragichissima Tragedia" by Zaccaria Vallaresso, an Arcadian known as Cattuffio Panchiano, with the title *Rutzvanscad il Giovine*, which seems, however, never to have been publicly performed in the city. The play attempted to combine the most characteristic elements of Greek tragedy and the alleged atrocities carried out by the Tartars, adopting the method of emotional rationalism and in many ways anticipating the ideas of Voltaire. In 1751 the translation of a French opera by Thomas-Simon Gueulette (1683-1766) was published in Venice with the title *Meravigliose avventure del Mandarino Fum-Hoam.*[26] In 1752 Carlo Goldoni (1707-1793) produced *La sposa persiana* and in the autumn of the same year his rival, Pietro Chiari

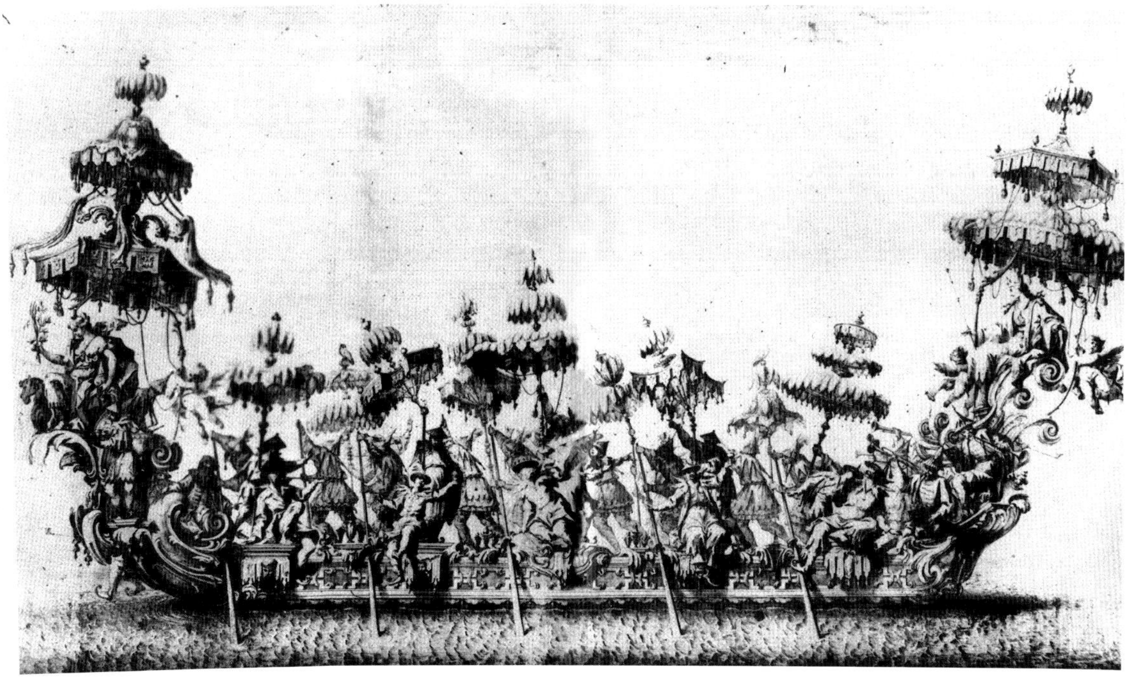

98. Alessandro Mauro and Andrea Zucchi, *Regatta barge "China arrives in triumph from Asia"*, Venice 1716. Venice, Museo Civico Correr.

This composition is a veritable icon of 18th century Venetian chinoiserie. The wistful oriental characters in languid poses, the cone-shaped coolie hats, the sunshades, are all features that would constantly reappear as the style continued to develop in Venice.

(1712-1785) presented *La schiava cinese* in the Sant'Angelo Theatre for the first time.[27] So successful was the performance that a year later Chiari produced a sequel, *Le sorelle cinesi*.[28]

In December 1749 at the San Cassian theatre Chiari had already presented an opera with an Eastern theme entitled *Alamena, principessa delle Isole fortunate*, based on Molière's *La princesse d'Élide*.[29] His 'Chinese' works drew their inspiration from the writings of Bartoli and from the *Storia moderna o sia stato presente di tutti i paesi e popoli del mondo* by Thomas Salmon (1679-1767), published in Venice in 1731.[30]

It is difficult to imagine the effect these performances had on the audience with their quite intriguing costumes and scenery. What kept the public glued to their seats was certainly not the historical aspect of the drama, still to a great extent based on Marco Polo's *Travels*, but the fantastic scenery, the mystery of the unknown and the general sense of frivolity that pervades the whole. Metastasio complained to his friend, Farinelli, "Greek and Roman plays are excluded because the nymphs are not allowed to show their chaste legs, so where possible oriental tales must be used because the pantaloons and cassocks worn by those nations envelope the bawdy parts of my actresses", and following the success of Chiari's plays in 1752 he produced his Italianized version of a Chinese theatrical text, transcribed by Father Du Halde, with the title *L'eroe cinese*.[31] The first performance was held in Schönbrunn in spring of that year. Just three years later on 20 August 1755, Voltaire presented his more famous version *L'Orphelin de la Chine* – one of the most successful theatrical performances of the 18th century and to a great extent the basis of that vision of a glorified Far East so widely accepted during the Age of the Enlightenment. In 1761 Carlo Gozzi presented his most famous opera, *Turandot*, which in both its original edition and revised by dramatists as famous as Schiller (1759-1805), Busoni (1866-1924) and Puccini (1858-1924), is still continually performed today.[32] Oddly, the China described in Gozzi's work is cruel and ruthless, entirely different to the benevolent and graceful vision of Metastasio. However, both interpretations were warmly received by the public and critics indicating that, at the time, exotic settings sent Venetians into raptures no matter what aspect was presented. Gozzi replied the following year with an exotic "tragicomic theatrical tale", *La donna serpente*, the story of which was clearly based on the idea of the *Thousand and One Nights*. The heroes of this new tale were the king of China, Ruzvanschad who had already appeared in Bettinelli's drama, and princess Cheheristani, and the tale took place first in Asia and then in Eldorado. This work too enjoyed great success, especially with the public; first presented by the Sacchi company at the Sant'Angelo Theatre in 1762 it was frequently performed and modified. Some time later Gozzi also wrote the drama *Marco Polo*,[33] while in 1768 Chiari published a tale entitled *Uomo di un altro mondo* in which the main character was Japanese.[34] The elements of novelty and surprise were thus the two factors that most contributed to the success of a 'Chinese' theme in the theatre. In 1762 (*Saggio sopra l'opera in musica*) Francesco Algarotti (1712-1764), a Venetian of many talents and enthusiastic supporter of the spread of the Enlightenment and its teachings in Italy, wrote of Chinese theatrical themes, "China again, that ancient birthplace of the arts and a colony – at least some believe – of Egypt, can supply endless lovely scenes".[35] Thus, despite his neoclassical education based on functionality and rationalism, quite the opposite of Rococo's decorative style, even Algarotti was seduced by the fanciful Cathay. This predilection was encouraged both by his experiences abroad, especially at the court of Frederick II of Prussia who was an enthusiast of chinoiserie, and his admiration for Voltaire with whom he held a constant and friendly correspondence. But Algarotti's passion for Chinese matters was cautious, rather flickering than truly ablaze, and his comments were formulated in a period when the theatre world, at least, was approaching "rejection from overuse" as Chinese settings were even used in situations that did not require them, "I do wish that here too we would not use pagodas and porcelain towers, unless the subject of the work is actually Chinese".[36] In 1762 Gaspare Gozzi, who had himself made use of the Chinese theme on many occasions, was even more adamant, stating, "The scenes are filled with Turkish or Chinese cloths that at first looked so attractive, but the actors have gradually used so many that there were no longer any Italian clothes in the wardrobe; and they went around in them so constantly that it became intolerable to see them".[37]

Interior Decoration

One of the best known examples of chinoiserie in the Veneto is the Foresteria designed by Giandomenico Tiepolo (1727-1804) in Villa Valmarana in Vicenza. This was the first occasion on which Giambattista (1696-1770) worked together with his eldest son, and while the father decorated the rooms of the main building with amorous scenes illustrating European poems, Giandomenico preferred to decorate the nearby Foresteria with a series of less formal frescoes, closer in spirit to the concepts of genre painting.[38] Goethe (1749-1832) clearly noted the differencc between the work of Giambattista and Giandomenico, although he was unaware that the younger Tiepolo was working on the site, as in a letter dated 24 September 1786 to Mme von Stein (1742-1827) he wrote, "Today I visited Villa Valmarana which Tiepolo has decorated giving free rein to all his virtues and vices. His lofty style is not as successful as his more natural subjects which are quite delightful; in general as a decorator he is full of gaiety and bravura".[39] Thus in the eyes of Goethe, Giandomenico's 'natural' painting seemed better than the 'lofty' style of the master, an opinion that was probably based on the more modern appearance of the young artist's painting and his ability to happily exploit the building's less formal function by making use of popular and fashionable themes to create "entertaining caprices". Tiepolo junior decorated the rooms of the Foresteria with rural,

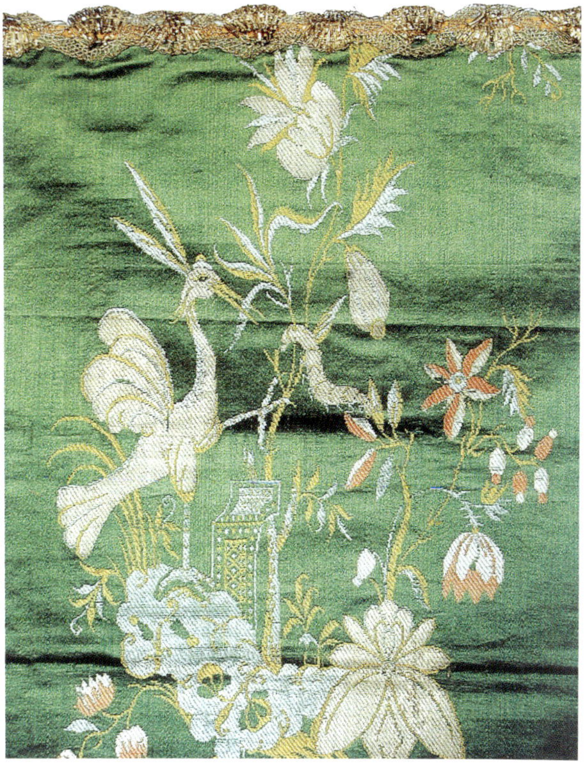

99. Fabric. Venice, mid 18th century. Venice, Istituzioni di Ricovero e di Educazione.

In the 1700s Venetian textile production made great use of oriental motifs derived from both original Far Eastern works and from European – especially French – chinoiserie repertories. Given the popularity of Asian motifs throughout the 18th century, the factories of Lyons and Tours, for example, often adapted them as fabric patterns.

popular and carnival scenes as well as set pieces with a rather 'gothic' appearance anticipating the eclectic style which evolved from the English trend of using medieval stylistic features during the mid-18th century. Giandomenico painted several rooms with varied themes in the Valmarana annex and the Chinese Room presents five different scenes with entirely Chinese subjects: *The Chinese fabric merchant, Two Chinamen with a vase, Chinese prince with a fortuneteller, The Mandarin's walk*, and lastly *Homage to a god*. The young Tiepolo, who also designed three chinoiserie compositions,[40] kept abreast of the developments in European chinoiserie especially on his travels to Germany and France, yet his Chinese works seem not to have drawn on any specific model. These Chinese vignettes are not only remarkable for the precision of the ornamental detail, whether on the coloured fabrics, fans or porcelain, but what is particularly striking is the essentially Venetian atmosphere, the quality of the light and the very expressions on the faces of the characters – features that instantly recall the artistry and culture of Venice.[41] This regional and temporal identity is typical of Giandomenico's art and is a contrast to the universal themes of Giambattista's work.[42] This, above all, is what makes Tiepolo's creations at Valmarana a synthesis of the entire and multifarious world of Venetian chinoiserie in the 18th century. However, in creating his chinoiserie, Tiepolo the younger must have drawn some inspiration from the frescoes that his father had painted about 1750 decorating the ground floor of Villa Corner at Merlengo. In a pamphlet written in 1751 in celebration of the wedding between Andrea Corner and Maria Foscarini, Saverio Bettinelli (1718-1808) mentions that for the occasion Giambattista had frescoed three rooms in the residence, one of which was decorated with a Chinese theme. Sadly, many of the frescoed paintings created by Tiepolo the elder in this villa have been lost.[43]

The most important chinoiserie produced by Andrea Urbani (1711-1798) is a room in Villa Vendramin Calergi Valmarana in Noventa Padovana, decorated with two scenes – *The judgement of the mandarin* and *The elephant procession*. Although stylistic similarities with paintings by Urbani dated 1772 would suggest the frescoes are of the same period, the 'official' biography written by his grandson Domenico in 1868 entitled *Andrea Urbani pittore-architetto veneziano,* states that the entire pictorial cycle of the villa was completed by Urbani in 1757 shortly before leaving for Russia to work on the interior decorations of the Winter Palace in St Petersburg.[44] This would therefore make Andrea Urbani's chinoiserie contemporary to Giandomenico's frescoes at Vicenza. In fact there are few similarities between the two, but they do, however, indicate how widespread chinoiserie was in the Veneto in the 1750s. The earlier dating of Urbani's frescoes to 1757 is confirmed by comparison with his decoration of the Chinese Room in Villa Giustiniani, dated 1771. Portrayed in this 'Saletta' are realistic images of mainly original oriental items such as ceramics and Chinese costumes, chosen by the artist

100.Giandomenico Tiepolo, *The Chinese fabric merchant*, 1757. Vicenza, Villa Valmarana.

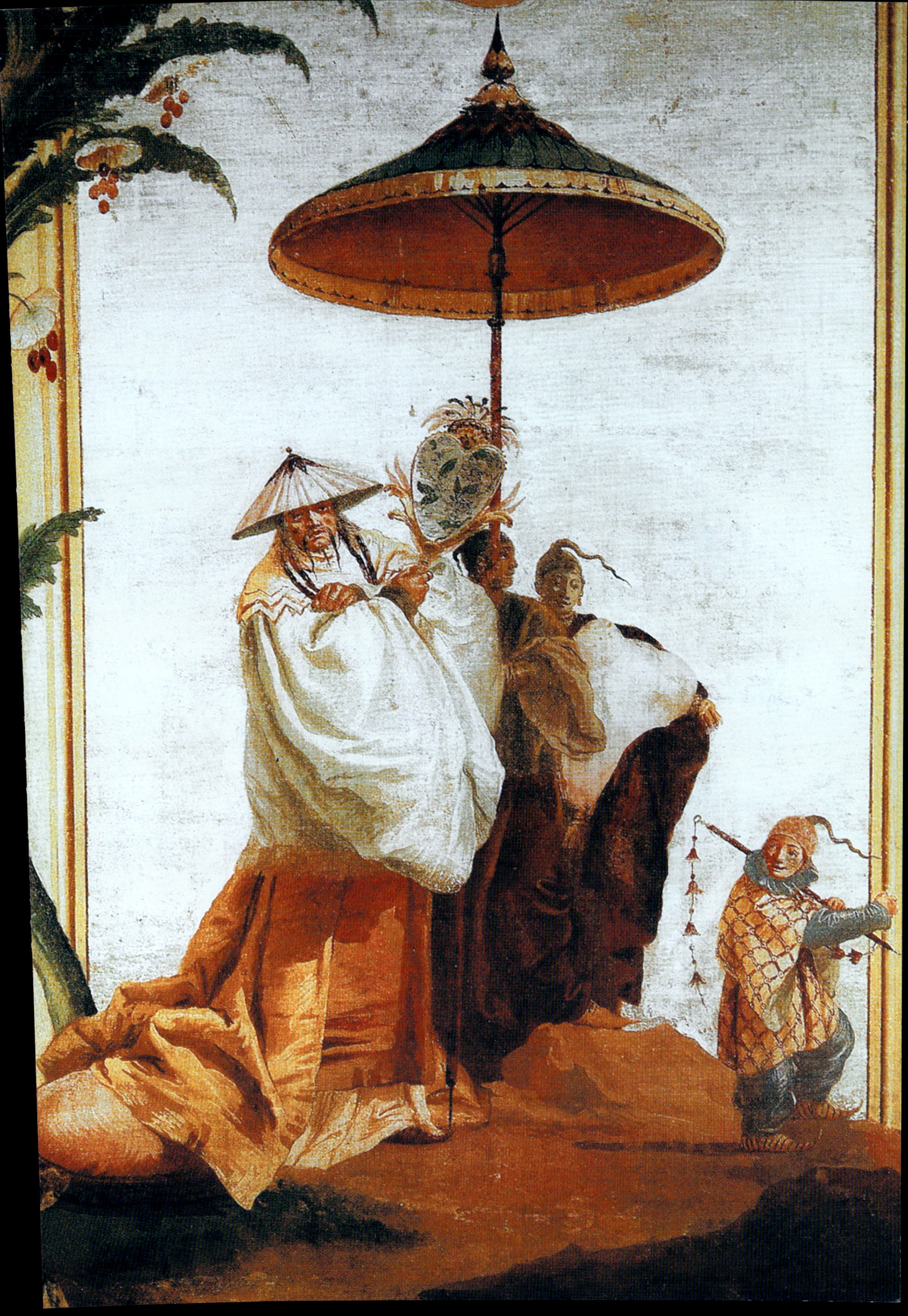

from exotic items in his own collection; even the architectural structures portrayed seem to be quite genuinely oriental.[45] His grandson also recalled that on his return from Russia in 1763, Urbani brought with him "those wonderful Chinese fabrics with trees, flowers and buildings made on blue, green and purple silk, and paper gilded on a background of dark orange satin, three sheets of which he guarded most jealously".[46] Still continuing his chinoiserie theme, and also in 1771, Urbani completed another work in Villa Giustinian-de Chantal. There are echoes of Tiepolo's works in these scenes, especially in the more 'popular' poses of the figures, while Pillement's pleasure in frivolity is also evident in some of the natural details surrounding the figures, the dreamy strangeness of the rocky structures and the languid droop of the leafy branches.[47] Chinoiserie is also present in one of the artist's last works – the decoration of rooms in the Castello Grimani-Marcello di Montegalda, completed before 1780.[48] Here he combined the rococo style with elements of neoclassicism, which was enjoying great popularity at the time. It has also been suggested that Urbani assisted with the scenery for *Lo sposalizio dell'Imperatore della Cina*, a ball performed in Padova in 1785 at the Teatro Nuovo, and although unconfirmed, he may well have been involved as he participated with Antonio Mauri and Guidolin in the competition for the decoration of the stage curtain at precisely this time.

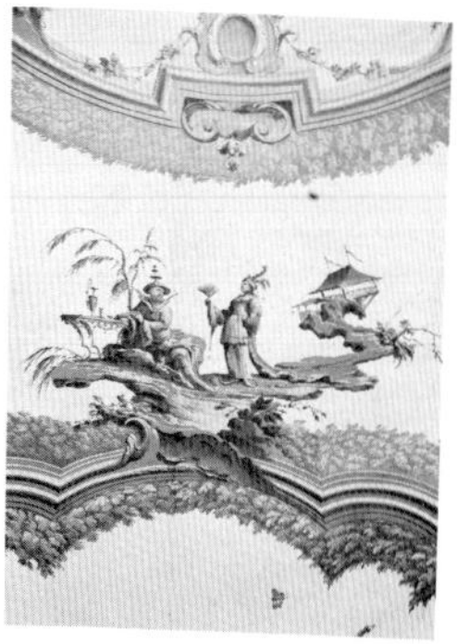

101. Andrea Urbani, Scene with Chinese figures, 1771. Noventa Padovana, Villa Giustinian De Chantal Destro.

Andrea Urbani designed this vignette late in his career, after having painted the frescoes with a Chinese theme in Villa Valmarana at Noventa Padovana. Compositions such as these clearly reveal the influence of Pillement's chinoiserie, especially in the ethereal setting with rocks and trees.

In his publication of 1961 Hugh Honour briefly mentions[49] that the painted stucco decorations in several of the rooms on the first floor of Villa Pisani, La Barbariga in Stra near Venice, are worthy of greater attention.[50] The design of these little scenes is of French derivation and reflects a delicacy and freshness perfected around the mid-1700s and diffused mainly through the engravings of works by Watteau, Boucher and Pillement.[51] The use of stucco for chinoiserie relief decoration is rare in Italy although the medium itself was frequently used to enhance Venetian interiors from about 1725. Two artisans in particular popularized the art - Abbondio Stazio (1663-1745) and Carpoforo Giacomo Maria Mazzetti Tencalla (1710-1775), who were skilled in reproducing Bérain's *rocaille*, with its more slender and sinuous grotesque décor, a forerunner of Rococo's later developments.[52] Exotic motifs were also used for the wall paintings in the salon on the first floor of Villa Negrelli in Pesina, decorated with chinoiseries by anonymous Veronese artists in the mid-18th century.[53]

Gaspare Diziani (1689-1767) was probably responsible for the delicate 'chinese scenes' which decorate the wood panels of cupboards and beams on the ceiling of a room in Palazzo Pisani Moretta in Venice.[54] In 1750 he was paid for having decorated some of the palace furnishings, probably in fact the delicate chinoiserie in gold with a few touches of colour on a lacquered brown background decorating the *boiseries* in the small salon in the apartment of Vettore, son of Chiara and Gerolamo Pisani, who owned the palace. Diziani was not new to decorative painting and had already been paid for frescoes in five rooms of the palace where internal renovations had begun

102. Andrea Urbani, *The elephant procession*, 1757 (?). Noventa Padovana, Villa Valmarana.

Urbani portrays a jolly procession with an elephant and group of Chinese musicians. To emphasize the oriental atmosphere, in the centre of the scene he has placed a diminutive figure with a Chinese porcelain vase on his head.

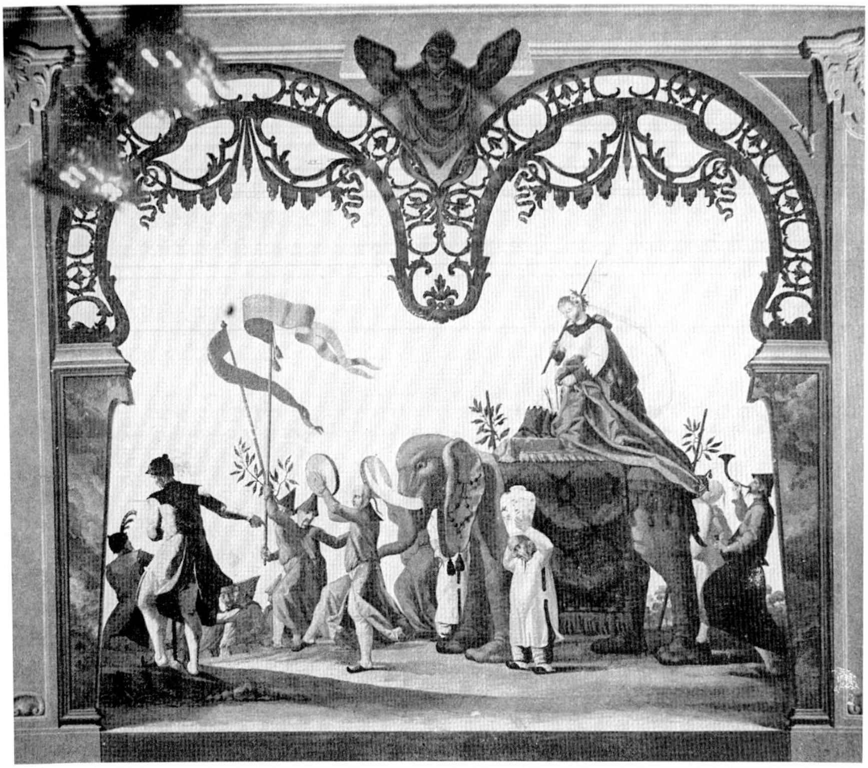

around 1742. Under the direction of the *trompe l'oeil* artist, Francesco Zanchi (1734-1772), stucco workers, carvers and painters such as Piazzetta (1683-1754) and Giambattista Tiepolo had worked on the palace interiors. Although there is some doubt concerning the attribution of the chinoiserie in Palazzo Pisani Moretta to Diziani, the excellent quality of the decorations indicates an artist of his standard while the style corresponds to the decorative tastes of the 1750s, the decade which produced the most fascinating of Venetian chinoiserie. The slender wafting figures portrayed in various poses, are certainly the work of a great artist such as Diziani, an expert in the effects of light and chiaroscuro with delicately traced forms, and the only artist capable of enhancing even the tiniest of details. Painted in the dim light of a candle, the motifs must have appeared quite stunning as their smoothly applied gold highlighted the reddish glow in which figures of Chinamen and Turks floated, fragile pavilions appeared from nowhere, foliage coiled around the decorative frames, interspersed with masks, cornucopia, exotic animals, trophies of arms and cameos of fair ladies. In 1754 the stucco worker Giovanni Andrea Rossi decorated a mezzanine room in Vettore's apartment in Palazzo Pisani Moretta, one of the most fascinating creations of the Venetian 18th century. The chinoiserie here takes the form of coloured motifs on a gold background arranged between the white stuccowork; the scrolls are in the most typical international rococo style and

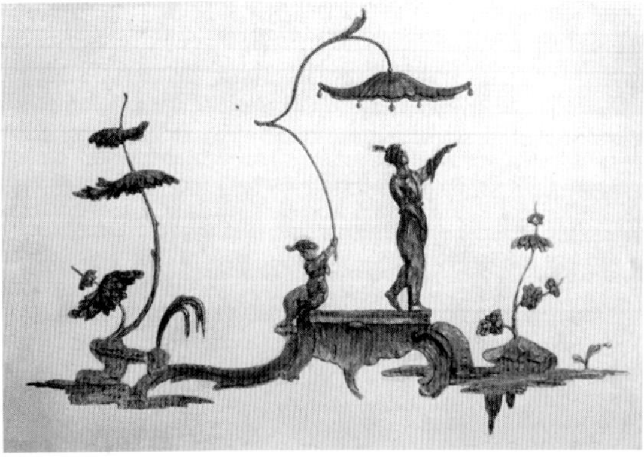

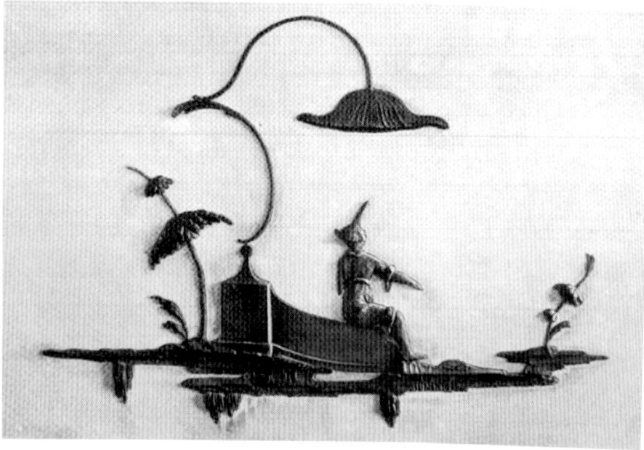

the decorative 'bizzarie' – winged dragons and lively groups of exotic flowers – are clearly derived from French *rocaille* chinoiserie designs.

103a,b. Anonymous Venetian stucco workers, Scenes with Chinese figures, After 1775. Stra (Venice), Villa Pisani.
The ethereal Chinese figures enhancing the white walls of a bedroom in Villa Pisani 'La Barbariga' at Stra are clearly derived from a mid 18th century European repertory of chinoiserie – most probably French. Created in painted stucco these delightful vignettes are redolent with a gentle melancholy.

The Venetian passion for chinoiserie is found too in the area of Padova where Urbani had also been active. The decoration of Palazzo San Bonifacio, dated between 1765 and 1770, is particularly interesting as is a room on the ground floor of a palace owned by counts Bonifacio and Antonio Borromei, described in *Descrizione delle pitture, sculture ed architetture di Padova*, published by Giovambattista Rossetti (1696-1785) in 1780: "almost all of the four walls are painted 'alla cinese' by Mr Giuseppe Nicoletti, and all the figures, quadrupeds and birds are most excellently painted by Mr A. Buttafuoco. It is a great pleasure to admire this room because – except for the windows – the chairs and all the other furnishings are so particularly inventive that no one could ever have dreamed of".[55]
Near Padova, the frescoes decorating two rooms on the second floor of Villa Savonarola-De Benedetti at Vaccarino are decorated with rather original chinoiserie frescoes revealing unusual stylistic elements compared to the general Venetian idiom. Gaetano Savonarola, the owner of the property, commissioned the interior decorations as part of a general renovation of the building which began in 1758; this richly painted decoration must be dated prior to his death in 1783.[56] The work of an anonymous artist, these exotic scenes are quite unlike the picturesque style of other Veneto painters who used the same themes, such as Tiepolo and Urbani. Compared to the other great chinoiserie cycles described here, the decorations at Vaccarino more obviously reflect the influence of both original Far Eastern items and European engravings of Chinese themes. The distant horizons of the marine-scapes portrayed in these frescoes are indeed almost entirely copied from the engravings in Du Halde's volume published in Paris in 1735. Moreover, the concise organization of the composition recalls the decoupage decorations of 'lacca povera', while the detailed gilding frequently highlighting the motifs is reminiscent of a miniaturist's skill and the creativity of the ceramic painters of Bassano del Grappa. There are indeed many similarities here to the decorative motifs of oriental porcelain and lacquer work, such as the

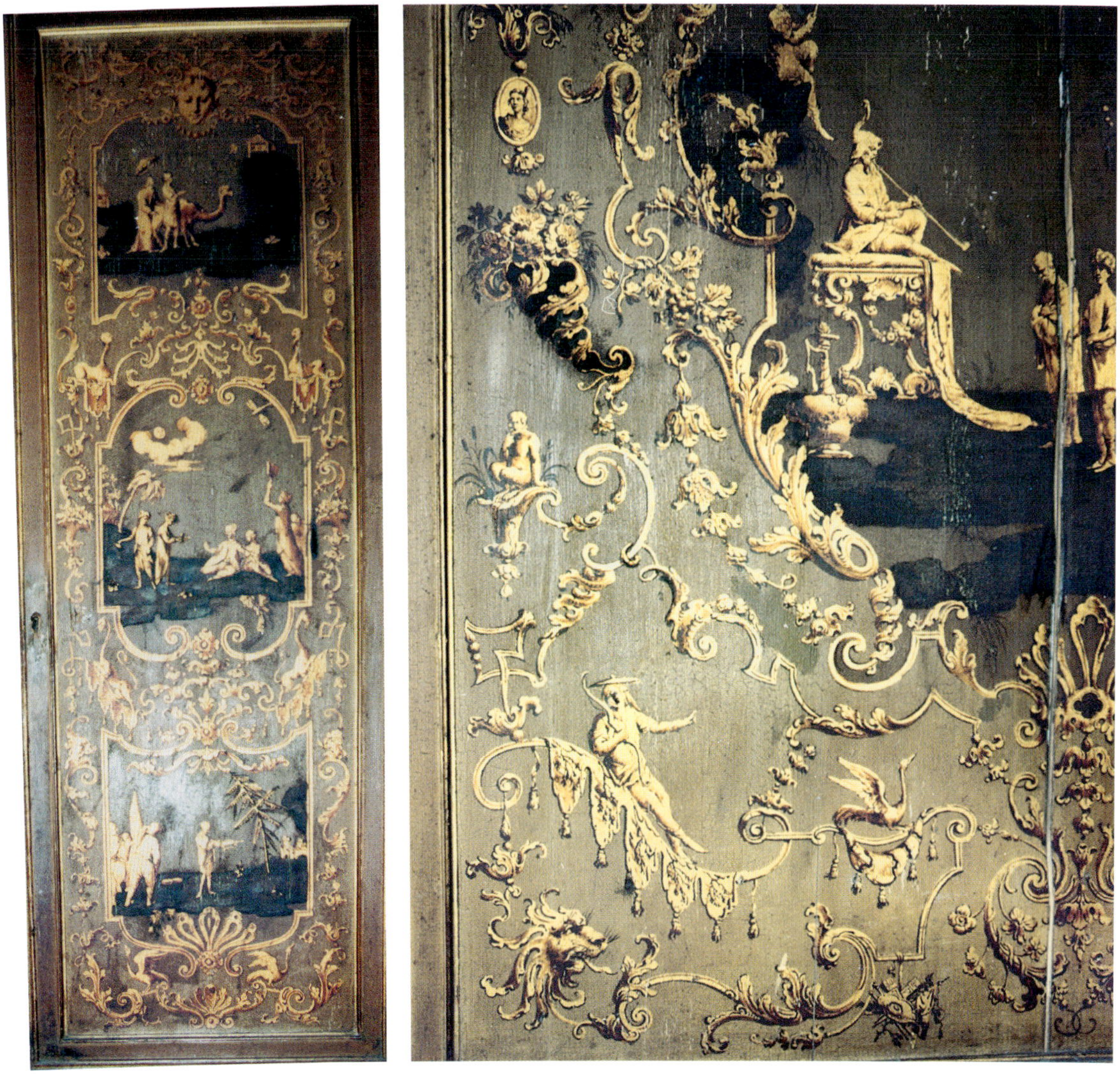

104a,b. Gaspari Diziani (?), Boiseries in the Chinese Room, c. 1750. Venice, Palazzo Pisani Moretta.

Perhaps the work of Gaspare Diziani, the gold chinoiseries that decorate the lacquered panels in this room are extremely elegant and meticulously detailed. The scenes, framed by elaborate grotesque decorations in the rococo style, are examples of a 'mixed' chinoiserie with references to both the Far East and the Islamic world. Possibly derived from the works of Paul Decker, the designs were explicitly for use on lacquer work (see Fig. 82).

elongated bodies, details of the clothing worn by the female figures, the extreme precision with which some of the objects are represented, suggesting they were copied from real models, the architecture of some of the buildings, and the freshness of the lakeside scenery arranged in sloping terraces – a typical stylistic feature of oriental art, particularly Chinese. The similarities between the Vaccarino scenes and Far Eastern motifs perfectly exemplify the comments on Chinese visual arts written by Francesco Milizia (1725-1798) in the same period, "They often place buildings, vases and other objects in a perspective that diminishes the further they are from the viewing point, and to make this trick more obvious, they apply a greener shading to the further sections of the composition, placing trees in the furthest parts of the scene, paler in colour and smaller in size than those that appear at the front. In this way, a scene that is really quite limited and confined takes on a broad and

spacious appearance" (*Principi di architettura civile*, 1785).[57] Francesco Milizia is responsible for the spread in the Veneto, and in Italy in general, of the eclectic style which first developed in England in the mid 18th century and which seems also to have inspired the anonymous artist of the Vaccarino frescoes – in particular the combination of chinoiserie with decorative elements of gothic art. The false terracing that defines the 'Chinese style' scenery, in particular recalls gothic motifs. "This art form has also been proposed by Brown, Chambers and Whateley. It seems that the English learned the art from China. In fact that excellent architect, Chambers, who once lived in the region, subsequently published a work on Chinese architecture as well as an important treatise translated into French, 'L'art de distribuer les jardins selon l'usage de Chinoise'" (F. Milizia, *Dizionario delle belle arti del disegno*, 1787, entry for "giardino").[58]
Milizia's reflections were based on the theories of Hirschfeld and referred explicitly to the spread in Italy of the informal landscape style of English garden. Carlo Lodoli (1690-1761), a forerunner of 'neoclassical enlightenment' who disliked the exaggeration of baroque and rococo decoration, had probably anticipated him. Lodoli had been the teacher of Algarotti and his theories were collected by a pupil named Andrea Memmo (1729-1793) in a volume entitled *Elementi d'architettura lodoliana, ossia l'arte di fabbricare con solidità scientifica e con eleganza non capricciosa*, published in Rome in 1786. The book also referred to Lodoli's presumed interest in the practical elements of gothic, Persian and Chinese architecture, though perhaps arbitrarily censured by Memmo.[59] Introduced to Freemasonry by Giacomo Casanova (1725-1798), Memmo was without doubt impressed by the English version of Chinese architecture currently in vogue. Appointed

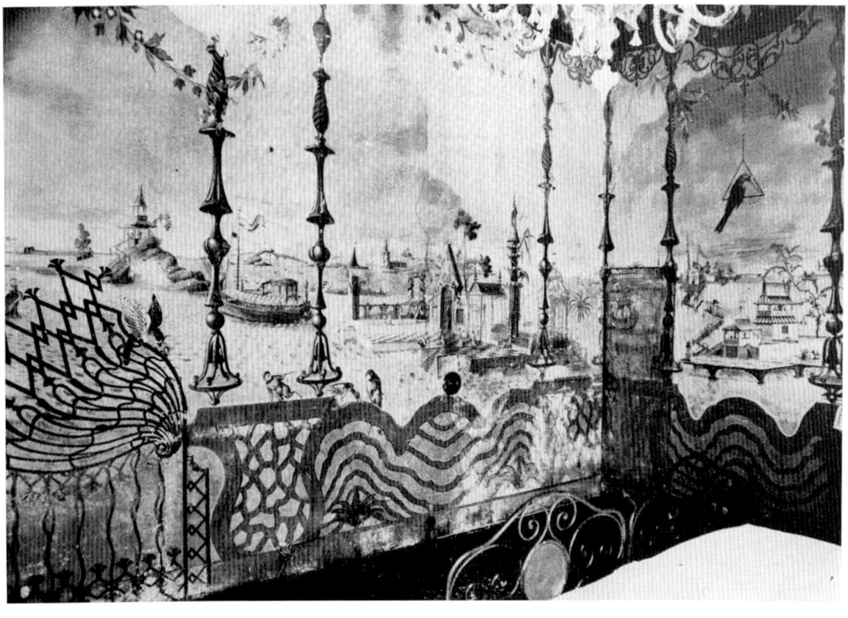

105. Anonymous Venetian artist, Frescoes in the Chinese Room, c. 1770. Vaccarino (Padova), Villa Savonarola-De Benedetti.

This detail demonstrates quite clearly the combination of a Chinese subject with some almost gothic ornamental features, such as the unusual latticework in the lower section of the wall. Greatly anticipating the revival of historic eclecticism in the 19th century, the author of this decoration may have been inspired by mid 18th-century English chinoiserie.

superintendent of Padova in 1771, his most important achievement was the reclamation of the surrounding marshlands which incidentally produced the surprising and innovative Prato della Valle. One of the architectural structures planned for this new area in 1789 was a rather controversial 'Chinese kiosque' to serve as a coffeehouse though, probably due to lack of finance, the project was never put into practice. Moreover, during this period a close working relationship existed between Superintendent Memmo and Gaetano Savonarola, President of Prato della Valle, coinciding with the latter's commission for the chinoiserie decorations of his villa at Vaccarino. Yet another 'anglo-chinois' garden in the Veneto was created by senator Angelo Querini (1721-1796) at Altichiero, just to the north of Padova towards Bassano.[60] A Venetian aristocrat, Querini adorned the gardens of this property (bought in 1765) with a series of buildings and features in various styles and succeeded in creating a harmonious mix of elegant geographical and historical features which was quite sweeping in its cultural references. Elements of the natural philosophy of Bacon (1561-1626) mingled with echoes of Masonic esotericism, and paradoxically with the most innovative ideas of the European Enlightenment. Scattered along the meandering paths of the Altichiero garden were classical sculptures or copies of classical models often arranged in allegorical groups, references to ancient Egypt and the Etruscan civilization, and various oblique hints at an awareness of Far Eastern cultures such as a Temple of Venus in the form of a *Pavillon Chinois* were not lacking. The structure – and the park – were destroyed after the Second World War, but were described in 1780 and again in 1787 by the French aristocrat Giustiniana Wynne (1737-1791), mistress of Memmo in her youth and subsequently wife to the Austrian ambassador in Venice, Philipp Rosenberg-Orsini (1692-1765). According to her, the building had a hexagonal plan, a cone-shaped roof with jutting and upward curving corners, on the tip of which was a decorative windmill with bells. The external walls were decorated with 'Chinese' subjects, although Giustiniana in fact compared them to the paintings at Herculaneum, which she thought had similarities with the principles of Far Eastern art, particularly in the succinct outlines of the figures and the colours used. (...) Lastly, the main building of the villa contained not only a series of 'Indian' idols housed in the 'curios' room, but also frescoes with "des habillement et usages des Orientaux, et autres sujets pareils..., qui arrêteur ceux qui aiment à réflechir sur les folis de tant prétendus sages".[61]

Lacquer

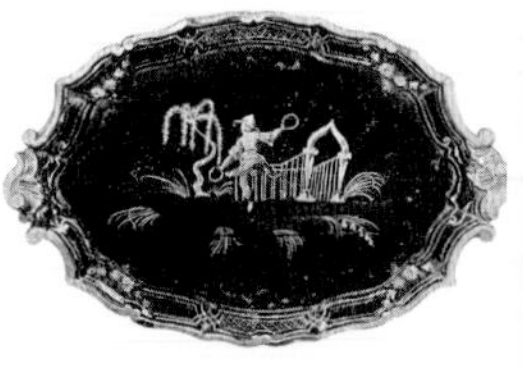

106. Lacquered tray. Venice, mid 18th century. Venice, Museo Correr.

The chinoiserie theme was used by Venetian lacquer masters in the 18th century to decorate a wide range of items of all shapes and purposes. In addition to large furnishings, many smaller items have survived such as this elegant tray with an undulating edge in the centre of which a carefree Chinaman appears in an Eastern landscape.

United in the same guild of 'depentori' since the 13th century, the official separation between artists and painters took place in 1691, thus enabling Venetian lacquer masters to continue their specialization independently.[62] However, artists of note did occasionally decorate lacquer furnishings thus provoking the anger of the lacquer workers. In 1771 a complaint was lodged with the 'Inquisitori delle Arti' reporting unfair competition on the part of the Artists' Guild for having transgressed regulations by undertaking work that was the responsibility of the 'depentori'. In addition to Diziani, lacquer decorations are known to have been carried out by at least Visantin, Fontebasso (1707-1769), Giovan Battista Crosato (1688-1758) – who made "a firescreen, four window enclosures, two doors and other works" for Palazzo Reale in Turin – and Guardi (1712-1793) who agreed to decorate panels for a church choir stall. Doubtless stimulated by the increasing amount of goods that arrived in Venice from the Far East, as well as European items in the oriental style, Venetian lacquer workers were well aware of the fashions most popular at European courts, but maintained a balance between their own decorative traditions and these external influences. Thus, within the guild of *depentori* the title of "painters in the Chinese style" came into being to describe the application of oriental decorations to lacquered works. In 1773 forty-nine craftsmen with this specialization were registered in the city, occupied in some thirty-five workshops.[63]

Not much is known about these 'painters' and even when a name has been traced it has not always been possible to identify his works. A document dated 1729 relating to work on the church of San Samuele, refers to a certain Iseppo Tosello a lacquer master specialized in chinoiserie décor,[64] and a record of the baptism of his son, Giobatta Vincenzo, dated 1740 mentions a certain Domenico Giuseppe Toselli who seems to have followed the same profession. It is, however, possible that he was employed as a decorator of ceramics, as the director of the Vezzi porcelain factory, Giovanni Vezzi, was also present at the baptism in the role of godfather. Around the same time Giacomo Locatelli, owner of a shop named "all'Insegna del Redentore in Merceria Venezia",[65] seems to have been specialized in 'lacca povera' decoration, while in 1771 Iseppo Rocco's workshop is recorded in the area of San Polo. Also in the second half of the 18th century, an account written by an aristocrat named Gabriello Marcello refers to a certain Agostino del Bene who not only produced furniture for sale abroad, but was also specialized in the importation of Chinese lacquer.[66] Lastly, a certain 'Vizzo' placed his signature on a cabinet, lacquered in black and decorated in gold, red and green with lively chinoiserie motifs.[67] This last item is representative of a style which was quite common in Venice throughout the 18th century and emulates a particular type of early 18th-century English and Dutch

107. Bureau. Venice, circa mid 18th century. Milan, Castello Sforzesco, Civiche Raccolte di Arte Applicata.

The Castello Sforzesco Museum houses two bureaux in this style. The chinoiserie decorating the pieces is derived from the oriental repertories most commonly used in northern Europe. The form too is that of early 18th-century Dutch and English models.

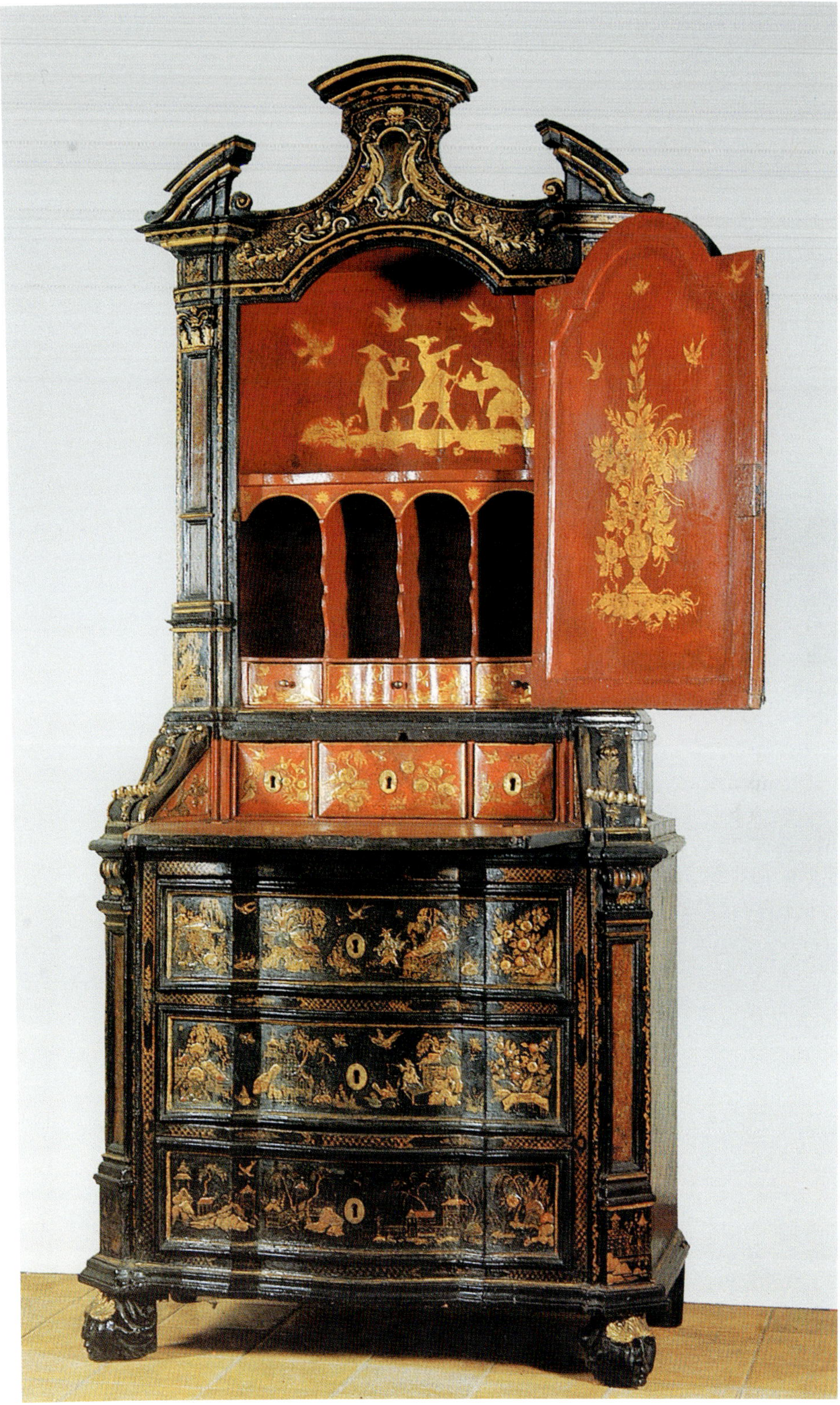

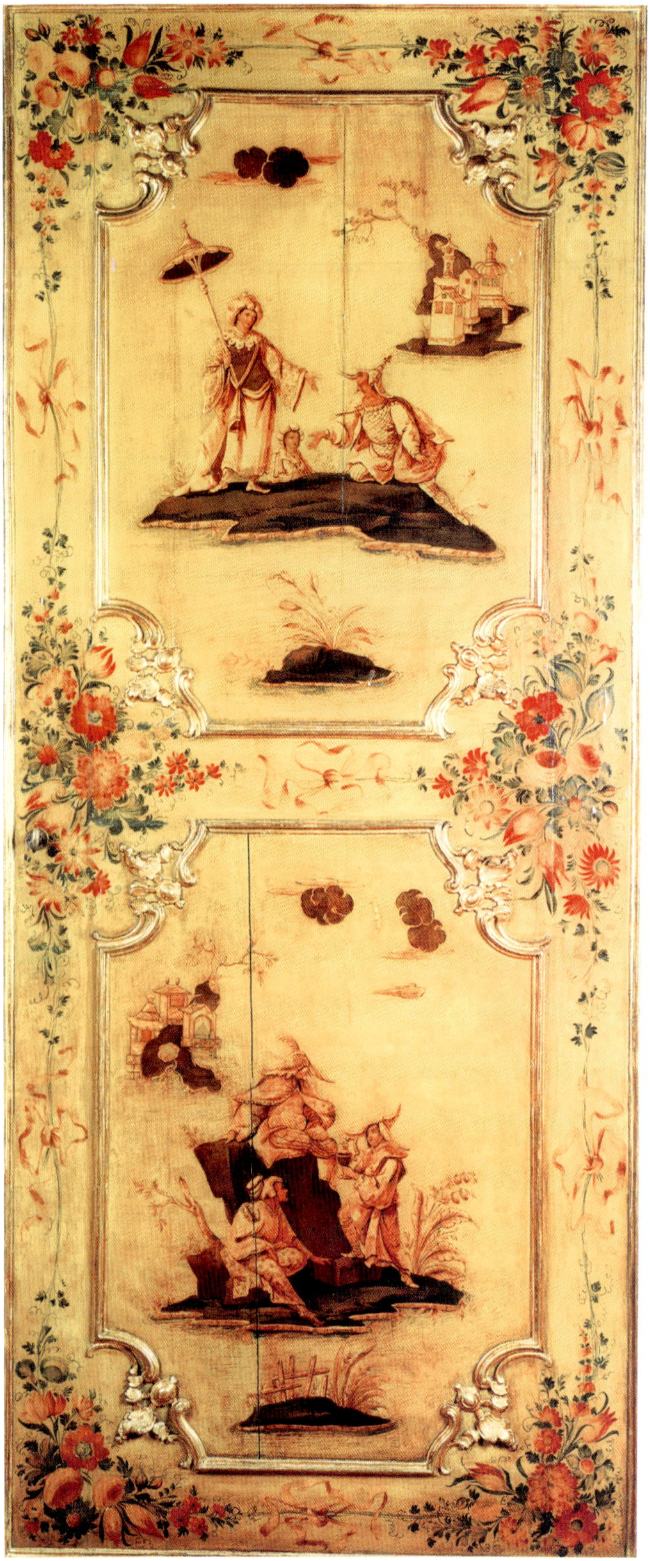

108a,b. Anonymous Venetian artist, Lacquered wood door with chinoiseries (*recto* and *verso*), c. 1758. Venice, Ca' Rezzonico.

Frequently published as a masterpiece of mid 18th century Venetian chinoiserie, the door and other lacquered panels of similar design and quality were made explicitly for a room in Ca' Rezzonico during the period when Giambattista Tiepolo and his son Giandomenico supervised the internal renovations. It is not impossible therefore that they were involved in designing the superb chinoiserie of these works.

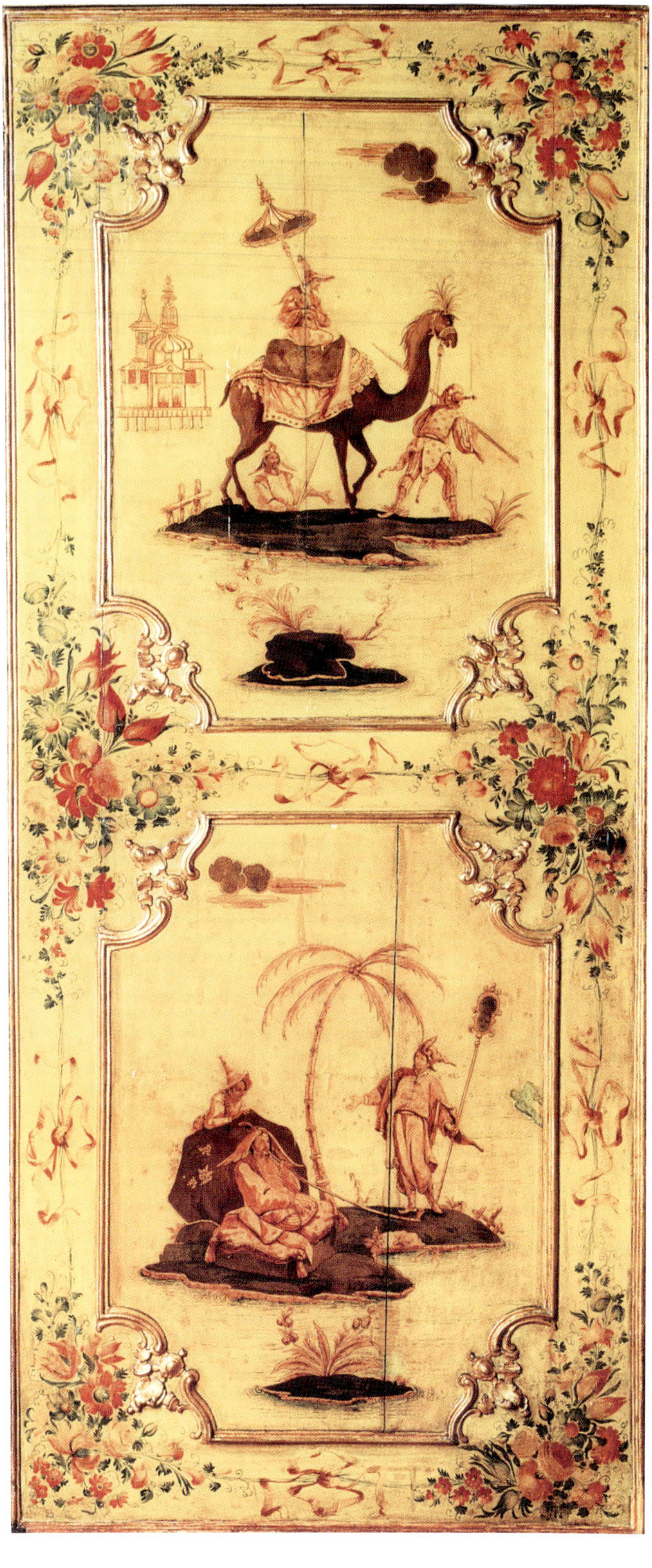

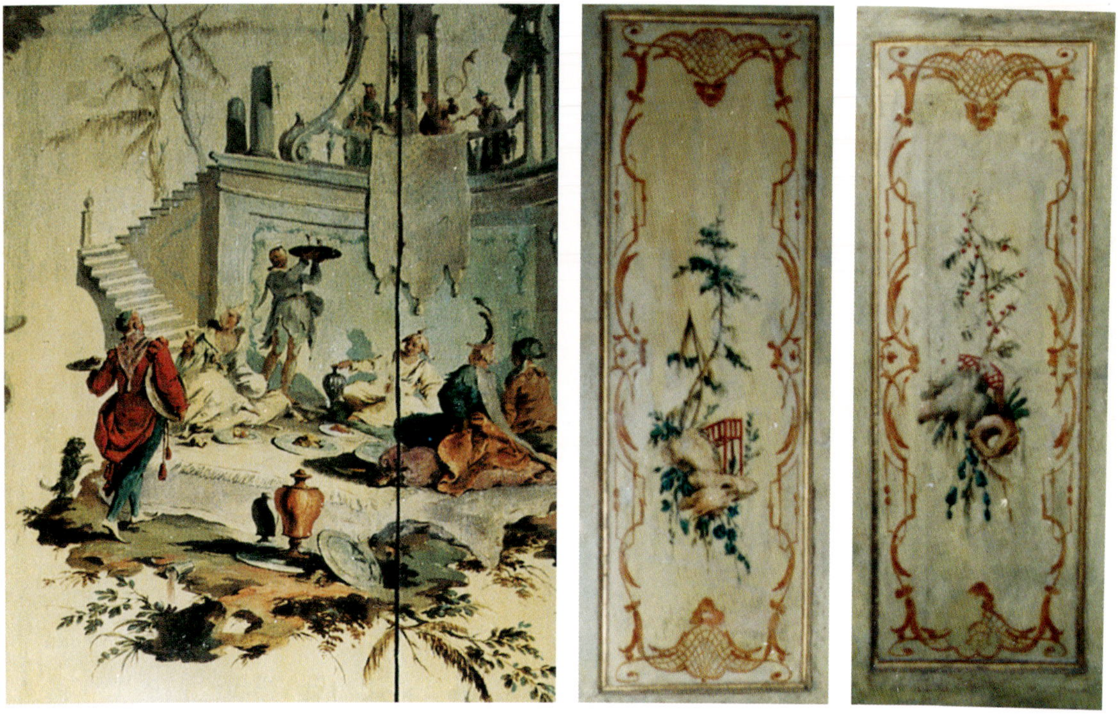

109. a,b,c,d. Anonymous Venetian artist, Details of boiserie decoration with chinoiserie scenes, third quarter of the 18th century. Stra (Venice), Villa Pisani.

furniture, both in form, combining a chest of drawers, desk and cabinet, and the lacquered backgrounds of red and very dark greenish black inset with delicate oriental landscapes inhabited by minute Chinese figures stuccoed in relief and painted in various colours. An excellent example of 18th-century Venetian furnishings is the door, now in the Ca' Rezzonico museum, made of deal, lacquered on both sides in yellow and decorated with scenes in the 'Chinese style' within floral *rocaille* frames.[68] The poupourri of cultural references evident in the figures portrayed completely represents the spirit of Venetian chinoiserie; dressed in long, flowing oriental-style robes, heads protected by the most classical cone-shaped hats, the characters ride unlikely camels or rest in the shade of occasional palm trees, receiving gifts or courting a lady beneath a parasol, all the while suspended in quite disparate times and places, above and detached from any terrestrial reference. The door is one of a series of similar items, all of excellent quality, now housed in both public and private collections. They were dispersed after 1935 when the last owner of the palace, count Lionello Hirschel De Minerbi, sold the group of doors to Loewi, an antiquarian, donating only one of them to the Accademia Gallery in Venice. It was later decided to exhibit the door in the new Museo del Settecento, located precisely in the palace of Ca' Rezzonico for which they had been made and housed for so long. The doors, and wainscotting of lacquered panels decorated with a similar chinoiserie composition (also in a private collection), were in fact made for two adjacent chinoiserie rooms on the first floor of the building, in the mid 18th century. Giambattista Tiepolo

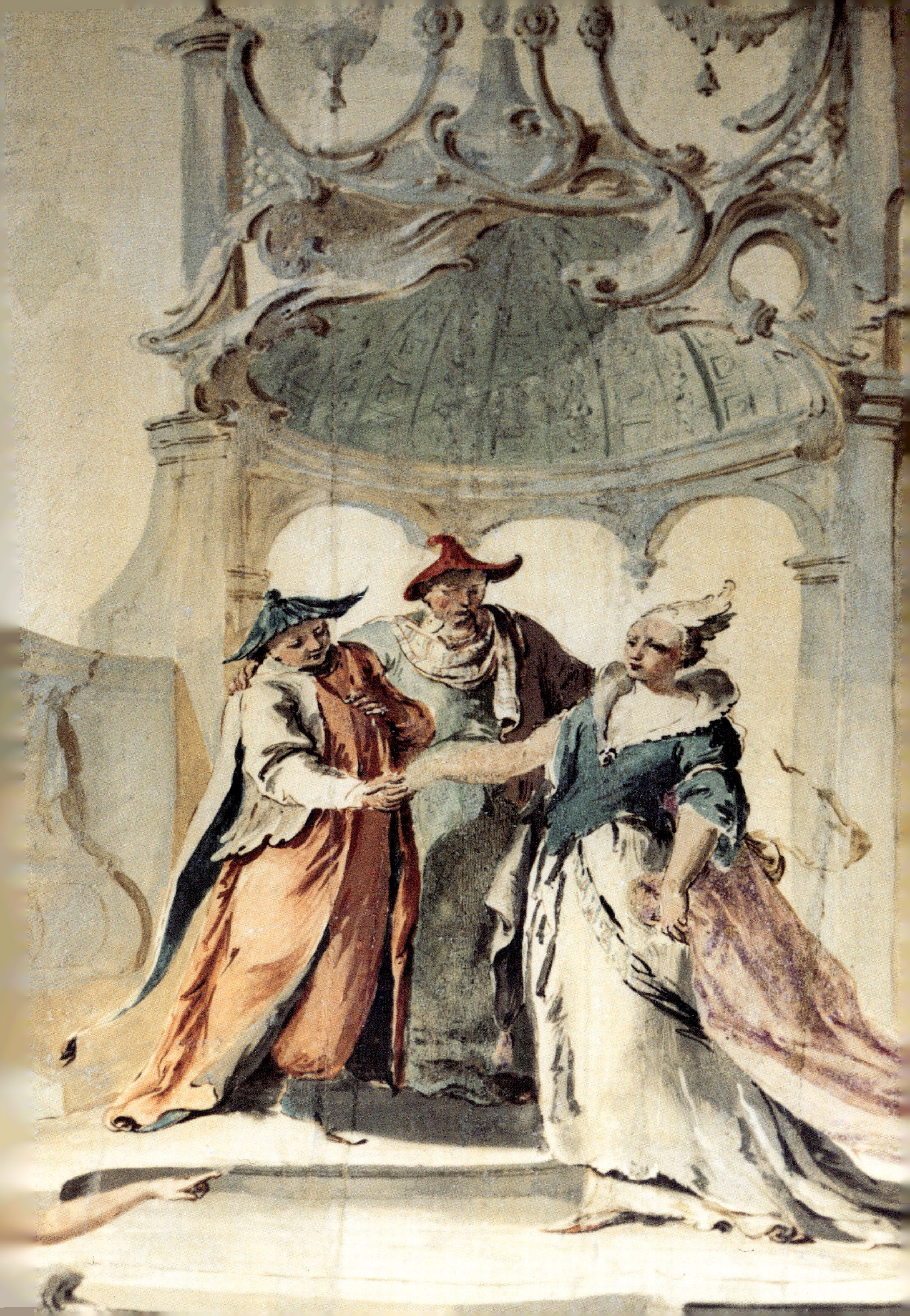

was director of the decorative works at the time assisted by his son, Giandomenico, and the *trompe l'oeil* artist, Girolamo Mengozzi Colonna (1688-1772). It is thought that Tiepolo the elder provided the essential suggestions for the decoration of the two Chinese rooms, probably supplying sketches which were then produced by an unknown "painter in the Chinese style". It is difficult to determine the role that Giandomenico might have had in this project as in 1757, the year in which he and his father were working on the frescoes of Ca' Rezzonico and the probable date of the lacquered chinoiserie doors, he was also busy completing the decoration of the Foresteria at Villa Valmarana in Vicenza. The two enterprises – the doors and the mural decorations in Vicenza – might well differ in form and technique, but the spirit behind their overall conception is clearly identical. Similarities can also be seen between these works by Tiepolo and the decorations on a series of lacquered panels now in Villa Pisani in Stra, not far from Venice. Dismantled from their original location – probably the complete wall coverings of a 'Chinese Room' or the doors of a large wall cupboard – the series of colourful chinoiserie scenes depicted on a pale green background have a pictorial appearance and arrangement. The scrolls and

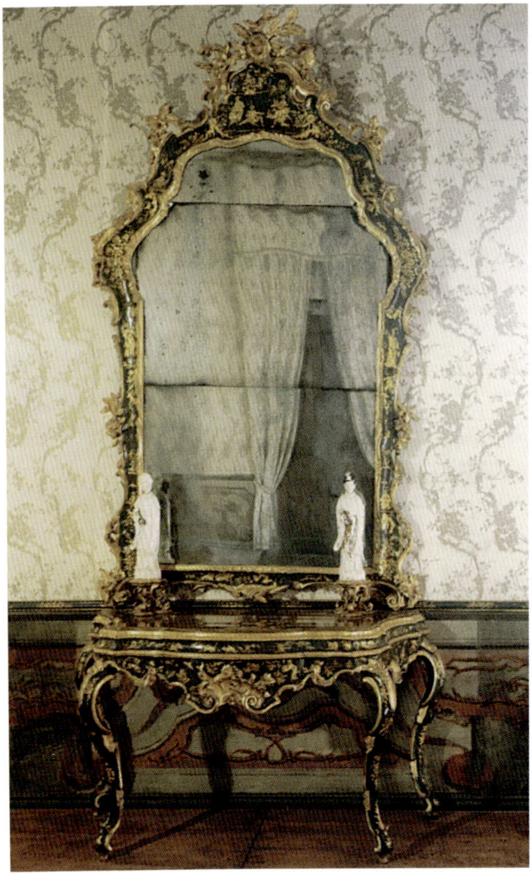

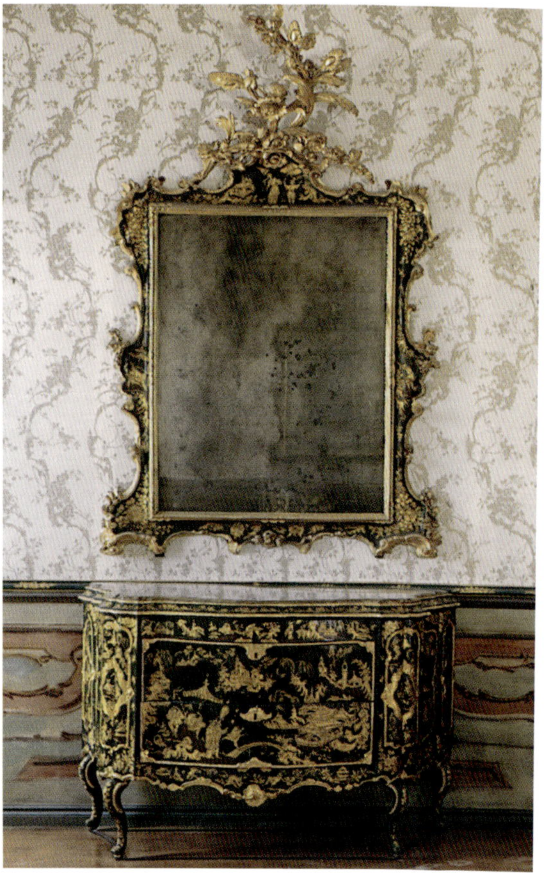

110a,b. Furniture in the Calbo Crotta Room. Venice, circa mid 18th century. Venice, Ca' Rezzonico.

This suite of furnishings is considered by many to be the greatest masterpiece of lacquer work with chinoiserie decorations produced in 18th-century Venice. All the pieces are decorated with Venetian-style oriental motifs in gold on a green lacquer background.

ornamental details are clearly derived from French *rocaille* designs popular around 1730-1770. There are also some similarities with Pillement's compositions, especially in the floral arrangements, which tend to suggest they date from the third quarter of the 18th century. The scenes containing oriental characters that tend to resemble refined Parisian ladies, form a series of cameos which fully complements the more picturesque scenes, creating a rather successful balance between a more linear decorative style and traditional Venetian painting. It is not impossible therefore that several artists may have collaborated on the work, under the direction of a more expert maestro. Although they were made for one of the numerous rooms in Villa Pisani, and were documented in the early 1800s as furnishings for "one of the ground floor rooms which were decorated in various manners: some were in the Turkish style, others were Chinese, and another with Persian

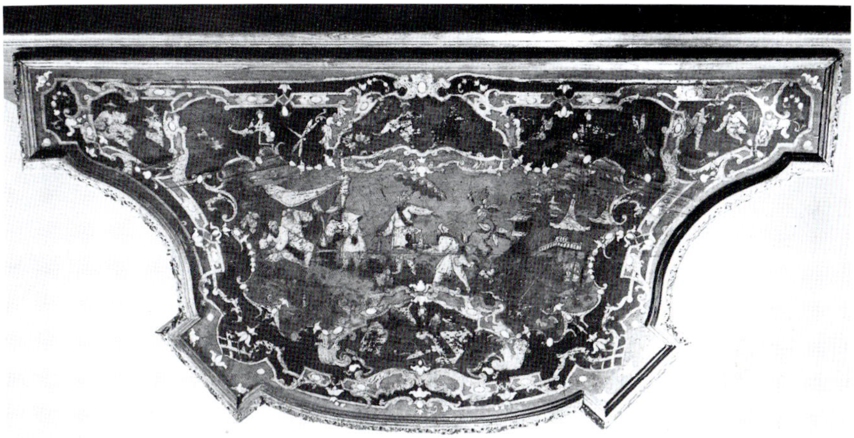

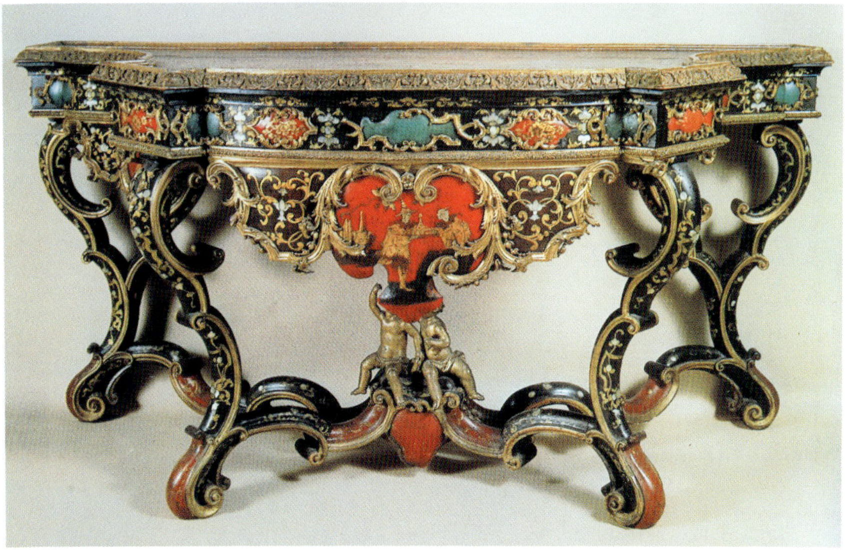

111.a,b. Table. Venice, after 1775. Vienna, Kunsthistorisches Museum.

Alvar González-Palacios presented this table, together with its matching pair in the same museum, to illustrate the Venetian practice of combining lacquer with mother-of-pearl inlay, describing it as "exemplifying all aspects of this kind of decoration, combining the severe magnificence of the 17th century with the gaiety and grace of the following century". Painted on a background of red lacquer, the chinoiserie scenes appear on various parts of the piece within cartouches framed by swirling rococo volutes of gilded wood. The Kunsthistorisches Museum also has two smaller tables originally *en suite* with these and all four were commissioned by the dukes of Modena.

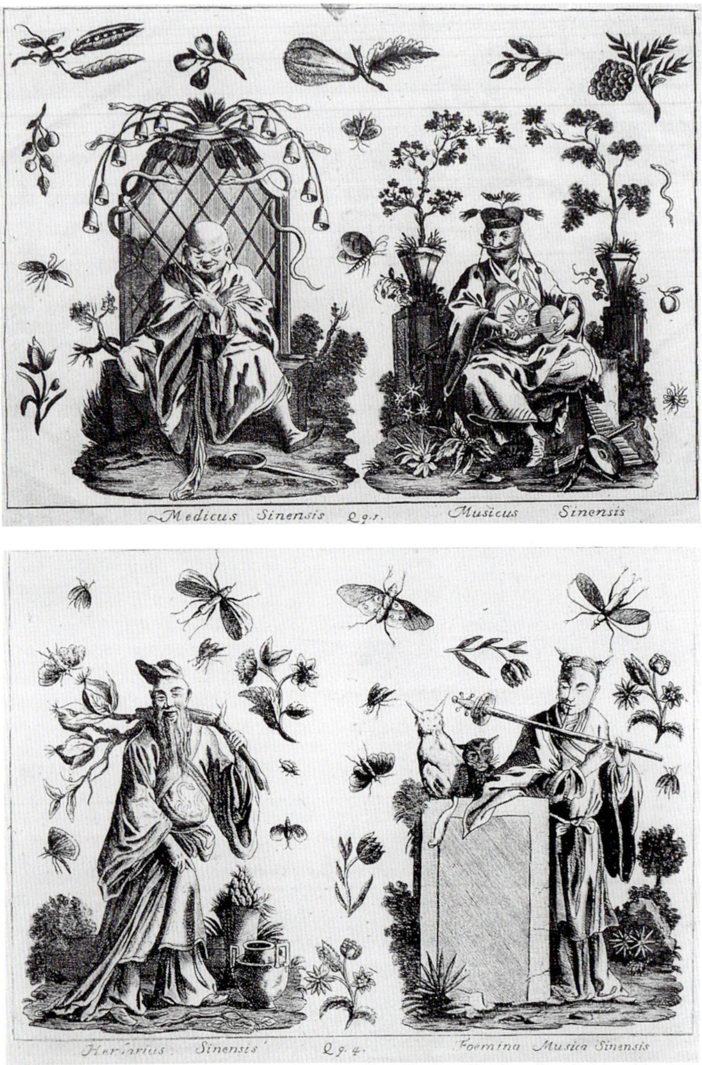

112a,b. Chinese figures. Remondini, 18th century, second half.

The Remondini company kept chinoiserie engravings in their catalogue throughout the second half of the 18th century. These were used primarily for decorations using the *lacca povera* technique. The oriental characters in these two prints derive from Boucher.

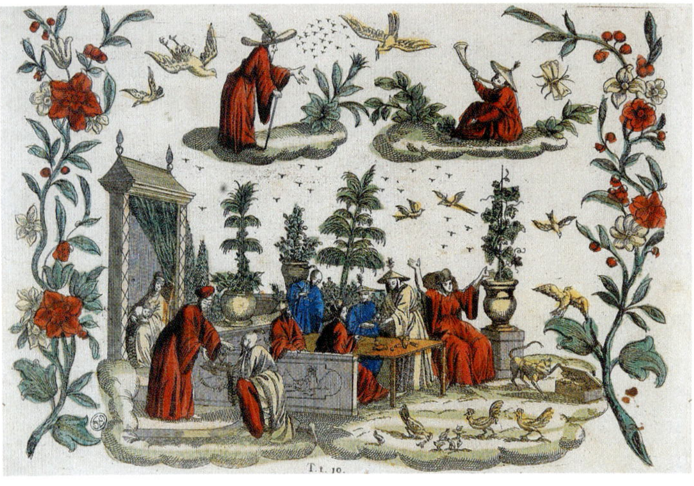

113. Chinoiserie. Remondini, after 1775.

It seems very likely that the Remondini managed to acquire some of the original copper plates engraved by Martin Engelbrecht, probably buying them from his heirs to be used in new compositions. An analysis of this print would seem to confirm this theory as there are many similarities to the work of Engelbrecht (see Fig. 81).

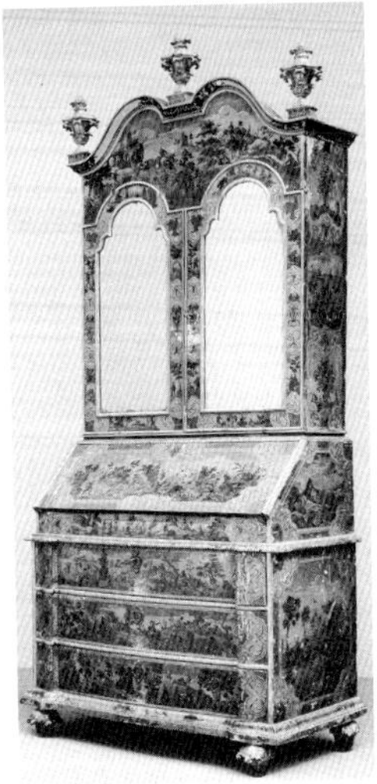

114. Bureau decorated with *lacca povera*. Venice, mid 18th century. New York, The Metropolitan Museum.

Based on English bureaux produced in the early 1700s, this piece is entirely decorated with *lacca povera*, or cut out prints applied to the surface. Numerous different subjects appear, including chinoiseries, one of which is based on a print by Martin Engelbrecht.

ornaments", little information is available concerning these panels. In 1761 Giambattista Tiepolo was working on the wall paintings of the villa and just a few decades later Jacopo (1720-1808) and Giuseppe Guarana (1709-1784) were responsible for further painted decorations. The internal decoration was, however, only the last stage in a long process of renovation of both the villa and the garden, begun around 1720 and only completed in 1756. Direction of the works, mostly commissioned by Almorò and Alvise Pisani (who was doge of Venice from 1735 to 1741), was first undertaken by Girolamo Frigimelica Roberti (1653-1732), followed by Francesco Maria Preti (1701-1774) from Castelfranco Veneto. Once the Pisani family's preferred summer residence, the villa was subsequently bought by Napoleon (1769-1821) in 1807 and then passed to the viceroy, Eugenio di Beauharnais (1781-1824). Numerous interiors of the building were decorated in the Chinese style and although they have now lost their original raison d'être, some traces of these are still visible even today. One such is a hanging, probably of French origin, of a printed fabric with floral motifs, clearly taken from a Chinese repertory, and probably placed in what is now referred to as the 'Bedroom of Eugenio di Beauharnais' (room 107) during the first renovation of the villa (1735-1740).[69] A series of thirteen original Chinese panels and a pair of screens made from painted papers, most probably bought by Alvise Pisani on one of his numerous visits to Paris or London during the mid 1700s, are also still among the furnishings of the villa. A further twenty-nine items of the same group are now kept in storage at the Palazzo Ducale in Venice. Another hanging with a naturalistic chinoiserie design, also most probably dating form the mid 1700s, is located in room 89, which was used by Vittorio Emanuele II of Savoy (1820-1878) from 1857 to 1866. The coverings of the chairs and the backs of the armchairs and couch in the room are in the same material.[70]

Without any doubt the most remarkable and famous example of Venetian furnishing lacquered and decorated with chinoiserie is the 'salotto' housed in the Ca' Rezzonico museum.[71] Originally in Palazzo Calbo Crotta agli Scalzi, in 1902 it was donated to the Musei Civici Veneziani and housed in the Correr Museum, until in 1936 it was transferred to Ca' Rezzonico. This 'salotto' is almost complete with two chests of drawers, a console table with its mirror, four *gueridon*, five *bonegrazie* for doors and windows, twelve chairs and frames. All the pieces have the soft, curving outlines of the rococo style with concave and convex forms entwining sinuously to create harmonious and elegant undulations. The pieces were first lacquered with a green background on which the chinoiserie decorations in gilded plaster were then arranged: delicate waterscapes with the soft fringes of willow trees and the curved roof of pavilions, the water rippling as little boats rock, rowed by Chinese figures. In other scenes the same characters are portrayed in their favourite pastimes of pleasant conversation or blissful relaxation representing the usual and varied repertory of Venetian chinoiserie. All the scenes, especially those on the more extensive surfaces of the front and sides of the drawers, are surrounded by gilded wood frames shaped with the soft curves most typical of French *rocaille*.

Decoupage, the technique of applying images cut out from engravings onto lacquered surfaces to create a decorative pattern, was closely related to the art of painting on lacquer. This procedure enjoyed some success in Venice where it was known as *lacca povera* indicating that its origins lay with the more noble form of decoration. Although the technique first began to be used in the early 17th century, it was during the 1700s that it became popular throughout Europe as dilettantes too began to experiment with the medium to satisfy their artistic leanings. The phenomenon lead to the publication of prints specifically designed for the purpose and indeed *The Ladies Amusement* was simply a repertory of images for the fans of *decoupage* and was not intended only for professional lacquer workers. Chinese motifs were obviously amongst the prints produced, especially as the technique originally developed to facilitate reproduction of the decorations that were applied to Oriental lacquered items. Chinoiserie designs could therefore be adapted from the engravings published in the oldest compendiums, or created *ex novo* from the prints now enthusiastically produced and made available by numerous publishers. Based in Bassano del Grappa the Remondini firm, for example, published sheets with 'Chinese' scenes and subjects to satisfy the passion for this popular hobby.[72] The company was established in the mid 1600s by Giovanni Antonio Remondini of Padova (1634-1711) and during the course of the 18th century his heirs, Giuseppe (1672-1742) and in turn his sons Giovanni Antonio (1700-1769) and Giambattista (1713-1773), enjoyed such success that not only did they produce a vast quantity of publications, but the quality of the engravings was of such a high standard that in 1790 Jérôme de Lalande (1732-1807) described the printers as the best of their kind in Europe. The Remondini factory produced numerous series of designs, mainly consisting of large print runs of individual motifs with popular subjects, while their oriental patterns fell into two categories: on the one hand 'Indian' floral subjects in the French style for the 'painted papers' to be used as wall decoration and, on the other, prints with 'Chinese' subjects frequently taken from the work of the Augsburg engravers, such as Martin Engelbrecht and Jeremias Wolff, made specifically for the *lacca povera* technique. Small scenes with a Chinese theme are listed under the heading "Chinesi" in the catalogue as early as 1751, such as "Chinese and European vases of flowers", "groups of figures and costumes from all nations", "Chinese reflections" and "various Chinese costumes". The catalogue of 1772 indicated that over two hundred sheets of Chinese subjects existed and were explicitly described as, "An assortment of prints with Chinese subjects on the finest paper to be cut out and used on fruit dishes, to decorate cabinets etc.".

Ceramics

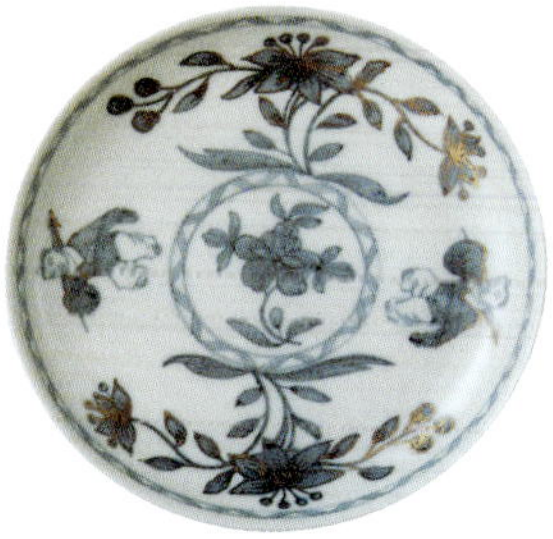

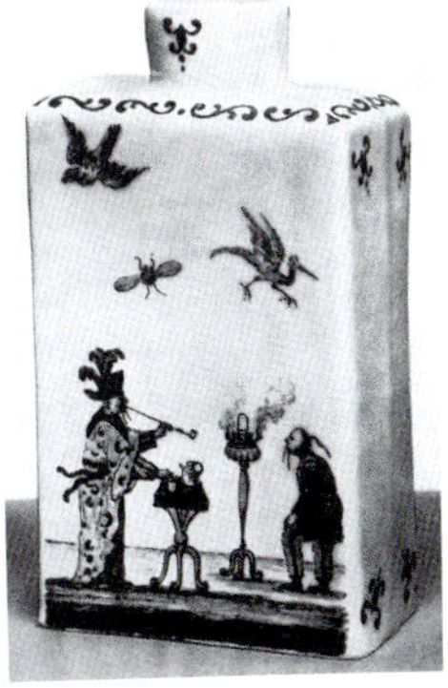

115. Small plate. Venice, Vezzi factory, before 1727. Sèvres, Musée National de Céramique.

The Vezzi factory also produced a variant of this design in which the cobalt blue is combined with iron red enamel. The decorative motif is based on Chinese porcelain produced in the second half of the 17th century, although the decorator working for Vezzi did not simply copy the original model, but rather provided his own interpretation. The flowers in particular do not belong to any Far Eastern repertory but are based instead on the 'Indian flowers' painted on the porcelain of Vienna and Meissen.

116. Tea flask. Venice, Vezzi factory, before 1727. London, Victoria and Albert Museum.

The chinoiserie decorating this flask made by Vezzi is taken from an engraving by Martin Engelbrecht (see Fig. 81).

The Vezzi Factory

After Meissen and Vienna, Giovanni Vezzi (1688-1746) founded the third most important porcelain factory in Europe in Venice on 5 June 1720.[73] Beset by problems, the factory only survived officially for seven years although during this brief period it was renowned for its high quality production. "You will be delighted by the quality of our porcelain, which is just as lovely as that of old Japan in transparency, weight and brilliance; in fact the right temperature has been found for firing all the different colours at the same time, as each colour requires its own specific temperature. The problem has been to discover which temperature is right for all the colours; our decorators are more skilled than the Chinese and you cannot imagine the effect of their lovely designs on this fine material. A service has been made for the pope, reproducing all his coats of arms, and they are even preparing a service as a gift for king Augustus to show him that the porcelain of Venice is far superior to that of Dresden. Madame Lecouvrer already owns several pieces which have been given to her by the count of Saxony and you will also have some as I intend to send you six cups and saucers. So I would ask you to send me your coat of arms or six little drawings by your son. They can be changed until they are to your liking, or relief decorations can be added, or gold can be mixed with the colours: all your suggestions can be produced. Quite gracefully shaped pagodas have been made. In conclusion, I would like to ask your opinion on some vases and figures that have recently been made...".[74]

Thus wrote the Abbé Conti (1677-1749) in a letter to Madame de Caylus (1672-1729) dated 4 January 1727. The policy of the Vezzi factory was therefore to reproduce the most significant characteristics of Chinese and Japanese porcelain, which at the time remained quite unequalled, and to achieve a standard of production and of ornamentation that could compete with the factory of Meissen. Evidently the first difficulty to be resolved was the use of the kilns. In the early stages of production, Giovanni Vezzi was assisted by an alchemist and friend of Böttger, Christian Conrad Hunger who was particularly skilled at applying gilding and subsequently worked for Du Paquier in Vienna. In this early phase, he sought mainly to emulate Far Eastern models, both the *blanc de Chine* produced by the Dehua factories in the southern province of Fujian, and the classic blue and white porcelain, although the influence of Meissen is also evident. The results obtained seem not to have satisfied Vezzi who sacked Hunger and in 1724 took over artistic direction of the kilns himself, employing two other less known German technicians, Gaspar Dietel and Matteo Margraiter. The factory also moved from its original location on the Giudecca to the Casin degli Spiriti, in the area of Madonna dell'Orto, while a retail shop was opened in San Marco. The second phase of production made greater use of colour compared to the first, and a wider variety of shapes was introduced, often based on contemporary metal ware items (the Vezzi family were traditionally gold and silversmiths). In addition, the pictorial and relief decoration became more varied and grotesque decoration in the style of Bérain was introduced to the repertory. Vezzi also made use of printed pattern books available at the time, such as the chinoiserie designs of Martin Engelbrecht.[75] The firm was officially closed in 1727 when Giovanni, burdened by debt, again sought help from his father who had already provided finance during the initial phase. This new stop-gap finance was only provided on the condition that the kilns would be destroyed. Despite not being able to produce new works, Vezzi was able to make use of a large amount of stock in his warehouse, much of which was undecorated and was subsequently painted with coloured motifs. In 1733 the shop in San Marco was still open and in 1740 Gaspar Goethe, son of Augustus III of Saxony mentioned that he had seen large quantities of Vezzi porcelain on market stalls set up for the Feast of the Ascension that year. A total of 1801 pieces of porcelain was listed in the inventory drawn up on the death of Giovanni in 1746. Vezzi's laudable initiative did not therefore bring him any economic benefit. One of the causes of his failure was the extremely high cost of primary materials, especially the clay from Schneeberg in Saxony (the same as was used at Meissen and Vienna), bought at exorbitant prices on the black market from two German merchants named Schnorr and Henningen. Moreover, the initial capital investment was insufficient and unreliable, partly provided by his father, Francesco, (who, indifferent to his son's financial problems, left the family fortune to a charity hospital on his death) and partly by the Zanoni cousins from Udine, who withdrew their investment on seeing the lack of profits, and claimed immediate reimbursement of their loan. Unable to obtain any cash, they began to requisition Giovanni's personal belongings, including the books which had provided Vezzi with valuable technical information at the time of establishing his factory.

117. Lantern. Venice, Vezzi factory, before 1727 (?), London, Sotheby's 23/09/1992.

Another version of this lantern exists in the Victoria and Albert Museum in London, painted in blue with touches of gold and without the cherub on the top. In comparison, the decoration of the 'red' version illustrated here is not of such a high quality and it may be one of the pieces produced before 1727 but decorated some time after the factory had closed. The style of both decorations is clearly based on Bérain's creations which were well known in Venice from the engravings of his work.

The Antonibon Factory of Bassano del Grappa

The closure of Vezzi's factory was not only a personal and family drama for its owner, but also directly involved the entire Republic of Venice. Naturally interested in developments in Europe, Venice considered that the existence of a ceramics factory on a level with other continental courts was indispensable for its prestige and useful for enriching the state coffers. Thus in 1728, just a few months after Vezzi had officially failed, the deputies of the Chamber of Commerce and the 'Cinque Savi della Mercanzia' (the five sages of merchandise) issued an order inviting Venetian citizens and foreigners to create new ceramics factories or to improve the efficiency and productivity of existing majolica factories. The challenge was accepted in 1732 by Gian Battista Antonibon (?-1738) who had been a partner of Giovanni Maria Moretto's factory at Rivarotta in 1719 and owner of a majolica and

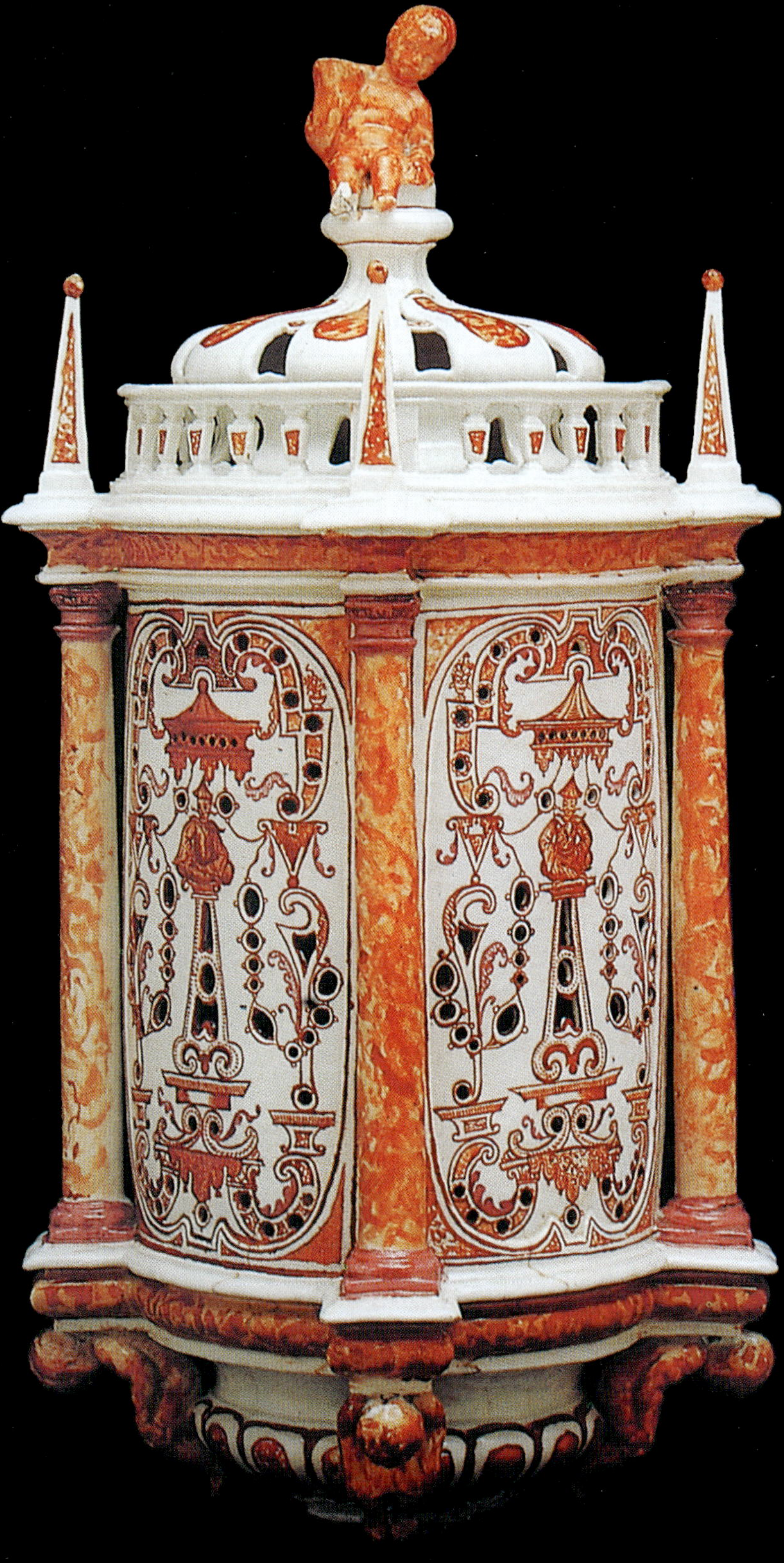

earthenware factory in Nove Vicentina near Bassano del Grappa since 1728. He was thus exempted from paying customs duties for twenty years and benefited from other economic and administrative concessions.
The Antonibon factory was well known for its production of ceramics which were often decorated with chinoiserie details.[76] Between 1728 and 1738, under the direction of the first director, Giovan Battista, early production was decorated with ornamental motifs – including chinoiserie – imitating the work of other more expert and famous European and Italian ceramic manufacturers, especially Rouen, Moustiers, Savona, Turin and Lodi. When Pasquale (?-1773) took over from his father, Giovan Battista, in 1737 a second and longer phase began during which the company experienced much greater artistic development and economic expansion. Chinoiserie patterns were more extensively introduced using a range of three colours (blue, green and yellow), extended at the specific request of the Venetian senate in 1755, by the use of a technique known as 'piccolo fuoco' (a third firing) which both Paul Hannong (1700-1760) in Strasbourg and Veuve Perrin in Marseilles had adopted a decade earlier. The decorative motifs were based on both original Chinese and Japanese porcelain works and compendiums of engravings containing the most popular chinoiserie designs in Europe at the time, such as those of Pillement. However, the motif of the "little bridge" (described in old records as the "Persian decoration"), without any doubt one of the most popular of the factory's chinoiserie designs, originated directly within the Antonibon workshops. Usually Chinese subjects were surrounded by 'European' motifs and the forms represented a typically western perception of the exotic style during the second half of the 18th century.
In the mid 1750s, the factory began to experiment with primary materials and the technique of manufacturing porcelain. At the end of the decade, following as series of poor results, Lorenzo Levatin began to achieve some success after being sent to the Vincennes factory from 1749 to 1752 at the expense of the Antonibon. Jean Pierre Varion, a French worker who moved to the Veneto from 1758 until 1765, also helped to improve production techniques. Porcelain production was still a matter of lively discussion in France at the time, thanks to the publication of the letters of Father d'Entrecolles (1712 and 1722),[77] diffusion of Du Halde's volume (1735), and the relative availability of *Le sécret des vraies Porcellaines de la Chine et de Saxe*, a little booklet contained in *L'Art de la Verrerie*, a French translation of a German original by Neri, Merret and Kunckel.[78] However, although the production of majolica continued for several decades, the Antonibon's attempts to produce porcelain were destined to remain incomplete; in 1764, just two years after having asked the senate to concede the same privileges to their porcelain products, Pasquale was taken seriously ill and was obliged to convalesce for a lengthy period in precisely the same year that the successful Cozzi factory began its production in Venice.

The Cozzi Factory

Born in Modena, Geminiano Francesco Antonio Cozzi (1728-1797) moved to Venice around 1754 after having learned the techniques of ceramic production in his home town.[79] A man of many talents, Cozzi's first steps towards founding his own ceramic factory were taken when he co-financed Natal Federico and Maria Dorotea Hewelcke, natives of Saxony, enabling them to establish their own factory in Udine, after having received the necessary privileges from the Venetian senate in 1758.[80] Cozzi's participation in the company was fundamental as attempts to make use of the clay available around Udine, which would have greatly reduced their costs, had failed and shortly before 1761 the couple decided to move their business to Venice. The economic difficulties immediately appeared to be insurmountable, however, and in 1763 they accepted Cozzi's assistance. The

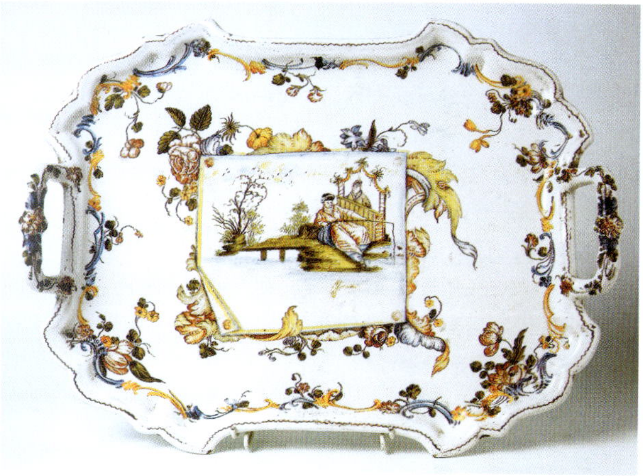

118. Tray. Nove (Vicenza), Antonibon factory, c. 1760-1790. Saronno, Giannetti Collection.

Faithfully reproduced in the centre is an engraving by Pillement with a 'Chinese' theme.
The surrounding flora arranged to enhance the irregular outline of the tray is entirely European.

arrival on the market of Pasquale Antonibon's porcelain was a lethal blow for the Hewelckes and in a matter of months they were forced to close down their business.

This brief experience with the Hewelckes and the employment of ceramists who had previously worked for Antonibon, provided Cozzi with the minimum knowledge necessary to profitably manage a ceramics business. The firm was founded in 1764 and the kilns were located in San Giobbe on the Fondamenta Canal Regio. Cozzi's first stroke of fortune was to use the clays found in the Veneto, signifying a considerable saving in costs; clay from the Tretto hills turned out to be particularly suited to the purpose. Unlike the Hewelcke's products, decorated predominantly with European motifs, Geminiano Cozzi made extensive use of 'Chinese style' decorations right from the start. Cozzi was, in fact, quite convinced that his porcelain would rapidly replace "Dutch porcelain" – the oriental ware imported by the Dutch East India Company, on which Venetians spent about 30,000 ducats every year. The extreme variety of his oriental motifs – both the painted decoration and the small figurines – is quite clear from an analysis of old records and the goods themselves. The decorators working for the Cozzi based their creations on original Chinese porcelain made for exportation to the European markets, sometimes reproducing them almost exactly, sometimes interpreting them more freely. Far Eastern motifs frequently used by the factory included the flowers of the 'famille rose' repertory and the 'Imari' colours of blue, red and gold. The Japanese 'Kakiemon' group of motifs was more rarely used and was mainly copied from imitations produced by other European factories. Indeed German and French manufacturers probably provided a further source for Cozzi's chinoiserie, inspiring both the formation of the landscapes and the physical features of the 'Chinese' figures. Models for these were found in engravings with chinoiserie themes available throughout Europe at the time, both German (Augsburg and its decorators) and French (especially Boucher and Pillement). It is, instead, difficult to trace any real influence by local painters and lacquer masters who were also developing chinoiserie motifs. However, Cozzi's porcelain also represents that entirely 'Venetian spirit' that is common to all chinoiserie produced in the city, no matter what the artistic medium was. Gaiety and vivacity of colour, elegantly conceived compositions, a combination of exotic motifs of various origin, suffused by a certain decadent melancholy – a cultural characteristic typical of the Venetian 18th century.

After his early success, Cozzi's factory too fell prey to an inexorable crisis. Despite having crushed competition from other factories, both Italian and European in a very short time, around 1780 he was faced with the problem of the highly competitive price of English earthenware, particularly the production of Wedgewood. Geminiano tried to counter the slump in sales by initiating production of 'English-style earthenware' and this policy was continued by his brother, Vincenzo (1740-1804) who took over direction of the factory in 1791. As Napoleon's troops entered the city just a few years later, bringing to an end the centuries of independence enjoyed by the Republic of Venice, Cozzi died hounded by his creditors, as too had Vezzi. His death coincided symbolically with the end of an epoch, the 18th century – often recorded as the century of porcelain and thus of the most elegant and lively chinoiserie.

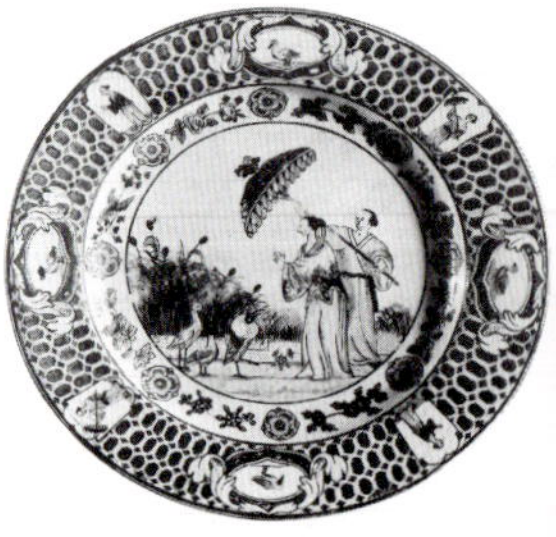

119. Plate. Venice, Cozzi factory, c. 1770-1780. Milan, Guido Rossi Collection.

The decoration of this plate is a copy of the design commissioned from Cornelius Pronk (1691-1759) by the Dutch East India Company to be reproduced by Chinese ceramists on dinner services for export to Europe. Despite enjoying commercial success, later repeated by Japanese producers, the pattern, known as the "Lady with the Parasol" was produced for only a very brief period.

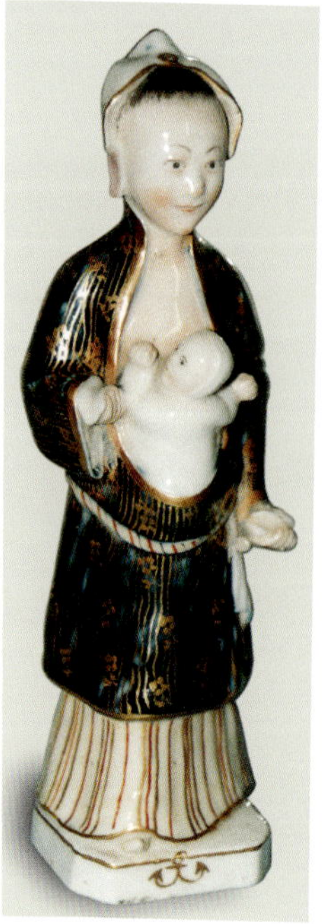

120a, b. Pair of Chinese figures. Venice, Cozzi factory, 1780. Naples, Museo Duca di Martina.

In addition to the inscription "Venice" the base of the male figure bears the date "1780" which is valid also for the female figure. A similar pair, with the same inscriptions, is housed in the Musée National de la Céramique in Sèvres. With their fine attention to detail and use of gold on the clothing, these highly elegant figures are a Venetian version of similar porcelain statuettes made in China for export to Europe throughout the 18th century.

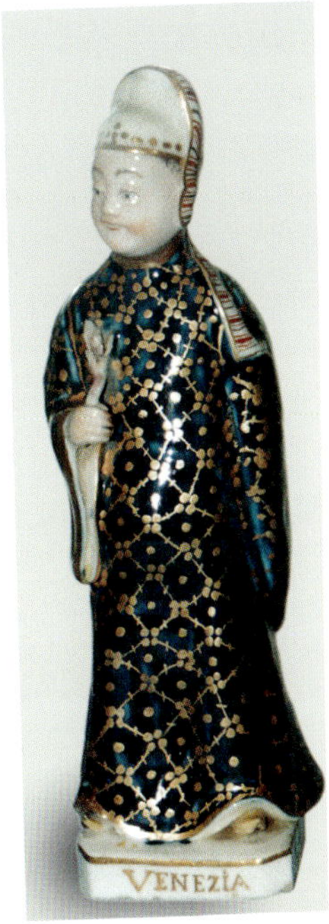

Glass

In the late 15th century Venice was renowned for its production of 'milk glass' – a form of white glass known as "porcellana contrafacta" and generally decorated with blue enamel, just like oriental porcelain. This traditional technique of glass making was revived in the 1700s and with the same purpose – to imitate the brilliance, hardness and transparency of real porcelain paste, both Chinese and European. Thus the decorative repertories of Venetian glass workers also included Chinoiserie motifs.[81] Using the procedure discovered by the physicist Réaumur (1683-1757), the glass factories of Murano revived the technique of milk glass immediately after the closure of the Vezzi company, precisely to satisfy the continuing demand for porcelain. Although it was generally known – as Abbé Francesco Griselini stated – that this substitute for porcelain was far from "having the characteristics and quality of Chinaware" the results were quickly evident and in January 1738 the Senate accepted the excellent quality of the products and conceded to the request for exemptions made by the glass producers, Gian Andrea and Pietro Bertolini.[82] The Bertolini also owned a small majolica factory specialized in reproducing Chinese and German porcelain and they filled a gap in the markets of the Veneto with their new high quality products at a reasonable price. They were also quite successful abroad and Horace Walpole (1717-1797) bought two pieces in 1741 (now in the British Museum).[83] The most distinctive feature of their decoration was the use of gold to which they had exclusive rights. The Miotti family was also specialized in the production of milk glass, often decorated with chinoiserie scenes in enamel.[84] They already had their own workshop on Murano in the 16th century but more concrete information is available from the end of the 17th century when milk glass was already listed in their catalogue. Active until 1805, their works are distinguished from the Bertolini's by a date and stamp.[85]

The chinoiserie motifs painted on 18th-century milk glass represent a varied and intriguing compendium of images. In many cases they consist of floral motifs or landscapes though figures too are included, portrayed with great flair and naturalness. Perhaps, having achieved the main aim of producing glassware that was a fair imitation of porcelain, the decorators felt entitled to give full vent to their artistic creativity, often ignoring the pattern books and thus producing equally attractive and effective results. In addition to plates, cups, small vases and teapots, the glass workers of Murano were renowned for their ability to make much larger items with different functions, such as chandeliers. Carlo Gozzi in a fine manuscript of *La Marfisa Bizzarra* mentions that on special occasions glass chandeliers were also used in the street and some were in the form of a pagoda.[86]

Coloured chinoiserie motifs were not only painted on milk glass but also transparent glass. Scenes of Chinese figures in a landscape embellished with

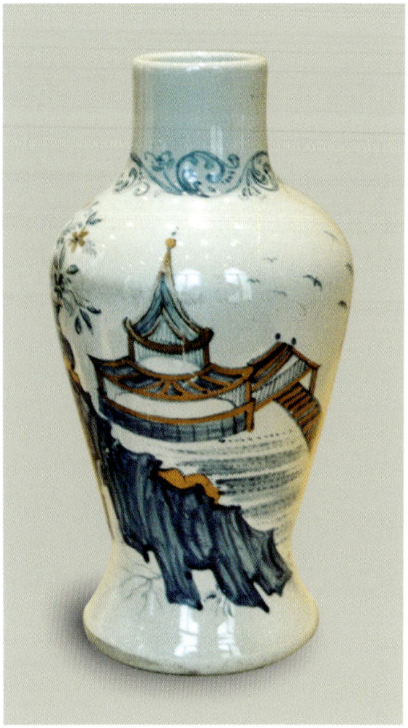

121. Milk glass vase. Venice, c. mid 18th century. Murano, Museo del Vetro.

This small vase is displayed paired with a similar one. In addition to the oriental motifs and the white vitreous paste, the use of blue enamel and gold to enhance various details reveals that the two pieces were intended to imitate Chinese porcelain or European pieces with chinoiserie designs.

little bridges, pavilions, exotic plants and animals were painted onto plates, flasks and glasses throughout the 18th century. This occurred in other European factories too, such as Kronstadt in Bohemia where the expert decorator Ignaz Preissler was employed on several occasions around 1730, Nurnberg where Anton Wilhelm Mänerl worked, and England. Indeed, Venetian chinoiserie motifs used to decorate transparent glass are stylistically similar to those used by the English and Bohemian factories.

1) Ericani 1982, pp. 97-98.
2) Ericani 1982, p. 96.
3) Ericani 1982, pp. 98-99.
4) Ericani 1982, pp.98-99.
5) Zoli 1984, p. 221.
6) Colle 2000, pp. 336-339; Belluno 2009, nos. 17-25.
7) Rotondi 1959, p. 49, figs. 4-5.
8) Zenone Padula 1992, note 40 at p. 82.
9) Semenzato 1966, pp. 49-51.
10) González-Palacios 1986, p. 313.
11) Morazzoni 1958, I, p. 24; Honour 1961 (1963), p. 140.
12) Alberici 1980, fig. 200.
13) Colle 2000, pp. 293-294, 332; Milan 2009, no. III.2.
14) Morazzoni 1958, I, pp. 15-17.
15) Morazzoni 1958., I, pp. 17-20.
16) Slomann 1953.
17) Miller 2006; Miller 2007.
18) Marot 1892.
19) Ericani 1982, p. 99, fig. 75.
20) Marini, in Ericani, Marini 1990, pp. 244-274.
21) Marini, in Ericani, Marini 1990, p. 257.
22) Montesquieu 1995, pp. 13-14.
23) Honour 1961 (1963), pp. 137-138.
24) Zoli 1974, p. 113.
25) Zoli 1974, p. 115.
26) Zoli 1974, p. 91.
27) Honour 1961 (1963), p. 139.
28) Turchi 1987, p. 535.
29) Catucci 2007, pp. 11-19.
30) Catucci 2007, p. 129.
31) Honour 1961 (1963), p. 139.
32) Honour 1961 (1963), pp. 139-140.
33) Zoli 1974, pp. 115-116.
34) Catucci 2007, p. 19.
35) Ericani 1976, p. 32.
36) Ericani 1982, p. 100.
37) Ericani 1982, pp. 99-100.
38) Mariuz 1971, pp. 54-60, pls. 110-117.
39) Mariuz 1971, p. 54.
40) Harvard 1970, no. 78.

41) Honour 1961 (1963), p. 142.
42) Mariuz 1971.
43) Pedrocco 2002, pp. 282-283, no. 214
44) Padova 1972, pp. 31, 40; Tiozzo 1972, pp. 50-53.
45) Padova 1972, p. 48.
46) Padova 1972, p. 48.
47) Padova 1972, p. 29; Tiozzo 1972, pp. 48-49.
48) Padova 1972, p. 65; Tiozzo 1972, pp. 66-68.
49) Honour 1961 (1963), p. 142.
50) Brunelli, Callegari 1931, pp. 67-79.
51) Bassi 1987, pp. 200-215.
52) Bassi 1987, pp. 200-215.
53) Affreschi ville venete 1978, I, pp. 212-213, no. 142.
54) Chiappini di Sorio 1983, p. 32.
55) Ericani 1976, p. 35.
56) Ericani 1976.
57) Ericani 1976, p. 34.
58) Ericani 1976, note 10 at p. 37.
59) Ericani 1976, p. 33.
60) Ericani 1983.
61) Ericani 1976, notes 14-15 at p. 38.
62) Rispoli Fabris 1974, p. 143.
63) Rispoli Fabris 1974, p. 144.
64) Alberici 1980, p. 204; Jarry 1981, p. 163.
65) Colle 2003, pp. 338-339.
66) Colle 2003, p. 336.
67) Colle 2003, pp. 334-336.
68) Santini 2003, pp. 57-67.
69) Ericani 1987-1988, pp. 81-82.
70) Ericani 1987-1988, p. 82.
71) Pedrocco 1998, p. 113, nos. 108-118.
72) Infelise 1980; Bassano del Grappa 1990; Zotti Minici 1994.
73) Melegati 1998.
74) Melegati 1998, p. 35.
75) Melegati 1998, p. 19, figs. 4-5.
76) Ericani, Marini 1990, pp. 277-350.
77) Coccolino 1998, pp. 151-187.
78) Stazzi 1982, p. 159.
79) Stazzi 1982.
80) Stazzi 1982, p. 22.
81) Dorigato 1981, pp. 7-13.
82) Barovier Mentasti 1982, p. 162.
83) Dorigato 1981, p. 12.
84) Dorigato 2002, pp. 164-166.
85) Dorigato 1981, p. 12.
86) Dorigato 1981, p. 10.

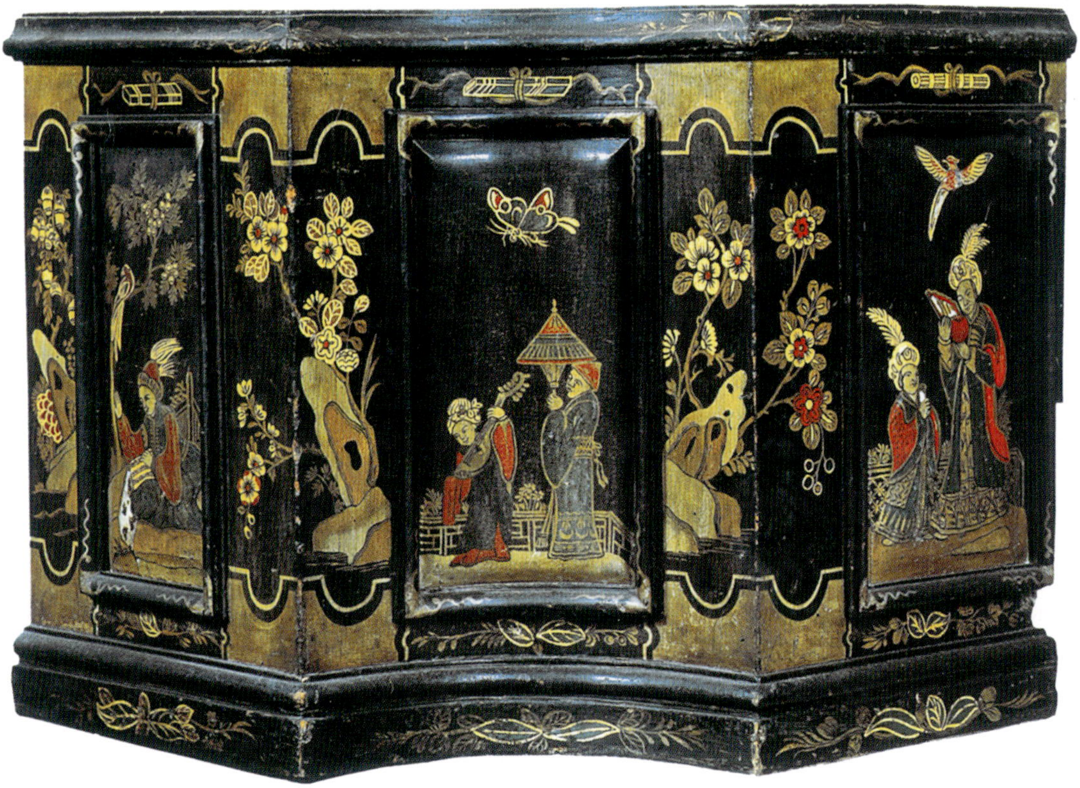

Piedmont and the Savoy

Under the rule of the Savoy family, Piedmont was one of the Italian kingdoms where the taste for chinoiserie was most eagerly indulged. Much favoured by both members of the royal family and the most influential members of the Savoy court, many examples of their passion have fortunately survived in the form of Chinese-style décor, Chinese furnishings and accessories, lacquer furniture, and ceramics in particular. The chinoiserie of Piedmont has recently been the subject of detailed study, the results of which were published in the volume *Villa della Regina. Il riflesso dell'Oriente nel Piemonte del Settecento* edited by Lucia Caterina and Cristina Mossetti.[1] The publication was issued on completion of a complex programme of restoration involving the entire magnificent structure of Villa della Regina following a near disastrous period of neglect. As part of this scrupulous task of renovation and reconstruction, specialists also worked on the Chinese Rooms still existing in the Villa and the expertise and knowledge acquired seemed to provide a suitable opportunity to re-examine and re-evaluate the other oriental-style rooms in the various royal and aristocratic residences of Piedmont. An unexpected quantity of works, all of a high standard, came to light, providing a fascinating and more complete history of chinoiserie during the Savoy period. Enthusiasm for chinoiserie was at its height during the 18th century and was greatly encouraged by an awareness of fashionable artistic developments in the other European courts. Family, commercial and cultural connections with neighbouring France clearly influenced the trends in Piedmont, which however, did evolve its own variants and characteristics.

The 17th Century

First indications of the Savoy family passion for the Orient date from the early 1600s when there was a vast increase in the amount of Far Eastern goods imported to Europe following the foundation of the English and Dutch East India Companies. Records dating from the period are variable and imprecise, and frequently documents may be open to differing interpretations, as in the case of those referring to oriental goods or describing European imitations of originals, possibly even made in Piedmont. However, the information provided does indicate the gradual growth of the style as it became one of the latest European fashions. The oriental theme was often in evidence when celebrations were staged, as for example, in 1608, on the occasion of the marriages of Carlo Emanuele I's

122. Pietro Massa, Lacquered wainscotting with chinoiserie, c. 1722. Turin, Palazzo Reale, Gabinetto del Poggiolo.

This is probably the first lacquer creation by Pietro Massa. In a career of over thirty years, Massa created many similar pieces and worked in most of the Savoy residences in Piedmont.

123. Fabric. Piedmont, c. 1720, detail. Riggisberg (Switzerland), Abegg-Stiftung.

The fabric was used for the canopy and hangings of a bed embroidered with designs and chinoiserie that recall the works of Bacqueville, Bérain and Marot. The detail illustrated here portrays one of the most frequent patterns of 17th and 18th-century European orientalism, with a deity (or emperor) between two supplicants.

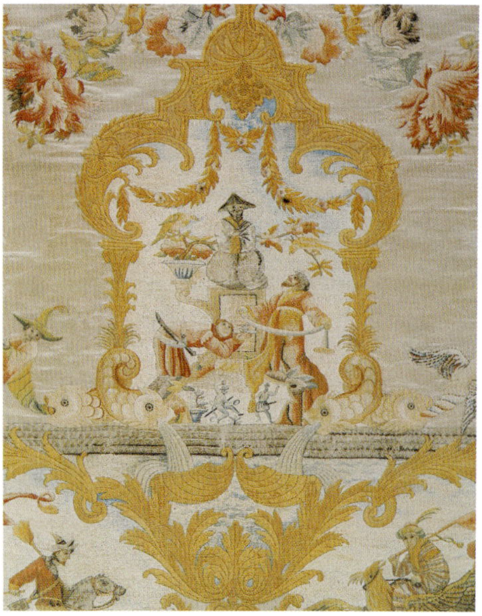

(who reigned from 1580 to 1630) two daughters when a 'Chinese banquet' was organized at the castle; in 1620 for the wedding of Vittorio Amedeo I (1587-1637) and Marie Christine of France (d. 1663), cardinal Maurizio (1593-1657, son of Carlo Emanuele I) acquired "robbe delle Indie" ("gifts from the Indies"); just a few months later, in February 1621, for the birthday of Marie Christine the *Balletto dei sette re de la China* with music by Sigismondo d'India (c. 1582-1629) was performed at cardinal Maurizio's 'Vigna' residence (later Villa della Regina). Furnishings too began to be influenced by the Orient: in 1637 the services of count Giovanni Antonio Turinetti, Marie Christine's banker, were used to acquire twenty pieces of Chinese fabrics for hangings; the inventory of the possessions of cardinal Maurizio's step brother, don Felice of Savoy (1604-1643), governor of Nice from 1625 to 1632 and of Savoy from 1634, records that Chinese textiles decorated the rooms of his residence, the castle of Chambéry; meanwhile the inventory of the possessions of Marie Christine dated 1644 describes in the 'flower room' of the Castello del Valentino, "a small table worked in the Chinese style with gold figures. Two more small tables decorated in the same way, with covers of embossed leather", while the Rose Room contained a "large cabinet from China", as well as a slightly smaller one, and two caskets of the same type. In 1662 in Marie Christine's 'Vigna' residence, a hanging of 'Chinese silk' was documented; in the 1664 inventory of Palazzo Madama, her furnishings included "a golden screen, of eight panels painted in the Chinese style, lined with "dark grey 'tabisso'", "two Chinese boxes, one inside the other", as well as fine 'Chinese-style' fabrics. In 1679 Ludovica (1629-1692), daughter of the duchess and widow of Maurizio who she married in 1642, is recorded as owning "a large Chinese-style desk with a frame" and a

"golden screen with Chinese figures". In Palazzo Reale the *Inventario mobili presso il Sig. Governatore de' Reali Palazzi Allemandi* dated 1682 records a number of items with "Chinese varnish", including drawers, desks, chests and two suits of armour complete with masks and silk linings. The first document referring to a room with Chinese décor dates from 1693 and records the payment of Andrea Rosso (also known as Pavia) "for Chinese miniatures" on six sections of *boiserie* in the New Pavilion of Palazzo Reale, a room leading to the courtyard terrace now known as "della Macchina".
At the end of the century a change in tastes and style was in full swing in Piedmont too as the baroque was progressively abandoned for a trend that would eventually evolve into international Rococo. The florid painted ceilings and the surfeit of gold that had dominated interiors were gradually replaced by a much lighter touch, characterised by a more sinuous and subtle appearance and a greater informality. The artists of Piedmont too began to discover unusual mannerist grotesques, frequently derived from the latest northern European examples and occasionally including oriental elements. Decorative models generally arrived from France, often reinterpreted by artists who had trained at the court of Louis XIV. Designers were able to consult numerous engravings of the works of ornamentalists such as Bérain, Paul Decker, Boulle (1642-1732), or René Chaveau (1663-1722) who had worked on the palace of count Tessin in Stockholm in 1697.

The Reign of Vittorio Amedeo II (1714-1730)

The passion for the oriental arts began to develop into a fully fledged style used in furnishings and décor during the reign (first as duke, then as king) of Vittorio Amedeo II (1666-1732) and his wife, Anne of Orléans (1669-1728), when the second "Madama Reale", Maria Giovanna Battista of Savoy-Nemours (1644-1724) was still alive. It was during this period that Filippo Juvarra (1678-1736) was made responsible for renovating all the Savoy residences. Juvarra was invited to Piedmont by Vittorio Amedeo II in 1714 and from then until 1735, when he left Italy for Spain, he modernised numerous palaces in the city and surrounding area. Once he had begun the renovations of the first and second floor of the Rivoli castle, Juvarra – an architect originally from Messina in Sicily – set to work on Palazzo Reale, Palazzo Madama, the Villa della Regina, Stupinigi, Rivoli and the Venaria Reale, bringing a truly international style to the art and architecture of Piedmont. During the 1600s the baroque style, magnificently interpreted in Turin by the architect Guarino Guarini (1624-1683), had been conceived to instigate a 'sense of wonder' and to some degree Juvarra continued this artistic concept. However, he also studied and creatively interpreted more modern French models introduced by a native of Turin, Juste-Aurèle Meissonier, who based his works on the engravings of Duvivier, Mondon, Pineau and Oppenordt. Juvarra, who had trained in Rome, invited the most

talented artists of the day – both Italian and foreign – to work in Turin and experts such as the cabinet-maker Pietro Piffetti (1701-1777), Andrea Boucheron, a goldsmith (1692-1761) and the bronze worker Francesco Ladatte (1706-1787) all spent time in the city, and frequently contributed to the oriental rooms so beloved by the Savoy.
Beginning in the France of Louis XIV and spreading throughout Europe, the new fashion for chinoiserie had already attracted royal attention when Juvarra began his work in Piedmont and even the theatre world had been affected. In 1716 *Teuzzone* had been performed – a musical drama with a Chinese setting by Apostolo Zeno (1668-1750). It had already been staged in Milan in 1706 and was the first play of its kind in Italy. *Teuzzone* was based on *Bajazet* by Jean Racine (1639-1699) and *Le comte d'Essex* by Thomas Corneille (1625-1709), but Zeno changed the original Turkish setting which had been used in France, perhaps because he could more easily avoid the severe criticism that had been directed at Racine for having little genuine knowledge of the actual location. At the time China was still a distant land and as it was generally quite unknown to Europeans Zeno therefore could rely on a degree of immunity from over meticulous scrutiny. In any case, his main intention in writing *Teuzzone* was to exalt the philosophy and values of the Far East, not to provide an ethnic and anthropological lesson on eastern Asia. He was obviously fond of the subject as he used the oriental theme on two further occasions, in *Ormisda* and *Gianguir*. However, his *Teuzzone* met with some success as it was performed in Vienna in 1735 at the same time as Metastasio's *Le Cinesi*, and its last public performance was held in 1751 in Livorno.
France's influence on the arts of Piedmont was particularly evident from the late 17th to the early 18th century. Indeed some of the most important members of the royal family were French by birth: queen Anne was the daughter of Philippe d'Orléans (1640-1701, brother of Louis XIV) and his first wife, Henriette Stuart (1644-1670), daughter of Charles I of England. Anne's sister, Marie-Louise, married the king of Spain, Charles II (1661-1700). Anne had spent her childhood and youth between Versailles and Saint-Cloud, where she had evidently appreciated the oriental style quite early on. She acquired various Far Eastern items for the Piedmont residences, organizing their importation with the help of members of her entourage such as Angelica Teresa Carron di San Tomaso (1673-1726), the queen's lady in waiting, and especially Ottavio Solaro di Govone (1645-1737), her knight of honour. Solaro acquired a series of important works of art for his own residence, the castle of Govone, and the collection was subsequently continued by his son, Giuseppe Roberto (c. 1695-1764), count of Breglio, and heir, the count of Favria (c. 1708-1789). During the period when he was the Savoy's diplomatic representative in Vienna, between 1720 and 1731, Ottavio Solaro bought Chinese papers which were used to decorate several rooms in his castle. Other members of Anne's social circle also indulged their

oriental tastes: count Antonio Maurizio Turinetti from Partengo (1664-1739), had several rooms in Villa Moglia near Chieri decorated with Chinese papers, and count Carlo Gaspare Graneri (1686-1768) commissioned two Chinese rooms in the family residence. In 1713 Anne probably acquired the 'Chinese style' taffeta hanging for one of the rooms in the Racconigi castle, made by Giovanni Andrea Grattapaglia who seems to have been specialised in painting oriental motifs on cloth. In 1715 she commissioned a room to be furnished with 'Chinese style' upholstery in the Masino castle.
A certain partiality to exotic décor is also evident in the inventories dated 1724 for Palazzo Madama, residence of the regent, Maria Giovanna Battista of Savoy-Nemours (widow of Carlo Emanuele II from 1675), which had been completely renovated at the end of the 17th century. Oriental items seem to abundantly populate the private rooms of the palace, appearing in the fabrics and the furnishings, while numerous lacquered boxes are scattered around. The most 'oriental' rooms, however, were the "small dressing room", the "room facing the grand stairway" and the "new room towards Piazza Castello", all located in the south wing of the palace and probably renovated at the same time as the work on Juvarra's staircase between 1720 and 1721. In addition to the 'bizarre' decoration on the ceilings, made by Domenico Guidobono and still visible today, many exotic items were recorded in these rooms including porcelain, lacquered cabinets and unusual curios.
Other Savoy residences in Turin and the immediate surroundings were also influenced by the Chinese style. In 1722 at the time of the marriage between the hereditary prince, Carlo Emanuele and Anne Christine Louise Gräfin von Sulzbach, their apartments on the second floor of Palazzo Reale were modernised. Work was directed by Juvarra and many artists, craftsmen and decorators were involved in the renovations. As part of this overall programme a first payment was made to Pietro Massa that year for "'Chinese' paintings in a room in the apartment of HRH in the New Palace". This could also have included the wooden wainscotting, lacquered in black and decorated with coloured paintings and mother of pearl inlay around the entire 'Gabinetto del poggiolo' (balcony chamber) originally known as the 'Gabinetto di toeletta in violac' (lacquered chamber). The scenes portrayed on the panels – a host of figures, animals, buildings and plants of all kinds – are framed vertically with compositions of rocks and flowers, while friezes extend along the horizontal sides forming semicircles containing cartouches of objects or small insects. This is a style of chinoiserie that is not found anywhere else in Piedmont and the images somehow exude an 'archaic' air. The exotic motifs are mixed – from China, the Indian sub-continent, and Persia – although in certain sections Chinese models predominate and were probably based on lacquered items to be found at the court, while the natural motifs that are also present were almost certainly taken from herbals. This Piedmontese craftsman seems to have been very up to date with the latest developments in international chinoiserie. In particular, echoes of late

17th-century northern European, and especially German, oriental decorative styles are evident. This commission at Palazzo Reale was to be only the first in Pietro Massa's lengthy career which continued until at least 1758. He was certainly one of the most important chinoiserie artists of Piedmont in the 18th century and his succession of works can be considered as an effective gauge of the development of the Savoy oriental style.
The grotesques painted by Filippo Minei between 1722 and 1724 on the ceiling of the 'Poggiolo' room are entirely of French derivation. There are clear references to the ornamentation of Bérain and Audran II, combined with a reinterpretation of early 16th-century Roman arabesques and a range of features derived from original oriental works, both Persian and Chinese. Also referred to by Honour in 1961 as one of the earliest interpreters of chinoiserie in Piedmont, Minei was paid for decorative work carried out on the Villa di Rivoli during the same period.[2]

The Reign of Carlo Emanuele III (1730-1773)

Vittorio Emanuele II initiated many works and these were continued and completed during the long reign of Carlo Emanuele III (1701-1773). Carlo Emanuele III was more a promoter of the arts than a collector, but he did decide to acquire part of the collection of oriental items which had belonged to prince Eugenio (1663-1736), a member of the Carignano branch of the Savoy family. One of the leaders, with Vittorio Amedeo II, of the struggle to liberate Turin from French occupation in 1706, Eugenio had subsequently been governor of the Austrian Low Countries. His collection of works of art was housed in his Viennese residence and contained many original oriental works. On his death in 1736 all his possessions were inherited by his niece, Vittoria of Savoy, who decided to sell them. Other items from his collection, including six porcelain chests and two lacquered cabinets, were bought by the Savoy of Turin in 1750 on the occasion of the marriage between Vittorio Amedeo III (1726-1796) and Maria Antonia Ferdinanda, Infanta of Spain (1729-1785). The acquisition was made with the intermediation of countess de Starhemberg (1722-1773) who had previously bought porcelain and lacquer from the prince of Carignano. Two Japanese lacquered cabinets which had belonged to the prince and later to Carlo Emanuele III are now in Palazzo Reale in Turin; in addition, both the Museo Civico di Arte Antica and Palazzo Madama have items known to have been in Eugenio's collection of orientalia – a lacquered panel decorated with gold scenes on a black background and a porcelain plate, both of which bear the prince's coat of arms and were made in China during the early 18th century. The most sumptuous example of chinoiserie belonging to Eugenio however, is without any doubt the famous set of fabrics made for a bed chamber and now in the Museum für Angewandte Kunst in Vienna; recently it has been suggested that the fabrics were specifically commissioned by Eugenio and were made in

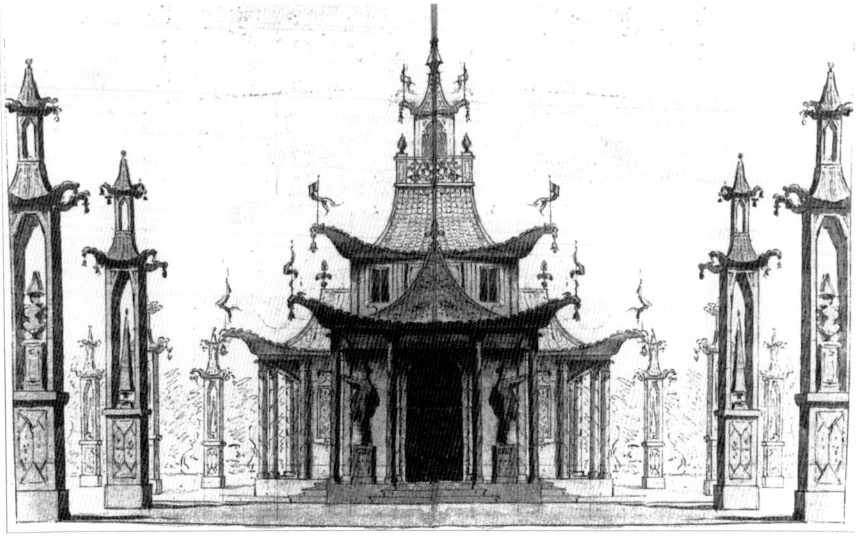

124. Giovannino Galliari, scenery for *L'orfano della China*, ballet by Gasparo Angiolini, Turin, Teatro Regio, 1790. Turin, Museo Civico d'Arte Antica e Palazzo Madama.

India to designs possibly created by Claude le Fort de Plessy.[3]
It was mainly the ladies of the Savoy household who were the most enthusiastic devotees of the oriental style at this time, especially Polyxena Landgräfin (1706-1735), second wife of Carlo Emanuele III whom she married in 1724, and Maria Antonia Ferdinanda of Spain. Various figures close to the two queens were also collectors of Far Eastern wares and enthusiasts of chinoiserie. Antonio Maurizio Solaro of Govone (d. 1765), the younger brother of Giuseppe Roberto, held several important posts in Vienna, Rome and lastly in Paris as the Savoy ambassador to France. Well known in Parisian society and esteemed by Voltaire, he decorated his dining room in Paris with "tenture de papier de la Chine montée sur toile", which was sold at auction following his death in 1765. Count Carlo Francesco Baldassarre Perrone di San Martino (1718-1802) and count Francesco Giuseppe Lascaris di Castellar (1729-1793) were both diplomats in the service of the Savoy court who commissioned grandiose chinoiserie works. On his estate at the old Abbey of Santo Stefano, Perrone had an "enclos à la chinoise" made, a large aviary in the shape of a pagoda, and in his palace at Ivrea he created an entire museum of oriental art, admiringly mentioned by Horace-Bénédict de Saussure (1740-1799) in his volume *Voyage dans les alpes* (1779-1796); in 1876 the museum became merged with the Museo Civico Pier Alessandro Garda in Ivrea. Lascaris di Castellar, Perrone's brother-in-law, was a diplomatic emissary in both Naples (1763-1770) and earlier, from 1754 to 1760, in the Hague from where he sent several consignments of 'pekins' to Turin.
Theatrical performances with Chinese themes were extremely popular around the mid 18th century, particularly following the success of the great carnival procession of the *Emperor of China* organised in Turin in 1749.[4] Metastasio's play *Le Cinesi*, was performed in the city from 1748 to 1750. In

the original production the "noble ladies" were represented in a "room in the Chinese style", but the setting had been transformed in this later version into "nymphs of the village" who were seen "sitting in the countryside". The scenery for *Arsinoe* performed at the Teatro Regio on 14 January 1758 was entirely in the 'Chinese style', while another play completely set in China was *Ghengis Khan*, presented on 18 January 1777. By an unknown author, *Ghengis* was an alternative version of *Arsinoe*, the principle differences being the title and some variations made to the arias and some of the actors' lines. The scenery for *Arsinoe* was created by Fabrizio (1709-1790) and Bernardino Galliari (1704-1794) who had arrived in Turin around 1743-44 and been responsible from 1748 for the stage settings of the Regio theatre, assisted by Stefano Marini who designed the costumes, and Francesco Ladatte. Inspired by the engravings of Chambers, the landscapes of Matteo Ripa, the tapestries of Beauvais and the original oriental artefacts at court, Fabrizio Galliari created an entire 'Chinese-style' stage set in which, "the towers, the roofs, the pagodas [...] the very trees and everything visible proclaim the differences, not so much of nature, but rather of the arts, in this world that is so very unlike ours" (Metastasio referring to his play *L'Eroe cinese*). Neither *Arsinoe* nor *Ghengis Khan* bear any reference to the philosophical vision underlying Metastasio's *L'eroe cinese* or Voltaire's *L'Orphelin de la Chine*, the two most important theatrical productions with a Chinese subject of the 18th century, but instead presented a romantic and mysterious image of old Cathay. Located in an unidentified "palais des Mandarins", the two dramas relate the story of the love between Ghengis Khan and Arsinoe, daughter of the Chinese emperor who has, however, chosen a different lover for her. Angered by the opposition of her father, Ghengis Khan decides to conquer Peking but restore the city to the emperor as a sign of his great love for Arsinoe. This act of generosity by the Mongol commander leads to the establishment of stable peace between the two countries. Thus the two operas are set in 1215, the year when Ghengis Khan's conquest of Peking actually took place. This precise and particular historic setting is the only connection between these two plays and *L'Orphelin* by Voltaire, presented at Carignano near Turin in 1761. This version, produced by Madame La Voie's company of Commediens Français ran for two whole years; there are no records on the other hand of performances of Metastasio's *L'eroe cinese* in Turin.

The Chinese Rooms of Villa della Regina

The four 'Chinese Rooms' of Villa della Regina were commissioned by Polyxena Landgräfin between 1732 and 1735 and Juvarra was assisted in the installation of his creations by Giovanni Pietro Baroni from Tavigliano. Designed by Ascanio Vitozzi (1539-1615) for cardinal Maurizio, the villa remained the property of his widow, Ludovica, until 1692 when it passed to Anne of Orléans, wife of Vittorio Amedeo II, on whose death in 1728 this late mannerist building and delightful gardens were bought by Polyxena. Not

125. Chinese Room, 1732-1735. Turin, Villa della Regina.

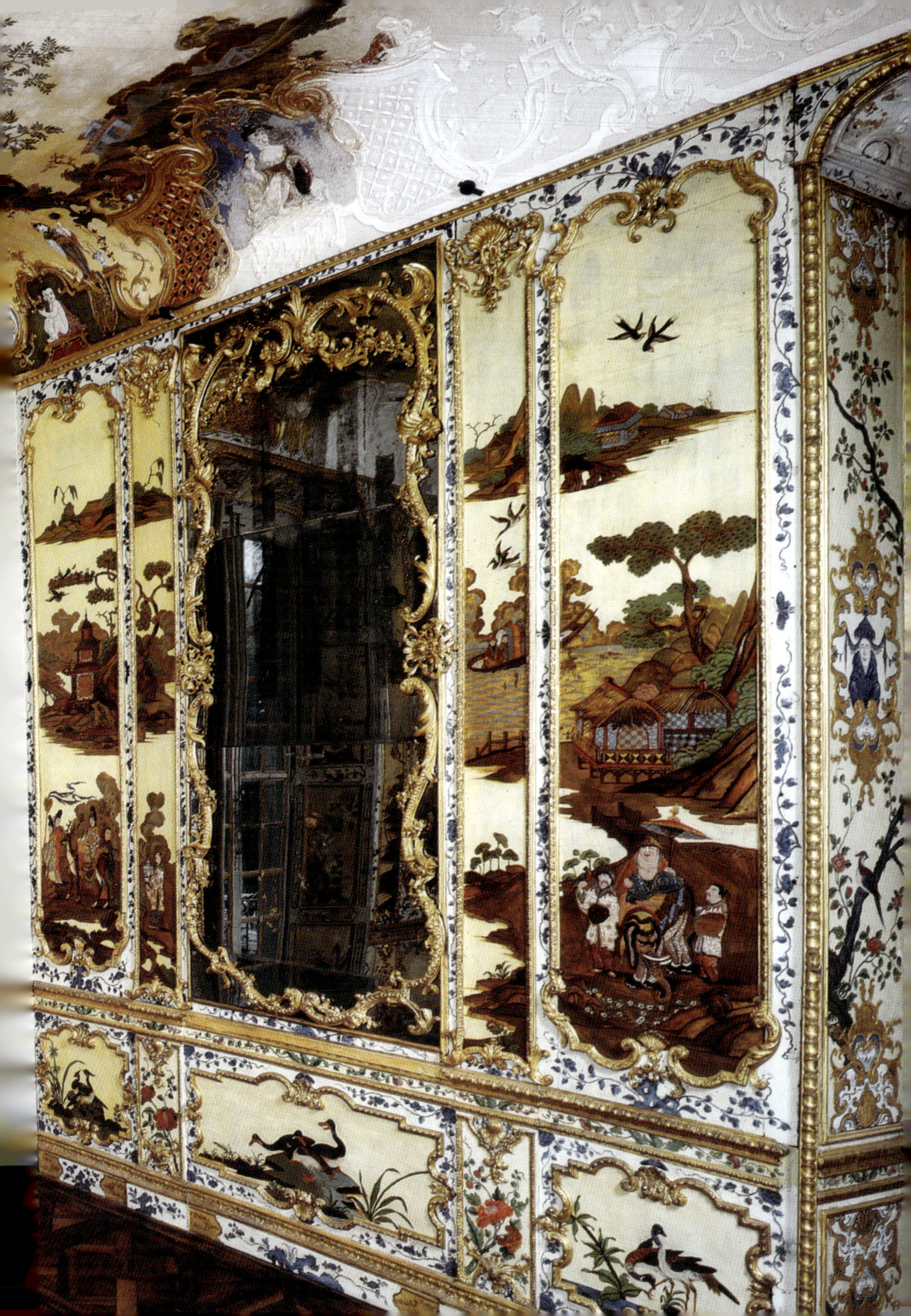

long after work on the Rivoli castle had begun, and contemporary to the renovations of Stupinigi in 1728-29, Juvarra presented his architectural plans for modernization of this Villa too. Work was finalized in 1737 in time for Carlo Emanuele's marriage to his third wife, Elizabeth Therese of Lorraine and most of the internal decorations, including those in oriental style, had also been completed by then. Almost twenty years later, in 1755, Antonia Ferdinanda of Spain and her husband, the hereditary prince Vittorio Amedeo inherited the residence and a complete and detailed inventory was carried out. This inventory was to provide the basis for the recently completed programme of restoration and for all research and study into chinoiserie in Piedmont. Designed by Filippo Juvarra, Villa della Regina is a magnificent example of harmonious planning of open spaces, architectural structure and interior décor and furnishings. Here Juvarra was able to devise a plan – combining aspects of classicism, Arcadia and exoticism, similar to the Parisian 'Menus Plaisirs' – that exploited the natural setting, adopting a more relaxed and flexible style compared to the city palaces where austere official events took place.

The four Chinese Rooms of Villa della Regina are at the furthest ends of the building, in the north and south towers. Three are still in place; the fourth was dismantled and transferred in 1867 to Moncalieri where it remained until 1888, when it was sent to Rome. In 1893, on the occasion of the visit of emperor Wilhelm II (1859-1941) and his wife Augusta Viktoria (1858-

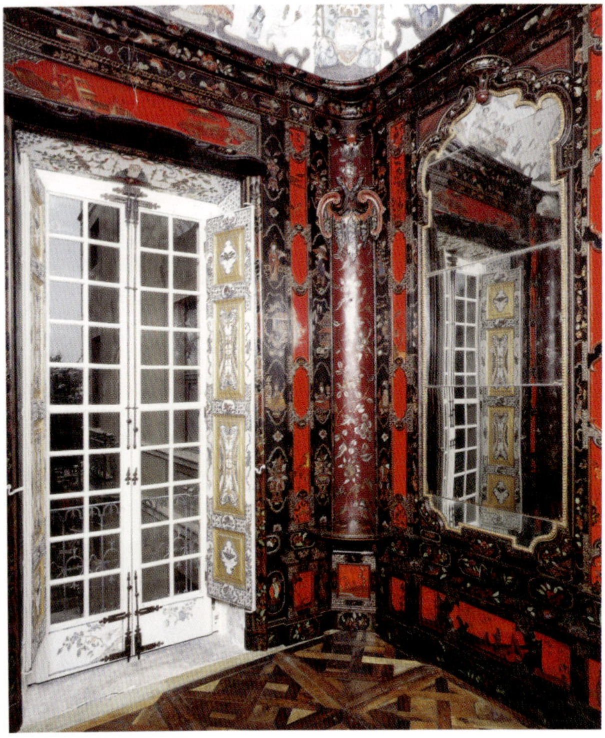

126. Chinese Room, 1732-1735. Turin, Villa della Regina.

1921), a bedroom in the Palazzo del Quirinale was decorated using the painted paper panels originally in the Chinese Room of Villa della Regina, a design of brightly coloured birds, trees and butterflies on a green background, framed with carved and gilded wood. The furniture too had already been sent to Rome from Moncalieri in 1876 and is still in the Quirinale. The room in Villa della Regina which originally housed the paper panels is now unfurnished, but the ceiling still has its original decoration of grotesque motifs and chinoiserie, probably painted by Filippo Minei at the same time as the panels and furniture were installed. Compared to the furnishings now in Rome, the other three rooms still in Villa della Regina – two in the king's apartment and one in the queen's – all have lacquered and decorated panels around the walls, a feature which the compiler of the 1755 inventory was careful to specify, using the term 'alla China' for these three rooms with *boiseries*. Pietro Massa, who had also worked in Palazzo Reale in 1722, was responsible for the decoration of all four Chinese Rooms, and his signature appears several times on some of the decorative details; the designs of the Chinese scenes enhancing the panels and the painted decorations of the ceilings are by him. Massa also coordinated the stucco workers, mainly craftsmen from Lugano, who made the decorations surrounding the wall paintings. One of these was Giovanni Maria Andreoli, known for his work with Giambattista Tiepolo in Udine, who was clearly abreast of the latest French grotesque inventions by Bérain and his contemporaries. Although there are only ten years between the 'Gabinetto del Poggiolo' in Palazzo Reale and the Chinese Rooms in Villa della Regina, Pietro Massa's chinoiserie has clearly developed stylistically and demonstrates a greater harmony. The images used are all obviously based on original Chinese models belonging to the Savoy collections – the figures, the arrangement of the landscapes into parallel diminishing levels, the objects portrayed, the flora and fauna, the choice of colours – are all decorative elements that closely recall designs on lacquer and porcelain, as is the frequent use of mother-of-pearl and blue on a white background, or gold on black and red. The compositions decorating the ceilings recall late 17th-century French designs – though the rustic touch is entirely Piedmontese.

The Chinese Rooms of Palazzo Reale

Chinoiserie decorations designed by Juvarra were introduced to Palazzo Reale at the same time as those of Villa della Regina. The 'Gabinetto del Pregadio' in the Queen's Apartment on the first floor (used by the king in the 1700s) is a supremely subtle combination of the skills of several specialised artists and craftsmen. The chinoiserie in the wainscotting and on the ceiling was made by the prolific workshop of Pietro Massa between 1732-33 using a selection of oriental images similar to those which appear in the Chinese rooms in Villa della Regina. On visiting Turin in 1749 Nicholas Cochin (1715-1790) found the *rocaille* décor of the palace a little overwhelming, "un mélange de

dorures et de glaces... un goût un peu mesquin". Known as the 'Gabinetto del Segreto Maneggio', another room contiguous to the king's bedroom was designed by Juvarra in 1730. Today there is nothing of the Orient about this room, but originally it was known as the 'porcelain room', as a selection of the king's vast collection of Far Eastern porcelain was displayed on tables, niches in the bookshelves and mirror frames, and decorative overdoors (made by Piffetti and Ladatte between 1732 and 1734). Portraying the *Virtues of a Monarch*, the ceiling was decorated by Beaumont (1694-1766). The décor of this 'Gabinetto' was an attractive example of the detailed and intimate style used by Juvarra in the smaller rooms of the palace to counterbalance the austerity and grandeur of the official reception rooms.
The Chinese Room in the King's Apartments on the first floor of Palazzo Reale was also mainly designed by Filippo Juvarra. Although it was not installed until 1736-37 when he had already left Piedmont for Spain, the initial plans date from 1732 when Juvarra was in Rome negotiating the commission for the sacristy of St Peter's, eventually awarded to Galilei by Clement XIII. While in Rome he visited the antique dealers of the city and, as he wrote in a letter of 8 March 1732, one had several "lacquer panels from China and Japan, which I can show to your Highness, a charming decoration for a room or chamber", adding that, "combined with

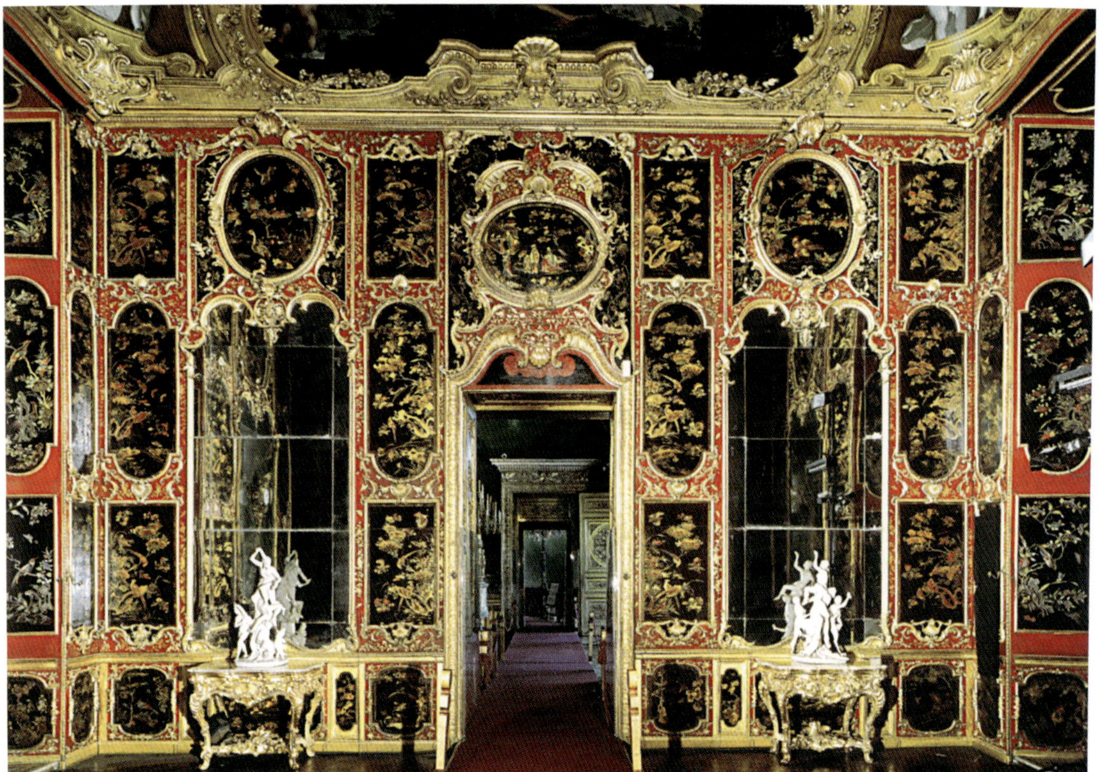

127. Chinese Room, 1736-1737. Turin, Palazzo Reale.

some of the abundant porcelain works in your Highness' collection, they would make a very fine decoration." Samples of the works were sent to Carlo Emanuele III and he agreed to acquire sixty panels from Barozzi (or Barassi) the antique dealer. Once shipment of the pieces had been arranged by Giovanni Battista Orengo, Juvarra set to designing the carved and gilded wood frames to surround the panels and mirrors of the room. The panels were deemed suitable for decorating the Queen's Dressing Room, which later became the office of Carlo Alberto's private secretary. Work must have begun in 1736 when Pietro Massa is documented as having received payment for "making the painted Chinese lacquer at the joints of the twelve panels to decorate the royal dressing room of the queen", as well as "making the painted Chinese lacquer at the joints of four panels for the coffers of the windows, for 86 other panels and inserts and to finish the boiserie ornamentation"; thus, in addition to the joints, he also made several panels decorated with chinoiserie for integration with the original pieces. Other craftsmen and artists worked on the room at the same time, such as the miniaturist Carlo Baroggio, the carvers Alessandro Omma, Carlo Matteo Bogetto, Giovanni Luigi Bosso and Pietro Giuseppe Valle, while the frescoed ceiling was by Beaumont and portrayed the *Judgement of Paris*. The Chinese Room in Palazzo Reale was one of the greatest achievements of the rococo period in Piedmont and is one of Filippo Juvarra's finest masterpieces. The gleam of the gold and the black sheen of the forty original Chinese lacquer panels decorated with delicate scenes of flowers and birds, blend perfectly with the delightful scenes devised by Pietro Massa and the superb wood carving framing both, while the four mirrors on the walls create intriguing reflections and illumination. Charles de Brosses (1709-1777, *Lettres historiques et critiques sur l'Italie, avec des notes relatives à la situation actuelle de l'Italie*), normally rather critical of the Savoy court which he pronounced to be endlessly boring with its rigid formalities, and unbearable for the bitter cold that gripped the palaces even in the springtime, could not avoid remarking – albeit laconically – in a letter sent to Madame de Neuilly on 3 April 1740 of the Chinese Room as "un cabinet tout vernis de la Chine, sur un fond noir; cela est magnifiquement triste". Oddly, as noted by Hugh Honour, the Count of Cork and Orrery (on a visit to Turin in 1754 and not an admirer of chinoiserie) did not mention Juvarra's masterpiece at all and on the contrary stated that "... not one effeminate toy, not one Chinese dragon, nor Indian monster is to be seen".[5]

Some of the Chinese lacquer panels bought by Juvarra in Rome in 1732 were used in 1749 to create another Chinese room on the second floor of Palazzo Reale, this time to provide a dressing room for the future wife of Vittorio Amedeo, Maria Antonia Ferdinanda of Spain. Pietro Massa was again commissioned to make additional panels decorated with chinoiserie scenes to integrate the originals, and the carpentry, carving and gilding were carried out by Carlo Baroggio, Giuseppe Gianotti and Bartolomeo Monticelli respectively. The room was designed by Benedetto Alfieri (1700-1767), architect and pupil of Filippo Juvarra whose example he followed closely. Carlo Emanuele III financed Alfieri to visit the main cities of Europe, studying the developments and innovations taking place, and from 1738 he became director of all new works in Turin, introducing an international style which reflects the lessons of both France and Germany (Cuvilliés, Ferdinand Plitzner, 1678-1724). Where, however, German decoration tended towards some exaggeration, Alfieri reduced the over-statement and was more circumspect, an approach that is particularly noticeable in the smaller rooms. In 1744 Pietro Massa was responsible for the light green lacquer decorated with chinoiserie motifs on the wainscot, doors and window shutters in the Galleria delle Battaglie in the King's Apartment on the first floor of Palazzo Reale. Here he relied on his by now 'classic' oriental repertory, ranging from floral compositions enlivened by birds and insects, to scenes with Chinese figures and motifs partly derived from original Far Eastern iconography and partly from the creativity of other European artists who were skilled chinoiserie designers, especially northern European and German. Carlo Baroggi was the carpenter while the delicate carving of the dado was by Giuseppe Marocco, and Giuseppe Stroppiana was responsible for the gilding, both completed between 1741 and 1742.

A much later work, dated 1789, was the Chinese room in the Apartment of the duchess of Aosta on the second floor of Palazzo Reale. The original Chinese lacquered panels covering the walls once formed screens and consisted of both painted and incised Coromandel pieces decorated with landscape scenes. These were integrated with wooden panels portraying the same subjects, painted in 1789 by Michele Antonio Rapous (1733-1819), an artist particularly well known for his floral compositions, often used on firescreens, dados and overdoors. The chinoiserie on the ceiling and the decorative details were completed by Giovanni Pietro (1713-1798), Pietro Antonio (1727-1788) and Giovanni Battista Pozzo working with Carlo Bellora, while a host of craftsmen was responsible for the carpentry, carving and gilding of both the fittings and the furnishings. Work on the Chinese room was directed by Giuseppe Battista Piacenza (1735-1818) who was responsible for modernising this wing of the palace where the duke of Aosta, Vittorio Emanuele (1759-1824) and his wife Marie Therese of Hapsburg-Este (1773-1832) were to live. Before the complete programme of renovation, begun in 1789, the room had been part of the apartment used by the king's sisters, and Giovanni Vignola had designed the fabrics of the décor. Active from 1750 to 1788, Vignola had created 'à la chinois' paintings on fabrics for Stupinigi in 1761, as well as the decorative paintings on white *gros de tours* and *crosi* fabrics, representing "images of Peking" and "a dissegno chinese" used as hangings, door coverings, and furnishing fabric, all of which were removed before the arrival of the dukes of Savoy. In 1788 Piacenza, working with Carlo Randoni (1755-1831), designed the Chinese room in the castle of Moncalieri, also decorated by the Pozzo family and Carlo Bellora the following year with chinoiserie patterns in a similar style to those of Palazzo Reale.

Rooms decorated with original Chinese lacquer panels, such as these of Piedmont, were also created in Spain in the Granja Royal Palace ("Dormitorio de los Reyes") and San Ildefonso ("Gabinete de los Espejos" or "Tocador de la Reina").[6] Not surprisingly these were also designed by Filippo Juvarra after leaving Piedmont in 1735 for Spain where he worked at the court of Philip V (1683-1746) and Elisabetta Farnese(1692-1766). The palace has yet another Lacquer Room made partly with original Chincse panels and partly with chinoiserie panels made by Spanish craftsmen, designed after 1723 by Andrea Procaccini (1671-1734).[7]

The Chinese Rooms in Other Residences of Piedmont

Between 1737 and 1741 Giovanni Francesco Fariano painted chinoiserie ceilings in the dressing rooms of the kings's and the queen's apartments in the Stupinigi Hunting Lodge designed by Filippo Juvarra in 1729. Fariano was also responsible for the chinioserie motifs on the dado, wainscotting and window shutters and, during the 18th century, the two rooms had wall hangings with oriental subjects in perfect keeping with the theme of the wall decoration. Giovanni Battista Morandi (1710-1767), a botanical artist from Milan who worked at the Botanical Gardens of the Valentino castle from 1732 to 1741 and author of three volumes with drawings of flowers and plants entitled *Academiae Taurinensis*, was paid between 1731 and 1733 for paintings of "arabesques and birds in the Chinese style" on furnishing fabrics

128a,b. Cabinet decorated with *lacca povera*. Piedmont, c. 1740. Turin, Museo Civico d'Arte Antica e Palazzo Madama (inv. 797/L).

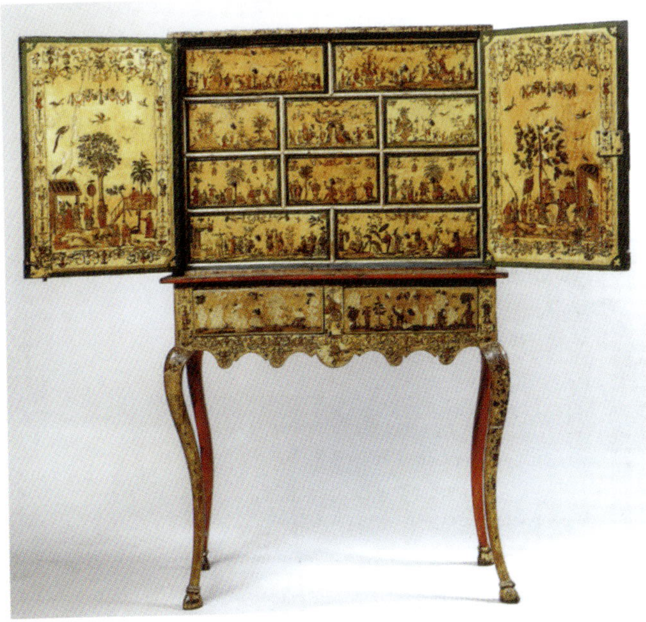

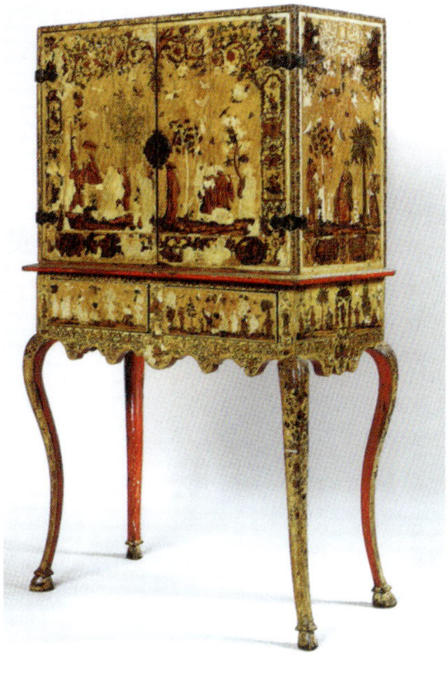

for Stupinigi. It was Fariano, however, who introduced the 'oriental' note to the decoration of the Lodge, successfully combining an ornamental style based on Far Eastern motifs with subjects of European origin. Born in 1681 and a pupil of Minei, Fariano is recorded as first working at Palazzo Reale in 1707, after which he worked on many different commissions in the Savoy residences. One such, in 1735, was the ceiling of the 'Gabinetto della Libreria' in Villa della Regina (now in the Quirinale in Rome), a work that clearly reveals the influence of Elias Baeck and the French ornamental style of the early 1700s. His work is documented until 1753.

Original Chinese lacquered panels were used in the decoration of the four Chinese Rooms in the Venaria Reale castle,[8] designed by Alfieri and made between 1753 and 1755 for the duke and duchess of Savoy, Vittorio Amedeo and Maria Antonia Ferdinanda of Spain. One of these rooms was described in 1764 (*Journey from Geneva to Rome*) "with panels of a fine Chinese lacquer" by the historian and scholar, Edward Gibbon (1737-1794) and by Jérôme De Lalande (*Voyage d'un François en Italie, fait dans les années 1765 et 1766*) who visited the residence in 1765 and commented "L'appartement du Duc de Savoie est très galant; le curieux en vieux laque y trouveront un beau cabinet dans ce genre; il y a aussi dans l'appartement de la Duchesse de Savoie un cabinet de toilete & un boudoir de pareille matiere: ce dernier est incrusté de pierre de lar". None of these Chinese rooms have survived today, but the artist and craftsmen responsible for their creation are known. Pietro Massa made the lacquer sections to integrate the Chinese panels with the help of Francesco Servozelli, active at the court from 1748 to 1758 and doubtless in possession of the 'secret of the lacquer', while the carpentry work was undertaken by various local craftsmen. The duke and duchess took up residence in 1775 and the onerous work of restoration and maintenance was undertaken by gilders Domenico Giardino and Giuseppe Benedetto, miniaturist Giovanni Gallinotti, the sculptor Giuseppe Maria Bonzanigo (1745-1820), and the artists Pietro Antonio Pozzo and Michele Rapous, who is recorded as the painter of various 'Chinese style' decorations. The four rooms were dismantled and moved with many of the furnishings of the Venaria castle in 1817 to the Moncalieri castle, where they were only partially reused. Several of the chinoiserie panels were subsequently sent to Rome in 1878 when Umberto of Savoy (1844-1900) and queen Margherita (1851-1926) took up residence in the Quirinale Palace, and in 1888 as part of the preparations for the arrival of emperor Wilhelm, they were used to create the 'Japanese Salon' in the 'Manica Lunga' of the Imperial Apartments. Work in Rome was directed by the architect Stramucci, while Luca Seri, a cabinet-maker, and Ignazio Perricci, a painter, adapted the panels to the new location. The ceiling was entirely covered with sheets of mirror painted with Japanese decorative motifs that had become popular in the late 19th century. Pietro Massa probably also made three doors and their frames for the Agliè castle in 1753. These are located in a room which, although only redecorated

129. Japanese Salon, 1888. Rome, Palazzo del Quirinale.

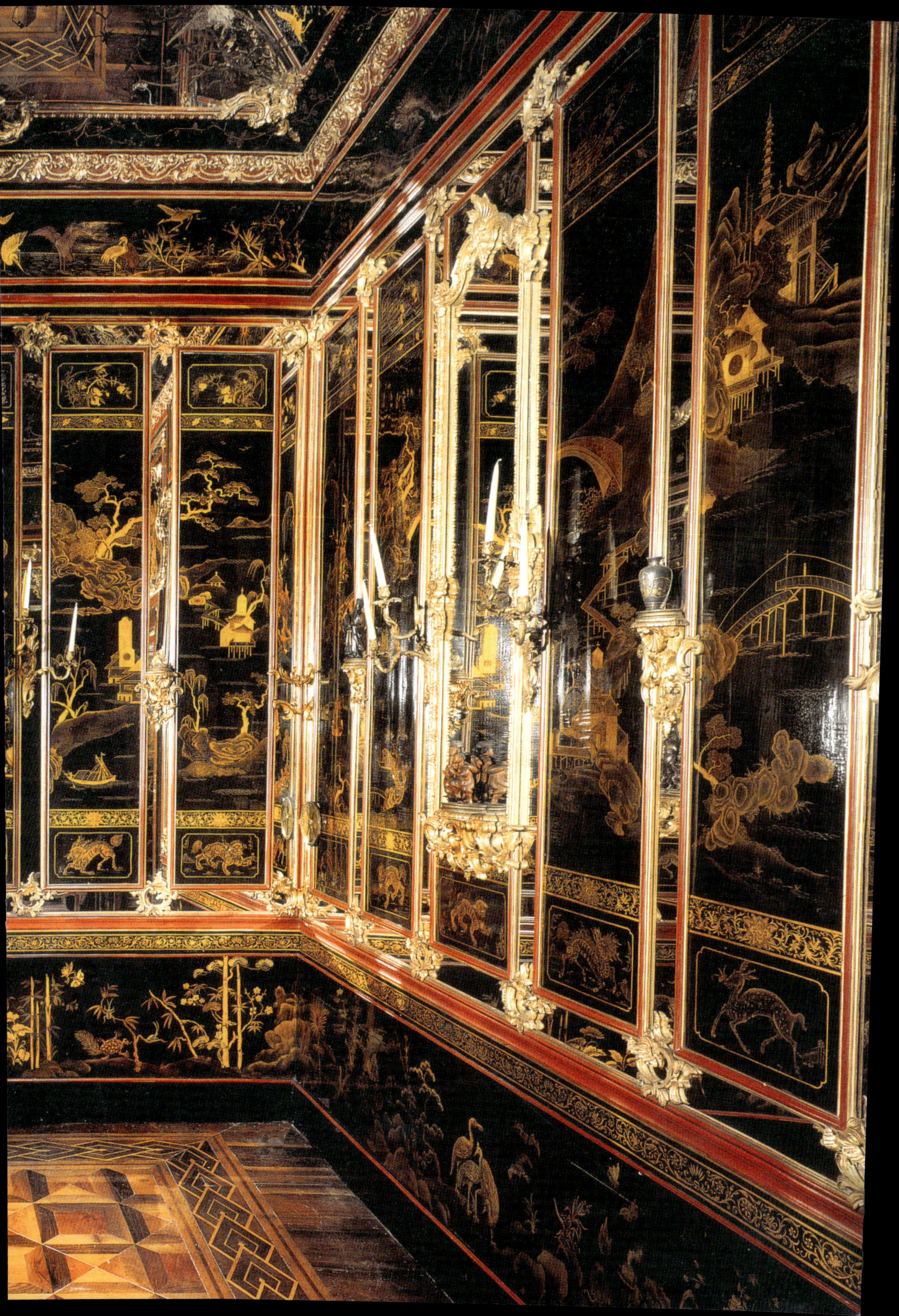

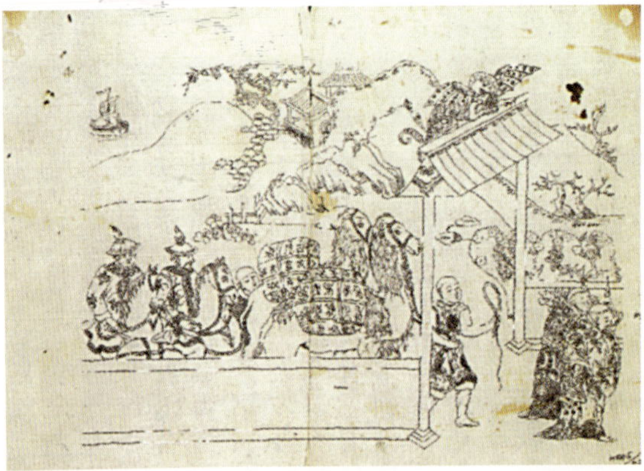
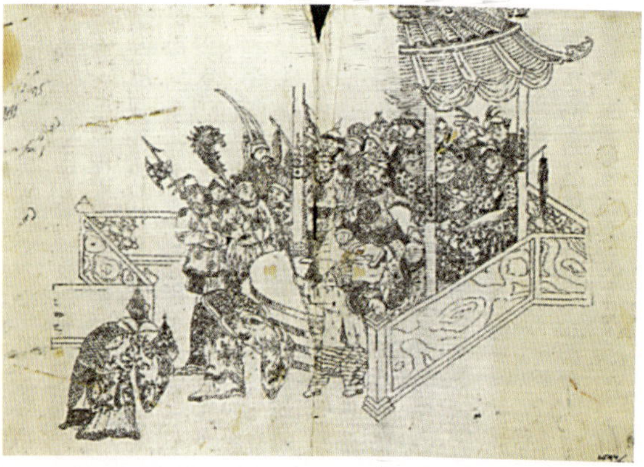

130a,b. Sketches from the *Wehrlin Album*. Turin, Museco Civico d'Arte Antica e Palazzo Madama.

with chinoiserie fittings in the mid 20th century, was originally furnished in oriental style in the 1700s. The castle was acquired by the Savoy in 1776 and was assigned to Benedetto Maurizio, duke of Chablais (1741-1808). Previously, at the time when the doors were made, the villa had been the hereditary seat of the San Martino family. Late 18th-century Savoy inventories record 'Chinese' furnishings in seven of the rooms on the second floor of the castle, all furnished with a great quantity of fabrics and chinoiserie objects, including "33 paintings for overdoors and 6 *sottofornelli*" made by Francesco Rebaudengo in 1775, portraying "flowers and animals in the Chinese style on paper applied to canvas". These six firescreens are still in their original locations.

Abundant evidence of Pietro Massa's prolific activity is also found in Turin in the Graneri palace, built by count De la Roche and designed by Gian Franco Baroncelli in the late 17th century. The palace was inherited during the 18th century by Carlo Gaspare Graneri of Mercenasco (1686-1768), an important member of the Savoy court who set about enhancing the residence with valuable paintings and furnishings to enhance the building. The marriage of his son, Giuseppe Luigi (1724-1786) to Teresa Felicita Cacherano in 1751, provided Carlo Gaspare with a suitable occasion to modernise the palace which originally had two Chinese rooms. One of these is still in place, while the other was acquired by the Kunstgewerbemuseum Staatliche Museen, Berlin in 1982 and was installed in the castle of Köpenick in 2004. Although no specific archival evidence exists, both the Chinese rooms – dating from 1740-50 – may be attributed to the workshop of Pietro Massa as there are strong stylistic similarities to his known works. The repertory of coloured motifs set on black, yellow and red backgrounds both on the boiserie and the ceiling of the room still in its original location, is that most frequently used by Massa and includes the 'flower and bird' compositions, or scenes filled with Chinese characters, portrayed in a style that clearly derived from original Far Eastern works.

Pietro Massa's career is documented until at least 1754 and it is most probable that the lacquered panels of the Chinese room in Villa Vacchetta at

Gerbido di Grugliasco belong to the latter phase of his activity. Bought from the Venetian antique dealer, Loewi in 1954, these are now in the Nelson-Atkins Museum of Art in Kansas City.[9] For the decoration of this room Massa used several compositions from the *Wehrlin Album*, housed in the Museo Civico d'Arte Antica e Palazzo Madama. Bought from Ettore Mentore Pozzi in 1932, the *Album* is a mixed collection of motifs including numerous Chinese themes and some markings and signs (dust shadows, divisions into squares, notes, etc.) would seem to indicate these were workshop materials used for transferring and adapting the decorative motifs. Some of the compositions with Chinese themes in the *Album* are taken directly from engravings in the *Livre de desseins chinois* by Jean-Antoine Fraisse and while not all the details are copied, they have been traced from the prints to be used as guidelines. Other designs in the book seem to be copies of decorations on original Chinese items, probably in the Savoy collections at the time. Fraisse's collection was probably brought to Turin by Gabriel Huquier who had published a new edition of the *Livre* from 1742 to 1750. Other original sources for the *Album* could include a series of drawings in the inventory of the Baroni di Tavigliano collection (1765), or the "various Chinese designs, some in sections" recorded in the possessions of the court painter Giovanni Adamo Wehrlin in 1777.

The son of Giovanni Adamo, Christian Wehrlin was best known in Piedmont as an 'oriental' decorator whose ornamentation of flowers and birds enhanced the walls, wainscot, doors and window shutters of the Games Room (known as the 'Camera Longa' in the 1700s) in the eastern apartments on the ground floor of the Stupinigi palace. The ceiling of the room was painted in the same year by Giovanni Pietro Pozzo, already author of the chinoiserie decorations ornamenting the ceiling of the 'Gabinetto di passaggio' on the ground floor of the Palace in 1761. Pozzo painted exotic birds amidst the Bérain-style arabesques of the ceiling; light and amusing with their brilliant colours and delicate touch, they harmonised perfectly with Wehrlin's compositions below. Wehrlin was particularly concerned that his works should have a natural appearance and his chinoiserie clearly reflects the example of French artists such as Boucher, Huquier and Pillement, but reinterpreted in the light of his botanical studies and artistic skills. A native of Vienna, in 1759 he had visited the Far East with Vitaliano Donati (1717-1762), a scholar from Padova, and no doubt was inspired by the original Chinese wall papers, made for exportation to Europe and already used in various residences of Piedmont in the first half of the 18th century.

Such Chinese wall papers were probably made in Canton and were transported to Europe on the ships of the East India Companies, most frequently as the private goods of the crew members. They were particularly easily identifiable by the themes that they portrayed: flowers and birds, life in a Chinese village with pavilions and figures, literary and theatrical themes, silk making, production of rice and tea, and porcelain manufacture. Rooms were decorated with Chinese papers not only in Stupinigi, where there were two in the east apartments where the Games Room was, but also in the castles of Govone and Racconigi, in the Villa d'Aglié, palazzo Lascaris in Turin (lost during the war), Villa Moglia in Chieri (partly recomposed in 1928 in the Museo Civico d'Arte Antica e Palazzo Madama in Turin), Palazzo Grosso in Riva di Chieri, Villa Il Maggiordomo at Gerbido di Grugliasco, the castle of Guarene, the castle of San Martino Alfieri, the castle of Masino, Villa Agnelli at Villar Perosa, Palazzo Doria di Ciriè, the Museo Civico di Carignano, and the Piossasco castle in Virle.

The 18th century also saw the use throughout Europe of painted silks from China to cover the walls of entire rooms, although paper was preferred as it was certainly less expensive. Only one example has survived in Piedmont, in the Castle of Cavour at Santena, where a salon on the ground floor is decorated with ten large silk panels painted with sprays of flowers framed with wood. Unfortunately the archival information available is not sufficient to explain their origin. An all-too-vague reference indicates that in 1773 Francesco Rebaudengo was paid by the count of Cavour for some work 'in the Chinese style'; similarly the Chinese décor of the main bedroom in the castle is also insufficiently documented. However, the bedroom was notable not only for the panels of Chinese paper, but also for the fabric that covered the bed, a silk with oriental floral motifs, manufactured in Piedmont during the 1760s. Similar Chinese silks are also found in two rooms of the Peterhof in St Petersburg, designed by the court architect, Francesco Bartolomeo Rastrelli (1700-1771) in 1750.

A painter specialized in Chinese style decoration, Francesco Rebaudengo, was active in the second half of the 18th century. Five rooms in the Chinese apartment on the first floor of the Racconigi castle are decorated with original Chinese papers brought from London in 1756 when modernization began and Rebaudengo's workshop may have been responsible for the matching painted papers used for overdoors, firescreens and above mirrors. Pietro Massa may also have participated in the renovation project, but it has not been possible to identify his work. A payment to Rebaudengo is recorded in 1771, but the artist's most prestigious commission was the decoration of Palazzo Chiablese in Turin. The residence was intended for the duke of Chablais, Benedetto Maurizio, son of Carlo Emanuele III and Elizabeth Therese of Lorraine in 1741. Modernization began in 1754 under the direction of Benedetto Alfieri, first on the 'piano nobile' and from 1775 on the rooms reserved for duchess Maria Anna. The panels for the duchess' dressing room on the first floor of the palace were painted with Chinese motifs of birds and flowers by Rebaudengo. The room was destroyed in 1943 but some period photographs have survived and Onorato Derossi described the design in his *Nuova guida per la Città di Torino* in 1781.

131. The Games Room, 1765. Stupinigi, Palazzina di Caccia.

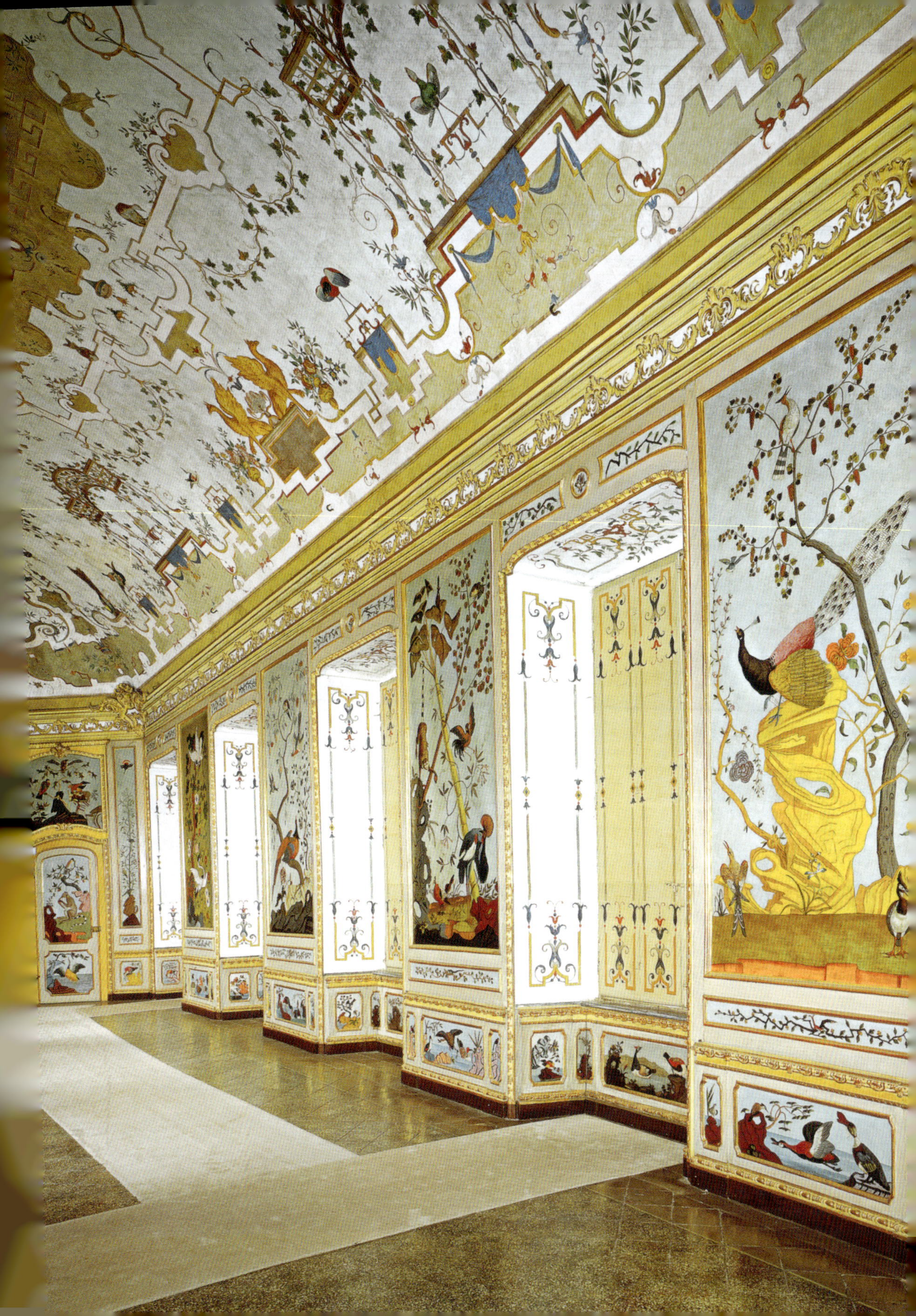

Neoclassicism

In 1767 the theatrical company of Antonio Sacchi presented Carlo Gozzi's 'romantic tragicomedy' *Turandot* which ran with success for two seasons. The Chinese theme was continued in 1771 when as part of the wedding celebrations for Giuseppina of Savoy (1753-1810) and the Count of Provence, the artistic director of the Teatro Regio, Filippo G. B. Nicolis di Robilant, designed four pavilions "dans le goût chinois" with four orchestras "pour l'amusement du Peuple"; an engraving of the event by Pietro Peiroleri (1741-1771) shows that the musicians too were in Chinese costume. Two decades later, at a ball held in 1791 in Palazzo Levaldigi, the musicians conducted by Gaetano Pugnani (1739-1798) were "all dressed in long silk robes and wore Chinese hats". The year before, on 23 January 1790, *L'orfano della China*, a ballet by Gasparo Angiolini (1731-1803), was performed at the

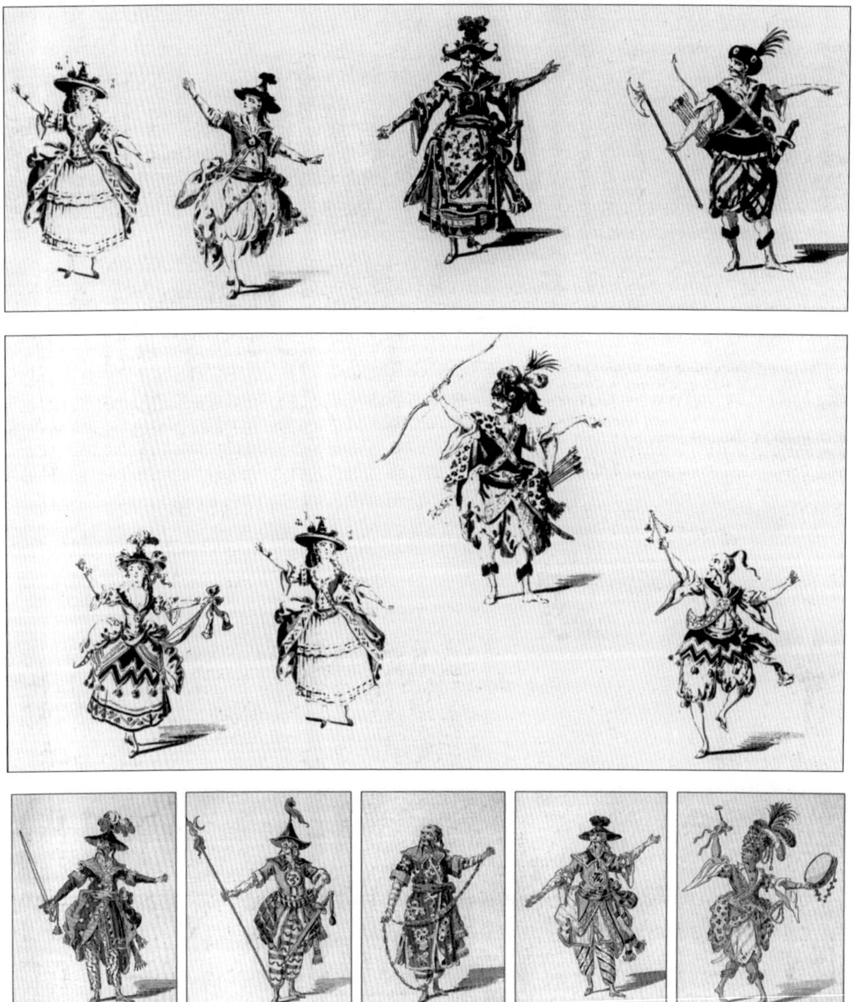

132a-g. L. Marini, Costume designs for *L'orfano della China*.

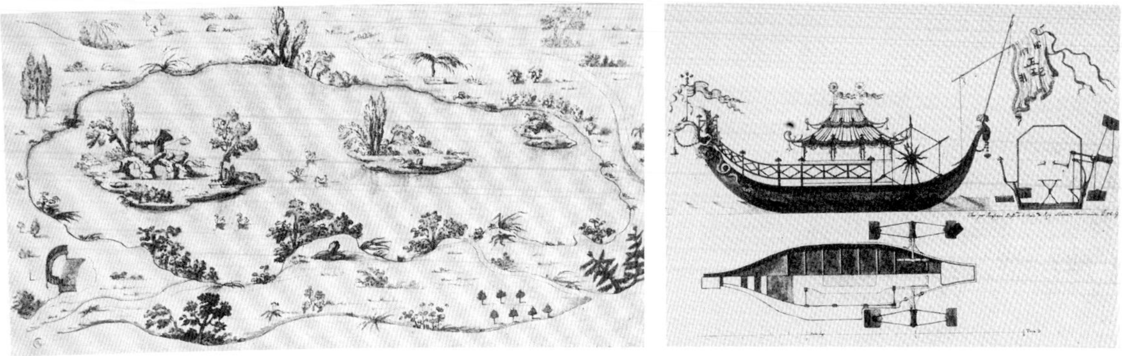

133a,b. Giacomo Pregliasco, Design for a 'Chinese style' garden in the Racconigi park, late 18th century. Private collection.

These two drawings were made towards the end of the 18th century when Giacomo Pregliasco was commissioned to redesign the Racconigi Park for Giuseppina of Lorraine, widow of Vittorio Amedeo, prince of Carignano. The style adopted was that of the eclectic 'anglo-chinois' garden so popular at the time.

Teatro Regio. Based on the play by Voltaire, the ballet had been performed in Vienna in 1774 and also in Turin in 1781, but in this particular period of strong social tensions, it reinforced the image of China as an egalitarian society and as an example for European nations. Sketches of the stage designs by Giovannino (1746-1818) and Giuseppe Galliari (1752-1817), and of the costumes by Leonardo Marini (1730-1789) for this later production have survived. Marini was the costume designer for the Teatro Regio from 1769, and during the last quarter of the 18th century – the period when classicism was regaining favour – was one of the most important innovators of decorative styles in Piedmont. Author of the volume *Studi diversi di decorazione inventati, disegnati ed in gran parte eseguiti di Leonardo Marini, disegnatore del Gabinetto del re di Sardegna, pittore professore della reale Accademia delle Belle Arti* (Turin, Biblioteca Reale), Marini also devised a "Chinese Room, ornamented with Chinese porcelain and shells. The remaining parts in lacquered boiserie", which recalls elements of Wehrlin with references to Chambers' compositions and the ornamentation of Jacques François Blondel (1705-1774) and Charles Delafosse (1636-1716). He also designed an exotic *boudoir* in 1780 for the princess of Carignano; the style chosen for the octagonal divan and the bulbous form of the buildings illustrated on the walls are clearly derived from Middle Eastern examples, although Marini himself specified that it should be "decorated with Chinese and Japanese porcelain".[10]

The balletic version of *L'orfano della China* was repeated at the Teatro Regio in 1805 by Giovanni Monticini and sketches of the costumes designed by Giacomo Pregliasco (1759-after 1823) also still exist. The decision to present the victory of the conqueror Ghengis Khan as opposed to Voltaire's original plot seems to have been a homage to Napoleon's contemporary successes. Pregliasco – "Dessinateur du Roi et de S.A.S. le Prince de Carignan" – was a firm enthusiast of the neoclassical style and in 1787 created a project for Maria Josepha of Lorraine (widow of Vittorio Amedeo, prince of Carignano) to transform part of the Racconigi park – made a century earlier by Le Nôtre – into an 'anglo-chinois' garden.[11]

Francesco Rebaudengo also worked on Villar Perosa and Villa Cravanzana in

Moncalieri, but his last piece of chinoiserie was the ceiling of the Chinese room in the apartment of the dukes of Aosta, Vittorio Emanuele and Marie Therese of Hapsburg-Este on the second floor of the Rivoli castle. Built between 1793-94 the room was designed by the architect Carlo Randoni and a plan for the decoration is housed in the Biblioteca Civica of Turin.[12] Rebaudengo's chinoiserie at Rivoli reflects the stylistic features and format of French 'Louis Seize' neoclassicism and represents the final phase of the oriental style in 18th-century Piedmont.

Ceramics

Ceramic production in Piedmont during the 18th century can be traced through the history of the Rossetti firm. In 1725 Giorgio Giacinto Rossetti was given official permission by Vittorio Amedeo II to establish a majolica factory in Turin. In 1727, however, he was excluded from the economic management of the business due to disputes with the other financiers and he left Turin for a brief but profitable period working in Lodi. In 1736 he was recalled by count Carlo Giacinto Roero di Guarene (1675-1749) who had become sole owner of the factory in 1728. During this period production was obviously very similar to that of Lodi, but was also influenced by the ceramics of Delft and the French factories of Moustiers, Rouen and Nevers, where decoration at the beginning of the 18th century relied heavily on the grotesques of Bérain.

In 1737 Carlo Emanuele III, in the hope of founding a factory similar to those of other European courts, gave Giorgio Giacinto Rossetti the royal right to produce porcelain, as well as a large loan to be repaid in twenty years.[13] Most probably the Rossetti family were in contact with Vezzi in Venice, although the factory had closed in 1727. Following an unsuccessful journey to Paris, Rossetti consulted specialists at the Du Paquier factory in

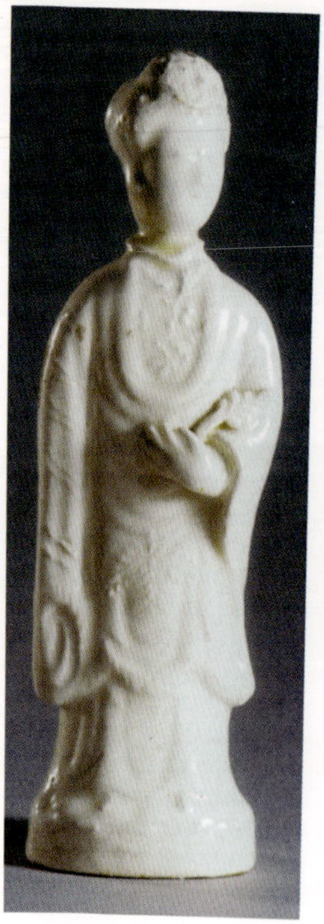

135. Porcelain Guanyin figure. Turin, Rossetti factory, 1737-1743. London, British Museum.

The paste and form of this small figure are of the highest quality. The statuette is one of the extremely rare pieces made during the few months when the Rossetti factory experimented with porcelain production. The figure also demonstrates that the ceramists of Piedmont were extremely knowledgeable about Far Eastern models: this European version of figures representing the Buddhist goddess Guanyin, is very close in style to the Chinese originals.

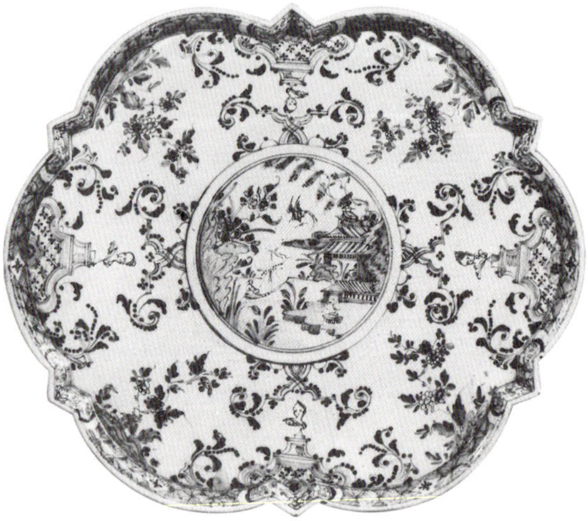

134. Large dish. Turin, Rossetti factory, second quarter of 18th century. Turin, Palazzo Madama.

A chinoiserie theme is present in the central image representing a lakeside scene with plants, a boat with fishermen and a pavilion on the right. The surrounding decorative motifs are early 17th century French, widely used on the ceramic works of Moustiers, Rouen and Nevers.

136. Large dish, last quarter of the 18th century. Vinovo factory. Turin, Palazzo Madama.

Decorated with a French-style chinoiserie scene, this dish is an example of Vinovo's ceramic production in the 1770s-80s. Towards the end of the century oriental themes were dropped from the factory's designs to make way for new patterns in the neoclassical style.

Vienna and in 1742, after difficult negotiations, succeeded in convincing the decorator Jakob Helkis, a pupil of Ignaz Bottengruber, and his colleague Anton Wagner to move to Turin. Production of porcelain was rapidly under way but continued only until 1743 when count Roero sold the factory to Carlo Giuseppe Bilotto, and by 1748 the Rossetti were forced to renounce their royal privileges due to the excessively high costs involved. Lasting a mere decade, only a few examples of Turin's porcelain production remain as evidence of the high standard and quality achieved by the Rossetti brothers. The works produced include 'blue and white' cups with floral motifs derived from oriental repertories and quite similar to those used at Meissen and Vienna, but also the traditional white figures portraying Chinese Quanyin produced by the Dehua factories in the south of the Fujian province.[14]
For almost two decades after the failure of the Rossetti factory, only foreign porcelain was used in Piedmont. Chinese and Japanese works were acquired from the Dutch, Portuguese and occasionally Viennese markets and European items were bought mainly from Meissen and later Vincennes and Nymphenburg. Rossetti continued to produce fine ware until 1765, the same year that Ardizzone's ceramic factory began production (though this too closed just six years later in 1771) and the Vische porcelain factory opened.[15] Vische moved to Vinovo in 1776 and its production tended to emulate French models, rarely resorting to Chinoiserie decorations.

1) Caterina-Mossetti 2005: where not otherwise specified, all references are taken from this text.
2) Honour 1961 (1963), p. 142.
3) Volker 2007.
4) Zoli 1974, p. 114.
5) Honour 1961 (1963), p. 137.
6) Lavalle-Cobo 2003.
7) García Fernández 2003.
8) Venaria Reale 2007.
9) Honour 1961 (1963), p. 143; Jacobson 1993, p. 115.
10) Colle 2005, p. 399.
11) Tagliolini 1988, pp. 330-332, figs. 225-226.
12) Colle 2005, pp. 430-431, no. 99.
13) Brosio 1973, p. 30.
14) Pettenati in Arte di Corte a Torino 1987, pp. 221-229.
15) Brosio 1973, p. 26.

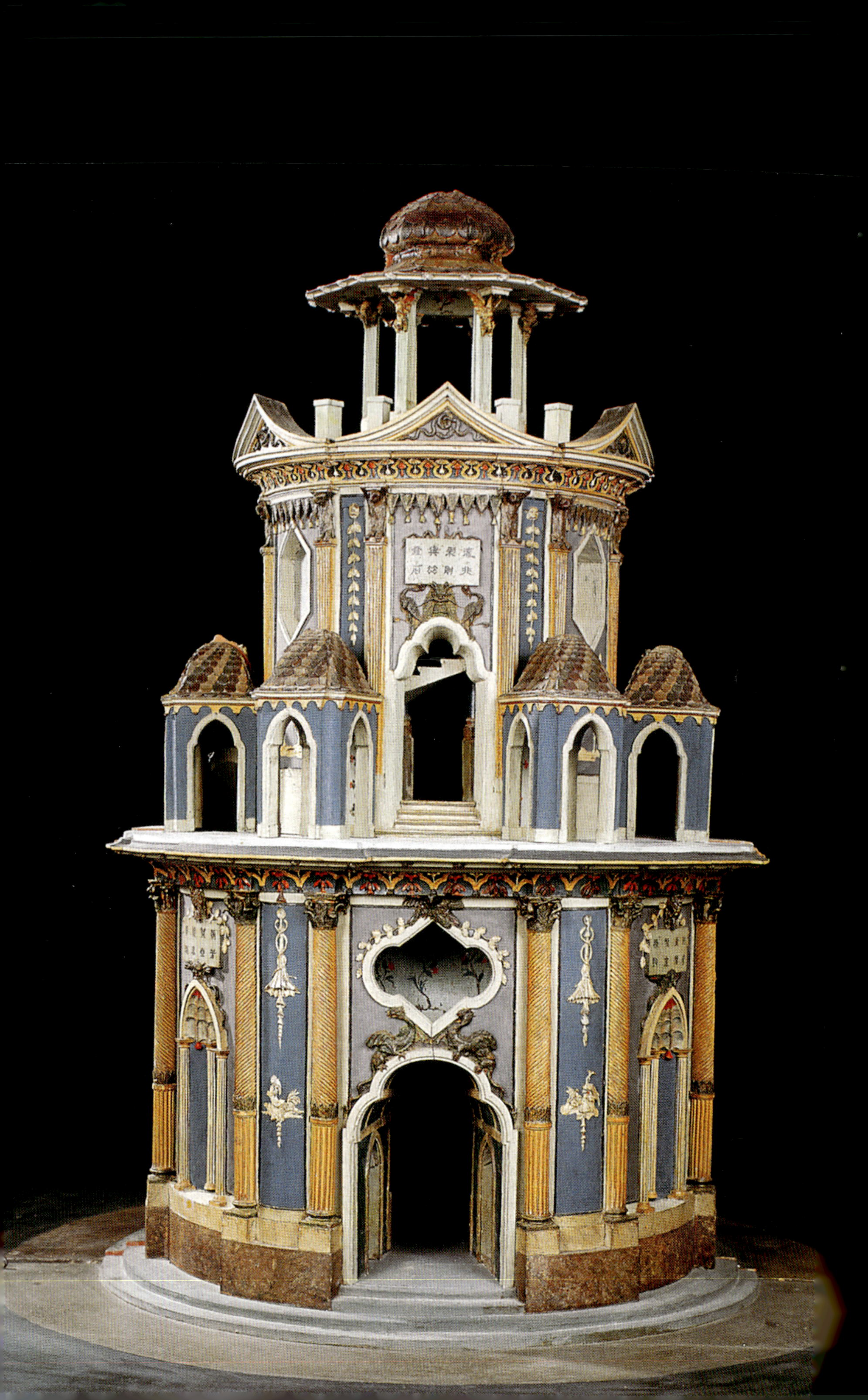

The Kingdom of Naples and Sicily

The 17th Century

A passion for the Orient and its art already flourished in Naples during the 17th century, although no artistic items of that period have survived to indicate just how the fashion evolved. And yet, as early as 1634 Giulio Cesare Capaccio (*Il Forestiero*) wrote that "the decorations that have come from China are wonderful", indicating that enthusiasm for Chinese style furnishings was already quite a widespread phenomenon.[1] Documents of the day contain many references to the style which developed during the first quarter of the 17th century when the merchant ships of northern European countries began to appear more frequently in the harbour of Naples, which at the time was capital of the Spanish protectorate. Thus all kinds of goods arrived in the city from distant eastern lands, delighting in particular the large community of Flemish merchants who had settled there, becoming altogether quite 'Neapolitan'.

The inventory of Gaspare Roomer, drawn up on his death in 1674, lists for example two trunks "in the Chinese style", a "writing desk with Indian decoration", another "with Chinese decoration" and "two trunks from China with gold leaf". His library too contained geographical texts and books that reveal his curiosity in far-flung lands, such as the *Relatione della gran monarchia della China* by Father Alvarez Ximenes.[2] A subject of the king of Spain, Gaspare Roomer (c. 1590-1674) had no difficulty in obtaining oriental goods, even in the 1630s shortly after his move to Naples.

The description of the items mentioned in the inventory is slightly ambiguous, but the document does differentiate quite precisely between 'Chinese style' furnishings and those 'from China' thus suggesting that he owned both original Chinese (or more generally oriental) items and reproductions, probably made in northern Europe although it is not impossible that Neapolitan craftsmen also copied the style. Despite the Chinese motif they bore, the thousands of pieces of majolica that Giovanni Andrea Bianchini from Savona sold to Giacinto Angiero in Naples were quite obviously from the factories of Liguria – as too were the "imitation porcelain of Genoa and of China" that the painter Marc'Antonio Ghirardi sent in 1675 to his father Bernardo in Naples. It would seem that 17th-century Ligurian ceramics decorated with Chinese designs were considered by these Neapolitans to be a more economic substitute and much easier to obtain than the rare Far Eastern wares.

137. Luigi Vanvitelli, Model for the Chinese Pavilion at the Palace of Caserta, c. 1760. Caserta, Reggia.

Although not particularly fond of chinoiserie, Luigi Vanvitelli – chief architect to the court of Naples – designed this pavilion to satisfy the Bourbon rulers and their passion for the Orient. Intended for the garden extending around the Caserta palace, unfortunately the Chinese-style structure was never built. Despite the presence of a mixture of eastern styles, including references to the Middle East, the overall structure of the building is classical, and thus still manages to reflect Vanvitelli's architectural preferences.

In the same period, writing desks 'from India' or 'Indian-style' were recorded in the inventory of the possessions of the princess of Sanza drawn up in 1662. Similar items are described in documents referring to the belongings of Troiano Spinelli (1676), duke della Torre, count del Carpio (viceroy from 1683 to 1687) and Stefano Carrillo Y Salsedo (1698). The inventory made on the death of Desiderio Gaulchier a dealer in jewellery from Lorraine included, "a tortoise shell writing desk with silver decoration", "nine stucco reliefs painted in the style of Brussels", "four large trunks of tortoise shell decorated with silver in the French style", "four stucco reliefs painted in the Chinese style and three smaller ones painted in the same fashion". Most probably all these items were made in Europe in an 'exotic' style and were imported to Naples from France. In 1683 the Neapolitan silversmith, Giuseppe D'Urso, was paid for making 26 'palmi' of an 'Indian-style' chain for two censers belonging to the church of Gesù. It would seem therefore that various factors combined to encourage the spread of an oriental fashion in Naples during the 17th century: the arrival of original items from the Far East, a demand for copies of oriental items made in Europe, and the adoption by local craftsmen of oriental decorative motifs and traditional techniques.

The exotic style continued to develop in Naples during the 1600s and the final years of the century saw the publication in 1698 of six volumes entitled *Giro del Mondo* by Francesco Gemelli Careri (1651-1725). Born in Reggio Calabria, Gemelli Careri was a jurist who held a series of administrative posts in the Kingdom of Naples. Between 1685 and 1687 he had journeyed widely in Europe and published his account of the trips in a volume entitled *Viaggio in Europa.* The experience encouraged him to depart again almost immediately, this time to travel around the world, leading to his next publication, *Giro del Mondo.* So well did both these books sell that they were reprinted just a year after their first edition. Despite being strongly criticised for plagiarism by the Jesuits in particular, Gemelli Careri's work, which included a set of descriptive plates, contributed greatly to an awareness of the Far East in Naples.[3] Without doubt the best-known of these plates illustrated the *Nanking Porcelain Pagoda*, which Careri had seen in the city in 1695 and represented in a style which was very similar to other 17th-century prints of China, especially those accompanying Nieuhoff's text (1665).[4] However, Gemelli Careri was possibly the first to express some negative opinions concerning the Chinese character and their public administration, leading to some xenophobic and anti-Chinese feeling during the course of the 18th century. This attitude was further encouraged by the publication of the book *Voyage Round the World* (London 1748) by George Anson (1697-1763), the travel diary of Loren Lange, a Swede in the service of Tsar Peter the Great (1721-22), the negative opinions of Montesquieu and Rousseau, and in Italy by the critical barbs of Abbots Roberti (1719-1786)and Stagni:[5] "If, in judging their disputes, the Mandarins did their duty according to the laws

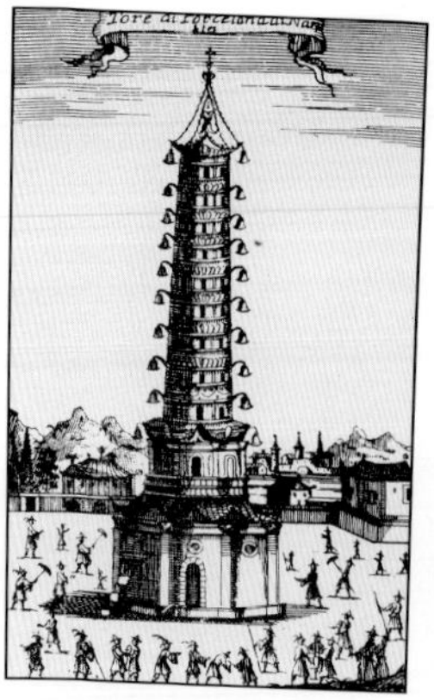

138. *The Nanking Porcelain Pagoda*, engraving from the *Giro del Mondo* by G.F. Gemelli Careri, Naples 1698.

The engraving of the Nanking porcelain tower in Gemelli Careri's book is one of the many heirs of the print contained in Nieuhoff's publication (1665). There can be no doubt that Vanvitelli also based his design for the Chinese pavilion on this image, re-utilizing the two lower floors (see previous illustration).

and intentions of the King, China would be the happiest place in the world and the best governed; but as much as they are rigorous observers of their ascribed external formalities, internally they are malignant, hypocritical and cruel" (Gemelli Careri 1698, from *Parte quarta contenente le cose più ragguardevoli vedute nella Cina*).[6]

The Austrian Vicereign

Naples enjoyed a rather prolific period of artistic output during the Austrian vicereign (1707-1734), partly due to a healthy patronage of the arts and crafts by the seven successive governors of the Kingdom. All forms of art and architecture benefited from this fertile climate; indeed, given that traditionally the initiatives of architects generally also stimulate the decorative arts, the early decades of the 1700s produced a more homogenous style as the external appearance of buildings reflected their contents and furnishings, establishing a degree of continuity.

Early in the century architects too seem to have been influenced by the oriental fashion. Domenico Antonio Vaccaro (1681-1745), whose vast output dates precisely from the period when baroque exuberance evolved into rococo caprice, was clearly aware of chinoiserie novelties as listed in the inventory made in the year of his death that recorded "two large Chinese-style bureaux with gilded carving and frame". Similar in style to many other cabinets made in Europe, these were described in 1751 as "decorated with Chinese figures and lacquered". Most probably chinoiserie details enhanced the frames which the prince of Tarsia commissioned in 1733 from an ornamentalist for several of Vaccaro's paintings, "quite certain that these will be in the latest fashion" and "of whimsical design".

Original Far Eastern works became increasingly available in Naples as elsewhere, encouraging the spread of the fashion. In 1709 the economist Paolo Mattia Doria (1667-1746), aware of the extent of the trend, strongly advised however continuing to invest in gold and silver, rather than in "pottery from the lands of China and Japan", which had become so common that "many rare things from China" could actually be bought on the stalls of local markets, as Raillard also mentions in his *Avvisi* in 1715. In his writings, on the other hand, Doria praised Chinese standards compared to the decadent western political and economic systems,[7] thus opposing the opinion of Giovan Battista Vico (1668-1744) who was quite critical both of the country and its practices, but also of the Jesuits;[8] Doria's considerations were later reinforced by Antonio Genovesi (1713-1769), a follower of Voltaire's enlightened teachings, although he was sceptical about the Chinese legislative system.[9]

Large quantities of goods in an oriental style are therefore recorded in many an aristocrat's inventory in the city, such as the possessions of Carlo Francesco Spinelli (1734), or the inventories of the Serra family. On the

whole, the items are porcelain 'of China' and 'Chinese style' lacquer, partly original items from the Far East, no doubt, but also examples of the creativity of European craftsmen, including those of Naples, in emulating techniques and motifs of oriental models. There is no doubt however, about the Italian origin of the five 'door screens' "with paintings of China in gold, with foliage and lacquer similar to that of China", which the prince of Cariati commissioned from Stefano Moricone of Palermo before 1729, "currently in Naples, and a painter of Chinese lacquer". This provides firm evidence that in Sicily too a tradition of chinoiserie décor had developed from quite an early date and continued to flourish during the 18th century.
Neapolitan chinoiserie was favoured not only in secular, but also religious circles during the 1700s. In the monastery of Santa Maria alla Stella, originally owned by the brotherhood of St Francis of Paola the first of two rooms that once housed the apothecary's shop was frescoed in 1707 with arabesques entwining around medicinal herbs, astrolabes and scenes with Buddhist, Chinese and Indian monks. Refurbished according to a design by Bartolomeo Granucci in 1729, both the internal and external decoration of the church of Santa Maria Vertecoeli have a strongly oriental flavour; meanwhile, it seems the nuns of the Santa Chiara convent specifically requested that their cells should be decorated in the 'Chinese style'.
Though it may seem strange that religious orders in Naples were enthusiastic about oriental themes, their interest is easily explained by the presence in the city of the Chinese College. The institution was founded in 1724 by Matteo Ripa (1682-1746) who had lived in China from 1710 to 1723, with the aim of educating the Chinese who had been converted in their homeland and followed Ripa on his return to Italy.
As early as 1715, when still in Asia as a missionary, Ripa seems to have decided to establish a Seminary in Naples and the opportunity presented itself when he left China to return home against, however, the orders of the Roman Curia. At the time political conditions had become dangerous to the point that the safety of European missionaries could no longer be guaranteed. The rise to power of emperor Yongzheng (1723-1736) lead to a violent resurgence of anti-Christian feeling in the country after a lengthy period of tolerance ratified by an edict of 1692 issued by emperor Kangxi (1662-1722), which had guaranteed freedom of worship and evangelization throughout the country. Subsequently relations between the Chinese government and the church of Rome, represented in Asia by numerous missionaries, had broken down over the 'Chinese Rites Controversy'.[10]
A certain tendency to a French-style absolutist approach, supported by the papacy, an increasing distrust of the Jesuits, opposition from the Portuguese who felt the church was a growing threat to their commercial interests in the Indian Ocean, were just some of the reasons why the efforts made since the beginning of the 16th century by the Jesuits, and especially Matteo Ricci, to achieve progress in China were completely destroyed in just a few years. The

successes obtained by missionaries in the Far East made an immense contribution to the development in Europe of that concept of a 'mythical China' expounded in various texts, especially the writings of Leibniz. Particularly in his *Novissima Sinica, historiam nostri temporis illustratura* published in Hanover in 1697, Leibniz proposes the theory that there is a degree of similarity between the teachings of Christ and those of Confucius. In Italy interest in Confucianism reached its height in 1660 with the first publication in Europe of the sayings of the Chinese philosopher translated by the Sicilian Jesuit Prospero Intorcetta (1626-1696).[11] Papal intransigence regarding the 'Chinese Rites' was at its most peremptory at the end of the 17th century. In 1673 Charles Maigrot, apostolic vicar of the southern province of Fukien, had rewritten and adjusted the rites and in 1704 pope Clement XI secretly promulgated an edict condemning this version.
In 1705 the pope sent cardinal Charles Tommaso Maillard de Tournon (1668-1710, one of the founders of Arcadia and the patriarch of Antioch) to China in order to deal directly with the *vexata quaestio*. The Jesuit fathers Filippo Grimaldi, Tommaso Pereira and Antonio Thomas succeeded in arranging a presentation with the emperor during which, however, Maillard de Tournon found he had to face the opposition not only of the Chinese court, but also of the Jesuits themselves. As a consequence in 1707 he made the papal edict of 1704 public in China. Cardinal Maillard was arrested at Canton and was subsequently transferred to a prison in Macao where he died in 1710. The controversy was only brought to an end during the papacy of pope Benedict XIV who promulgated the two bulls *Ex Quo Singulari* (1742) and *Omnium Sollicitudinum* (1744), subsequent to the bull *Ex Illa Die,* published in 1715. The rigid stance of the church of Rome concerning Chinese customs effectively brought to an end a lengthy period during which Europeans, mainly following the judicious example of the Jesuits, had attempted a low-key approach based more on a desire to communicate and collaborate than on a tactic of confrontation, force or imposition. The situation became increasingly difficult until it degenerated into violent episodes during the 19th century.[12] The presence in Naples of the Chinese College founded by Ripa stimulated the cultural debate regarding the situation in the Far East, while artistically it also influenced the work of many Neapolitan craftsmen who ventured into the realms of chinoiserie. This Jesuit priest donated his collection of Far Eastern items to the institute, including many pieces of Chinese and Japanese porcelain.[13] Ripa was an adept painter and cardinal Tournon had sent him to Peking as an artist at the court of Kangxi where the Chinese sovereign commissioned him to illustrate thirty-six views of imperial palaces and gardens. These became known throughout Europe and provided a source of inspiration for the creation of 'anglo-chinois' gardens.[14]

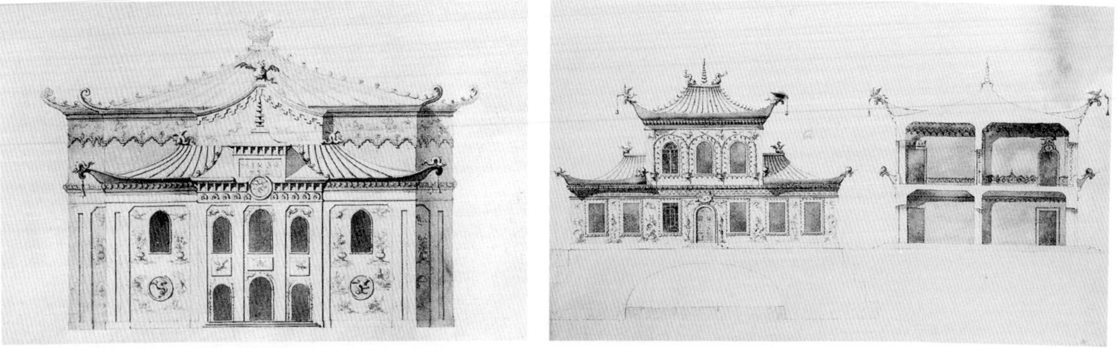

139a,b. Antonio Rinaldi, Designs for the Chinese Theatre and the Chinese Pavilion in Tsarskoe Selo, c. 1775. St Petersburg, Hermitage Museum.

Antonio Rinaldi was responsible for a series of structures in the Chinese style for the park of the imperial residence at Tsarskoe Selo, known as the 'Russian Versailles', commissioned by Catherine II in the 1770s. The buildings in fact constituted a fully fledged village with numerous 'Chinese' buildings arranged around an octagonal square. Rinaldi's designs were later built by Neelov and Cameron.

The Reign of Charles III of Bourbon (1734-1759)

Charles of Bourbon arrived in Naples in 1734, leaving for Spain in 1759, and throughout the entire period of his reign artistic and architectural patronage continued to flourish. Charles was a natural heir to the splendours of the Farnese and to the prolific traditions of the Medici and he initiated a series of projects in the capital, both renovating existing buildings and constructing entirely new palaces, from Palazzo Reale to those at Portici and Capodimonte, from rural villas such as Astroni, Carditello, Persano and Castellammare, to the palace of Caserta, designed and built by Vanvitelli in 1750. Moreover, Charles established a series of artistic workshops – semi-precious stones, tapestries, a porcelain factory, glass works – creating a ferment of activity in the city which also benefited the numerous workshops of Naples from cabinet makers to carvers, jewellers, silversmiths and tortoise shell workers. The arrival in town of the Bourbon court also happened to coincide with a renewal of the decorative repertories used by architects, artists and craftsmen, who were now increasingly keen to keep abreast of stylistic innovations taking place in other European courts, especially French and German. This did, in effect, correspond to a move away from baroque designs towards a gradual lightening of decorative motifs, approaching an international *rocaille* style. In the 16th-century palazzo in Piazza San Domenico Maggiore, bought by duke Agostino Saluzzo di Corigliano in 1732, the 'Gabinetto' made between 1739 and 1741 and designed by Filippo Buonocore, an architect and stage designer, provides an early and elegant example of this new decorative tendency in Naples. Entirely Rococo, the whirls and scrolls of the superb wood carving that clambers around the duke's Gabinetto (possibly designed and made by the architect and sculptor Bartolomeo Granucci) are highlighted by the mirrored walls which brilliantly – and perfectly – reflect the gilding of the decoration. Some oriental touches are entwined amidst the decorative woodwork, while fifty pieces of porcelain displayed on as many little shelves provided a more obvious element of chinoiserie in the original arrangement.

Even Luigi Vanvitelli (1700-1773), who was not altogether an enthusiast of chinoiserie, was inevitably affected by the spread of a taste that at times

reached the level of a veritable mania in Naples. Queen Maria Amalia (1724-1760) commissioned him to design a 'Chinese style' pavilion for the park of the Portici villa – an idea that he did not approve of, but an offer that he could not refuse – and he accepted, assuring the queen that for her he would by all means transform himself into "a Chinese architect". Although the pavilion was never built, a model of it, made by Vanvitelli, exists in the palace of Caserta. He succeeded in designing a building which, despite its rather classical layout with a hexagonal form and columns with Corinthian capitals, has numerous oriental features, such as the characteristic decorative motifs of dragons, exotic birds and inscriptions in ideograms, and some of the structural elements, such as the emphatically pointed windows and doors, the six small pavilions with curving roofs situated on the terracing, and the open structure at the top of the building. Even if only in embryonic form, this is the only example of 'Chinese' architecture produced in Naples in the 1700s. Usually an advocate of sombre and rational architecture, Ferdinando Fuga (1699-1782) – who devised the decoration of the Chinese Room in the Castel Gandolfo residence of pope Benedict XIV – designed the "Casina chinese" for the Granili residence, built between 1775 and 1790 and destroyed during the Second World War, but despite its name the pavilion was rather restrained and really had very little of the exotic about it either decoratively or structurally, although perhaps the onion-shaped roof was intended to provide the eastern element. In the 19th century, the scholars Alvino (1843) and Chiarini (1860) declared that "it is called the Chinese casino for the architecture that would embarrass the Chinese themselves".[15] Yet the oriental style continued to be used in Neapolitan architecture during the 19th century with buildings such as the Pagoda at Villa Roccaromana (post 1814) and the Pagoda d'Angri (1833), both located in Posillipo.
The influence of Vanvitelli's architecture can be seen in the work of Antonio Rinaldi (1709-1794), although his most important projects were realised in St Petersburg where he worked from 1756 to 1790, after a period in the Ukraine in 1752 where he worked on various commissions for prince Razumovskij (1709-1771), a favourite of the empress Elisabeth (1709-1762).[16] A pupil and assistant of Vanvitelli in Rome, Ancona and Caserta, Rinaldi provided a fundamental contribution to the programme of modernization in St Petersburg, initiated by the Tsarina. Catherine II was a quite passionate devotee of chinoiserie, writing in 1762 "I love to distraction gardens in the English style, the curving lines, the gentle slopes, ponds like lakes, groups of little islands and I hold in contempt straight lines, *l'anglomanie domine dans mon plantomanie*". Some of Rinaldi's more obviously oriental-style creations were the Chinese House and another two storey building both in the Petrovskij park in the fortress of Peterstadt, built between 1756 and 1762 for Catherine's husband, Peter the Great (1728-1762), and destroyed in 1778, as well as the Chinese palace, the Chinese Kitchen, the Chinese Pavilion and the Pavilion of the Sloping Mountain in

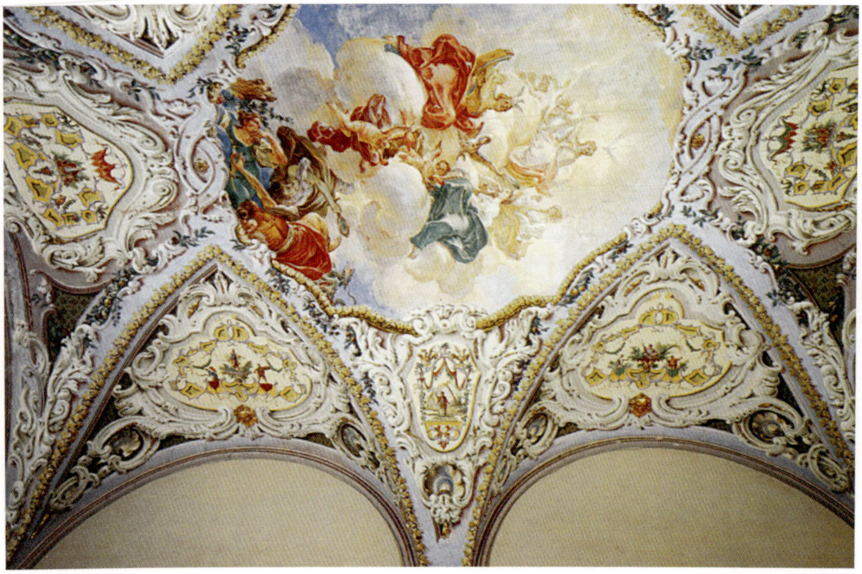

140a,b. Chinese Room (Prior's Library), wall paintings. Naples, mid 18th century. Naples, Certosa di San Martino.

Built to house the library of the prior at the Charterhouse of St Martin, the room is decorated in quite brilliant colours. Delicate little chinoiserie scenes surround the central fresco with a religious theme in the vault of the ceiling, the work of Crescenzo Gamba.

the large park of Oranienbaum, where work continued from 1762 to 1774.[17] Lastly in the Chinese village in Tsarskoe Selo he designed the Creaking Pavilion and the Chinese Theatre, completed in 1777 by the Russian architect Neelov. There are many parallels between Rinaldi's architecture and Vanvitelli's, especially the classical appearance of the structures, but Rinaldi also embraced international models including elements based mainly on the French Rococo and English picturesque styles. This combination is clearly visible in the numerous 'Chinese' buildings designed for the Russian sovereign, one of the most typical being the Chinese Palace at Oranienbaum. A classic of 18th-century European oriental architecture, the building combines the sobriety of neoclassicism with richly florid baroque interiors, created by famous Italian artists such as Tiepolo, the Barozzi brothers, Torelli, Bonazza, Marchiori, Molaiter and Goretti, and quite charmingly blending with the original Chinese furnishings ordered directly from the craftsmen of the Celestial Empire.

Interior Decoration

Painters specialised in Chinese style ornamentation of interiors were active in Naples in the mid 18th century. Recorded in documents of the day as "painters of papers and Chinese decorations" for their skill in using cut-out motifs, they produced numerous interiors that have long since been lost. Descriptions of some of these have survived, however, such as the 'little lantern room' housing some 3,025 Chinese figures in the Palazzo alla Sanità owned by Bartolomeo Di Maio, recorded in an inventory of 1748. Other interiors included a decoration with trees, parrots and "other kinds of Chinese birds" painted by Domenico Galietti in Palazzo Bonito, under the direction of Ferdinando Sanfelice (1675-1748), an architect and designer

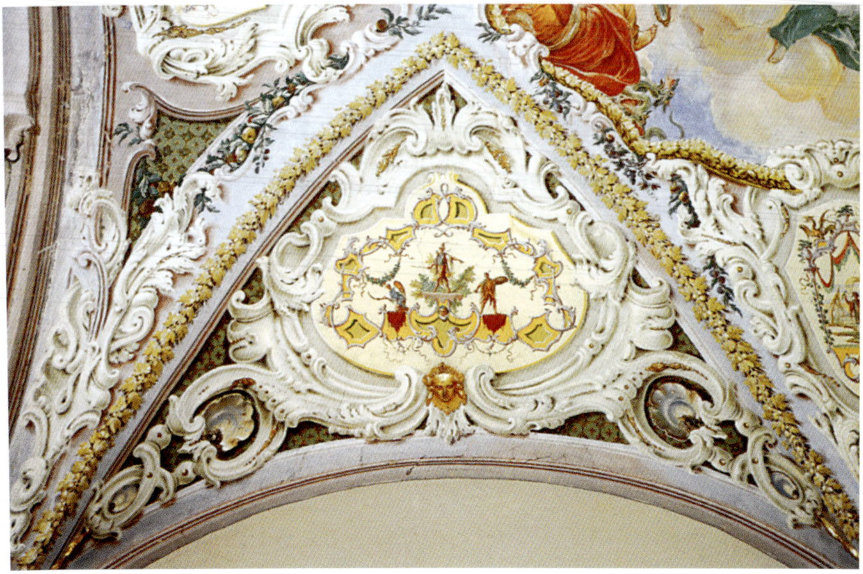

who, on the occasion of the festivities to celebrate the birth of the Infanta, created a large temporary scenario with a *Gran Macchina* vaguely similar to the *Nanking Tower* illustrated in Gemelli Careri's book. Many more exotic furnishings are recorded such as a "Chinese cover to use for a fireplace in the 'Gabinetto nobile'" made by Carmine Allio for prince Rocca in 1750; doors lacquered and decorated by Antonio Camisa and commissioned by Lorenzo Greco, while similar ones were also made for Palazzo Carafa di San Lorenzo under the supervision of Gabriele Preziosi; a room commissioned in 1750 by count Vallelonga, entirely decorated with 'Chinese' figures and ornamentation created by the painter Giovanni Fiorelli; and finally chinoiserie decorations designed in 1760 by the architect Nicolò Tagliacozzi Canale (1680-1764) for the residence of count Rossi in Porta San Gennaro. Tagliacozzi Canale also renovated the 'Quarto' at the Certosa di San Martino for its prior Giovanni Vernucci. The Library, also known as the 'Porcelain Room', is decorated with paintings of allegorical subjects by Crescenzo Gamba (*Triumph of the Virtues of the Chartreuse Order*); within sinuously scrolling frames the scenes are surrounded by elegant chinoiseries of jugglers and slender oriental figures painted in lively colours on a light background, probably the work of the decorator Gaetano Magri. Magri is also the author of another design with a Chinese theme housed in the Neapolitan Società di Storia Patria. The ceiling of a neighbouring room at the Certosa is decorated with similarly 'exotic' subjects painted on a base of gilded papier-maché. The chinoiserie scenes are surrounded by jagged frames interspersed by masks, the domes of pavilions, facing dragons and classical style busts, each of which is enclosed by the scrolls of a cartouche fitted into the corners of the ceiling. In many cases the central figure is flanked by two servants, a composition frequently found in the European chinoiserie repertory and best known from

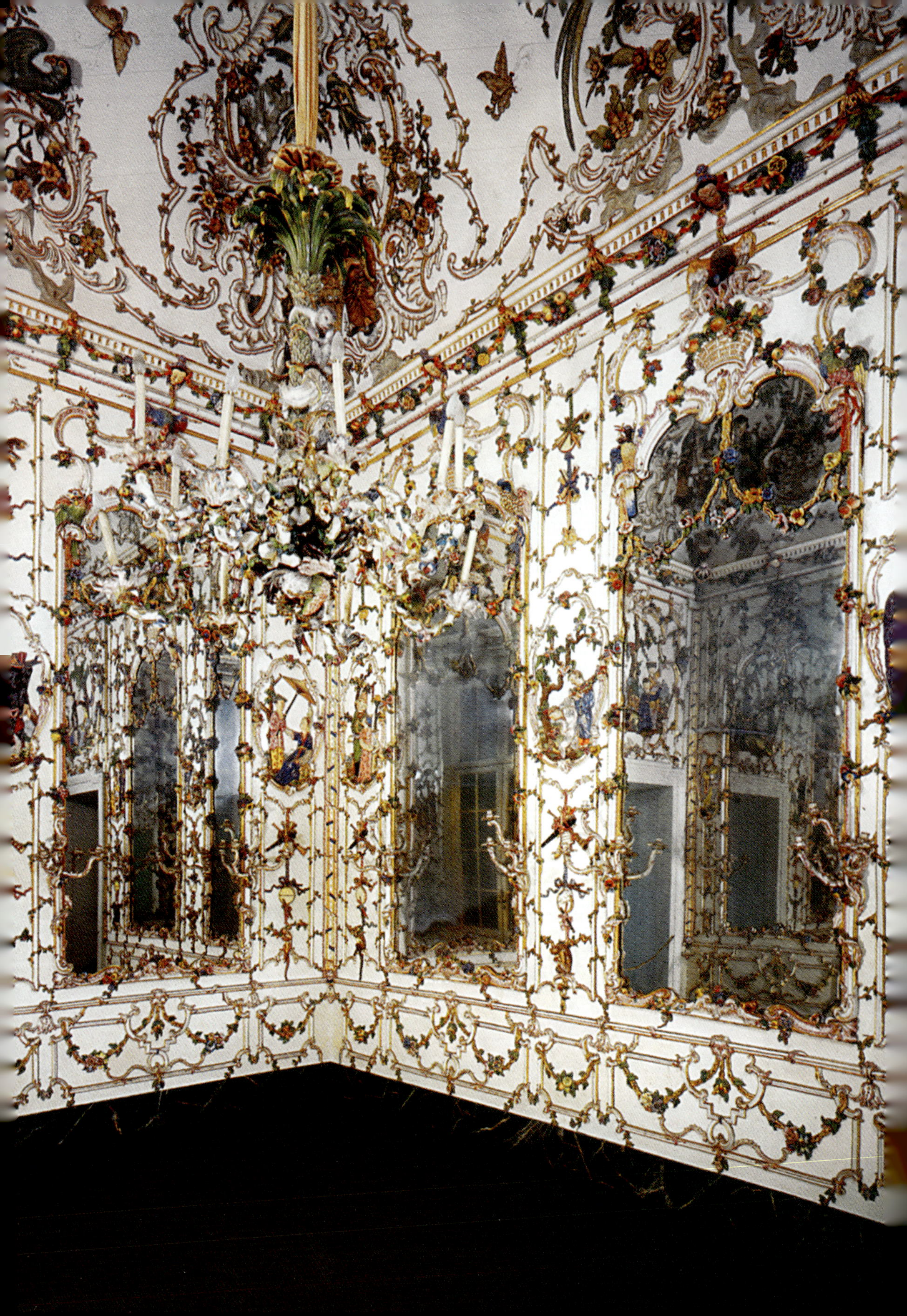

141. The Porcelain Room, Naples. Naples, Capodimonte factory, c. 1757. Naples, Capodimonte Museum.

One of the greatest masterpieces of international Rococo and without doubt the most ambitious work produced by the Capodimonte factory.

142. The Porcelain Room, detail. Naples, Capodimonte factory, c. 1757. Naples, Capodimonte Museum.

The models for this and the other compositions that adorn the walls and ceiling of the Porcelain Room at Portici were provided by early and mid 18th-century compendiums of European chinoiseries. The influence of French artists specialised in the genre, such as Watteau and Boucher, is particularly evident - that of original Far Eastern items less so.

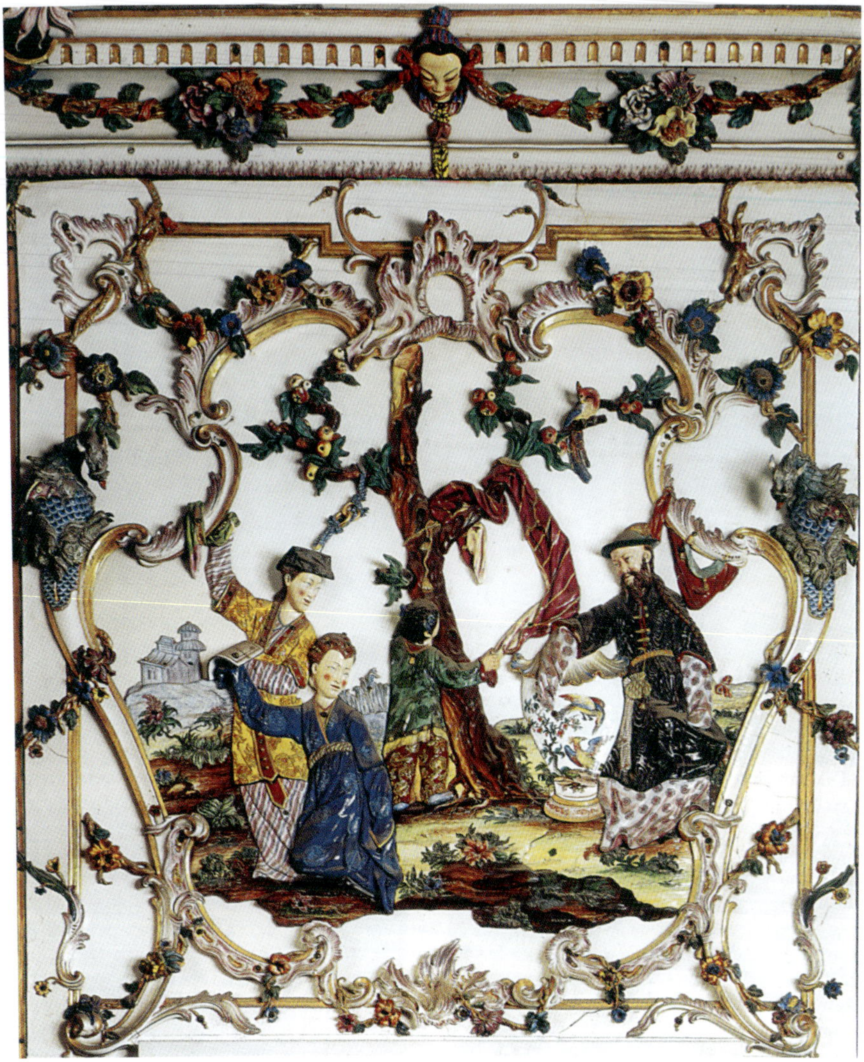

Watteau's version, illustrated in the decorations of the Muette castle. The beautiful flooring of majolica tiles with a trellis pattern is by Giuseppe Massa and an inscription shows that it was made in 1741.
Chinoiserie continued to be appreciated in the religious institutes of Naples. Directed by the architect Ferdinando Fuga, Chinese ornamentation, both painted and sculptural, appeared in some interiors in Santa Chiara, and in 1767 the ornamental decorator, Gennaro Pierro produced two works for the chamberlain of the monastery, one of which was painted 'in the Chinese style' and the other with flowers and birds.

Porcelain

Located in the gardens of the Royal Palace, the Royal Porcelain Factory began production in 1741 under the direction of two Florentine alchemists, Livio Vittorio Schepers and his son, Gaetano, and the painter and decorator

Giuseppe Caselli from Piacenza. In 1743 the workshops were transferred to buildings located in the woods of Capodimonte and specifically designed for the purpose by the architect Ferdinando Sanfelice. Other artists and craftsmen began to collaborate with the factory such as the Florentine modeller, Giuseppe Gricci (1700-1770), and Giuseppe della Torre, a painter and possibly of Spanish origin. From 1744 to 1759 the factory was managed by Gaetano Schepers, who was responsible for the paste, together with Giuseppe Gricci and Caselli; following the death of Caselli in 1753, Giovanni Sigismondo Fischer took over his responsibilites, later followed by Cristiano Adler of Vienna. Work ceased however, in 1759 when Charles III moved to Madrid where he decided to establish the Buen Retiro factory promptly transferring not only most of the workers at the Capodimonte factory, but also the moulds and even the prepared paste, and to avoid his son making use of the machinery left behind, he ordered it to be destroyed. Despite this, in 1770 Ferdinando founded the Royal Porcelain Factory in Naples, though as far as Neapolitan chinoiserie was concerned Charles's factory was much more important, as it came into being and developed during the mid 18th century when the oriental style was most passionately indulged by the sovereign, his court and artistic circles.

The Royal Factory's greatest masterpiece and one of the most elaborate pieces of chinoiserie in all of Europe is the Porcelain Room made for the royal villa at Portici between 1757 and 1759 in the apartment of queen Maria Amalia.[18] The entire room was transferred to Capodimonte in 1866, except for the painted and stuccoed ceiling and the chandelier which were only moved to Naples in 1955-57.[19] A dating for the room is provided by a letter written by Luigi Vanvitelli to his brother Urbano on 17 June 1758 in which he reports having seen, still at the Capodimonte factory, "a complete Room of Porcelain, including the floor, the dado, and the walls with Chinese-style frames and bas reliefs, and as I say, quite everything is in Porcelain except for six large glass mirrors which must have come from France". The room must have been completed and installed by July 1759 when the workers presented their bill for payment. The entire arrangement was designed by Giovan Battista Natali from Piacenza, probably sent for by his fellow townsman, Giuseppe Caselli. Giuseppe Gricci was responsible for the sculptural aspect of the decoration, and the painting is by Sigismondo Fischer and numerous assistants, followed on his death in May 1758 by Luigi Restile. The Marquis de Sade (1740-1814) saw the Porcelain Room during his famous journey to Italy in 1775 and provided a lively description, adding that the walls of the adjoining room in the queen's evening chambers were hung with "cloth from the Indies with large patterns".[20]

The room is a quite superb creation and only one notable example existed earlier, though of inferior quality, commissioned by count Dubsky in 1730 for his residence at Brunn, and now in the Museum für Angewandte Kunst in Vienna. The Naples 'Gabinetto' is decorated with eighty-one square

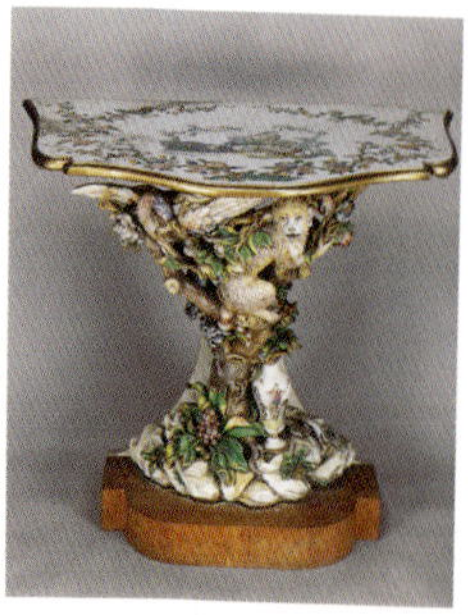

143. Small porcelain table. Naples, Capodimonte factory, c. 1757. Sèvres, Musée National de Céramique.

This highly sophisticated table would seem to be unique in European ceramic production. The unusual piece also demonstrates that decorators working for the Neapolitan ceramic factory made use of French chinoiserie compositions.

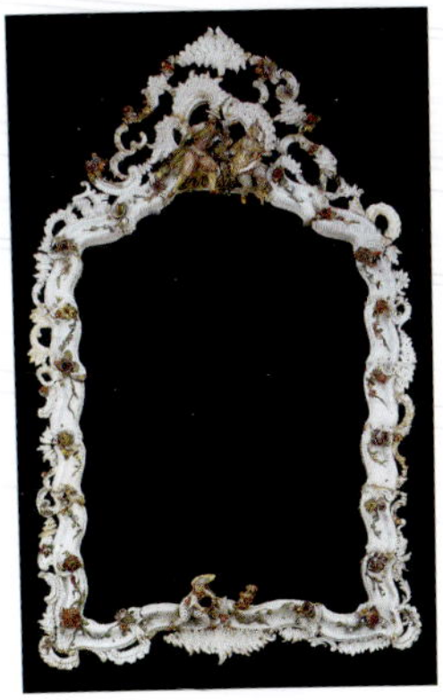

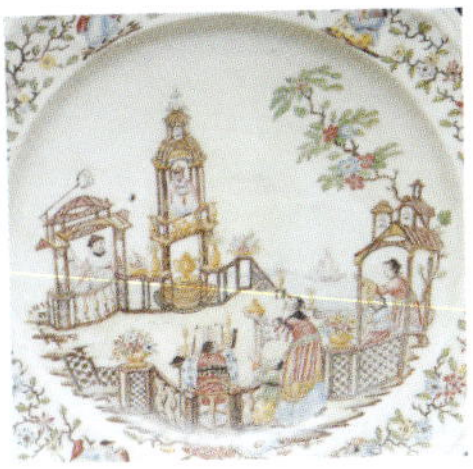

144. Mirror. Naples, Capodimonte factory, c. 1757. Naples, Museo Duca di Martina.

145. Plate, detail. Naples, Capodimonte factory, c. 1748-1750. Zurich, Andreina Torré collection.
The decorative style of this plate recalls German chinoiserie, known throughout Europe from widely available collections of engravings. Neapolitan artists were greatly inspired by the decoration of Viennese and Meissen porcelain, as can be seen from the floral motif around the border.

metres of coloured porcelain panels arranged in a pre-established sequence, entirely covering the walls of what amounts to a fair-sized room. The ceiling, created under the supervision of Mattia Gasperini, is of stuccowork painted with motifs "like those used on porcelain", and the flooring may also have been of porcelain, or perhaps simply painted with similar designs, though according to Lady Blessington (1789-1849) writing in 1839, it was removed by the French in 1779; during the 19th century, however, the flooring of the room consisted of an antique mosaic pavement from Herculaneum. The coloured decoration in high-relief is on a white background and is arranged in parallel vertical rows divided by rocaille frames, interspersed with trophies of musical instruments, monkeys, exotic birds, masks shaped like oriental faces, dragons, female faces – all entwined with festoons of flowers and bunches of ribbons. Towards the ceiling gilded frames linked like a series of scrolls surround various scenes with figures, generally portraying two Chinamen in the most genteel pursuits and poses entirely in keeping with 17th-century Europe's vision of old Cathay. The craftsmen who worked on the 'Gabinetto' clearly had access to original oriental items as is revealed by the presence of traditional musical instruments of exclusively Chinese origin, the precision of the hairstyles and clothing of the figures, and indeed many of the Chinese inscriptions in the décor can be perfectly well translated.[21]
Although there are some errors of transcription, the decorators must have had the help of an expert in the Chinese language, probably one of the brothers from the nearby Chinese Seminar. There are stylistic similarities between the scenes with figures and French chinoiserie of the first half of the 18th century (Watteau, Boucher, Huet and Huquier), and it is probably no coincidence that in 1747 Caselli asked that the prince of Ardore, the Neapolitan ambassador in France, should "send from Paris five or six dozen papers printed with Chinese designs with figures, landscapes and flowers, all in that exact style, however".
A design reproduced on a vase set into the base of a small table now in the Sèvres Porcelain Museum, demonstrates the use of French chinoiserie prints at the Royal Factory of Naples.[22] The source of the composition was *La Déesse THVO CHVU dans l'isle d'Haïnan*, devised by Antoine Watteau for the castle of Muette in 1709, engraved by Aubert and published in *L'Oeuvre Gravé* in 1726. Created by Giuseppe Gricci in the same period that the Porcelain Room at Portici was made, the table is another fine example of Neapolitan artistry and its design was based on the 17th-century naturalistic decoration invented by Bernini, Parodi and Brustolon.
The top is a single large slab and is also decorated with a chinoiserie scene, probably based on an engraving in *L'Oeuvre gravé*. Dating from the same period is a mirror, now in the Duca di Martina Museum in Naples, with full relief Chinese figures at the top and bottom edges, and with the highly unusual feature, at least for Italian decorative arts, of asymmetrical scrolls in the frame.[23]

'Exotic' motifs and subjects that were more specifically 'Chinese' were also used by Neapolitan ceramists on earthenware in the mid 1700s. The sources of inspiration during the early years were both original Chinese works – especially the floral motifs in high relief decorating the porcelain of Dehua, although the influence of the colourful 'famille rose' designs can also be seen – and versions of these designs that had been produced by the Meissen factory. The unusual floral decoration known as 'Korean Flowers' derived from the Meissen repertory although it was in fact based on Kakiemon porcelain made in Japan. The best example of this Meissen oriental-style floral decoration produced in Naples is the famous *Augustus Rex* vase in the Floridiana Museum in Naples. In the second decade of its existence, the Capodimonte factory entered a new phase of chinoiserie decoration when themes derived from original oriental works, or from versions of these produced in Germany, were gradually replaced by European 'Chinese style' designs. The Capodimonte decorators certainly referred to the works of both French and German artists available in printed compendiums, although in some cases the models seem also to have evolved out of traditional 18th-century Neapolitan patterns, typically representing scenes redolent with bucolic naturalism.

Although it was made between 1761 and 1765, some years after the Capodimonte factory had closed, the Porcelain Room in the royal residence of Aranjuez is in many ways an offspring of the Portici room. It is in fact the

146. The Porcelain Room. Madrid, Buen Retiro factory, 1761-1765. Aranjuez, Palacio Real.

Larger than the Porcelain Room in Portici, the Aranjuez room is the finest masterpiece of the Buen Ritiro ceramic factory, established by Charles III in Spain immediately on his arrival from Naples.

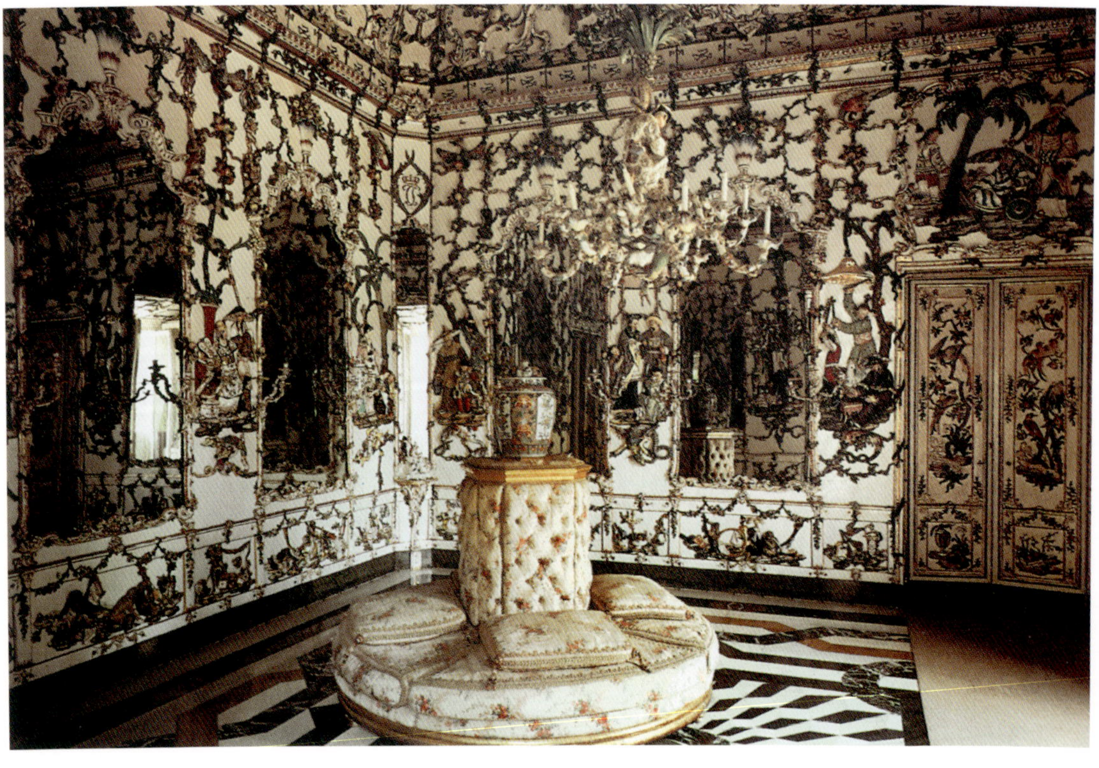

most important creation of the Buen Ritiro factory, established by Charles III in 1759, after he had left Naples to become king of Spain.[24] The work was designed and made by the same craftsmen as the room at Portici, in particular Giuseppe Gricci (who actually signed one of the panels). Hugh Honour saw the hand of Gian Domenico Tiepolo in the decorative paintings of the Aranjuez room and the artist was indeed in Spain at that time working on several commissions for Charles III's residences in Madrid.[25] The artists of the Spanish factory also made the porcelain room in the Palacio Real in Madrid between 1763 and 1771, though the decoration painted on ceramic plaques like those of Portici and Aranjuez, had a Bacchanalian theme.[26]

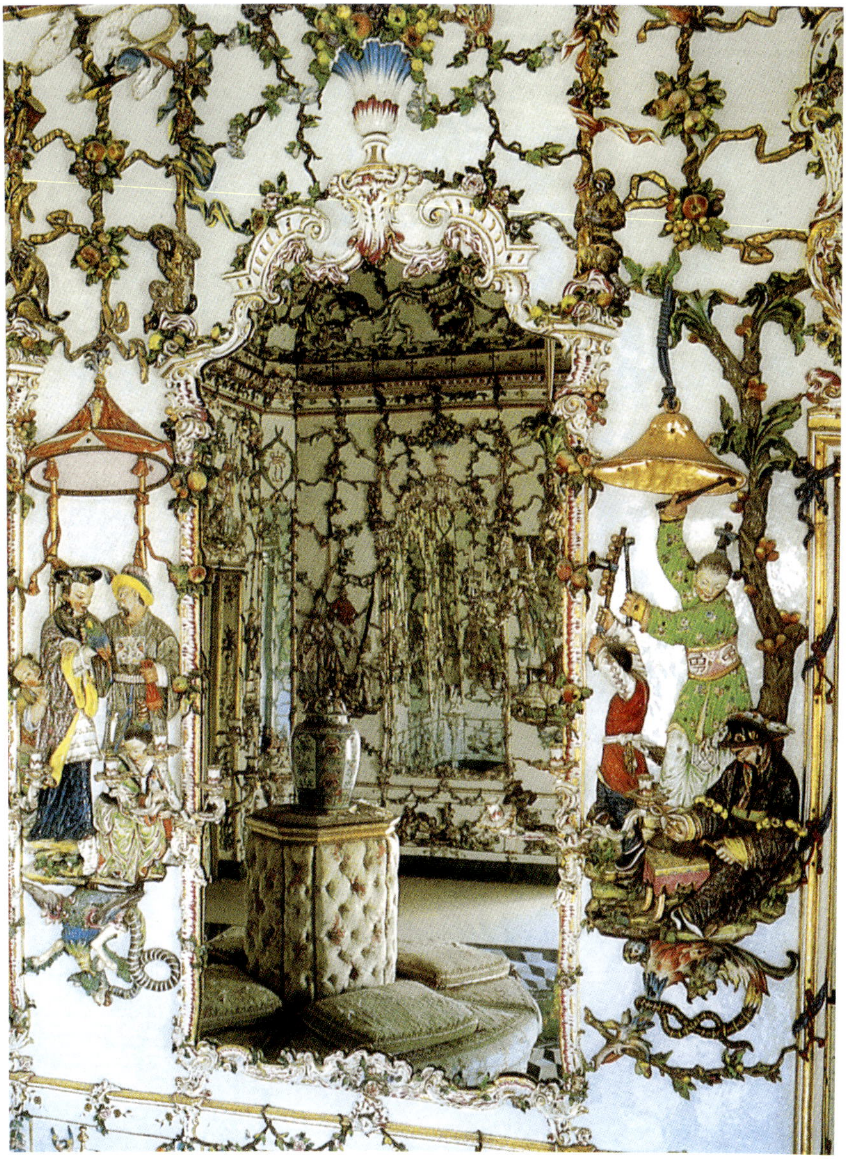

147. The Porcelain Room, detail. Madrid, Buen Retiro factory, 1761-1765. Aranjuez, Palacio Real.

The chinoiserie of the Aranjuez room must have inspired Mattia Gasperini, an Italian decorator who created a similar style of stucco work in the vault of the Salon in Charles III's Apartment in the Palacio Real in Madrid.

Lacquer

In addition to the porcelain room at Portici documents refer to at least three rooms decorated with lacquer panels which existed from the time of Charles until the late 18th century when, in the early years of the Napoleonic period, it was decided to dismantle them.[27] The lacquered panels in the room referred to as the "Gabinetto blò di S.M. il Re" in an inventory of 1799 were made by Guillaume-Jean Martin, one of the famous family of lacquer masters who worked for the king and aristocracy of France. Born in 1713, Guillaume-Jean worked in Naples as a "peintre de Sa Majesté le roi des deux Siciles" until at least 1754, the same period that Mattia Gasperini, a "Venetian japanner" also specialised in making and applying the varnish, was working for Charles III. Martin therefore probably made the lacquer panels for Portici around mid century. The room was briefly described by Abbé Richard and the marquis de Sade in 1770 and 1776 respectively and the inventory of 1799 records the room as decorated with panels painted with a blue lacquer (a rather characteristic feature of the Martin family's work) and ornamented with "figures, animals and glided motifs in bas relief, with Chinamen". The room also contained "thirty-four groups in white porcelain", probably arranged at different heights on the walls, while the ceiling was painted with "playful cherubs, pleasantly done", a description

148a,b. Table. Naples, mid 18th century. Naples, Capodimonte Museum.

One of a pair in the Capodimonte Museum, this table is an excellent example of the skill of Neapolitan furniture makers and decorators in the 18th century. The Chinese figure that appears at the joint of the struts joining the four legs is of painted terracotta.

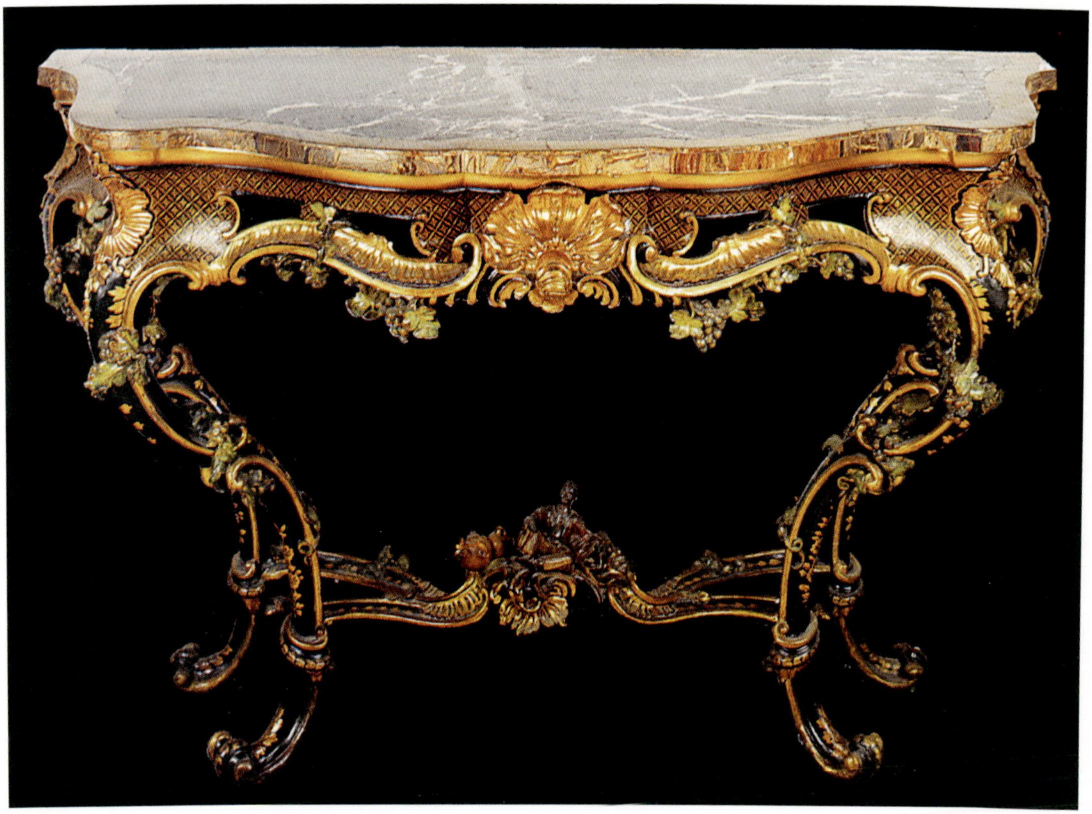

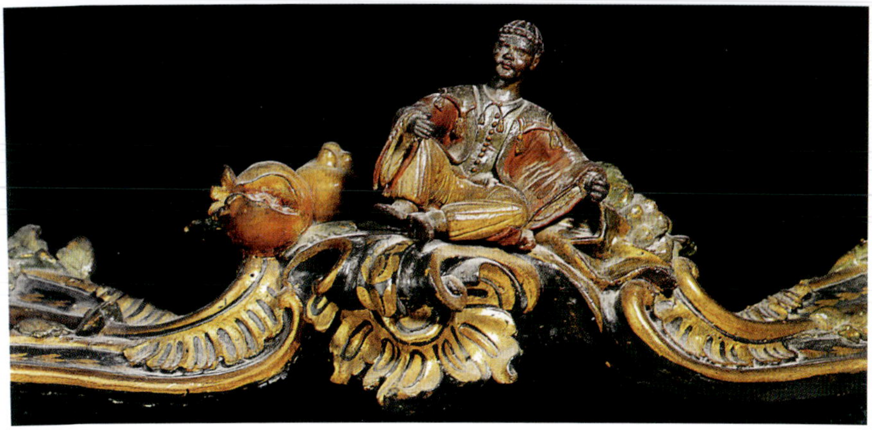

that recalls the work of Clemente Ruta (1685-1767), still now enhancing the ceiling of one of the rooms in the palace. Martin was also responsible for at least one of the two other lacquer rooms located in the neighbouring queen's apartments. Here, the French lacquer master used a light green background for his work, another colour that frequently appeared in the Martin family's palette, but the subjects portrayed on these panels were not Chinese and the porcelain chosen to decorate the room was entirely from the Meissen factory. The third room was also in the queen's apartment, but unfortunately it is not known who created it, although the panels were described as decorated with "Chinese bas-reliefs in gold", and in keeping with the walls, all the furniture was also lacquered.

During Charles's reign chinoiseries were used to decorate wooden furnishings made by local craftsmen. The existence of similar works made outside Italy stimulated a taste for this kind of lacquered furniture in Naples. English furniture, for example, graced the Portici palace throughout the entire 18th century; probably acquired by Charles and now in the Capodimonte museum, the furnishings have been attributed by González-Palacios to the English cabinet maker and carver, Giles Grendey (1693-1780).[28] In addition, De Lalande who visited Italy from 1765 to 1766, referred to the Portici palace as housing, "des ouvrages en vernis faits à Londres, à Venise & à Paris; comme ils sont tous du plus beau choix, on peut y juger, par comparaison, du degré de perfection où le vernis a été porté dans ces trois villes; il m'a paru qu'on donnoit, sans balancer, la préférence à celui de Martin fait à Paris". Mid 18th-century documents contain numerous references to Chinese decorations on European wood furniture, sometimes specifically Neapolitan such as "a harpsichord with carved figures in the Chinese style" described in the inventory of doctor U.I. Nicola Coccorese dated 28 January 1741 or the 'Chinese' furnishings carved by Antonio Bozzaotra (or Vozzaotra) to designs commissioned in 1745 from the architect Felice Bottiglieri by prince Bartolomeo of Capua for both his town residence and the villa at Portici.[29] In 1751 count Vincenzo Maria Mazzara paid Giovanni Buonocore, a desk maker, for two "Bureaux covered with leather ... with Chinese lacquer decorated with figures and highlighted in gold"; in 1756 the master ornamentalist Nicola Finamore delivered a 'Chinese lacquer' carriage to Raimondo Diaz; a year later, in 1757, the maestro Domenico Basile received payment for a carriage with the sides "painted with figures and natural landscapes, with six coats of fine Chinese lacquer". Lastly, recorded in Ignazio Fortini's inventory of 1762 are a "walnut desk, the top painted in the Chinese style" and "four small paintings with images of fountains and some Chinese figures".

Some Neapolitan lacquered furnishings decorated with chinoiserie have survived, including the two magnificent console tables in the Capodimonte museum, considered "the finest examples of late baroque Neapolitan furnishings, both for the decorative style and their technical perfection".[30] The oriental influence is seen not only in the dark blue background of the lacquer, enlivened by the geometric motifs in gold, but also the painted terracotta Chinese figure sitting at the juncture of the struts that join the legs; the table tops are further enhanced by the use of antique marble and oriental alabaster. Two corner cabinets with Chinese-style gold motifs on a dark blue-green lacquered background, also in the Capodimonte museum, may well have been made in Naples, though many of the stylistic elements are typical of northern European works. However, the sedan chair now in Amalfi cathedral, decorated with Chinese scenes, framed with elaborate floral festoons, is certainly the work of an anonymous Neapolitan craftsman.[31] Made during the mid 18th century as part of the renovation of the cathedral carried out under Monsignor Bologna, the structural and stylistic features of this elegant work abundantly reveal its Neapolitan origins. Moreover, sedan chairs were a speciality of Neapolitan wood workers and were frequently decorated by renowned artists, as noted by the Spaniard Leandro Fernández de Moratín (1760-1828) in 1793-1794, "the carriages of Naples can compete with those of any other city both for their lightness and attractive design and for the excellent taste of their painting and decoration, or the beauty of the lacquer". The corner cabinet in the Correale Museum of Sorrento is also a fine mid-18th century piece made in Naples, lacquered in yellow with two standing Chinese figures decorating the two doors.[32]

Chinoiserie also influenced the decorations on majolica produced at the Caserta factory, and even book bindings, while tortoiseshell works with gold, silver and mother-of-pearl inlay were particularly esteemed. Tortoiseshell items had been produced in the area of Naples for quite some time and in the 1600s this unusual material was widely used in church decoration. In the 18th century such items were mainly made for secular purposes and the elegance of their design was highly esteemed. Neapolitan craftsmen specialised in making tortoiseshell items had generally trained as gold or silver smiths and the high quality of artistry and production was closely linked to the techniques and skills of this art. The decorations on

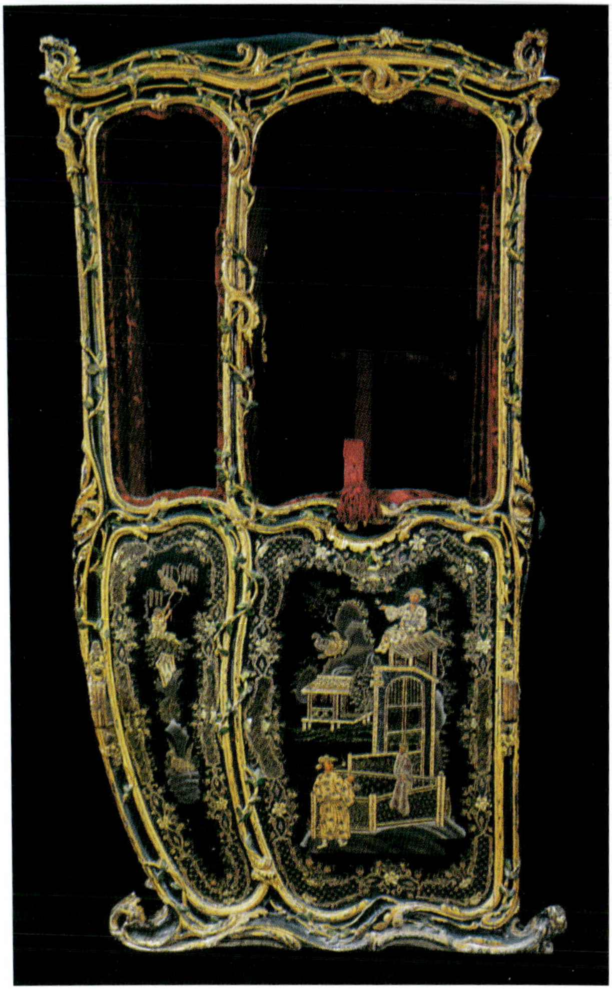

149. Sedan chair. Naples, third quarter of the 18th century. Amalfi, Cathedral.

Neapolitan sedan chairs were greatly appreciated abroad, as well as in Italy, for the quality of the lacquer and the elegant decoration. The detailed chinoiserie scenes on this example in the cathedral of Amalfi seem to have been based on French compositions known from engravings that were widely available in Naples too.

tortoiseshell works were frequently chinoiseries, occasionally combined with classical motifs which came into fashion in Naples following the discoveries at Herculaneum and Pompei. Tortoiseshell was often used in Asia to produce items destined for exportation to Europe, and was an intrinsically 'exotic' material with a gloss similar to that of Far Eastern lacquer. Neapolitan works were often decorated with inserts of mother-of-pearl and little silver or gold friezes. Some of the craftsmen who were skilled in the production of tortoiseshell items during the 1700s are known to us.[33] Nicola De Turris, a silversmith, and Gennaro Sarao were both active in 1735, and on the occasion of celebrations for the return of Charles III from Sicily, were vying with each other in the piazza in front of Palazzo Reale where, "glittering with splendid light in front of the walls of the Palagio Vecchio were the two workshops of the most important masters of tortoiseshell and mother-of-pearl production, Niccolò de' Turris and Giuseppe Sarao, who competed to best illuminate their works, all decorated with gold and silver and expensive

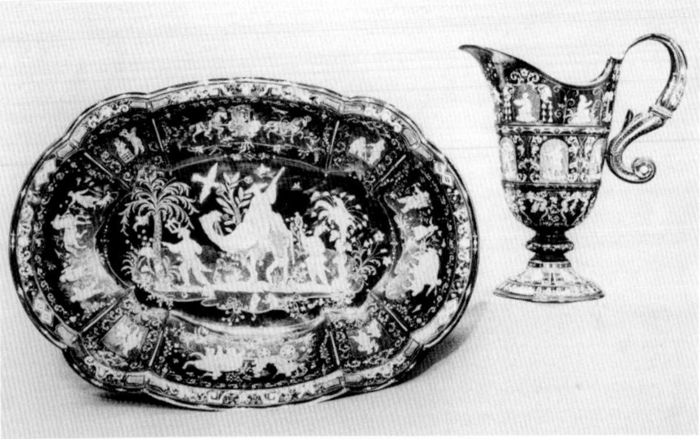

150. Jug with tray. Naples, mid 18th century. London, Victoria and Albert Museum.

Chinoiserie was one of the favourite subjects for Neapolitan tortoiseshell workers in the 1700s, often combined with a classical form of decoration. These two pieces present a mixture of oriental motifs, combining Far Eastern and Islamic iconography.

gems".[34] Several of De Laurentis' works have been found in London and Paris, while the princess of Angri commissioned two rare caskets from Gennaro D'Avino. Sarao, active until at least 1777 when he apparently held an administrative post at the Capodimonte factory, created some particularly interesting pieces. Some of the items made in his workshop were decorated with chinoiserie motifs, framed by a decoration that is still baroque, rather than rococo. Examples of these are the mirror with the coat of arms of Elisabetta Farnese and Filippo V dated between 1734 and 1746,[35] a casket sold at auction by Sotheby's in London in 1967,[36] and lastly a small table now in the Hermitage Museum in St Petersburg with the emblems of João V and his wife Marie Anne of Austria.[37]

The Reign of Ferdinando IV (1759-1825)

Ferdinando IV (1751-1825) became king in 1759 when his father Charles left for Spain. Although his lengthy reign is mainly remembered artistically for a revived interest in classical decorative elements stimulated by the archaeological discoveries at Pompei and Herculaneum, chinoiserie continued to enjoy great popularity. In 1767 the 'opera buffa' *L'Idolo Cinese* – by Giovanni Paisiello (1740-1816) with a libretto by Giambattista Lorenzi – enjoyed great success at the theatre.[38] Inventories of the residences of both the royal and aristocratic families are indicative of the widespread presence of 'Chinese-style' items, especially lacquered furniture decorated with Chinese scenes and porcelain, whether original works made in the Far East or items made in Europe, including Naples, by craftsmen specialized in copying oriental motifs. In 1768 for example, on the occasion of the marriage of Ferdinando and Marie Caroline of Austria (1752-1814), a lacquered writing desk with gilded framing was acquired, although in the exchange of correspondence between the minister Bernardo Tanucci (1798-1783) and abbé Galiani (1728-1787) who negotiated the deal, it is mentioned that the king would appreciate the work even though at the time furnishings of the kind were so widely available that they no longer represented a novelty.

Many documents dating from the 1760s and 1770s describe rooms that were entirely decorated in the Chinese style. The ornamentalist Giuseppe Funaro made a series of decorative paintings for prince Della Rocca in 1767; a decade later several rooms were entirely frescoed *à la chinois* in the palaces of the Brienza Caracciolo; in 1770 Alessandro Fischetti, a painter, was paid by the minister Giovanni Acton (1736-1811) for having restored "a wall in the Chinese style to be used in his new residence" near to Palazzo Reale; an inventory of the possessions of princess Cellammare dated 1772 records numerous small paintings "with figures painted in the Chinese style, and gilding"; in 1774 the painter Pietro Turco was responsible for the Chinese decoration of four rooms in the Chiaia palace, owned by the prince of Ischitella. In 1781 Turco also frescoed Villa Caracciolo at Torchiarolo with Chinese and Pompeian designs and at approximately the same time the little known "Chinese painter", Antonio Cipullo, was responsible for the tempera decoration in the Billiard Room of the palace at Portici, no longer in existence. The chinoiserie frescoes in the 'Gabinetto' of the duke of Casacalenda in his palace in Piazza San Domenico Maggiore also date from the 1770s. This oriental decoration could have been the work of Giuseppe and Gaetano Magri who had previously created similar ornamentation in the 'Quarto del Priore' at San Martino.
Although the Casacalenda frescoes and the decorations in the Chinese Room in the Portici palace are contemporary, the two styles are quite different. While the chinoiserie scenes depicted by the Magri have a rather European flavour, especially noticeable in the classical arrangement of the compositions, the frescoes in the room at Portici seem, on the other hand, to have been based on original Far Eastern works, both for the layout of the decoration and for many of the details. The anonymous painter of the eight large frescoes with smaller compositional inserts and an ethereal floral decoration in the ceiling, was clearly a highly skilled artist who decided not only to make use of Chinese themes on this occasion, but also to adopt some of the more characteristic techniques, thus abandoning the subtleties of shading and rules of perspective. The subjects of the frescoes include dancers, musicians, an audience with the emperor, and a large crowd of Chinese characters including ladies, men and children, evoking a happy, imaginary and carefree world, a perfect representation of that 'vision of Cathay' so typical of 18th-century European chinoiserie.
A similarly idealized portrayal is found in the frescoes of the vestibule, which has a pavilion roof, and a smaller bathroom, both in Villa Lauro Lancellotti, also in Portici. As in the frescoes of the Palace, here too the unknown artist has created a narrative composition portrayed in an uninterrupted sequence. The horizontal series of floral festoons and little bells and the vertical rows of twisted columns create a sort of stage set within which the dreamy Chinese figures drift nonchalantly around the scene.
At Caserta too new 'Chinese-style' features appeared. Laid out by Graffer in

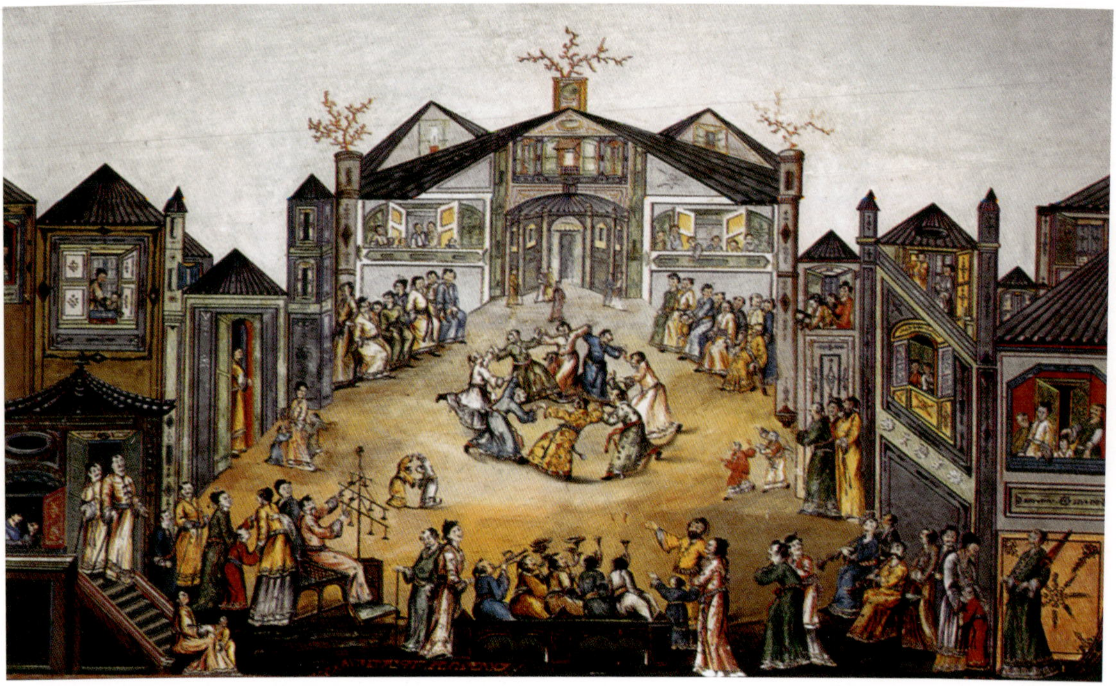

151a,b. Anonymous Neapolitan artist, Detail of wall paintings in the Chinese Room, c. 1775. Portici, Palazzo Reale.

The delightful scenes that decorate the Chinese Room in Palazzo Reale at Portici depict an ideal land where men, women and children lived together harmoniously, enjoying their earthly pleasures. In keeping with the ideas of enlightened thinkers such as Voltaire, in the second half of the 18th century, some intellectuals maintained that China provided an example of perfect government to which Europe should look to prevent its progressive decline.

the English style popular at the time, the park had an informal landscape arrangement where Vanvitelli's pavilion was to have been located.[39] In addition, in 1775 the royal engineer Nicola Fiore designed a chinoiserie room with frescoes by Giovan Battista Rossi; made at the time when Carlo Vanvitelli was responsible for the palace decorations, this 'Country Room' was destroyed at the end of the 19th century, but a drawing in the Cooper Hewitt Collection in New York provides us with an image of it.[40] Chinoiserie designs dating from about the 1790s also decorated some backrooms at the palace, though the style was heavily influenced by the neoclassicism then in fashion. In 1790 Ferdinando bought a group of furnishings from the Parisian antiquarians Daguerre and Lignereux which were made by the cabinet maker Adam Weisweiler and decorated with lacquered Chinese panels enhancing Louis Seize forms. Intended for the king's private studio, they were partly replaced by copies made in 1887 while the originals are now divided between the Metropolitan Museum of Art in New York and a private collection.[41] Not far away from the palace, an impressive example of the late 18th-century taste for chinoiserie popularized by Ferdinando in Naples before his forced exile in Sicily is found in the Villa Favorita at Portici. In a splendid location overlooking the sea, the Portici royal residence – once owned by Stefano Reggio di Gravina who had, in his time, installed some rooms in the oriental style – was radically renovated from 1796, just three years before the revolutionary outbreaks. Yet in this brief period numerous decorative projects were completed and the furnishings too were almost all in place.[42] According to the inventory drawn up in 1799, the work on the 'Stanza Lunga alla

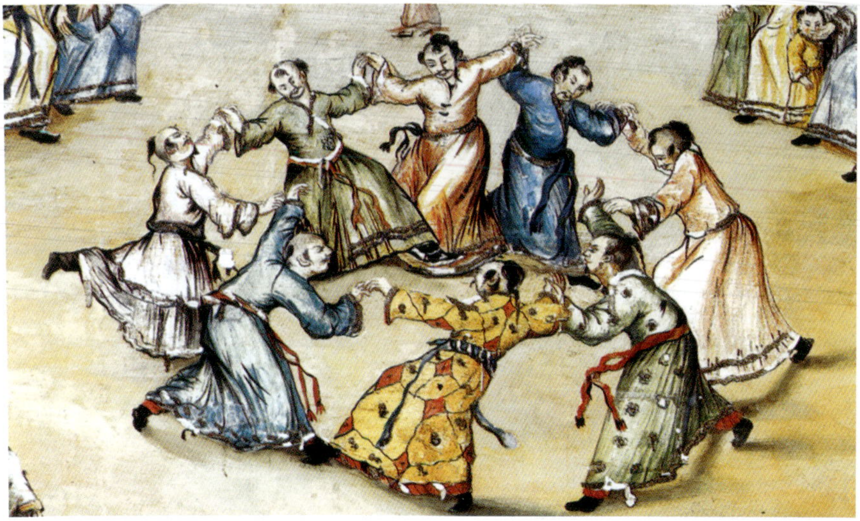

Chinese' was also near completion. The walls were certainly already decorated with murals and despite the poor state of conservation they are still visible today. Both the ceiling and the walls are painted, the walls with a series of scenes with full-length Chinese figures, simply standing or intently fishing or playing musical instruments, images that in some cases are copied from the engravings in Du Halde's publication of 1736. In 1785 Abbé Grosier had revived these scenes in his *Atlas général de la Chine, pour servir à la description générale de la Chine*, a copy of which was in the Palatine Library in Naples together with thirteen volumes of the *Histoire générale de la Chine* (1777-1783) by Grosier himself and a complete collection of *Mémoires concernant l'histoire, les sciences, les arts, les moeurs et les usages des Chinois* (1776-1791) by Abbé Batteaux. A tempera painting on paper applied to canvas, the decoration on the ceiling is sparser, painted in lighter colours on a bright background, and only two scenes are portrayed along the two longer sides, with figures between bamboo pergolas, balustrades and delicate floral garlands. This room at Portici is a good example of the changes that took place in Neapolitan chinoiserie after 1775. It is in fact more measured and less fanciful than the earlier rococo style and closer in concept to neoclassicism which was becoming popular throughout Europe at the time. The overall impression is therefore of an elegant, bright and sophisticated décor with a series of intriguing cultural references. This important chinoiserie work was created by the Neapolitan ornamentalist Lorenzo Giusto who was responsible for the figures, and his father Andrea,[43] who painted the flora and fauna. Numerous other rooms of the Villa Favorita at Portici were also decorated in the oriental style, both on the first and second floors, where one of the rooms had a ceiling decorated with "flowers and birds in the Chinese style, painted in natural colours". Other rooms are decorated with Moorish designs and date from the late 19th century when,

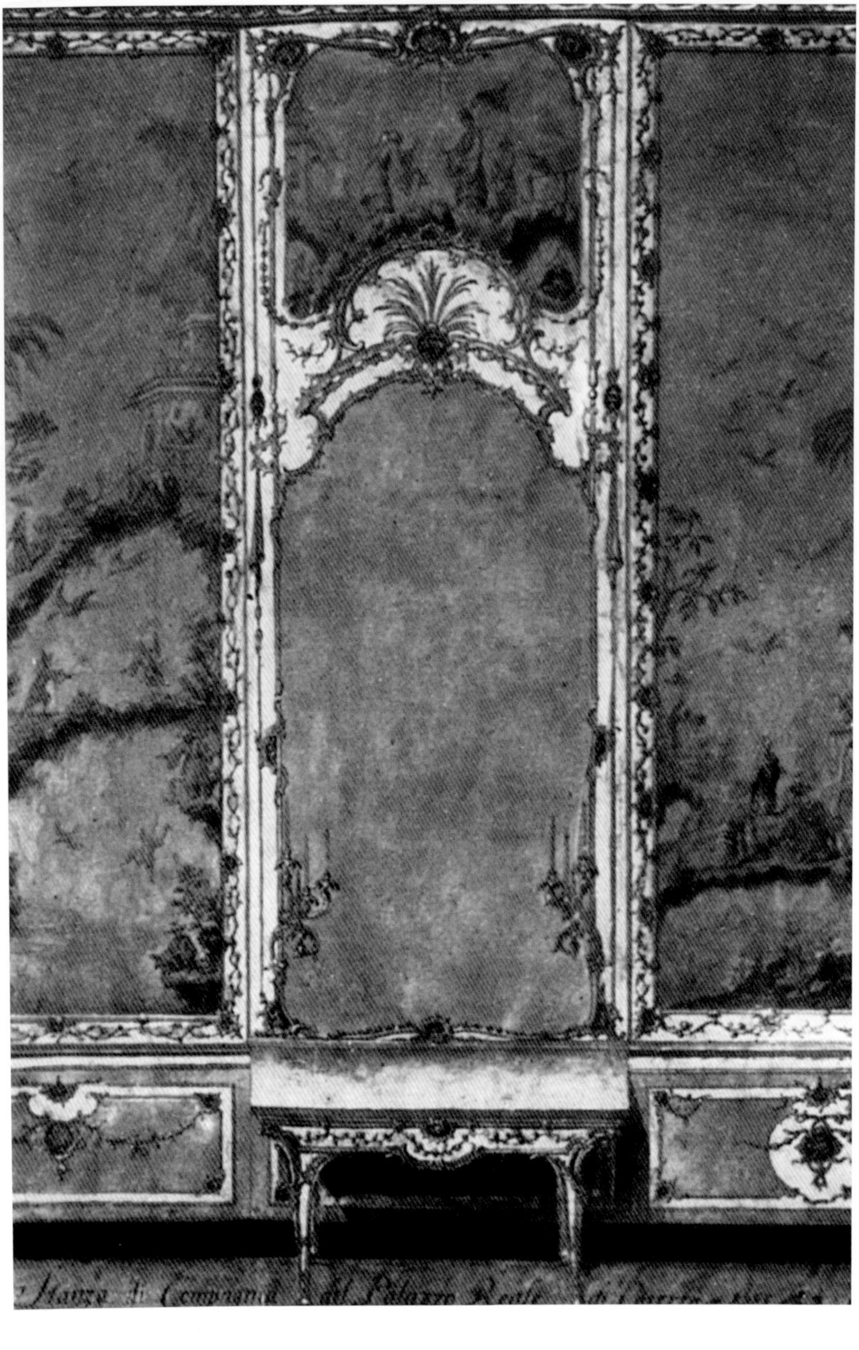

152. Nicola Fiore, Design for a Chinese Room in the palace of Caserta, 1775. New York, Cooper Union Museum for the Arts Decoration.

This drawing is the only remaining evidence of a Chinese room created in the palace of Caserta around 1775 and destroyed in the early 19th century. The arrangement of the decoration is neoclassical, evident especially in the harmonious distribution of the scenes on the walls.

153. Andrea and Lorenzo Giusto, Wall paintings in the Chinese Room, 1796-1799. Resina, Villa La Favorita.

Chinoiserie dominated much of the design and furnishings of the Villa Favorita. It was created just before the turbulent period of the French occupation however, and was destined to be abandoned, falling into a severe state of neglect. In 1821 Lady Morgan (c. 1776-1859) described it as "an ordinary building, miserably furnished, with nothing new or splendid ...".

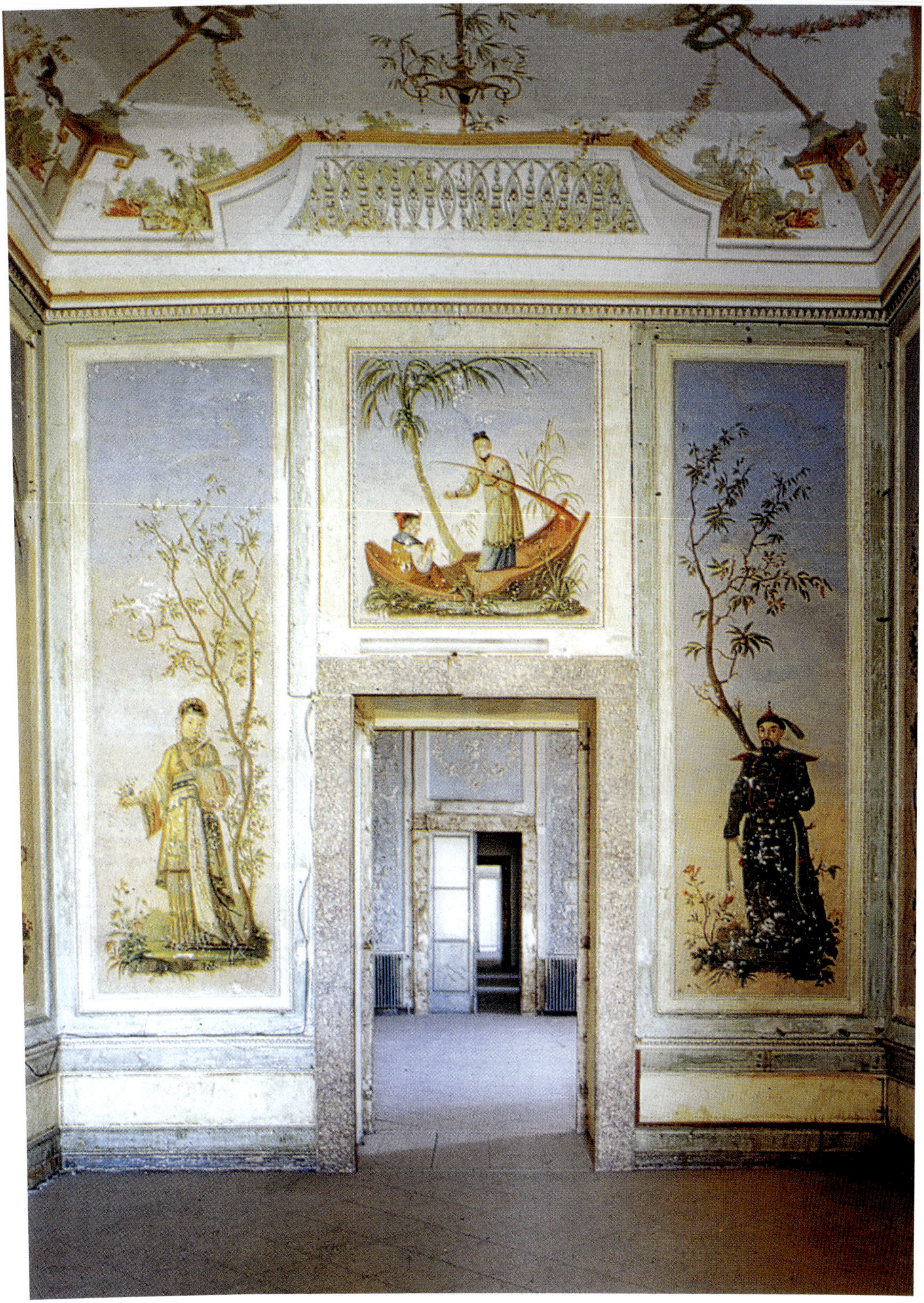

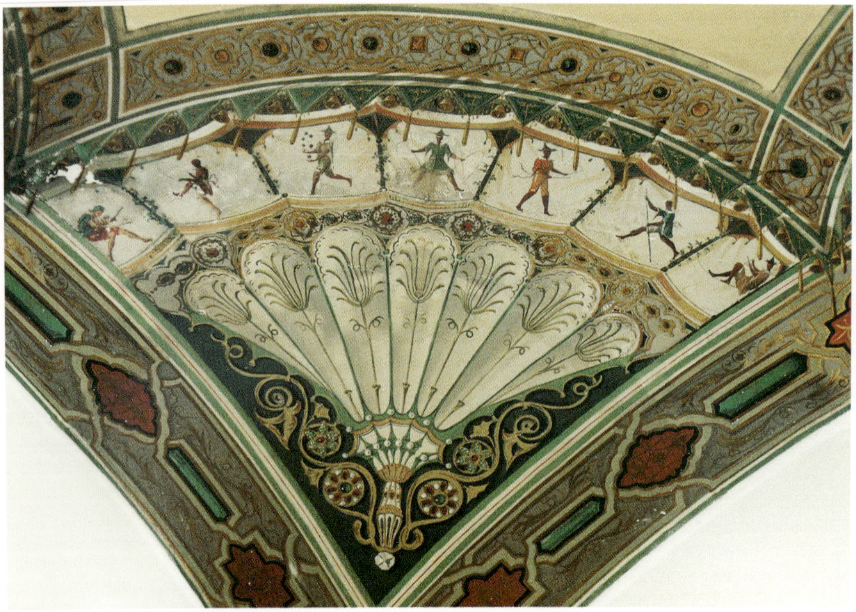

154a,b. Salvatore Giusti (?), Detail of a ceiling with 'Chinese style' decorative motifs, 1840. Naples, Palazzo Reale.

The decorative motifs surrounding the chinoiserie figures in this small room in Palazzo Reale are emphatically neoclassical. The décor is therefore a 19th century interpretation of the exotic style that was so popular in Naples in the 18th century. The work is attributed to the Neapolitan decorator Salvatore Giusti (1773 – after 1845) and is dated 1840.

for a brief period, the villa became the residence of the exiled viceroy of Egypt, Ismail Pascià (1830-1895). The two portraits of a *Mandarin* and a *Chinese Lady* now in Palazzo Reale may also be attributed to Lorenzo Giusto in the period around 1797, given the similarities to the figures at Portici, and indeed most probably they are the "two Chinese figures" which were recorded in the Villa Favorita before 1799.[44]

Of a much later date are the frescoes decorating the ceiling of a room on the ground floor of Palazzo Reale in Naples. The highly ornamental pattern is composed of Chinese jugglers, friezes of circular and pointed geometric motifs, stylized dragons and plants and glimpses of classical landscapes. The arrangement of the ornamental decoration is typical of late neoclassicism and dates from the mid 1800s when this entire section of the palace, housing the guest apartments and court offices, was entirely renovated by the court architect, Gaetano Genovese (1795-1875). The rooms were decorated principally with motifs from Pompei and Herculaneum.[45]

Almost of the same period is a small salon on the piano nobile of Villa Signorini in Herculaneum, decorated in an unusual Chinese style which combines late baroque elements with the use of clearly 'Pompeian' colours and some echoes of the exotic oriental lacquer motifs. Culturally and artistically this eclectic mix suggests a dating in the mid 19th century, when the Moorish decorations of Villa de Gregorio at Barra were also created.[46]

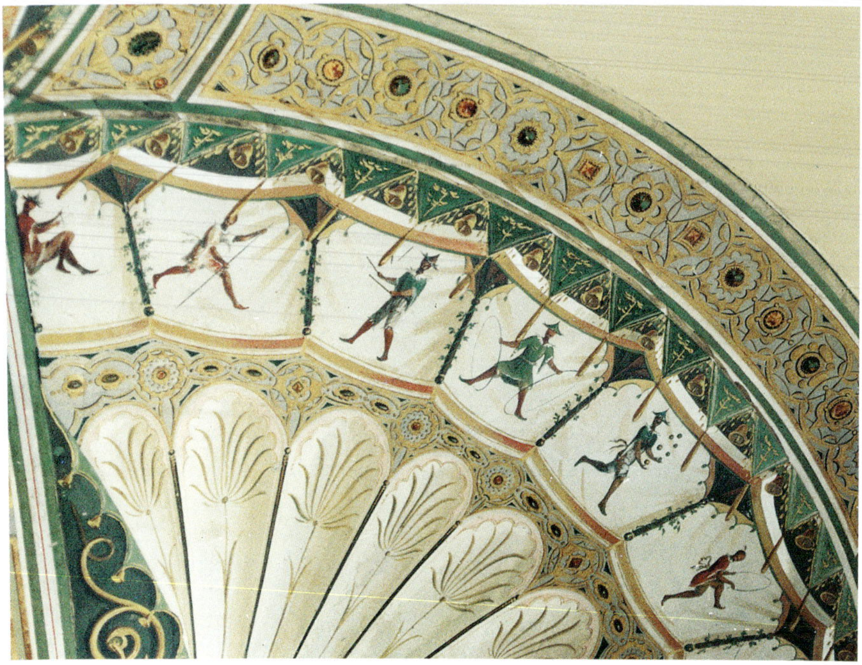

Sicily

Artistic and decorative styles and inspiration arrived directly from France in 18th-century Sicily, and the oriental fashion certainly did not bypass the island. *Rocaille* decoration was also in vogue therefore, though Sicilian craftsmen, traditionally accustomed to the more exuberant and elaborate Spanish style, interpreted it in their own way. [47] Use of the oriental style is first reported in Palermo in the mid-18th century (1752-1753) when the painters Michele Latino and Vincenzo Salerno produced some works in "prospettiva, gruttesco e figurista [alla] chinesa" (perspective, grotesque and in the Chinese style) in Palazzo Castelnuovo, a property owned by prince Carlo Filippo Cottone (1679-1763) [48] The furnishings of the Palermo residence of the prince of Butera, Nicolò Placido, reflected the latest innovations embracing the international oriental style. The building today preserves at least one example of this development in decorative styles, dating from the second half of the 18th century – a carved wooden door engraved and gilded with floral motifs, rocaille and chinoiserie, attributed to Giacomo Garretti and Francesco Guicciardi (or Licciardi) who clearly based their design on Pillement's compositions. Although the intention was French, a strongly local element is particularly evident in the lower section of the door where chinoiserie mingles with an abundance of other motifs.[49]

The two *poudreuses* at the far end of the Hall of Mirrors in Palazzo Valguarnera Gangi in Palermo (near the Kalsa) are decorated with delicate little Chinese scenes portraying figures of ladies surrounded by birds and trees, painted and lacquered on wood panels with a yellow background and framed by carved and gilded scrolls of leaves. The Chinese appearance is completed by the arrangement of numerous pieces of Far Eastern porcelain on small shelves within wooden frames. The Hall of Mirrors and the two *poudreuses* were made from 1757-1758 to a design by a young architect from Trapani, Andrea Gigante (1731-1787). The project was commissioned by prince Pietro Valguarnera (d. 1779) who not only followed the progress of the works personally but seems also to have provided the designs for the carvings in the two smaller chinoiserie rooms, superbly executed by Giuseppe Melia and Giovanni Battista Rizzo. Gaspare Serenario was the artist who designed the pictorial décor, and the walls, stuccowork and carvings were painted by Pietro Berardi.[50] The Hall is one of the masterpieces of Sicilian baroque, a delightful early interpretation of French Rococo, where the influence of

155. Sicilian artists, *Poudreuse* in the Hall of Mirrors, 1757-1758. Palermo, Palazzo Valguarnera Gangi.

One of two small powder rooms, the wealth of decoration recalls the exuberance of Venetian chinoiserie. References to the Far East are seen in the paintings on the walls but also in the arrangement of Chinese and Japanese porcelain on the small shelves set into the sinuous outlines of the wood frames.

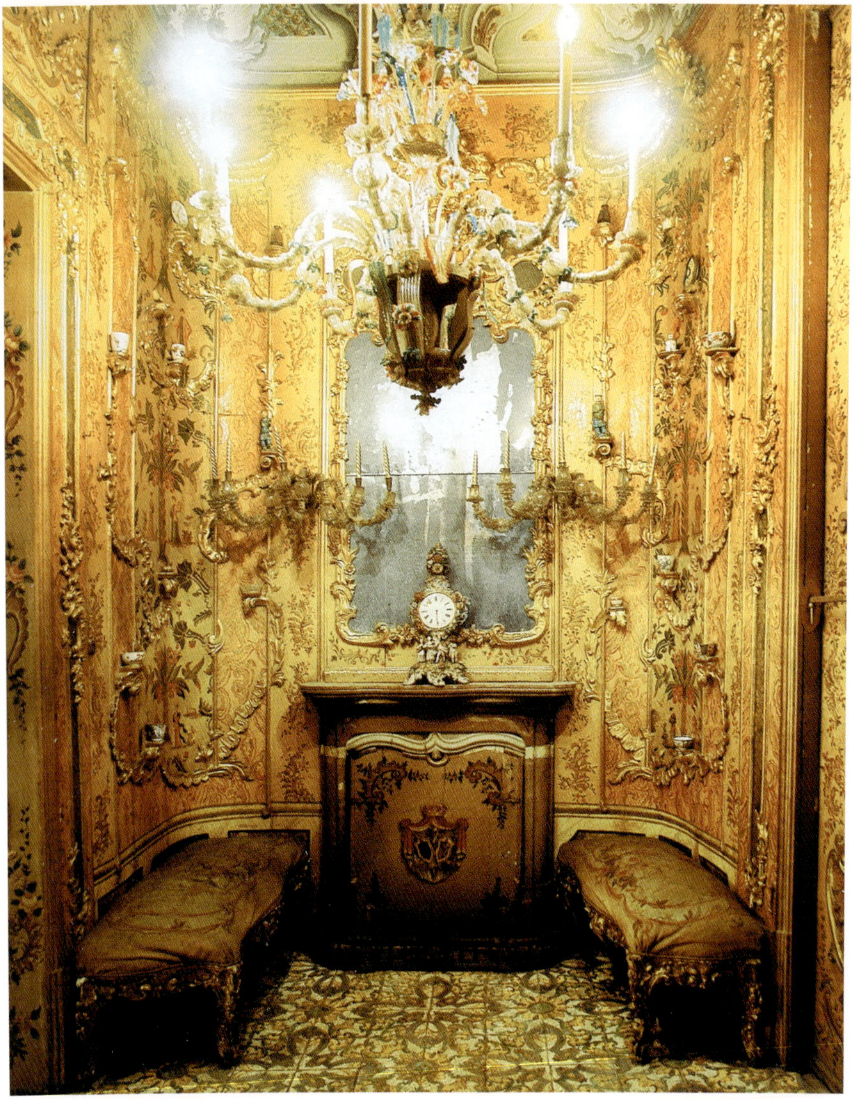

156. Sicilian artists, Gallery of Birds, c. 1766. Catania, Palazzo Biscari.

A splendid example of Sicilian Rococo showing two types of chinoiserie: on the one hand scenes with Chinese figures in the vault and on the other, compositions with exotic birds painted on the walls. Both cases represent a highly original interpretation of the oriental motifs popular throughout Europe in the early 1700s.

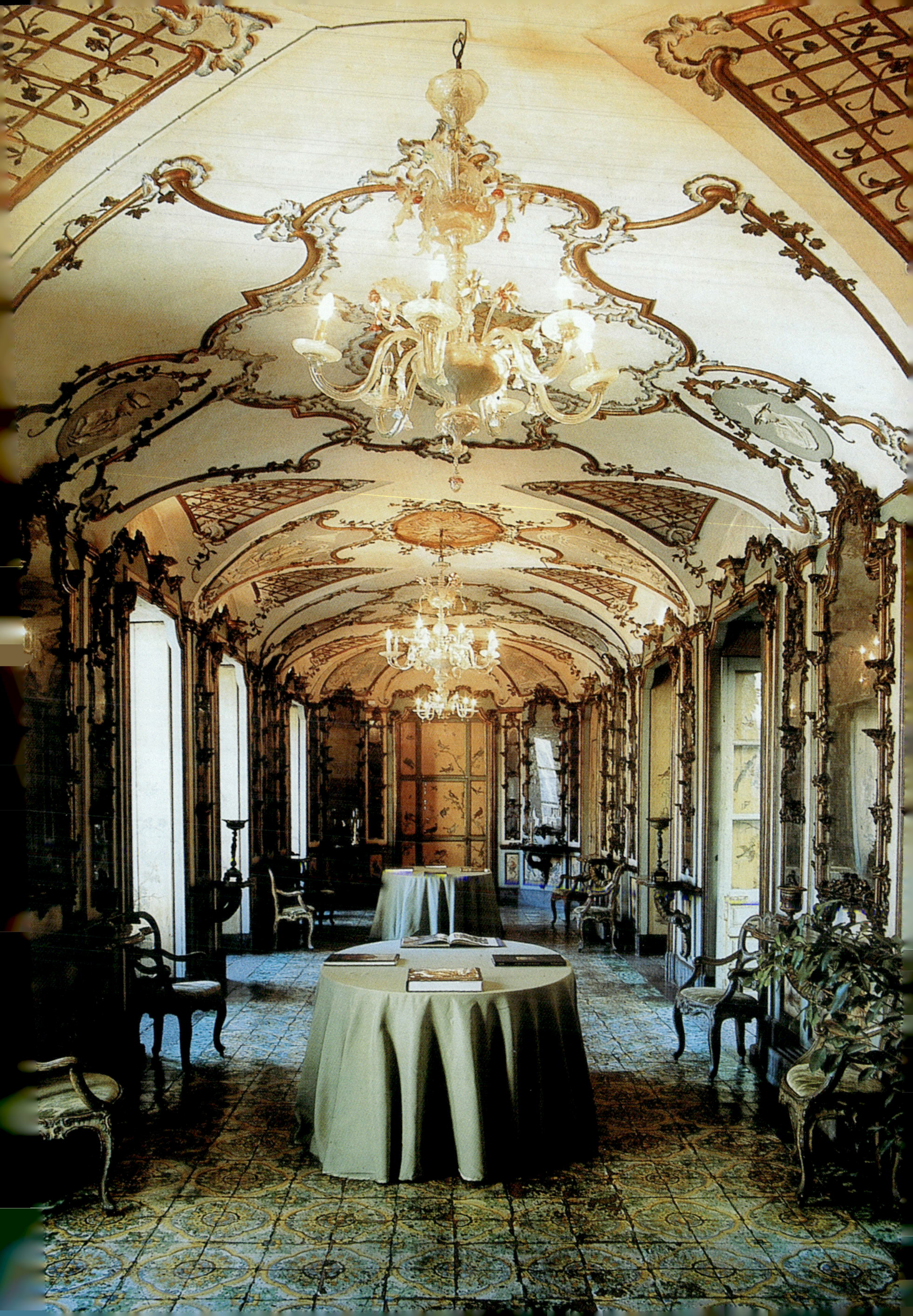

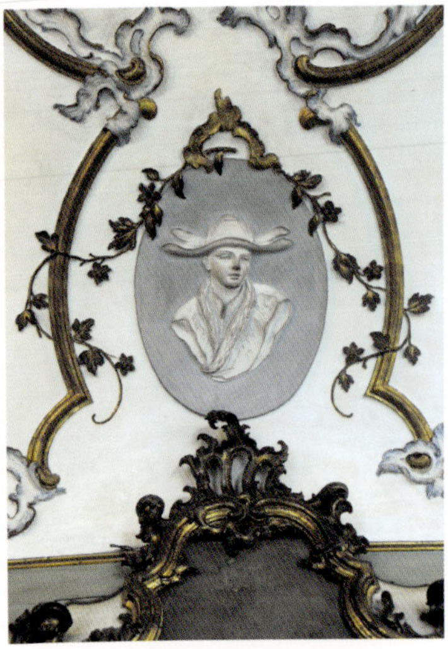
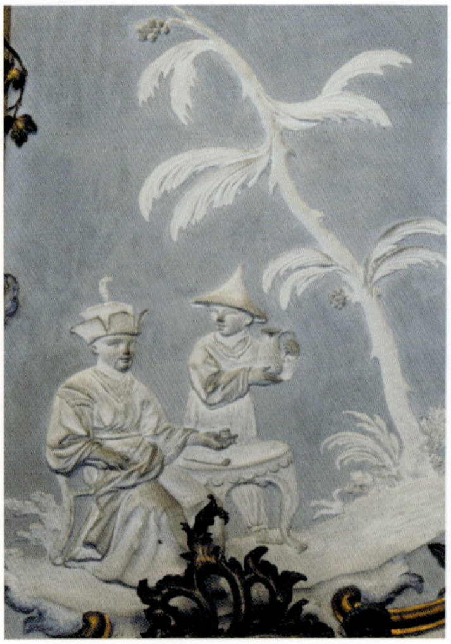
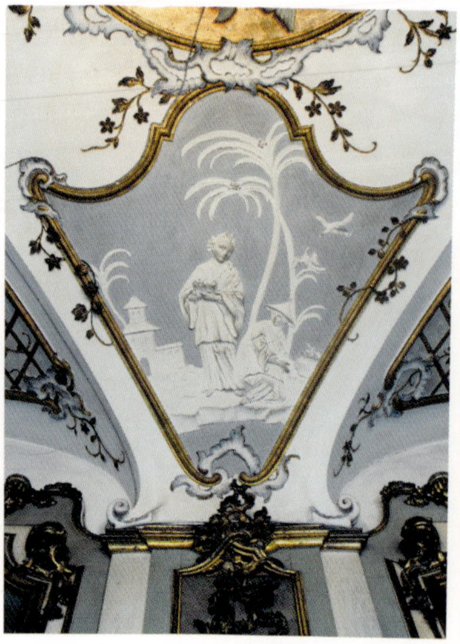

157a,b,c. Sicilian artists, Gallery of Birds, details of ceiling, c. 1766. Catania, Palazzo Biscari.

Picked out in white stucco on a turquoise background, these vignettes clearly reveal the influence of French compositions with an oriental theme – especially Watteau, Boucher and Pillement, whose works were known from engravings available in Sicily too.

contemporary Venetian works is also felt, especially in the decorative design of the two small chinoiserie rooms.[51]

Just slightly later than the chinoiserie of Palazzo Valguarnera Gangi in Palermo, the two Chinese rooms of Palazzo Biscari in Catania have been described as "one of the finest examples of chinoiserie in the entire island".[52] The two rooms are known as the "Gallery of Birds" and the "Don Quixote Room". The vault of the former is decorated with stuccowork in which slender gilded frames surround oriental scenes in relief. Along the walls, mirrors and console tables alternate with doors and panels painted with birds of all kinds. Documents dated 1766 record the acquisition in Naples of ceramic tiles and Japanese porcelain as well as "porcelain statuettes from India" and "from China and the factory in Paris, all in the latest style", to be arranged on the numerous shelves and brackets of the Gallery. The same date is engraved on the stuccowork that decorates the vault of the Don Quixote Room – also known as the 'conversation room' – where the ornithological theme, inspired by the eclectic imagination of prince Ignazio, is continued. The subject here however, is represented by a series of canvases portraying the adventures of Don Quixote, the work of Sebastiano Lo Monaco (c. 1730-c. 1775).[53] These two rooms were created around 1766 when the entire building was completely renovated, a complex operation which began in 1702, became more intense after 1743 under the guidance of Giuseppe Palazzotto, an engineer, and continued in the rococo style after 1764 when prince Ignazio Paternò Castello (1719-1786) commissioned the architect Francesco Battaglia. The prince was a man of great culture, a theatre lover, art collector and financier of numerous archaeological expeditions. His visitors were frequently renowned personalities including Goethe (2 May 1787) who was particularly fascinated by the collection of ambers in the room of the elderly princess, mother of Ignazio, but provided no information whatsoever regarding the two splendid 'Chinese' rooms.[54]

158. Sicilian artists, Gallery of Birds, detail, c. 1766. Catania, Palazzo Biscari.

The designs with birds appear alongside the wood carvings that decorate the walls, echoing the wooden structures of the chairs furnishing the room.

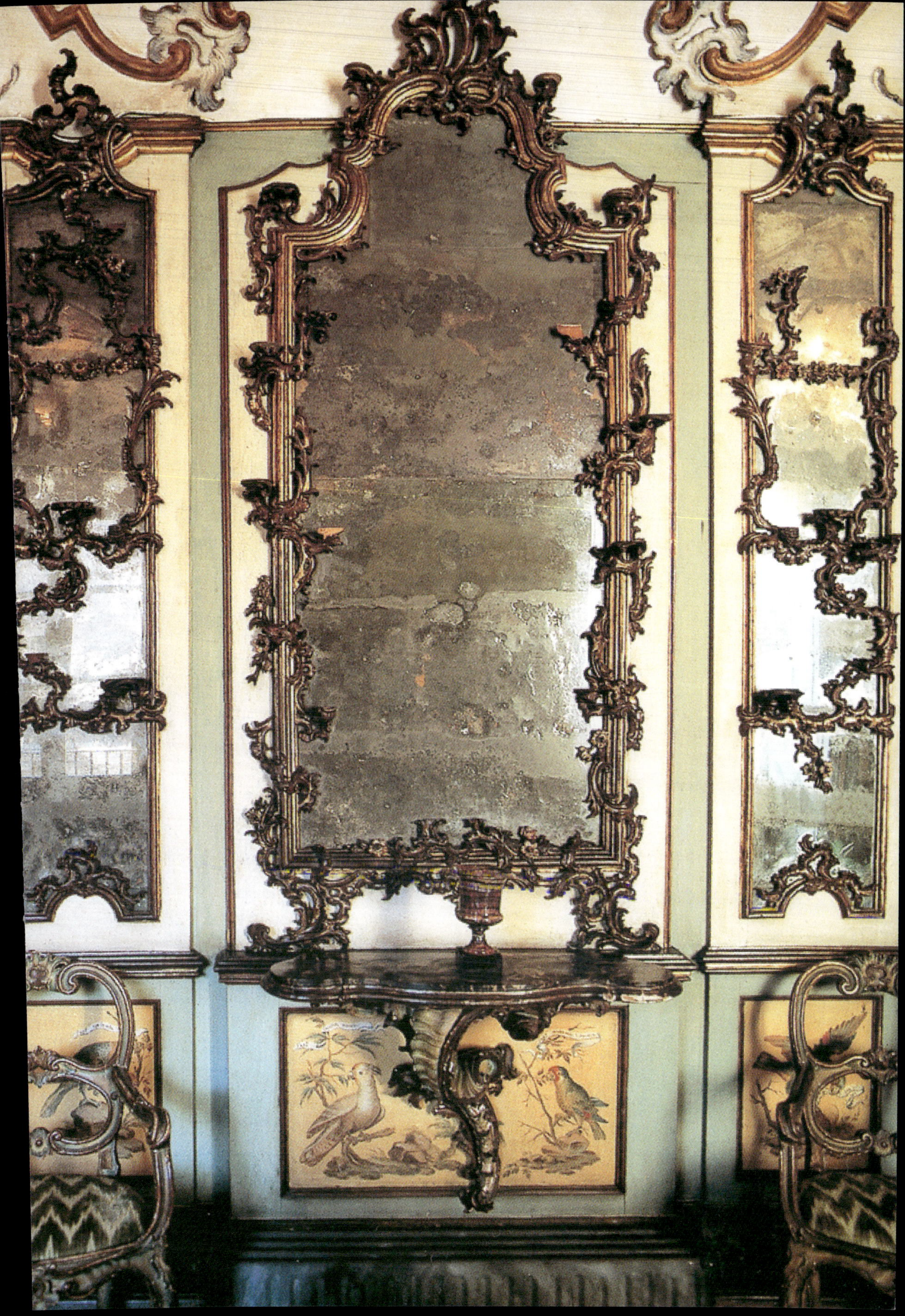

The apartment furnished in the Chinese style on the first floor of count Airoldi's villa on the slopes of Monte Pellegrino in Palermo dates from just slightly later. It is mentioned in the volume *Breve relazione di una casa fatta al monte Pellegrino per ordine del marchese Stefano Airoldi* by Michele Torcia (1736-1808), published in Palermo in 1784, slightly before the neoclassical reinterpretation of chinoiserie reached its height with the arrival in Sicily of the Bourbon.

The construction that best exemplifies Sicilian chinoiserie is the 'Palazzina Cinese' in the Favorita park in Palermo. It may also be considered the final phase in the development of the oriental fashion in the Kingdom of the Two Sicilies in the 18th century.[55] The villa was built for Ferdinando IV and his wife, who had been obliged to flee from Naples in 1798 due to the revolutionary uprisings. The couple purchased a huge area of land at the foot of the hills to the north of Palermo, close to the residences of the most important families of the Sicilian aristocracy, where they hoped to spend their exile as enjoyably as possible. In creating the 'Favorita' at Portici not so very long before, the sovereigns had included many oriental elements and in Palermo too there was ample opportunity to develop the Chinese theme. The project was entrusted to Giuseppe Venanzio Marvuglia (1729-1814), who based the project on an earlier building he had designed in the very same park, a hereditary property of the Lombardo-Lucchese family.[56] This original building was a rather modest wooden affair, illustrated in a watercolour by Pietro Martora in Palazzo Reale, constructed after 1790 according to the architect Léon Dufourny (1754-1818) who visited the site that year. By 1798 work on this ephemeral structure must have been complete as count Villabianca described it then as "a structure completely in wood, the planks of the balconies are attached to the wooden beams with ropes, it is round in shape and is decorated in the Chinese style with domes over all the bells which swing and chime in the wind so that it is called the House of Bells", adding that "it seems to me an eccentric building without any splendour, and that is destined to be short lived". With the arrival of the Bourbons work rapidly recommenced both on the structure and on the decorations, and the park and gardens were also involved in the general overhaul with the installation of several white marble pools with 'Chinese style' artificial grottos, made in 1800 by the marble worker Giosuè Durante. The grounds also contained a "cafeaos", a small octagonal pavilion later destroyed and known only from a tempera attributed to Gioacchino Martorana, now in Caserta's Palazzo Reale. It is quite clear from this painting that the structure in the Palermo park was inspired by the pavilion designed by Rambonillet and illustrated in one of Le Rouge's volumes in 1784. Giuseppe Marvuglia's son, Alessandro Emmanuele, was the author of the preparatory drawings for the wall paintings representing Chinese subjects which decorated the interior of the Villa's "cafeaos", though these were later lost.[57] Work on the 'Palazzina' continued under the direction of Alessandro between 1802 and 1806 when

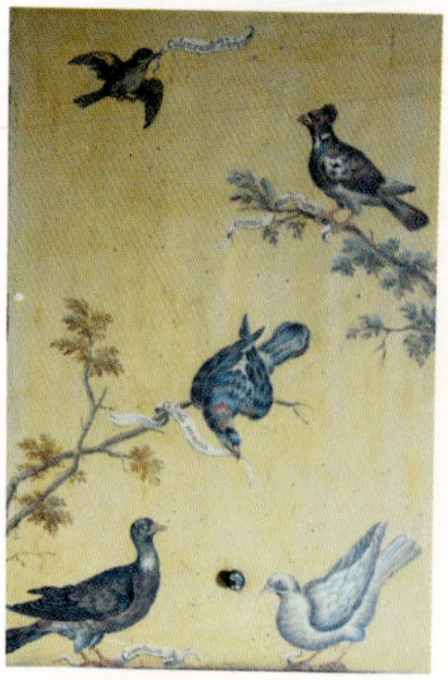

159. Sicilian artists, Gallery of Birds, detail, c. 1766. Catania, Palazzo Biscari.

The natural appearance of these compositions would seem to indicate that the Sicilian decorators were familiar with this theme from fabrics and painted papers produced in China for export to Europe. The precision with which the various species are depicted suggests that the artists used illustrations from ornithological texts as their models.

160. Sicilian artists, The Don Quixote Room, 1766. Catania, Palazzo Biscari.

The exotic compositions with various species of birds alternate here with a series of canvases portraying episodes from the adventures of Don Quixote.

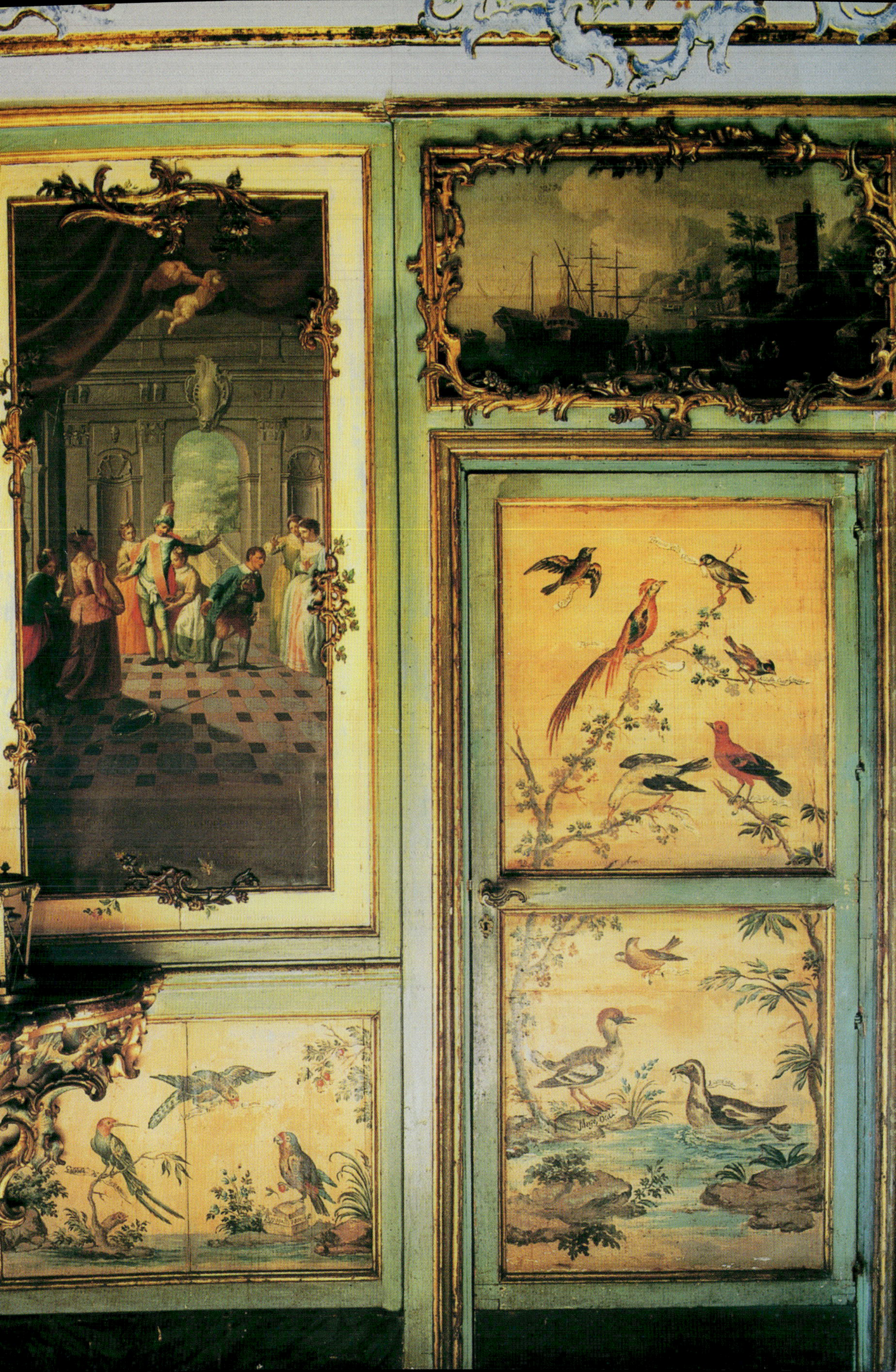

Ferdinando and his retinue were allowed to re-visit Naples and must have been complete by the time the court returned to Sicily in 1807. In contrast to the original structure, the final version of the Palazzina Cinese successfully combines elegance and dignity. Marvuglia skilfully handled the difficult task of emphasising the Chinese features of the building while, however, intelligently applying them to a neoclassical concept of the whole. Having studied under Vanvitelli in Rome as a young man, Marvuglia assiduously utilized classical elements in numerous buildings in Sicily and did not altogether abandon them even in the design of the Favorita. Despite this, the resulting structure is effectively one of the most characteristic examples of the European fashion for chinoiserie. Completed between 1805 and 1815, decoration of the villa interiors combined various stylistic revivals, an approach frequently found in the décor of the time. Surprizingly coexisting, instead of clashing, were oriental elements, references to Vesuvian classicism, echoes of the late baroque period and anglo-chinois features which somehow combined to create appealing chinoiserie despite the brilliant colours, pretty and attractive despite the geometric symmetry of the painted panels, far removed from wayward oriental Rococo. One of the artists involved in the Chinese decorations in the Favorita was Giuseppe Velasco (1750-1827), who was paid for various wall paintings in 1806. The ornamental painters included Rosario Silvestri and Benedetto Cotardi, as well as Vincenzo Riolo

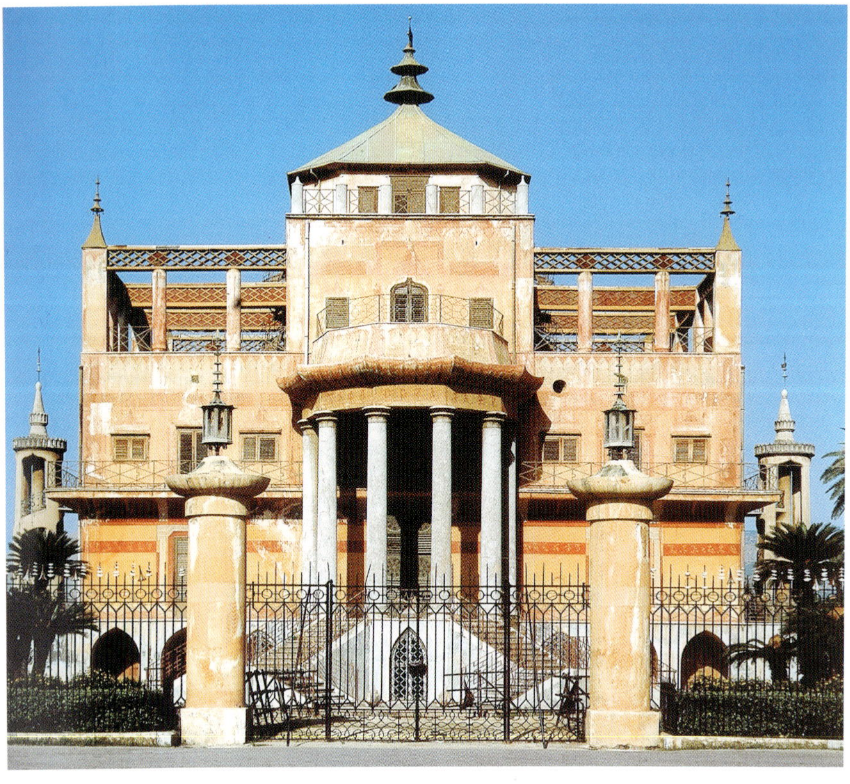

161. The Chinese Palace, 1798-1807. Palermo, Parco della Favorita.

Designed by Giuseppe Marvuglia and built over a pre-existing wooden structure, the Palazzina is one of the most fascinating Italian chinoiseries; the exotic theme blends perfectly with the neoclassical architectural forms.

162. Pietro Martora, Watercolour of the 'first' Chinese Palace, 1790-1797. Palermo, Palazzo Reale.

This watercolour provides an image of the ephemeral wooden structure which existed on the site where Ferdinando IV's Chinese Palace would subsequently be built. While Marvuglia was probably inspired by this earlier building he succeeded in creating a decidedly more harmonious structure worthy of the royal couple.

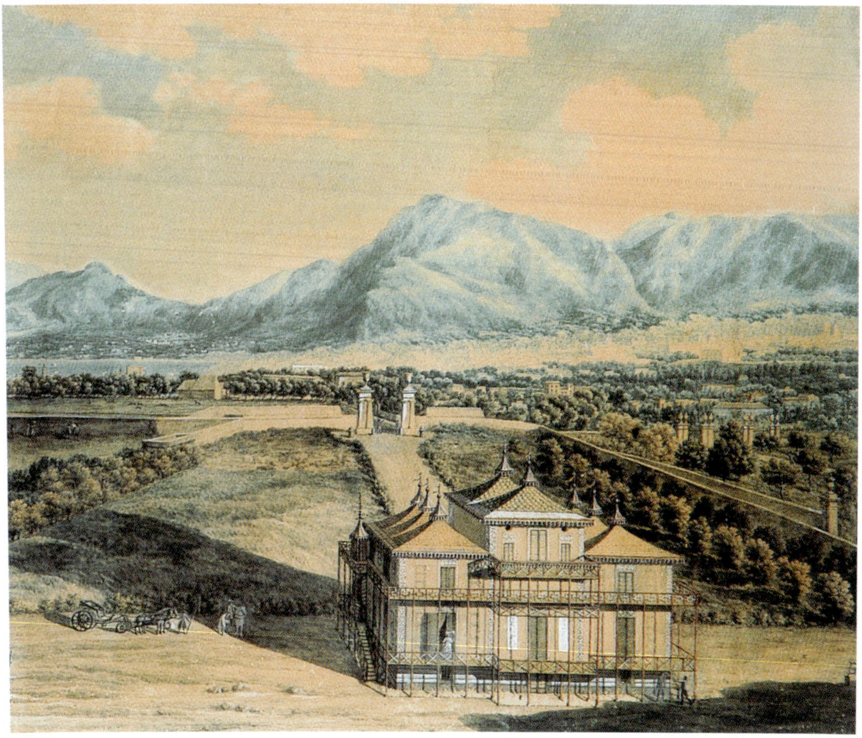

who worked on both the silk wall hangings on the piano nobile and the chinoiserie ceiling in the reception hall, where he collaborated with Rosario Silvestri. Although his painted works reveal a relationship with the themes and styles of Rococo, Velasco is considered the most important representative of neoclassicism in Sicily and was frequently called on by Marvuglia.[58] In the course of his long career the Favorita was the only occasion on which he undertook oriental themes and although he achieved some pure chinoiserie on the ceiling of the bedroom in the royal apartment, where he worked with Cotardi, even here his classical roots are fairly evident. Furnishings for the Villa were brought from the Portici Favorita and included numerous small original Chinese paintings.[59]

The scenes decorating the ceiling of the Chinese salon in Palazzo Mirto in the old Kalsa district in the centre of Palermo are later than the paintings in the Favorita.[60] For the occasion the anonymous artist of the tempera decorations designed a fantastical perspective of a loggia seen from below, where ethereal oriental figures stroll. This ghostly group provides the oriental element of the composition which, apart from this, has a rather classical appearance especially in the neo-Renaissance colonnade and even the fretwork of the balustrade, although this particular feature would seem to be derived from mid 18th century English chinoiserie. More obviously oriental are the original Chinese silks on the walls, painted with scenes derived from the *Silk Manufacture Set*, and the furniture lacquered in red and black with

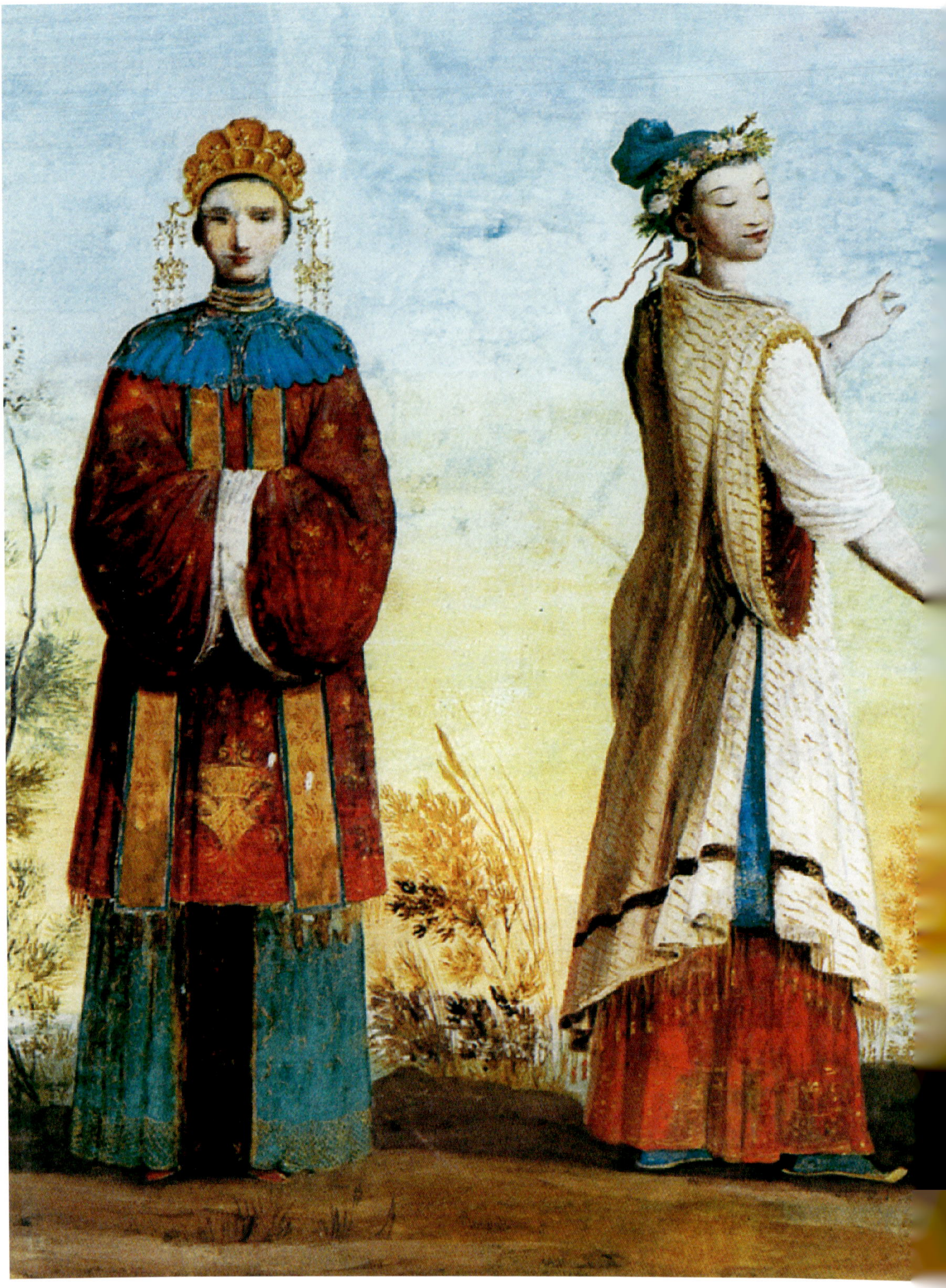

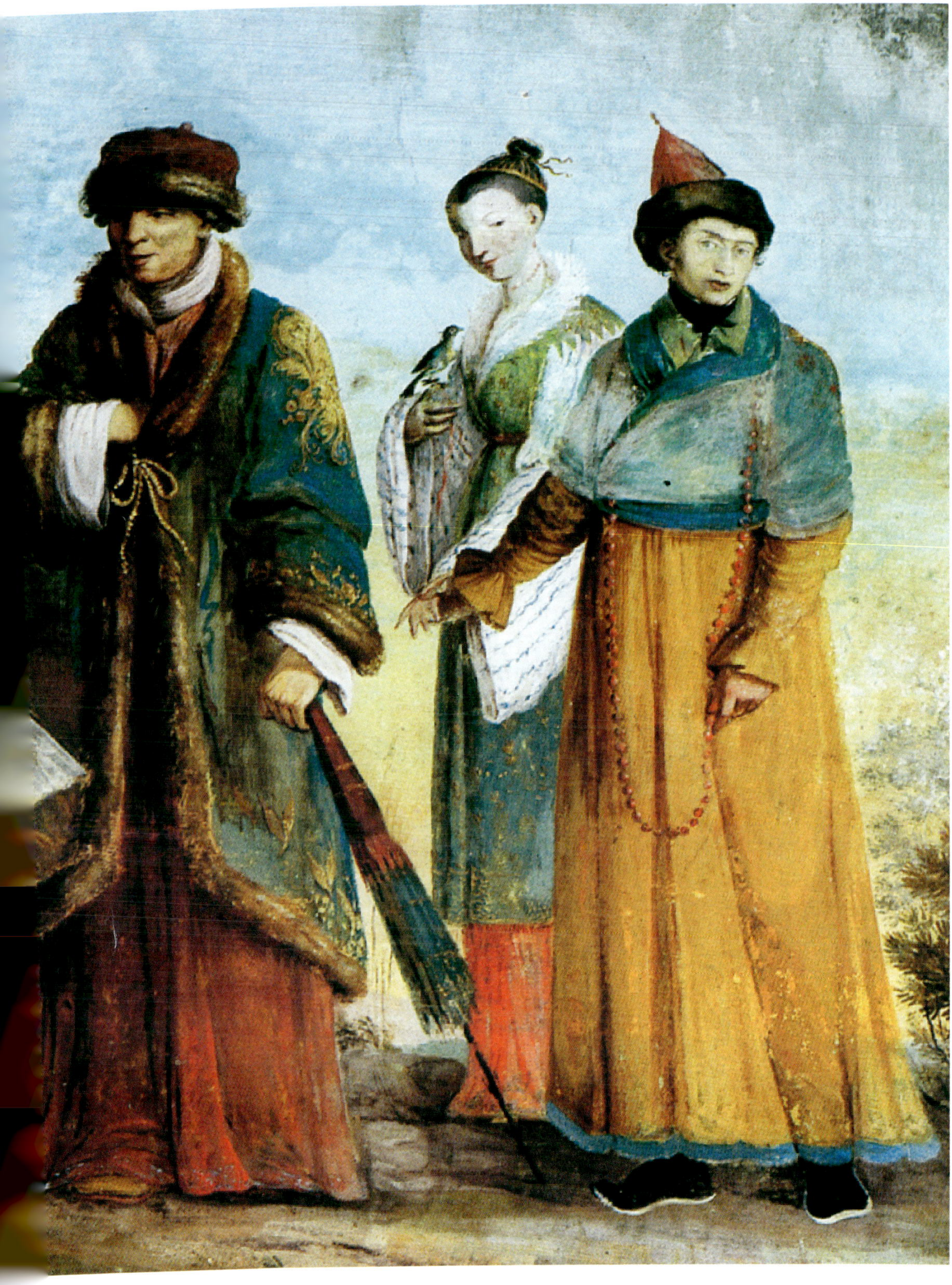

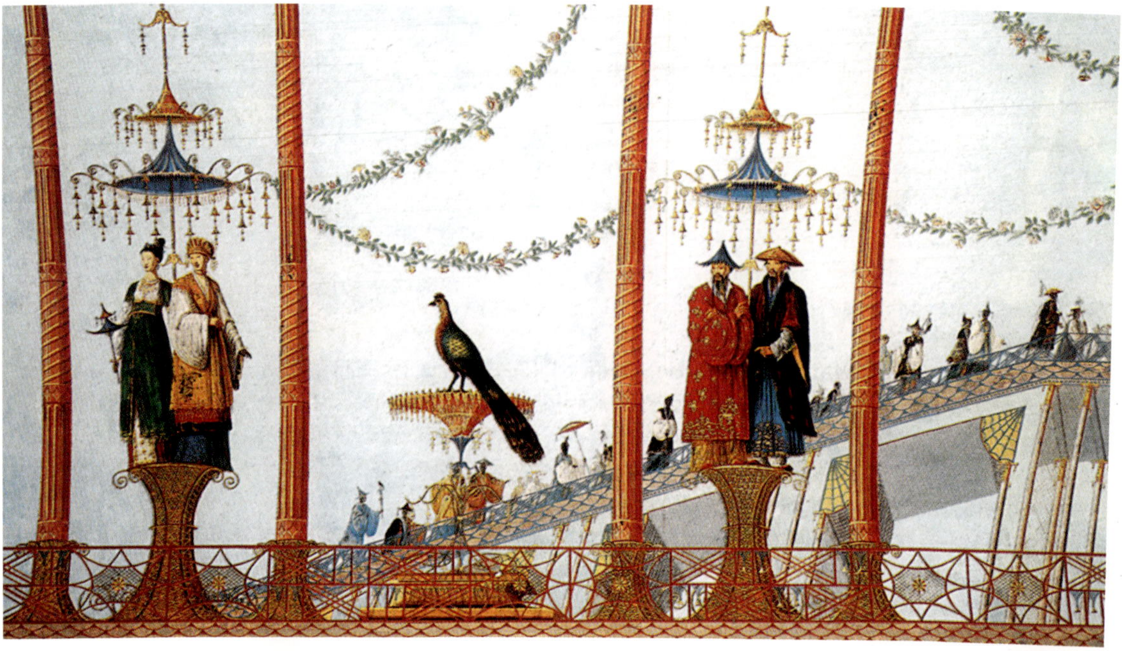

Previous pages, above and following page:

163a,b,c. Anonymous Sicilian artists, Details of the Chinese-style wall paintings, c. 1805-1815. Palermo, Palazzina Cinese.

The mural paintings in the Chinese Palace represent an elegant and sophisticated orientalism, strongly influenced by neoclassical harmony. The figures are generally portrayed in tranquil poses that indicate, however, a degree of romantic idealisation of the oriental character. The compositional panels are large and airy and the lively colours have been intelligently used.

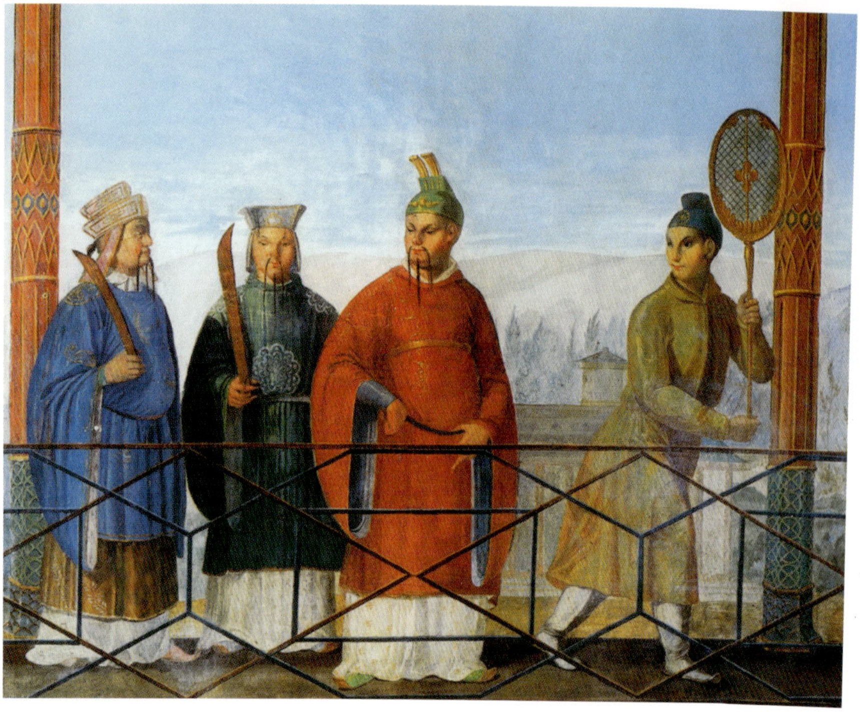

164. Giovanni Patricolo, Chinese scene, 1835. Palermo, Palazzo dei Normanni.

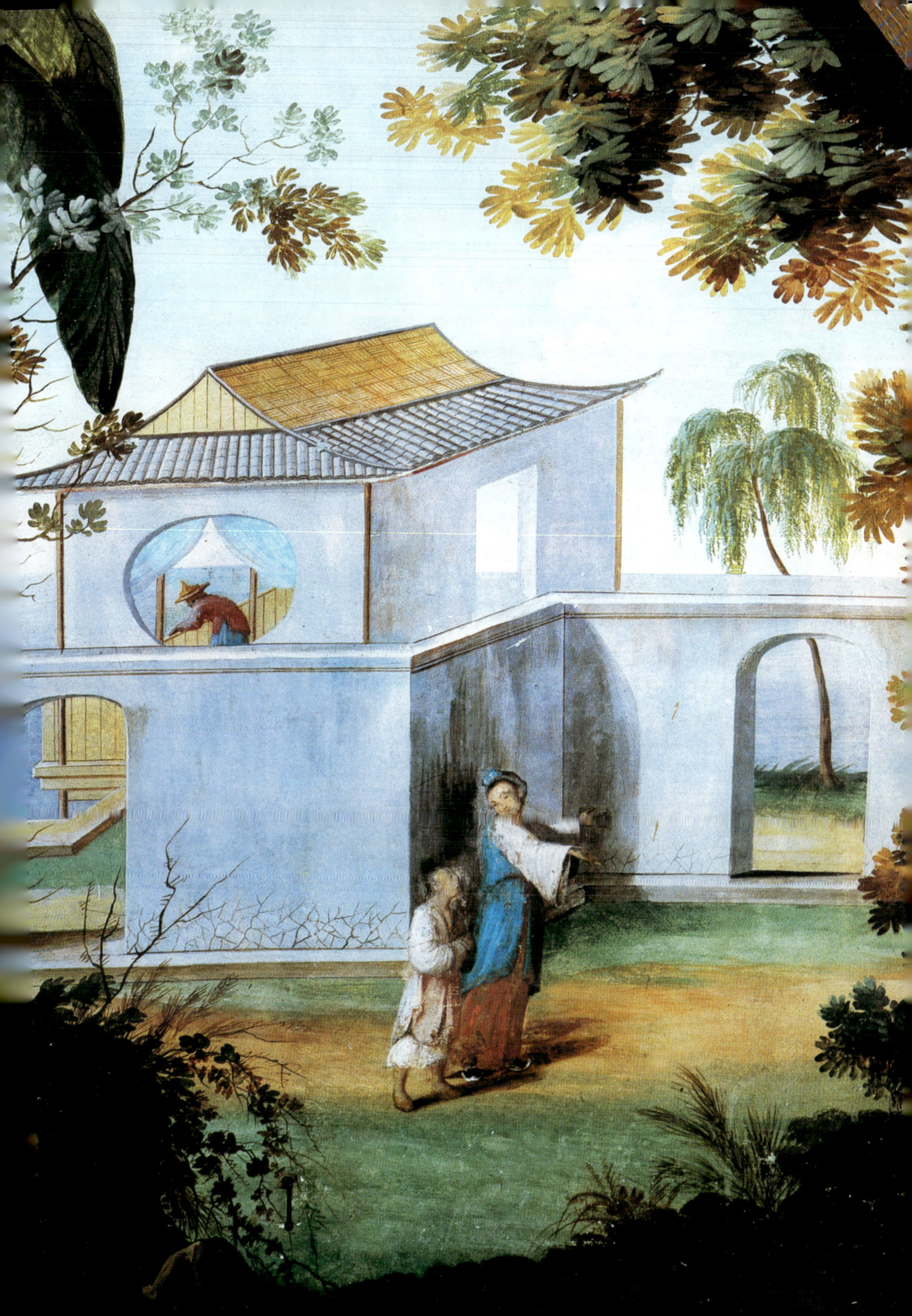

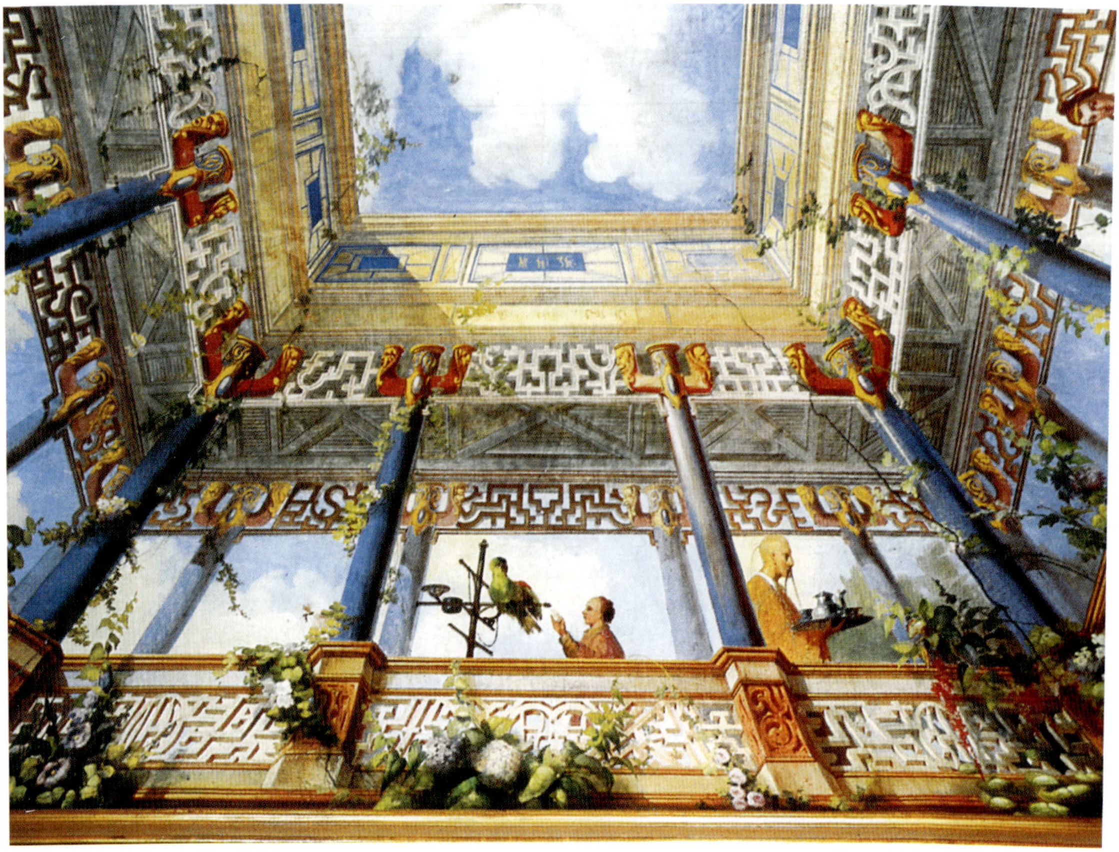

165. Anonymous Sicilian artist, Wall paintings in the Chinese Room, 19th century. Palermo, Palazzo Mirto.

Ghostly figures of Chinamen drift along behind the columns on the lower level of this perspective view designed for the ceiling of the Chinese Room in Palazzo Mirto.

Chinese motifs in gold, probably made between 1891 and 1892 and recently attributed to Antonio Catalano, a craftsman from Palermo.[61] An extensive programme of internal renovation was commissioned in 1793 by Bernardo Filangeri e Montaperto, prince of Mirto and count of San Marco, a member of the family who had owned the building since the 1600s. The present appearance of the palace still substantially reflects the many alterations made at the time when the Chinese salon was also installed.

Although much later compared to the decorations in the Palazzina Cinese, the paintings with oriental subjects in Palazzo Reale in Palermo are similar in style and composition to earlier works. The Chinese-style scenes in Palazzo dei Normanni were painted by Giovanni Patricolo (1789-1861) about 1835, when much of the ancient building was modernised and the current decorative schemes were established.[62]The decorations in Palazzo dei Normanni indicate that chinoiserie remained persistently popular in Sicily, continuing throughout at least the first half of the 19th century. In 1831 the Palermo edition of the 'Traditions of China' edited by Giulio Ferrario (1767-1847) was published and its precise descriptions and references to the architecture and interior furnishings of the country must have reflected, and possibly perpetuated, widespread interest in the oriental style.[63]

1) Catello E. 1992, *passim*: where not otherwise specified the information in this chapter is taken from this work.
2) Ruotolo 1982, p. 7.
3) Naples 1984, II, p. 476, no. 6.23.
4) Santuccio 1992, pp. 35-36.
5) Zoli 1974, p. 30; Zoli 1984, pp. 215-217.
6) Zoli 1984, p. 218.
7) Zoli 1984, pp. 224-228.
8) Zoli 1984, p. 229 and ff.
9) Zoli 1974, pp. 45-56; Zoli 1984, pp. 239-243.
10) Zoli 1974, pp. 8-13; Zoli 1984, pp. 215-216.
11) Lightbown 1969, p. 265.
12) Fatica 1984, pp. 171-175.
13) Tamburello 2003, p. 232.
14) Wittkower 1989, p. 189.
15) Di Mauro 2002.
16) Buccaro, Kjučarianc, Miltenov 2003.
17) Honour 1961 (1963), p. 136; Jacobson 1993, pp. 106-110.
18) Honour 1961 (1963), p. 143; Jacobson 1993, pp. 116-118.
19) Giusti 1986.
20) Sade 1996, p. 309.
21) De Martini in Naples 1979, II, p. 123.
22) Naples 1986, pp. 256-257; Paris 2007, p. 154.
23) Morazzoni 1960, II, pl. 301.
24) Wilson Frothingham 1955; Mañueco Santurtún 2003.
25) Honour 1961 (1963), p. 144.
26) Cerrada Clemente, Sánchez Hernández 1998.
27) Porzio 2005.
28) González-Palacios in Naples 1979, II, no. 432; Morroni 2001, p. 30.
29) Colle 2003, p. 29.
30) González-Palacios in Naples 1979, II, no. 438.
31) González-Palacios 1984, p. 295, figs. 507-508.
32) Putaturo Murano 1977, p. 75, nos. 80-81, pl. XXXVI.
33) González-Palacios 1984, pp. 323-324, figs. 531-537.
34) Arbace 1994, p. 23.
35) González-Palacios 1984, p. 324, fig. 531, pl. XLII.
36) González-Palacios 1984, p. 324, fig. 530, pl. XL.
37) Arbace 1994, p. 30 and fig. at p. 33.
38) Zoli 1974, p. 114.
39) Tagliolini 1988, pp. 324-325.
40) Honour 1961 (1963), p. 145, fig. 91.
41) González-Palacios 2003.
42) González-Palacios 1984, pp. 363-380.
43) Porzio 2001, pp. 12-13.
44) Porzio 2001, p. 13
45) Porzio 1994, pp. 95, 104-105.
46) Catello A. 1998, p. 90.
47) Palazzotto 2002; Palazzotto 2008.
48) Palazzotto 2008, p. 535.
49) Giarrizzo, Rotolo 2004, p. 54 and fig. 29 at p. 41.
50) Zalapì 1998, p. 172.
51) Giarrizzo, Rotolo 2004, fig. 21 at p. 34; Piazza 2005.
52) Zalapì 1998, p. 186.
53) Zalapì 1998, p. 186.
54) Giarrizzo, Rotolo 2004, pp. 48-50.
55) Giuffrida, Giuffrè 1987.
56) Bufalino, Di Cristina 1984.
57) Palazzotto 2008, pp. 24-25.
58) Palazzotto 2008, p. 558 and figs. 21, 22.
59) Caterina, Porzio 2001.
60) Palazzo Mirto s.d.
61) Palazzotto 2002, pp. 32-33.
62) Palazzo dei Normanni 1991, fig. III. 27 and no. 19 at p. 210; Zalapì 1998, p. 44.
63) Giuffrida, Giuffrè 1987, p. 94.

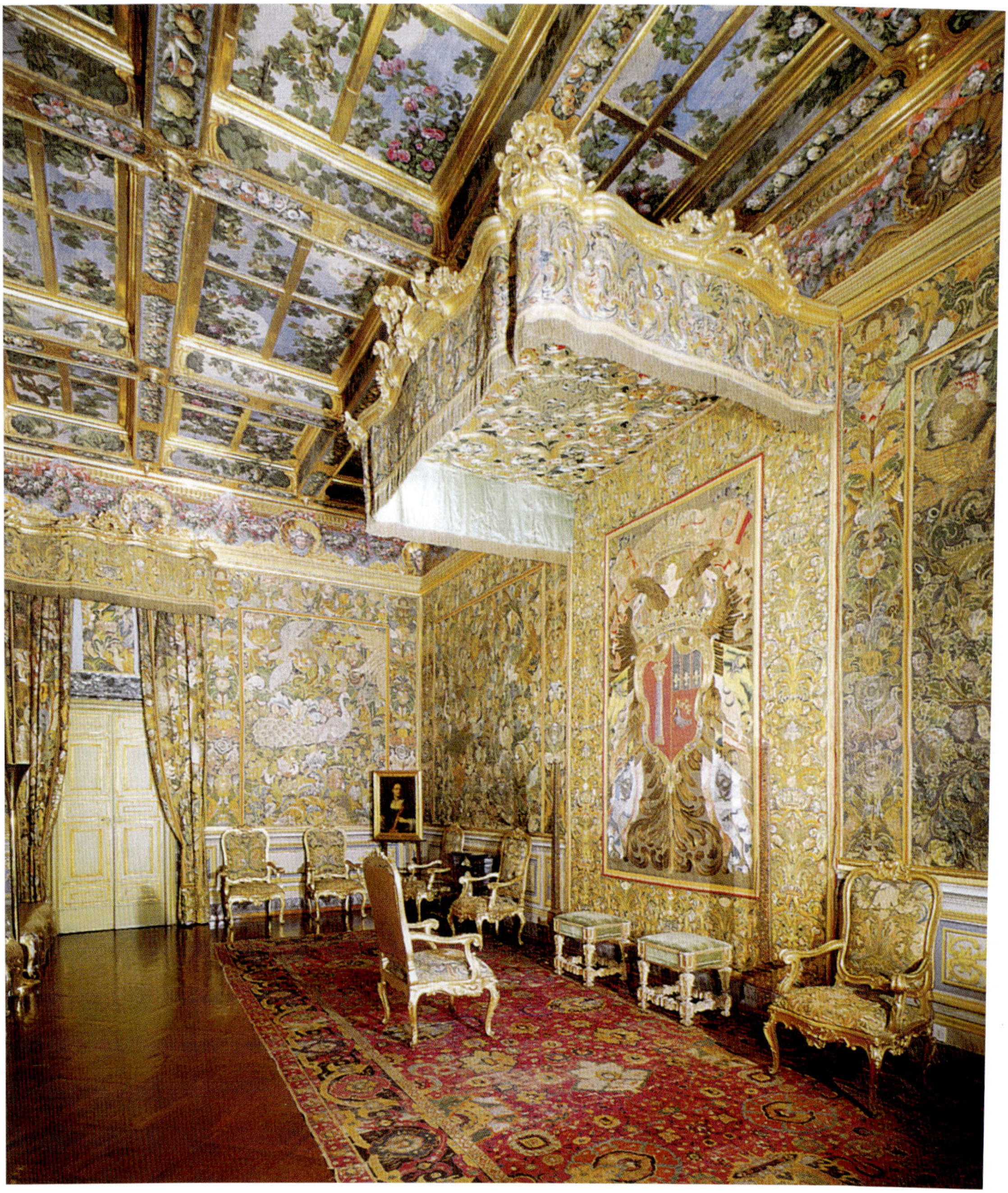

166. Roman textiles fabrics embroidered in the exotic style, late 17th century. Rome, Palazzo Colonna, Apartment of Olimpia Pamphilj.

The embroidery decorating the walls and furnishings of this room perhaps represents the only surviving example of textiles with 'Indian-style' motifs made in late 17th-century Rome. Documents of the period reveal that this style of furnishing was highly fashionable.

Rome and the Vatican State

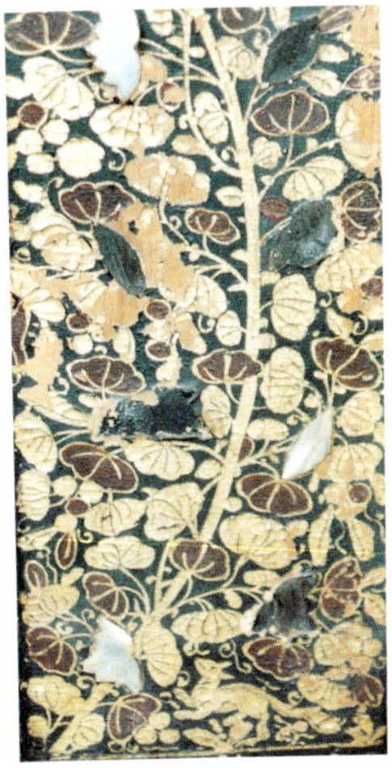

167. Japan (?), Detail of a column of a bedstead, late 16th-early 17th century. Rome, Palazzo Colonna, Apartment of Olimpia Pamphilj.

In rather a poor state of repair, the two columns are decorated with gold, some paintwork and inserts of mother-of-pearl on a background of black lacquer. The style and technique of the decoration recall Japanese items known as *Nanban* (meaning "the barbarians of the south"), made from the 1550s for export to Europe.

The presence of the Vatican and the pope – the highest authority of the Christian faith – was a crucial factor in stimulating the arrival in Rome of goods from the distant Orient at quite an early date. During the 13th and 14th centuries, the initiative of several popes had succeeded in establishing direct and continual relations between Europe and Mongol China. Although not officially involved, from the beginning the church participated actively in the colonial expansion of the European nations. Portugal and Spain were, after all, the most Catholic countries in Europe and their trade on the other side of the world was given the blessing of the papacy in the hope that the teachings of Christ would eventually penetrate the mysteries of oriental idolatry and thus create a barrier in the East to the increasing spread of the Islamic culture. Many priests and brethren – especially Jesuits, but also Franciscans, Dominicans, and others – travelled on Portuguese and Spanish ships, courageously undertaking the long journey to the Far East where they lived for years, sometimes remaining there for the rest of their lives. The accounts of these missionaries, sometimes sent from China, sometimes written on their return home, provide an inexhaustible source of information on the eastern cultures, as useful and informative as the descriptions of the Orient written by English and Dutch scholars in the 17th century. In many ways these missionaries' reports, both published and unpublished, constituted a unique papal resource, encouraging and facilitating the manufacture of items in an 'exotic' style. Moreover, the final destination of most diplomatic missions organised by Far Eastern countries was in fact the Vatican and envoys arrived with numerous gifts for the pope and his entourage. Legations first arrived in the 13th and 14th centuries and again in the 16th and 17th centuries, when two arrived from Japan (in 1585 and 1615) and at least one from China in 1652. A few portraits of these Japanese diplomats have survived and doubtless contributed to establishing a somewhat more accurate image of the Orient and its peoples:[1] a painting kept in the Gregoriana University in Rome, the fresco in the library of the Vatican Museums, paintings in the Teatro Olimpico in Vicenza, five drawings by Urbano Monte in the Biblioteca Ambrosiana in Milan are preserved, while in the Quirinale a fresco by Agostino Tassi provides another portrait. Further images are found in a private collection in Rome, and in a volume by De Grevembroch (*Gli abiti de' Veneziani di quasi ogni età con diligenza raccolti e dipinti nel sec. XVIII).*

The 17th Century

The publication of *China Illustrata* by Athanasius Kircher in 1667 brought greater awareness and more accurate knowledge of the Far East to Rome. A Jesuit, Kircher was also the creator and founder of a museum established in the Roman College where original artefacts from China, Japan and Asian countries in general were exhibited. His famous publication also contained descriptions of the principal eastern artistic techniques which he had formulated from his own studies of ancient texts and from information provided by his fellow brethren on return from the East. Kircher's description of original oriental lacquer was based on Martino Martini's earlier account in *Novus Atlas Sinensis* dating from 1655, but the recipe for the varnish was supplied by the Augustinian father Eustache Jamart which, although "it was not Chinese, was highly regarded and much appreciated".[2]

Lacquered furniture with 'Chinese' decorations was already being produced in Rome in the early 1600s. In a letter of 1616 to the count of Arundel, Thomas Howard (1585-1646), the English japanner William Smith comments that Chinese lacquer was very popular among the princes and cardinals of the city.[3] References to lacquered items increase in Rome in the later 17th century[4] as they were imported by the East India Companies, and in 1666, for example, there was even a "small study in the Indian style, entirely inlayed with mother-of-pearl" in Palazzo Pamphilj in Piazza Navona, while "a small table of Indian woods, decorated with animals and figures on horseback and other similar Indian motifs" was recorded in the possessions of princess Rossano on her death in 1682. Cardinal Flavio Chigi (1631-1693) was the owner of an interesting collection of curios consisting of numerous original Chinese and Japanese items, including a "round vase of lacquered wood with gold arabesques". Although there are no known examples of oriental style lacquered items made in Rome during the 17th century it is, however, probable that most of the objects in the Chigi collection were made in Europe and perhaps even in Rome.

In his book *Le traité de la décoration intérieure*, published in 1717, but based on his two journeys to Rome in 1673 and 1688, the Swedish architect, Nicodemus Tessin the Younger (1654-1728) stated that Roman palaces were then at the height of their artistic splendour flaunting unparalleled magnificence.[5] Generally harmonious, the ornamentation was designed to be theatrical in appearance, the various elements combining to create an overall impression of opulence. The most important Roman palaces were crowded with colourful frescoes, painted and gilded stucco and almost sculptural furniture, sumptuously carved with scrolls and curlicues. Walls were covered with hangings, embossed leather and crimson brocades with gold embroidery. Perhaps the only surviving example of embroidered fabric wall coverings is in Palazzo Colonna in the second backroom of Olimpia Pamphilj's apartment, second wife of Filippo II Colonna (1663-1714). Also covering the backs and seats of the chairs and the bed canopy – in the centre of which is the Colonna-Pamphilj coat of arms – this vast embroidered creation is a riot of exotic motifs with parrots, peacocks, flowers and foliage, all highly original and brilliantly coloured. At the end of the 17th century Diego Casale, an embroiderer, is documented as having designed "wall hangings in the Indian style with flowers and animals and fruits ... made by the countess Stella". Thus the wall coverings still existing in Palazzo Colonna reproduced the decorative style of many Asian works imported to Europe at the time, but were entirely made in Rome.[6] Previously housed in the 'Guardaroba', the five large embroidered panels must have been installed in Olimpia's apartment immediately after the death of Filippo Colonna in 1714, and although the wooden structure of the furniture was restored in 1750, their original 'oriental' fabric was reused.

The present furnishings of the room also include two small columns which must originally have belonged to a bed or a sedan chair, made of black lacquered wood decorated with gold and mother-of-pearl inlay where birds and small monkeys appear amidst the floral arabesques. In 1714 these works were described in the possessions of Filippo Colonna as "four small columns of black wood decorated in gold with Indian motifs, and a dish on top to hold candles". . In addition to numerous paintings of all kinds, the room where they were housed was furnished with other Eastern items[7] such as a 16th century Isfahan rug (now in the Sala della Fontana on the first floor of the Palace), eight chairs, two small tables with two pairs of porcelain vases and two sets of wooden drawers with trays, two mirrors, an oval clock beneath which were some Spanish vases, a firescreen, and an ebony case inside which were more pieces of porcelain (presumably Chinese or Japanese). Like the two columns, these furnishings were nearly all, "wood varnished in black, painted in the Indian style with gold flowers", and many were also enhanced with mother-of-pearl inlay. The entire room is obviously a prime example of the 'Indian style' furnishings that gained some popularity in Rome in the late 1600s. It has been suggested in the past that the two small columns may have been made in Turkey in the 17th century.[0] Excluding the possibility of Chinese, Japanese or Indian manufacture, it is quite possible that they were made in Europe, reproducing a style generically referred to as 'Indian'. In 1683 a bill was sent to the Colonna by a certain Giovan Battista De Pedibus, "a painter in the Indian style in via de' Coronari", for the decoration of eighteen chairs, painted "in the Indian style, lacquered and decorated with gold" - perhaps providing a suggestion for the origin of these works.[9]

Rococo

In the early 1700s trade in exotic products was flourishing in Rome. In 1701, for example, Anton Giulio Brignole bought Chinese lacquer items in Rome for his palace in Genoa and in 1732 a Roman antique dealer supplied Filippo Juvarra with the lacquer panels that were subsequently used to decorate the Lacquer Room in the Royal Palace in Turin. Demand for original oriental items, especially Chinese and Japanese porcelain and lacquer, grew enormously towards the middle of the century. Original oriental items were used to create 'Chinese' interiors, but these were supplemented by reproductions, quite frequently made by specialised Roman craftsmen. The walls and furnishings of Maria Camilla Pallavicini's Music Room were decorated in the 'Indian style', described in the inventory of Palazzo Rospigliosi di Zagarolo drawn up in 1710,[10] and in 1720 pope Clement XI (1700-1721) received from China a gift of a screen "with Chinese paintings of the liveliest and most brilliant colours that art can invent. Portrayed on the front are various scenes of lakes, hills and plains, with ships and boats, trees and Chinese houses, surrounded by a pretty arabesque".[11] In 1725 prince Ruspoli sent a tray as a gift to the family of the pope, "of Indian varnish and with a porcelain service for chocolate and coffee".[12] Now destroyed, in 1726 the Villa Patrizi at Porta Pio had a complete 'Chinese' room decorated with Venetian lacquered panels on which Chinese scenes were depicted, while all the furnishings (chairs, mirror frames, fireplace and shelves for porcelain) were in the oriental style.[13] In 1727 the Chinese emperor sent a gift to pope Benedict XIII of "various caskets, tables, shelves, chests and lacquered dishes from Japan, plates and small leather boxes";[14] and in 1732 a salon in an apartment in the Quirinale palace was entirely decorated in the Chinese style.[15] Meanwhile pope Benedict XIV (1740-1758), who in 1756 had issued the papal bull *Ex Quo Primum* against the "Chinese rituals", acquired a large collection of oriental items, including "an enamelled writing desk with its Chinese cover and a Chinese tray", a gift from monsignor Barzia in 1743;[16] on his death Benedict donated much of this collection to the Institute of Sciences in Bologna, his birthplace.[17] Benedict also installed a Chinese Room adjoining the Gallery in his residence at Castel Gandolfo, using panels of original Chinese-made paper and Roman furniture decorated with chinoiseries.[18] Clement XIV commissioned the Roman carver Giovanni Crespi to make six wooden pedestals bearing his coat-of-arms for six monumental Chinese porcelain vases, now housed in the Quirinale Palace.[19] The residence in Rome of Emmanuel Pereira de Sampajo, ambassador of the Portuguese king João V, was abundantly decorated with lacquered furnishings in the oriental style, some of which were clearly acquired on his behalf by Portuguese merchants in the Far East, though others may well have been reproductions made in Rome.[20] The Portuguese diplomat also owned collections of porcelain, displayed in both his private rooms and in the Chinese Room where tables "with Chinese figures carved in wood from Portugal" were just some of the many oriental furnishings.[21] Porcelain items, both Chinese and in "Chinese style", appear in great numbers in the inventory of the possessions of cardinal Silvio Valenti Gonzaga (1690-1756, secretary to Benedict XIV), drawn up on his death in 1756.[22] Moreover, the cardinal bought a Villa at Porta Pia in 1756 from Prospero Colonna Sciarra – also an enthusiast of orientalia – where he created a room decorated with portraits of characters from all the world's nations, as well as three rooms with Chinese papers bought in Holland. These rooms did not survive the renovations carried out in the 19th century, but two descriptions were written by Saverio Bettinelli (1758) and Francesco Cancellieri (1813) and provide valuable information regarding the furnishings and rich ornamentation.[23] Chinese papers were also used to cover the walls of the salon in the Villa Aldobrandini, Frascati, which was probably decorated during the 18th century.[24]

The desire to imitate foreign models, and the French in particular, was doubtless one of the main contributing factors to the popularity of Chinese decoration among the Roman aristocracy. The *Chinese Masquerade* staged for the carnival of 1735 by the students of the French Academy of Arts in honour of the duke of Saint Aignan, special ambassador to Rome of the king of France, must have been a wonderful and impressive sight. Portrayed in the

168.Jean-Baptiste Pierre, '*Mascarade Chinoise faîte a Rome le Carnaval de l'année MDCCXXXV Par MFs le Pensionaires du Roy de France en son Academie des Arts dediée a Son Excellence Mong. Le Duc de S.t Aignan Pair de France Chevallier des Ordres du Roy et Son Ambassadeur Extraordinaire a Rome*', 1735.

This carneval float paraded in the streets of Rome in 1735 and is not unlike the Chinese regatta barge decorated for the arrival of Augustus II the Strong in Venice in 1716 (see Fig. 98).

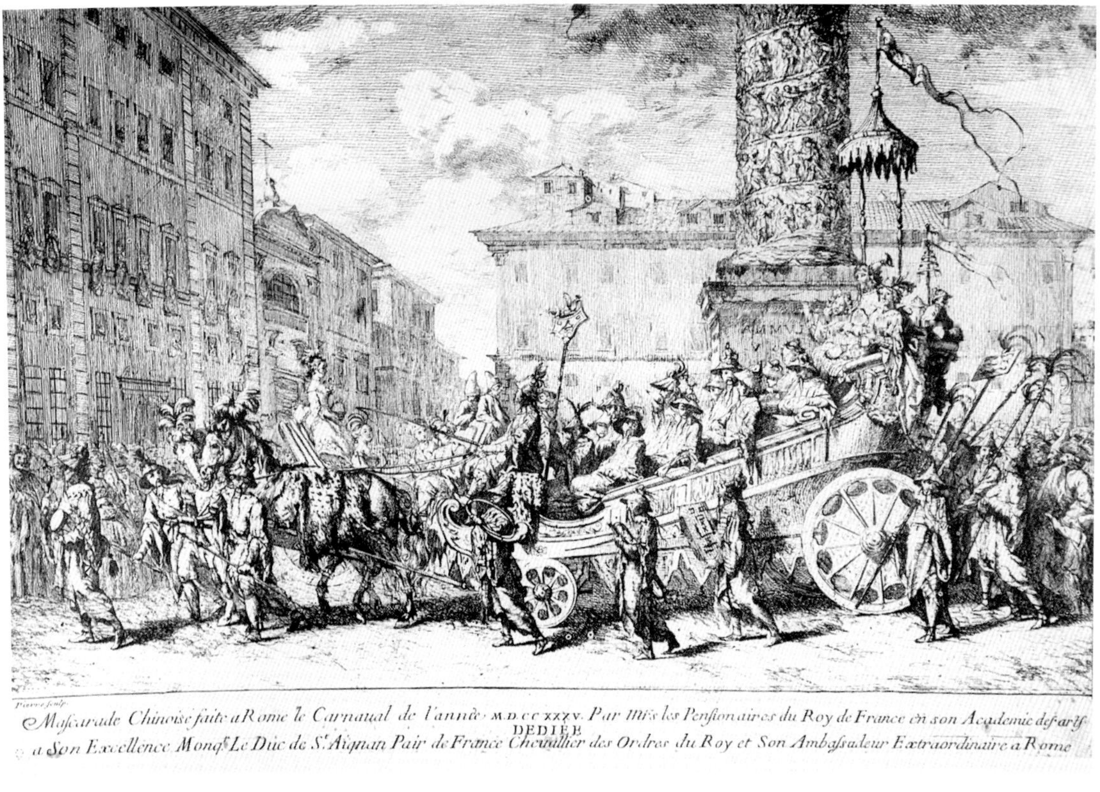

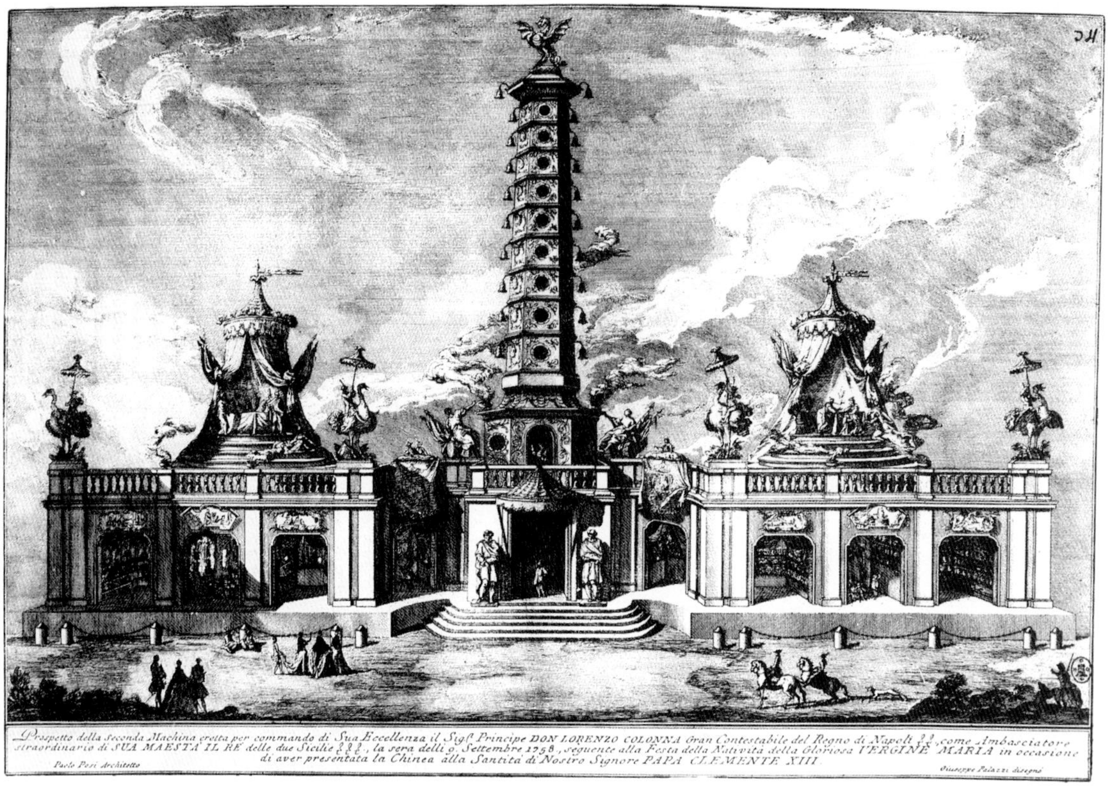

169. *Prospetto della Seconda macchina eretta per la festa della Chinea, 9 settembre 1758, arc. Paolo Posi, dis. Giuseppe Palazzi*, engraving from the *Raccolta di tutte le Machine de Fuochi Artifiziali*, pl. 74. Rome, Biblioteca Casanatense.

The Nanking Pagoda, the parasols, the pavilions with domes, the bells: this engraving dated 1758 illustrates some of the most typical features in the European chinoiserie repertory, popular ever since the 1650s.

smallest detail in a print published by Jean Baptiste Pierre (1714-1789) the same year,[25] the float is represented as it passes Trajan's column entirely filled with rows of characters dressed in Chinese costume with voluminous robes, drooping moustaches and cone-shaped hats. Further figures, similarly dressed, surround the carriage, some playing instruments, some bearing items that appear to be Chinese, while others carry plumes of feathers as an enthusiastic public watches the entertainment in a lively and festive atmosphere. Some years later, for the carnival of 1748, the *pensionnaires* of the French Academy devised another exotic masquerade, this time based on the theme of the *Sultan's Caravan to Mecca.* About forty people participated in the masquerade, mostly dressed in Middle Eastern costume, although there was also a *Chinese Ambassador* (interpreted by Simon Challes, 1719-1765, one of the students) and the event is recorded in various prints and drawings, mainly produced by the Academy's scholars, including some drawings by Joseph-Marie Vien (1716-1809).[26]
In 1758, on the occasion of the Chinese festival, organised every year by the Kingdom of the Two Sicilies to symbolise their obediance to the pope, Paolo Posi (1707-1776) an architect from Siena who was responsible for staging the festivals from 1751 to 1775, invented a pyrotechnic structure of wood and papier-mâché which, according to the account in the *Diario Ordinario* (published by *Chracas*) that year represented, "that Tower near Nanking in

China so greatly celebrated by Travellers, and called the porcelain tower around which a Market was created, or a Fair in the custom of that country. The Tower was octagonal in form, entirely painted like lovely porcelain, and had a winged Dragon at its summit, the symbol of that Imperial land; and from each of the nine storeys, becoming narrower as they rose, some small gilded bells stuck out, poised so that with every slightest breeze they rang out in joyful, though dissonant tunes. Flanking the Tower on either side were two sophisticated buildings, the lower part of which was divided into various stores and workshops, some full of Porcelain and some kinds of lacquered objects that are produced for trade in those countries, and others fitted out for the most suitable use of Porcelain, while the upper part extended into a broad loggia with balustrades shaped in the Chinese fashion, and in the middle of these two loggias stood a pretty pavilion in the same style, for the entertainment of the Mandarins, with ostriches ridden by men and Chinese ladies in the corners, their umbrellas opened against the sun [...]". A preparatory sketch of the arrangement and the structure by Posi has survived (London, Trinity Fine Art Ltd) as well as an engraving by his pupil, Giuseppe Palazzi (1740-1810).[27]

Salons in the 'Chinese Style'

Of all the 18th-century rooms in oriental style to have survived in the palaces of the Roman nobility, the Room of Mirrors on the second floor of Palazzo Sciarra is one of the most interesting, especially for the originality of its design.[28] It was in place by 1750, when modernization of the building, initiated by cardinal Prospero Colonna in 1743 (1707-1765), was finally completed. Luigi Vanvitelli directed the renovations, his most important architectural intervention being the 'Libraria'. He may also have been involved at the planning stage of the adjoining Room of Mirrors, though it is not attributed to him.

The Room is quite small and squarish in shape, with a rather low ceiling; the decorative designs are a mixture of purely oriental motifs and obviously European elements (allegorical images, still lifes, mirrors painted with cherubs and ruins, late baroque wood carving, blue and white tiles probably made in Delft in the 17th century and decorated with land- and sea-scapes, a pavement in coloured majolica made in Naples). Chinese scenes are painted on the six doors and two wall panels lacquered in green, with numerous small shelves for displaying oriental porcelain from the cardinal's considerable collection.

The chinoiserie decoration is attributed to Stefano Pozzi (1699-1768) and assistants as there are strong similarities between this and his work documented in Palazzo Colonna.[29] The influence of French chinoiserie on Pozzi's designs in Palazzo Sciarra is evident and has provided the underlying inspiration not only for the characteristic poses of his figures, which are also similar to Callot's work, but also the reinterpretation of the 16th-century

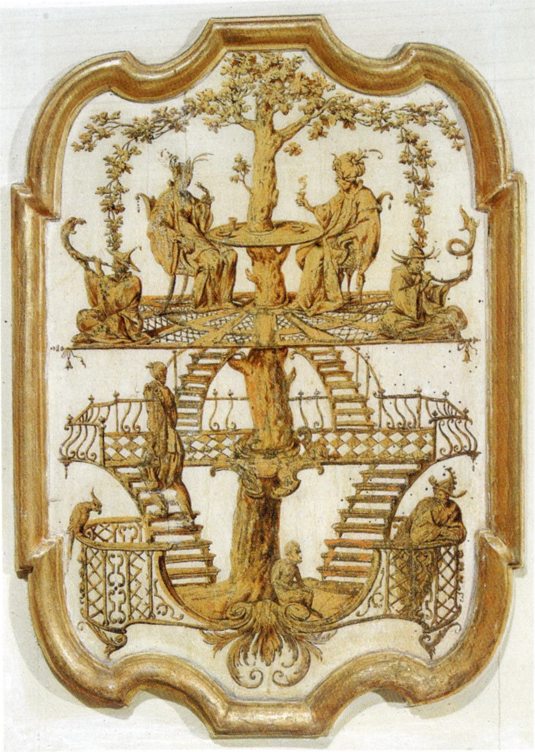 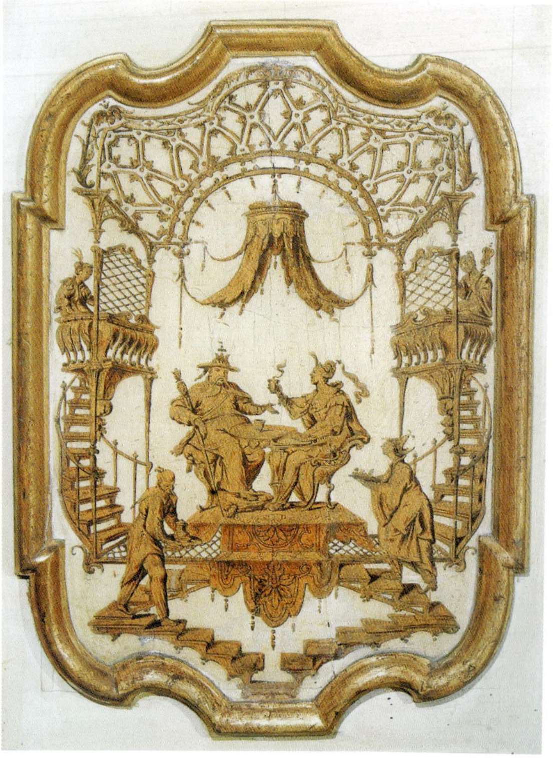

170a,b. Stefano Pozzi, Chinoiseries, before 1750. Rome, Palazzo Sciarra, Room of Mirrors.

For this decoration Pozzi was inspired by compositions with an oriental theme designed in France in the first half of the 18th century. The decorative quality and painting is of a high standard despite the debt to French models.

grotesques devised by Bérain and Audran III. The more famous French chinoiserie compositions of the earlier 18th century – Watteau, Huet, Boucher and Pillement – are also present, derived from the numerous engravings available in Rome.[30]

The influence of French *rocaille* can also be seen in the decoration of the 'Sala dell'Aurora' on the second floor of Palazzo Colonna, named after the subject of the painting enhancing the ceiling.[31] Apart from some landscapes by Andrea Locatelli, the entire decorative cycle may be attributed to Stefano and Giuseppe Pozzi, who were commissioned by Girolamo Colonna and completed the work between 1758 and 1760. The two painters and their assistants had been responsible for the chinoiseries of Palazzo Sciarra a decade earlier and this time they sought inspiration from the designs published by Cesare Vecellio in 1598, and much more recent sources such as the works of Watteau, Boucher and Pillement. The motifs chosen by the Pozzi must also have been quite strongly influenced by the oriental décor in the villa of cardinal Valenti Gonzaga, described by contemporary sources as including images of costumes from distant lands. The closest comparisons to this Roman *boudoir* are Cristophe Huet's decorative *Singerie* in the castle of Chantilly (1735) and Hôtel de Rohan in Paris (1749-1752), but especially the *Salon Chinois* at Champs, completed in 1747. Both Huet's work and the 'Sala dell'Aurora' by the Pozzi used Boucher's chinoiserie as their primary

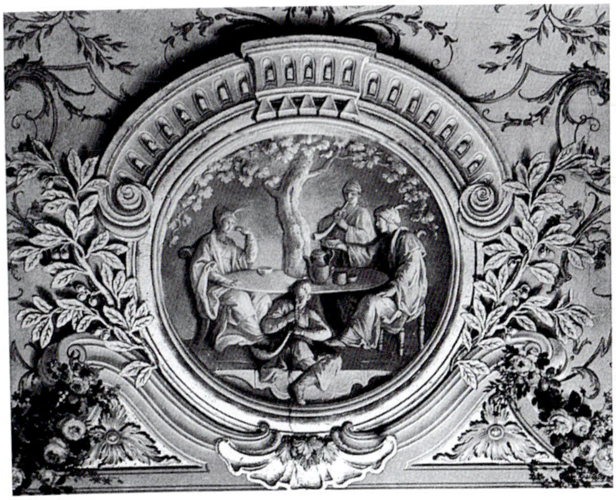
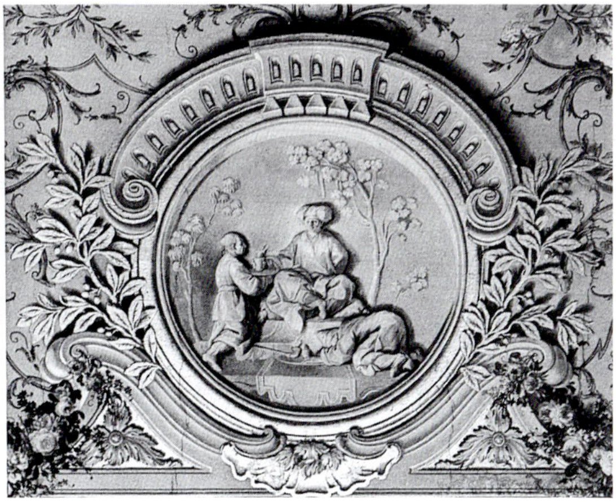

171a,b,c,d. Stefano and Giuseppe Pozzi, Decorations in the Chinese style, c. 1758-1760. Rome, Palazzo Colonna, Sala dell'Aurora.

A decade after completing work on Palazzo Sciarra, the Pozzi returned to the chinoiserie theme for the decorations of a room in Palazzo Colonna. The vignettes in the medallions are derived from the same models and can be traced to French creations with an oriental theme.

source for the oriental detail, but stylistic similarities can also be seen in the arrangement of the ornamentation – figures inserted amidst the slender meanderings of the *rocaille* volutes, and similar colour schemes, where bright and pastel shades contrast with the gilding of the carved wooden frames. A series of monochrome medallions containing oriental scenes taken from compendiums of both Near and Far Eastern images appear both on the ceiling and along the top of the walls.[32]

There are similiarities between the decorations of the 'Sala dell'Aurora' in Palazzo Colonna and wall panels decorating one of the rooms on the second floor of Palazzo Borghese, where the apartment of the younger princes, Giacomo (1698-1766) and Paolo (1704-1792) was located. The use of French *rocaille* seems to provide the only element that could be defined as 'exotic' however, as the images portrayed in the centre of the panels are allegories of the Arts - not exactly an oriental theme. Yet this kind of decoration was generally described as 'alla cinese', probably a reference to the fashions of France. Although the sequence of the renovations, begun in the 1740s and completed by 1770, is not clear, it is known that the Pozzi were

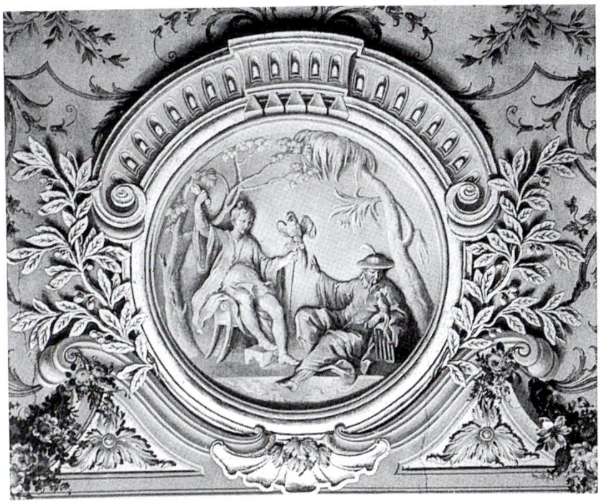
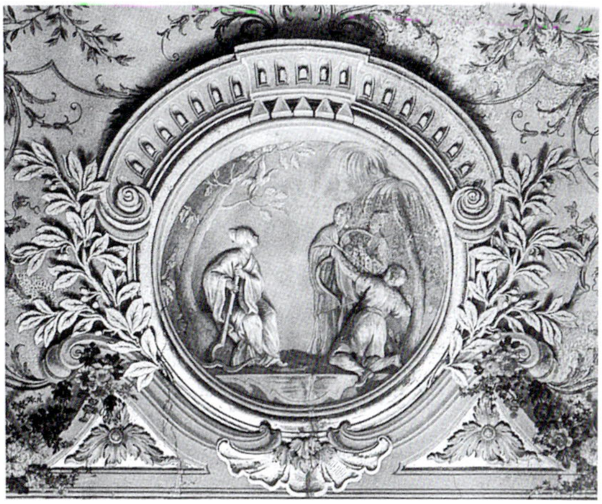

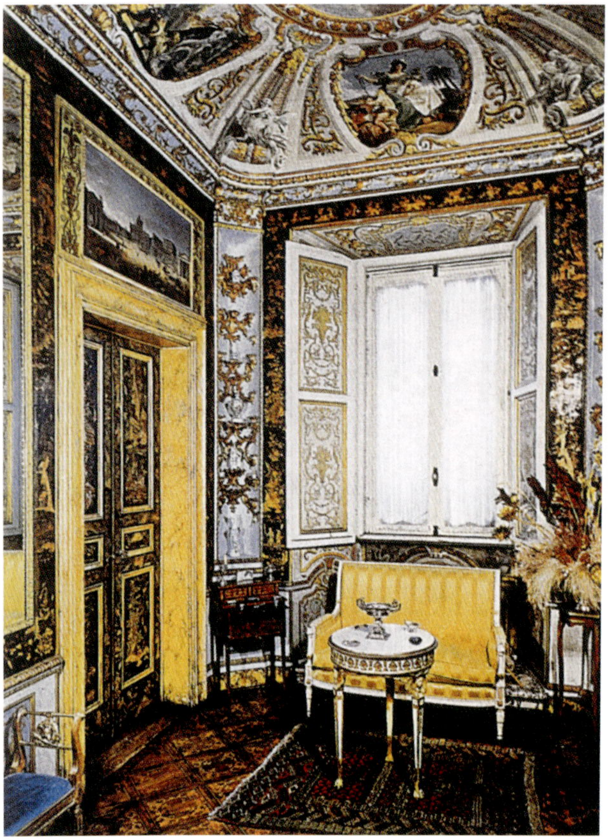

172. Lacquer Room. Rome, mid 18th century. Rome, Palazzo Borghese.

Highly fashionable in Europe and the rest of Italy, the trend to create lacquer rooms did not catch on in Rome in the 1700s, despite the fact that there was a flourishing market for Far Eastern goods. This room in Palazzo Borghese and one in Villa Albani (see Fig. 181), are two of the few remaining examples.

involved in the project and thus the paintings in the 'Chinese' room could probably be attributed to their workshop.[33]

Palazzo Borghese also boasts a 'Lacquer Room', though this is only known to us from an image published in 1965.[34] Although it is quite difficult to tell, it would seem that the lacquered panels decorating the walls and the door and framing the mirrors and window embrasures are not of oriental manufacture, but European, successfully imitating both the technique and decorative themes of Chinese and Japanese lacquer work. The room was described more recently as "decorated with dark green Chinese lacquer on the doors of the corner cabinet and mirror frames and doors themselves, portraying scenes of peasants at work ... in addition to the lacquer and the mirrors, the corners of the room were filled with carved shelves (still in place today) on which porcelain was displayed".[35] The discrepancy between the oriental style of the room's décor and the subject of the fresco on the ceiling – *The Cardinal Virtues* – painted by Corrado Giaquinto (1703-1706) in 1743, is explained by the original purpose of the room which served as a chapel until 1745 when it was converted into a study. Both Giacomo and Paolo were interested in developments in French fashions, especially Paolo who had spent a period in Paris as a young man, and their apartments seem to have intrigued and

173a,b,c,d. Chinese Room, 1763-1770. Rome, Palazzo Barberini, 18th century apartment.

The silk fabric that decorates the walls of this room is decorated with delicate floral motifs of clearly oriental inspiration. Similar fabrics were produced by almost all the European factories during the 18th century. In Italy, the main producers were in Genoa and Milan.

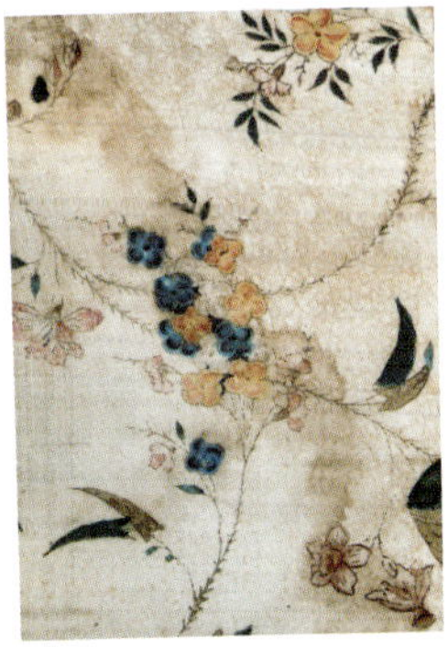

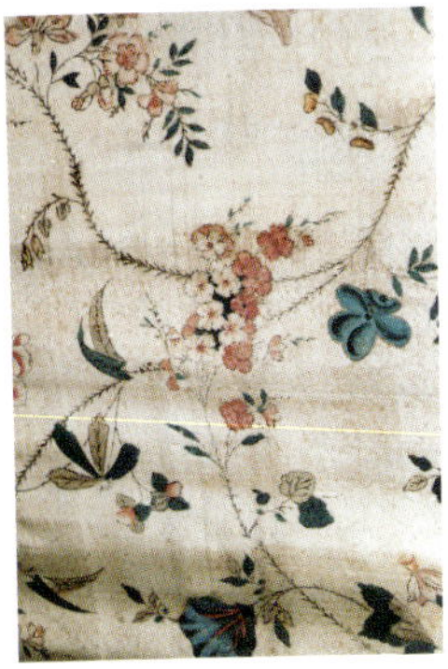

delighted visitors, as in 1754 Giuseppe Vasi (*Magnificenze di Roma*) described them as "charming and filled with singular ornaments", perhaps referring to the abundance of oriental items displayed there. The antique dealer Ridolfino Venuti provided more detailed information in 1766 writing that in Giacomo's apartment there was "a room with walls decorated in the Persian style" and that the "Gabinetto, full of the finest porcelain and mirrors, has a ceiling painted by Corrado; all the floors are of inlayed wood and everything is resplendent with unusual metals and marble, especially the quite unique Porcelain from Saxony, with mounts of gilded metal, which grace all the side tables".[36] This description refers to the Lacquer Room where, as far as Venuti was concerned, the pieces of Meissen were the main oriental feature, while the lacquer panels themselves passed uncommented. Two rooms decorated with oriental motifs in the 18th-century apartment on the second floor (right wing) of Palazzo Barbarini provide a good example of the pivotal moment when Rococo was in decline and Neoclassicism began to develop. The series of rooms in this apartment illustrates the rapid progress from the more dated style of *rocaille* to Piranesi's revival of classical ornamentation. This evolution occurred in the seven-year period when work was completed – between 1763 and 1770.[37] Moreover, from the structural point of view the Barberini apartment provides an excellent example of the 18th-century preference for smaller, more intimate rooms, reflecting the French fashion for the *boudoir* – a reaction to the magnificence and grandeur

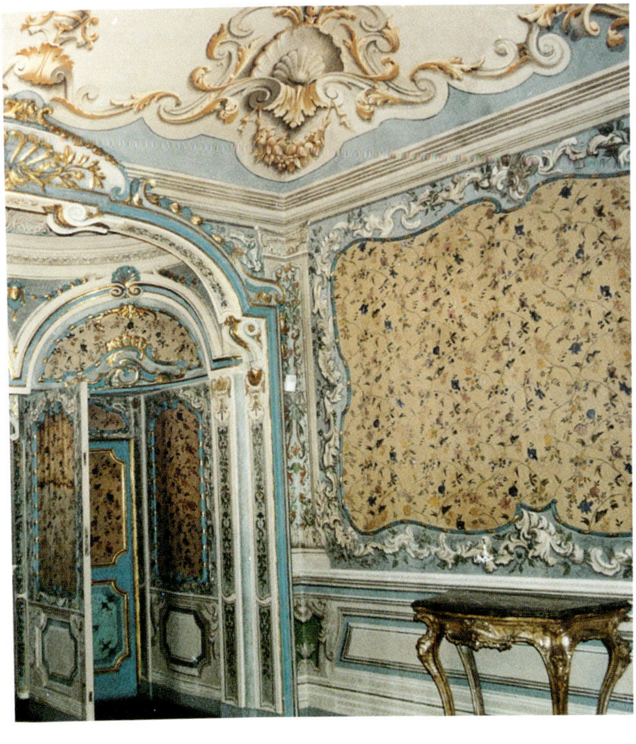

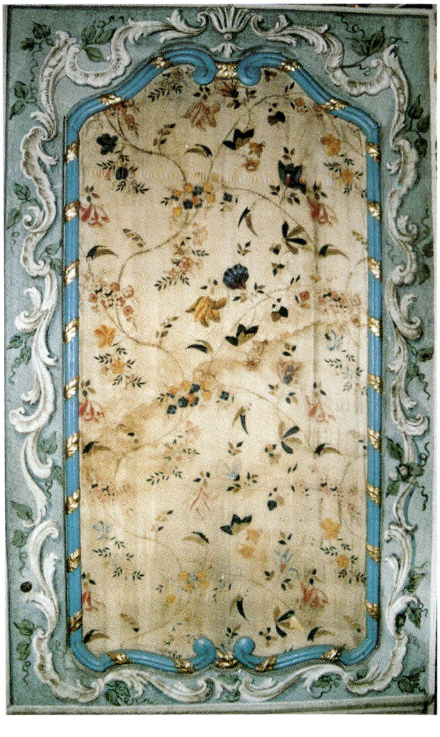

of baroque structures. Ironically it was precisely in this palace, once inhabited by pope Urban VIII (1568-1644), that this moment of splendour had reached its height with the works of Bernini, Borromini and Pietro da Cortona. The new decoration on the second floor was commissioned by princess Cornelia Costanza Barberini (1716-1797) and her husband, Giulio Cesare Colonna di Sciarra, who succeeded in creating a more comfortable and intimate area in the palace for themselves and close family. The choice of decorating two rooms in this apartment with oriental silks was not surprising as chinoiserie was still very much in vogue in Italy at the time, though it might have seemed rather eccentric to use exotic silks to decorate the chapel too. However, at least in the area around Naples it was quite common to decorate rooms reserved for religious functions with Chinese motifs. Moreover, although the motif of little flowers scattered over the fabric is pretty and lively, the design is not really a distraction for the penitent spirit in prayer and reflection. On the contrary the informal pattern is well suited to the spiritual atmosphere of a family gathering – more tranquil and

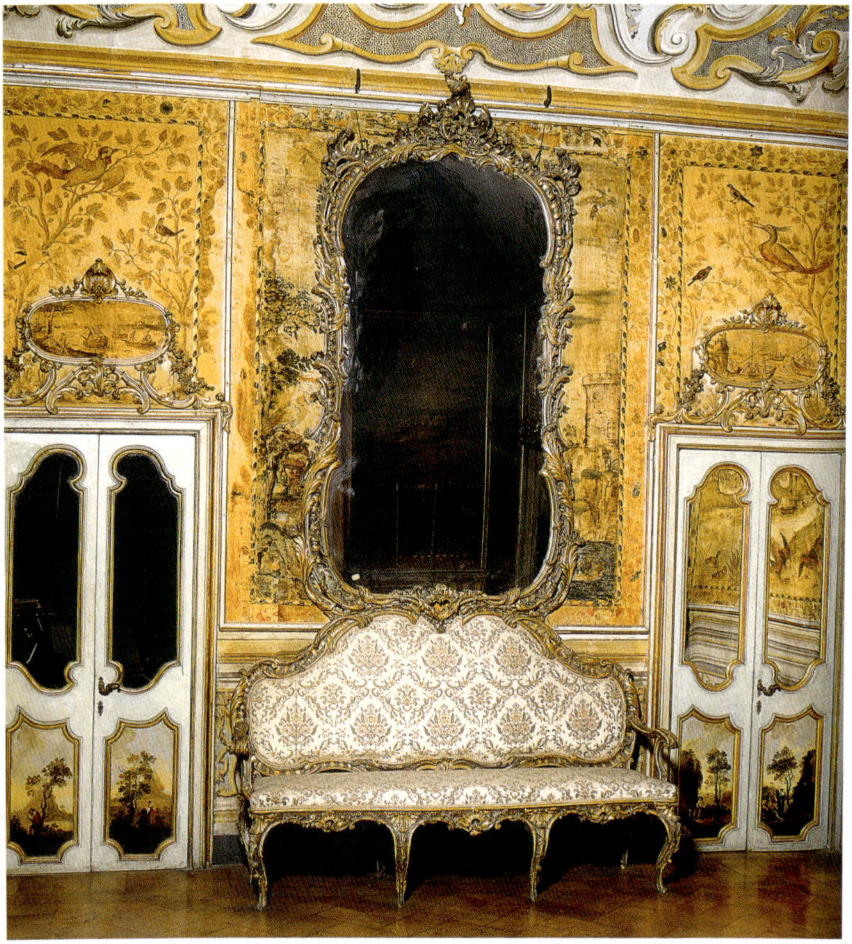

174 a,b. The Silk Room, 1763-1770. Rome, Palazzo Barberini, 18th century apartment.

The silks decorating the walls of this room are painted with North American scenes, but chinoiserie motifs can be seen in the sections with 'bird and flower' designs which are quite similar to the patterns on fabrics and painted papers made in eastern Asia during the 1700s for export to Europe.

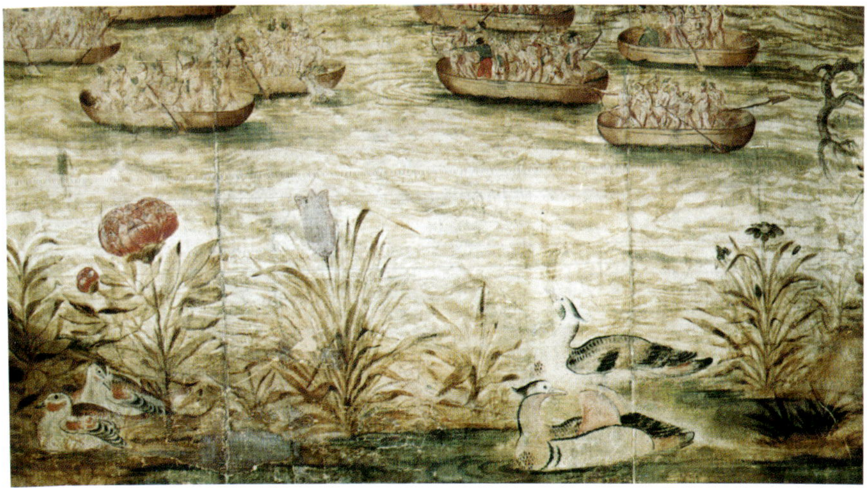

intimate and less austere and declamatory. In any case, the room was actually used as a private salon for most of the day and the small altar on one side of the room was simply concealed by closing the two doors. The original fabric – clearly of oriental inspiration – was painted with delicate and colourful flowers irregularly arranged amidst slender entwining fronds; two pieces remain on the inside of the doors that conceal the altar. Originally, before being replaced in the 19th century with paper painted in a similar design but of much poorer quality, the entire room was covered with this fabric, arranged in large panels with softly curving *rocaille* frames painted blue.
Adjoining the chapel-salon is the 'silk room' – named after the fabrics that cover the walls almost entirely, except for the area occupied by mirrors, the doors, the geometric dado and the splendid furniture. Both the scenes portrayed on a light background, and the frames of bands of flowers are painted on silk; the subject however, is not chinoiserie but represents rather the designs and motifs of the 'western Indies' – in other words the Americas – also quite popular in 18th-century Europe.[38] The scenes are filled with Indians in canoes, totems and tribal dances, images derived from the numerous engravings that accompanied texts on the subject, mainly published by the Jesuit missionaries and widely available in Europe since the 16th century. Despite the 'American' theme, chinoiserie is not altogether absent and the flowers and birds decorating the scenes are in fact the same as those always used in 'Chinese' scenes.
Outside Rome the Umbrian residence of the Serego Alighieri family provides an example of rococo chinoiserie.[39] The themes of the tempera paintings on walls and furnishings are obviously taken from oriental compendiums, but despite being much nearer to Rome evidently the local craftsmen looked to contemporary developments in Venice for their models and inspiration in designing both the lacquer work and the Chinese style fabrics.

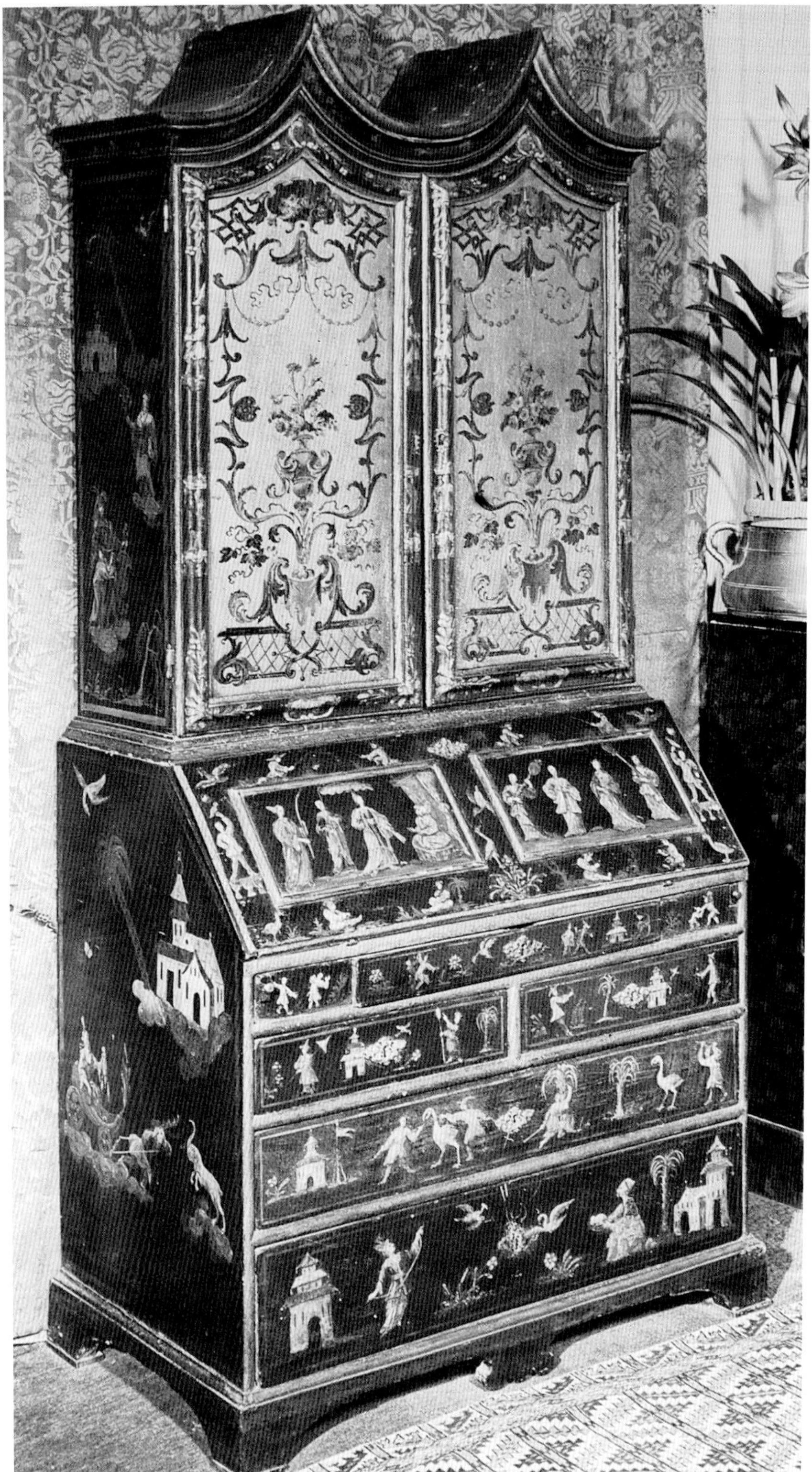

175. Bureau. Rome, early 18th century. Florence, Villa La Pietra.

A 'mixed' form of chinoiserie decorates this piece of furniture, with purely Chinese images sharing the scene with Middle-Eastern elements. Based on English, Dutch and German models of the late 17th and early 18th centuries, the motifs used are quite early inventions.

Lacquer

In 1720 the Jesuit intellectual and conservator of the *Musaeum kircherianum* in the Roman College, Filippo Bonanni (1638-1725), published his *Trattato sopra la vernice detta comunemente Cinese.*[40] A French translation of the work was prepared by 1723, a new edition appeared in Rome in 1731, and a later edition was produced by Lelio della Volpe in Bologna in 1786. Bonanni had attempted – without any success – to produce the lacquer according to the instructions given by Louis Le Comte in 1687, using the original primary materials brought to Italy for the Tuscan grand duke Cosimo III. He therefore decided it was time to write a manual "to produce some type of Varnish with qualities and properties similar to the Chinese", based on the information provided by Kircher as well as reports from the missionaries who had returned to Europe from China and his own personal experiments. Bonanni collected together a large number of recipes for making lacquer, and described the process with quite simple instructions so that, as he himself said, anyone would be able to try the craft. This was a popular approach that other manuals on the subject had also adopted and which Parker and Stalker had begun in 1688. The fame of Bonanni's *Trattato* continued throughout the 1700s and influenced other publications on the same subject, such as the *Metodo facile per formare qualunque sia sorta di vernici della Cina, e del Giappone praticato in Francia ed in Inghilterra* by Alberto Guidotti published

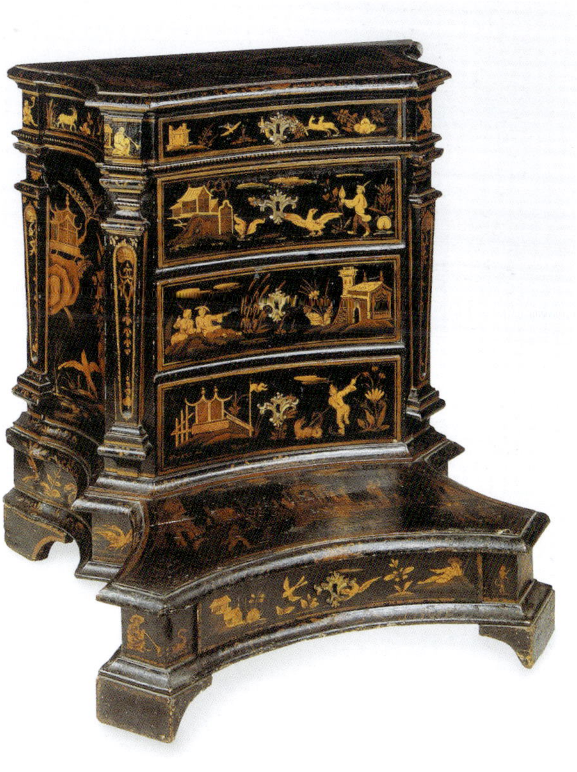

176. Prie-dieu. Rome, c. 1725. Rome, Palazzo Pallavicini.

This item demonstrates that in Rome too chinoiserie motifs were used in a religious context. Chinese vignettes based on northern European examples, are picked out in gold on a dark green background.

in Rimini in 1784 and the *Trattenimenti sulle vernici ed altre materie utili e dilettevoli sparse nelle opere di molti accreditati autori, particolarmente nel trattato assai stimato di P. Filippo Bonanni* by Filippo Agricola (Ravenna 1788). In a publication of 1772, Jean Félix Watin also referred to Bonanni's manual, although he claimed that it was "full of mistakes, wrong concepts and abundant inconsistencies".[41]

From Bonanni we also learn that at the time of his *Trattato* the lacquer workshops were concentrated in the area around Via de' Coronari where the japanner Giovan Battista De Pedibus, who worked for the Colonna, was active. Also in this period a certain Mario Nuzzi became renowned as a maker of lacquered furniture for the Borghese family; particularly well-known in artistic circles for his skill as a floral painter, he was nicknamed 'Nuzzi dei fiori' and presumably the lacquer ware he decorated was adorned with floral motifs too. In the early 1700s Lorenzo Molinari also worked for the Borghese family, producing two lacquered chests of drawers decorated with chinoiserie that was derived from more or less contemporary English works. These masters were succeeded by Rocco Zandevelt, probably of Dutch origin, who had a workshop in Piazza di Spagna and produced "Chinese style" lacquer work for Benedict XIII in 1730.[42] In the Barberini Collection is a microscope of a slightly later date made by the Jesuit Father

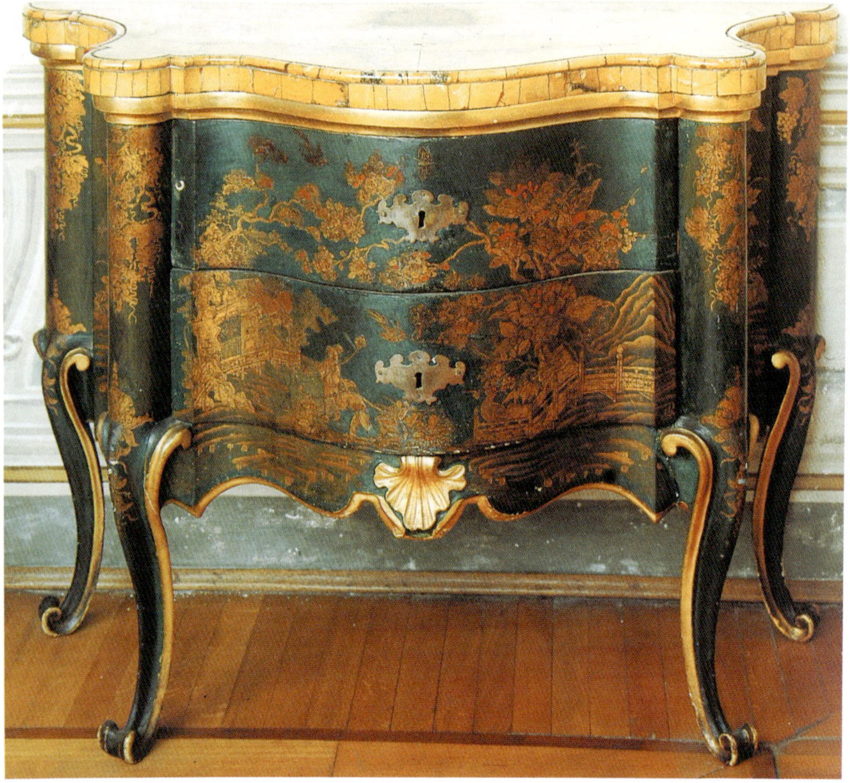

177. Commode. Rome, mid 18th century. Private collection.

This sophisticated piece is decorated with a chinoiserie pattern covering the front and sides. Compared to similar Roman items, the design here seems to have been derived from original Chinese lacquered items, especially evident in the arrangement of the landscapes.

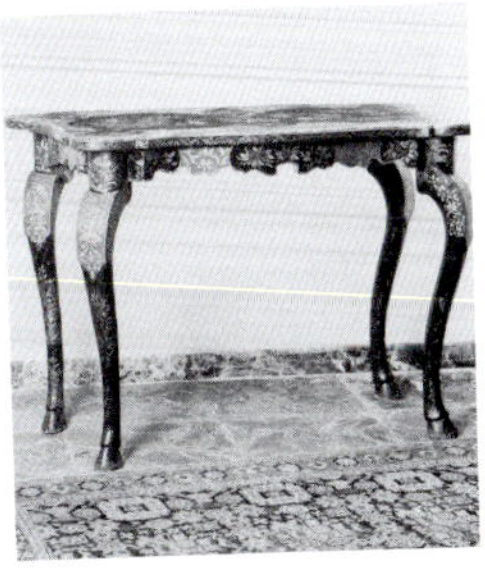

178. Pietro Rotati (?), Small table, c. 1769. Previously antiquarian market.

Alvar González-Palacios attributed this table to Pietro Rotati, a Roman craftsman who specialised in decorating furniture with motifs usually applied to porcelain. Obviously the description "ad uso di porcellana" was accepted to mean Far Eastern designs, but his particular skill lay in creating Chinese style decorations.

Paulus Maria Petrini (1704-1773) and decorated with black lacquer, although the gold motifs bear little reference to the Far East.[43] In 1724 Rocco Fanduel made two lacquer trays for the Pallavicini and in 1743 he was paid for a cabinet most probably identifiable as one that is still in the Pallavicini collection. The cabinet was registered in an inventory of 1784,[44] and was formerly believed to be of English origin,[45] though it was later confirmed as Roman.[46] The collections in Palazzo Pallavicini Rospigliosi include both lacquer furniture produced in Europe and oriental porcelain, probably acquired before 1752 and displayed in their residence in Monte Cavallo.[47] Fortunately, as well as the Pallavicini cabinet quite a large amount of mid 18th-century lacquered furniture decorated with chinoiserie motifs, yet produced in Rome has survived. Many of these works are actually rather similar to English pieces produced earlier in the century. Specific forms – such as cabinets for example – were more frequent, while black and red lacquer was quite common and a wide range of 'exotic' motifs was employed, including those of China, the Indian sub-continent, the Middle and Far East, and of course European chinoiseries. A bureau in Villa La Pietra in Florence is frequently published as a typical example of Roman chinoiserie dating from the mid 1700s, identified by an unusual technique whereby the

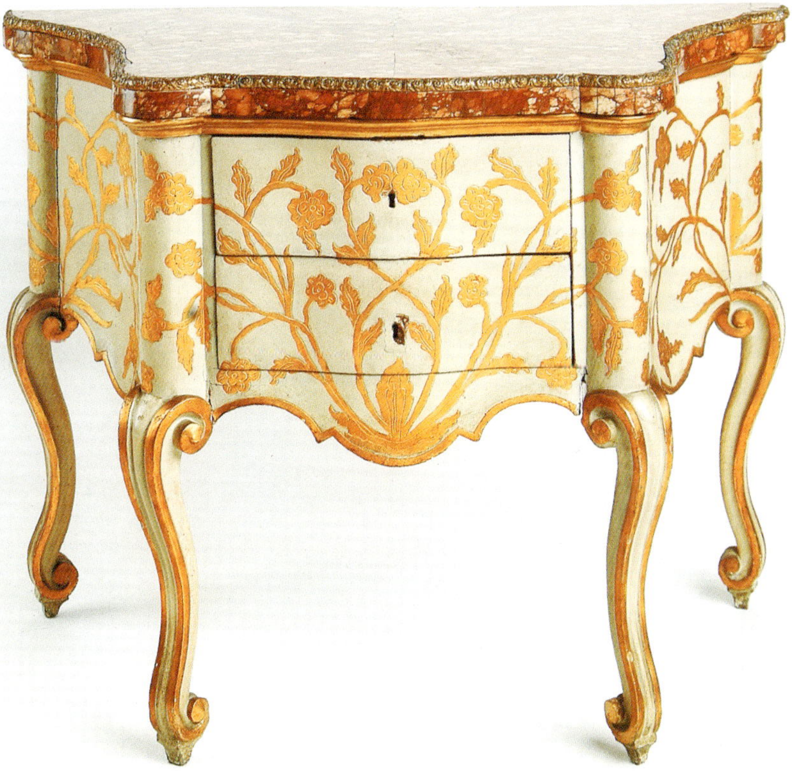

179. Commode. Rome, mid 18th century. Rome, Palazzo Pallavicini.

Alvar González-Palacios noted that the decoration of this and various other Roman items appears to be derived from Japanese textile patterns imported to Europe during the 18th century by Dutch merchants, although in lesser quantities than Chinese fabrics.

figures were raised from the lacquered surface by the application of papier-mâchè and then painted.[48] A similar bureau with a splendid still-life painted on the upper section and a background of fine white lacquer covering part of the surface has also survived.[49] Yet another piece is housed in Palazzo Sacchetti in Rome, decorated with red lacquer on the outside and black on the inside, also dating from the mid 18th century.[50]

Other works produced in Rome in the same period present similar features: a dresser with a prie-dieu in Palazzo Pallavicini is late Baroque, a form that was fairly common throughout the first half of the 18th century;[51] two chests of drawers originally in Villa Borghese in Frascati, dated after 1760[52] have a dark blue lacquered background with gold chinoiserie motifs in relief, a style that is repeated on a piece of furniture in the collection of prince Urbano Barberini.[53] The decoration of these items is more extensive compared to the items described above, spreading over the entire surface and not enclosed within specific areas, such as the drawer fronts.

A similarly unrestrained arrangement of design is also seen in two sets of drawers in Palazzo Pallavicini, probably originally in Palazzo Barberini[54] and perhaps acquired in the mid 18th century by Cornelia Costanza Barberini.[55] The floral decoration executed in gold is the most oriental feature of this item – more so than the blue-grey background of the entire piece which has little in common with lacquer apart from the transparent protective varnish. The inspiration for this floral decoration was not so much provided by other lacquer items, as by the oriental fabrics that were imported in quantity to Europe and Italy and often imitated by the European factories. The decoration of a matching chest of drawers and small table, consisting of an inlayed floral design elegantly picked out in darker woods on a lighter background, was also derived from oriental patterns on fabric.[56]

Pietro Rotati was another Roman craftsman specialised in the production of lacquered furnishings. Working for cardinal Flavio II, he was paid in 1769 for "having painted four sofas with many swags and festoons which entwine around the sitter both at the feet and on the arm rests, the swags and cascades are like fronds and bellflowers are painted like porcelain motifs in bright and varied colours". The description could also be applied to the other furnishings in the room which included a 'tremò', a small table and shelves, all of which were painted with Chinese motifs.[57] Rather than patterns on ceramics, the designs 'painted like porcelain motifs' were actually more similar to the ornamentation used on Chinese and Japanese lacquer works, interpreted according to Roman tastes.[58]

Also made in Rome are two candle holders dated after 1725 and now in Palazzo Altieri.[59] Some 177 centimetres in height, the two figures are carved in wood in the round, painted, lacquered and gilded, and represent two Chinamen stepping forward with the dish to hold the candle in their hands. Purely decorative pieces, González-Palacios noted some similarities with the figures that decorate the exterior of the Tea House in the park at Potsdam,

180a,b. Two torchère with Chinese figures. Rome, c. 1725. Rome, Palazzo Altieri.

The pose of these two statuettes in particular strongly reflects a French influence, rather similar to the chinoiseries of Watteau; engravings of his works were widely available throughout Europe.

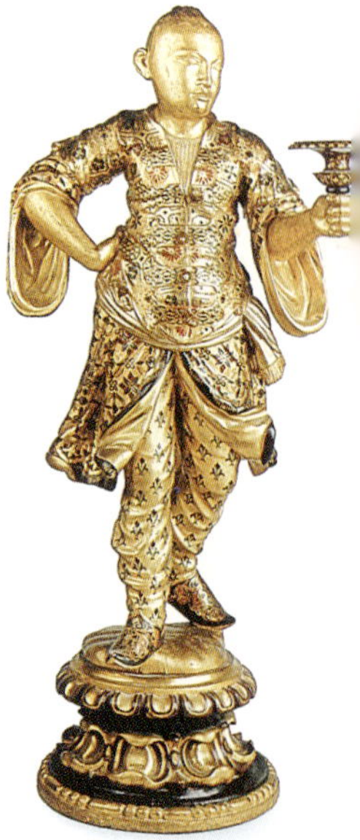

and with porcelain works produced at Nymphenburg, or perhaps the Chelsea factory in England. Such similarities suggest that the pieces may not be Italian although their history and especially the form of their pedestal entirely reflect the style of mid 18th century Roman works.

Neoclassicism

During the latter years of the 18th century the revival of classical designs introduced a new and more sombre phase to Roman chinoiserie, replacing the splendours of Rococo. But before the complete demise of the style, Francesco Bettini (1737-c.1815) created an 'anglo-chinois' garden for cardinal Giuseppe Doria Pamphilj (1751-1816), in the park of his villa, beyond the Pinciana gate. Although the area was not large, Bettini, a garden designer, succeeded in exploiting all possible perspectives of the Roman landscape, creating a series of viewpoints that the visitor would come across while walking in the Doria garden. He also had a wooden bridge and a Chinese garden and fortress built.[60] Bettini, who described himself as "clever with gardens" had discovered the new trend towards landscaped gardens during his many travels throughout Europe, including lengthy periods both in England, where he worked for Lord Lucan between 1776 and 1778, and in Paris, where he was part of the entourage of the apostolic nuncio, Giuseppe Doria. In Paris Bettini met Le Rouge who esteemed his work and described him as "plein de génie" and indeed the drawings that Bettini supplied for engravings in volumes produced by Le Rouge provide us with important information concerning the development of his career. He designed his first garden for prince Mocenigo; in 1780 he was commissioned to provide a series of plans for the Venetian ambassador, Andrea Dolfin and this was followed by the Doria Pamphilj Roman garden. Bettini's designs are perfect examples of the evolution of the great European debate concerning styles in garden layout, although quite clearly he was much more interested in their practical creation than in contributing to such discussions. Many of Bettini's original designs include 'Chinese' motifs devised to be used in the context of a landscape – pagodas, pavilions, bridges – all quite international in style and reflecting the contemporary and more famous English, French and German inventions.

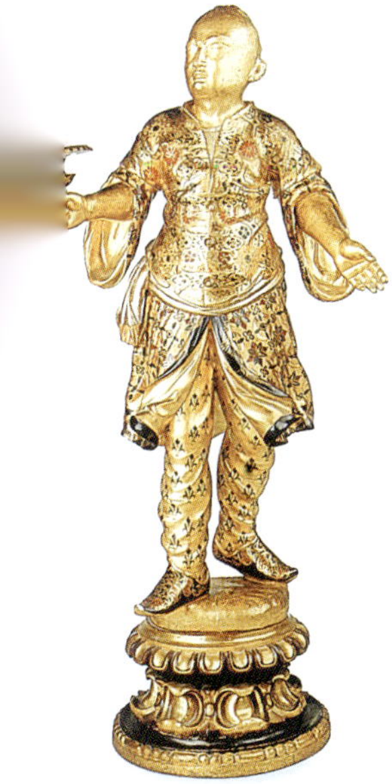

The Lacquer Room in Villa Albani is an important example of neoclassical chinoiserie in Rome and clearly indicates the continuing popularity of oriental features, even in contexts where ornamentation has altogether abandoned the whims of Rococo. Moreover, the Chinese Room in Villa Albani is a prime example of the archaic style which was a constant aspect in Roman cultural circles during the second half of the 18th century, the period in which this particular room appears to have been installed.[61] Twelve panels of black lacquer are arranged vertically around the walls, each surrounded by a frame of grotesque motifs and candelabra derived from the most classic repertories of Italian ornamentation, both Renaissance and antique. Along the lower edge of each of these panels a carved and gilded wooden shelf was used to display valuable collectors' items. A further fourteen black lacquer panels are set horizontally into the dado, and lastly a larger lacquered panel was placed in the centre of the ceiling. Since the mid 1600s oriental lacquer had been used purely as furnishings or fitments, but here the role is radically altered as the arrangement highlights each single lacquered item in such a way that the observer's attention is concentrated on the individual panels as though they were paintings. The lacquerwork is of mixed provenance, some panels clearly being Japanese, others Chinese, though most are European imitations. All however were heavily retouched with bright colours by the decorators who installed the works.[62]

Even in the early decades of the 19th century the taste for chinoiserie continued in Rome. The Chinese Room on the second floor of Palazzo Braschi is located in a corner linking the east and the west sides of the floor. Almost an oval, the white background of the ceiling is decorated with tempera paintings of Chinese figures, exotic birds, dragons and geometric motifs amidst highly stylised slender fronds of foliage while below, a pair of friezes with geometric motifs and little pagodas runs around the walls of the room. A series of inscriptions in characters that imitate Chinese ideograms surround large empty spaces where most probably the long vertical oriental prints or paintings, known as *kakemono* in Japanese, were to have been hung. The Chinese Room is the last in a series of rooms in Palazzo Braschi occupied by duke Luigi from 1812; the overall decoration was commissioned from Liborio Coccetti (1739-1816) who had already designed the ornamentation of the third floor.[63] The rooms on the second floor were decorated in Empire style in honour of Napoleon and tended to favour mythological and eclectic archaeological themes. The areas preceding the Chinese Room include the Egyptian Room, the Etruscan Room, the Apollo

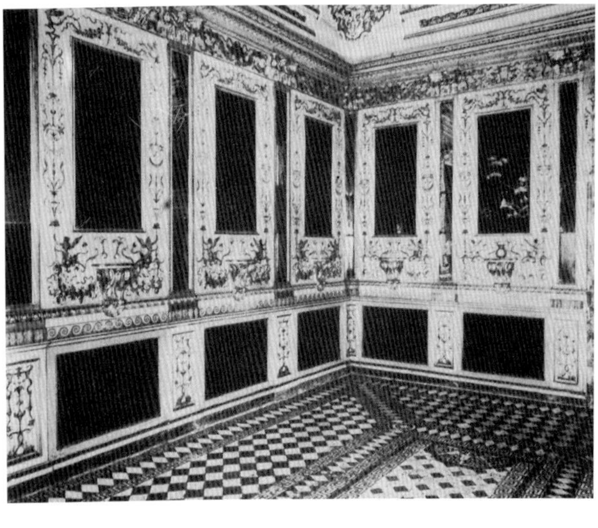

181. Chinese Room, 18th century, second half. Rome, Villa Albani.

Decidedly neoclassical in style, this lacquer room is one of only a very few created in Rome in the 18th century.

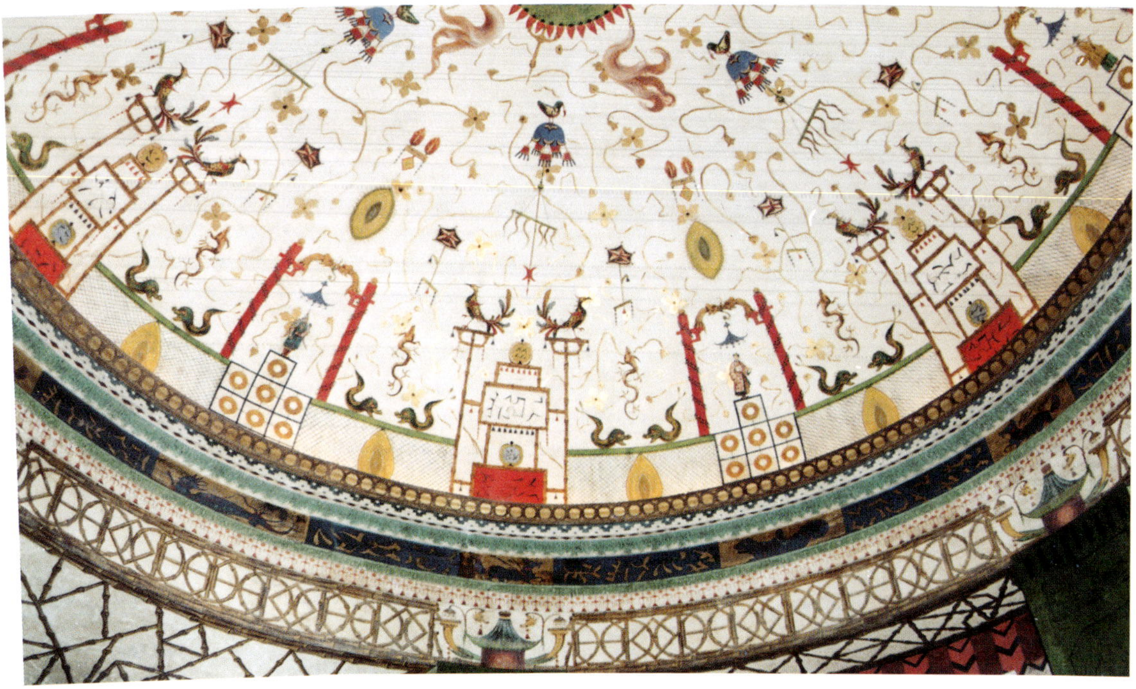

182. Chinese Room, after 1816. Rome, Palazzo Braschi.

An eclectic mixture here combines the chinoiserie theme with other styles – such as Etruscan, classical, Egyptian – producing a rather original decoration.

Room, the Salome and Queen of Sheba Room. Coccetti however was not responsible for the tempera painting in the Chinese Room which is quite different in style from his known works and it was completed after his death in 1816, when it was still described as being undecorated.[64]

Another 19th-century Chinese room is located in Palazzo Besso, also known as Palazzo Strozzi as from 1636 to 1763 it was the Roman residence of the aristocratic Florentine. The walls of the 'Stanza dei Lumaconi' are decorated with a series of oriental paintings first mentioned in an inventory dated 1843 – probably also the year in which they were executed – when the residence was still rented to the Giorgi family.[65] The room is decorated with motifs of flowers, birds, trees, plants, monkeys, rocks, butterflies, all painted in brilliant colours on a background where some relief work is partly gilded and partly painted in yellow-gold. These compositions are especially delightful for the high decorative quality of the subjects and the brilliance of the golden-yellow tones and were obviously inspired by original oriental items, especially screens, both Chinese 'Cormandel' style and Japanese. Acquired in 1905 by Marco Besso, a book collector and dealer, Palazzo Besso's complex history can actually be quite easily traced in the ornamental features of the 'Stanza dei Lumaconi' where elements of earlier schemes have survived. The ceiling, for example, is decorated with paintings of shells of all kinds, arranged within a square grid; just below this runs a frieze with pairs of Nereids and Tritons with a cherub and seascapes. The marine paintings might be the work of Domenico De Marchis known as 'il Tempestino' (1646-1713), but the figures were almost certainly painted by Giacinto

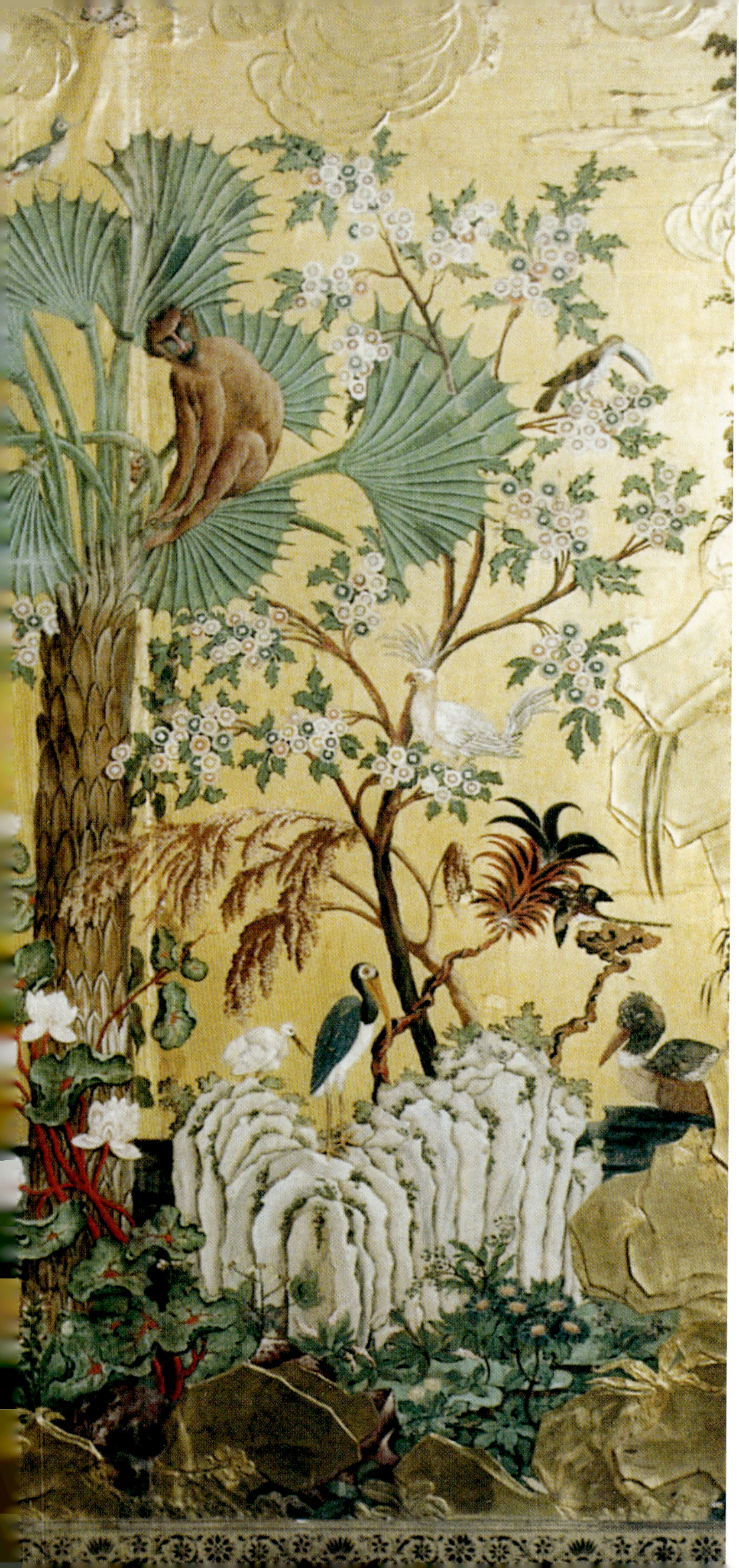

183. 'Stanza dei Lumaconi', c. 1840. Rome, Palazzo Strozzi.

The decoration of this room could be considered a late blossoming of European chinoiserie, just before Japanese orientalism began to come into fashion in the mid 19th century.

Calandrucci (1646-1707) who completed them and the entire décor of the room before 1702.[66] The precision with which the anonymous artist painted the shells decorating the wooden ceiling of the room suggests that he copied examples from the vast collection of *naturalia* housed in the palace at the time. A member of the aristocratic Florentine family, Leone Strozzi (1657-1722) was highly respected for his learned interests and the collections he created.[67] As early as 1680 Leone Strozzi's 'Museum of Wonders', which contained items of ethnographic interest and oriental porcelain, was widely renowned and could almost rival the museum in the Roman College which re-opened about this time under the direction of Filippo Bonanni. In 1708 it was fully described in *L'Arcadia* by Giovanni Mario Crescimbeni (1663-1728).[68] Moreover, in 1748 a room containing 'fine porcelain' was installed where not only a large quantity of Chinese works was displayed, but also Chinese-style furnishings and oriental paintings.[69]

Ceramics

The Majolica of Faenza

The ceramic factory owned by the counts of Ferniani in Faenza is known to have produced majolica decorated with oriental designs at least as early as 1731, when a document in the factory's archive records an order for "three regal plates with lacquer figures", although it is quite probable that the craftsmen had developed this decorative style some years earlier.[70] Customers of the day were clamouring for Chinese and Japanese porcelain and the factory simply responded to demand. In order not to be excluded from the market – both Italian and international – the historic factory of Faenza could not simply rely on its glorious past and was thus obliged to adapt to the latest fashions. Annibale Ferniani (d. 1784) therefore travelled to France and Germany before assuming direction of the family business, to study ways of improving the factory's productivity. On his return Ferniani brought with him new knowledge and information, but also some oriental porcelain services that he had acquired on his travels around Europe. Still in the family collection, these items were used by the porcelain painters as models for a series of new 'Chinese style' decorations which appeared on Ferniani's works from the middle to the end of the 18th century. The Chinese porcelain services were made in the factories of Jingdezhen for export and were sold, sometimes partly decorated, in the markets of Canton destined almost exclusively for Europe. In the 19th century various names which are now familiar came into use to describe the ware according to the colours used: blue and white, famille vert, Imari and famille rose.
The designs described in documents of the period as "alla Pagoda", "little house", or "Japanese" were very similar to the original Chinese prototypes and represented a pavilion, a lakeside scene with trees, rocks, flowers and aquatic plants. The motifs were reproduced on a wide range of items that

were much in use in the mid century – trays, plates, coffee pots, baskets, incense burners. Faenza majolica with these motifs was mainly produced around 1750-1775 and during this period the decorators tended to faithfully reproduce the oriental models, although some rather more local motifs crept in, especially in the flowers and plants that are perhaps natives of Emilia Romagna more than the Orient.[71] The 'pagoda' motif was only produced for a few years and seems not to have met with great commercial success as it was replaced by other, predominantly floral, chinoiserie decorations – the 'Lotus Flower', 'Peonie', 'Tulip', 'Garden with balustrade', 'Purple flower' and 'Bunch of flowers'.[72] The most famous motif in Faenza's 18th-century chinoiserie repertory was the 'Carnation', a floral compositon with a large flower vaguely resembling the traditional oriental carnation. This was surrounded by smaller bunches of the same flower and a trellised band of obviously Chinese derivation. This was, in fact, one of Faenza's most successful inventions, despite having little in common with original oriental works and using typically Faentine colours – red, green, yellow, blue, purple, black – vigorously applied to produce shades quite unlike either those of China or those used in other Italian and European factories. So popular was the carnation motif that it is still one of the most frequently used in Faenza.

The Majolica of Bologna

Originally from Vienna, Giuseppe Finck (1735-1789) first worked with the Antonibon in Nove and later moved to Parma where he was employed by the 'Royal Majolica Factory'. In 1764 with Bartolo Franzosi, a modeller, and Giovanni Antonio Rolandi, a painter from Verona he established a small business in Bologna near to Porta San Vitale in a property belonging to senator Hercolani.

Even in the early days of its existence the company produced ceramics of high aesthetic quality and was able to compete directly with the Ferniani factory in Faenza.[73] Finck and Rolandi also acquired the Colle Ameno factory in Sasso Marconi, founded by count Ghislieri in 1759, and for a short period until 1765, successfully managed both this and their Bologna business.[74] By 1767 their profitable collaboration had come to an end, however. Rolandi continued to work successfully in the factory that he had shared with Finck who, with the help of a series of large financial loans, established a new business in Via San Felice.[75]

In the meantime, Jean Pierre Varion (1737-1781), a Parisian who had worked at Vincennes from 1749 to 1752 and subsequently with Pasquale Antonibon at Bassano del Grappa, established the first porcelain factory in Bologna, also with the help and support of senator Hercolani. It seems not to have been at all successful, however, as it only survived for about two years (1765-1767).[76] By 1781 both the Finck and Rolandi factories had acquired the technique of third firing thus enabling them to work with an entirely new range of colours. At the same time Finck – rapidly pursued by Rolandi

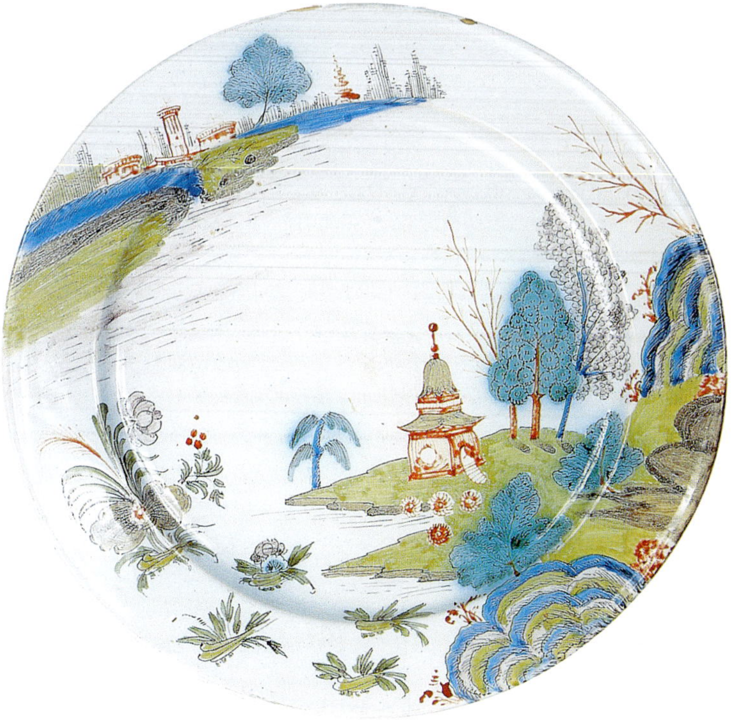

184. Plate with the 'alla Pagoda' motif. Faenza, third quarter of the 18th century. Faenza (Ravenna), Museo Internazionale delle Ceramiche.

The ornamentalists of Faenza clearly based this composition on original Chinese porcelain produced in the mid 18th century. The theme of the lakeside view with pavilions and trees was quite common in Far Eastern ceramics, including pieces for export to Europe.

185.Plate with the 'carnation motif'. Faenza, Ferniani factory, third quarter of the 18th century.

The 'carnation motif' is one of the most original chinoiseries of Italian ceramic production. Although there are obvious references to the decoration of original Chinese porcelain, the design is so recognizable that it is almost a trademark of the Ferniani factory.

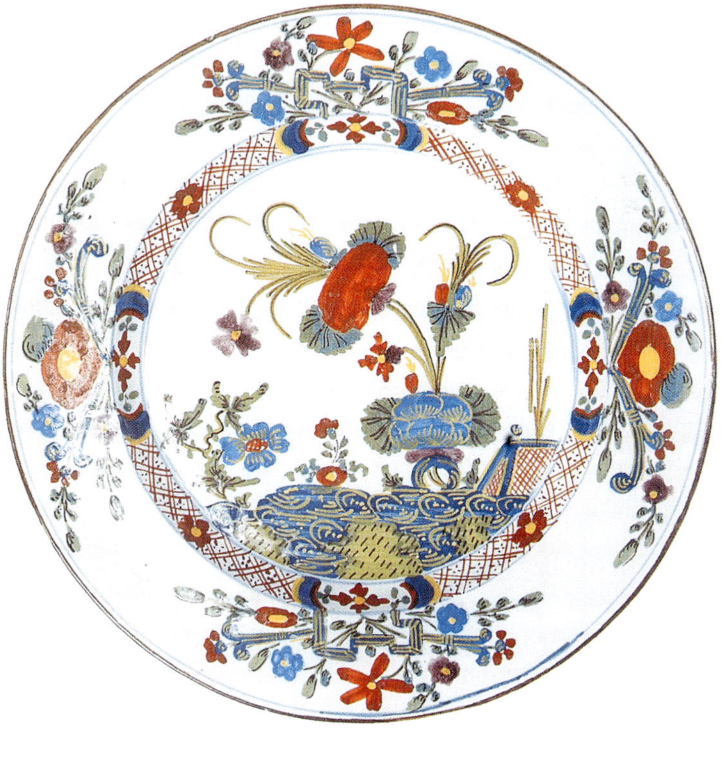

– sent a series of requests to cardinal Ignazio Boncompagni Ludovisi (1743-1799), the Apostolic envoy to Bologna, to obtain the exclusive right to produce 'English-style' earthenware.[77] Despite a series of problems, Finck's factory was quite successful and when Giuseppe died in 1789 his brother Leopoldo took control, continuing production until 1797 when Napoleon's troops were on the threshold of the city.[78]

By 1811 however, Finck's son-in-law, Gaetano Gozzi, the last owner of the factory was forced to sell all his possessions in an attempt to pay off his many creditors.[79] As for his rival, Rolandi suddenly departed in 1785 on an unexpected trip to the Canaries, apparently on factory business; he never returned however, and died there some ten years later in 1795.[80] The company was managed for a further decade by his wife, Caterina Casalgrandi, but did not survive the arrival of the French army in 1796.[81]

While the Colle Ameno factory produced majolica with white enamel and blue motifs that were partly derived from oriental works,[82] the repertory used by Finck's company consisted principally of 'Chinese' compositions. The inventory made of the majolica remaining in the workshop in 1796 records that among the items "decorated with gold and surrounded with yellow" were "No. 2 bowls with 'Barba alla Chiné" – a coloured enamel decoration with bunches of flowers, edged with 'Meissen lances' (also typical of Chinese porcelain made for export in the 18th century) and with a scene in the centre of rocks, plants, birds, glimpses of pavilions in oriental style and two Chinamen.[83]

This style is obviously not based on original Chinese porcelain but is derived rather from French majolica in the second half of the 18th century, especially

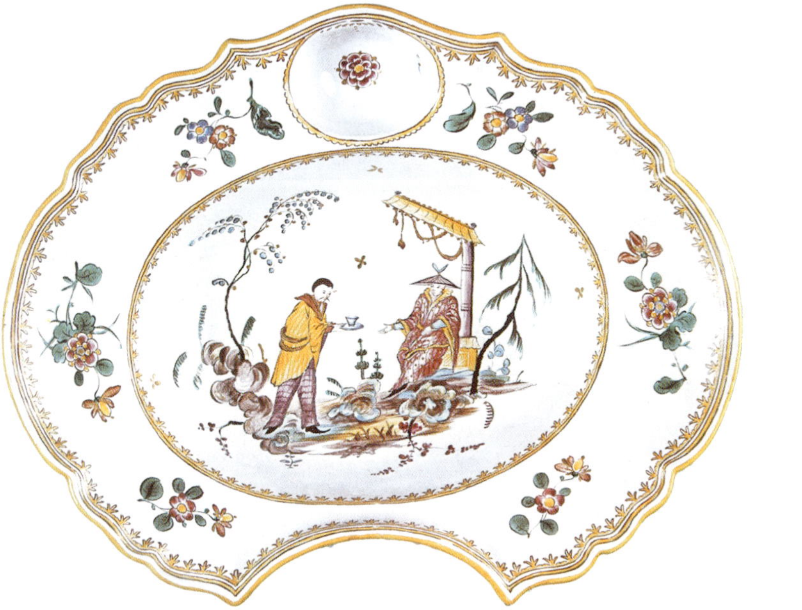

186. A 'beard' dish. Bologna, Finck factory, after 1775. Modena. Private collection.

This kind of dish or bowl is clearly described in the inventory of majolica wares in the Finck factory in Bologna dated 1796: "*Cattini da Barba, alla Chiné*".

that produced in La Rochelle, Strasbourg and Lunéville. The same is also true of the 'Chinese flower and bird' decoration which quite frequently appeared in Finck's catalogues, rather skilfully executed with a pleasing use of colour.[84] In a later inventory dated 1806 when the factory was managed by Gozzi, a series of items decorated in the 'Japanese style' that did not appear in the previous lists of 1796 is also briefly described. Precisely what these were is not altogether clear, although it is is quite possible that the design was an early 19th-century revival of a motif used during Finck's management of the factory.[85] Oriental decorations must also have appeared on some of the items produced by Rolandi's factory, and the "General inventory of fine majolica existing in the factory of Gio. Antonio Rolandi at Porta S. Vitali" drawn up in 1897 includes four "large Chinese vases".[86]

The Majolica of Pesaro

Pesaro had become part of the Vatican State after the death of the last duke of Urbino, Francesco Maria II Della Rovere in 1631. The town already had a long tradition of majolica production at that time, equal to that of other important centres nearby such as Urbino, Casteldurante and Gubbio. The change in the political situation and the distance from the papal government were the principle causes of the progressive decline that struck ceramic production in the Marche throughout the 17th and for most of the 18th century. Not until the mid 18th century did some enlightened local intellectuals, including Giannandrea Lazzarini (1710-1801), who had lived in Rome for a long period, and Giovan Battista Passeri, a doctor, think of reviving Pesaro's ceramics trade in the hope of resolving the disastrous economic situation affecting most of the local population. Thus in 1757 the first of several experiments to teach arts and ceramics began on the initiative of Passeri who employed Giuseppe Bartolucci, a ceramic worker from Urbino, assisted by the Fattori brothers. In addition to everyday items the newly created factory also produced a 'fine majolica' for wealthier customers, including the papal envoy, Monsignor Ludovico Merlini. It was rumoured during this period that Lazzarini hoped to start producing porcelain, but this first experiment to revive production directed by Bartolocci was unsuccessful. The factory's heavy reliance on traditional local decorative themes proved to be detrimental; what was really required was radical renewal both from the technical and the aesthetic point of view, with the aim of creating a more international product. In 1760 Filippo Antonio Callegari and Antonio Casali, both from the Ferretti factory in Lodi, were invited by Passeri to join the group directed by Bartolucci. With them they brought fresh expertise and knowledge, in particular the technique of a third firing. In 1763, following the failure of Bartolucci's direction, they established their own company, intending to produce 'fine majolica' as near as possible in appearance to porcelain, a form of production that had already obtained excellent results some decades earlier in France.[87]

This early phase of Callegari and Casali's production saw the invention of a motif that became known as 'the daisy style' or 'the whim' and even '*blanser*', representing bunches of flowers, one of which is usually portrayed sprouting out of a rock and placed to the edge of the composition. Although quite similar to a pattern used by the Antonibon factory in Bassano, it has also been suggested that it could have originated from the stylised daisy, or other decorations, on Kakiemon Japanese porcelain.[88] There are also convincing similities to Pillement's *Fleurs persiannes* or at least to the range of exotic floral motifs that frequently appeared in *rocaille* ornamentation in the mid 18th century. References to original Chinese porcelain are also evident in the blue and white 'Bérain-style' decoration used by Callegari and Casali from the early years of their production, although there are also many similarities to the ornamentation first used in France at Nevers, Rouen and Moustiers, and later at Lodi and Turin.[89]
In 1765 Pietro Lei, a painter from Sassuolo who had created a series of fine quality pieces, joined the Pesaro firm. The dish signed by him and dated 1765, now in the Ashmolean Museum, Oxford[90] already shows a strong Chinese influence both on the border with diamond shapes and the style of flowers and birds on the sides. Lei was also responsible for the coloured decoration on a vestibule vase decorated with chinoiserie and based on a print by Martin Engelbrecht, which had already been used some forty years earlier by Vezzi to decorate a flask.[91] When Lei retired to his home town in 1782, his place was taken by Antonio Scacciani, one of his pupils and a native of Pesaro. Although he tended to prefer the highly popular 'rose' motif, Scacciani also digressed into the Chinese style, such as in the case of two dishes dated 1787 now in the Museo Civico in Pesaro, copies of an original Chinese famille rose decoration. There are also clear references to the Milanese majolica of Clerici and Rubati.[92] Casali and Callegari's factory achieved many artistic and economic successes and only ceased production in 1810 following the death of Callegari.

1) Malena 2003.
2) Bonanni 1720, pp. 5-6.
3) Huth 1967, p. 336.
4) González-Palacios in Rome 1991, p. 169
5) Colle 2000, p. 81.
6) Valeriani in Safarik 1999, p. 257.
7) Safarik 1996, pp. 297-298.
8) Valeriani in Safarik 1999, p. 256.
9) Valeriani in Safarik 1999, p. 256.
10) Pacia 1990, p. 153.
11) González-Palacios 2004, p. 151.
12) González-Palacios 2004, p. 151.
13) Pacia 1990, p. 153.
14) De Angelis 2008, pp. 63-80
15) De Angelis 2008, p. 34.
16) Morena 2006, pp. 43-44.
17) González-Palacios 2004, p. 151.
18) González-Palacios 2004, p. 151.
19) Ghidoli in Rome 2005, pp. 276-277.
20) González-Palacios in Rome 1991, pp. 168-170.
21) Colle 2003, p. 96.
22) Cormio Ricci 1991-1992.
23) Pacia 1990, p. 114.
24) Ciotola 2008.
25) Bassano del Grappa 1983, pp. 56-57, no. 134.
26) Loire in Rome 2005, pp. 267-268, no. 165a-d; Parigi 2007, p. 144.
27) Santuccio 1992, pp. 38-42.
28) Pietrangeli 1986, pp. 284-308; Pacia 1990, pp. 91-107.
29) Pacia 1990, p. 92.
30) Pacia in Michel, Pacia, Susino 1987, pp. 153-155, nos. 45-45A.
31) Pacia 1990, pp. 108-124.
32) Pacia in Michel, Pacia, Susino 1987, pp. 150-151, no. 43F.
33) Fumagalli 1994, p. 128, fig. 148.
34) Trionfi Honorati 1965, p. 83, no. 5.
35) Fumagalli 1994, p. 113.
36) Fumagalli 1994, p. 111.
37) Magnanimi 1984.
38) Honour 1976.
39) Cantelli 1993, p. 18, figs. 161, 165, 175.
40) Bonanni 1720.
41) Gheroldi 1995.
42) De Angelis 2008, p. 73.
43) Huth 1967, p. 337, fig. 1.
44) Di Castro in Di Castro, Pedrocchi, Waddy 1999, p. 335, no. 56.
45) Huth 1971, pl. 57.
46) González-Palacios 1984, p. 68.
47) Di Castro in Di Castro, Pedrocchi, Waddy 1999, p. 293.
48) González-Palacios 1984, fig. 151.
49) González-Palacios 2004, pp. 176-177.
50) Colle in Schütze 2003, p. 158.
51) González-Palacios in Rome 1991, pp. 168-170.
52) González-Palacios 2004, pp. 178-179.
53) Huth 1971, p. 60, pls. 141-142.
54) Huth 1967, p. 338; González-Palacios in Rome 1991, p. 171, no. 109, pl. LVIII.
55) Di Castro in Di Castro, Pedrocchi, Waddy 1999, p. 336, no. 58.
56) Lizzani 1970, fig. 201; González-Palacios in Rome 1991, p. 180, nos. 124-125; González-Palacios 2004, pp. 210-211.
57) González-Palacios 1984, I, p. 68.
58) González-Palacios 1984, II, pl. 150.
59) González-Palacios in Rome 1991, p. 171, nos. 106-107, pl. LII; González-Palacios 2004, p. 180.
60) Tagliolini 1988, p. 29, fig. 222; Heimbürger Ravalli 1981.
61) Pacia 1990, p. 152.
62) Pacia 1990, p. 151.
63) Honour 1961 (1963), p. 216.
64) Leone 1998.
65) Guerrieri Borsoi 2004, p. 102.
66) Guerrieri Borsoi 2004, pp. 101-102.
67) Guerrieri Borsoi 2004, pp. 26-36.
68) Guerrieri Borsoi 2004, pp. 278-280.
69) Guerrieri Borsoi 2004, p. 111.
70) Ferniani Paolucci 1991, p. 20.
71) Ravanelli Guidotti 1998, pp. 605-606.
72) Ravanelli Guidotti 1998, pp. 621-633.
73) Bertocchi, Liverani 1981, p. 34.
74) Bertocchi, Liverani 1981, pp. 35-36.
75) Bertocchi, Liverani 1981, pp. 37-38.
76) Bertocchi, Liverani 1981, pp. 38-41; Bertocchi 1988.
77) Bertocchi, Liverani 1981, p. 42.
78) Bertocchi, Liverani 1981, pp. 45-46.
79) Bertocchi 1987, pp. 7-12.
80) Bertocchi, Liverani 1981, pp. 44-45.
81) Bertocchi, Liverani 1981, p. 47.
82) Bertocchi, Liverani 1981, nos. 7-20.
83) Bertocchi, Liverani 1981, nos. 25-26.
84) Bertocchi, Liverani 1981, nos. 46, 58, 62-65, 70-71.
85) Bertocchi 1987, pp. 13, 15, 18.
86) Bertocchi, Liverani, *Documenti*.
87) Giardini 1995, pp. IX-XXII.
88) Biscontini Ugolini 1986, pp. 60-65; Giardini 1995, pp. XXIII-XXIV.
89) Biscontini Ugolini 1986, pp. 55-59.
90) Giardini 1995, p. XXIV, fig. at p. XXI.
91) Biscontini Ugolini 1986, pp. 76-77, figs. at pp. 80-81.
92) Biscontini Ugolini 1986, p. 107, no. 88; Giardini 1995, pp. 52-53, nos. 43-44; Giardini 1996, p. 138, nos. 455-456.

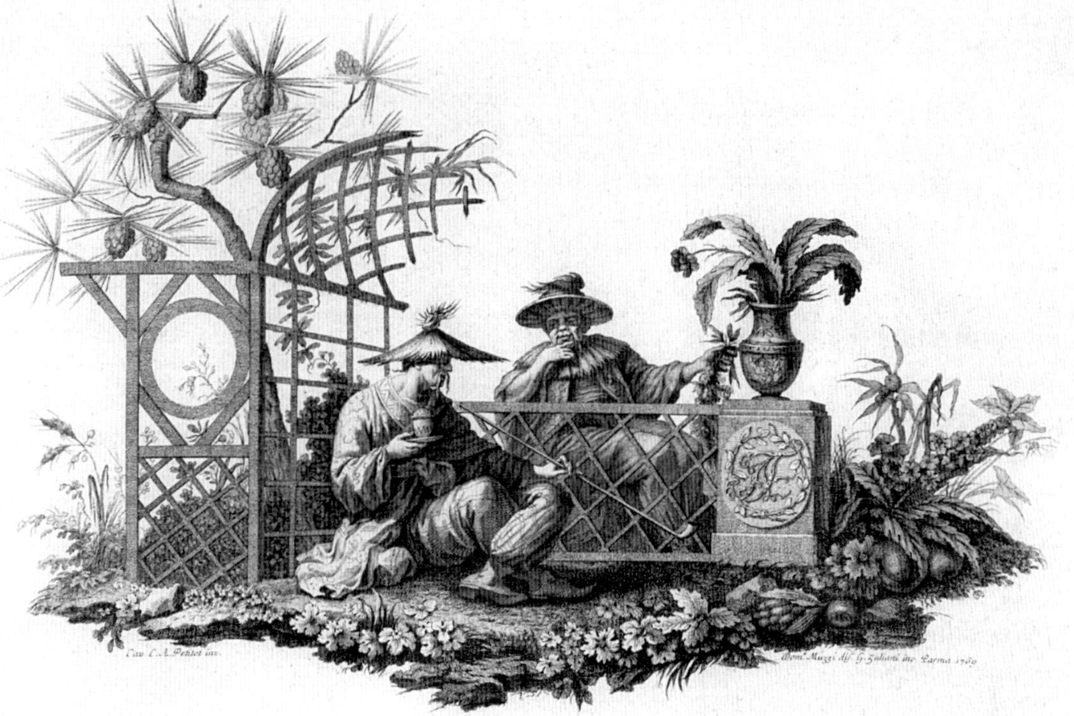

187. *Two Chinamen in a garden*. Drawing by Domenico Muzzi, after a design by Ennemond Alexandre Petitot, engraving by Giuliano Zuliani on page 73 of *Descrizione delle feste celebrate in Parma l'anno 1769 per le auguste nozze di S.A.R. Don Ferdinando colla Reale Arciduchessa Maria Amalia*, Parma, Stamperia Reale, 1769. Florence, Biblioteca Nazionale Centrale.

The Duchy of Parma

The Oriental Tastes of the Bourbon

"But the paragon of all chinoiserie festivals was that held at Colorno in 1769 to celebrate the marriage of Don Ferdinando, Duke of Parma, with the Archduchess Maria Amalia, daughter of Maria Theresa. A handsome elephant folio, printed by Bodoni and illustrated with engravings after the French architect and master of ceremonies Ennemond Petitot, was published to commemorate the occasion and presents a very full account of the various junketings. After having experienced the thrills of a Gothic tournament and indulged the pastoral delights of an Arcadian *fête champêtre*, the wedding guests were diverted with the spectacle of a Chinese fair. Round a piazza, specially built for the evening's entertainment, were ranged a number of shops lit by flickering Chinese lanterns, well stocked with oriental rarities and served by young men and women in Chinese garb. On benches in front of each counter squatted children dressed as pagods, some burning perfume in casolettes or puffing at long clay pipes, others tinkling bells and clanging triangles. The centre of the piazza was given up to a brightly clad crew of charlatans, puppet masters, acrobats, musicians, and men with dancing monkeys and bears. When the courtiers had inspected this lively scene, caravans began to arrive from Tartary, Japan, Java and even China itself, with porters staggering under vast bundles of merchandise labelled in outlandish characters. 'The musicians of each caravan placed themselves on arrival in the corners of the piazza and discoursed singular music', the contemporary description records. All at once, the puppets acted and danced, the players on musical glasses performed their tunes, and the children jumped over their casolettes or walked on tightropes while at the same time sounding their bells above their heads It must have seemed as if a whole volume of prints by Pillement had suddenly come to life".[1]

This amusing account was written by Hugh Honour who in turn based it on the entertaining description that appears in the magnificent volume *Descrizione delle feste celebrate in Parma l'anno 1769 per le auguste nozze di S.A.R. Don Ferdinando colla Reale Arciduchessa Maria Amalia*. Published in 1769 by Giambattista Bodoni (1740-1813), director of the Royal Printworks of Parma, the volume contains illustrations of Ennemond Alexandre Petitot's (1727-1801) designs drawn by Domenico Muzzi (1747-1812), and others and engraved by Benigno Bossi (1727-1792) and numerous assistants, including Giuliano Zuliani (1730-1814).[2] Such thorough organization, meticulous even in the geographically inspired ornamentation of the caravans, could only have been conceived and produced by designers who were quite familiar with the Orient in all its various facets. It is not difficult to imagine therefore that the ducal court of Parma had nurtured a passion for China and other far-flung lands some time before the organization of the event.

The most important collection of *orientalia* in the duchy in the early 1700s belonged to the abbé Giovanni Antonio Baldini (1654-1725) who created a museum of Far Eastern artifacts in Piacenza in 1716. Although entirely dispersed on Baldini's death, the original contents of the collection were described in a catalogue compiled in 1722 by the naturalist Antonio Valliesnieri (1661-1730) of Padova, also a collector of exotic items. Baldini had acquired most of his collection during periods spent in northern Europe as a diplomat in the service of the Farnese.[3]

The Farnese had ruled the duchy of Parma for an extremely long period and collections of orientalia almost certainly existed,[4] while the fashion for Chinese and Japanese wares, especially porcelain and lacquer, continued to be eagerly indulged by Don Filippo Bourbon (1720-1765) and his wife, Louise Elisabeth (1727-1759). The duke, son of the Spanish rulers, Felipe V and Elisabetta Farnese, and the duchess, daughter of Louis XV, took up residence in Parma in 1748. Their first concern was to entirely refurbish the residences where they were to live, as they had been almost stripped bare by Charles of Bourbon, Don Filippo's brother, who had moved to Naples in 1734 taking with him most of the furnishings and works of art in the Farnese collections. Under the keen supervision of the duchy's first minister, Guillaume Du Tillot (1711-1774), Filippo and Louise Elisabeth began a radical programme to renovate the ducal palaces, especially the residences in Parma and Colorno, which were to be respectively their winter and summer abodes. Furnishings and accessories were acquired quite frenetically, mainly on the initiative of the duchess who not only had her own healthy income, but could also rely on the generosity of her father. Between 1748 and 1759 she travelled to Paris three times returning with vast quantities of paintings, furnishings, fabrics and porcelain, many of which were gifts from her father, Louis XV, though more often they were acquired through the services of Du Tillot and his agents in France, Claude Bonnet (1711-1772) and Testard.

Following the unification of Italy (1860), this precious heritage was totally dispersed as the collections of Parma were transferred to other Italian palaces in Turin, Florence, Rome, Genoa and Venice, between 1862 and 1868. However, research by various scholars into the original collections has, to some degree at least, recreated an important impression of the size, fine quality and immense variety of these possessions, which included tapestries,[5] French[6] and Italian furniture,[7] French porcelain,[8] German porcelain,[9] and paintings.[10] Many of the oriental works were transferred to Florence in the 19th century and are still located there.[11] Despite the lack of any firm documentary evidence, it is more than likely that many of these items once belonged to Don Filippo and Louise Elisabeth, or to their son and heir Don Ferdinando (1751-1802) whose marriage to Maria Amalia of Austria (1745-1804) was celebrated with the famous *Fête Chinoise*. Both the dating of the pieces and the style of the porcelain and lacquer, which is entirely mid 18th century French, support this suggestion.[12]

Petitot and the Chinese Rooms at Colorno

From the beginning Colorno was Filippo's favourite residence, especially as it was well suited for him to indulge his favourite pastimes, which included hunting. Elisabeth too was delighted by the palace, confident that here she could at least partially recreate the magnificence of those French and Spanish palaces to which she had been accustomed since her youth.[13] Basic repairs and rebuilding of the villa and large garden were completed by 1752 and the following year modernization of the interiors began, leaving the general structure of the rooms unaltered.[14]

The creation of a Chinese Room near the duchess' apartment in the wing of the palace facing the garden probably dates from this first phase. The walls are covered with original Chinese paper painted with outdoor scenes in which figures busy themselves in various occupations, surrounded by wood frames painted in light green, echoing the colour of the *rocaille* stucco work that decorates most of the rooms in this wing. Two of these panels, both the same

188a,b. Chinese Room, third quarter of the 18th century. Colorno (Parma), Palazzo Ducale.

The painted papers decorating the walls of this salon at Colorno were produced in China and can be dated to the 1730s or '40s. This style of paper was quite widely available in Europe, arriving on the ships of the various East India Companies.

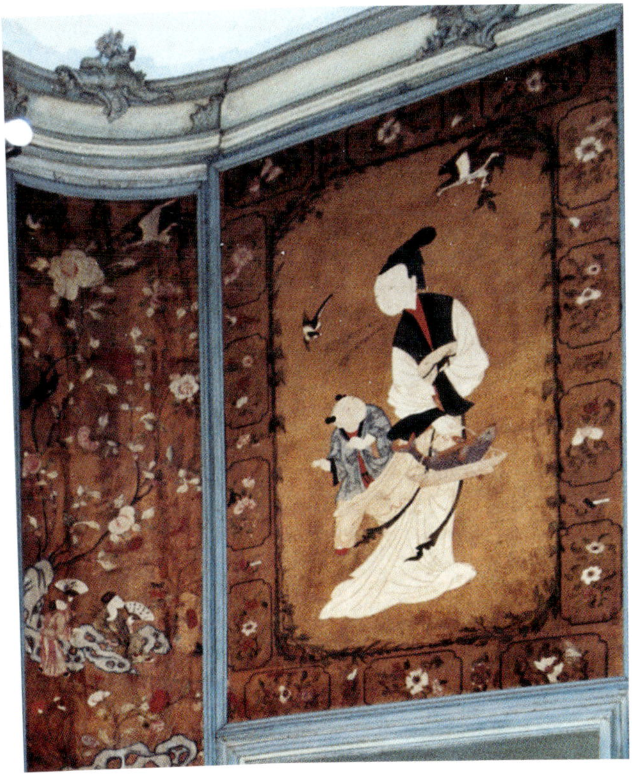

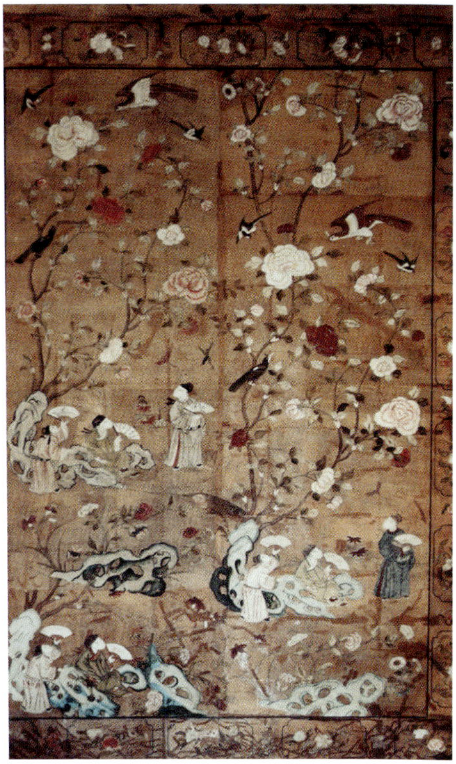

size and used as overdoors, are particularly lovely, decorated with a scene of a child and lady who is carrying on her arm a basket containing a fish, a Chinese symbol representing good fortune and wealth. The paper was produced in southern China for export to Europe and can be dated to the period 1725-50, though the painting has been slightly retouched, most probably by craftsmen in Parma who were asked to enliven the colouring a little. Aldo Raimondi (1902-1998)made a watercolour painting of the room in 1929 (Parma, Museo Glauco Lombardi) showing some Chinese-style furniture which must originally have been here.

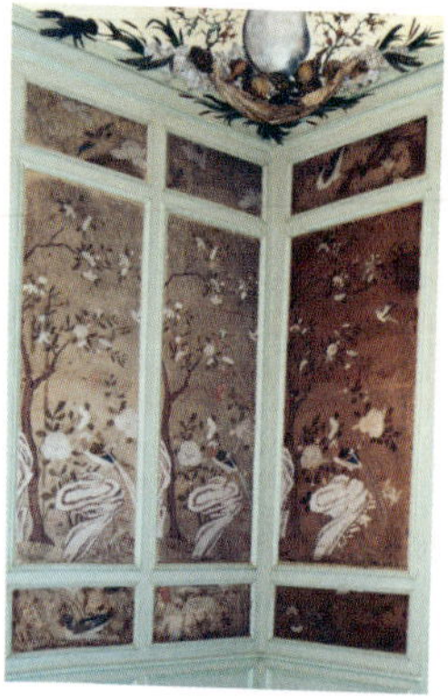

Subsequent interior designs at Colorno were commissioned from the young Petitot, who arrived in Parma in 1753 instantly becoming the duchy's principle doyen of the arts. Born in Lyons, he attained the Grand Prix of the Parisian Accademie in 1745, and moved to Rome in 1746 as a member of the French Academy there, directed at the time by Jean-François de Troy (1679-1752). Petitot remained in Rome until 1750 and thus experienced at first hand the revival of classical models that took place among artists and intellectuals, mainly stimulated by the work of Piranesi (1720-1778), also a member of the French Academy. A portrait made by de Troy in 1748 shows Petitot dressed as an 'Indian Chief' with a scimitar and turban on the occasion of the famous Middle Eastern masquerade described earlier as an exuberant example of mid 18th-century Roman chinoiserie. Despite being an early enthusiast of Neoclassicism, the young Petitot was also attracted to the charms of the Orient, although in this case he is closer to Turkey than China.[15] When his Roman sojourn came to an end in 1750 he returned to France and remained there until 1753 working with count Caylus (1692-1765) on the design of plates for the *Recueil d'antiquités*. Petitot thus arrived in Parma as a well-experienced architect, soon becoming part of an important group of artists and intellectuals who aspired to the ideal of transforming Parma into a "second Athens", a paragon among the European courts representing the ideals of Ancient Greece.[16] This cultural circle was skilfully guided by Du Tillot and the perspicacious Abbé Frugoni (1741-1797), a famous Arcadian who in 1737 had written the long poem *Per la nobile mascherata fattasi in Parma nel carnevale del 1737 rappresentante varie nazioni* and from 1752 was secretary of the Accademia di Belle Arti.[17] This worthy 'classical project' culminated in the creation of the Sala Grande in Palazzo Ducale (1755-1756)[18] and while Petitot participated enthusiastically he did so with a touch of irony, often introducing novel and different ideas. Not only did he design, for example, the nine plates of the *Mascarade à la Grecque* in 1771, a clear satire on the presumed supremacy of Greece, but he was also responsible for creating various more or less ephemeral productions 'in the Chinese fashion', some of which are documented in his own drawings.[19]
Petitot was able to fully express his artistic and creative potential at Colorno, indulging as far as possible the duke and duchess' aspirations; accustomed to the grandiosity and scale of Versailles, the couple frequently acquired

189a,b. Chinese Room, formerly the Porcelain Room, third quarter of the 18th century. Colorno (Parma), Palazzo Ducale.

Another Chinese Room at Colorno decorated with original Chinese painted papers dated 1730s or '40s. The 'birds and flowers' decoration is also typical of Far Eastern works produced for export to Europe.

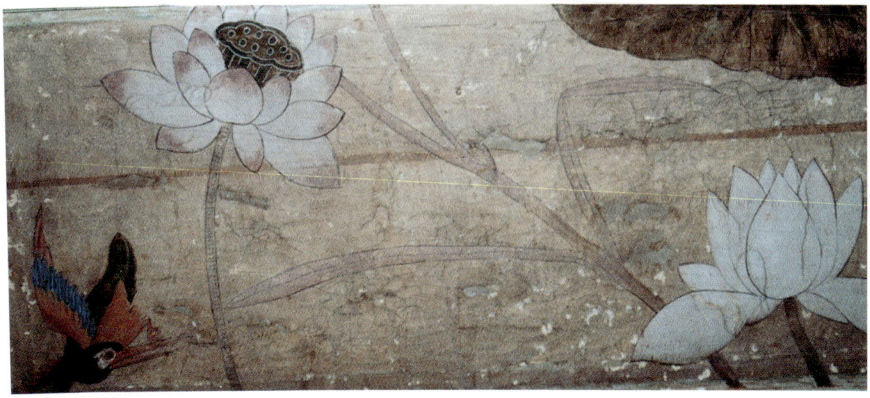

chinoiserie items. An upholstery fabric for furnishings (or perhaps a hanging) in "moëre de Soye blanche peint à la Chinoise" must have been especially rare as seven upholsterers worked on it for 284 days in 1756.[20] In the same period 'works in the Chinese style' were commissioned from the gilder Francesco Remoneda, such as the gilding on the "iron bars for the 'Chinese' bed in the apartment of Madame Infante" – Louise Elisabeth.[21] In 1752 Parma also acquired the tapestries of the *Chinese Suite* which had been designed by Boucher for the Beauvais factory, now housed in Palazzo Reale in Turin,[22] and lastly Testard acquired some Chinese-style firedogs on behalf of the dukes in Paris in 1754 and 1760; two of these are now among the furnishings of the Quirinale Palace.[23]

Shortly after 1753, a second Chinese room was completed in the villa, also located in the wing overlooking the garden, but this time in the duke's apartment, almost diagonally opposite the room on the duchess' side. In this second room Petitot designed the painted high relief stucco still lifes of shells, grasses, a snail and a crab, that appear above the cornice in the four corners of the room, and in the centre of the ceiling. These wonderfully bizarre groups are a magnificent example of Petitot's creative fantasy and skill as an architect and perfectly illustrate his ability to combine explicit references to the world of nature with the rigorous symmetry of early neoclassical models. Recently a preparatory drawing of these naturalistic ornaments has been published, confirming his contribution to the design of the room; written in his hand is a note that they were for the 'Gabinetto delle Porcellane'.[24] It would seem that the ducal couple had decided to use this room to display part of their porcelain collection, including the oriental pieces, however, it is not known if the project was ever realised nor how it might have been installed. Arranged inside panels in two rows, one above the other with the larger ones above and the smaller ones below, were identical Chinese papers painted with a motif of flowers and birds – probably also retouched by local artisans. There is no sign that any shelves or brackets were ever attached along the edges of the wood frames, however. Thus if the porcelain room ever was created, the pieces could only have been displayed inside cases and cabinets and not on shelves. It is

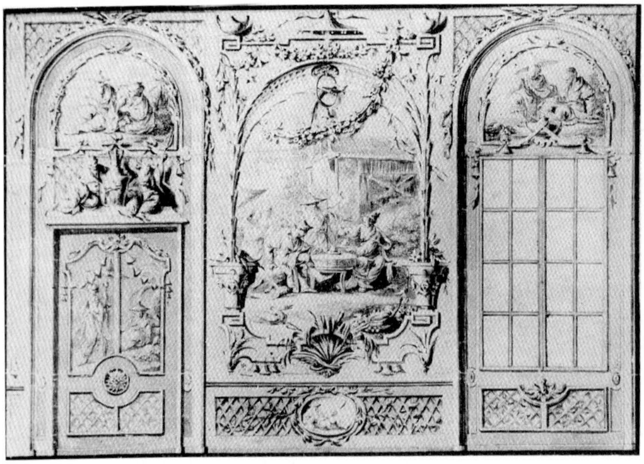

190. Benigno Bossi, Design for a Chinese Room at the Colorno Villa, 18th century, second half. Berlin, Kunstbibliothek.

Set within neoclassical frames, the Chinese scenes devised by Bossi appear to be based on Bouchet's oriental compositions. The *Second Chinese Suite* of tapestries made at Beauvais and designed by Boucher belonged to the Bourbon collections.

also uncertain exactly when the papers were installed; apart from the different themes portrayed, they are similar to the papers in the first Chinese Room and both also have the same light green framing, perhaps indicating that Petitot made the still lifes on the ceiling after the room had been decorated with the papers.

Further evidence of chinoiserie at Colorno is seen in a general plan by Petitot of the magnificent shelves in the Sala Grande, each supporting a 'trumpet-shaped' porcelain vase, made in Europe and imitating Asian models, if not in fact Chinese or Japanese. Described in an inventory of 1825 as "Four Large Porcelain Vases from Japan", it has been suggested that they were actually made at Parma's royal majolica factory which began production in 1759.[25] A watercolour sketch by Benigno Bossi, a stucco worker and engraver who also made the plates for Petitot's *Suite de Vases* of 1764 and *Mascarade à la Grecque*, most probably represents yet another oriental room in Colorno, decorated with scenes of Chinese figures in various poses and activities, surrounded by neoclassical frames.[26]

Petitot also contributed to the design of the Chinese Fair held on 5 and 6 September 1769. Two drawings, later engraved, show the outline plan and his design for the shorter side of the market to be created in the Ducal Gardens. The second in particular shows his skill in combining basic architectural elements with more casual and natural features.[27] The most oriental touches are the ephemeral pavilions on the two sides of his design and the groups of items laid out ready for the beginning of the Fair. These designs represent the apogee of Petitot's eclectic creativity, both in his clever use of the baroque, rococo and early neoclassical styles, and the themes of the celebrations, which seem to happily embrace elements of Ariosto, Egypt, ancient Greece, Arcadia, and of course, China.

It is quite possible that Petitot and his assistants also drew their inspiration for the Chinese Fair from the *Second Chinese Suite* of tapestries that had arrived in Parma in 1752.[28] Not entirely in keeping with early 18th-century fashions, they remained in storage for a period until duchess Maria Luigia (1791-1847

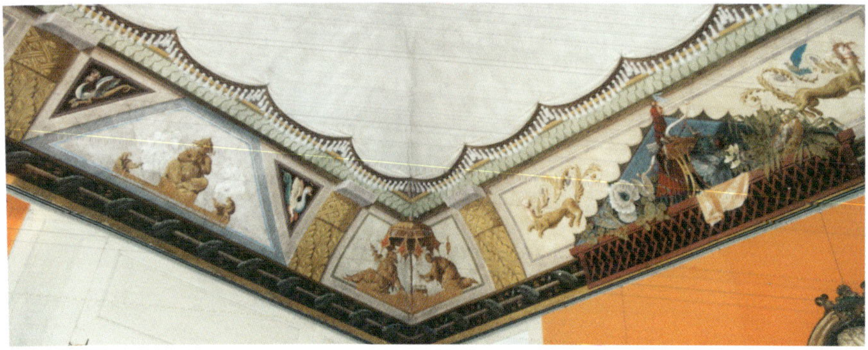

191a,b. Anonymous artist from Parma, Chinoiserie frescoes, 19th century, first half. Colorno (Parma), Palazzo Ducale, dining room.

Dated after 1815, this frieze represents a late comeback of chinoiserie at the court of Parma. The scene of supplicants with a deity illustrated here is one of the most characteristic motifs of the oriental fashion; it first appeared about 1650 and was constantly reproduced throughout the 1700s.

decided to use three to decorate the walls of the Dining Room at Colorno, before they were transferred to Turin in 1862. The Dining Room reflects the late revival of Chinese style furnishings in the duchy of Parma. In addition to the tapestries, the lower section of the ceiling is decorated with painted Chinese motifs. Dated after 1815, in the centres of the frieze on all four sides are still life compositions of various objects, such as Chinese porcelain and a large closed parasol, alongside entirely European military trophies. Moreover, these alternate with smaller scenes painted in yellow and grey, portraying Chinese deities and supplicants, reminiscent of compositions that had continually appeared in European chinoiserie since the days of Nieuhoff.
The taste for chinoiserie was not restricted only to Parma's ducal court. The Chinese Room in Palazzo Pallavicino[29] is decorated with late examples of French chinoiserie. Dated towards the end of the 18th century, when the revival of neoclassical principles began to displace the frivolity of *rocaille*, the oriental elements of the room consist mainly of figures of Chinamen in the corners of the ceiling, and a harmonious design of fantastic animals, birds and small monkeys sparingly arranged within the neatly understated scrolls of volutes and arabesques.[30]

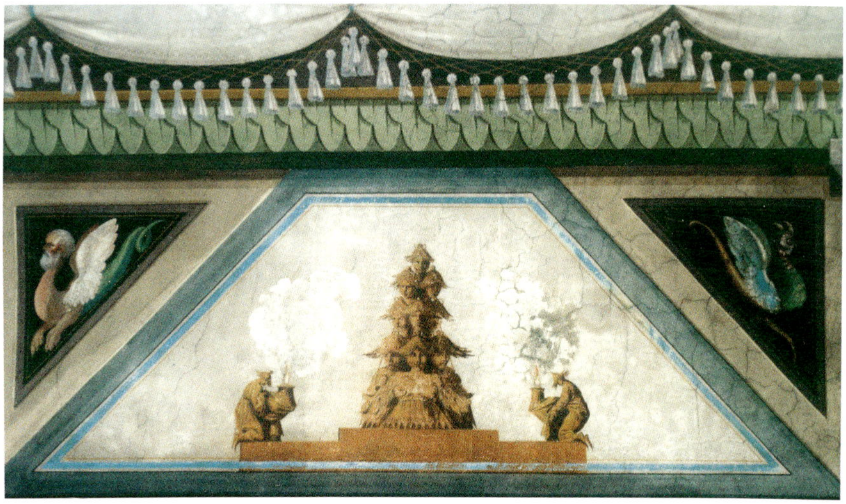

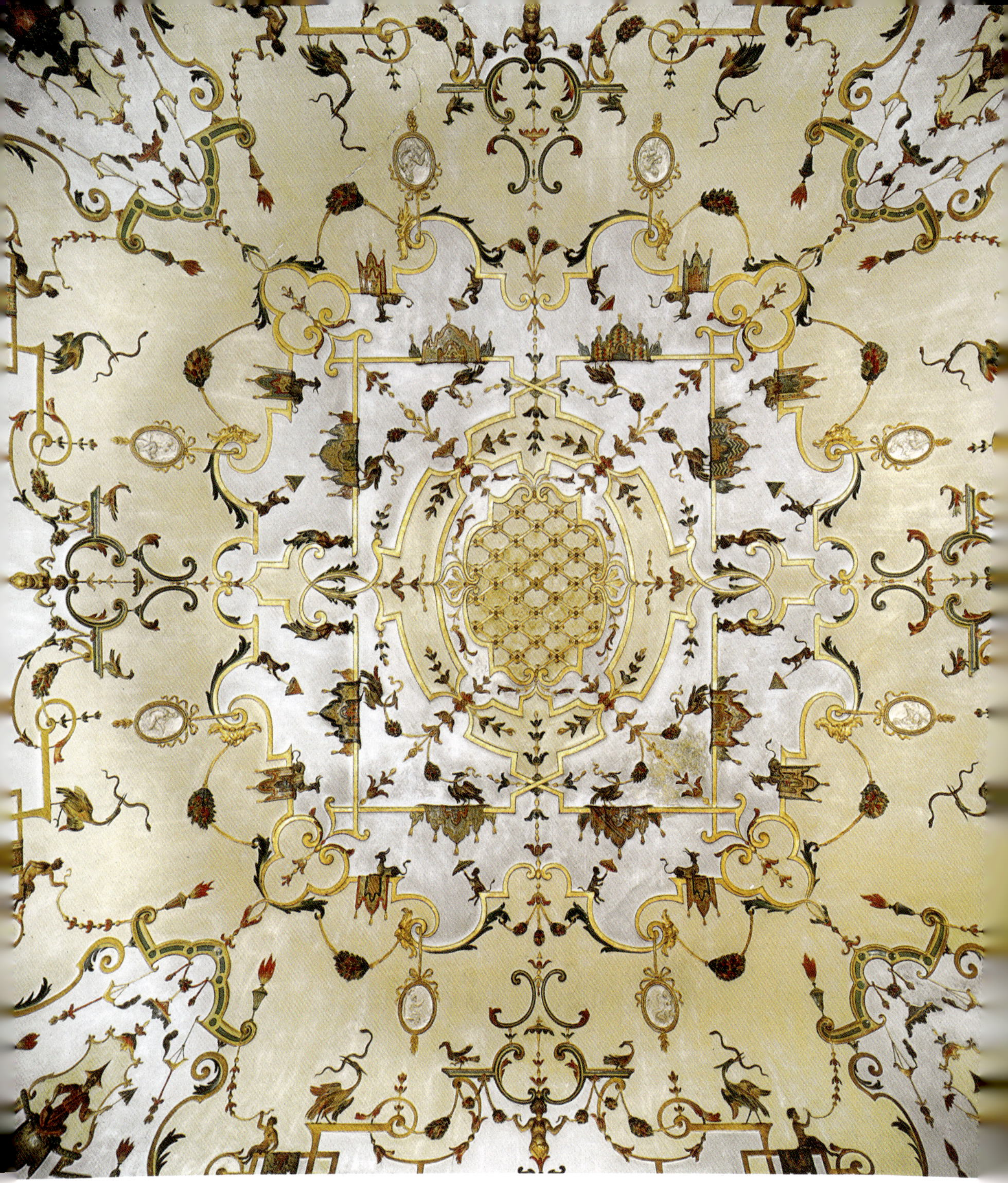

Furniture in the Chinese Style

Although criticized by Alvar González-Palacios,[31] the most recent publication specifically on Emilian furniture was published in 1983 and was written by Giuseppe Cirillo and Giovanni Godi; the text is accompanied by illustrations of furniture decorated with chinoiseries, both inlayed and painted on a lacquered background.[32] The table in figure 225 (p. 99: Venice, Unesco HQ) passed uncommented by González-Palacios, perhaps because he accepted the authors' attribution as one of the earliest examples of 'Chinese-style' furniture in Parma. In fact the authors do not propose many attributions, and in the introduction (p. 11) merely comment that the oriental fashion was popular even during the latter decades of the Farnese dukes, citing the example of "twenty Chinamen painted on planks of wood and carved" described in Palazzo Sanvitale between 1715 and 1727. Cirillo and Godi also mention two other tables, one in storage in the Villa at Stra, and another sold at auction by Christies' in 1980. The table reproduced in a drawing in their book (fig. 226: Parma, Archivio di Stato, Mappe e Disegni, v. 11, no. 87) could – given the stylistic similarities to contemporary French production – also be dated to the same period (1715-1730). The authors cautiously suggest the work of a Parma craftsman influenced by the French style. The well-defined little Chinese figures in the two halves of the cartouche below the table top and in the frieze around the edge on the right reveal some similiarities to late 17th-century 'Chinese' motifs derived from the engravings of Nieuhoff, Montanus and Kircher and highly popular in both France and Germany in the late 17th and early 18th century.

The attribution of two items from the Soragna castle illustrated by Cirillo and Godi in figures 227-228 (p. 100), remains ambiguous. The first is a small desk which the two authors identify in the 1743 inventory of the castle where it is described with its "ink pot and dredger". The second is a cabinet with a glass case and several similar items are mentioned in the same inventory including "a wood bureau with black lacquer, illuminated with gilded figures", two similar corner cabinets in the "turquoise room" on the ground floor, and a "Chinese-style bureau with figures and decorations in gold". This latter piece was located in the "room of her Ladyship", where a half table and two corner cabinets were similarly decorated – thus creating a complete 'Chinese' interior. Cirillo and Godi suggest that the two items were made by local craftsmen who based their designs on Venetian models (especially the writing desk, the square shape of which is typical of the furniture of Parma), though this is rejected by González-Palacios who proposes instead Venetian, or even English, origin. As it is known that the owners of the castle were particularly partial to Venetian furnishings, especially after the marriage in 1691 of Niccolò (1666-1748) to the Venetian Cecilia Loredan,[33] this could be a valid proposal. The furnishings of the Soragna residence included a magnificent support for a vase, carved and gilded with late baroque volutes (possibly first half of the 18th century) on top of which was a complete five-piece Japanese

192. Anonymous decorators from Parma, Ceiling of the Chinese Room, late 18th century. Parma, Palazzo Pallavicino.

The exotic elements of this chinoiserie design (Chinamen, birds, dragons and monkeys) are placed symmetrically among neoclassical volutes and medallions.

'Imari' porcelain *guarniture de cheminée*, dated late 17th or early 18th century. As similar porcelain items, both Chinese and Japanese, were usually placed on the broad shelves of fireplaces during the winter or inside the unlit chimney during the summer, we can easily imagine how rare the item must have been. González-Palacios recalls having seen two chinoiserie lacquered desks similar to those of Soragna in the Medici Villa at Poggio a Caiano before the theft in 1969 of several chairs, a desk with a folding top and a divan, all belonging to the same suite. Perhaps Venetian, the divan was illustrated by Cirillo and Godi in their publication (fig. 341) as it seems to have formerly been in the villa at Colorno. Bought by the last Bourbons in the mid 1800s, similar furnishings had already been recorded in the ducal residence in 1802.[34] The divan is also seen in Aldo Raimondi's watercolour representing a possible reconstruction of a Chinese Room in the Colorno Villa.

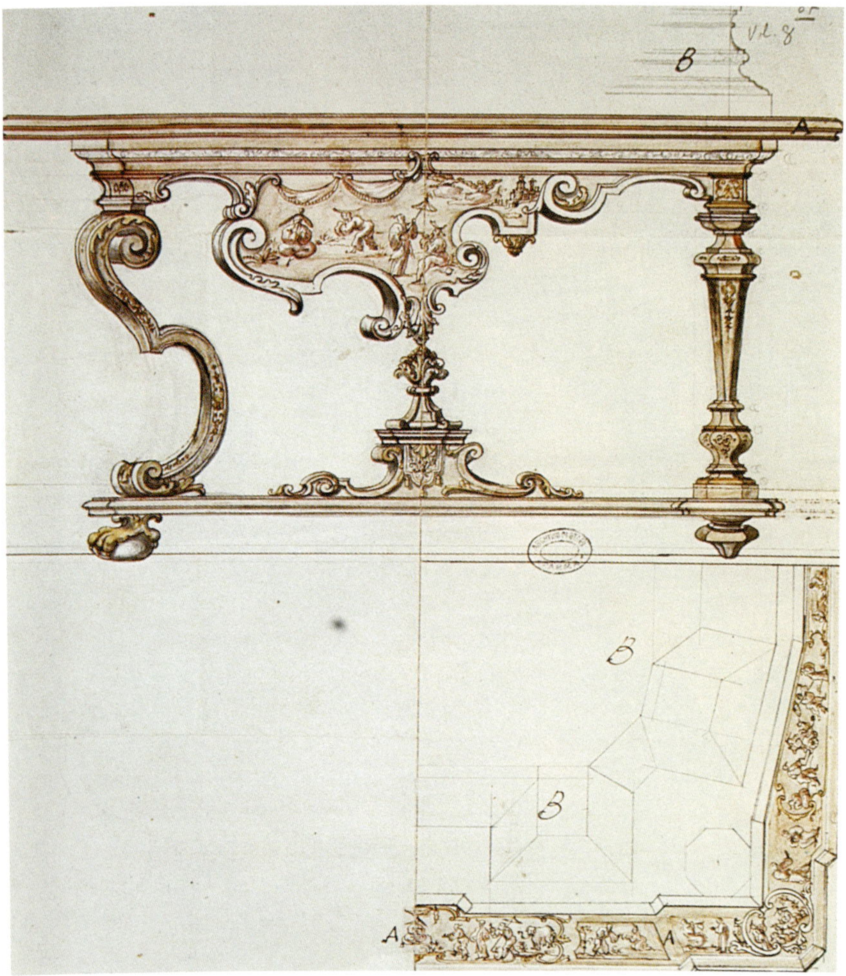

193. Design for a console table. Parma, 18th century, first half. Parma, State Archive.

Both the form and the chinoiserie decoration of this console table are clearly influenced by early 18th-century French works. Some details of the oriental vignettes seem to be derived from Dutch repertories published during the second half of the 17th century (Nieuhoff, Montanus, Dapper, etc.).

1) Honour 1961 (1963), pp. 138-139.
2) Mignardi in Rome-Parma-Lyons 1989, p. 111.
3) Lightbown 1969, pp. 265-279.
4) Martino 1996.
5) Colorno 1998.
6) González-Palacios 1995.
7) Colle 1992.
8) Eriksen 1973; González-Palacios 1995.
9) Clarke, D'Agliano 1999.
10) Bertini 2005.
11) Morena 2005, pp. 337-432.
12) Morena 2005, p. 338.
13) Lavalle, Cobo 2003.
14) Pellegri 1981, p. 88.
15) Parma 1997, p. 12.
16) Zoli 1974, note 1, p. 113.
17) Parma 1997, pp. 17-18.
18) Bertini 1974.
19) Cirillo 2002, figs. 144 bis, 144 tris, 219.
20) Briganti 1977, p. 384.
21) González-Palacios 1986, p. 210.
22) Colorno 1998, pp. 194-201.
23) Briganti 1977, pp. 387-388.
24) Cirillo 2002, pp. 60-61, fig. 63.
25) Cirillo in Parma 1997, pp. 301-302, no. 50.
26) Berlin 1973, pp. 302-303, no. P18; González-Palacios 1986, I, pp. 210-211; II, fig. 481.
27) Rome-Parma-Lyons 1989, pp. 121-122, nos. 143-144.
28) Forti Grazzini in Colorno 1998, p. 198.
29) Gambara, Pellegrini, De Grazia 1971, pp. 367-368.
30) Colle 2003, p. 287 and fig. on p. 289.
31) González-Palacios 1986, pp. 239-246.
32) Cirillo, Godi 1983.
33) Cirillo, Godi 1983, pp. 10-11.
34) Cirillo, Godi 1983, p. 136, no. 341.

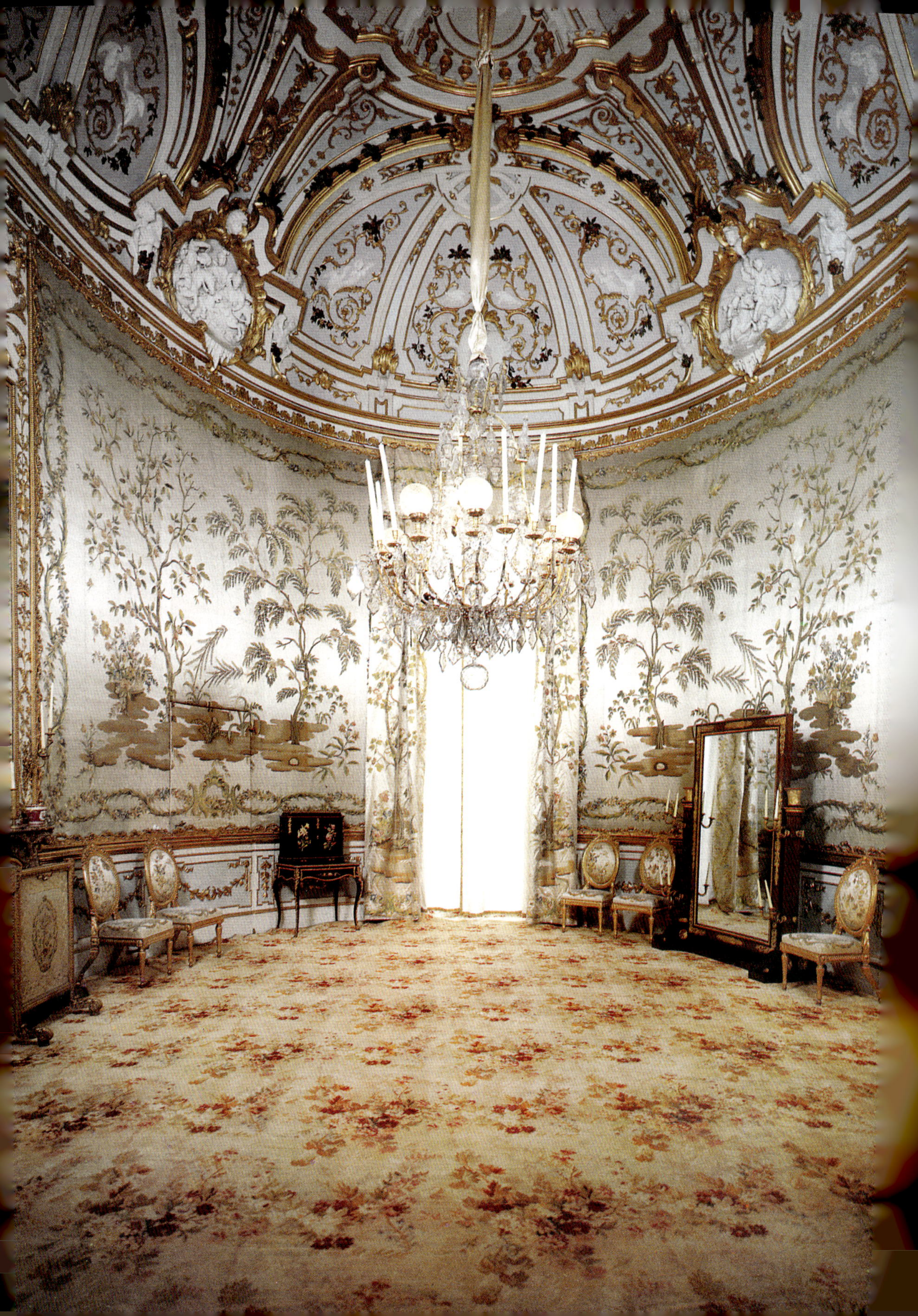

The Tuscan Grand Duchy

Exoticism at the Court of the Last Medici

Between 1712 and 1713 the extrovert and unconventional writer Girolamo Gigli (1660-1722) wrote a play entitled *Il Gazzettino*.[1] The theme of the play was based on the amusing consequences caused by the arrival of a letter from 'Gionata VII' (an inexistent king of China) seeking thc hand of the pope in marriage. Gigli's irony may have derived from the theatre of Molière, but its irreverent hilarity was entirely Tuscan and the misunderstandings that arise from this comic situation gave him plenty of opportunity to make barbed quips against the aristocracy and the priesthood, the Jesuits in particular. Gigli included some quite fanciful descriptions for the Chinese customs in his text but on this particular occasion the setting of China seems to have been entirely coincidental to the plot of the melodrama and the author had no intention or interest in describing these distant lands. However the choice of China to fulfil the role of a mysterious, distant and exotic land in the context of *Il Gazzettino* is perhaps not altogether coincidental. In fact, in the early 18th century there was a lively interest in the Far East in Tuscany, and especially at the court of the grand dukes. In 1688 for example, as part of the festivities for the marriage between Ferdinando de' Medici (1663-1713) and Violante Beatrice of Bavaria (1673-1731) a fabulous procession was staged at the court, at the head of which was the "King of China", who had travelled to Tuscany with his retinue to render homage to the Medici. The event is immortalized in a painting on silk, seven metres long, on which all those who participated in the masquerade are identified.[2]

Even from the early days of their power, from at least the 15th century until the final extinction of the dynasty in 1743, the Medici dukes had been avid collectors of Chinese and Japanese items.[3] The last representatives of the house, from Cosimo III (1642-1723, grand duke from 1670) to his children Ferdinando, Gian Gastone (1671-1737, grand duke from 1723) and Anna Maria Luisa (1667-1743), truly the last of the Medici – all were passionate collectors of Far Eastern works of art. Chinese and Japanese porcelain was their greatest passion and was used both practically as tableware and to create various Porcelain Rooms located, for example, in the corridor on the second floor of the Uffizi, in almost all the Medici villas surrounding the city and especially in Palazzo Pitti. Indeed at Pitti the Electress Palatine commissioned a 'Gabinetto' where more than three thousand porcelain items – mostly oriental – could be displayed, most of which she had acquired in Holland

194. 'Gabinetto Ovale'. Florence, Pitti Palace, Royal Apartments.
The floral design of the magnificent decorations covering the walls was, without any doubt, derived from the patterns on Chinese wall papers used for two of the four Chinese rooms created in the Poggio Imperiale villa before 1780. The decorative motif of the Tree of Life appeared on all manner of items in China and India (though especially fabrics) and was one of the most popular oriental designs in Europe. In the 17th century versions of this motif that were more satisfactory to European tastes, were sent to the Far East to be reproduced by highly skilled Asian craftsmen.

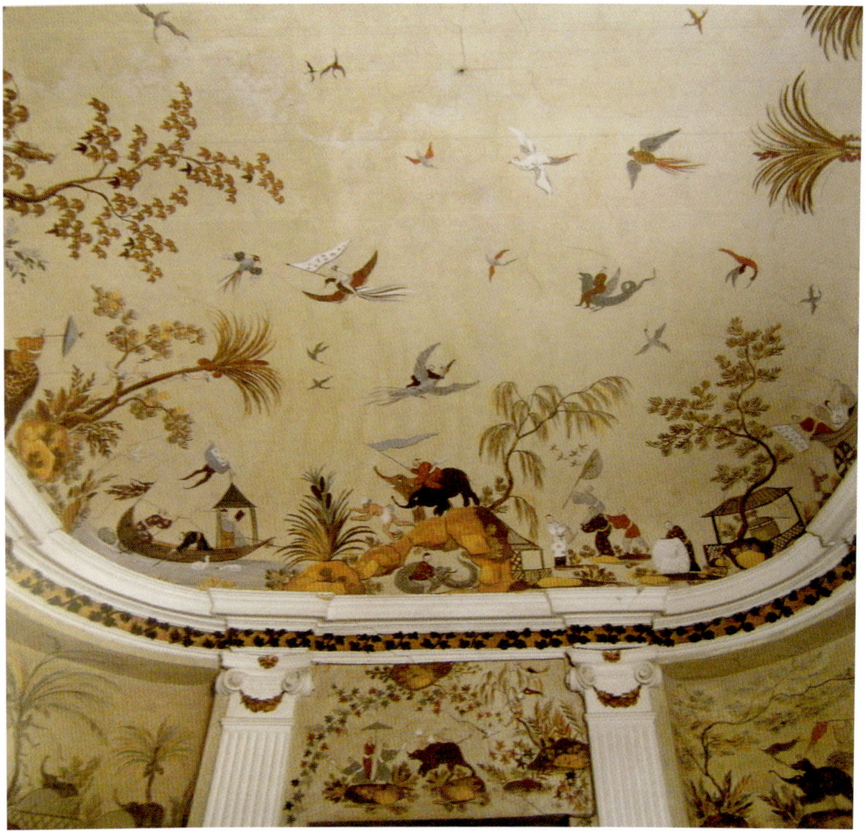

195. Marino Benaglia, Chinoiserie, circa 1702. Bagno a Ripoli (Florence), Hunting lodge at Lilliano, the 'Indian' Room.

when, following her marriage to Johann Wilhelm von der Pfalz-Neuburg (1658-1716) the Elector Palatine, she had lived in Düsseldorf.[4] But in addition to porcelain the collections of the later Medici also included lacquered objects, painted papers, natural curios, printed books – a complete range of assorted items that represented a compendium of the arts and culture of these distant Asian lands. Other aristocratic Florentine families could also boast oriental porcelain works, such as the Gerini who De Brosses recorded in 1738 as owning "antique Japanese porcelain, of quite unusual size".[5]
The popularity of porcelain amongst collectors encouraged the Medici to try to reproduce original oriental items in Florence. Ferdinando I had already made an attempt in the 16th century when he established the 'Medici porcelain' factory. At the same time wood workers and furniture makers had begun to specialize in 'Indian-style' decoration. In the late 1600s, or early 1700s, grand duke Cosimo III set up workshops to experiment with varnishes to imitate oriental lacquer, and detailed information about these experiments was provided by Filippo Bonanni in his *Trattato*: "After having received this direct information I was able to try it out, as His Royal Highness of the Grand Duchy of Tuscany Cosimo III, had received from that kingdom a considerable quantity of the above-mentioned Chiaràm, and oil, not mixed, but separate in different jars and I was able to have a small flask of each and

test them according to the rules sent to me in the letters mentioned, and with the practical assistance of someone who had arrived in Rome from there ...".[6] Thus, although we do not know how or from where, Cosimo had succeeded in obtaining the resin of the *Rhus Vernicifera*, known in Portuguese as *Chiaràm*, in an attempt to understand its composition and reproduce it. Bonanni, as director of the Kircher Museum, also had an interest in understanding the properties of Chinese lacquer and was recruited to assist. Although it would be interesting to speculate that the grand duke supported further experiments with the intention of establishing a specialised lacquer workshop in Florence, this seems to have been an isolated incident and, moreover, unsuccessful. Not a single item made in Tuscany during the late 17th and early 18th centuries provides any evidence of the existence of locally produced lacquer.

Without any doubt the most spectacular chinoiserie decoration dating from the period of the Medici Grand Duchy is the 'Indian' room in the Lilliano residence, not far from Florence. The walls and ceiling of the room are painted with eastern subjects and themes. The scenes reflect an imaginary Orient, in which Chinese, Moorish and south American characters pursue their favourite activities, mainly in the open air. The landscape is formed of rocks, various species of trees, pavilions, lakes and rivers plied by little boats, while the human figures are accompanied in their occupations by a selection of elephants, tortoises and birds. The decorative style is clearly derived from that of northern Europe – in particular England and Holland – and the closest reference is Stalker and Parker's *Treatise* of 1688. There are, moreover, similarities with the chinoiserie decorations found on 17th-century English and Dutch lacquer work, while some features are drawn directly from original Oriental wares such as the large Tree of Life depicted on one of the walls, clearly reflecting a subject that decorated many Indian textiles of the 17th century produced for exportation to Europe. The author of this early Italian chinoiserie has recently been identified as Marino Benaglia who produced this décor around 1702.[7] At this time the hunting lodge at Lilliano was one of the properties belonging to cardinal Francesco Maria de' Medici (1660-1711) and was an annex to the nearby Villa di Lappeggi. Fascinated by the exotic style and an important collector of oriental items, in the late 17th and early 18th centuries, Francesco Maria initiated an intense programme of rebuilding and refurbishing his favourite properties at Lappeggi and Lilliano. He therefore chose an 'exotic' style of decoration for many of the rooms in the two buildings: as well as the 'Indian' room at Lilliano he used a similarly effusive form of decoration in the Kaffeehaus located in the garden of Lappeggi. No longer existent, the cardinal enjoyed welcoming his guests here, offering them the fashionable drinks of the day – tea, coffee and chocolate.[8] Benaglia also worked on this structure, principally on the oriental-style lacquer on some of the items. It would seem in fact that, Venetian by birth and training, he was specialized in the technique of varnishing and documents appear to suggest that he had worked in Holland for a while. This would certainly explain the style of the decoration at Lilliano, which reflects the influence of late 17th-century English and Dutch chinoiserie.

The Lorraine Grand Duchy

With the extinction of the Medici dynasty the international powers decided that the Duchy of Tuscany should pass to Francis Stephen (1708-1765), duke of Lorraine and married to Maria Therese of Hapsburg (1717-1780). In fact, the new sovereign was elected emperor of the Holy Roman Empire in 1745 and only visited Florence once in 1739, promptly entrusting the government of the duchy to prince de Craon (1679-1754), who was succeeded by count Emmanuel de Richecourt (1694-1768) and lastly marshal Adorno Botta (1688-1774). In 1765 Francis Stephen's son, Pietro Leopoldo (1747-1792), was nominated grand duke of Tuscany; he moved to Florence in the same year, taking up residence in Palazzo Pitti and introducing a period of enlightened government despite a degree of austerity and thrifty management of public money. At the same time, however, he encouraged a revival of traditional Tuscan arts, clearly preferring a neoclassical style of décor.[9] The theories expounded by Voltaire and Quesnay (1694-1774) on China's exemplary government were quite widely known in Tuscany through the writings of Abbé Alfonso Longo (1738-1804) (*Istituzioni economico politiche*, 1773) and Ferdinando Paoletti (1717-1801), a physiocrat (*I veri mezzi di render felici le società*, 1772). Financed by the reformist state councillor Angelo Tavanti (1714-1782), a satirical novel (London 1768) written by Gabriel François Coyer (1707-1782) and translated by the Tuscan economist Giuseppe Sarchiani appeared in 1770 with the title *Chinki, Istoria Concinese che può servire ancora ad altri paesi.*[10]

Chinoiserie in Tuscany enjoyed rather mixed fortunes during both the 'Regency' (1737-1765) and Pietro Leopoldo's rule (1765-1792). On the one hand the collections of orientalia created by the Medici over three hundred years were entirely dispersed; as they were not mentioned in Anna Maria Luisa's famous *Family Pact* ensuring that the Lorraine would not remove the Medici's art collections from Florence, the porcelain works were almost all sold in a series of public auctions including thousands of lots, between 1772 and 1773.[11] On the other hand, Pietro Leopoldo seems rather to have favoured other forms of chinoiserie. De Lalande, for example, wrote that the procession organised for the St John's day celebrations in 1766 was lead by a 'machine' in the form of a pagoda. Two years later, in 1768, when Marie Caroline of Austria passed through Florence on her way to Naples to marry Ferdinando IV, a fancy-dress ball was organised in the Cascine park, opened by Pietro Leopoldo and the grand duchess in Chinese costume, accompanied by fifteen other couples similarly attired.[12] Oriental costumes must also have been used in 1775 when *L'orfano della China* was performed in the city

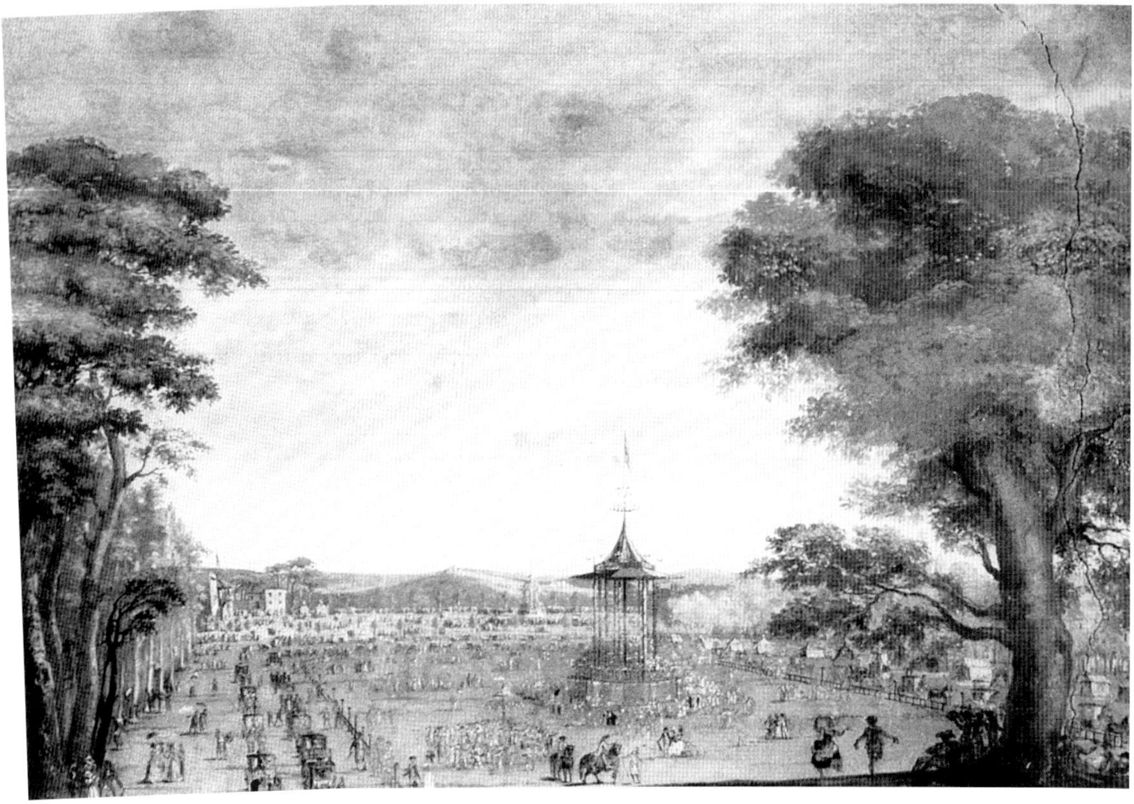

196. F. Mulinelli, *Carriage race in the Cascine park to celebrate the wedding of archduchess Maria Teresa, 9 September 1787.*

"The celebrations were most interesting as they were designed in the new Chinese fashion [...]. The promenade of carriages was held in the large field known as the 'Quercione' and the carriages were obliged to proceed around the sides of the field behind a fencing of columns made in the Chinese style and decorated with torches, flowers and plumes. An orchestra played in the centre of the fenced-off area".

theatre during the interval of the opera *Perseus and Andromeda*, attended by a quite bored and very disappointed marquis De Sade.[13]

While paradoxically Pietro Leopoldo was responsible for the sale of the porcelain collections, he did however commission the decoration of various rooms in the grand ducal residences in a pure and thorough oriental style. Altogether nine rooms were fitted out in the 'Chinese style' in the Poggio Imperiale villa, the residence preferred by the grand duke, while Palazzo Pitti continued to be used for representational purposes. Four of these rooms were decorated with original Chinese papers and in a smaller adjoining room numerous small framed examples of painted papers were displayed, many of which were bought by Pietro Leopoldo between 1786 and 1787 from Micali in Livorno.[14] 'Flower and bird' compositions decorate the walls of two of these rooms, while the other two are enhanced by landscapes with buildings and figures busy in various pursuits. The remaining four 'Chinese rooms' in the villa were decorated with Indian chintz with floral motifs. These painted papers and silks were ordered by the countess of Rosenberg from François de Rens, a merchant in Brussels, and arrived in Florence in 1770. The court upholsterer, Giuseppe Marechal, was responsible for the decoration of the rooms but soon realised that the materials were insufficient and travelled personally to Brussels to acquire additional quantities. Work on the rooms began on his return and was completed by 1780.[15] It is perhaps unusual that

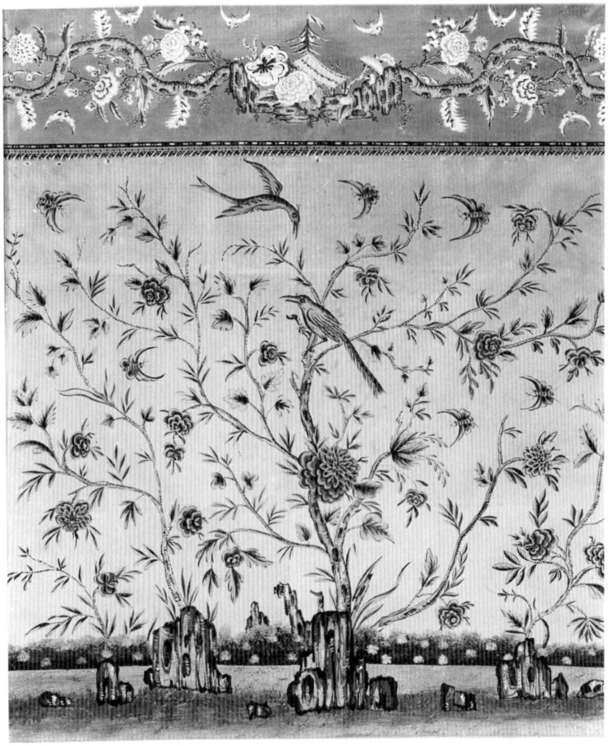

197. Werkruis and Saller, 'Chinese' decoration, c. 1775-1780, detail. Florence, Villa del Poggio Imperiale.

One of the overdoors made by the Genoan painters, Werkruis and Saller, who were specialized in Chinese style decorations. The overdoors were prepared for four rooms in the Poggio Imperiale villa to complete and integrate the wall covering of original Chinese papers. The religious symbolism of the Tree of Life motif had existed in the Orient since the fourth millenium BC and was used in China, and especially India where it appeared as a pattern on printed furnishing fabrics known as *palampore* – mostly produced for export to European markets.

the rooms decorated with painted papers in villa Poggio Imperiale are one of the very few surviving examples in Tuscany of a fashion which elsewhere – both in other Italian states and abroad – enjoyed immense popularity. To complete the decoration (especially the overdoors and windows) strips of painted papers with the same motifs of 'flowers and birds' and 'Chinese scenes' were made by Werkruis and Saller, painters in Genoa who were specialised in the reproduction of oriental motifs.[16]
At about the same time the *Kaffehaus* in the Boboli Gardens at the Pitti Palace was under construction and, supervised by the architect Zanobi del Rosso (1724-1798), was completed in 1774. Although referred to in documents of the time as a 'Chinese pavilion' – a description merited only by the unusual circular shape of the dome covered with sheets of copper – the building has little of the Orient about it either architecturally or decoratively, and is rather more evidently late Viennese Rococo in style. However, it is a good example of a type of garden structure which was highly fashionable in the most important European courts in the mid 1700s, such as the *Petit Trianon* at Versailles and the *Teehaus* at Potsdam, although the design and decoration of these was not always strictly 'oriental'.[17]
The 'flower and bird' motifs of the painted Chinese papers in Poggio Imperiale most certainly provided the inspiration for Paolo Migliorati when he designed the richly embroidered white satin wall covering in the 'Gabinetto Ovale' (or Queen's Boudoir) in the Royal Apartments of Palazzo

198. Chinese Room, late 18th century, detail. Geggiano (Siena), Villa Bianchi Bandinelli.

This printed French fabric is decorated with chinoiserie motifs taken from the *The Ladies Amuseument*, published in London in 1760 by Robert Sayer; it was used to cover the walls and furniture of this room in the late 1700s.

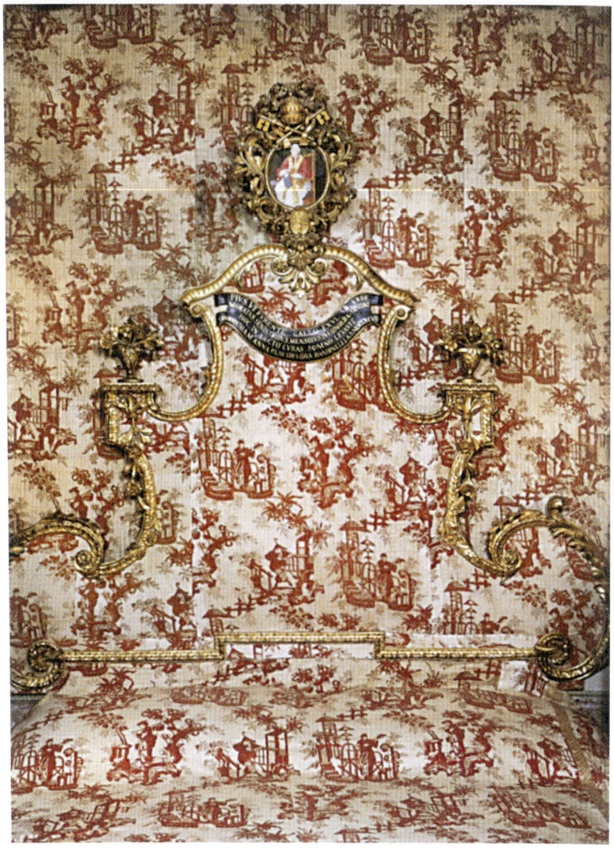

Pitti.[18] Commissioned by Pietro Leopoldo's wife, grand duchess Maria Luisa (1745-1792), the work was undertaken by Rosa Migliorati, Paolo's wife, who, with her assistants, completed it in 1783 after three years of what must have been an exhausting effort. But this was not the only elegant fabric with oriental motifs chosen for the grand duchess' apartment adjoining the boudoir. Sent to Florence by empress Maria Therese as a present for her son, Pietro Leopoldo, and her daughter-in-law, white satin decorated with an oriental floral design covered the walls of a room adjoining the grand duchess' bedroom. A similar chinoiserie floral pattern was also used on the fabric made in Florence around 1770, decorating the walls of the 'Yellow Room' nearby, though later transferred to the antechamber of the king's apartment where it is still to be seen. Another fabric in the same style was originally acquired to decorate the grand duchess' apartment, but in 1840 it was used to decorate the grand duke's antechamber on the second floor of the palace and was subsequently transferred to the king's studio in 1899. This material too was made about 1770, almost a decade before the decoration of the 'Gabinetto Ovale' was completed. These three sets of wall coverings are a unique example of 18th-century Florentine textile production with oriental motifs. The grand dukes had in fact established both an Academy for the design of hangings and a Royal and Imperial Factory, thus providing an economic incentive that was essential to the survival of one of Florence's finest arts, at the time facing rapid decline due to strong competition from the factories of Lyons.[19]

Rolls of paper painted with an exuberant and colourful decoration of 'flowers and birds' decorating a room in Villa Medici in Fiesole are more or less contemporary to the painted papers in the Poggio Imperiale villa (third quarter of the 18th century) and indicate that a taste for chinoiserie was not limited to the Lorraine court in the 1700s. Although the exact date of this decoration is unknown, when the historic villa was owned by the countess of Oxford, Lady Margaret Rolle Walpole in 1781, several rooms were decorated with "hangings fixed to the walls", one of which could well be the room still in existence.[20] Another room in the villa is also decorated with oriental style flowers and furnished with a red lacquer bookcase on which oriental figures are picked out in gold, designed by Cecil Pinsent (1884-1963) in 1919.[21]

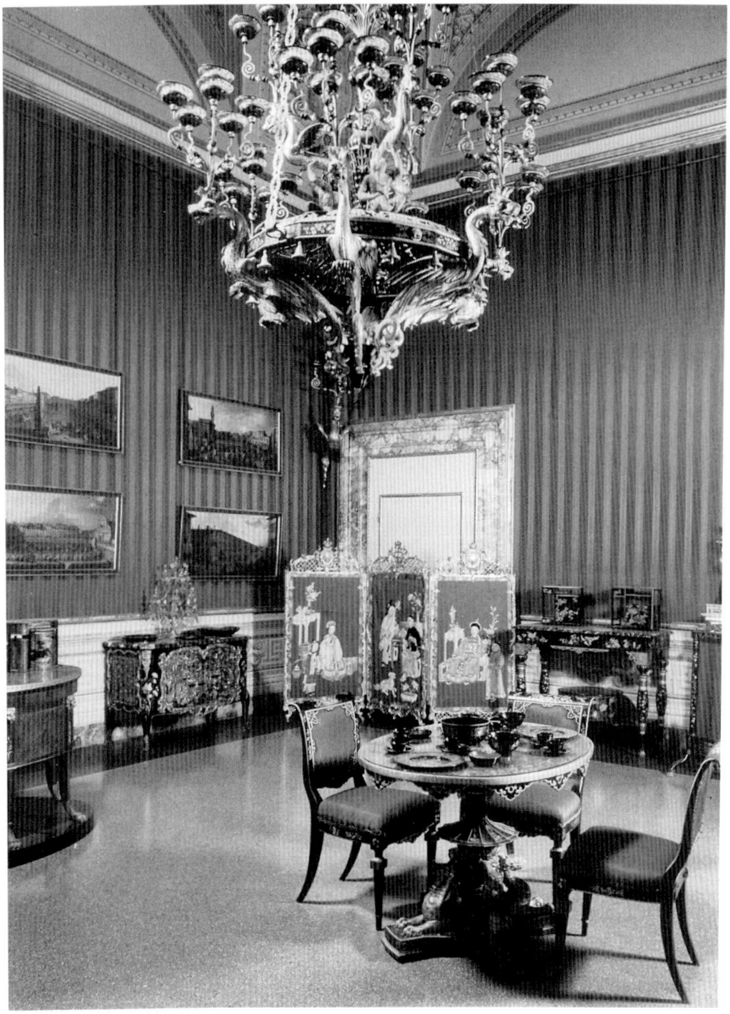

199. Chinese Room, 1833. Florence, Pitti Palace, Winter Apartments.

The furnishings were made by Florentine craftsmen in 1833 when, elsewhere in Europe, chinoiserie had already become outmoded. The original Chinese and Japanese items still exhibited in the room were selected from many belonging to the Medici collections.

Hugh Honour[22] has described the 'cardinal's bedroom' on the first floor of Villa Bianchi Bandinelli at Geggiano (Siena) as the best surviving example of a *cabinet chinois* decorated with *toile de Jouy.* The late 18th-century chinoiserie décor – dated between 1780 and 1790 – has remained almost intact. The ancestral home of the Bianchi Bandinelli family, the noted archaeologist, Ranuccio, took up residence in the villa and wrote an account of the history of the room. Bandinelli recounts that the name of the room actually refers to the colour of the decoration, rather than to any cardinal who might have been a guest there, and dwells in much greater length on the story of the bed required for pope Pius VI in 1798 during his flight from Rome to France, where he later died.[23] Bianchi Bandinelli confirms that the fabric printed with chinoiserie on the walls is original and was also used more recently for the furnishings and bedcover. The rusty brown background of the fabric is decorated with little Chinese vignettes of figures, trees and buildings, clearly derived from Pillement's motifs published in the *The Ladies Amusement.* Honour suggests that the fabric is of French manufacture, produced about 1790,[24] and this is supported not only by the style of the pattern and the history of the villa and its residents, but also by the presence of a French paper produced by the firm 'Au grand Balcon' which decorates another room in the villa and dates from the same period.

Of altogether a different character is the 'Chinese Room' on the second floor of Palazzo Pitti (the 'Quartiere d'Inverno' or duchess of Aosta's apartment) created in 1833 at the explicit request of grand duchess Maria of Saxony (1796-1865), who became Ferdinando's second wife in 1821 and his widow in 1824. The furnishings of the room (divans, seats, chairs, tables, a mirror, a chandelier, wall lights, a large circular table and the firescreen) were all made by the court craftsmen. The walls are decorated with narrow red and black stripes and arranged around the room are original Chinese and Japanese porcelain and lacquer works as well as oriental style European pieces.[25] Made in Florence, the black lacquer furniture was decorated with red, green and gold painting and a generous sprinkling of mother-of-pearl incrustations, a further reminder of Far Eastern techniques. The painted decorations are mainly floral, though pagodas and exotic birds are also featured, while dragons put in an appearance as sculptural elements on the foot of the circular table and the supports for the dishes on the chandelier. The form of the furnishings is late neoclassical, the style which was most prevalent when the entire room was designed and arranged. While many neoclassical chinoiserie interiors are rather attractive, on the whole this 'Chinese Room' really has little of the Orient about it and is simply an uncomfortable offspring of a taste that was already well past its prime – and indeed decline.

Ginori Porcelain

The ceramic factory established at Sesto Fiorentino, near Florence, by count Carlo Ginori (1702-1757) began its production in 1737 – the year of the death of Gian Gastonc, the last of the Medici grand dukes. Unlike other important European factories active at the time, such as Meissen and Vienna, Ginori received no royal subsidies to facilitate his business and, as with Vezzi in Venice, had to rely exclusively on his own financial resources. It was not until 1741 (25 January) that Ginori finally succeeded in obtaining the much desired twenty-year monopoly with its relevant and indispensable financial advantages.[26] Ginori identified the right clays to make a good porcelain paste, mixing together some found naturally in Tuscany and others from the Tretto valley near Vicenza which had been used not only by the Medici in the 16th century, but also by Vezzi until 1727 and then by Cozzi. This done, the count travelled to Vienna where he remained for a lengthy period, sent as a representative of the Florentine senate to the new sovreigns of the grand duchy, Francis Stephen and Maria Therese of Austria.[27] This Viennese sojourn was of critical importance for the future of the Ginori factory as here the count had ample opportunity to study the techniques used at the Du Paquier factory, acquire samples and especially to recruit some expert workers. These included the painter Carl Wendelin Anreiter von Ziernfeld who, having acquired excellent experience as a *Hausmaler* in Vienna and great familiarity with the traditional decorations of Saxony, played a vital role during his period at the Ginori factory from 1738 to 1746. Anreiter is known to have utilised some chinoiserie motifs while working in Vienna,[28] but it is not clear whether he also used the same themes while working at Ginori. He did however decorate some original Chinese porcelain cups made in the Dehua factory in the province of Fujian – albeit with traditionally European designs.[29]

This particular type of ceramic production was also known as 'blanc de Chine' in Europe and had been imported from the Orient in great quantities since the early 17th century, becoming one of the most imitated by European factories. Meissen, Vienna and Venice all produced 'blanc de Chine' items and Ginori too added this style to his range in the 1740s, described in the factory's lists as "white with flowers and leaves in relief". Imitating the original Chinese style, the items were not painted with decorations but very often had a floral ornamentation in high relief, especially branches of cherry blossom, one of the most recognizable features of the Dehua output. Fujian porcelain was, moreover, used as a model for the complex latticework technique which was a frequent product of the Doccia factory in the mid 1700s. This style was also known as a "double mould" and consisted of a normal inner form covered by a second latticework moulding which not only served the practical purpose of protecting ones hands from the heat of the drinks, but also had quite a pretty appearance.[30] During the 1750s this white 'Chinese' porcelain

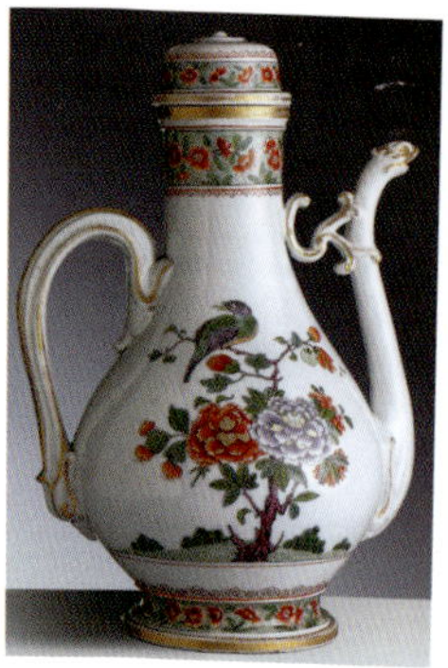

200. Carafe. Sesto Fiorentino, Ginori factory, c. 1745. Private collection.

This shape was frequently used by the Ginori factory: the decoration of this piece was clearly inspired by the designs on Chinese *famille verte* porcelain, so named for the predominance of shades of green, produced in the late 17th and early 18th centuries almost exclusively for export to Europe.

was produced at Sesto in both typically European and oriental forms.[31] Around 1740 the small statuettes portraying the Buddhist deity Guanyin were also in produced at Sesto, based on similar items made in Dehua and exported to Europe in quantity during the mid 17th century.[32]
The influence of Chinese porcelain is also quite evident in the motifs made using stencils. The decorative motif was cut out of sheets of paper, copper or parchment and the colour was applied to the porcelain over the resulting stencil to create a painted composition. The oriental designs produced in this way were mainly floral, but also included the blue motifs painted on a white background. However, in homage to the 'Medici porcelain' produced in the late 16th century, the symbol of the dome of the Florentine cathedral used at

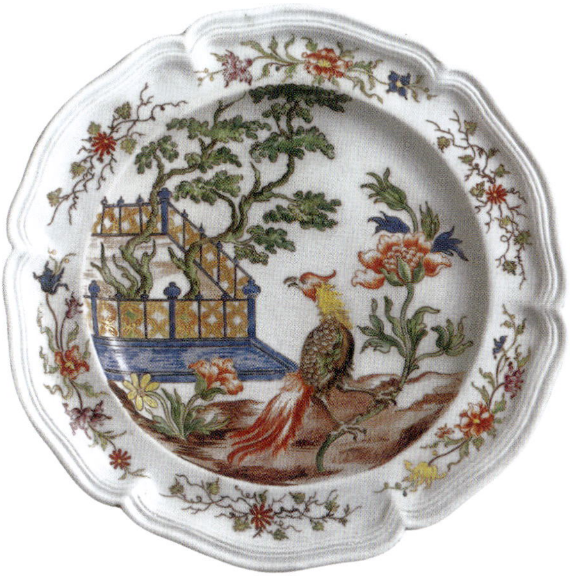

201. Plate. Sesto Fiorentino, Ginori factory, c. 1745. Sesto Fiorentino (Florence), Richard Ginori Museum of the Doccia factory.

Although the decoration of this piece is similar to the designs used on *famille rose* pieces destined for the European markets from the 1730s on, there seems to be no original Far Eastern equivalent. Ornamentalists at the Ginori factory invented the design themselves using various motifs found on Chinese porcelain.

that time also appears on many of these 18th-century pieces.[33]
The Ginori factory also used the 'famille verte', 'famille rose' and Imari oriental motifs as models in the mid century and there are clear echoes too of the decoration found on Japanese 'Kakiemon' porcelain, easily recognizable for its brilliant red, yellow, blue and green colours. As with other factories, the influence of original models gradually evolved, starting as a direct copy, then an imitation, developing into an 'interpretation' and concluding in autonomous designs which reveal some knowledge of oriental porcelain, although it is impossible to identify a direct source.[34] References to oriental subjects are found in the factory's lists dated 1757: "blue Chinese-style flowers", "Chinese-style flowers in various colours with ornaments and birds", "Chinese palaces" – all styles recognisable on items that still exist from that period.[35] Ginori's ornamentalists were particularly fond of using floral motifs and other natural designs on their oriental porcelain – the tulip and the peony

especially were constantly used after 1745, while the chrysanthemum, pine tree, willow, carnation, and rocks also appear, though less frequently.[36] The cockerel design was used from the early days of production at Doccia and is also of Asian origin, a pattern often associated with the decorator Ferdinando Campostrini.[37]

Ginori's porcelain chinoiserie designs were also influenced by the oriental motifs of other factories active in Europe at the time, especially Meissen and Du Paquier in Vienna. Carl Wendelin Anreiter probably introduced patterns from the Meissen factory as, previous to arriving in Tuscany, he had had ample opportunity to learn the 'Chinese' decorations used in Augsburg by decorators working for Meissen, especially in the workshops of Seuter and Auffenwerth. Close similiarities to German chinoiseries, especially those derived from Höroldt's compositions, are seen for example in the designs with oriental landscapes and figures of Chinese dignitaries "all richly painted in gold", which may well have been painted by Anreiter himself. A recent exhibition held at the Liechtenstein Museum has highlighted the extremely close artistic relationship that existed between the Viennese factory and Sesto, especially during the early stages of Ginori's production. During Anreiter's lengthy career at Sesto Fiorentino the styles in fashion at the imperial court in Vienna increasingly influenced the decisions and choices of count Ginori.[38] Both factories preferred, for example, a 'soft' range of colours, and both referred to a similar repertory of late baroque designs, including floral and figurative motifs.

On the death of his father Carlo, the factory passed to Lorenzo (1735-1791), who decided to use kaolin (china clay) extracted from quarries in Tuscany. This drastically reduced costs, but the quality of the ceramic paste obtained was much poorer, a problem resolved by applying an enamel that had a brilliance not dissimilar to that of porcelain. Chinese wares continued to influence the decorative style and while older motifs were still used, new patterns were also introduced. During the 19th century, at the request of the Lorraine grand dukes who wished to replace original items that had been broken, Ginori reproduced the decorative motifs of other ceramic factories. The designs of Viennese and Meissen porcelain were therefore copied exactly and, in one case at least, some original Japanese porcelain was so perfectly imitated that it looks almost identical to the genuine article.[39]

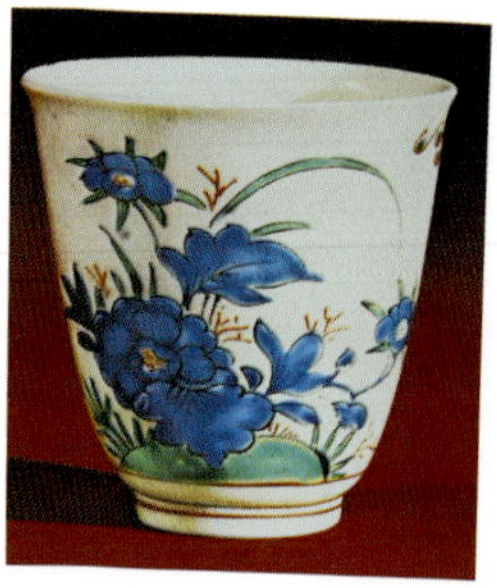

202. Coffee cup. Sesto Fiorentino, Ginori factory, c. 1750. Sesto Fiorentino (Florence) Richard Ginori Museum of the Doccia factory.

The decorative style and choice of colours used for this small cup recall Japanese *Kakiemon* items. This kind of porcelain was imported in large quantities in the later 17th century and was highly popular for the purity of the white paste and brilliance of the colours used. As at Meissen and Vienna, the Doccia factory too produced items emulating *Kakiemon* decorations in the early stages of production.

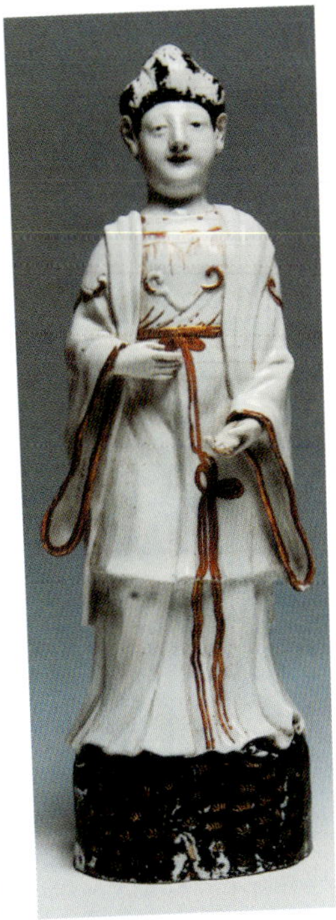

203. *Guanyin*. Sesto Fiorentino (Florence), Ginori factory, c. 1740. Rome, Galleria Lukacs & Donath.

43 cm in height, this figure is the Tuscan version of similar items produced at Dehua in the Fujian province in the 17th century and exported to Europe in large quantities. D'Agliano (1996, p. 8, no. 1) has suggested that, as such figures do not appear in catalogues of the factory, this piece was commissioned by the Gerini family of Florence who already owned numerous pieces of oriental ceramics. The application of cold painted coloured details is also unusual in Ginori production. Some small Chinese figures are also housed in the Pitti Palace, produced by the Medici workshops and also enlivened with touches of colour around 1720.

1) *Il Gazzettino di Gerolamo Gigli* 1864.
2) Allegri 1989, pp. 27-29, no. 11.
3) Spallanzani 1978; Spallanzani 1994; Morena 2005.
4) Morena 2006a.
5) Colle 1992, p. 14.
6) Bonanni 1720, p. 41; Huth 1971, p. 22; Gheroldi 1995, p. 39.
7) Maccioni 2007, pp. 168-175.
8) Barbolani di Montauto, 2007, pp. 145-146.
9) Colle 2005, p. 165 ff.
10) Zoli 1974, pp. 83-94; Zoli 1984, p. 251.
11) Morena 2005, p. 297.
12) Morena 2005, p. 301.
13) Sade 1996, pp. 35-37.
14) Morena 2005, pp. 300, 330-335, nos. 298-307.
15) Orsi Landini 1987.
16) Colle 1992, p. 190, no. 133.
17) Morena 2005, pp. 301-302.
18) Orsi Landini 1993, pp. 196-197.
19) Orsi Landini 1993, p. 197.
20) Mazzini 2004, pp. 181-182 and figs. 65, 87.
21) Mazzini 2004, p. 50, figs. 60-61.
22) Honour 1961 (1963), p. 113.
23) Bianchi Bandinelli 1985, pp. 26-29.
24) Honour 1961 (1963), p. 113.
25) Morena 2005, pp. 305-307.
26) Biancalana 2005, p. 16.
27) Ginori Lisci 1963, p. 25.
28) Vienna 2005, p. 106, fig. 2.
29) Vienna 2005, pp. 306 nos. 139-140; p. 359, no. 208; p. 369, no. 223; p. 375, no. 231; p. 378, nos. 235-236.
30) Ginori Lisci 1963, p. 41; Lucca 2001, p. 81, no. 8.
31) Lucca 2001, pp. 75-85, nos. 1-13.
32) D'Agliano 1996, p. 8, no. 1.
33) Ginori Lisci 1963, p. 41.
34) Pisa 1998.
35) Ginori Lisci 1963, p. 38.
36) Casprini 2000, pp. 180-190.
37) Biancalana in Lucca 2001, p. 102, no. 33.
38) Vienna 2005.
39) Morena 2005, pp. 238-239, no. 172.

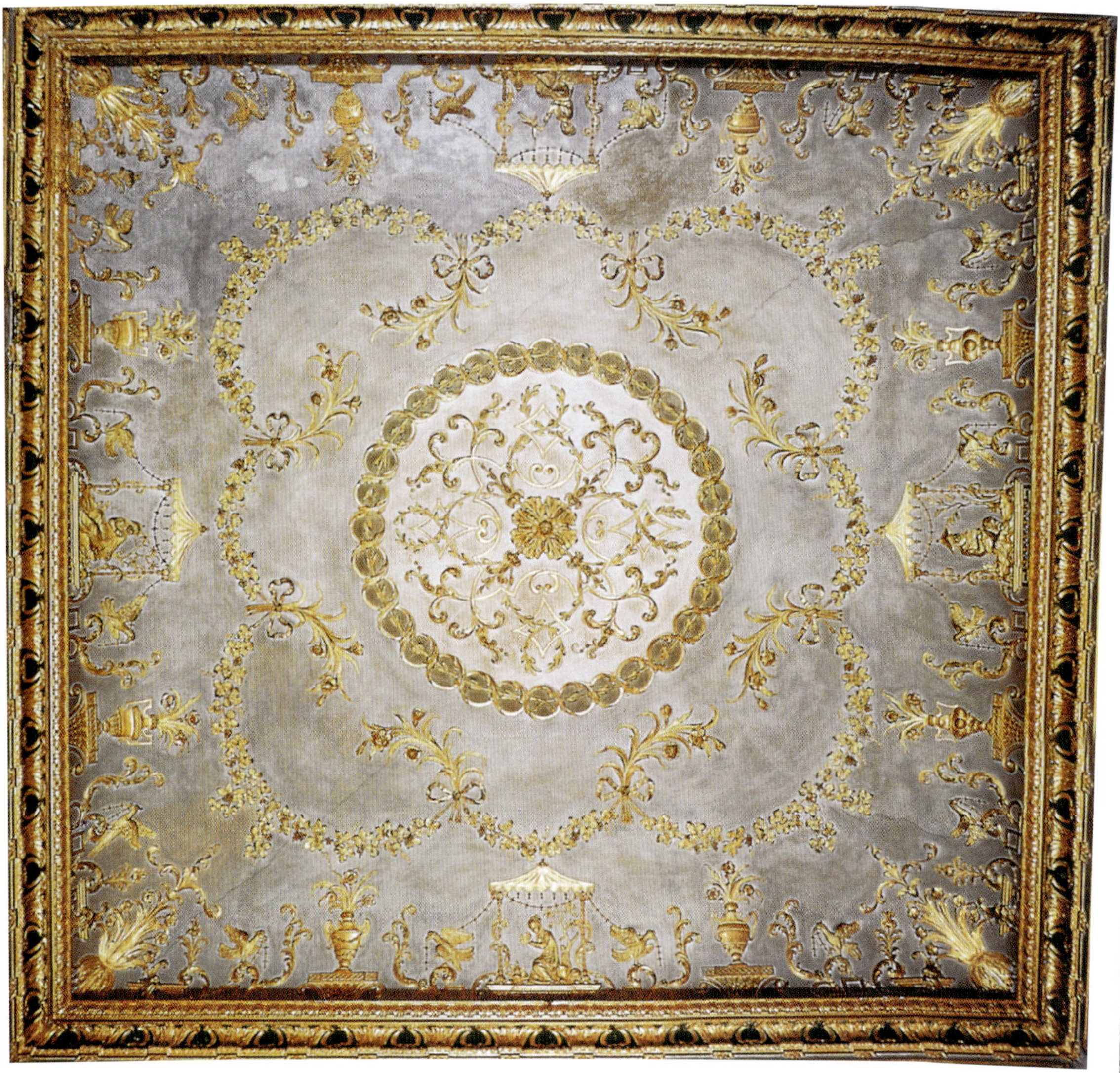

204. Andrea Tagliafichi, Decoration in the ceiling of the Chinese Room, c. 1775. Genoa, Palazzo Cristoforo Spinola in Strada Nuova.

Tagliafichi made full use of the French high neoclassical style for the decoration of this ceiling in the Chinese Room. The exotic element is limited to the oriental figures seated beneath a canopy in the centres of all four sides and rather isolated compared to the gentle meanderings of the floral motifs.

The Republic of Genoa

Rococo

In the 13th and 14th centuries the city of Genoa played a fundamental role in promoting cultural exchanges between Italy and the Far East. Both Genoa and Venice functioned as important distribution centres not only for goods arriving from Asia, but also for information about the region. Just as Marco Polo had voyaged from Venice, Genoans too left their home town, travelling to the ends of the earth to seek their fortune – and often finding it. Though greatly diminished, signs of the city's glorious past as a major trading port lasted throughout the 16th and 17th centuries and indeed in 1647 an attempt was made to establish direct commercial links from Genoa "to open routes and mercantile traffic with the Eastern Indies, especially with Japan, its neighbours and other open and accessible places". It may have been a good idea, but the results were disastrous. The Republic of Genoa had two ships built in Amsterdam from where they set forth for Batavia (Indonesia) to take delivery of a shipment of porcelain and other oriental rarities. The expedition was lead by a Dutch fleet and was financed by St George's Bank which enlisted the support of Portugal. But just as they were about to set sail on the return journey to Italy, they were attacked by Dutch ships and – relieved of their cargo – sunk. Attempts by the Genoan ship owners to retrieve at least part of the goods met with no success – the experiment had failed and an enterprise of this kind was never again considered.[1]

Thus the Genoans continued to acquire their oriental goods from the European ports of London, Amsterdam and Marseilles where the ships of the English, Dutch and French East India Companies arrived regularly. Items from the Far East began to be imported to Genoa more consistently during the 17th and 18th centuries,[2] such as the six lacquer boxes 'from China' that arrived in 1663 on board the 'Carlo Quinto'. Far Eastern items, mainly Chinese porcelain, arrived from Amsterdam between 1699 and 1712, sent by Biliotti and Sardi, two agents resident in Holland. In the late 17th and early 18th centuries Cesare Sardi maintained a continual correspondence with the grand duke of Tuscany, Cosimo III, informing him, among other things, of the dates on which public sales of goods from China were to take place in Holland.[3] In 1718, 1725 and 1741 porcelain 'from China' and 'from Japan' was acquired on behalf of important members of the Genoan aristocracy, including Giovan Francesco II Brignole Sale, but it was in the second half of the 1700s that the acquisition of porcelain items was at its most intense. In

1772 an entire Chinese porcelain service (now in the collections of Palazzo Durazzo Pallavicini) was sent directly from Canton to an aristocratic family of Genoa by Onofrio Villani, a Jesuit who acted as agent in the transaction.[4] The presence of such original Far Eastern items and an awareness of contemporary artistic developments in the rest of Europe were the two most important factors that stimulated the taste for chinoiserie in Genoa, becoming the height of fashion especially during the latter half of the 18th century.

The construction of Palazzo Durazzo Bombrini at Genoa-Cornigliano began in 1752 under the direction of the military architect, Pierre Paul de Cotte. This was to be the *maison de plaisance* or summer residence of the Durazzo family who already owned a splendid palace on Via Balbi in the city. The structure and décor of the interiors strongly reflected the influence of French *rocaille*, though this was later modified by the designs of Tagliafichi who adapted the arrangement to more modern neoclassical tastes after 1778. Giacomo Filippo II (1672-1764) commissioned the work and the property was inherited by his son, Marcello (1703-1787). Not only was structural work carried out on the building, but the decoration and furnishings of the interiors were also modernized. The Durazzo family commissioned craftsmen to make furniture painted in soft shades in the contemporary French fashion and the same tones were used on the walls and for the stuccowork. Between 1756 and 1757 the painter Agostino Favale worked on a range of furniture and a series of "overdoors in the Chinese style", two of which are still in their original location.[5] Surrounded by undulating frames these delightful compositions portray scenes of what was imagined to be everyday life in China, such as figures of musicians and acrobats, animal tamers, women with children, a man on a donkey lead by a servant – all surrounded by groups of rocks with flowers. Favale's work has a pleasant ingenuity about it making it difficult to identify a model, though he most probably made use of engravings of oriental subjects, perhaps Dutch or German compendiums, interpreting them with a lively spirit and original decorative style. Many of the rooms in this residence appear to have been decorated with bright colours, often provided by unusual fabrics, including "walls covered in cloth from Lyons with a Chinese pattern of flowers on a green background".[6] Moreover, in 1753 some 30 sheets of "Chinese painted paper" were bought to be used in 1755 for two "rooms with Chinese-style papers", unfortunately no longer in existence, though it is known they were part of a larger "Chinese apartment".[7] The Durazzo also ordered "Chinese papers" to be bought in Paris on several occasions around 1760 for their residence in Via Balbi; a small screen made of Chinese paper painted red and gold on a black background still exists, the wood frame of which is decorated with particularly interesting chinoiserie motifs.[8]

Neoclassicism

Both the Accademia Ligustica (founded in 1751) and the Società Patria di Arti e Manifatture (1786) were responsible for encouraging a return to classical ideals, with a more modern French interpretation. Both institutions offered instruction and information about the "new way of decorating" for artists as well as for local manufacturers.[9]

Andrea Tagliafichi (1729-1811) was a Genoan architect of humble origins who had trained at the Accademia Ligustica and who developed a style similar to that of the French architect Pierre Le Pautre (1660-1744). His contribution to the shift in styles from Rococo to neoclassical in Genoa was fundamental and is best represented by his work on the town residence of Agostino Lomellini in 1769 (1709-1792). Lomellini was doge of Genoa from 1760, but already in the 1750s was an important personage in the cultural circles of the city, a member of the scientific and enlightened society which looked to France for its model and adhered to principles opposed to the whims and fancies of Rococo. Lomellini himself recognised the young Tagliafichi as the artist most capable of introducing the more modern and international Neoclassicism to Genoa.[10] The critical moment when rococo whim was abandoned in Genoa and neoclassical harmony was introduced is perfectly synthesized in Palazzo Spinola in Via Garibaldi, renovated between 1770 and 1778 and described as the "Palais du Soleil" for its magnificence in 1785 by Charles Dupaty.[11] Modernization of the town residence was commissioned by Cristoforo Spinola and in 1780, just two years after Andrea Tagliafichi and the more famous French architect, Charles De Wailly (1730-1798) had completed their project, Spinola unexpectedly decided to sell the entire building to Domenico Serra. Not surprisingly the decorative style was predominantly French, influenced not only by De Wailly (who had arrived in Genoa on a visit in 1771) but also by Spinola who, as the Republic's ambassador in Paris and Durazzo's agent there, was familiar with the latest fashions in French décor. To ensure that the palace interiors would be exquisitely French in appearance, Spinola specifically sent Tagliafichi to Paris in 1774[12] where he also frequented auctions in order to procure suitable furnishings for Luca Durazzo.[13] One of Tagliafichi's most successful creations was the "charming Chinese room, a quite harmonious example of a fashion which, although it had been used for some time in furnishings and décor, now became a means of definitively breaking with the designs of the past". While the oriental theme had been one of the essential characteristics of Rococo, it was used here to implement a more modern decorative scheme of a quite different concept. The elements are arranged delicately, to create a balanced setting within which oriental figures and pavilions reside quite gracefully. In a geometric arrangement, vases of flowers alternate with the ephemeral houses of Chinamen, birds and scrolls with palmettes, to create one of the most typical instances of neoclassical chinoiserie in Italy or elsewhere. Spccifically in Genoa, this pattern is often seen along the borders of the printed cotton spreads discussed below. Tagliafichi was probably also responsible for the design of the neoclassical gilded bronze mounts that enhance several oriental porcelain vases in palazzo Spinola. The style of the mounts is similar to French works dated after the mid 1700s, and as Tagliafichi coordinated the entire decorative scheme of the palace on behalf of Spinola[14] he was almost certainly their author. Silverware too felt the impact of chinoiserie themes in the late 1700s as can be seen in a candlestick with two arms and central support in the form of a pagoda, within which sits a Chinaman. First published in 1950 by Morazzoni,[15] Hugh Honour presented it as an example of a typically bizarre Italian neoclassical chinoiserie with a particularly odd blend of 'Chinese' elements and the classical figure of Pan squatting on top.[16]

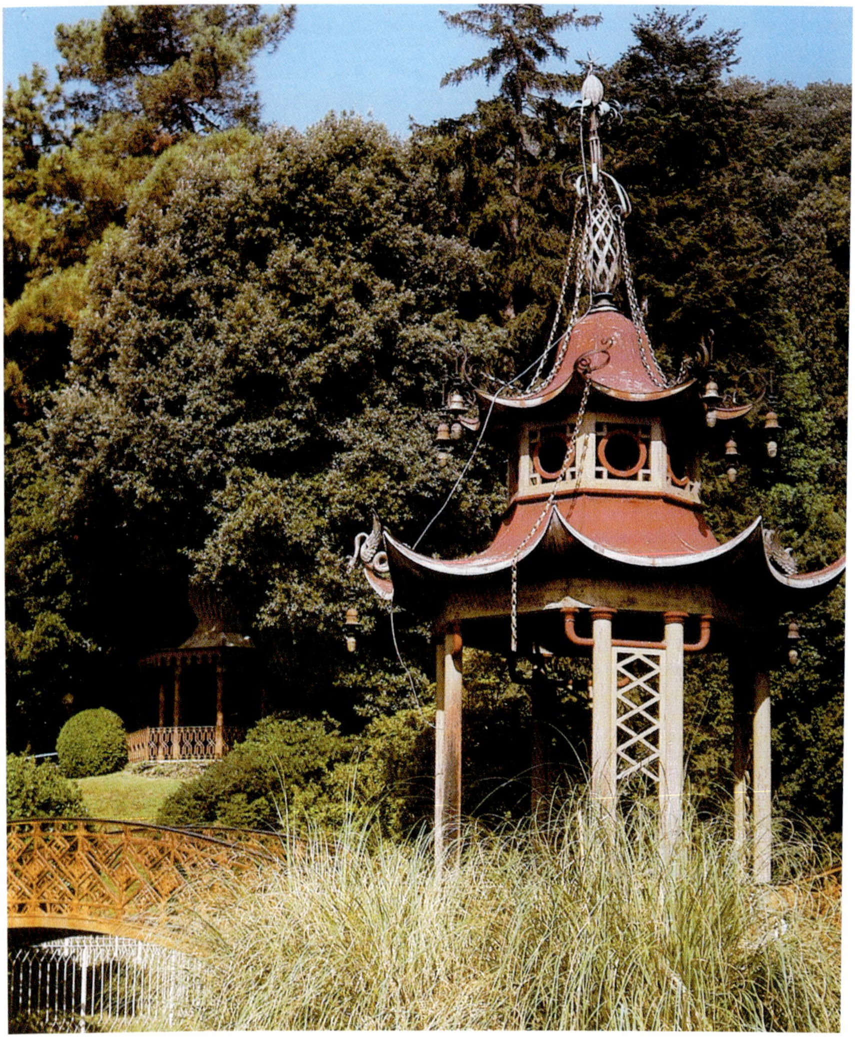

205. Michele Canzio, Chinese Pavilion, 1837. Pegli.

Few Chinese garden pavilions have survived in Italy. This structure in Pegli represents a later phase in the development of chinoiserie and is a perfect example of some of the main characteristics of this 'oriental-style' architecture, highly fashionable in 18th-century Europe.

Andrea Tagliafichi was also responsible for the design of the 'anglo-chinois' garden at the residence of Agostino Lomellini in Pegli which was nearing completion in 1775.[17] Claude Henri Watelet (1718-1786), author of the famous text *Essai sur les jardins* published in 1772, had visited Lomellini in 1763 and his horticultural principles presumably influenced the decision to base the design of his garden on 'picturesque' and 'romantic' concepts. Various buildings and features, some of them oriental, were dotted throughout the park. An enlightened thinker, Lomellini considered China, and other Asian countries, not as mysterious, fabled countries, but as an example of "an ideal moral philosophy".[18] In particular, the park in Pegli contained a "Chinese Temple", with "a hexagonal structure with columns and capitals, and an architrave with heiroglyphs ... that give a genuine idea of the tastes ... of the ancient land of Confucius". This description was written by count Luigi de Isengard who wrote an introduction to a volume of Lomellini's poetry in 1786.[19] Sadly, no trace remains of the structures that once stood in Lomellini's park. Another 'romantic' garden has partly survived in Pegli, however, including some few remaining 'exotic' structures such as a little bridge with a small pagoda alongside. This park was commissioned by Ignazio Pallavicini in 1837 and the layout, clearly inspired by the older botanical garden nearby created by Clelia Grimaldi Durazzo, was designed by Michele Canzio (1788-1868), a painter and stage designer.[20]

The artistic and cultural context had fully evolved into Neoclassicism by 1785 when a celebration for the arrival of the rulers of the Kingdom of the Two Sicilies was organised at Acquaverde. The trend that affected many of the Italian courts to associate grand festivities with Chinese Pavilions was repeated in Genoa too.[21] In 1815 a Chinese Fair was organised in the city in honour of the visit of queen Maria Theresa of Savoy (1803-1879). The scenes and settings were devised by Carlo Barabino, professor of architecture at the Accademia Ligustica di Belle Arti, and the celebrations took place mainly in the garden of Palazzo Doria.[22] From the description of the event it is obvious that various neoclassical elements had now infiltrated the rococo style, especially those many eclectic variants that characterised the exotic theme during the late 18th and early 19th centuries: flanking the Chinese figures, porcelain, monkeys and pavilions with upswept roofs, are features derived from Greek, Roman, Etruscan and even Egyptian classical repertories.

Lacquer

Although very few pieces of lacquer work made in Genoa with chinoiserie decorations have survived, such furnishings were highly popular in the city in the 18th century. Many of these were produced in Liguria as De Lalande commented when he visited Genoa in 1765, "Lacquered boxes are made quite well in Genoa; some twenty years ago the workshop of a *vernisseur* in front of the Maddalena church enjoyed such prestige that people still refer to *la vernice della Madalena* just as in Paris one speaks of *le vernis de Martin*".[23] Lalande was therefore referring to a period just before 1750, yet various documents contain numerous references to 'Chinese-style' lacquer in the palaces of Genoa, much earlier in the 18th century. In Rome in 1701, for example, Anton Giulio II Brignole Sale bought two mirrors with "Chinese varnish" as well as "two tables, candle holders and vases, all with Chinese lacquer".[24] Probably these are the same items that appear in a document dividing the assets of Gio Francesco and Gio Giacomo Brignole Sale in 1717[25] described as "mirrors", two "sideboards", "small table tops", two "vases", "four small round tables with their stands", a "table stand", a "large tray" and four smaller ones, and "small boxes", all decorated with "Chinese varnish".[26] The same inventory also lists "red chests with Chinese gilding and mirrors", a "black chest as above", and a "mirror of the same kind",[27] while in 1710 Antonio Giulio had bought himself a "small table in coral coloured lacquer with a mirror and all its trimmings".[28] It is highly probable that at least some of the items belonging to the Brignole Sale family originated from Rome where, in the early 1700s production of 'Chinese-style' lacquered furnishings was flourishing.[29] Unfortunately there is no way of knowing if maestro Piantanida, paid by count Durazzo in 1729 for applying "fine coloured lacquer to the carriage", was also capable of decorating his work with exotic motifs.[30] In an inventory dated 1755 the furnishings of Palazzo Rosso are more carefully described, such as the "walnut screen for a fireplace, painted in the Chinese style",[31] or in the list of Livia Centurione Pallavicini's possessions drawn up in 1758 including a "Chinese bureau" and a "Chinese table with a box and mirror, and 18 other boxes inside", all of which were lacquered and decorated with oriental motifs.[32] The inventory of Palazzo Rossi dated 1775 and two others recording the furnishings of the Brignole Sale family's country houses (1774) all record Chinese-style lacquered furnishings.[33] Even later, references still appear to painted furniture in the country house of Isabella De Mari Doria (1785), in the residence of Giorgio Doria (1793), and in inventories recording the possessions of both Bartolomeo Lomellini (1801) and Clelia De Mari Lomellini (1801),[34] while recorded in the possessions of Marcello Durazzo in 1787 are "three small Chinese tables".

A particular feature of Genoan lacquer is the fineness of the underlying layer of plaster and glue and of the lacquer applied. The range of colours used –

206. Commode. Genoa, third quarter of the 18th century. Private collection.

The form, colours and decorative theme of this piece are clearly influenced by late French Baroque. The slightly heavy forms and stiff postures of the oriental figures recall designs by French masters, especially Pillement and his repertory of 'exotic' subjects.

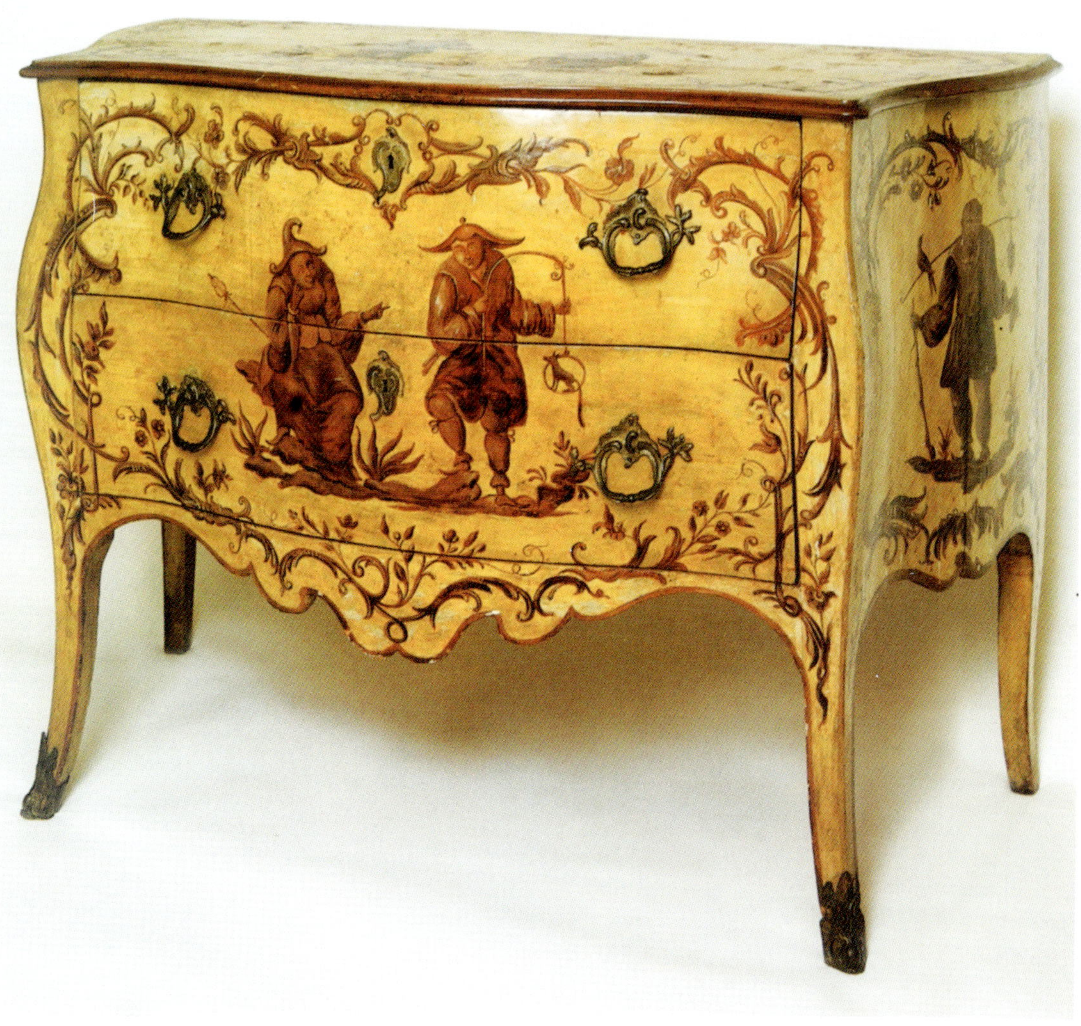

mainly based on subtle shades of ivory, light green and pink – are those of the late French Baroque. Very few pieces of Genoan lacquered furniture decorated with chinoiseries still exist, but in 1996 González-Palacios published a chest of drawers dating from the late 18th century, decorated on the front and sides with a series of vignettes with Chinese figures, framed within floral scrolls painted in red and purple on an ivory background.[35] In 1949 a cabinet was published by Morazzoni.[36] Although not decorated with chinoiserie motifs, certain French furnishings lacquered in black and enhanced with original Japanese and Chinese lacquered panels, doubtless served as models for some mid 18th-century Genoan furnishings.[37] The use of 'gold on black', a traditional characteristic of lacquer, was clearly inspired by both French and oriental items.

The most interesting 18th-century work with chinoiserie decoration produced in Genoa is the famous sedan chair in Palazzo Durazzo Pallavicini.[38] Painted with a dark background similar to lacquer, the most interesting feature of the chair is the decoration, applied to the entire external surface, of

207. Sedan chair. Genoa, c. 1770-1780. Genoa, Palazzo Durazzo Pallavicini.

The chinoiserie decoration of this fine sedan chair recalls the ornamentation designed by Tagliafichi for the Chinese room in Palazzo Spinola (see Fig. 204). Made in Genoa in the 1770s, the style of the composition derives principally from French Neoclassicism.

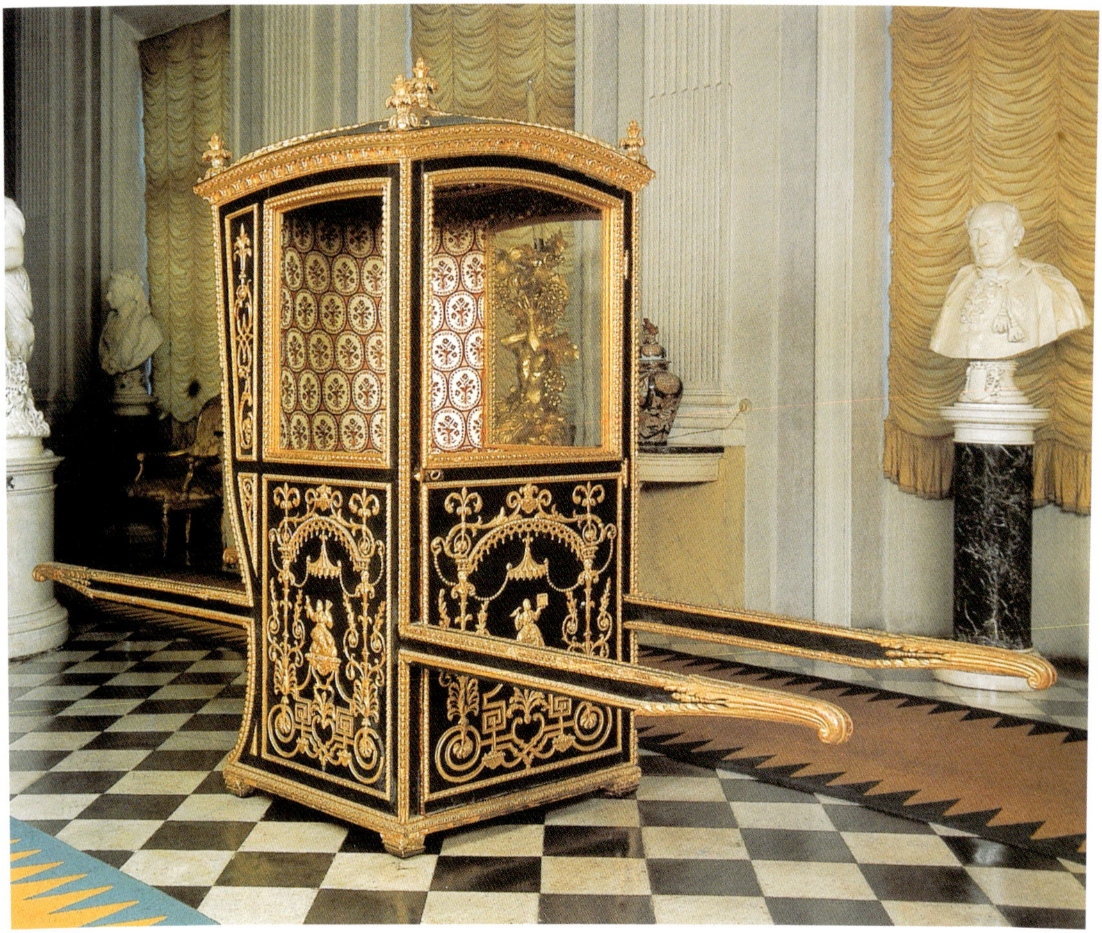

gilded wood in the form of candelabra and floral arabesques. Amidst the scrolls on all four sides is a Chinese figure just beneath the dome of an 'oriental' pavilion. The style clearly reflects the new international neoclassical taste in decoration which began to appear in Genoa from about 1770. The sedan chair belonged to Clelia Durazzo, wife of Marcello, and was later inherited by her son, Giacomo Filippo III.[39]

'Mezzari' – Printed Cotton Spreads

Production in late 18th century Genoa of fabrics printed with oriental motifs is relatively well documented, but the origins of this particular art lie much earlier. Oriental fabrics, known as 'mezzari', were imported to Genoa as earlyas the 16th century. Mainly produced in India, the cloths arrived from Portugal and Venice, the primary destinations for Asian goods that travelled along the Egyptian route. The Spanish ambassador of Carlo V to the Republic of Genoa from 1529 to 1549, Gomez Soarez de Figueroa, owned two "Indian 'meizari'", while in 1577 the inventory of Leonardo Cattaneo, doge of Genoa from 1541 to 1543, records a "deep blue mezzaro", "three cotton mezzari" and a "mezzaro of dark red silk". Two red *mezzari* appear in the inventory of Agostino Carroccio's possessions in 1584, and in the inventory of the furnishings belonging to Gio Batta Pittalunga, also 1584, a "*mezzaro* from the Levant" is recorded. Numerous oriental fabrics are listed in the inventory of the possessions of prince Gio Andrea Doria drawn up the year of his death in 1606, two of which are described in detail as, "cloths from the Indies and Portugal and Holland, all quilted with a white silk backing, with a yellow border and four bows and buttons in the centre, one of which is fourteen and one third 'palmi' long and twelve wide, ornamented with many animals, the other being twelve 'palmi' long and ten and one third wide", a description that recalls the fabrics of Bengal decorated with animals. As commercial trading intensified between Europe and the East Indies during the 17th century, Asian textiles became more generally available, arriving in particular from Aleppo and Smyrna, cities with which Genoa regularly traded, or from Marseilles and Livorno. Descriptions of these materials appear in documents of the Durazzo family in 1665 for example, and in earlier inventories relating to the possessions of Francesco Garbarino (1654) and of Francesco Imperiale, a local aristocrat (1658).[40] Moreover, the inventories of the wardrobes of Caterina Durazzo Adorno (1672) and Paola and Luchino Adorno (1687) reveal that "indiane" were also used to make 'housecoats'.[41] Oriental fabrics, used both for clothing and for furnishings, were so widely available in Genoa that, following the example of his fellow Armenians in Marseilles some years earlier, Gio Batta De Georgiis opened a factory in 1690, producing fabrics printed with bright colours, of just as good quality, he claimed, to those of Persia.[42]

In the early decades of the 18th century his initiative lead to the establishment of more textile factories, anxious to acquire a share of the profitable market which until then had benefitted exclusively importers of oriental goods and other European textile factories that produced similar patterns. Fortunately a quite unique description of the early 18th-century cloths made in Genoa is provided in a volume entitled *Echantillons d'étoffes de manufactures etrangères recuillés par le maréchal de Richelieu*. This compilation by duke Louis François de Richelieu (1696-1788) covered a wide range of examples of textiles produced in Europe and, in the case of Italy, particularly Genoa where he lived in 1740. The volume includes "indiennes fines" and "indiennes de seconde qualité" "imprimé à Gennes" and their derivation from oriental designs is clear to see.[43] De Richelieu also mentions that the factories specialized in producing this kind of printed fabric in Genoa at the time were in fact French, with Italianized names, such as Matteo Ruelle and Enrico Giuliani.[44] About 1730 it became fashionable in Genoa to wear a kind of cotton scarf that covered just the head and shoulders; this custom gradually became one of the most characteristic features of women's costume in Genoa, often referred to in literature (by both Casanova in his *Memoires* dated 1767, and De Lalande in 1768, for example), and was also illustrated in engravings and paintings of the day.[45]

In the wake of the success obtained by this kind of cloth, shortly after mid century other local entrepreneurs began to produce fabrics printed with 'exotic' motifs. Paolo David, for example, had specialized in "dying Indian stuffs" since 1760, and from 1785 until 1820 the business was continued by his son, Luigi.[46] Of Swiss origin, Giovanni Speich was the first of his family to open a series of textile factories and in 1787 he requested the senate of the Republic of Genoa to grant him the right to produce "Calancà, Mezzari, Scarves and other printed Fabrics". With the help of his many relations, Speich remained active in various kinds of textile production, until at least the mid 1800s. The family tradition was continued by Luigi Testori who married into the Speich family.[47]

The most characteristic decorative motif on Genoan *mezzari* is the design with a large central tree, brightly patterned with coloured flowers and birds, and always surrounded by a decorative border on all four sides. This tree motif – including the variations with two trees or flowers scattered over the entire surface – is directly derived from the *palampore*, a printed fabric made in India as early as the 16th century, mainly for export to Europe where it remained in favour until the 19th century. Used predominantly for furnishings in Europe these large cotton spreads were described as "large enough for an English bed" in 1633, and indeed the term *palampore* might be a European corruption of the Hindu or Persian word *palangpush* meaning "bed cover".[48]

The Tree of Life design was very often used by Chinese factories to decorate various items intended for export to Europe, such as papers and fabrics for wall coverings. Without embarking on a discussion of the specific origins of

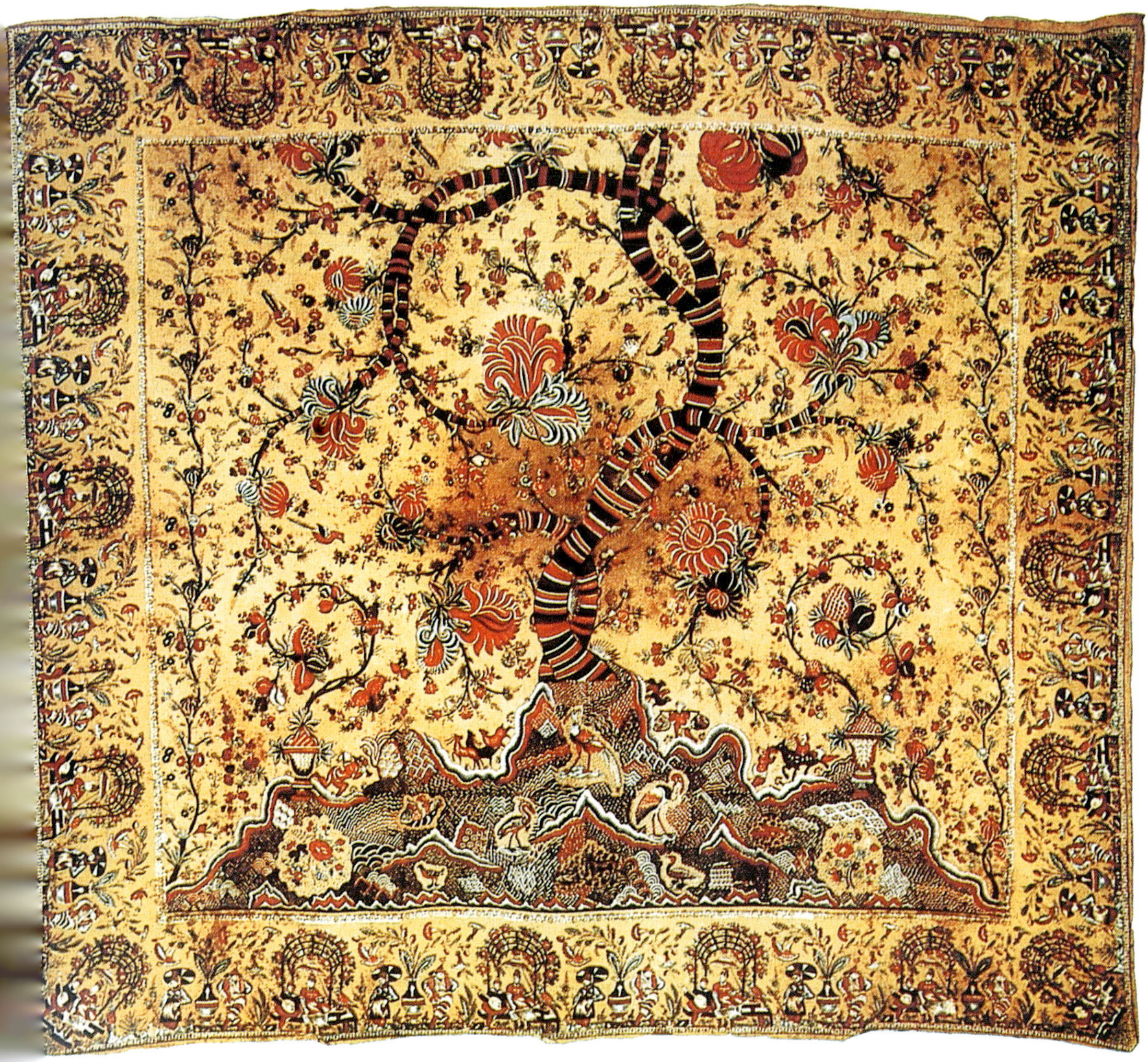

208. Printed cotton spread. Genoa (?), Speich factory (?), late 18th century. Genoa. Private collection.

This spread may possibly have been made in Genoa in the late 18th century. More than in other examples of these printed spreads, a specific reference to chinoiserie themes is evident in the external border around all four sides. The Tree of Life in the centre also has Eastern origins but became known in Europe in the early 16th century when painted textiles began to be imported from the Indian subcontinent.

this motif, whatever its derivation Europeans appreciated its 'Chinese style' and specially ordered the design directly from eastern craftsmen. The borders of some of the Genoan *mezzari*, however, present designs that are more recognizably chinoiseries, such as the border around the 'hunting' design illustrated by Margherita Bellezza Rosina and Marzia Cataldi Gallo.[49] They tentatively attribute this work as being of Genoan origin, dated late 18th century (and perhaps made by Speich),[50] pointing out that both the specific layout of the tree in the centre of the composition and the chinoiserie border around it also appear in contemporary French and Swiss items. The unusual appearance of the tree trunk, which is not unlike bamboo, the large flowers blossoming on the branches and the vases on either side of the tree are all fairly typical of Indian items intended for exportation to Europe. However, the chinoiserie scenes along the edges with female figures and musicians amidst vases, canopies, umbrellas and a scattering of flowers are entirely European in style. These vignettes are obviously derived from Boucher and Pillement although this does not necessarily indicate French provenance, as the style was equally popular in Genoa at the time.[51] Leaving aside the 'ambivalent' motifs which could be either of Indian or Chinese origin, some elements of pure chinoiserie can be detected in the vast 'Indian' repertory of the *mezzari*. Bellezza Rosina and Cataldi Gallo, for example, illustrate a spread with a 'chestnut tree' pattern (figure 125 in their book); this, more than other examples, emphatically recalls chinoiserie patterns, especially the group of vases with pomegranate sprigs and the cockerel that appears in the composition of fruit and vases. The design of this Genoan *mezzaro* is based on a fabric printed in Jouy in 1780 with a decoration of *Fleurs et vases chinois,* derived in its turn from a Chinese wood template which provided various individual prints.[52]

In the 18th century printed cotton spreads based directly on Indian *palampore* designs were produced in many European countries, especially France, but also Switzerland. England produced its own version of 'exotic' motifs, though these were somewhat different from oriental designs, and as Holland placed no restrictions on the importation of textiles from Asia, Indian, Chinese and even Japanese goods were widely available. Thus Genoa's direct competitors both in the use of similar techniques and of comparable decorative patterns, were the factories of France and Switzerland.[53]

1) Fossati 1992, pp. 16-17.
2) Zenone Padula 1992, pp. 38-42.
3) Morena 2005, p. 157.
4) Zenone Padula in Palazzo Durazzo Pallavicini 1995, pp. 368-370, no. 210.
5) Bonora 1991, p. 73, figs. at pp. 78-79.
6) Bonora 1991, p. 73.
7) Bonora 1991, pp. 75, 91.
8) Baccheschi in Palazzo Durazzo Pallavicini 1995, p. 35.
9) Colle 2005, p. 367.
10) Gavazza, Magnani 2000, pp. 191, 196.
11) Colle 2005, p. 369.
12) Gavazza, Magnani 2000, p. 197.
13) Zenone Padula 1992, p. 80.
14) Zenone Padula 1992, pp. 80-81.
15) Morazzoni 1950, no. 206.
16) Honour 1961 (1963), p. 214 and fig. 132.
17) Gavazza, Magnani 2000, p. 197.
18) Magnani 1987, p. 214.
19) Magnani 1987, p. 214.
20) Tagliolini 1988, pp. 358-359, pl. XLII.
21) Zenone Padula 1992, p. 41.
22) Zenone Padula 1992, pp. 42-43.
23) González-Palacios 1996, p. 211.
24) Tagliaferro 1995, p. 94.
25) Tagliaferro 1995, note 89, p. 119.
26) Zenone Padula 1992, pp. 35, 38-39; Tagliaferro 1995, p. 316.
27) Tagliaferro 1995, p. 328.
28) González-Palacios 1996, p. 211.
29) González-Palacios 1996, p. 211.
30) González-Palacios 1996, p. 211.
31) González-Palacios 1996, p. 214.
32) González-Palacios 1996, p. 211.
33) Zenone Padula 1992, pp. 36, 41.
34) Gonzàlez Palacios 1996, pp. 211, 214.
35) González-Palacios 1996, p. 215, fig. 246.
36) Morazzoni 1949, pl. LXXXVI.
37) Caumont Caimi 1995, p. 25 and fig. VII on p. 27; González-Palacios 1996, pp. 212-213, figs. 243-245.
38) Baccheschi in Palazzo Durazzo Pallavicini 1995, pp. 357-360, no. 205.
39) Baccheschi in Palazzo Durazzo Pallavicini 1995, pp. 359-360.
40) Bellezza Rosina, Cataldi Gallo 1993, p. 70.
41) Cataldi Gallo in Milan 1988, p. 26.
42) Cataldi Gallo in Milan 1988, p. 25.
43) Cataldi Gallo in Milan 1988, pp. 29-32.
44) Bellezza Rosina, Cataldi Gallo 1993, pp. 74-77; Bellezza Rosina 2000, p. 127.
45) Bellezza Rosina, Cataldi Gallo 1993, pp. 88-89.
46) Bellezza Rosina, Cataldi Gallo 1993, p. 77; Bellezza Rosina 2000, p. 127.
47) Bellezza Rosina, Cataldi Gallo 1993, pp. 80-82, 113.
48) Bellezza Rosina, Cataldi Gallo 1993, pp. 9-10, 16.
49) Bellezza Rosina, Cataldi Gallo 1993, p. 151, no. 142.
50) Cataldi Gallo in Milan 1988, pp. 90-91.
51) Bellezza Rosina, Cataldi Gallo 1993, p. 150.
52) Bellezza Rosina, Cataldi Gallo 1993, p. 130.
53) Bellezza Rosina, Cataldi Gallo 1993, pp. 38-49; Bellezza Rosina 2000, pp. 131-132.

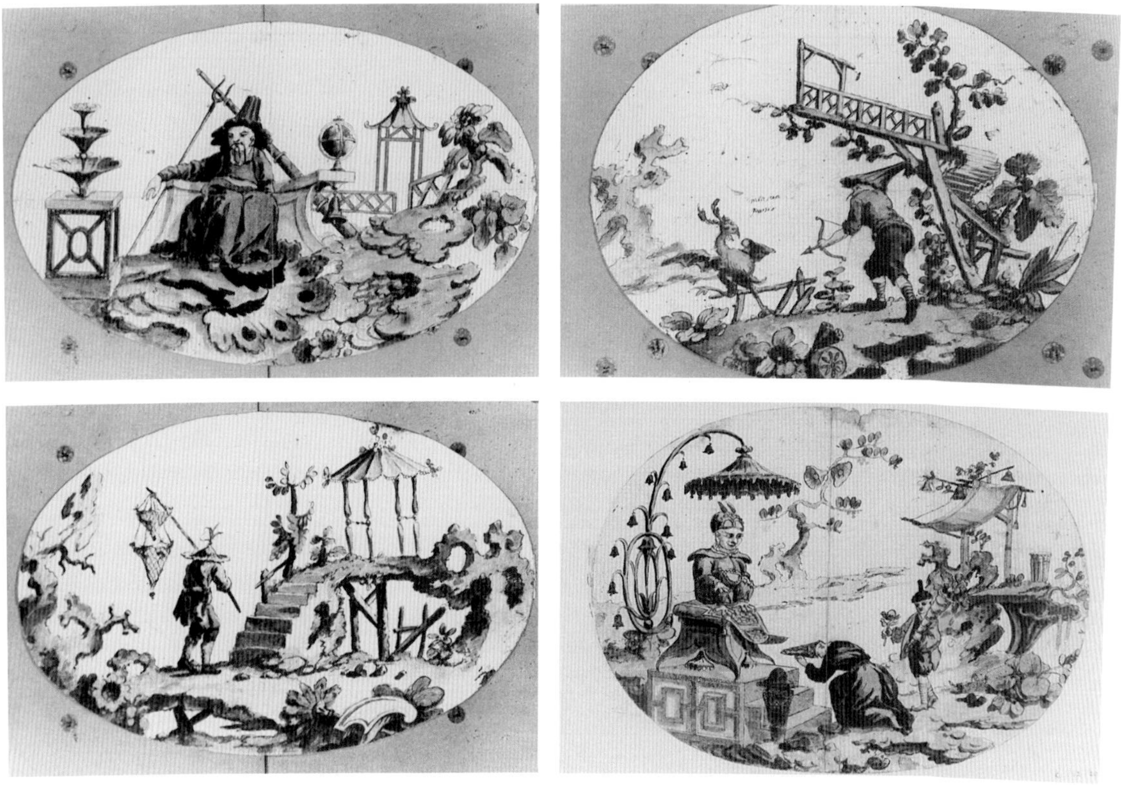

209a,b,c,d. Giuseppe Levati, Chinoiseries, c. 1770. Milan, Castello Sforzesco, Civiche Raccolte d'Arte Applicata e Incisioni.

The oval format of these compositions indicates that Giuseppe Levati created them specifically for the cabinet maker Giuseppe Maggiolini to use as a decoration for the desk commissioned by duke Ferdinando as a gift for his mother, empress Maria Theresa (see Fig. 211). The scene with a supplicant and deity also appears in an inlay decoration on the sides of a pair of commodes housed in Villa Reale at Monza.

Hapsburg Lombardy

Rococo

Chinoiserie was at its most popular in Milan and throughout Lombardy from 1750-1775, almost exactly the same period during which Vienna and the court of empress Maria Theresa were captivated by the rage for exoticism. Most of the Chinese interiors still visible in the castle of Schönbrunn were in fact commissioned by the empress. Following the treaties of Utrecht and Rastadt (1713-1714), Lombardy had become a protectorate of the Hapsburg empire and consequently the arts and culture of the duchy were affected by its influence.[1]

The start of this period of Hapsburg rule in Lombardy coincided with the progressive demise of the baroque style, which had dominated the arts under the Spanish Bourbons, and the spread of the more modern forms of Rococo which was greeted with enthusiasm, and perhaps relief, as they spread from France and Germany. The foremost families of Milan quickly conformed to the new fashions and redecorated their residences employing famous artists, such as Tiepolo, as well as local painters skilled in interpreting the new trends, such as Giuseppe Antonio Castelli (1650-1723) from Monza, more usually nicknamed 'Il Castellino'.[2] Numerous engravings of German ornamentations derived from French models were available in artistic circles in the mid 1700s and their influence continued to increase despite opposition from many of the most important intellectuals in Lombardy who rejected the extravagances of *rocaille* in favour of a return to classical harmony.[3]

There was, however, a lively interest in 'exotic' subjects in Lombardy even before the Austrian empire came to power. Apostolo Zeno's play *Teuzzone,*

210a,b. Andrea Appiani, Chinoiseries, c. 1770. Milan, Castello Sforzesco, Civiche Raccolte d'Arte Applicata e Incisioni.

These two vignettes of Chinese subjects were designed by an extremely young Andrea Appiani; Giuseppe Maggiolini used them to decorate a commode with an inlay of rare woods (see Fig. 212), made before 1773. A collection of papers that once belonged to Maggiolini contains not only these designs by Appiani but also two sheets for dusting over the stencil of the composition used on the commode.

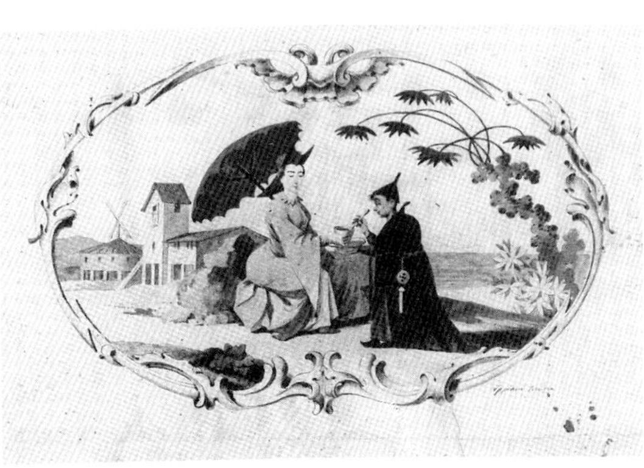

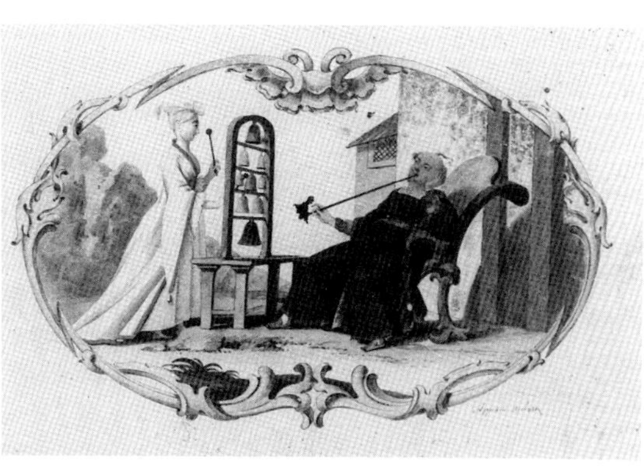

set to music and located in China, had its first Italian performance in Milan in 1706 and was presented in Turin ten years later. *Zoe, imperatrice d'Oriente*, a play with music by Silvani, was performed in 1737 in Mantova where, in 1782, the ballet *Il Teatro italiano della China* accompanied two comic operas presented by the Sacco company.[4] Records also show that in 1717 the fifteen mysteries of the Rosary in the church of the Rose in Milan were supported by carved plaiting 'in the Chinese style'.[5] Some decades later, around the mid 1700s, the fashion for oriental themes even reached the cabinet makers of Milan who began to enhance their furniture with chinoiseries.

An example of this particular speciality is the tallboy with a drop door, dated mid 18th century in a private collection published. The floral decoration of this piece is clearly based on the motifs seen on oriental lacquer, especially Japanese. However, the scenes with figures, the winding tendrils of the leafy garlands, and especially the arrangement of the applied scrolling borders (which are quite unrelated in style to the painted decorations within) are all elements that belonged to the repertory of Lombardy furniture makers. The influence is explicitly German and is especially reminiscent of the workshop of Abraham Roentgen (1711-1793) and his son David (1743-1807) in Koblenz.[6]

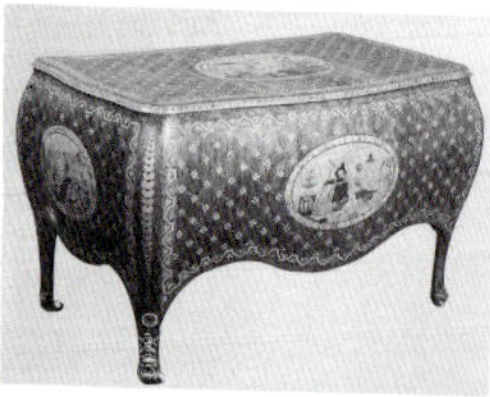

211. Giuseppe Maggiolini, Desk, c. 1773. Vienna, Bundesmobiliensammlungen.

The structural severity of this piece is only slightly relieved by the Chinese vignettes. Maggiolini clearly made the desk at a time when the sinuosity of Rococo was being replaced by the more sombre lines of Neoclassicism.

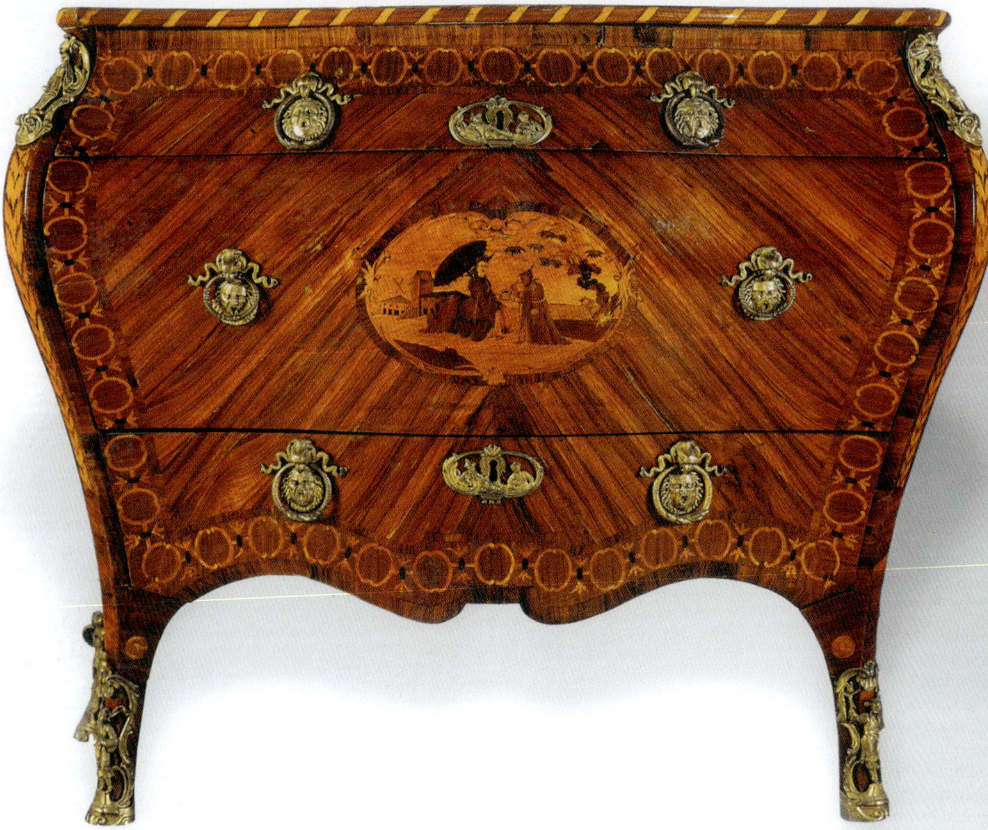

The marriage of empress Maria Theresa's son, archduke Ferdinando (1754-1806), to Maria Beatrice d'Este (1750-1829) in October 1770 provided a suitably fashionable occasion to be celebrated in grand oriental style. Four years later (1775), in the publication 'Milano', Giuseppe Parini (1729-1799) provided an account of the event entitled *Descrizione delle feste celebrate in Milano per le nozze delle Altezze Reali*. In the centre of the garden where the celebrations took place was "a great table divided in three, large enough for four hundred and fifty people, above which was ... a ... parterre designed in the Chinese style with various unusual curios and whims", while the floats that formed the parade were all decorated in a decidedly exotic manner, particularly prominent in the costumes of the participants, who wore, "clothes designed and adorned in the Chinese style. The largest float was especially notable for its eccentric and charming originality. It was ornamented in gold on a background of white enamel and fanciful paintings decorated it ... On top of the cart was a Chinaman holding a beautiful large bird. Below this, positioned on a small loggia, was a large porcelain vase containing lofty, broad leaves and beside this were two Chinamen joking with each other and holding umbrellas made of feathers. Below this again,

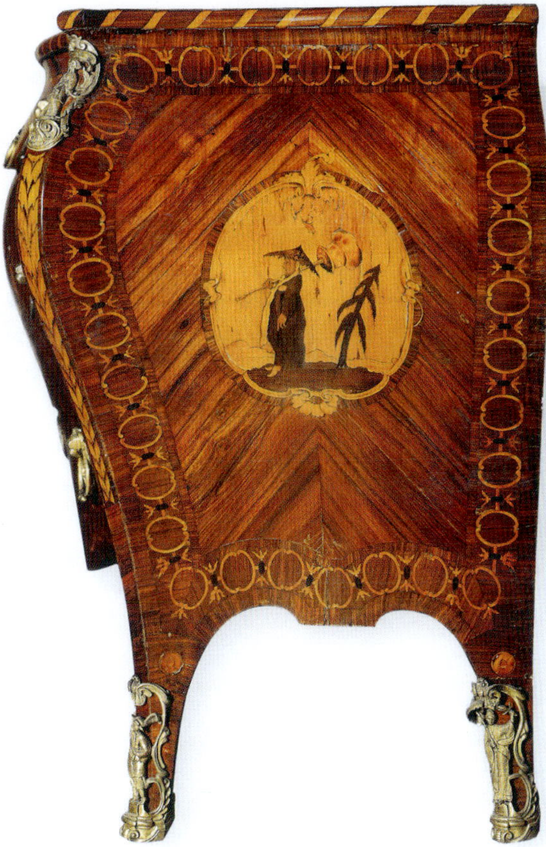

212a,b. Giuseppe Maggiolini, Commode, c. 1773. Milan, Castello Sforzesco, Civiche Raccolte d'Arte Applicata e Incisioni.

The minimalist and simplified style of these inlays is ideal for reproduction as an inlay of various woods and clearly demonstrates that Appiani devised his chinoiseries so that they could be used by Maggiolini to decorate this piece.

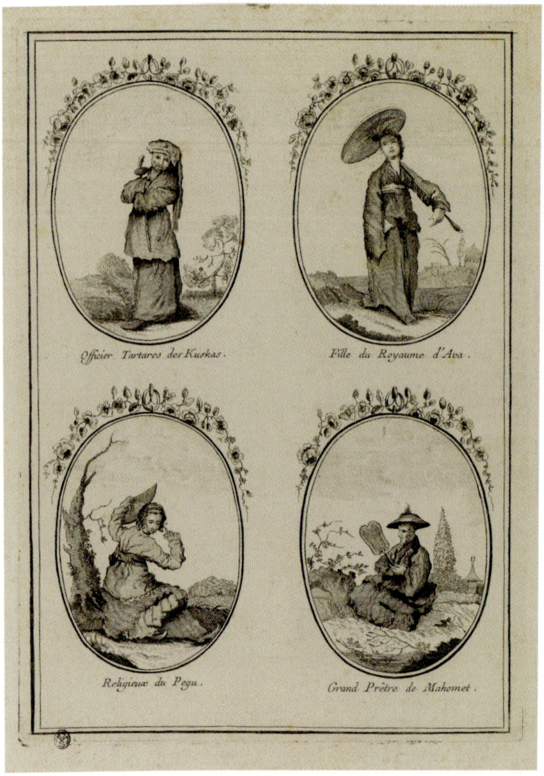

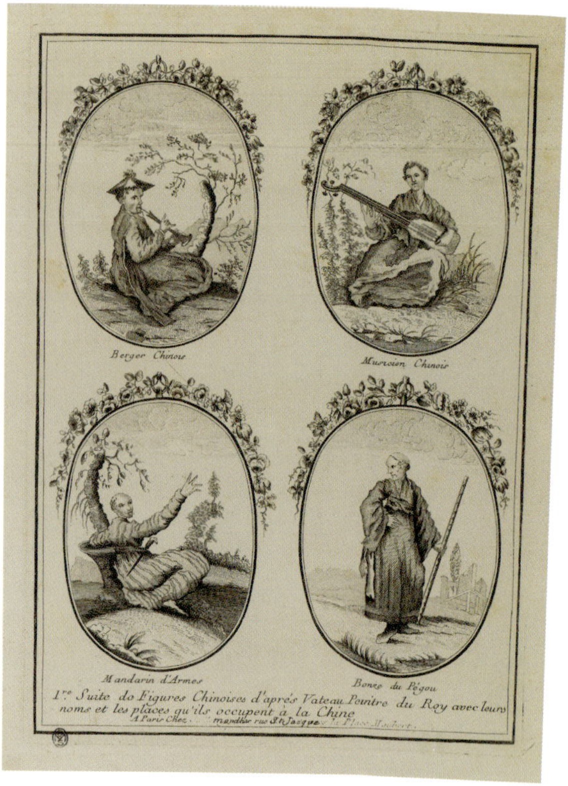

213a,b,c,d. Four pages from the '*Ière Suite de Figures Chinoises d'aprés Vateau Peintre du Roy avec leurs noms et les places qu'ils occupent à la Chine*', 18th century, second half. Milan, Castello Sforzesco, Civiche Raccolte d'Arte Applicata e Incisioni.

Maggiolini re-elaborated Watteau's compositions so that they were suitable for use by the craftsmen of Lombardy who wished to create chinoiserie works. The scenes are framed by an oval the upper part of which is adorned with a garland of flowers. He used two of these images on the two sides of the commode in Fig 212.

sitting on a pedestal with steps leading up to it, was a Chinese deity whose head nodded underneath a large green and gold coloured parasol. Around him four other figures were joking, also holding umbrellas and feathers of various kinds. At the front was a Chinaman in a capricious pose. The eight horses pulling the float also had umbrellas made of feathers on their heads...".[7]

About the same time Giuseppe Levati (1738-1828), an architect and decorator, produced a series of four oval drawings each with an oriental theme (Milan, Castello Sforzesco, Gabinetto dei Disegni, Maggiolini collection). These designs appear in the decoration of a desk made by the cabinet maker Giuseppe Maggiolini (1738-1814), commissioned by archduke Ferdinando as a gift for his mother, empress Maria Theresa, and completed in 1773.[8] This famous desk, now housed in the Bundessammlung Alter Stilmöbel in Vienna, is quite beautifully proportioned and Levati's designs were portrayed in a sophisticated inlay of various precious woods surrounded by irregular frames which serve to separate the compositions on the veneered rosewood surface. Based mainly on the chinoiseries of Watteau and Boucher, as well as Pillement's oriental anthologies, Levati obviously created these designs in close collaboration with Maggiolini who was, at the time, teetering between the curlicues of rococo decoration and the rigidity of nascent Neoclassicism which was soon to become his definitive style.

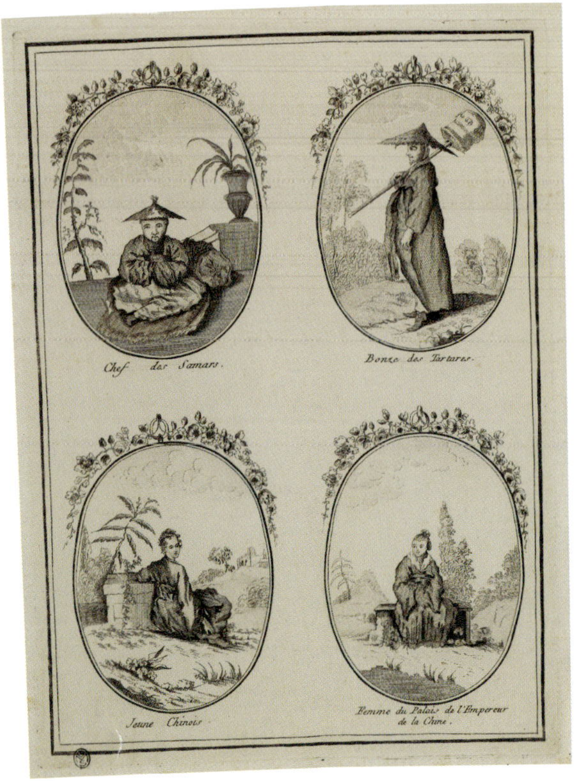

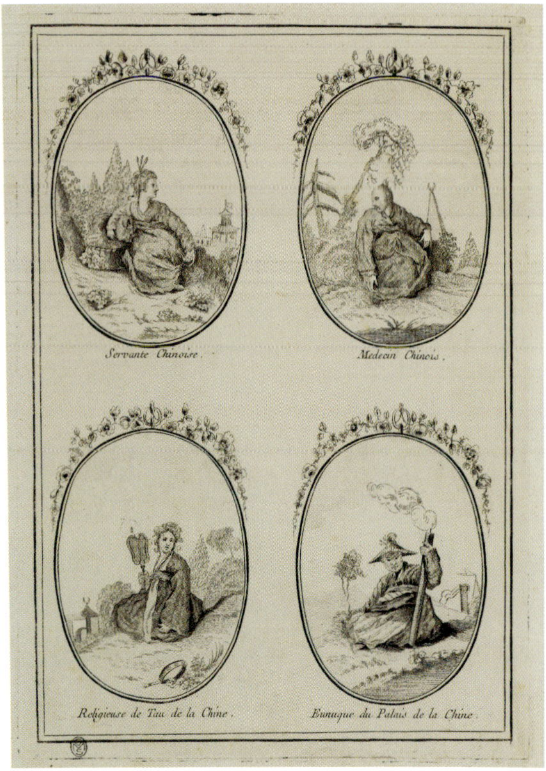

Two Chinese vignettes (Milan, Castello Sforzesco, Gabinetto dei Disegni, Maggiolini collection) attributed to Andrea Appiani (1754-1817) were obviously also designed to be produced in wood inlay. Both the compositions are enclosed by a frame of slender linked volutes almost identical to the surround that appears on the chest of drawers made by Giuseppe Maggiolini and decorated with Appiani's chinoiserie.[9] Similar in form to the desk in Vienna, and also datable to about 1773, this work too is of extraordinarily high quality, highlighted by the delightful bronze ornamentation, particularly on the feet where a design of male and female Chinese figures mingles with leafy scrolls. Various other items of furniture dating from the same period in Lombardy were enhanced with similar bronze details and Chinese figures.[10]

These two chinoiseries by Appiani are based on designs made by Antoine Watteau in 1709 for the castle of La Muette, extensively known throughout Europe from the engravings published in *L'Oeuvre Gravé*.[11] Doubtless Maggiolini owned some of Watteau's chinoiserie prints, since he himself had made sketches for four engravings with sixteen vignettes in oval frames, two of which provided the design for the inlay on the sides of a chest of drawers in the Sforzesco castle (*Bonzes des Tartares* and *Officiers tartares des Kuskas*). Each of the characters portrayed is identified by a title, though only one of the sheets bears an explanatory inscription, "Ière Suite de Figures Chinoises d'aprés Vateau Peintre du Roy avec leurs noms et les places qu'ils occupent à la Chine".[12]

Textiles too began to be affected by the increasing popularity of chinoiserie during the mid 1700s. The Rho brothers, Cipriano and Carlo Francesco, opened a factory in 1755 to produce printed fabrics known as 'Indian cloth' or 'calancà', imitating the eastern fabrics – mainly imported from India – that were so popular in Europe at the time.[13] Located in the Cavalchina district, the textile workshops effectively began production in 1756, and on 15 October 1760 the factory was granted a twenty-year monopoly. The two brothers began by buying Indian cloth – of a higher quality than that manufactured in Europe – in the markets of France, Switzerland and Holland and hired professional foreign experts who were gradually replaced by Milanese craftsmen.[14] The brothers went their separate ways in 1766, each trying to establish their own business. However, Cipriano's business failed almost immediately, while Carlo Francesco persevered with the production of *calancà* right up until 1782 when foreign competition forced him to close. So few examples of the material produced have survived that very little is known about the factory's production. Records of the day show that his firm offered a wide range of decorative motifs, many of them floral, including one named "alla porcellana" - an explicit reference to the oriental style from which it derived.[15] In 1782 Carlo Francesco's business was taken over by Giovanni Adamo Kramer, an innovative entrepreneur whose 'Indian' printed fabrics were marketed cheaply although the quality of the designs suffered. Kramer's heirs continued to manage the company until it finally closed in 1844.[16]

Neoclassicism

Those same artists and craftsmen that produced the finest chinoiserie in Lombardy in the 1760s were to become the firmest supporters of the classical revival in the last quarter of the century. According to the decorator and archaeologist Agostino Gerli (1744-1821), the decisive shift from a whirling rococo style to the harmony of Neoclassicism occurred about 1776 precisely with the works of Levati and Maggiolini. Naturally other artists contributed to the stylistic evolution, such as Appiani, Giuseppe Piermarini (1734-1808), who seems to have been involved with the 'Chinese' inventions for the duke's marriage in 1771, and Giocondo Albertolli (1744-1817). Writing in 1785 (*Opuscoli*), but referring to the situation at least a decade earlier, Gerli opined that "No one in fact, entering any one of the more recently decorated noble apartments, is so terribly fond of that muddle known as the 'French style' that they do not prefer the more modern order and rigour" – a clear case of "classical perfection" compared to "caprice and disorder".[17] Yet despite the impact of the new classical trend on the artists of Lombardy, chinoiserie still remained in favour and managed to survive quite happily even within the more austere decorative environment at the end of the century.

Published in Monza in 1811 by an anonymous author, a volume entitled *Descrizione della villa Silva in Cinisello* recounts that the residence of count Ercole Silva (1756-1840) in Cinisello Balsamo included an apartment of five rooms (two rooms and three smaller studies) decorated in the Chinese style. Silva commissioned the decorative scheme from Giuseppe Levati and the work was carried out by the painters Carlo Caccianiga and Agostino Gerli who, despite his earlier comments on the style, on this rare occasion abandoned himself to the delights of oriental themes.[18] The description of the apartment, possibly written by count Silva himself, tells us that "the first room is painted with a Chinese landscape, the work of that fine artist, Carlo Caccianiga; the coffered ceiling contains various images of Chinese rites and customs, as do the overdoors made by the painter Gerli. The table tops are supported by sea rocks and shells with coral attached, some of which is real. The other bedroom is similar in style and so too are the studies. All the decor, furniture and accessories of this apartment reflect our notion of the arts of that country; there is even a small rickety ladder in one of the studies, leading up to a landing, reminiscent of that style".[19] Ercole Silva commissioned the alterations in 1787 on his return from a long period abroad as part of the retinue of archduke Ferdinando; the interiors of the building, and the surrounding park in particular, were renovated while the existing architectural structure remained substantially untouched.

Although the furnishings and collections have been almost totally dispersed it has been possible to partially reconstruct the late 18th century décor of the villa. Unfortunately none of the wall decorations have survived, except for painted frames of flowers and exotic birds in the 'Sala degli Amorini' (not therefore in the Chinese apartment on the ground floor), described in the text of 1811 and attributed to the ornamentalists Felice Alberti and Caimi.[20] The two designers clearly based their work on Carlo Antonio Raineri's slightly earlier decorations with the same theme in the Chinese Room of the nearby Monza Villa, where they are known to have worked as assistants to Levati.[21] Some of the furniture belonging to the villa's Chinese rooms was recognised by Morazzoni who noted them together with a second, similar set of armchairs and divans in a private collection in Genoa;[22] these were subsequently published by Alberici.[23] In a later study of the furnishings, now recognised as designed by Levati,[24] Alvar González-Palacios defined the divan as "one of the most original interpretations of chinoiserie by an Italian; it is interesting to note moreover, the curious mixture achieved here of exoticism and Neoclassicism"; he also published a design by Levati for the decoration of the Sala Grande in the villa, in which oriental features appear on the right side.[25] More recently Enrico Colle has recognised a chair in the Museum of Fine Arts in Boston as another example of furniture once belonging to this superb interior. The style of this piece is identical to a console table previously illustrated by González-Palacios and Colle, leaving little doubt as to its provenance.[26] Carved and painted with figures of Chinamen, the wood furniture once owned by Ercole Silva (armchairs, chairs, two types of divan, tables and perhaps a chest of drawers) have a geometric design which is purely neoclassical. The oriental style had coincided with the development of Rococo throughout most of the 1700s, but here in contrast it has become a distinct stylistic choice. Perhaps this was the only way in which chinoiserie could survive, especially in the context of Lombardy where the renewed severity of decorative tastes based on classicism was almost unanimously approved.

Ercole Silva was also responsible for introducing landscape gardens *à l'anglais* in which exotic features played an important role. An expert in both natural history and law, in 1801 count Silva published a book entitled *Dell'arte dei giardini inglesi*, in which he outlined the theories already propounded by Kent, Hirschfeld and Walpole. The work included a series of illustrations engraved by Gaetano Riboldi, some designed by Levati, and provided both an explanation of the concept and – especially – practical advice for the use of natural and architectural elements according to the English style. At the beginning of his treatise Silva also included a section on the Chinese garden and most probably it was those 'Chinese rocks' which had appeared continually since the days of Nieuhoff that inspired him to build the "accessible cliffs" in his park in Cinisello – a path leading through artificial caves to the "extensive oak wood".[27] Silva's publication on gardens emphasised in particular the role of the artist-gardener who developed a feeling for nature – as opposed to the rigidity of the architect – and was the first Italian work to genuinely understand the principles of the 'anglo-chinois' garden, compared to earlier texts by Francesco Milizia (1787),

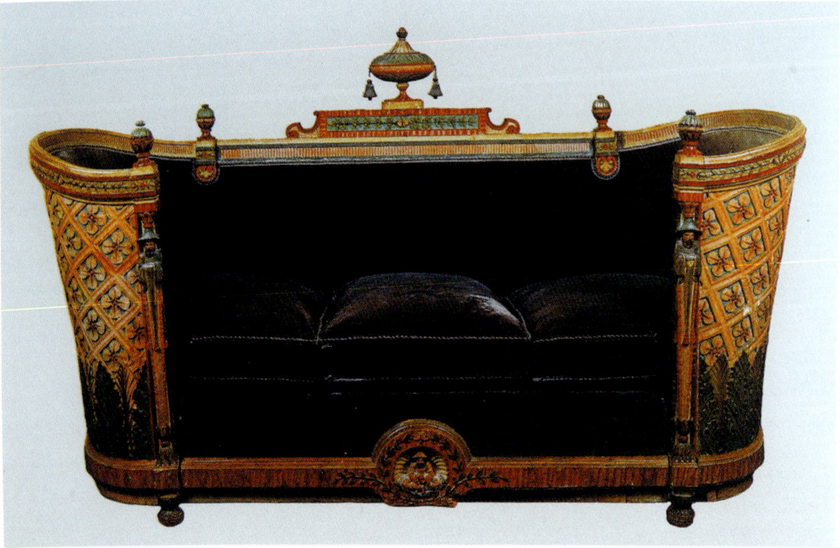

214. Settee, Milan, late 18th century. Private collection.

Originally part of the furnishings in Villa Silva at Cinisello Balsamo. The unusual form of this piece belongs to the neoclassical repertory of design enhanced, however, by the appearance of some 'exotic' details, satisfying Ercole Silva's penchant for oriental motifs.

Ippolito Pindemonte (*Dissertazione sui giardini inglesi e sul merito in ciò dell'Italia*, 1792) and Luigi Mabil (*Sopra l'indole dei giardini moderni*, 1796).[28]

At the end of the century Giuseppe Levati was one of the most important artists capable of using chinoiseries in a neoclassical context without corrupting the sobriety of the style. He was probably responsible for designing some of the furniture – showing great similarities to the items once in Villa Silva – published by Morazzoni in reference to the artist's work.[29] In the mid 20th century these furnishings were in Villa Litta Modignani in Lainate, suggesting that they were originally commissioned by count Antonio Greppi (1722-1799), owner of the villa in the late 1700s. Greppi was a passionate enthusiast of the exotic style and a room in his town residence in Via Sant'Antonio in Milan, renovated by Piermarini, was decorated with Chinese wall papers in 1776.[30] Levati also designed an arcade decorated with exotic motifs in an imaginary landscape, formed by a mosaic of coloured pebbles in the nymphaeum of Villa Litta in Lainate. This novel feature was part of the alterations made by Pompeo Litta (1727-1797) to the 16th-century building which had formerly belonged to the Visconti Borromeo.[31] The decoration of a study with "wallpapers from China with borders of green and white" and a room with "Chinese wallpapers" in palazzo Cusani in Via Brera in Milan dates from the last quarter of the 18th century. The second room also had a "chimney piece in two parts, with a coloured Chinese decoration". The descriptions seem to indicate that there was a difference between the paper coverings of the two rooms: the study was probably decorated with original Chinese works, while the other was Chinese in style, but actually made in Europe, possibly even in Milan. Renovation of the entire palace was begun in 1774, commissioned by Ferdinando Cusani

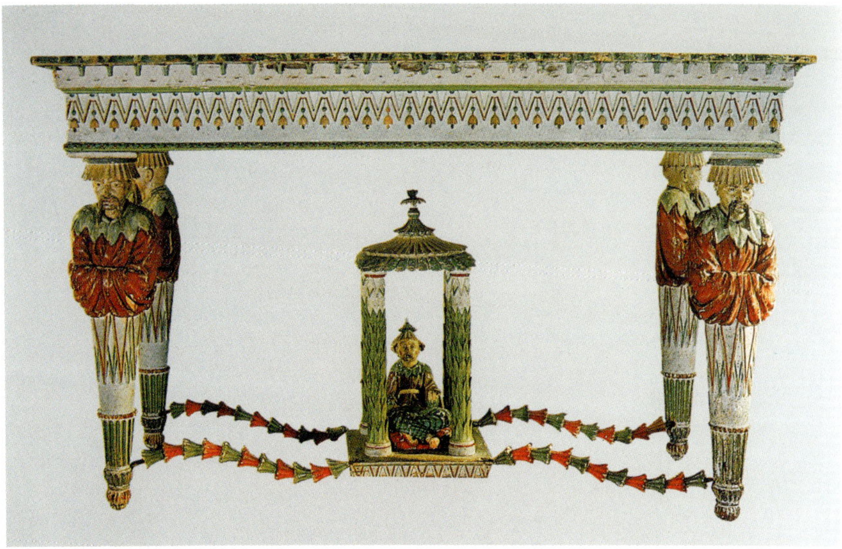

215. Table. Milan, c. 1780. Private collection.
Also originally part of the furnishings in Villa Silva, González-Palacios has compared this table with a piece housed in Buckingham Palace, formerly in Carlton House, dated around 1780 and of uncertain provenance (France or England); he noted in particular the use in both pieces of Chinese figures to support the table top.

(1737-1815), an influential personage connected to the Austrian court; in 1808 his son, Luigi, sold the building to the state administration.[32]
Decoration of the interiors of Palazzo Reale at Monza was completed about 1790. The painted silk panels in the 'Salotto Chinese' were probably installed about that time, and were certainly in place before the arrival of the French in 1796.[33] This room was part of the "appartamenti di società", most of which were planned by Levati and decorated by Albertolli and ornamentalists employed by Piermarini. Begun in 1777, both the architectural and the decorative works were directed by Piermarini and were sufficiently advanced in 1780 as dances and theatrical performances were held there in June that year. Furniture arrived continually from Vienna and the park too was almost completed – designed by Piermarini in the most fashionable style of an English landscape garden. The furniture of the 'Salotto Chinese' was designed by either Levati or Albertolli, though it is almost certain that Levati alone invented the Chinese scenes that decorated the fabric on the chairs and divans.[34]
The compositions of flowers and birds on the fabric covering the walls of this room are by Carlo Antonio Raineri (1765-1826), a painter specialised in natural subjects.[35] Chinese art is one of the most evident sources of inspiration for the wall decoration in the Salotto of Villa Reale, as it was for many other works attributed to Raineri. The artist was evidently extremely familiar with the Chinese papers painted with scenes of 'flowers and birds' that had arrived in Europe, Italy and, of course, Milan, constantly since the early 1700s. These papers were particularly popular in neighbouring Piedmont where they were often used to cover the walls of 'oriental' rooms, many of which have survived. Christian Wehrlin, for example, worked for the Savoy rulers, and in 1765 had been responsible for scenes with chinoiserie themes in the 'Camera longa' in the Stupinigi Hunting Lodge, and there are strong similarities between these and Raineri's inventions. He was, however, also inspired by illustrations in the many volumes of natural history that were published in the 18th century, such as the *Histoire naturelle générale et particulière* by Georges Louis Leclerc, count Buffon (Paris 1770-

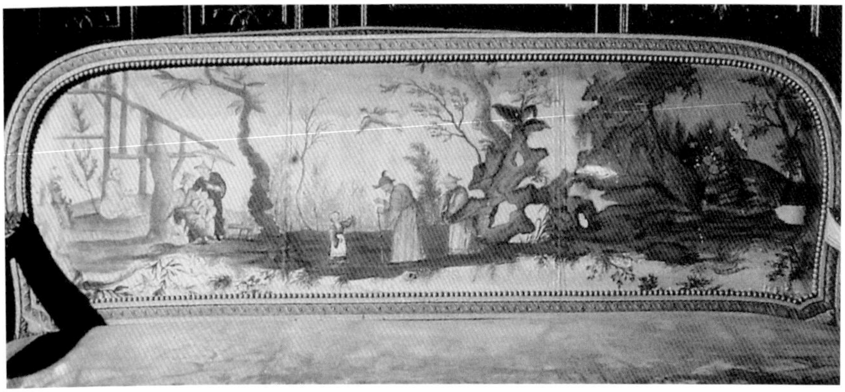

216. Upholstery for settee. Milan, late 18th century. Monza, Villa Reale, Chinese Room.

The chinoiserie designs and scenes adorning the upholstery of the furnishings in the Chinese Room in Villa Reale in Monza can almost certainly be attributed to Giuseppe Levati who had previously invented oriental scenes (see Fig. 209).

1786), especially the volumes dedicated to the *Histoire naturelle des oiseaux* illustrated by Martinet.[36] Working with other artists, Raineri was also responsible for the decoration of Palazzo Perego, unfortunately destroyed, and in 1788 he made several panels in the 'Animal Room' in Palazzo Anguissola. In the 1790s he moved to Genoa and here, as in Milan, he created a series of oriental-style works not designed for a residential context.[37] His son, Vittorio Raineri (1797-1869?), produced the same kind of themes executed in such a similar style that it is often difficult to attribute their undocumented works to father or son.[38]
Active throughout the early decades of the 1800s, the architect Rodolfo Vantini (1792-1856) lead the revival of the neoclassical style in Brescia. Towards the end of the 18th century, during the period when the sobriety of neoclassical design was at its height, the rooms of Palazzo Averoldi, owned by the Chizzola family were completely redecorated under the direction of Giuseppe Manfredini (1795-1796). The Chizzola also requested that one room should have panels of oriental lacquer and the Chinese motifs and scenes were painted by Giuseppe Teosa (1760-1848).[39]

Ceramics

The Coppellotti Factory, Lodi
The factory was founded by Giovanni Coppellotti in 1641. Little is known of this early phase of production and recent specialized studies have succeeded in identifying only pieces dating from the 18th century – the period in which the use of chinoiserie decorative themes was most prolific.[40] The factory was particularly active under Antonio Maria's management which lasted from 1703 to 1740 when he was succeeded by his son Bassano, who continued the family tradition until 1770.[41] Chinoiseries appear continually in all the various subjects created by Coppellotti's decorators and modellers. In the early 18th century they successfully imitated French motifs derived from Bérain which appeared on the ceramics of Rouen, often in cobalt blue on a white surface; from the 1750s chubbier oriental figures were portrayed in the midst of landscapes, strongly reminiscent however of the Italian countryside. In all cases Coppellotti's 'international' innovations were copied by many other Italian producers, especially when their workers moved on to the Clerici factory in Milan or the Antonibon in Bassano del Grappa. The illustrations accompanying Ferrari's study of production in Lodi demonstrate the evolution of chinoiserie decoration at the factory. The examples of oriental themes, painted in cobalt blue or with coloured enamels, mostly date from the third or fourth decade of the century, and present motifs which are very similar to those used at Nevers and Rouen in France.[42]

The Rossetti Factory, Lodi

Although Giorgio Giacinto Rossetti first opened a factory in Turin, events subsequently lead to the establishment of a second factory in Lodi. The Turin ceramic factory was established in 1725 by Rossetti with crucial finance from both his uncle Giovanni Battista and the Piedmont sovereign. Additional investors arrived in 1727 but Giorgio Giacinto was excluded from management of the company and was relegated instead to directing the department of ornamentation. Rossetti therefore left Turin and moved to Lodi where he set up his own business, joined by his brother, Giovanni Battista, in 1732. The company rapidly achieved success, and was already so well-known in 1736 that Rossetti was recalled to Turin by count Roero who, in the meantime, had become sole owner of the original factory.[43] Thus Rossetti's period of production in Lodi dated only from 1729 to 1736, but in this brief interval Giorgio Giacinto had experimented with a range of grotesque motifs, a style that had developed in France at the end of the 17th century. The majolica produced by Rossetti at Lodi was mainly painted with blue monochrome decorations although a few rare examples were also coloured and are very similar to the styles of Rouen, Nevers and especially Moustiers. Decorative motifs designed by ornamentalists such as Bérain and Audran III were exploited by the Moustiers factory in particular, but Rossetti's interpretation is more creative and less inhibited. Giorgio Giacinto's fondness for Bérain's grotesques may even be related to his birthplace near Pinerolo, which for long periods of its history had belonged to the French. Although not impossible, there is no evidence to prove that Rossetti had actually worked in the Moustiers factory in his youth.[44] Chinoiseries decorate some of Rossetti's Lodi majolica, but are always dominated by a more generous use of Bérain's motifs. The juxtaposition of the two styles becomes more obvious when the oriental element consists of small figures surrounded by grotesques or amidst floral compositions.[45] In other cases, and in particular when no figures are present, the designs of original Chinese porcelain are more rigidly interpreted and the French influence is less evident. Felice Ferrari has illustrated a good example of this demonstrating a fair imitation of early 18th-century Chinese porcelain made for exportation, except for the lobed edge which is totally unrelated to the standard designs of oriental wares[46].

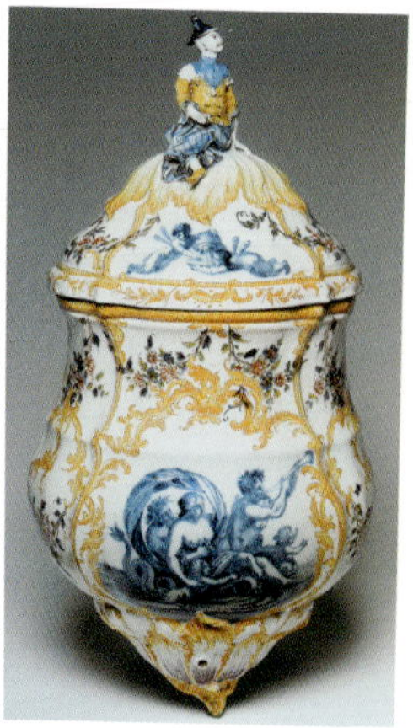

217. Wall fount. Lodi, Ferretti factory, c. 1765. Lodi, Museo Civico.

This majolica wall fount is certainly one of the masterpieces produced by the Ferretti factory in the 1700s. Almost entirely classical in both the decorative scheme and form, the little Chinese figure in full relief crowning the cover is an excellent example of Italian ceramic sculptural works with an oriental theme.

The Ferretti Factory, Lodi

Chinoiserie was a constant feature in the decorative style of the Ferretti factory, established in 1725 when Sempliciano bought an old kiln in the town of Lodi, establishing his new factory there. One of the very few pieces of this early phase of production to have survived is a teapot[47] decorated with floral motifs and rocks, inspired by wares from the Far East. The piece is also important for the contemporary use of blue with colours including red, green, yellow and purple, emulating Chinese porcelain produced during the second half of the 17th century. Following the death of Sempliciano, his son Antonio assumed management of the business between 1748 and 1750, continuing until his death in 1810. Coinciding with Antonio's management, Ferretti was at its most successful from the 1750s on producing a variety of high quality items, both technically and artistically. Although the factory was the first in Italy to adopt the 'Strasbourg flowers' design which gradually replaced the 'Indian flowers' (Chinese, in other words), Ferretti too had plenty of chinoiseries in their repertory. A statuette of a Chinese figure decorating the cover of the beautiful fountain in Lodi's Civic Museum dates from about 1765; the decorative style is almost entirely classical rather than exotic, but the figure is clearly based on characters seen in the oriental scenes invented by Boucher.[48] Dating from the late 1770s, a large set of plates, mostly housed in the Museo Civico of Milan, is decorated with oriental figures portrayed in a variety of occupations and is without any doubt the work of just one highly skilled painter.[49] These delightful scenes are painted with such freedom of artistic expression that it is very difficult to identify any specific source, but the cultural climate in which they were designed is easier to determine. Certainly Pillement's later designs for *divertissments* were in vogue and the first signs of neoclassical harmony were beginning to emerge, influencing the chinoiseries of Giuseppe Levati about the same time.

The Clerici and Rubati Factories, Milan

During the 18th century two majolica factories in Milan were of particular importance for Italian chinoiserie – Felice Clerici, founded in 1745, and Pasquale Rubati, which opened in 1756. While it is true that the two firms

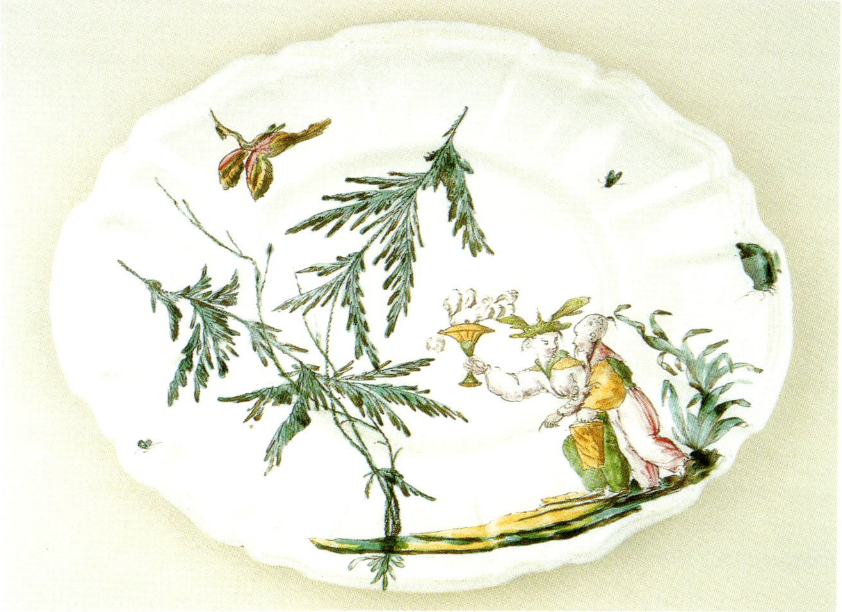

218. Plate. Lodi, c. 1770-1780. Milan, Castello Sforzesco, Civiche Raccolte d'Arte Applicata e Incisioni.

This dish is one of a series created by a single highly talented decorator who worked for one of the ceramic factories in Lodi during the second half of the 18th century. The quality of the work is extraordinary, especially the painting which is so delicate it looks almost like a watercolour.

had individual characteristics, their decorative styles are so similar that it is not altogether mistaken to consider them together as equally representative of 18th-century Milanese ceramics.

Before establishing his own factory, Rubati had worked for Clerici for a period, but his career as a ceramist had begun in Turin, where he is recorded as working for Giorgio Giacinto Rossetti from 1737 to 1740. Chinoiserie patterns were some of the most brilliant motifs to be used by Clerici and Ferretti, and their declared aim was to produce majolica with a paste and enamel as similar as possible to that of porcelain. The oriental motifs of the two factories can be divided into several groups depending on whether their primary derivation was based directly on original Chinese works, or European 'Chinese-style' creations. Both Clerici and Rubati literally plundered the ornamental decoration of Far Eastern – and especially Chinese – porcelain, producing precise copies of original works based predominantly on the items and designs most commonly produced for exportation in the first half of the 1700s.

The designs fall into several categories: the traditional 'blue and white', especially floral patterns; the 'Batavia' style in which at least part of the surface (usually the exterior) is painted entirely with a 'caffelatte' light brown colour; a monochrome background (usually blue, but occasionally light brown) with sections framed by irregular borders – a style particularly popular during the second half of the long reign of emperor Kangxi (1662-1722) and identified in the registers of the two factories as "enamelled landscapes in blue sections"; Chinese and Japanese Imari style in red, blue and gold, though the latter was often replaced with yellow to reduce costs; coloured famille rose, the design and layout as well as the shades of which were so expertly imitated by the artists that genuine oriental pieces can only be differentiated from the imitations by direct comparison. Moreover, ornamentalists of the two factories frequently designed floral compositions which are very similar to the decorations of Chinese porcelain, but are more imaginative and liberal in their interpretation.

The factories produced yet another group of decorative ware, distinguished by the use of French chinoiserie. The most plausible source for these designs are Watteau and Boucher's compositions and in at least two cases the Milanese decorators reproduced prints from *Diverses figures chinoises*, a series of engravings by Boucher of Watteau's drawings.[50] Workers employed by both Clerici and Rubati continually received engravings and other printed sources from Paris, Augsburg and Bassano del Grappa and indeed their chinoiseries are more or less evidently based on the compositions of Martin Engelbrecht, Jean-Baptiste Pillement and the Remondini.

These sources are clearly seen in vignettes referred to at the time as "a chinesi coloretti"; this kind of decoration usually consists of a scene with oriental figures and a floral detail, referred to as "fioretti coloretti". In fact, Morazzoni suggested that this design did not derive from oriental porcelain, but was

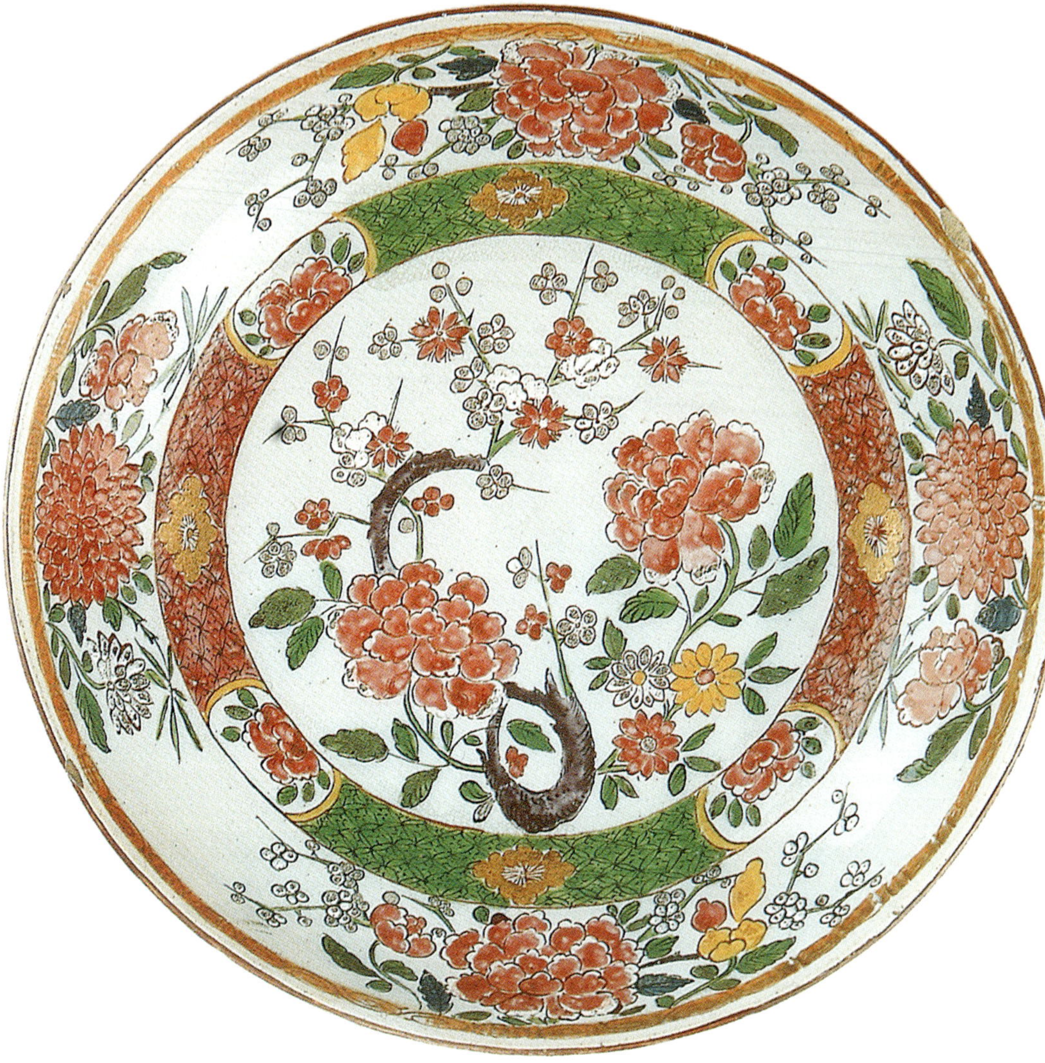

219. Plate. Milan, Clerici factory, c. 1760-1780. Milan, Castello Sforzesco, Civiche Raccolte d'Arte Applicata e Incisioni.

An almost exact copy of peonie and cherry blossom flower motifs, typical of *famille rose* Chinese porcelain produced in the mid 18th century explicitly for export to Europe. Both the Clerici and Rubati factories were specialised in transposing Far Eastern porcelain motifs onto majolica, producing such fine imitations that they could only be told apart by comparing the transparency of the glaze.

based on "most probably a fine piece of cotton printed 'alla cinese' which was produced by Kramer in Milan with great success".[51]

Lastly, both Clerici and Rubati invented some entirely original scenes with a Chinese theme – a group of works that perhaps best represents the development of chinoiserie in Milan. While these still reveal the influence of Chinese porcelain and international chinoiseries, their concept is quite markedly Milanese. A good example of this combination is the motif referred to as "della pagoda", though also occasionally as "del carabiniere". Both the format and the colours used undoubtedly recall Chinese models, but the style of painting is 'condensed', crisper and more fluid, revealing an ease that the painter could only achieve from a long familiarity with the subject. An entirely original feature of these scenes is the portrayal of a western character

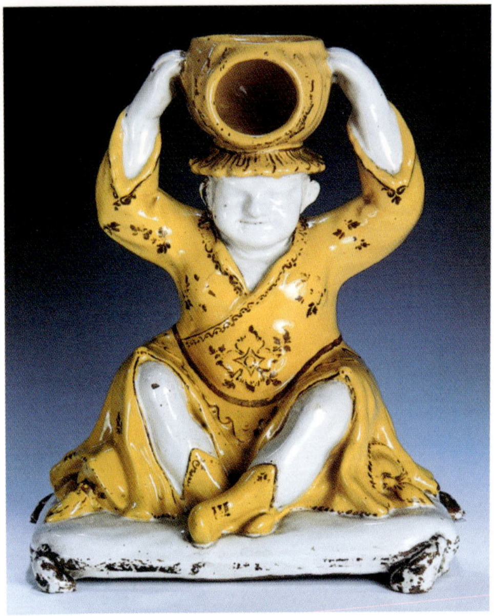

220. Figure of a Chinaman. Milan, Clerici factory, c. 1745-1790. Saronno, Giannetti collection

Madeleine Jarry published a similar figure to this, in the Museo del Castello Sforzesco in Milan, as representative of Italian majolica works with a chinoiserie theme, and noted similarities with sculptures made in the French factories of Saint-Cloud, Chantilly and Lille.

alongside an oriental figure as if to better emphasise that the entire composition is, in fact, a chinoiserie. Mid century Felice Clerici introduced a group of statuettes to his catalogue which further represents this stylistic evolution. Two such figures represented a "pagò", or a pagod, and "Chinese ladies". The first figure was a Chinese child seated with his legs crossed and a vase on his head with an opening on the front where a perfectly functioning watch was housed. Inspired by Chinese porcelain works portraying the chubby Buddhist monk, Budai Heshang, such figures were produced in the 1700s by many European ceramic factories including Saint-Cloud, Chantilly and Lille,[52] but the Milanese edition is rather more original – particularly his function as a watch stand. Carlo Martinelli was most probably the author of the moulds for these figures as he is listed among the employees of Clerici as a 'figurista' from 1754 to 1759. The female figure is closer to the oriental original, especially the Buddhist deity Guanyin produced at the Dehua

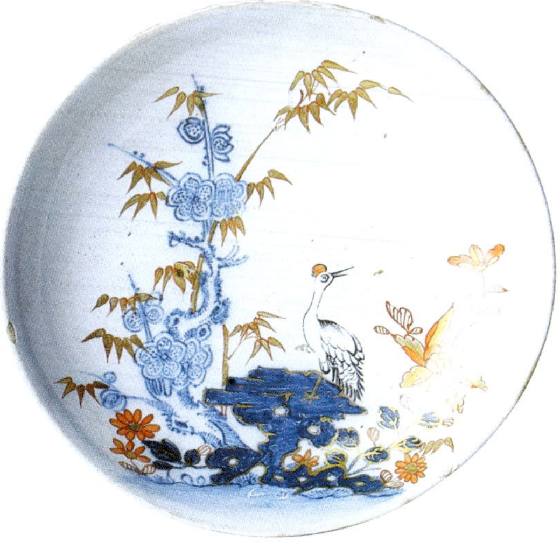

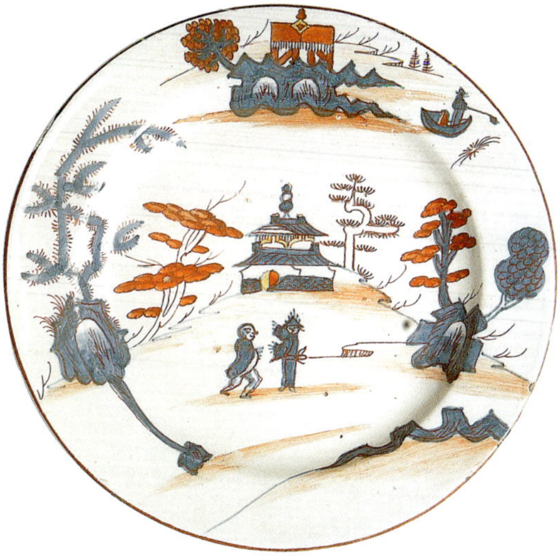

221. Plate. Milan, c. 1770-1790. Saronno, Giannetti collection.

With few variations, the decoration of this plate (diam. cm. 13.3) is a close copy of an 18th-century Chinese plate also belonging to the Gianetti Collection in Saronno (inv. 98/1) and an example of the Imari style with three colours (cobalt blue, iron red and gold).

222. Plate. Milan, 1745-1780. Milan, Castello Sforzesco, Civiche Raccolte d'Arte Applicata e Incisioni.

This style of decoration was known as 'alla pagoda' or alternatively, 'del carabiniere' and was the most famous chinoiserie design created by the Clerici and Rubati factories. The motif was used on all kinds of tableware (plates, cups, coffeepots, etc.) and must have been extremely popular as it is found in almost all museums exhibiting the historic ceramics of Lombardy.

factory in a white porcelain known in Europe as 'blanc de Chine'. Easily distinguished from descriptions found in sources of the day, these two Chinese figures were accompanied by others of similar style and technique, though sometimes sparingly coloured.[53]

1) Venturelli 1987.
2) Colle 2003, pp. 367-369.
3) Colle 2003, pp. 367-380.
4) Zoli 1974, pp. 113-114.
5) Venturelli 1987, note 11, p. 280.
6) Colle 2003, pp. 388-391, no. 89.
7) Venturelli 1987, pp. 271, 273.
8) Witt Dorring 1980; Beretti 1994, pp. 42-49.
9) Colle 2003, pp. 396-399, no. 92.
10) Pettorelli 1926, pp. 242-243, pls. CLXVII-CLXIX, figs. 298-305.
11) Baccheschi 1969.
12) Venturelli 1987, p. 274 and figs. 350-353; Beretti 1994, pp. 36-37.
13) Venturelli 1987, p. 277.
14) Bellezza Rosina, Cataldi Gallo 1993, pp. 53-54.
15) Bellezza Rosina, Cataldi Gallo 1993, pp. 54-59.
16) Bellezza Rosina, Cataldi Gallo 1993, pp. 59-61.
17) Venturelli 1987, p. 279; Colle 2005, pp. 285-303.
18) Venturelli 1987, pp. 274, 276.
19) Mazzocca in Mazzocca, Morandotti, Colle 2001, p. 356.
20) Guerci 2000, p. 46.
21) Mazzocca in Mazzocca, Morandotti, Colle 2001, p. 355.
22) Morazzoni 1955, p. 42, pls. CCLXXI-CCLXXII.
23) Alberici 1969, pp. 220-221.
24) Beretti 1998.
25) González-Palacios 1986, I, p. 256, pls. XLI-XLII; II, figs. 557-559.
26) Colle 2005, pp. 362-363, no. 85.
27) Guerci 2000, p. 80.
28) Tagliolini 1988, pp. 322-323.
29) Morazzoni 1955, p. 42, pls. CCLXXIII-CCLXXV.
30) Morazzoni 1955, p. 42; Venturelli 1987, p. 274.
31) Morandotti in Mazzocca, Morandotti, Colle 2001, p. 85 and fig. at p. 95.
32) Venturelli 1987, p. 277.
33) Della Seta, Massari in Casalzuigno 1994, p. 20.
34) Venturelli 1987-1988; Colle in Mazzocca, Morandotti, Colle 2001, p. 154 and fig. at p. 164.
35) Venturelli 1987, p. 276.
36) Della Seta, Massari in Casalzuigno 1994, p. 18.
37) Della Seta, Massari in Casalzuigno 1994, pp. 19-27.
38) Della Seta, Massari in Casalzuigno 1994, pp. 27-31.
39) Colle 2005, p. 292, fig. at p. 295.
40) Ferrari 2003, p. 36.
41) Ferrari 2003, p. 37.
42) Ferrari 2003.
43) Ferrari 2003, pp. 47-49.
44) Ferrari 2003, pp. 45-46.
45) Ferrari 2003, pp. 183-184, nos. 114-115.
46) Ferrari 2003, p. 197, no. 134.
47) Ferrari 2003, p. 222, no. 161.
48) Ferrari 2003, pp. 230-231, nos. 174-176.
49) Ferrari 2003, pp. 364-373.
50) Ausenda 1995, nos. 2-3.
51) Morazzoni 1948, p. 26.
52) Jarry 1981, p. 94.
53) Ceramiche 2001; Ausenda 1996, pp. 23-215, nos. 1-141.

Bibliography

This bibliography includes both the sources mentioned in abbreviated form at the end of each chapter as well as other works consulted by the author while writing this volume, though not referred to specifically.

Ackermann 2000
H.C. Ackermann, *Seidengewebe des 18. Jahrhunderts. I. Bizarre Seiden*, (Die Textilsammlung der Abegg-Stiftung), Riggisberg 2000

Affreschi ville venete 1978
Gli affreschi nelle ville venete dal Seicento all'Ottocento, 2 vols., Venice 1978

Alberici 1969
C. Alberici, *Il mobile lombardo*, Milan 1969

Alberici 1980
C. Alberici, *Il mobile veneto*, Milan 1980

Albisola Superiore 1989
Ceramica in banca. 50 maioliche liguri della Cassa di Risparmio di Genova e Imperia, exhibition catalogue, edited by A. Cameirana, Albisola Superiore (Savona) 1989

Alessandro Valignano 2008
Alessandro Valignano S.I. Uomo del Rinascimento: ponte tra Oriente e Occidente, Rome 2008

Alinari 1987
A. Alinari, *Maioliche marcate di Cafaggiolo*, Florence 1987

Allegri 1989
E. Allegri (ed.), *La Fondazione Carlo Marchi: raccolta d'arte e arredi*, Florence 1989

Alverà Bortolotto 1981
A. Alverà Bortolotto, *Storia della ceramica a Venezia dagli albori alla fine della Repubblica*, Florence 1981

Apollonj Ghetti 1991
F.M. Apollonj Ghetti, *Giapponesi a Roma nel primo Seicento. Il mio concittadino Hasekura*, 'Strenna dei Romanisti', 1991, pp. 17-32

Appartamenti imperiali 1998
Gli appartamenti imperiali nella manica lunga, Rome 1998

Arbace 1994
L. Arbace, *L'arte della tartaruga a Napoli nel Settecento*, in *L'arte della tartaruga. Le opere dei musei napoletani e la donazione Sbriciolo-De Felice*, exhibition catalogue, Naples 1994, pp. 23-37

Arbace 1998
L. Arbace, *Il Museo Artistico Industriale di Napoli*, Naples 1998

Arizzoli-Clémentel 1990
P. Arizzoli-Clémentel, *Le Musée des Tissus de Lyon*, Paris 1990

Arte di corte a Torino 1987
Arte di corte a Torino da Carlo Emanuele III a Carlo Felice, edited by S. Pinto, Turin 1987

Ausenda 1995
R. Ausenda, *'Figure' e 'Chinesi'. Maioliche milanesi di Felice Clerici*, exhibition catalogue, Milan 1995

Ausenda 1996
R. Ausenda (ed.), *Ceramiche della collezione Gianetti. Maioliche settecentesche. Milano e altre fabbriche*, Saronno (Varese) 1996

Avignon 1997
Brocarts célestes, exhibition catalogue, Avignon 1997

Baccheschi 1969
E. Baccheschi, *Cineserie rococò nell'ambiente maggioliniano: Appiani e Watteau*, 'Arte Lombarda', 1969, XIV, 2, pp. 147-150

Baccheschi, Levy 1966
E. Baccheschi, S. Levy, *Ferri battuti italiani*, Milan 1966

Balboni Brizza 1992
M.T. Balboni Brizza, *Vetri millenari nelle collezioni del Museo Poldi Pezzoli*, 'CeramicAntica', II, 1992, 7, pp. 20-33

Baldwin Beer 1970
A. Baldwin Beer, *Trade Goods, a Study of Indian Chintz*, Washington D.C. 1970

Ballardini 1919
G. Ballardini, *Alcuni cenni sull'influenza mongolo-persiana nelle faenze del secolo decimosesto*, 'Faenza', V, 1919, III-IV, pp. 49-59

Bandera 1972
L. Bandera, *Il mobile emiliano*, Milan 1972

Barber 2006
P. Barber, *Medieval Maps of the World*, in *The Hereford World Map. Medieval World Maps and their context*, edited by P.D.A. Harvey, London 2006, pp. 1-44

Barbolani di Montauto 2007
N. Barbolani di Montauto, *La villa di Lappeggi: il Tempo e la Fama nelle stanze del cardinale*, in *Fasto di corte: la decorazione murale nelle residenze dei Medici e dei Lorena*, vol. III: *L'età di Cosimo III de' Medici e la fine della dinastia (1670-1743)*, edited by M. Gregori, Florence 2007, pp. 141-161

Barbolini Ferrari 2004
E. Barbolini Ferrari (ed.), *Mobili dipinti. Tempera, lacca ed arte povera nelle botteghe italiane da XVII al XVIII secolo*, Modena 2004

Barovier Mentasti 1982
R. Barovier Mentasti, *Il vetro veneziano*, Milan 1982

Bassano del Grappa 1983
Il capriccio nell'incisione francese del Seicento e del Settecento, exhibition catalogue (Bassano del Grappa), edited by P. Morel and C. Nissirio, Rome 1983

Bassano del Grappa 1990
Remondini. Un editore del Settecento, exhibition catalogue (Bassano del Grappa), edited by M. Infelice and P. Marini, Milan 1990

Bassi 1987
E. Bassi, *Ville della provincia di Venezia*, Milan 1987

Beevers 2008
D. Beevers, *'Mand'rin only is the man of taste'. 17th and 18th Century Chinoiserie in Britain*, in *Chinese Whispers: Chinoiserie in Britain 1650-1930*, exhibition catalogue, Brighton 2008, pp. 13-25

Belevitch-Stankevitch 1910
M. Belevitch-Stankevitch, *Le Goût chinois en France au temps de Louis XIV*, Paris 1910

Bellezza Rosina 2000
M. Bellezza Rosina, *Indiane europee e mezzari genovesi*, in *Arte e lusso della seta a Genova dal '500 al '700*, exhibition catalogue, edited by M. Cataldi Gallo, Turin-London, 2000, pp. 124-135

Bellezza Rosina, Cataldi Gallo 1993
M. Bellezza Rosina, M. Cataldi Gallo, *Cotoni stampati e mezzari dalle Indie all'Europa*, Genoa 1993

Belluno 2009
Andrea Brustolon 1662-1732: "Il Michelangelo del legno", exhibition catalogue (Belluno), edited by A.M. Spiazzi, M. De Grassi, G. Galasso, Milan 2009

Beretti 1994
G. Beretti, *Giuseppe e Carlo Francesco Maggiolini. L'officina del Neoclassicismo*, Milan 1994

Beretti 1998
G. Beretti, *I mobili all'ultima moda nella villa di campagna dei signori Silva*, in *Ercole Silva (1756-1840) e la cultura del suo tempo*, edited by R. Cassanelli and G. Guerci, Cinisello Balsamo (Milan) 1998, pp. 89-92

Berlin 1973
China und Europa. Chinaverständnis und Chinamode im 17. und 18. Jahrhundert, exhibition catalogue, Berlin 1973

Berti 1986
F. Berti, *La maiolica di Montelupo. Secoli XIV-XVIII*, Milan 1986

Berti 1998
F. Berti, *Storia della ceramica di Montelupo. Uomini e fornaci in un centro di produzione dal XIV al XVIII secolo.* Vol. II: *Le ceramiche da mensa dal 1480 alla fine del XVIII secolo*, Montelupo Fiorentino (Florence) 1998

Bertini 1974
G. Bertini, *La sala grande del Palazzo Ducale di Colorno*, 'Arte Lombarda', XIX, 1974, pp. 163-170

Bertini 2005
G. Bertini, *Ritratti provenienti dai palazzi ducali conservati presso istituzioni parmensi: note documentarie*, in *Principi in posa. Ritratti del Settecento alla Galleria Nazionale di Parma. Nuove acquisizioni e restauri*, exhibition catalogue (Parma), edited by D. Gasparotto and M. Giusto, 2005, pp. 17-21

Bertocchi 1987
G. Bertocchi, *La fabbrica di ceramiche Finck in Bologna. Decadenza e fine*, 'Il Carrobbio', XIII, 1987, pp. 5-18

Bertocchi 1988
G. Bertocchi, *La porcellana di Bologna. Una sconosciuta avventura dell'arte ceramica del Settecento*, 'Il Carrobbio', XIV, 1988, pp. 37-46

Bertocchi, Liverani 1981
G. Bertocchi, F. Liverani, *Ceramiche bolognesi del Settecento*, Bologna 1981

Bertuccioli, Masini 1996
G. Bertuccioli, F. Masini, *Italia e Cina*, Bari 1996

Biancalana 2005
A. Biancalana, *La storia della manifattura Ginori: 1737-1791. Il periodo di Carlo Ginori e quello di suo figlio Lorenzo*, in *Quando la manifattura diventa arte, le porcellane e le maioliche di Doccia*, conference proceedings (Lucca 2003), edited by A. Biancalana, Pisa 2005, pp. 9-30

Bianchi Bandinelli 1985
R. Bianchi Bandinelli, *Geggiano*, Montepulciano (Siena) 1985

Biscontini Ugolini 1986
G. Biscontini Ugolini, *Ceramiche pesaresi dal XVIII al XX secolo*, Casalecchio di Reno (Bologna) 1986

Blunt 1959
C. G. E. Blunt, *Venetian Fabrics*, (The World's Heritage of Woven Fabrics), Leigh-on-Sea (Great Britain) 1959

Blunt 1961
C. G. E. Blunt, *Sicilian & Lucchese Fabrics*, (The World's Heritage of Woven Fabrics), Leigh-on-Sea (Great Britain) 1961

Boesen 1979
G. Boesen, *'Chinese' Rooms at Rosenborg Castle*, 'The Connoisseur', CC, 1979, 803, pp. 34-39

Bonanni 1720
F. Bonanni, *Trattato sopra la Vernice detta comunemente Cinese*, Rome 1720; ed. consulted: Cremona 1994

Bonito Fanelli 1981
R. Bonito Fanelli (ed.), *Five Centuries of Italian Textiles: 1300-1800. A Selection from the Museo del Tessuto Prato*, exhibition catalogue, Prato 1981

Bonora 1991
F. Bonora, *Il palazzo Durazzo Bombrini in Cornigliano. Un'architettura francese a Genova*, Genoa 1991

Boothroyd, Détrie 1992
N. Boothroyd, M. Détrie, *Le Voyage en Chine. Anthologie des voyageurs occidentaux du Moyen Âge à la chute de l'empire chinois*, Paris 1992

Briganti 1969
C. Briganti, *Curioso itinerario delle collezioni ducali parmensi*, Milan 1969

Briganti 1977
C. Briganti, *Documents sur les arts à la cour de Parme au XVIIIème siècle*, 'Antologia di Belle Arti', 4, 1977, pp. 380-401

Brighton 2008
Chinese Whispers: Chinoiserie in Britain 1650-1930, exhibition catalogue, Brighton 2008

Brosio 1973
V. Brosio, *Rossetti Vische Vinovo. Porcellane e maioliche torinesi del Settecento*, Milan 1973

Brunelli, Callegari 1931
B. Brunelli, A. Callegari, *Ville del Brenta e degli Euganei*, Milan 1931

Bruno 1998
I. Bruno, *Giuseppe Velasco alle soglie dell'età neoclassica*, 'Kalos', X, January-February 1998, supplement to No. 1

Buccaro, Kjučarianc, Miltenov 2003
A. Buccaro, G. Kjučarianc, P. Miltenov, *Antonio Rinaldi architetto vanvitelliano a San Pietroburgo*, Milan 2003

Bufalino, Di Cristina 1984
G. Bufalino, U. Di Cristina, *Palermo delle pagode*, 'FMR', 20, 1984, pp. 77-100

Buss 1992
C. Buss, *Collezione Antonio Ratti. Seta oro e argento. Le sete operate del XVIII secolo*, Milan 1992

Bussagli 1986
M. Bussagli, *La seta in Italia*, Rome 1986

Cameirana 2004
A. Cameirana, *Influenze orientali nella maiolica 'bianco-blu' ligure del XVI e XVII secolo*, in *Bianco-blu. Cinque secoli di grande ceramica in Liguria*, exhibition catalogue, edited by C. Chilosi and E. Mattiauda, Genoa 2004, pp. 25-29

Campori 1879
G. Campori, *Maiolica e porcellana di Ferrara nei secoli XV e XVI*, Pesaro 1879; Bologna 1980

Cantelli 1973
G. Cantelli, *Il mobile umbro*, Milan 1973

Cartari 2004
V. Cartari, *Immagini delli Dei de gl'Antichi*, preface by A. Grossato, Milan 2004

Casalzuigno 1994
Gli uccelli dei Raineri. Arte, natura e decorazione tra Settecento e Ottocento, exhibition catalogue (Casalzuigno, Varese), Milan 2004

Caserta 2004
Casa di Re. Un secolo di storia alla Reggia di Caserta 1752-1860, exhibition catalogue (Caserta), edited by Rosanna Cioffi, Milan 2004

Casprini 2000
L. Casprini, *Dove sbocciano i fiori. I giardini e le porcellane di Carlo e Lorenzo Ginori*, Florence 2000

Casprini Gentile, Liscia Bemporad 2008
L. Casprini Gentile, D. Liscia Bemporad (eds.), *Il gusto esotico nella Manifattura di Doccia*, Florence 2008

Cassidy-Geiger 1996
M. Cassidy-Geiger, *Graphic Sources for Meissen Porcelain: Origins of the Print Collection in the Meissen Archives*, 'Metropolitan Museum Journal', 31, 1996, pp. 99-126

Cataldi Gallo 1999
M. Cataldi Gallo 1999, *Galleria Nazionale di Palazzo Spinola. Tessuti*, Genoa 1999

Cataldi Gallo 2000
M. Cataldi Gallo (ed.), *Arte e lusso della seta a Genova dal '500 al '700*, exhibition catalogue, Turin-London 2000

Catello A. 1998

A. Catello, *Riflessi dell'esotico nella decorazione delle ville vesuviane*, in C.F. Attanasio, *Ville vesuviane e siti reali*, Naples 1998, pp. 85-90

Catello A. 1999
A. Catello, *Arredo fisso e arredo mobile. Il gusto dell'esotico*, in S. Attanasio, *I palazzi di Napoli. Architetture e interni dal Rinascimento al Neoclassico*, Naples 1999, pp. 119-123

Catello E. 1992
E. Catello, *Cineserie e turcherie nel '700 napoletano*, Naples 1992

Caterina, Mossetti 2005
L. Caterina, C. Mossetti (eds.), *Villa della Regina. Il riflesso dell'Oriente nel Piemonte del Settecento*, Turin 2005

Caterina, Porzio 2001
L. Caterina, A. Porzio (eds.), *'Quadretti' cinesi di collezione borbonica dalla 'Favorita' di Napoli e di Palermo*, exhibition catalogue, Naples 2001

Caterina Proto Pisani 1996
R. Caterina Proto Pisani (ed.), *Il Museo di*

Santa Maria all'Impruneta, Florence 1996

Catucci 2007
M. Catucci, *Il teatro esotico dell'abate Chiari. Il mondo in scena tra décor e ragione*, Rome 2007

Caumont Caimi 1995
L. Caumont Caimi, *L'ebanisteria genovese del Settecento*, Parma 1995

Cecchi 2001
A. Cecchi (ed.), *Simone Martini e l'Annunciazione degli Uffizi*, Cinisello Balsamo (Milan) 2001

Ceramiche 2001
Museo d'Arti Applicate. Le ceramiche. Tomo secondo, Milan 2001

Cerrada Clemente, Sánchez Hernández 1998
M.D. Cerrada Clemente, M.L. Sánchez Hernández, *El Gabinete de Porcelana de Madrid*, 'Antologia di Belle Arti. Studi sul Settecento', N.S., 1998, 55-58, pp. 86-93

Chiappini di Sorio 1983
I. Chiappini di Sorio, *Palazzo Pisani Moretta. Economia, arte, vita sociale di una famiglia veneziana nel diciottesimo secolo*, Milan 1983

Chiappori 1981
M.G. Chiappori, *Riflessi figurativi dei contatti Oriente-Occidente e dell'opera poliana nell'arte medievale italiana*, in *Marco Polo. Venezia e l'Oriente*, edited by A. Zorzi, Milan 1981, pp. 281-288

Ciatti 1996
M. Ciatti, *I paramenti e i mantellini della chiesa di Santa Maria all'Impruneta: note storiche*, in R. Caterina Proto Pisani (ed.), *Il Museo di Santa Maria all'Impruneta*, Florence 1996, pp. 169-183

Cionini 1993
N. Cionini, *I fiori del Catai. Introduzione alla figura e all'opera grafica di Jean-Baptiste Pillement e i suoi rapporti con la contemporanea produzione di tessuti d'arte in Europa*, 'Rassegna di studi e di notizie', XVII, 1993, pp. 21-55

Ciotola 2008
D. Ciotola, *Carte cinesi nella Roma del Settecento. Villa Aldobrandini a Frascati*, 'Art e dossier', XXIII, 242, 2008, pp. 44-47

Cirillo 2002
G. Cirillo, *Ennemond Alexandre Petitot. Lyon 1727, 1801 Parma*, Parma 2002

Cirillo, Godi 1983
G. Cirillo, G. Godi, *Il mobile a Parma fra barocco e neoclassicismo, 1600-1860*, Parma 1983

Clarke 1974
T.H. Clarke, *Lattimo. A Group of Venetian Glass Enamelled on an Opaque-White Ground*, 'Journal of Glass Studies', XVI, 1974, pp. 22-56

Clarke, D'Agliano 1999
T. Clarke, A. D'Agliano, *Le porcellane tedesche di Palazzo Pitti*, Ferrara 1999

Coccolino 1998
G. Coccolino, *Incontro con le porcellane cinesi di epoca Ch'ing prodotte dai laboratori imperiali e dai forni privati dal periodo K'ang Hsi all'epoca della Repubblica*, Pinerolo (Turin)1998

Cole 1899
A. S. Cole, *Ornament in European Silks*, London 1899

Colle 1992
E. Colle, *I mobili di Palazzo Pitti. Il primo periodo lorenese 1737-1799*, Florence 1992

Colle 1993
E. Colle, *Arredi dalle dimore medicee*, Florence 1993

Colle 1996
E. Colle, *Museo d'Arti Applicate. Mobili e intagli lignei*, Milan 1996

Colle 1998
E. Colle, *I tesori della collezione Mosca. Scrigni e stipi*, 1998

Colle 2000
E. Colle, *Il mobile barocco in Italia. Arredi e decorazioni d'interni dal 1600 al 1738*, Milan 2000

Colle 2003
E. Colle, *Il mobile rococò in Italia. Arredi e decorazioni d'interni dal 1738 al 1775*, Milan 2003

Colle 2005
E. Colle, *Il mobile neoclassico in Italia. Arredi e decorazioni d'interni dal 1775 al 1800*, Milan 2005

Collezione Gianetti 2000
Ceramiche della collezione Gianetti. Porcellane italiane europee e orientali, Saronno 2000

Colorno 1998
Gli arazzi dei Farnese e dei Borbone. Le collezioni dei secoli XVI-XVIII, exhibition catalogue (Colorno), edited by G. Bertini and N. Forti Grazzini, Milan 1998

Conner 2008
P. Conner, *Chinese Themes in 18th Century Gardens*, in *Chinese Whispers. Chinoiserie in Britain 1650-1930*, exhibition catalogue, Brighton 2008, pp. 55-63

Conner 2008a
P. Conner, *Chinese Style in 19th Century Britain*, in *Chinese Whispers. Chinoiserie in Britain 1650-1930*, exhibition catalogue, Brighton 2008, pp. 65-73

Cora, Fanfani 1982
G. Cora, A. Fanfani, *La maiolica di Cafaggiolo*, Florence 1982

Cora, Fanfani 1986
G. Cora, A. Fanfani, *La porcellana dei Medici*, Florence 1986

Cordier 1910
M. Cordier, *La Chine en France au XVIII siècle*, Paris 1910.

Cormio Ricci 1991-1992
S. Cormio Ricci, *L'inventario degli arredi del Cardinale Valenti Gonzaga*, 'Antologia di Belle Arti', 39-42, 1991-1992, pp. 148-166

Cornice italiana 1992
La cornice italiana. Dal Rinascimento al Neoclassico, edited by F. Sabatelli, Milan 1992

Curatola 1990
G. Curatola, *Venezia, la via della seta e le arti orientali*, in *Le vie della seta e Venezia*, Rome 1990, pp. 41-55

D'Agliano 1996
A. d'Agliano, *Settecento Europeo e Barocco Toscano nelle porcellane di Carlo Ginori a Doccia*, exhibition catalogue, Rome 1996

Daidone 2005
R. Daidone, *La ceramica siciliana. Autori e opere dal XV al XX secolo*, Palermo 2005

Davanzo Poli 1997
D. Davanzo Poli (ed.), *Seta & Oro. La collezione tessile di Mariano Fortuny*, Venice 1997

Davanzo Poli, Moronato 1994
D. Davanzo Poli, S. Moronato, *Le stoffe dei veneziani*, Venice 1994

De Angelis 2008
M.A. De Angelis, *Il Palazzo Apostolico di Catel Gandolfo al tempo di Benedetto XIV (1740-1758): pitture e arredi*, Rome 2008

De Jonge 1969
C.H. de Jonge, *Delfter Keramik*, Tübingen 1969

Della Seta, Massari 1994
R. Della Seta, *Gli uccelli dei Raineri. Arte, natura e decorazione tra Settecento e Ottocento*, in *Gli Uccelli dei Ranieri. Arte, natura e decorazione tra Settecento e Ottocento*, exhibition catalogue (Casalzuigno, Varese), Milan 2004, pp. 15-35.

De Moura Carvalho
P. De Moura Carvalho, *Oriental Export Lacquerwares and Their Problematic Origin*, in *Esotica. Portugals Entdeckungen im Spiegel fürstlicher Kunst- und Wunderkammern der Renaissance. Die Beiträge des am 19. und 20. Mai 2000 vom Kunsthistorischen Museum Wien veranstalteten Symposiums*, 'Jahrbuch des Kunsthistorischen Museums Wien', 3, 2001, pp. 247-261

Den Blaauwen 1966
A.L. Den Blaauwen, *Keramik mit chinoiserien nach stichen von Petrus Schenk Jun.*, 'Keramos', 31, 1966, 66, pp. 2-18

Devoti 1974
D. Devoti, *L'arte del tessuto in Europa*, Milan 1974

Devoti 1976
D. Devoti, *Storia dei tessuti in Italia e in Spagna*, in *Etoffes Merveilleuses du Musée Historique des Tissus, Lyon. Tome III. Tissus de l'Orient, de l'Italie et de l'Espagne*, Tokyo 1976, pp. XIII-XVIII

Devoti 198
D. Devoti (ed.), *La seta. Tesori di un'antica arte lucchese*, exhibition catalogue, Lucca 1989

Di Carpegna 1969
N. Di Carpegna, *Le armi Odescalchi*, Rome 1969

Di Castro, Pedrocchi, Waddy 1999
D. Di Castro, A.M. Pedrocchi, P. Waddy, *Il Palazzo Pallavicini Rospigliosi e la Galleria Pallavicini*, Turin 1999

Di Mauro 2002
M. Di Mauro, *La fabbrica dei Granili e la Casina Cinese*, 'Napoli Nobilissima', quinta serie, vol. III, fascicolo V-VI, September-December 2002, pp. 215-222

Dorigato 1981
A. Dorigato (ed.), *Vetri di Murano del '700*, exhibition catalogue (Venice), Milan 1981

Dorigato 2002
A. Dorigato, *L'arte del vetro a Murano*, Venice 2002

Ducret 1966
S. Ducret, *Die vorbilder zu einigen chinoiserien von Peter Schenk*, 'Keramos', 31, 1996, 66, pp. 19-28

Durante, Martellotti 1982
E. Durante, A. Martellotti, *L'Arpa di Laura. Indagine organologica, artistica e archivistica sull'arpa estense*, Florence 1982

Eidelberg, Gopin 1997
M. Eidelber, S.A. Gopin, *Watteau's chinoiseries at La Muette*, "Gazette des Beaux-Arts', CXXX, 1997, 1542-1543, pp. 19-46

Ericani 1976
G. Ericani, *Gaetano Savonarola architetto e committente*, 'Antichità Viva', XV, 1976, 1, pp. 32-39

Ericani 1982
G. Ericani, *L'"Impero della China" sulla scena e nella festa veneziana tra Sei e Settecento*, in *La scenografia barocca*, edited by A. Schnapper, (Proceedings of the 24th Conference of the Comité International d'Histoire de l'Art, Bologna, 10-18 September 1979), Bologna 1982, pp. 95-104

Ericani 1983
G. Ericani, *La storia e l'utopia nel giardino del senatore Querini ad Altichiero*, in *Piranesi e la cultura antiquaria. Gli antecedenti e il contesto*, Conference Proceedings. 14-17 November 1979 (Rome), Rome 1983, pp. 171-192

Ericani 1987-1988
G. Ericani, *I parati murari e le tappezzerie della Villa Pisani ora Nazionale di Stra*, in *Le tappezzerie nelle dimore storiche. Studi e metodi di conservazione.* Conference proceedings. Florence 13-15 March 1987, Turin 1987-1988, pp. 80-89

Ericani, Marini 1990
G. Ericani, P. Marini, *La ceramica nel Veneto. La terraferma dal XIII al XVIII secolo*, Verona 1990

Eriksen 1973
S. Eriksen, *Le porcellane francesi a Palazzo Pitti*, Florence 1973

Fani 2008
F. Fani, *Influssi estremo-orientali nella porcellana europea: la Manifattura Ginori di Doccia nel XVIII secolo*, in L. Casprini, Gentile, D. Liscia Bemporad (eds.), *Il gusto esotico nella Manifattura di Doccia*, Florence 2008, pp. 39-53

Farris 2004
G. Farris, *Per una storia della ceramica torinese del '600*, 'Faenza', XC, 2004, 1-6, pp. 61-107

Fatica 1984
M. Fatica, *Prolegomeni ad un discorso storico su Matteo Ripa*, in *La conoscenza dell'Asia e*

dell'Africa in Italia sei secoli XVIII e XIX, Naples 1984, vol. I, pp. 171-209

Ferniani Paolucci 1991
M.T. Ferniani Paolucci, *Le porcellane orientali alla base della rinascita faentina nel '700*, 'CeramicAntica', I, 1991, 1, pp. 19-24

Ferrari 2003
F. Ferrari, *La Ceramica di Lodi*, Azzano San Paolo (Bergamo) 2003

Fido 2007
F. Fido, *L'Oriente sui palcoscenici veneziani del Settecento: età dell'innocenza?*, in L'*Oriente: storia di una figura nelle arti occidentali (1700-2000)*, edited by P. Amalfitano, L. Innocenti, 2 vols., Rome 2007, vol. I: *Dal Settecento al Novecento*, pp. 127-144

Fiocco, Gherardi 1994
C. Fiocco, G. Gherardi, *La ceramica di Deruta dal XIII al XVIII secolo*, Perugia 1994

Fitz-Gerald 1963
D. Fitz-Gerald, *Juste Aurèle Meissonnier and Others*, New York 1963

Fitz-Gerald 1964
D. Fitz-Gerald, *An unpublished 'Chinoiserie' by Jacques de Lajoue (1686-1761) with some Thoughts on the Evolution of the 'Genre Pittoresque' in 18th-Century France (Part 1)*, 'The Connoisseur', 157, October 1964, 632, pp. 109-113

Fitz-Gerald 1964a
D. Fitz-Gerald, *An unpublished 'Chinoiserie' by Jacques de Lajoue (1686-1761) with some thoughts on the evolution of the 'Genre Pittoresque' in 18th-Century France (Part 2)*, 'The Connoisseur', 157, November 1964, 633, pp. 156-161

Florence 1997
Magnificenza alla corte dei Medici. Arte a Firenze alla fine del Cinquecento, exhibition catalogue, Florence 1997

Florence 2005
Maria de' Medici (1573-1642), una principessa fiorentina sul trono di Francia, exhibition catalogue, edited by C. Caneva and F. Solinas, Florence 2005

Fondazione Roberto Longhi 1980
La Fondazione Roberto Longhi a Firenze, Milan 1980

Fontein, Den Blaauwen 1966
J. Fontein, L. Den Blaauwen, *"Pictura sinicae ac surattenae" von Petrus Schenk sr*, 'Keramos', 31, 1966, pp. 29-40

Fossati 1992
G. Fossati, *I commerci tra Oriente e Occidente nel tempo*, in L. Zenone Padula (ed.), *Viaggio in Occidente. Porcellane orientali nelle civiche collezioni genovesi*, exhibition catalogue (Genoa), Milan 1992, pp. 11-19

Franzoi 1990
U. Franzoi, *L'armeria del Palazzo Ducale a Venezia*, Dosson (Treviso) 1990

Frugoni 2002
C. Frugoni (ed.), *Pietro e Ambrogio Lorenzetti*, Florence 2002

Fuhring 1999
P. Fuhring, *Juste-Aurèle Meissonnier. Un genio del rococò, 1695-1750*, 2 vols., Turin 1999

Fuhring 2005
P. Fuhring, *Designing the Decor. French Drawings from the Eighteenth Century*, exhibition catalogue, Lisbon 2005

Fumagalli 1994
E. Fumagalli, *Palazzo Borghese, committenza e decorazione privata*, Rome 1994

Gagliardi Mangilli 2008
E. Gagliardi Mangilli (ed.), *L'arte di fabbricare l'Indiane all'uso d'Inghilterra e di comporre tutti i colori, e buone tinte proprie e convenienti alle medesime. Opera del Sig. Delormois*, Saonara (Padova) 2008

Gambara, Pellegrini, De Grazia 1971
L. Gambara, M. Pellegrini, M. De Grazia, *Palazzi e casate di Parma*, Parma 1971

García Fernández 2003
M. S. García Fernández, *Muebles y paneles decorativos de laca en el siglo XVIII*, in *Oriente en Palacio. Tesoros asiáticos en las Colecciones Reales españolas*, exhibition catalogue, Madrid 2003, pp. 338-344

Gatti 1997
A. Gatti (ed.), *Museo degli Strumenti Musicali*, Milan 1997

Gavazza, Magnani 2000
E. Gavazza, L. Magnani, *Pittura e decorazione a Genova e in Liguria nel Settecento*, Genoa 2000

Il Gazzettino di Gerolamo Gigli 1864
Il Gazzettino di Gerolamo Gigli. Nuova edizione corretta col riscontro del codice della Biblioteca di Siena per cura di L. Bianchi, Milan 1864; anastatic reprint, Milan 1974

Genoa 2004
Bianco-blu. Cinque secoli di grande ceramica in Liguria, exhibition catalogue, edited by C. Chilosi and E. Mattiauda, Genoa 2004.

Gheroldi 1995
V. Gheroldi, *Le Vernici al principio del Settecento. Studi sul "Trattato" di Filippo Bonanni*, Cremona 1995

Giardini 1995
C. Giardini, *Ceramica pesarese nel XVIII secolo. La manifattura Casali e Callegari (1763-1816)*, exhibition catalogue (Pesaro), Ferrara 1995

Giardini 1996
C. Giardini, *Pesaro. Museo delle ceramiche*, Bologna 1996

Giarrizzo, Rotolo 2004
M. Giarrizzo, A. Rotolo, *Il mobile siciliano dal Barocco al Liberty*, Palermo 2004

Ginori Lisci 1963
L. Ginori Lisci, *La Porcellana di Doccia*, Florence 1963

Giuffrida, Giuffrè
R. Giuffrida, M. Giuffrè, *La Palazzina Cinese e il Museo Pitrè nel Parco della Favorita di Palermo*, Palermo 1987

Giusti 1986
P. Giusti, *Il salottino di porcellana di Portici*, in *Le porcellane dei Borbone di Napoli. Capodimonte e Real Fabbrica Ferdinandea 1743-1806*, exhibition catalogue, edited by A. Carola-Perrotti, Naples 1986, pp. 47-56

González-Palacios 1984
A. González-Palacios, *Il tempio del gusto. Le arti decorative in Italia fra classicismi e barocco. Roma e il Regno delle due Sicilie*, 2 vols., Milan 1984

González-Palacios 1986
A. González-Palacios, *Il tempio del gusto. Le arti decorative in Italia fra classicismi e barocco. Il granducato di Toscana e gli stati settentrionali*, 2 vols., Milan 1986

González-Palacios 1995
A. González-Palacios, *Il patrimonio artistico del Quirinale. Gli arredi francesi*, Milan 1995

González-Palacios 1996
A. González-Palacios, *Il mobile in Liguria*, Genoa 1996

González-Palacios 1996a
A. González-Palacios, *Il patrimonio artistico del Quirinale. I mobili italiani*, Milan 1996

González-Palacios 2003
A. González-Palacios, *Daguerre, Lignereux and the King of Naple's Cabinet at Caserta*, 'The Burlington Magazine', June 2003, pp. 431-442

González-Palacios 2004
A. González-Palacios, *Arredi e ornamenti alla corte di Roma, 1560-1795*, Milan 2004

González-Palacios 2007
A. González-Palacios, *Lacche e chinoiseries:noterella italiana*, in *L'Oriente: storia di una figura nelle arti occidentali (1700-2000)*, edited by P. Amalfitano, L. Innocenti, 2 vols., Rome 2007, vol. I: *Dal Settecento al Novecento*, pp. 231-239

Gordon-Smith 2000
M. Gordon-Smith, *The Influence of Jean Pillement on French and English Decorative Arts. Part One*, 'Artibus et historiae, an art anthology', 41 (XXI), 2000, pp. 171-196

Gordon-Smith 2000a
M. Gordon-Smith, *The Influence of Jean Pillement on French and English Decorative Arts. Part Two: Rappresentative Fields of Influence*, 'Artibus et historiae, an art anthology', 42 (XXI), 2000, pp. 119-163

Gordon-Smith 2004
M. Gordon-Smith, *Jean Pillement at the Imperial Court of Maria Theresa and Francis I in Vienna (1763 to 1765)*, 'Artibus et historiae, an art anthology', 50 (XXV), 2004, pp. 187-213

Gordon-Smith 2005
M. Gordon-Smith, *Jean Pillement at the Court of King Stanislaw August of Poland (1765-1767)*, 'Artibus et historiae, an art anthology', 52 (XXVI), 2005, pp. 129-163

Götz 2007
E. Götz, *The Pagodenburg in the Park of Nymphrenburg Palace*, in *A Taste for the Exotic: Foreign Influences on Early Eighteenth-Century Silk Designs*, edited by A. Jolly (Riggisberger Berichte 14), Riggisberg 2007, pp. 175-186

Grimm 2007
U. Grimm, *Favorite, A Rare Palace Exluding the Spirit of an Age when Chinoiserie Reigned Supreme*, in *A Taste for the Exotic. Foreign Influences on Early Eighteenth-Century Silk Designs*, edited by A. Jolly (Riggisberger Berichte 14), Riggisberg 2007, pp. 77-90

Griseri 1988
A. Griseri, *Un inventario per l'esotismo. Villa della Regina 1755*, Turin 1988

Grube 2006
E.J.Grube, *Le "laque" vénitien et la reliure au XVIe siècle*, in *Venice et l'Orient 828-1797*, exhibition catalogue (Paris-New York 2006-2007), Paris 2006, pp. 230-243

Gruber 1984
A. Gruber, *Chinoiserie. L'influence de la Chine sur les arts en Europe XVIIe-XIXe siècle*, exhibition catalogue, Bern 1984

Gruber 1985
A. Gruber, *Grotesques. Un style ornamental dans les arts textiles du XVIe-XIXe siècle*, exhibition catalogue, Bern 1985

Gruber 1996
A. Gruber, *Chinoiserie*, in *The History of Decorative Arts. Classicism and the Baroque in Europe*, New York-London-Paris 1996 (first published in Paris 1992)

Guerci 2000
G. Guerci (ed.), *Villa Ghirlanda Silva. Guida storico-artistica*, Cinisello Balsamo (Milan) 2000

Guerrieri Borsoi 2004
M. B. Guerrieri Borsoi, *Gli Strozzi a Roma. Mecenati e collezionisti nel Sei e Settecento*, Rome 2004

Hansmann 2002
W. Hansmann, *Die Schlösser Augustusburg und Falkenlust in Brühl*, 2 vols., Worms 2002

Harris 2007
The Drottningholm China House and its Place in European Garden Chinoiserie, in *L'Oriente: storia di una figura delle arti occidentali (1700-2000)*, edited by P. Amalfitano, L. Innocenti, 2 vols., Rome 2007, vol. I: *Dal Settecento al Novecento*, pp. 257-263

Hartkamp-Jonxis, Smit 2004
E. Hartkamp-Jonxis, H. Smit, *European Tapestries in the Rijksmuseum*, Amsterdam 2004

Harvard 1970
Tiepolo. A Bicentenary Exhibition, 1770-1970. Drawings, mainly from Amercan Collections, by Giambattista Tiepolo and the Members of his Circle, exhibition catalogue, Harvard 1970

Hasselink 2002
R. H. Hasselink, *Memorable Embassies: the secret history of Arnoldus Montanus Gedenkwaerdige Gesantschappen*, in www.brill.nl/qua

Heimbürger Ravalli 1981
M. Heimbürger Ravalli, *Disegni di giardini e opere minori di un artista del '700, Francesco Bettini*, Florence 1981

Helmecke 2001
G. Helmecke, *Byzantinische und orientalische Seidenstoffe. Grabfunde aus der Sepultur der Bamberger Domherren*, Bamberg 2001

Hong Kong 1997
From Bejing to Versailles. Artist e Relations between China and France, exhibition

catalogue, Hong Kong 1997

Honour 1961 (1963)
H. Honour, *Chinoiserie. The Vision of Cathay*, London 1961; Italian ed.: *L'arte della cineseria*, Florence 1963

Honour 1976
H. Honour (ed.), *The European Vision of America*, exhibition catalogue, Cleveland-Paris 1976

Huth 1967
H. Huth, *Lacquer in Rome*, 'Apollo', LXXXV, May 1967, 63 (N.S.), pp. 336-339

Huth 1971
H. Huth, *Lacquer of the West. The History of a Craft and an Industry. 1550-1950*, Chicago 1971

Impey 1977
O. Impey, *Chinoiserie. The impact of Oriental styles on Western art and decoration*, Oxford 1977

Innocenti 2007
L. Innocenti, *Falsi orientali*, in L*'Oriente: storia di una figura nelle arti occidentali (1700-2000)*, edited by P. Amalfitano, L. Innocenti, 2 vols., Rome 2007, vol. I: *Dal Settecento al Novecento*, pp. 15-29

Infelise 1980
M. Infelise, *I Remondini di Bassano. Stampa e industria nel Veneto del Settecento*, Bassano del Grappa 1980

Irwin, Brett 1970
J. Irwin, K.B. Brett, *Origins of Chintz*, London 1970

Jacobson 1993
D. Jacobson, *Chinoiserie*, London 1993

Jarry 1981
M. Jarry, *Chinoiseries. Le rayonnement du goût chinois sur les arts décoratifs des XVIIe et XVIIIe siècles*, Fribourg 1981

Kisluk-Grosheide 1996
D.O. Kisluk-Grosheide, *Cutting up Berchems, Watteaus, and Audrans: A* Lacca Povera *Secretary at the Metropolitan Museum of Art*, 'Metropolitan Museum Journal', 31, 1996, pp. 81-97

Kjellberg 1977
P. Kjellberg, *El Palacio Real de Madrid*, 'Connaissance des arts', 310, 1977, pp. 68-77

Klesse 1967
B. Klesse, *Seidenstoffe in der italienischen Malarei des 14. Jahrhunderts*, Bern 1967

Kopplin 2001
M. Kopplin, *Les laques du Japon. Collections de Marie-Antoinette*, exhibition catalogue (Versailles-Münster 2001-2002), Paris 2001

Krása 1983
J. Krása, *The Travels of Sir John Mandeville*, New York 1983

Kühn 1973
M. Kühn, *Leibniz und China*, in *China und Europa. Chinaverständnis und Chinamode im 17. und 18. Jahrhundert*, exhibition catalogue, Berlin 1973, pp. 30-36

Lacquer 1984
Lacquer. An International History and Collector's Guide, Malborough 1984

Lavalle, Cobo 2003
T. Lavalle, Cobo, *El coleccionismo oriental de Isabel de Farnesio*, in *Oriente en Palacio. Tesoros asiáticos en las Colecciones Reales españolas*, exhibition catalogue, Madrid 2003, pp. 211-214

Leone 1998
R. Leone, *Cultura dell'abitare e gusto decorativo a Palazzo Braschi. II*, 'Bollettino dei Musei comunali di Roma', XII, 1998, pp. 45-73

Levy 1967
S. Levy, *Lacche veneziane settecentesche*, 2 vols., Milan 1967

Lightbown 1969
R.W. Lightbown, *Oriental Art and the Orient in Late Renaissance and Baroque Italy*, 'Journal of the Warburg and Courtauld Institutes', XXXII, 1969, pp. 228-279

Lisbon 1994
A Influência Oriental na Cerâmica Portuguesa do Século XVII, exhibition catalogue (Lisbon), Milan 1994

Liverani 1967
G. Liverani, *Il Museo delle Porcellane di Doccia*, Sesto Fiorentino (Florence) 1967

Lizzani 1970
G. Lizzani, *Il mobile romano*, Milan 1970

London 1998
Kensington Palace and the Porcelain of Queen Mary II, exhibition catalogue, edited by M. Hinton and O. Impey, London 1998

London 2004
Encounters. The Meeting of Asia and Europe, 1500-1800, exhibition catalogue, edited by A. Jackson and A. Jaffer, London 2004

Lo Sardo 2001
E. Lo Sardo (ed.), *Athanasius Kircher. Il Museo del mondo*, exhibition catalogue, Rome 2001

Lucca 2001 *Lucca e le porcellane della Manifattura Ginori. Commissioni patrizie e ordinativi di corte*, exhibition catalogue, various authors, Lucca 2001

Macchia, Montagni 1968 G. Macchia, E.C. Montagni, *L'opera completa di Watteau*, Milan 1968

Maccioni 2007
P. Maccioni, *Il Ritiro di Lilliano*, in *Fasto di corte: la decorazione murale nelle residenze dei Medici e dei Lorena*, vol. III: *L'età di Cosimo III de' Medici e la fine della dinastia (1670-1743)*, edited by M. Gregori, Florence 2007, pp. 162-175

Magagnato 1983
L. Magagnato (ed.), *Le stoffe di Cangrande. Ritrovamenti e ricerche sul 300 veronese*, exhibition catalogue, Verona 2003

Magnani 1987
L. Magnani, *Il tempio di Venere. Giardino e villa nella cultura genovese*, Genoa 1987

Magnanimi 1984
G. Magnanimi, *The Eighteenth-Century Apartments in the Palazzo Barberini*, 'Apollo', CXX, 1984, 272, pp. 252-261

Malena 2003
C. Malena, *Le ambascerie giapponesi in Italia (1585, 1615) e il loro lascito nell'editoria e nelle arti*, in *Italia-Giappone: 450 anni*, edited by A. Tamburello, 2 vols. Rome-Naples 2003, vol I: pp. 41-51

Mantova 2000
La collezione Chigi Saracini di Siena. Per una storia del collezionismo italiano, exhibition catalogue (Mantova), Florence 2000.

Mañueco Santurtún 2003
C. Mañueco Santurtún, *La presenzia de Oriente en la Manufactura del Buen Retiro*, in *Oriente en Palacio. Tesoros asiáticos en las Collecciones Reales españolas*, exhibition catalogue, Madrid 2003, pp. 331-337

Marco Polo 1981
Marco Polo. Venezia e l'Oriente, edited by A. Zorzi, Milan 1981

Maresca 2004a
P. Maresca, *Giardini, mode e architetture insolite*, Florence 2004

Maresca 2004b
P. Maresca, *Giardini incantati, boschi sacri e architetture magiche*, Florence 2004

Markowsky 1976
B. Markowsky, *Kunstgewerbe Museum der Stadt Köln. Europäische Seiden gewebe des 13.-18. Jahrhunderts*, Cologne 1976

Mariuz 1971
A. Mariuz, *Giandomenico Tiepolo*, Venice 1971

Marot 1892
Das Ornamentwerk des Daniel Marot in 264 Lichtdrucken nacgebildet, Berlin 1892

Martino 1996
L. Martino, *Dalla "Galleria delle cose rare" di Parma al Museo di Capodimonte. Gli oggetti d'arte di Casa Farnese*, in *La Collezione Farnese. Le arti decorative*, Milan 1996, pp. 119-129

Marzinot 1987
F. Marzinot, *Ceramica e ceramisti di Liguria*, Genoa 1987

Mazzini 2004
D. Mazzini (ed.), *Villa Medici a Fiesole, Leon Battista Alberti e il prototipo di villa rinascimentale*, Florence 2004

Mazzocca, Morandotti, Colle 2001
F. Mazzocca, A. Morandotti, E. Colle, *Milano neoclassica*, Milan 2001

Melegati 1998
L. Melegati, *Giovanni Vezzi e le sue porcellane*, Milan 1998

Michel, Pacia, Susinno 1997
G. Michel, A. Pacia, S. Susinno, *I Pozzi*, Bergamo 1997

Mignini 2005
F. Mignini (ed.), *Padre Matteo Ricci. L'Europa alla corte dei Ming*, exhibition catalogue (Rome), Milan 2005

Milan 1988
I mezzari tra Oriente e Occidente, exhibition catalogue (Milan), edited by M. Cataldi Gallo, Genoa 1988

Milan 2009
Magnificenza e progetto: cinquecento anni di grandi mobili italiani a confronto, exhibition catalogue, edited by L. Settembrini, E. Colle, M. De Giorgi, Milan 2009

Miller 1996
S. Miller, *Jean-Antoine Fraisse, "Gravé par Huquier"*, in 'Metropolitan Museum Journal', 31, 1996, pp. 127-130

Miller 2001
S. Miller, *Images of Asia in French Luxury Goods. Jean-Antoine Fraisse at Chantilly, c. 1729-36*, 'Apollo', CLIV, November 2001, 477, pp. 3-12

Miller 2006
S. Miller, *Disegni* bizarres *per tessuti di seta. 1680-1710*, in R. Orsi Landini (ed.), *Seta. Potere e glamour. Tessuti e abiti dal Rinascimento al XX secolo*, exhibition catalogue (Caraglio), Cinisello Balsamo (Milan) 2006, pp. 83-109

Miller 2007
S. Miller, *Europe Looks East: Ceramics and Silk 1680-1710*, in *A Taste for the Exotic: Foreign Influences on Early Eighteenth-Century Silk Designs*, edited by A. Jolly (Riggisberger Berichte 14), Riggisberg 2007, pp. 155-173

Modelli Meissen 1981
I modelli di Meissen per le cineserie Höroldt, 2 vols., Florence 1981

Montesquieu 1995
Montesquieu, *Viaggio in Italia*, edited by G. Macchia and M. Colesanti, Bari 1995

Morazzoni 1948
G. Morazzoni, *Le maioliche di Milano*, Milan 1948

Morazzoni 1949
G. Morazzoni, *Il mobile genovese*, Milan 1949

Morazzoni 1950
G. Morazzoni, *Argenterie genovesi*, Milan 1950

Morazzoni 1955
G. Morazzoni, *Il mobile neoclassico italiano*, Milan 1955

Morazzoni 1958
G. Morazzoni, *Mobili veneziani laccati*, 2 vols., Milan 1958

Morazzoni 1960
G. Morazzoni, *Le porcellane italiane*, 2 vols., Milan 1960

Morena 2005
F. Morena, *Dalle Indie orientali alla corte di Toscana. Collezioni di arte cinese e giapponese a Palazzo Pitti*, Florence 2005

Morena 2006
F. Morena, *Arte cinese e giapponese nel Museo Civico Medievale di Bologna: una ricognizione*, 'DecArt', 2006, 5, pp. 40-4

Morena 2006a
F. Morena, *La Stanza delle Porcellane dell'Elettrice Palatina a Palazzo Pitti*, in *La pricipessa saggia. L'eredità di Anna Maria Luisa de' Medici Elettrice Palatina*, exhibition catalogue, edited by S. Casciu, Florence 2006, pp. 78-83

Morena 2006b
F. Morena, *La collezione Scalabrino: porcellane orientali e maioliche europee*, Livorno 2006

Morena 2007
F. Morena, *Sur les traces de la chinoiserie italienne du XVIIIe siècle*, in *Pagodes et dragons. Exotisme et fantaisie dans l'Europe rococo 1720-1770*, exhibition catalogue, Paris 2007, pp. 63-70

Morroni 2001
F. Morroni, *Arredi di Giles Grendey per il Re di Napoli*, 'Antologia di Belle Arti. Studi sul Settecento II', 2001 (2000), 59-62, pp. 30-33

Mottola Molfino 1976
A. Mottola Molfino, *L'arte della porcellana in Italia. Il Veneto e la Toscana*, Busto Arsizio (Varese) 1976

Mottola Molfino 1977
A. Mottola Molfino, *L'arte della porcellana in Italia. Il Piemonte, Roma e Napoli*, Busto Arsizio (Varese) 1977

Naples 1979
Civiltà del '700 a Napoli, 1734-1799, exhibition catalogue, 2 vols. (Naples 1979-1980), Florence 1979

Naples 1984
Civiltà del Seicento a Napoli, exhibition catalogue, 2 vols., Naples 1984

Naples 1986
Le porcellane dei Borbone di Napoli. Capodimonte e Real Fabbrica Ferdinandea 1743-1806, exhibition catalogue, edited by A. Carola-Perrotti, Naples 1986

New York-Detroit-Paris 1986-1987
François Boucher, 1703-1770, exhibition catalogue, Paris 1986

Novasconi, Ferrari, Corvi 1964
A. Novasconi, S. Ferrari, S. Corvi, *La ceramica lodigiana*, Lodi 1964

Odorico da Pordenone 1982
Odorico da Pordenone, *Relazione del viaggio in Oriente e in Cina (1314?-1330)*, Pordenone 1982

Orsi Landini 1987
R. Orsi Landini, *I parati orientali della Villa del Poggio Imperiale*, in *Le tappezzerie nelle dimore storiche. Studi e metodi di conservazione*, Centro Italiano per lo Studio della Storia del Tessuto, Sezione Toscana, 4th conference, Turin 1987, pp. 146-157

Orsi Landini 1993
R. Orsi Landini, *Il Quartiere delle Stoffe*, in *Gli Appartamenti Reali di Palazzo Pitti. Una reggia per tre dinastie: Medici, Lorena e Savoia tra Granducato e Regno d'Italia*, edited by M. Chiarini, S. Padovani, Florence 1993, pp. 195-201

Orsi Landini, Niccoli 2005
R. Orsi Landini, B. Niccoli, *Moda a Firenze 1540-1580. Lo stile di Eleonora di Toledo e la sua influenza*, Florence 2005

Pacia 1990
A. Pacia, *Esotismo decorativo a Roma fra tradizione rococò e gusto neoclassico*, 'Studi sul Settecento Romano. Temi di decorazione. Dalla cultura dell'artificio alla poetica della natura', Rome 1990, pp. 91-156

Padova 1972
Andrea Urbani (1711-1798) scenografo e frescante, exhibition catalogue, edited by L. Grossato, Padova 1972

Palazzo dei Normanni 1991
Palazzo dei Normanni, Palermo 1991

Palazzo Durazzo Pallavicini 1995
Il Palazzo Durazzo Pallavicini, Genoa 1995

Palazzo Mirto n.d.
Palazzo Mirto. Cenni storico-artistici ed itinerario, Palermo [n.d.]

Palazzotto 2002
P. Palazzotto, *Chinoiserie di Sicilia*, 'Salvare Palermo. Giornale della fondazione salvare Palermo onlus', September-December 2002, pp. 32-33

Palazzotto 2008
P. Pallazzotto, *Riflessi del gusto per la cineseria e gli esotismi a Palermo tra Rococò e Neoclassico: collezionismo, apparati decorativi e architettura*, in *Argenti e cultura rococò nella Sicilia centro occidentale 1735-1789*, exhibition catalogue, edited by S. Grasso, M.C. Gulisano (Lübeck), Palermo 2008, pp. 535-561

Paris 1911
La chinoiserie en Europe au XVIIIe siècle: tappisseries, meubles, bronzes d'ameublement, ceramiques, peintures et dessins, exhibition catalogue, edited by J. Guérin, Paris 1911

Paris 2007
Pagodes et dragons. Exotisme et fantaisie dans l'Europe rococo 1720-1770, exhibition catalogue, Paris 2007

Paris-New York 2006-2007
Venice e l'Orient 828-1797, exhibition catalogue (Paris-New York 2006-2007), Paris 2006

Paris, Sydney, Ottawa 2003, 2005-2006
François Boucher et l'art rocaille dans les collections de l'École des beaux-arts, exhibition catalogue, (Paris-Sydney-Ottawa 2003, 2005-2006), Paris 2003

Parma 1997
Petitot un Artista del Settecento europeo a Parma, exhibition catalogue, Parma 1997

Pedrocco 1998
F. Pedrocco (ed.), *'700 Veneziano. Capolavori da Ca' Rezzonico*, exhibition catalogue (Rome), Venice 1998

Pedrocco 2002
F. Pedrocco, *Giambattista Tiepolo*, Geneva-Milan 2002

Pedrocco 2003
F. Pedrocco, *Paolo Veneziano*, Milan 2003

Pellegri 1981
M. Pellegri, *Colorno. Villa Ducale*, Parma 1981

Pessa 2005
L. Pessa (ed.), *Le ceramiche liguri*, Cinisello Balsamo 2005

Pettorelli 1926
A. Pettorelli, *Il bronzo e il rame nell'arte decorativa italiana*, Milan 1926

Piazza 2005
S. Piazza, *Il palazzo Valguarnera-Gangi a Palermo*, Palermo 2005

Piccolpasso Durantino 1879
C. Piccolpasso Durantino, *I tre libri dell'arte del vasajo*, Pesaro 1879; Bologna 2003

Pietrangeli 1986
C. Pietrangeli, *Palazzo Sciarra*, Rome 1986

Pisa 1998
La Manifattura toscana dei Ginori, Doccia 1737-1791, exhibition catalogue, edited by M. Burresi, Pisa 1998

Porcellane Capodimonte 1993
Porcellane di Capodimonte. La Real Fabbrica di Carlo di Borbone 1743-1759, Naples 1993

Porzio 1994
A. Porzio, *Arte e storia in Palazzo Reale*, in *Il Palazzo Reale di Napoli*, Naples 1994, pp. 39-109

Porzio 2001
A. Porzio, *Da Palazzo Reale alla Favorita di Resina, sulle tracce della cineseria 'neoclassica' a Napoli*, in L. Caterina, A. Porzio (eds.), *'Quadretti' cinesi di collezione borbonica dalla 'Favorita' di Napoli e di Palermo*, exhibition catalogue, Naples 2001, pp. 7-14

Porzio 2005
A. Porzio, *Un 'verniciaro francese' alla corte di Napoli: Martin a Portici*, in L. Caterina, C. Mossetti (eds.), *Villa della Regina. Il riflesso dell'Oriente nel Piemonte del Settecento*, Turin 2005, pp. 98-101

Prinz 1993
W. Prinz, *I Tatari nella pittura italiana del Trecento*, in *Studi di storia dell'arte sul Medioevo e il Rinascimento nel centenario della nascita di Mario Salmi, Atti del Convegno Internazionale. Arezzo-Firenze, 16-19 Novembre 1989*, Florence 1993, pp. 415-429

Pugliatti 1977
T. Pugliatti, *Agostino Tassi tra conformismo e libertà*, Rome 1977

Putaturo Murano
A. Putaturo Murano, *Il mobile napoletano del Settecento*, Naples 1977

Ravanelli Guidotti 1998
C. Ravanelli Guidotti, *Thesaurus di opere*

della tradizione di Faenza nelle raccolte del Museo Internazionale delle Ceramiche in Faenza, Faenza 1998

Rispoli Fabris 1974
A. Rispoli Fabris, *L'arte della lacca*, Milan 1974

Romano 1994
M. C. Romano, *Il Senmurv*, in *La Seta e la sua Via*, exhibition catalogue, edited by M. T. Lucidi, Rome 1994, pp. 135-137

Rome 1991
Fasto Romano, dipinti, sculture, arredi dai Palazzi di Roma, exhibition catalogue, edited by A. González-Palacios, Rome 1991

Rome 1994
La seta e la sua via, exhibition catalogue, edited by M.T. Lucidi, Rome 1994

Rome 2005
Il Settecento a Roma, exhibition catalogue (Rome), edited by A. Lo Bianco and A. Negro, Cinisello Balsamo (Milan) 2005

Rome-Parma-Lyons 1989
Feste Fontane Festoni a Parma nel Settecento. Progetti e decorazioni disegni e incisioni dell'architetto E.A. Petitot (1727-1801), exhibition catalogue, edited by P. Bedarida, (Rome-Parma-Lyons), Rome 1989

Rothstein 1990
N. Rothstein, *Silks Designs of the Eighteenth Century in the Collection of the Victoria and Albert Museum, London. With a Complete Catalogue*, London 1990

Rotondi 1959
P. Rotondi, *Filippo Parodi maestro dell'intaglio*, 'Bollettino d'Arte', XLIV, 1959, 1, pp. 46-56

Ruotolo 1982
R. Ruotolo, *Mercanti-collezionisti fiamminghi a Napoli, Gaspare Roomer e i Vendeneynden*, in *Ricerche sul '600 napoletano*, 1982

Sade 1995
D-A-F. Marquis de Sade, *Viaggio in Italia*, Turin 1996

Safarik 1996
E.A. Safarik, *Collezione dei dipinti Colonna. Inventari 1611-1795*, Munich 1996

Safarik 1999
E.A. Safarik, *Palazzo Colonna*, Rome 1999

Safarik 2002
E.A. Safarik, *Palazzo Colonna. La Galleria. Guida*, Rome 2002

Santangelo 1959
A. Santangelo, *Tessuti d'arte italiani dal XII al XVIII secolo*, Milan 1959

Santini 2003
C. Santini, *Le lacche dei veneziani. Oggetti d'uso quotidiano nella Venezia del Settecento*, Venice 2003

Santuccio 1992
G. Santuccio, *Curiosità e fantasmagoria dal Celeste Impero, "...la tanto da Viaggiatori celebrata Torre presso Nanckin nella Cina, detta delle porcellane..."*, 'CeramicAntica', II, 1992, 9, pp. 35-42

Sassuolo 2000
Le ceramiche dei duchi d'Este: dalla Guardaroba al collezionismo, exhibition catalogue (Sassuolo), edited by F. Trevisani, Milan 2000

Schlosser 1908
J. Von Schlosser, *Die Kunst- und Wunderkammern der Spätrenaissance*, Leipzig 1908; Italian ed. Milan 2000

Schütze 2003
S. Schütze (ed.), *Palazzo Sacchetti*, Rome 2003

Schwarm 2007
E. Schwarm, *Tapestries in the Indian Style: Remarks on the Chinoiserie Interior of The Holländisches Palais at Dresden*, in *A Taste for the Exotic: Foreign Influences on Early Eighteenth-Century Silk Designs*, edited by A. Jolly (Riggisberger Berichte 14), Riggisberg 2007, pp. 91-104

Semenzato 1966
C. Semenzato, *La scultura veneta del Seicento e del Settecento*, Venice 1966

Simmons 1948
P. Simmons, *Chinese Patterned Silks*, New York 1948

Simmons 1956
P. Simmons, *Some Recent Developments in Chinese Textile Studies*, 'The Museum of Far Eastern Antiquities. Bulletin', 28, 1956, pp. 18-44

Slomann 1953
V. Slomann, *Bizarre Designs in Silks. Trade and Traditions*, Copenhagen 1953

Sommariva 2004
G. Sommariva, *Palazzi nobiliari di Palermo*, Palermo 2004

Spallanzani 1978
M. Spallanzani, *Ceramiche orientali a Firenze nel Rinascimento*, Florence 1978

Spallanzani 1994
M. Spallanzani, *Ceramiche alla corte dei Medici nel Cinquecento*, Modena 1994

Stazzi 1982
F. Stazzi, *Le porcellane veneziane di Geminiano e Vincenzo Cozzi*, Venice 1982

Stein 1996
P. Stein, *Boucher's chinoiserie: some new sources*, 'The Burlington Magazine', CXXXVIII, September 1996, 1122, pp. 598-604

Surdich 2007
F. Surdich, *La Via della Seta: missionari, mercanti e viaggiatori europei in Asia nel Medioevo*, Genoa-Trento 2007

Tagliaferro 1995
L. Tagliaferro, *La magnificenza privata*, Genoa 1995

Tagliolini 1988
A. Tagliolini, *Storia del giardino italiano. Gli artisti, l'invenzione, la forma dall'antichità al XIX secolo*, Florence 1988

Tamburello 2003
A. Tamburello, *La componente giapponese nella chinoiserie italiana: porcellane e lacche giapponesi e loro imitazioni in Italia*, in *Italia-Giappone: 450 anni*, edited by A. Tamburello, 2 vols., Rome-Naples 2003, vol. I: pp. 231-235

Tanaka 1984
H. Tanaka, *Giotto and the Influences of the Mongols and the Chinese on his Art*, 'Art History', 6, 1984, pp. 1-15

Tanaka 1985
H. Tanaka, *Fourteen Century Sienese Paintings and Mongolian and Chinese influences. The Analysis of Simone Martini's Works and Ambrogio Lorenzetti's major works*, 'Art History', 7, 1985, pp. 1-57

Tanaka 1994
H. Tanaka, *La testimonianza estremorientale nella pittura italiana nell'epoca di Giotto*, in *La Seta e la sua Via*, exhibition catalogue, edited by M. T. Lucidi, Rome 1994, pp. 129-132

Thornton 1998
P. Thornton, *Form & Decoration. 1470-1870. Innovation in the Decorative Arts*, London 1998

Tiozzo 1972
C.B. Tiozzo, *Andrea Urbani pittore. Opera completa*, Vicenza 1972

Trionfi Honorati 1965
M. Trionfi Honorati, *Un appartamento in Palazzo Borghese*, 'Antichità Viva', IV, 1965, 4, pp. 79-87

Trionfi Honorati 1982
M. Trionfi Honorati, *La decorazione dell'arpa estense*, in E. Durante, A. Martellotti, *L'Arpa di Laura. Indagine organologica, artistica e archivistica sull'arpa estense*, Florence 1982, pp. 65-72

Turchi 1987
R. Turchi (ed.), *Il teatro italiano. IV. La commedia del Settecento. Tomo primo*, Turin 1987

Ulrichs 2007
F. Ulrichs, *Johan Nieuhof's and Olfert Dapper's Travel Accounts as Sources for European Chinoiserie*, in *A Taste for the Exotic: Foreign Influences on Early Eighteenth-Century Silk Designs*, edited by A. Jolly (Riggisberger Berichte 14), Riggisberg 2007, pp. 45-56

Vado Ligure-Genoa 2004
Bianco-blu. Cinque secoli di grande ceramica

in Liguria, exhibition catalogue (Vado Ligure-Genoa), Milan 2004

Venaria Reale 2007
La Reggia di Venaria e i Savoia: arte, magnificenza e storia di una corte europea, exhibition catalogue , edited by E. Castelnuovo, (Venaria Reale)Turin 2007

Venturelli 1987
P. Venturelli, *Cineserie: il nuovo esotismo europeo nella cultura artistica lombarda*, in *Civiltà di Lombardia. La Lombardia delle riforme*, Milan 1987, pp. 271-281

Venturelli 1987-1988
P. Venturelli, *Le tappezzerie della Villa Reale di Monza: sete dipinte e velluti di gusto esotico*, in *Le tappezzerie nelle dimore storiche. Studi e metodi di conservazione. Atti del convegno. Firenze 13-15 marzo 1987*, Turin 1987-1988, pp. 17-30

Vercellin 1990
G. Vercellin, *Storie di viaggiatori e mercanti sulle vie della seta*, in *Le vie della seta a Venezia*, Rome 1990, pp. 25-36

Vienna 2005
Baroque Luxury Porcelain. The Manufactories of Du Paquier in Vienna and of Carlo Ginori in Florence, exhibition catalogue (Vienna), edited by J. Kräftner, Munich-Berlin-London-New York 2005

Völker 2007
A Völker, *An Indian Chinoiserie from an Austrian Palace: The Textile Furnishing for Prince Eugene's State Bedroom in Schlosshof*, in *A Taste for the Exotic: Foreign Influences on Early Eighteenth-Century Silk Designs*, edited by A. Jolly (Riggisberger Berichte 14), Riggisberg 2007, pp. 57-76

Von Strasser, Spiegl 1989
R. Von Strasser, W. Spiegl, *Dekoriertes Glas. Renaissance bis Biedermeier. Meister und Werkstätten ; Katalog Raisonné der Sammlung Rudolf von Strasser*, Munich 1989.

Wilson 2005
V. Wilson, *Chinese Textiles*, London 2005

Wilson Frothingham 1955
A. Wilson Frothingham, *Capodimonte and Buen Retiro Porcelains : period of Charles III*, New York 1955

Witt Dorring 1980
C. Witt Dorring, *Ein Schreibtish von Giuseppe Maggiolini*, 'Alte und moderne Kunst', 1980, January, pp. 38-39

Wittkower 1989
R. Wittkower, *Selected Lectures of Rudolph Wittkower: The Impact of non-European Civilizations on the Art of the West*, edited by D.M. Reynolds, Cambridge 1989

Whitehouse 1966
D. Whitehouse, *Chinese Porcelain from Lucera Castle*, 'Faenza', LII, 1966, IV-VI, pp. 90-93

Zalapì 1998
A. Zalapì, *Dimore di Sicilia*, Venice 1998

Zenone Padula 1992
L. Zenone Padula (ed.), *Viaggio in Occidente. Porcellane orientali nelle civiche collezioni genovesi*, exhibition catalogue (Genoa), Milan 1992

Zoli 1974
S. Zoli, *La Cina e l'età dell'Illuminismo in Italia*, Bologna 1974

Zoli 1984
S. Zoli, *La Cina nella cultura italiana del settecento*, in *La conoscenza dell'Asia e dell'Africa in Italia nei secoli XVIII e XIX*, Naples 1984, vol. I, pp. 211-257

Zotti Minici 1994
C.A. Zotti Minici, *Le stampe popolari dei Remondini*, Vicenza 1994

Photo Credits:

Accademia Chigiana, Siena

Civiche Raccolte d'Arte, Gabinetto dei Disegni, Castello Sforzesco, Milan

Civiche Raccolte d'Arte, Raccolta delle Stampe 'Achille Bertarelli', Milan

Collezioni d'Arte di Banca Carige, Genoa

Fondazione di Studi di Storia dell'Arte Roberto Longhi, Florence

Fondazione Torino Musei

Giovanna e Lorenzo Moncada, Catania

Ministero per i Beni e le Attività Culturali, Archivio di Stato di Parma

Monte dei Paschi di Siena

Musée des Beaux-Arts et d'Archéologie, Besançon (France)

Museo Poldi Pezzoli, Milan

National Gallery of Art, Widener Collection, Washington D.C.

Palazzo Madama, Turin

Photo archive of the Author

Réunion des Musées Nationaux, Paris

Soprintendenza per i Beni Architettonici e per il Paesaggio per le Province di Milano, Bergamo, Como, Lecco, Lodi, Pavia, Sondrio e Varese; Villa Reale di Monza

Soprintendenza per i Beni Culturali e Ambientali di Palermo

Soprintendenza per il Patrimonio Storico, Artistico ed Etnoantropologico e per il Polo Museale della Città di Firenze

Sotheby's, London

The Walters Art Museum, Baltimore (Maryland)

Villa La Pietra, New York University, Florence

The publisher will be grateful for information concerning the sources of photographs without credits and will be pleased to acknowledge them in future editions.